Lecture Notes in Computer Science 16332

Founding Editors

Gerhard Goos
Juris Hartmanis

Editorial Board Members

Elisa Bertino, *Purdue University, West Lafayette, IN, USA*
Wen Gao, *Peking University, Beijing, China*
Bernhard Steffen, *TU Dortmund University, Dortmund, Germany*
Moti Yung, *Columbia University, New York, NY, USA*

Masaaki Kurosu · Ayako Hashizume
Editors

HCI International 2025 – Late Breaking Papers

27th International Conference on
Human-Computer Interaction, HCII 2025
Gothenburg, Sweden, June 22–27, 2025
Proceedings, Part II

 Springer

Editors
Masaaki Kurosu
The Open University of Japan
Chiba, Japan

Ayako Hashizume
Hosei University
Tokyo, Japan

ISSN 0302-9743   ISSN 1611-3349 (electronic)
Lecture Notes in Computer Science
ISBN 978-3-032-12384-8   ISBN 978-3-032-12385-5 (eBook)
https://doi.org/10.1007/978-3-032-12385-5

This Springer imprint is published by the registered company Springer Nature Switzerland AG
The registered company address is: Gewerbestrasse 11, 6330 Cham, Switzerland

If disposing of this product, please recycle the paper.

Foreword

The HCI International (HCII) conference was founded in 1984 by Gavriel Salvendy (Purdue University, USA, Tsinghua University, P.R. China, and University of Central Florida, USA) and the first event of the series, "1st USA-Japan Conference on Human-Computer Interaction", was held in Honolulu, Hawaii, USA, on 18–20 August. Since then, HCI International has been held jointly with several Thematic Areas and Affiliated Conferences, with each one under the auspices of a distinguished international Program Board and under one management and one registration. Twenty-seven HCI International Conferences have been organized so far (every two years until 2013, and annually thereafter).

Last year, we celebrated 40 years since the establishment of the HCII conference, which has been a hub for presenting groundbreaking research and novel ideas and collaboration for people from all over the world. Over the years, this conference has served as a platform for scholars, researchers, industry experts, and students to exchange ideas, connect, and address challenges in the ever-evolving HCI field. The conference has evolved itself, adapting to new technologies and emerging trends, while staying committed to its core mission of advancing knowledge and driving change.

The 27th International Conference on Human-Computer Interaction, HCI International 2025 (HCII 2025), was held as an 'on-site' conference at the Gothia Towers Hotel and Swedish Exhibition & Congress Centre, in Gothenburg, Sweden, on June 22–27, 2025, with the additional option for 'on-line' participation. It incorporated the 21 thematic areas and affiliated conferences listed below.

A total of 7972 individuals from academia, research institutes, industry, and government agencies from 92 countries submitted contributions. 1430 papers and 355 posters (as short research papers) were included in the volumes of the proceedings published just before the start of the conference. Additionally, 439 papers and 104 posters were included in the volumes of the proceedings published after the conference, as "Late Breaking Work". The contributions thoroughly cover the entire field of human-computer interaction, highlight the evolving role of computers in diverse contexts, and demonstrate how HCI research is shaping and improving user experiences across a wide range of domains, influencing technological progress and its effective integration into various sectors. The volumes constituting the full set of the HCII 2025 conference proceedings are listed on the following pages.

I would like to thank the Program Board Chairs and the members of the Program Boards of all thematic areas and affiliated conferences for their contribution towards the high scientific quality and overall success of the HCI International 2025 conference. Their manifold support including paper reviews (via a single-blind review process, with a minimum of two reviews per submission), session organization, and their willingness to act as goodwill ambassadors for the conference is most highly appreciated.

This conference would not have been possible without the continuous and unwavering support and advice of Gavriel Salvendy, founder, General Chair Emeritus, and Scientific Advisor. For his outstanding efforts, I would like to express my sincere appreciation to Abbas Moallem, Communications Chair and Editor of HCI International News.

September 2025   Constantine Stephanidis

HCI International 2025 Thematic Areas and Affiliated Conferences

- HCI: Human-Computer Interaction Thematic Area
- HIMI: Human Interface and the Management of Information Thematic Area
- EPCE: 22nd International Conference on Engineering Psychology and Cognitive Ergonomics
- AC: 19th International Conference on Augmented Cognition
- UAHCI: 19th International Conference on Universal Access in Human-Computer Interaction
- CCD: 17th International Conference on Cross-Cultural Design
- SCSM: 17th International Conference on Social Computing and Social Media
- VAMR: 17th International Conference on Virtual, Augmented and Mixed Reality
- DHM: 16th International Conference on Digital Human Modeling & Applications in Health, Safety, Ergonomics & Risk Management
- DUXU: 14th International Conference on Design, User Experience and Usability
- C&C: 13th International Conference on Culture and Computing
- DAPI: 13th International Conference on Distributed, Ambient and Pervasive Interactions
- HCIBGO: 12th International Conference on HCI in Business, Government and Organizations
- LCT: 12th International Conference on Learning and Collaboration Technologies
- ITAP: 11th International Conference on Human Aspects of IT for the Aged Population
- AIS: 7th International Conference on Adaptive Instructional Systems
- HCI-CPT: 7th International Conference on HCI for Cybersecurity, Privacy and Trust
- HCI-Games: 7th International Conference on HCI in Games
- MobiTAS: 7th International Conference on HCI in Mobility, Transport and Automotive Systems
- AI-HCI: 6th International Conference on Artificial Intelligence in HCI
- MOBILE: 6th International Conference on Human-Centered Design, Operation and Evaluation of Mobile Communications

Conference Proceedings – Full List of Volumes

85. CCIS 2772, HCI International 2025 — Late Breaking Posters: Part II, edited by Constantine Stephanidis, Margherita Antona, Stavroula Ntoa, George Margetis and Gavriel Salvendy
86. CCIS 2773, HCI International 2025 — Late Breaking Posters: Part III, edited by Constantine Stephanidis, Margherita Antona, Stavroula Ntoa, George Margetis and Gavriel Salvendy

https://2025.hci.international/proceedings

27th International Conference on Human-Computer Interaction (HCII 2025)

The full list with the Program Board Chairs and the members of the Program Boards of all thematic areas and affiliated conferences of HCII 2025 is available online at:

http://www.hci.international/board-members-2025.php

HCI International 2026 Conference

The 28th International Conference on Human-Computer Interaction, HCI International 2026, will be held jointly with the affiliated conferences at the Montréal Convention Centre (Palais des congrès de Montréal), in Montreal, Canada, 26–31 July 2026. It will cover a broad spectrum of themes related to Human-Computer Interaction, including theoretical issues, methods, tools, processes, and case studies in HCI design, as well as novel interaction techniques, interfaces, and applications. The proceedings will be published by Springer (part of Springer Nature) in a multi-volume set. More information will become available on the conference website: https://2026.hci.international/.

General Chair
Constantine Stephanidis
University of Crete and ICS-FORTH
Heraklion, Crete, Greece
Email: general_chair@2026.hci.international

https://2026.hci.international/

Contents

Human–AI Interaction and Generative AI in Design

Ethics, Privacy and Sustainability in Digital Systems

Robotics, Embodied Agents, and Human-Robot Interaction

Design of a Child Language Learning Robot Based on AI Agent

Yibing Chen$^{(\boxtimes)}$

Beijing University of Posts and Telecommunications, Beijing, China
564669787@qq.com

Abstract. Language learning plays a crucial role in children's growth process. However, children's language learning is facing problems such as unbalanced distribution of educational resources and insufficient family support for language education. At the same time, the traditional teacher-centered teaching method lacks interactivity and fun, making it difficult to attract children's interest. For this reason, this study designs an AI Agent-based language learning robot for children. Throughout the study, we pay special attention to the second language (English) learning needs of non-native English-speaking children because English, as a globally accepted language, is of great significance for children's future development. This study relies on the natural language processing capability of the Doubao Big Model, integrates speech recognition and synthesis, multimodal sentiment analysis technology, and uses the Arduino hardware platform to realize embodied interaction. At the same time, we designed personalized teaching content that is suitable for different age groups and provides real-time learning progress tracking feedback. We invited 20 non-native English-speaking children in kindergartens to take the test, and through user interviews to understand their feelings and feedback on this new learning method. The results showed significant improvements in vocabulary growth, language expression, and self-confidence. The children felt that this design greatly increased their interest and engagement in learning English. In addition, the project will be a long-term experiment in the hope of providing more children with a quality learning experience.

Keywords: Learning Education · Child Language Learning · AI Agent · Human-Computer Interaction · Human-Robot Interaction

1 Introduction

Language proficiency is the core foundation of children's cognitive development, social integration, and emotional expression [1]. With the acceleration of globalization, children in non-native-speaking environments have an increasingly prominent need to learn a second language (especially English), and the early acquisition of English, as the most widely used language in the world, is not only about vocabulary accumulation but also has a direct impact on children's future academic competitiveness and cross-cultural adaptability [2]. However, the shortage of professional English teachers in kindergartens in developing countries and the reliance of non-English speaking families on fragmented

M. Kurosu and A. Hashizume (Eds.): HCII 2025, LNCS 16332, pp. 3–14, 2026.
https://doi.org/10.1007/978-3-032-12385-5_1

digital tools have resulted in a lack of contextual coherence and personalized guidance for children's language input [3].

In the traditional teacher-centered teaching model, children's opportunities for active language output occur less than three times per lesson on average [4]. Furthermore, most instruction lacks a multi-sensory design [5], which hinders the activation of embodied thinking and may lead to frustration due to mismatched difficulty levels. Although numerous digital tools such as apps and educational websites have been developed to enhance learning through gamification, their reliance solely on screen-based visual and audio interaction makes it difficult to simulate the non-verbal cues of real social settings. Prior studies have found that the emotional feedback provided by such tools is weak, which can result in a loss of children's attention even with continued use [6]. Moreover, fixed and pre-programmed interaction flows fail to adapt to individual differences among children, causing a decline in interest due to the lack of real-time dynamic adjustment [7].

Advances in Artificial Intelligence (AI) technology offer new pathways for improving children's language learning experiences. For example, one study demonstrated that children learning with a robot exhibited significantly increased functional connectivity in the theta band of the brain, which was positively associated with improved second-language acquisition outcomes [8]. Another experiment found that when robots interacted with children in a "peer role," both vocabulary retention and the frequency of active speech improved significantly [9]. However, current AI educational robots still face limitations, including restricted interaction modes, poor adaptability, and lack of physical interactivity. Most products only support voice-based dialogues or fixed animation feedback, and they are unable to perceive children's real-time emotional or physical states, often relying on preset teaching scripts throughout the instructional process.

This study aims to improve the participation and effectiveness of language learning for non-native English-speaking children through an AI-based agent. Specifically, it addresses the following aspects: 1. How to bridge the gap caused by the lack of emotional feedback in traditional teaching using speech emotion recognition technology, enabling dynamic adaptation to children's emotional states and learning guidance strategies. Additionally, how to realize embodied interaction through Arduino hardware to stimulate interest in independent learning and creative expression. 2. How to build a scenario-based interactive environment using camera-based visual recognition, allowing children to acquire language naturally in real-life-like situations—for example, by recognizing toy images and movements to trigger corresponding English dialogues. 3. How to analyze children's language proficiency data through AI models and provide age-specific adjustments to the difficulty level of learning content. This project constructs a three-dimensional interaction mechanism—combining speech emotion recognition, visual scene interaction, and dynamic difficulty adjustment. It integrates multimodal data collection and embodied feedback devices via the Arduino hardware platform and leverages the intelligent decision-making capabilities of the Doubao large language model to realize a closed-loop system from "perception of children's state" to "generation of personalized guidance strategies."

Initial testing with 20 non-native English-speaking kindergarteners showed significant gains in vocabulary, language expression, and interest in learning, validating the effectiveness of the AI-driven learning model.

Future research will further optimize the robot's real-time responsiveness and content adaptability and plans to expand the sample size and conduct long-term follow-up experiments to validate its sustained impact on children's language development.

2 System Design

The solution proposed in this study consists of three parts: 1. Designing a bionic form based on a parrot as a prototype, enabling physical companionship and scene interaction through shoulder-mounted magnets, camera perception, and screen-less multimodal feedback (e.g., wing servo, vibration). 2. Constructing a three-layered architecture of "Sensing–Intelligence–Execution", integrating speech emotion recognition, visual scene analysis, and dynamic difficulty adjustment algorithms. Arduino is used to complete data acquisition and provide physical feedback. 3. Developing learning modes of contextualized speech interaction and stepped auditory reinforcement and outputting customized content.

2.1 Exterior Structural Modeling

To enhance children's sense of participation and interactivity in the language learning process, this study modeled the parrot as a prototype in the appearance design. The image of the robot "Little Parrot" not only meets children's visual preferences but also skillfully fits the theme of language learning. The white color of the robot's body, together with the yellow feathers and pink cheeks on the top of its head, is in line with the children's love for cute images and brings them closer to the children's emotional distance (see Fig. 1).

Fig. 1. The overall appearance of the "Little Parrot" robot in its default posture.

To enhance the convenience and fun of interaction, the robot is equipped with a magnetic device on the bottom of its feet, allowing children to easily attach it to their clothing shoulder. This way, the robot can accompany the study in an anthropomorphic "standing on the shoulder" posture. This design not only frees up children's hands, making it easy for them to interact with the robot at any time during the activity but also realizes real-time language guidance nearby, making the learning process more immersive (see Figs. 2 and 3).

Fig. 2. The "Little Parrot" robot in its shoulder-mounted mode.

In terms of environment perception and feedback, the robot's eyes have a built-in miniature wide-angle camera (resolution 1080P), which, because it is worn on the shoulder, has a viewing angle that is highly consistent with the child's natural line of sight and can accurately capture things in the child's current field of vision, such as the environment they are in, the toys they are holding, and so on. After analyzing the scene content through visual recognition technology, the robot can trigger the corresponding English vocabulary teaching or situational dialogue promptly, realizing the intuitive learning effect of "what you see is what you learn". In addition, the robot's wings are designed with bionic joints and a built-in micro servo drive, which can convey emotions through dynamic movements such as opening closing, and fluttering. For example, when a child answers a question correctly, the wings open and close quickly to simulate happy emotions (see Fig. 3); when a child says a wrong word or grammar, the wings move gently and slowly to convey encouragement and support. The yellow feather on the top is designed as a physical button switch, which can be pressed to turn on or turn off the device. The feather is warm yellow and lights up when the device is turned on and dims out when the device is turned off, which enhances the intuition of the operation feedback through the change of light (see Fig. 3).

Due to the consideration of children's eyesight protection, the robot is not designed for screen interaction but rather builds a learning scene through multimodal interactions such as voice guidance, wing swinging, motor vibration, and so on. This auditory and

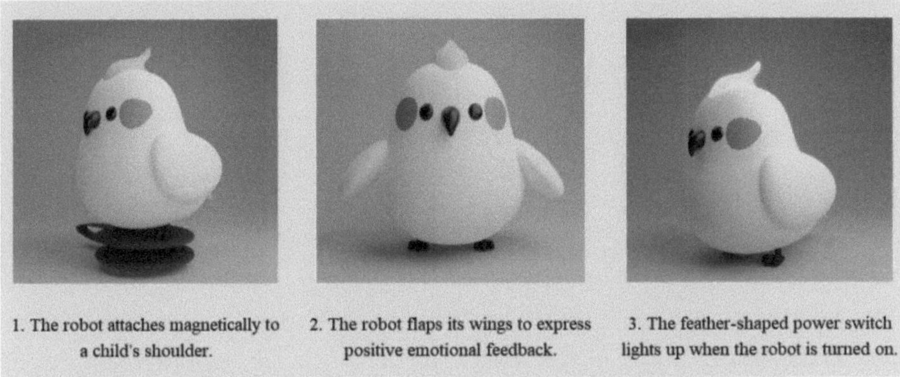

Fig. 3. Schematic diagram of the "little parrot" robot's functional appearances.

tactile design not only reduces the potential harm to children's eyesight caused by continuously looking at the screen but also improves the efficiency of children's reception and comprehension of linguistic information through the multidimensional interaction of "auditory guidance - tactile response - visual scene linkage", which is more in line with the characteristics of preschool children's sensory development [10].

This study aims to deeply integrate the bionic concept with the educational function in the design of the appearance structure and transforms the technological product into a trustworthy "learning partner" for children through anthropomorphic interaction, which not only enhances the emotional connection but also provides the carrier support for the realization of the subsequent technological framework and learning mode.

2.2 Technical Framework

This research constructs a three-layer technology architecture of "perception layer-intelligence layer-execution layer", taking the big model of beanbag as the core intelligence hub, integrating modules of speech emotion recognition, visual scene analysis, dynamic difficulty adjustment, etc., and realizing the driving and control of physical interaction devices through Arduino hardware platform (see Fig. 4), forming a complete closed loop from environment perception, state analysis It forms a complete closed loop from environment perception, state analysis to interaction feedback (see Fig. 5).

Perception Layer: Multimodal Data Acquisition and Preprocessing. In this study, the core data acquisition is accomplished through a microphone and camera. The robot's built-in MEMS microphone array is responsible for collecting children's speech, applying the MFCC (Mel Frequency Cepstrum Coefficient) feature extraction algorithm to perform noise reduction and endpoint detection on the speech, obtaining acoustic features such as fundamental frequency, energy value, and so on [11], and combining with the ResNet neural network model to construct a speech emotion classifier, which can recognize six emotional states such as "happy", "confused", "frustrated" and six other emotional states.

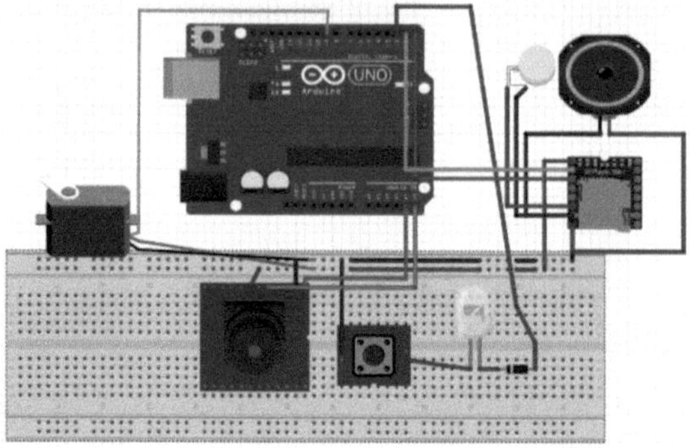

Fig. 4. Schematic diagram of Arduino hardware connection.

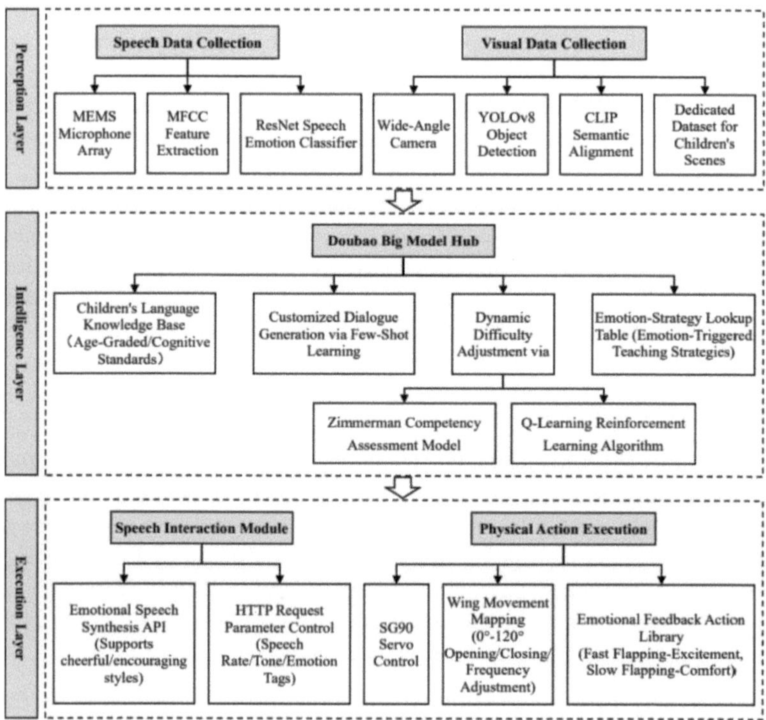

Fig. 5. Schematic diagram of the technical framework (Perception Layer - Intelligence Layer - Execution Layer).

Visual information is collected by a miniature wide-angle camera built into the eyes of the robot. The acquired RGB images are processed by the YOLOv8 target detection algorithm to quickly recognize common objects in children's learning and living scenes, such as toy blocks, picture books, and stationery. Together with the CLIP model to realize the semantic alignment of images and text, accurate semantic labels of the scene are generated, for example, "apple" when recognizing apples and "bear doll" when recognizing dolls. For example, when recognizing a doll, it is labeled as a "bear doll". The object recognition system is optimized by constructing a dedicated dataset containing over 100,000 images of children's scenes. It is further enhanced by data augmentation methods such as rotation, scaling, and adding noise to ensure stable operation under complex lighting and multi-angle shooting conditions. This provides accurate visual information for subsequent intelligent decision-making.

Intelligence Layer: Beanbag Big Model-Driven Decision Hubs. Relying on the Beanbag Big Model, this study constructs a knowledge base of children's language development, covering vocabulary, grammatical structure, and cognitive level standards of different age groups (refer to "Milestones of Child Language Development in the United States"), and realizes personalized learning strategy generation and dynamic adaptation based on multimodal data. In terms of language comprehension and generation, this study uses the Few-shot Learning (FSL) technique [12] to generate customized dialogue content based on children's historical interaction data, e.g., using simple sentences ("It's an apple, apple") for 3-year-olds, and introducing compound sentences for 5-year-olds ("Look, the red apple is hanging on the tree, apple is red"). The dynamic difficulty adjustment algorithm is based on Zimmerman's self-regulation learning theory [13], which establishes a model for assessing children's language proficiency, calculates real-time proficiency values (0–100 points) based on vocabulary correctness, fluency, etc., and divides the learning content into "Comfort Zone-Challenge Zone-Panic Zone," and adopts the Q-Learning (Q-Learning) method to assess children's language proficiency. Q-Learning is used to dynamically adjust the teaching difficulty: if the conversation is completed without vocabulary and grammatical errors for 10 consecutive times, the vocabulary complexity will be increased (e.g., from "cat" to "kitten"); if consecutive incorrect answers are given, the difficulty will be returned to the previous level and encouragement and guidance will be added. If there are consecutive wrong answers, the difficulty level will be returned to the previous one, and encouragement and guidance will be added. In addition, the study also established an "emotion-teaching strategy contrast table" in the intelligence layer. For example, when the child is recognized as "happy", the robot increases the dialogue interaction and reinforces positive motivation; when the child is recognized as "frustrated", it triggers encouraging actions; when the child is recognized as "happy", it triggers encouraging actions. When the child is recognized as "frustrated", the robot triggers encouraging actions, such as wing fluttering and corresponding voice soothing.

Execution Layer: Embodied Interaction and Multimodal Feedback. The execution layer realizes the closed loop of "perception-decision-execution" through the multichannel feedback of physical movement, voice, and touch. In the speech synthesis and interaction module, this study considers that the solution of directly calling third-party API services does not require the construction of a complex deep learning environment, does not require a large amount of arithmetic and data support, has a short development cycle, and the quality of the synthesized speech is stable and the pronunciation accuracy is high, so we decided to adopt this solution, which is a simple HTTP request for the input of text, and then set the parameters of the voice style, speech rate, intonation, etc., and then quickly obtain the synthesized audio file. The synthesized audio file is obtained quickly by passing in the text content through a simple HTTP request and setting parameters such as voice style, speech speed, and tone. Since the platform supports preset emotion parameters, such as "happy", "sad", "encouragement", etc., the robot can realize that when a child completes a learning task, it can pass in an emotion parameter such as "success". "success" when the child completes a learning task and outputs a cheerful voice feedback full of encouragement. In terms of physical action execution, this study uses the Arduino development board to drive the SG90 micro-servo to realize the precise control of the opening and closing angle (0°-120°) and vibration frequency of the wings, e.g., set the wings to open and close rapidly (80°/sec) to express excitement, and to flap slowly (20°/sec) to simulate the state of comforting and encouraging the child. This technical framework provides an immersive and personalized language learning environment for children through multimodal fusion decision-making, dynamic personalized adaptation, and embodied intelligence, constructing an AI learning partner with emotional understanding and dynamic response capabilities [14], laying a technical foundation for the validation of the effectiveness of the subsequent learning model.

Among them, the multimodal data fusion realizes the precise understanding of children's state, the real-time analysis capability of Doubao's big model guarantees the exclusive customization of learning paths, and the Arduino hardware platform, with its low-cost and high-expandability advantages, makes the technology more feasible on the ground and is especially suitable for the promotion of kindergartens in developing countries.

2.3 Learning Models and Processes

The children's language learning robot learning model designed in this study is based on contextualized, personalized, and multimodal interaction as the core, integrating dynamic feedback and adaptive mechanisms to form a coherent learning closed loop (see Fig. 6).

In the contextualized voice interaction mode, the robot visually identifies the scenes and objects (e.g., toys, daily necessities) that the child is in, and triggers the teaching of corresponding English vocabulary or contextual dialogues in real-time, e.g. actively outputs apple-related dialogues when it recognizes apples, and builds coherent learning scenarios by combining different environments, such as indoor and outdoor environments. At the same time, the robot will change emotional voice tones (e.g. excitement, gentle tone) with the children's emotions to enhance the sense of immersion in the interaction and bring them closer to each other.

The stepwise auditory reinforcement model builds a step-by-step content system based on children's age and cognitive level: it matches the learning content related to basic nouns and simple sentences for children with a weak foundation in English learning, and provides a low level of difficulty for them to get started; as children's comprehensive mastery of English vocabulary and grammar improves, it begins to guide them to contact with verbs, adjectives, and compound sentences, and improves their ability to utilize the language through situational dialogues and other means. The learning path follows the logic of "input-imitation-application-consolidation" spiral reinforcement: firstly, children's songs and stories are listened to establish speech perception, then the

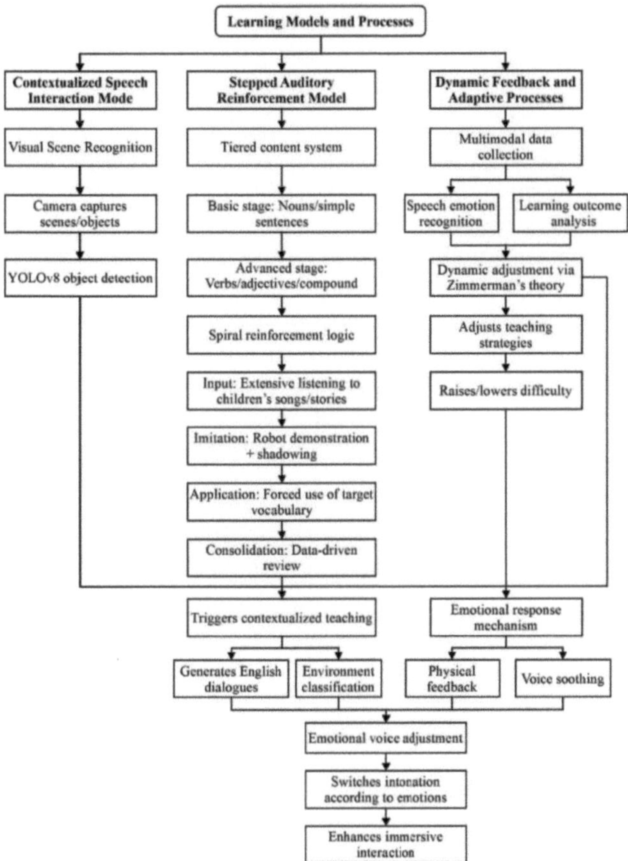

Fig. 6. Flowchart of the learning model (with dynamic feedback and adaptive mechanisms).

robot demonstrates pronunciation and guides the children to follow along, and in the application stage, the application of the target vocabulary is guided through dialogues; finally, according to the personalization of the learning data, the children are added to the follow-up dialogues to consolidate what they have learned. Consolidation of learned content.

Dynamic feedback and adaptive processes are precisely adjusted through multimodal data collection. The robot captures children's voice emotions and learning outcomes in real-time and dynamically adjusts teaching strategies based on Zimmerman's self-regulated learning theory. The emotional response mechanism synchronizes physical feedback and voice soothing.

3 Evaluation User Study

3.1 Participants

Usability evaluation is an important method to validate the functionality of a product or system and help iterate on it [15]. To assess the effectiveness of the robot in facilitating children's language learning, researchers used usability evaluation methods. In this study, 20 non-native English-speaking kindergarten children (10 males and 10 females) were recruited to participate in a usability test of an AI Agent-based language learning robot for children. The participants were between 4 and 6 years old (Mean = 5.2, SD = 0.8), all from the same kindergarten, and had no prior exposure to similar AI learning devices. Thirteen of the children had parents with basic or unsystematic English proficiency, and seven had a small amount of experience reading picture books in English. All participants passed the screening for vision and hearing, were at normal developmental levels, and had basic language comprehension and expression skills.

3.2 Usability Assessment

All 20 non-native English-speaking kindergarten children participated in a complete usability evaluation, which included a pre-introduction, learning experience, question-naire completion, and interviews. The testing process was as follows: before the test, the researchers explained the purpose, process, and safety precautions to the children and their guardians, briefly introduced the role of the robot "Little Parrot", and demonstrated its functions such as voice dialog, wing movements, camera recognition, and magnetic attraction for children to wear. The learning experience was based on the theme of "fruits." Children picked up the experimentally prepared fruits, triggering the robot to start English vocabulary teaching, while the robot gave real-time correction of pronunci-ation and voice rewards. Finally, the vocabulary memorization was consolidated through a multimodal approach. At the end of the experience, the researchers arranged for the children to independently talk to the robot or repeat the session of interest and observed and recorded the frequency and content of the active interactions.

The interviews centered on the dimensions of robot appearance attractiveness, inter-active format fun, and task difficulty suitability. The following is an outline of the questions:

1. Do you think the robot "Little Parrot" looks good?
2. Do you find it interesting when you learn English with the robot "Little Parrot"?
3. Was today's learning task difficult for you?
4. Does the robot "Little Parrot"'s speaking voice sound comfortable?
5. Would you like to study with the robot "Little Parrot" next time?

4 Results

The quantitative results indicated a notable improvement in children's language learning effectiveness. The mean number of correctly recognized words increased from 1. to 3.8 after the interaction with the robot, representing a 217% improvement. Similarly, the mean number of active verbal interactions rose from 0.5 to 2.3 per 15-min session. In the interview feedback, children positively evaluated the following:

1. "The robot 'Little Parrot's' wings move, like real birds."
2. "I like to put it on my shoulder so it can walk with me."
3. "When I get it right, it dances! That's so funny!"
4. "It talks to me! It knows my name!"
5. "It makes learning fun, like a game!"
6. "I want to play with him again tomorrow!"
7. But at the same time, we get some improvement ideas like:
8. "Kind of boring, longer wait time for robot to respond."
9. "Sometimes it doesn't understand me."
10. "It's a bit of a rush to answer until it finishes talking."
11. "It gives me easy words. I want harder ones too."

Vocabulary acquisition and conversational engagement varied by age. Children aged 4 years (N = 7) showed a mean vocabulary increase of 2.1 words and 1.8 active conversations. In contrast, children aged 5–6 years (N = 13) demonstrated a higher vocabulary gain (Mean = 4.3 words) and more active conversations (Mean = 2.7). Additionally, the 5- and 6-year-olds showed greater engagement during the role-playing sessions, with a mean of 1.5 instances of actively switching roles, and paid more attention to the challenge posed by the game rules. These differences may be related to developmental differences in understanding abstract vocabulary and rule-based activities. This usability evaluation shows that the AI Agent-based children's language learning robot is highly usable, interesting, and of significant educational value for non-native English-speaking kindergarteners and that its multimodal interaction, contextualized learning, and dynamic adaptation mechanisms can effectively enhance children's language learning participation and effectiveness. Although the product still needs to be optimized in terms of technical stability and content richness, it has demonstrated its potential as an auxiliary teaching aid for English language learning in kindergartens. In the future, we can further expand the sample size, extend the testing period, explore the in-depth integration with the existing curriculum (e.g., synchronizing the themes of teaching materials), and develop the function of the parent terminal to build a "classroom-family" learning ecosystem, so that non-native English-speaking children can be provided with more targeted support for language learning.

5   Conclusion and Future Work

In this study, we designed a child language learning robot based on AI Agent, integrating speech recognition, multimodal sentiment analysis, and Arduino hardware interaction to construct a three-dimensional dynamic adaptation mechanism. The effectiveness of AI technology in children's language enlightenment was confirmed by 20 non-native English-speaking kindergarten children.

In the future, we will optimize and iterate on the issues of technical response speed and content diversity exposed in the test, expand the samples for long-term tracking, and cooperate with educational institutions to explore large-scale application scenarios, so as to further validate the product's sustained impact on children's language proficiency development, and provide innovative solutions to the inequality of educational resources and the pains of the traditional teaching model.

References

1. Nelson, K.: Language in Cognitive Development: The Emergence of the Mediated Mind. Cambridge University Press, Cambridge (1998)
2. Diaz, R.M.: Chapter 2: Thought and two languages: the impact of bilingualism on cognitive development. Rev. Res. Educ. **10**(1), 23–54 (1983)
3. Huttenlocher, J., Waterfall, H., Vasilyeva, M., Vevea, J., Hedges, L.V.: Sources of variability in children's language growth. Cogn. Psychol. **61**(4), 343–365 (2010)
4. Zohrabi, M., Torabi, M.A., Baybourdiani, P.: Teacher-centered and/or student-centered learning: English language in Iran. English Lang. English Lang. Lit. Stud. **2**(3), 18 (2012)
5. Baines, L.: A Teacher's Guide to Multisensory Learning: Improving Literacy by Engaging the Senses. ASCD, Alexandria (2008)
6. Golonka, E.M., Bowles, A.R., Frank, V.M., Richardson, D.L., Freynik, S.: Technologies for foreign language learning: a review of technology types and their effectiveness. Comput. Assist. Lang. Learn. **27**(1), 70–105 (2014)
7. Hsin, C.-T., Li, M.-C., Tsai, C.-C.: The influence of young children's use of technology on their learning: a review. J. Educ. Technol. Soc. **17**(4), 85–99 (2014)
8. Alimardani, M., van den Braak, S., Jouen, A.-L., Matsunaka, R., Hiraki, K.: Assessment of engagement and learning during child-robot interaction using EEG signals. In: *Social Robotics: 13th International Conference, ICSR 2021, Singapore, November 10–13, 2021, Proceedings*, pp. 671–682. -Springer, Cham (2021)
9. Engwall, O., Lopes, J.: Interaction and collaboration in robot-assisted language learning for adults. In: Computer Assisted Language Learning 35(5 Computer Assisted Language Learning, vol. 35(5-6), pp. 1273–1309 (2022)
10. Cosentino, G.: Exploring multi-sensory interaction to enhance children's learning experience. In: Proceedings of the 20th Annual ACM Interaction Design and Children Conference, pp. 644–647. ACM, New York (2021)
11. Ittichaichareon, C., Suksri, S., Yingthawornsuk, T.: Speech recognition using MFCC. In: International Conference on Computer Graphics, Simulation and Modeling, vol. 9, p. 2012 (2012)
12. Parnami, A., Lee, M.: Learning from few examples: a summary of approaches to few-shot learning. arXiv preprint arXiv:2203.04291 (2022)
13. Zimmerman, B.J., Martinez-Pons, M.: Construct validation of a strategy model of student self-regulated learning. J. Educ. Psychol. **80**(3), 284 (1988)
14. Panagiotidis, P.: Personal learning environments for language learning. Soc. Technol. **2**(2), 420–440 (2012)
15. Branaghan, R.J., O'Brian, J.S., Hildebrand, E.A., Bryant Foster, L.: Usability evaluation. In: Branaghan, R.J., O'Brian, J.S., Hildebrand, E.A., Bryant Foster, L. (eds.) Humanizing Healthcare - Human Factors for Medical Device Design, pp. 69–96 . Springer, Cham (2021). https://doi.org/10.1007/978-3-030-64433-8_4

Will You Be My Playmate? Children's Robot Acceptance and Teachers' Roles in Preschool Classrooms with Social Robots

Soojung Kim[1] (ID), Hyejun Park[1(✉)] (ID), and Boram Lee[2] (ID)

[1] Seoul National University, Seoul, Republic of Korea
hyejun@snu.ac.kr
[2] Daegu University, Gyeongsan, Republic of Korea

Abstract. This case study examines children's acceptance of social robots and the role of teachers in two preschool classrooms: a 5-year-old *Grass* class (one teacher, 12 children) and a 4- and 5-year-old *Apple* class (one teacher, 19 children), both of which had used robots for 7 months prior to observation. Between September and November 2023, each class conducted 14 observations, totaling 28 observations. Additional data from teacher interviews, parental questionnaires, photographs, and teacher documents were thematically coded and analyzed based on de Graaf et al.'s (2017) framework. In the *Grass* class, children's interest declined due to frequent technical errors encountered during conversation with the robot but later revived with the introduction of a movement function. Over time, their robot use declined but they developed an understanding of robots as artifacts lacking autonomy. In the *Apple* class, children actively explored robot functions with teacher's scaffolding, and integrated coding as a means of enhancing play. Ultimately, children personalized their engagement by naming robots and incorporating them as playmates. These results indicate that children adapted to robot functions based on their ease of use and applicability to play. They formed emotional bonds with the robots, engaging with them as social partners while still understanding them as artificial objects. Finally, when teachers encouraged child-led exploration rather than merely transmitting knowledge, children more thoroughly integrated robots into their classroom.

Keywords: Child-robot Interaction · Role of Preschool Teacher · Long-term Acceptance of Social Robots

1 Introduction

AI technology has recently been integrated into various aspects of children's daily lives. In response to its growing influence, the Korean Ministry of Education has outlined an AI education policy that enables preschool children to engage with AI through play (Ministry of Education, 2020). As part of this initiative, several regions in Korea have begun offering rental services of social robots to preschool institutions.

A social robot is an AI-equipped machine that mimics human cognition. Unlike traditional robots, they can make context-sensitive judgments and respond according to

M. Kurosu and A. Hashizume (Eds.): HCII 2025, LNCS 16332, pp. 15–35, 2026.
https://doi.org/10.1007/978-3-032-12385-5_2

individual preferences and characteristics (Papadopoulos et al., 2020). These features have drawn attention to their potential in educational settings (Belpaeme et al., 2018). Numerous studies have demonstrated their educational benefits, including enhanced learning motivation (Kory-Westlund et al., 2015), computational thinking (Lee et al., 2025), and vocabulary acquisition (Gordon et al., 2016; Kory-Westlund & Breazeal, 2015).

1.1 Need for Naturalistic Observations Through a Multiple-Case Study

Previous research has primarily focused on demonstrating the educational effectiveness of social robots, often imposing technological constraints. For example, most researchers manipulated the robot's speech and behavior (Breazeal et al., 2016; Gordon et al., 2016) or observed child-robot interactions involving predefined tasks, typically in one-on-one interactions (Belpaeme et al., 2018). Although such studies contribute to exploring educational potential of social robots, they offer limited practical insights into real-world implementation. In preschool classrooms, children will engage in spontaneous conversations with robots, which must operate without technological intervention. Consequently, frequent errors may occur, creating a different interaction context from those observed in previous studies. To address this gap, this research aims to observe how preschool children interact with social robots in classrooms.

A deeper understanding of children's experiences with social robots requires not only naturalistic observation but also long-term engagement (Kanda et al., 2007; Sung et al., 2010). Research on long-term child-robot interactions suggests that children initially exhibit high interest, actively explore the robot and even compete for its use (Ioannou et al., 2015; Tanaka et al., 2007). However, findings on how children's interest evolves over time vary. Some studies indicate that the novelty effect diminishes, leading to decreased engagement (Kanda et al., 2007). Conversely, others suggest that children incorporate the robot into their play or that teachers integrate it into group activities and free play to maintain children's interest (Crompton et al., 2018; Kim et al., 2023). These findings imply that the integration process of social robots into classrooms differs based on their context. Yet, previous studies have mainly focused on single-classroom observations, limited in identifying variations in child-robot interaction across different settings. To bridge this gap, this study adopts a multiple-case approach to analyze the integration process of social robots across different preschool classrooms.

1.2 A Phased Framework for Long-Term User Acceptance of Social Robots

This study applies De Graaf et al. (2017)'s phased framework to systematically examine long-term interactions between children and social robots in classroom. This theoretical framework illustrates how individuals accept interactive technology, such as social robots, in the domestic environment from a long-term perspective. Specifically, robot acceptance occurs in four stages after the introduction of robots: *adoption, adaptation, integration,* and *identification.* In the *adoption* phase, individuals explore new technology and gradually become accustomed to it. During the *adaptation* stage, they recognize its limitations and adjust their usage. Technology becomes embedded in daily life to the extent that it is used regularly in the *integration* stage. In the *identification* phase, people develop an emotional attachment to technology beyond its functional purpose. However, these stages do not necessarily progress in a fixed order. For instance, a user may remain in one stage for an extended period, or multiple stages may occur simultaneously (de Graaf et al., 2017).

1.3 Teacher's Role in Integrating Social Robots into Preschool Classrooms

In preschool classrooms, while children are the primary users of robots, teachers are the ones who determine how these robots are introduced. Also, they guide children in using robots by demonstrating functions, addressing technical issues, and integrating them into various classroom activities, helping sustain engagement beyond the novelty phase (Arnott, 2016; Plowman & Stephen, 2007). Despite teachers' significant role in robot integration, most studies have focused solely on child-robot interactions (Conti et al., 2020; Kanda et al., 2007), overlooking their role in shaping these experiences. To address this gap, the present study examines the role of teachers in integrating social robots into early childhood education.

1.4 Current Study

This study investigates the integration of social robots into preschool classrooms, considering child-robot interactions and teachers' roles in a long-term perspective. Adopting a multiple-case study and de Graaf et al. (2017)'s phased framework, this research aims to capture the diverse classroom contexts and how this relates to children's robot acceptance. Accordingly, the research question follows: **"How do child-robot interactions and the role of teachers evolve in classrooms with social robots?"**.

2 Methods

2.1 Multiple-Case Study

This study adopted a multiple-case study to explore the process of children's robot acceptance in two preschool classrooms where social robots had been introduced. The case study approach enabled an in-depth understanding of the phenomenon by drawing on rich, longitudinal data from multiple sources (Creswell & Poth, 2016). This study aimed to examine the unique characteristics of each classroom while also generating a more comprehensive understanding through cross-case comparison (Merriam, 2002).

2.2 Research Settings and Participants

This study selected two research sites: the 5-year-old *Grass* class at a private daycare center and the mixed-age of 4- and 5-year-old *Apple* class at a workplace daycare center. In the *Grass* class, parental consent was obtained for 11 out of 12 children, while all 19 children in the *Apple* class participated. Consequently, the total participants included 2 teachers and 30 children (8 four-year-olds, 22 five-year-olds).

This study applied purposeful sampling. To ensure the active use of social robots in early childhood classrooms, teachers should cultivate values, beliefs, and assumptions through firsthand experience with them (Castro et al., 2018). Thus, G City was chosen as the recruitment region for research participation, because it implemented a social robot rental project from 2021 to 2023 to explore ways to integrate robots into early childhood education. Unlike Seoul or Gyeonggi Province, where robots were rented for only one month, G City provided robots for over a year. Both institutions participated in G City's social robot rental project and participating teachers were awarded for their successful integration of social robots into early childhood curriculum.

The Grass Class. The *Grass* class had one social robot and two AI-powered robots designed to read books. The daily schedule balanced free play and teacher-led activities, where children gathered to talk about their weekends or participate in group activities.

Children. Children in *Grass* class usually interacted with the robot through voice commands, such as playing songs or asking about unfamiliar words. Initially, the researcher focused on all children's use of robots. However, as certain children frequently engaged with robots, the observation gradually centered on three children (*Jennifer*, *James*, and *John*) who demonstrated a high frequency of robot interaction.

Teacher. The teacher had ten years of experience as a homeroom teacher. Initially, she introduced the social robot into the classroom because of the director's request. Despite being passively involved in robot integration without personal initiative, she maintained a positive attitude toward using robots. For instance, when parents expressed concerns about the potential negative impact of robot interaction on children's socio-emotional development, the teacher acknowledged the importance of human relationships but emphasized the value of offering meaningful technological experiences in digital society.

She also showed an interest in robot coding and anticipated that, although young children may struggle with coding by themselves, they would understand the concept of coding by observing how robots move during coding activities. Furthermore, viewing coding as a valuable skill for children growing up in a technology-driven society, she tried robot coding with children in the classroom. Due to the lack of institutional support, she used her personal laptop, which was accidentally damaged by the children. As she bore the repair costs herself, the activities were suspended pending discussions with the director about securing appropriate equipment.

The Apple Class. The *Apple* class owned two social robots and a tablet PC with the financial support of its affiliated workplace. The daily routine of the class featured a relatively high proportion of free play time and included coding activities as special sessions. These coding sessions began in April 2023, occurring once a week for 30 min every Monday. Designed as play-based activities, allowing children to physically engage and experience coding concepts. In addition to the social robots, the Apple class was equipped with eight programmable robots named 'Curie', which were utilized in the coding sessions.

Children. Children in *Apple* class primarily used the robots' conversation function to play songs; however, frequent errors led them to rely more on touch-interface use. Since they interacted with robots through tablet PCs, they sometimes explored the coding function on their own. However, due to difficulties in reading letters and understanding the structure of coding blocks, they showed little interest in robot coding. As in the *Grass* class, the researcher focused on children with high robot interaction frequency, specifically *Emily* (4-year-old), *Emma* (4-year-old), *Ethan*, *Evan*, and *Eric*.

Teacher. The teacher had 13 years of experience as a homeroom teacher. The institution to which she belongs was open to coding activities in response to increasing technological influence. Within this environment, she participated in the social robot rental project and received positive recognition for facilitating meaningful child-robot interaction. Her efforts in integrating robot coding programs and organizing group activities aligned with the play-based curriculum, fostering enjoyable learning experiences.

Her experience with social robots in the classroom sparked a growing interest in AI technology, leading her to visit a science museum where she learned about its basic principles. Inspired by the enjoyment she personally felt, she wanted to offer children similar experiences. She came to see coding education not just as controlling robot movements, but as a way to introduce deeper concepts such as machine learning. Also, rather than positioning coding activities as a *"task"* imposed by the teacher, she envisioned play-based learning environments where children could explore and engage with robots to build an intuitive understanding of AI through robot coding.

2.3 Social Robot: Alpha-Mini

The robot used in this study is the Alpha-Mini, approximately 6 inches wide, 4 inches long, and 10 inches high. It can be operated through voice commands or touch-based apps, with different functions available depending on the mode. With 14 servomotors and sensors built in, it can express human-like movements and expresses more than 100 emotions through eye displays. It also exhibits attention-seeking behaviors such as sitting on one knee or sneezing when the user does not use the robot for a certain period.

2.4 Procedure

All research procedures were approved by the Seoul National University Institutional Review Board (SNUIRB) (IRB No. 2308/001–034).

Recruitment of Participants. To recruit research sites, official recruitment documents were distributed to daycare centers in G City. Teachers who voluntarily expressed interest were recruited on a class-by-class basis. With consent from both the center directors and participating teachers, recruitment letters were then sent to children's homes. Research manuals and consent forms were provided only to families who expressed willingness to participate.

Date Collection. This study used triangulation, which collects various types of data to increase the reliability of the research results.

Observation. A total of 28 participatory observations—14 in each of the two classes—were conducted over eight weeks, from September 12 to November 3, 2023. Each observation session lasted between 1 h and 1 h and 30 min. During observations, the researcher minimized intervention in children's play, except when requested. Also, the researcher responded to inquiries about robot functions and coding programs and assisted in resolving technical issues. Additionally, in the latter half of the observation, the researcher provided each class with five 30-min sessions of robot utilization programs except in observation time.

The researcher documented observation records detailing child-robot interaction including time, facial expressions, gestures, and utterances. Since these records contained personal identifiers, names were converted into alphanumeric codes. In addition to written observations, the researcher attached a recorder to the robot to capture conversations between children, robots, and teachers, ensuring comprehensive data collection. The audio files were deleted immediately after transcription to ensure ethical research practices. Also, interactions involving the assistant teacher and non-participant children were documented only in a general sense, with their names, statements, and behaviors excluding from observation and transcription records.

Teacher Interviews. Teacher interviews were conducted twice—once at the beginning of participatory observation and once during the final session. Each interview lasted approximately 30 min to 1 h. A semi-structured questionnaire was prepared, covering topics such as teachers' experiences and perceptions of social robot use, as well as their values and ideologies regarding early childhood education.

Parent Survey. The parent survey was carried out twice, once in the first week and once in the last week of observation. Questionnaires were distributed to households and collected within one week. The initial survey examined children's prior experiences with robots as well as media ownership and usage at home, while the last survey focused on children's experiences with social robots in the classroom.

Other Data Collection. Photographs were taken of children interacting with robots in the classroom, as well as their robot-related drawings and coding projects. Additionally, with the consent of parents, teachers, and the institution's director, document data—including curriculum plans and observation diaries—were collected.

Data Analysis. The collected data were reviewed multiple times, with key concepts summarized into words or short phrases through an iterative coding process to assess the validity of the themes and their interrelationships. To ensure the reliability of the findings, peer researchers reviewed the analysis, minimizing researchers' bias. Additionally, the results were shared with teacher participants to verify whether they accurately reflected the characteristics of the research site.

3 Results

3.1 Robot Acceptance in *Grass* Class

Getting to know the robot

Talking to the robot with clear pronunciation. Children in the *Grass* class primarily used the robot to ask about unfamiliar words or concepts during teacher-led group activities. Rather than independently formulating and expressing their questions, they simply repeated the sentences provided by the teacher.

(Ahead of Hangul Day, *which commemorates the creation of the Korean alphabet,* the class is learning the meanings of pure Korean words.)

Teacher: What date is Hangul Day? (**Children**: October 9!) That's right, October 9. Let's ask Clova. Who wants to ask Clova today? (*John* raises his hand.) John, go ahead and ask. (Whispering to John) Hey Clova, when is Hangul Day?

John: Hey Clova. (**Robot**: Yes?) When… When is the…Han… Hangul Day?

(The robot does not respond.)

Teacher: John, look—what do you think? When you hesitate, Clova takes longer to process, which makes it harder to find an answer. *[…]* What does the fourth meaning of 'beot'— which means 'friend' in Korean — refer to? (*John* raises his hand.) John, go ahead and ask. (Whispering to John) Say "Hey Clova, what does 'beot' mean?

John: Hey Clova. (**Robot**: Yes?) (Carefully enunciating each word) What does 'beot' mean?

Teacher: John, well done! That was a great way to ask Clova.

(Audio record of the first observation session, 2023.10.04)

As seen in the scene above, the child asked the robot using the exact sentences provided by the teacher. However, the robot often struggled to understand the speech. In response to these errors, the child adjusted by deliberately articulating their words more clearly. Some children in the *Grass* class had unclear pronunciation due to prolonged mask-wearing during the COVID-19 pandemic. Therefore, the teacher perceived robot errors as valuable learning experiences, prompting children to improve their pronunciation.

Disappointing Conversations with the Robot. Children tried to resolve errors in conversations with the robot, but due to its technical limitations, interactions did not always go smoothly. When the robot error occurred, children made simple adjustments by replacing certain words with synonyms or clarifying their pronunciation when the robot failed to understand them. However, restructuring sentences in entirely new forms required a more advanced level of language modification. As a result, they relied on the teacher's guidance to explore different phrasing and elicit desired responses from the robot. Due to these challenges, children rarely engage in conversations with the robot, instead limiting their interactions to simple, standardized requests like "Play the song".

Re-exploring the robot

Renewed Interest in the Moving Robot. As the children showed little interest in using the robot, the teacher linked it to a mobile phone app, enabling them to activate its motion functions. The motion feature allowed users to press icons on the app screen to make the robot perform corresponding movements.

Seeing the robot move fascinated the children, and they eagerly shared their excitement with peers (*"Come here! It's working out!"*). Also, the children actively expressed their desire to choose movements (*"Let's do Kung-fu!"*), showing strong enthusiasm for the motion feature. In other words, the robot's movements not only surprised them but also reignited their interest due to its variety of options, and immediate responsiveness. Children's interest in the moving robot was further reflected in a parent survey.

Q. Does your child often talk about robots at daycare?

A. "They say the robot greets them and can even dance.", "Whenever they talk about their daily activities, they always mention the robot— 'I played and danced with the robot!'".

(Parent survey after finishing the observation)

For the children, the moving robot left such a strong impression that they shared their experiences about it at home. Moreover, at the beginning of play time, they frequently approached the teacher to borrow the phone and used the motion feature, maintaining their interest in the robot. As they observed the robot's movements, they began expressing affection toward it—exclaiming *"Cute!"* as they watched, gently stroking its head as if it were a person or even giving it soft kisses on the cheek.

Increased Peer Interaction. Children's interest in robots increased, but since only one robot was available in the classroom, they naturally gathered around it and used it together. To ensure fair use, they determined the order through rock-paper-scissors and explained the movements associated with different icons when their peers selected them on the app screen. Additionally, they engaged in physical play by imitating the robot's movements, fostering active peer interaction mediated by the robot.

Recognizing the Robot as an in-between. In the later stages of observation, the children came to perceive the robot as a social entity that could build relationships and foster bonds, yet also as an artificial being lacking independent movement or speech—an intermediary being that embodied characteristic of both living and non-living things.

Classmate. As time passed, the children grew tired of the movement function and used the robot less. When they played with it, they often engaged in caregiving activities, such as putting the robot to sleep or feeding it. This shift suggests that children became more interested in the presence as an object rather than the robot's function, and this change can also be observed in Fig. 1.

Fig. 1. A female Clova drawn by a child, a four-leaf Clova.

Figure 1 is a drawing of 'Four-Leaf Clova,' a female 'Hey Clova' drawn by Sarah. Each time a child starts a conversation with the robot, they must call it 'Hey Clova'.

Since she perceived the robot as a male, she created a female version by drawing 'Four-Leaf Clova.' This implies that the child personalized their relationship with the robot by assigning it a familiar name, imagining its gender, and shaping its specific appearance. In other words, the child's anthropomorphizing serves as an attempt to understand it as an entity and to enhance their sense of intimacy with it (Epley et al., 2007). For the child, the robot is not merely an object but an emotionally connected being. This relationship between the child and the robot is also evident in the next observation scene.

(Children gathered for their monthly seat assignment, where each child selected a number to determine their designated seat.)

Teacher: Number 8, Victoria. Number 9, Jennifer. Number 10, Mathew. Number 11, Ethan.

Jennifer: Why doesn't Hey Clova get a seat?

Teacher: What number should Hey Clova takes? This friend is the teacher's partner. (**Children:** Zero!) Shall we go with zero? Alright, Hey Clova will be assigned to the teacher's desk as seat number zero.

(Audio record of the 13th observation session, 2023.11.01)

In the *Grass* class, children had a monthly seat assignment to prepare for elementary school, where sitting at designated seats would become a daily habit. Each child would sit in their assigned seat, which symbolized their unique place within the classroom. Jennifer's suggestion to assign a seat for the robot demonstrates how the children perceived it not just as a tool but as a member of their class. They built a sense of connection with the robot, accepting it as a social entity that shared their classroom environment and relationships.

Programmed Machine. In the later phase of observation, the institution affiliated with the *Grass* class provided a laptop for robot use. Also, the researcher shared robot coding program materials, leading the teacher to begin incorporating robot coding into curriculums. For example, the teacher programmed the robot to give questions in a quiz game with the children and used it to assist the class activity.

(Children gathered for their monthly seat assignment, but some children were engaged in conversation with their peers. While the teacher attempted to regain their attention, the robot, which had not been used for a while, suddenly said, "I'm tired now" and sat down.)

Teacher: Oh dear, this little friend is tired from waiting! You've been talking for a while, and this friend's legs must be sore from standing too long, so now it's sitting down.

Thomas: Teacher, didn't you touch the computer to control the robot?

Teacher: I didn't touch anything! Look, my hands are up in the air. Did I press anything? No, right? This friend is waiting just like you until everyone is ready!

(Audio record of the 13th observation session, 2023.11.01)

The robot's movement was designed to regain user attention when left unused for a certain period. The teacher explained its behavior as though the robot had been standing and waiting for the children to finish talking, portraying it as a psychological entity capable of reasoning and experiencing fatigue. However, the child questioned whether the teacher had controlled the robot via the computer. His question indicates that the children understood the robot was not truly autonomous and that its speech and behavior were manipulated by pre-programmed inputs.

How did the children recognize that the robot's seemingly intelligent behavior was merely a result of programmed responses? They observed that the robot would only speak after the teacher had interacted with the computer, leading them to infer that its speech was triggered by external commands. To reinforce this understanding, the teacher demonstrated that she had not touched the laptop, proving she was not actively controlling the robot at that moment. Through these observations, the children realized that the robot was simply a programmed entity rather than an independent thinker.

3.2 Robot Acceptance in *Apple* Class

Getting to Know the Robot

Immersive Touch Interface. Children in *Apple* class primarily used the robot through a table PC, intuitively pressing icons and buttons on the screen and observing the robot's immediate movements, which enabled them to understand which actions correspond to each symbol. They become deeply engaged with the robot through touch interfaces, sometimes manipulating the robot to move to their peers as destinations for over 15 min. On the contrary, when using robots through voice commands, the robot often failed to respond, leading the children to prefer operating the robots via tablet PCs.

Rich Observation and Experimentation. Since 19 children had to share two robots, the Apple class established a rule where each child could take turns using the robot for 10 min. During their turns, most children engaged with it alongside their peers or teachers rather than exploring the robot alone. For example, when a child who was able to read explored the coding function, the teacher explained how the robot operated according to the coding sequence. Other children, including those who could not read and thus had difficulty engaging with the coding function directly, became curious and gathered to observe. By watching the robot move under the teacher's guidance, they realized that coding enabled them to control the robot as they wished, thereby fostering interest in the robot coding.

Meanwhile, the children were deeply interested in the remote-control function and frequently used it. While observing the children's controlling the robot, the teacher prompted deeper engagement. For example, when she posed a question comparing two different types of robots (*"Who would win in a battle between Alpha-Mini and Curie? Which one is faster?"*), the children initiated a competition between robots to find an answer. They placed both robots face-to-face, observing that Alpha-Mini—lighter and slower than Curie—ultimately lost. Lucy, who had been watching this competition, later said, "*Just like cars are faster than people running, Curie, with wheels, moves faster than Alpha Mini, which has legs.*" Through this experiment, the children approached robotics like scientists, testing and observing results to deepen their understanding.

Using the robot in play.

Play Involving a Moving Robot.   As children frequently used remote control and became aware that they could control the robot 'remotely', they enjoyed a play where they moved the robot while hiding to surprise others.

When Daniel took the robot outside the classroom into the hallway, saying "I want to prank someone!". He placed the robot near the entrance of the kitchen and prepared to control it remotely. At that moment, Geroge, who was in the hallway, warned, "You'll get caught! Hide!" Following the advice, Daniel hid behind a signboard near the kitchen entrance and controlled the robot to move toward where the kitchen staff were.

(Field notes of the 8th observation session, 2023.10.11)

The children hid themselves and remotely controlled the robot, creating the impression that the robot was moving on its own. In other words, they understood that the robot was not capable of autonomous movement and looked forward to surprising others by creating the illusion of an "impossible" event.

Robot Coding as a Play Tool.   As previously mentioned, only a small number of children who could read were able to use the coding due to the text-based program. However, even these children encountered difficulties understanding abstract terms like "variable" and "function," limiting their ability to use the robot coding. To address this issue, the teacher devised a coding program in which the robot posed quiz questions and displayed the correct answers as text through its eyes.

For this activity, the teacher prepared the coding in advance, in contrast to the earlier phase in which children explored the coding function to create their own sequences. That is, coding was initially an object for exploration, but in this quiz game, it served as a material for the play. Through this shift in the meaning of robot coding, children came to perceive the robot as an interactive play object that could be freely manipulated in accordance with their interests and needs. Some even expressed enthusiasm to try coding themselves to create their own quiz questions. Ultimately, coding was no longer viewed as a subject to be learned, but rather as a tool that enabled playful engagement.

Playing with the Robot

Playmate.   As described earlier, children surprised others by remotely controlling robots while hiding their bodies during free play. They also engaged in playful activities like staging face-to-face robot battles and creating barriers to prevent robots from moving. Over time, robots became an essential part of play in the class.

Reflecting their interests in the remote-control function, the researcher conducted a robot program to find treasure by controlling a robot on a maze. After the activity, the teacher provided a large paper for children to draw their own maze. The children began to draw a maze, saying the robot should pass quickly through sections where monsters were chasing or fire was falling. In other words, the children added various elements to their maze, constructing a story of the robot escaping. This maze escape game with the robot continued in the following observation sessions.

(As the researcher entered the classroom for observation, a maze was spread out on the floor for the robot to navigate. Ethan was controlling the robot, while Evan, William, Daniel, and George stood nearby.)

Evan: Hey, Ethan! This is a shortcut. Let's make it (the robot) hold a hammer in one hand.

Daniel: And a sword in the other!

George: Hey, but why aren't we drawing a shield?

Evan: We'll draw one! (Shows a tiny shield drawn on paper) Look, a super small shield!

(The children each drew weapons on paper and attached them to the robot. [...] Ethan continued maneuvering the robot through the maze.)

Evan: *(As the robot approached a specific point in the maze)* Hey! There's a super strong enemy here. We can't beat it. Ethan, stop for now!

William: Stop, stop!

Daniel: Ahhh! Don't come over here!

Ethan: *(Pauses the robot)* What is happening? Seriously!

William: Isn't this Batman? It totally looks like Batman!

Evan: Yeah, it's the Batman! Wait, let me draw a hammer! *(Looking at the robot)* I'll attach it to your hand, so stay still.

George: If you go over there, you'll get attacked!

(Audio record of the 12th observation session, 2023.10.26)

The children excitedly discussed equipping the robot with various weapons, so it could pass through the maze filled with enemies. They eagerly called out different weapons, drew them on paper, and attached them to the robot, showing their enthusiasm for preparing it for battle. They screamed for the robot to stop before the powerful enemy and hurried to equip it with even stronger weapons. In this way, they treated the robot as a character within the imaginary play which they had created. By assigning the robot a role and identity that aligned with their play, the children brought it to the center of their play, solidifying its place in shared narrative.

After outfitting their robotic companion, Evan suggested naming it "Yellow warrior" as shown in Fig. 2. In other words, he replaced the robot's original name, 'Alpha-Mini,' with the new name 'Yellow warrior,' emphasizing its unique identity distinct from other robots. By giving the robot a unique name, the child demonstrates the close bond formed through play in the classroom.

Game with a Smart Fool.   Rather than teaching children how to code, the teacher shifts the focus to introducing coding within the context of play. Also, she previously believed that children should be fully involved in every coding process. However, she recognized that it is more effective for the teacher to *"prepare the foundation"* for coding while allowing children to explore coding and its outcomes freely based on their interests. As a result, the teacher prepares coding in advance to structure robot play, enabling children to participate selectively according to their interests.

Fig. 2. A Yellow warrior's maze escape play.

(As the teacher and Emily explored a robot designed to distinguish between similar-looking animals, such as otters and sea otters, Daniel sat nearby.)

Robot: Let me try to distinguish between an otter and a sea otter.

Emily: (Showing a picture of a sea otter searched on the teacher's phone) Sea otter!

Robot: This is an otter.

Emily: But it's a sea otter!

Robot: Let me try to distinguish between an otter and a sea otter. *(After recognizing the teacher's face through the camera)* This is an otter.

Teacher: But that's my face! Try showing it Emily's face this time. Let's see what it says about Emily (**Emily**: Otter!) Alright, here we go *(Turns the camera toward Emily.)*

Robot: Let me try to distinguish between an otter and a sea otter. This is an otter.

Teacher: Huh? It says you're an otter!

Emily: No way! That doesn't make sense! *(Laughs)*

(Audio record of the 13th observation session, 2023.10.31)

The child conducted an experiment to test whether the robot, trained to recognize images of otters and sea otters, could accurately distinguish between the two. However, when the robot saw the teacher's face and mistakenly identified it as an otter, it revealed a limitation of supervised learning, a type of machine learning where models select answers only from predefined categories. In other words, while the robot was designed to be "smart" enough to differentiate between otters and sea otters, it struggled when presented with an untrained category—such as a human face—forcing it to choose an answer within its limited dataset. This resulted in a "foolish" response.

Recognizing this unexpected flaw in AI through play, the teacher encouraged further experimentation while the children questioned the robot's accuracy. Through this experience, the children realized that AI technology is not perfect and began critically assessing its results. Building on their understanding, the children also proposed ideas for creating their own AI technology tailored to their needs and interests. For example, Daniel suggested creating a robot that could distinguish between dragons and 'yong (Korean dragons)', inspired by the robot that differentiated between otters and sea otters. For him, dragons and yong share similar appearances, but they are distinct creatures, differing in the presence or absence of wings. To help the robot differentiate between the two, Daniel and the teacher trained the robot to recognize images of both. He described this process as *"teaching the robot about dragons and yong"*, demonstrating the children's understanding that creating a 'smart' robot requires a learning process in which they transfer their knowledge to the robot. Through this experience, he actively engaged with AI technology, developing their own AI based on their understanding.

4   Conclusion

4.1   A Comparative Analysis of Robot Acceptance in Two Preschool Classrooms

Children in the *Grass* class initially learned how to communicate with the robot through teacher-driven activities. However, technical errors during conversation led to reduced interest in the robot (***adaptation phase***). In response, the teacher introduced a movement function. Children showed an interest in the robot that performed the movements they had chosen (***adoption phase***), leading to frequent peer play using the robot (***integration phase***). However, because of the limited range of movements, children lost interest again. Instead, they began to care for the robot, perceiving it as a member of the classroom. Additionally, with a device support from the institution, the teacher worked with the children on coding. This collaborative effort led to a deeper understanding among the children that robots, as artifacts, lack the ability to think and act independently (***identification phase***). This process is summarized in Fig. 3.

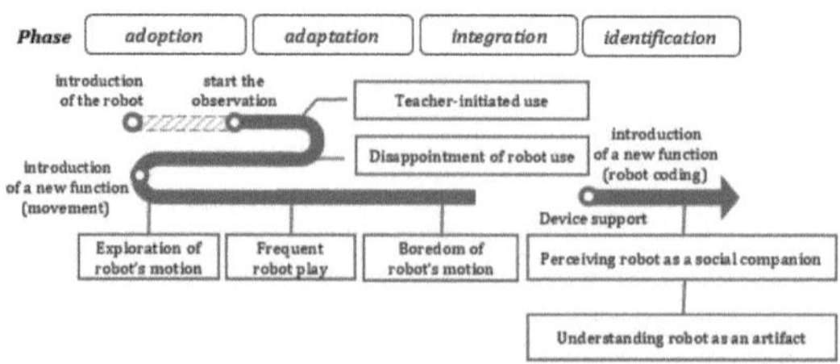

Fig. 3. Robot acceptance in the Grass classroom.

Children in the *Apple* class preferred using robots with tablet PCs due to fewer errors than the voice conversation (***adoption phase***). With the teacher's scaffolding, the children actively explored its functions, particularly using remote-control function to play with robots in various ways (***adaptation phase***). Moreover, when the teacher used coding, not as a means for the children to learn coding itself, but as a tool to facilitate their play, the children came to understand the intelligent characteristics of the robots through play. Based on their understanding of robot coding, the children suggested creating the robots they desired and fully integrated them into their play (***integration phase***). Also, they personalized their relationships with the robots by treating them as playmates and giving them names (***identification phase***). This progress is illustrated in Fig. 4.

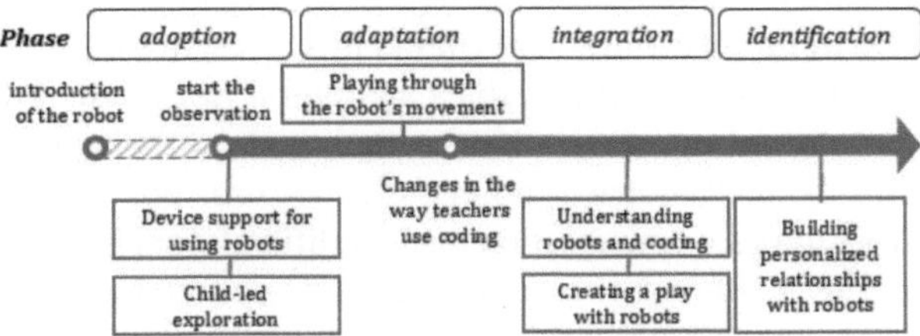

Fig. 4. Robot acceptance in the *Apple* classroom.

Child-Robot Interaction. The commonalities and differences in child-robot interactions across the two classrooms are as follows. *First*, children actively explored the various functions of robots, familiarizing themselves with their use. Over time, they adjusted their interaction based on ease of use and the applicability in the context of play. This aligns with previous research showing that adults explore new technology and subsequently modify their use according to their needs (Sung et al., 2010). However, this study extends prior work by emphasizing that, for technology to be sustained in children's classrooms, it should be intuitively usable without adult guidance and adaptable to a variety of play contexts.

Looking at the detailed characteristics of the functions, frequent errors in voice recognition limited children's use of robots. This aligns with previous research indicating that voice recognition technology remains impractical for young children (Belpaeme et al., 2018; Kennedy et al., 2017) and those frequent errors discourage continued use (Aliasghari et al., 2021). In contrast, remote-control function sustained children's interest continuously, as it enabled them to move robots freely across various contexts, thereby facilitating its integration into diverse forms of play. This expands previous child-robot interaction research by highlighting how robots are creatively used in a play context rather than executing conventional instructional roles.

Second, as children used robots, their connection extended beyond functional use—they started perceiving robots as social beings. For example, children in the *Grass* class accepted robots as classroom members, while children in the *Apple* Class treated them as playmates. This aligns with studies showing how long-term interaction with robots fosters friendship-like social behaviors, such as expressing affection or sharing secrets through physical contact (Gordon et al., 2016; Kory-Westlund & Breazeal, 2015). Moreover, robots became facilitators of peer interaction. This is consistent with studies showing that robots foster positive social connections, as children collaborate, use robots together, and engage in shared play experiences (Yoon & Hyun, 2012).

Lastly, although children treated robots as social beings, they simultaneously acknowledged their mechanical nature—understanding that robots are controlled by humans rather than autonomous beings. Through hands-on experience, they recognized the limitations of robots, such as imprecise communication and inability to accurately recognize similar things. In this way, children accepted robots as "in-between"—having both living and non-living characteristics. These findings align with studies showing that long-term robot use helps children develop an accurate understanding of robots' cognitive abilities (Kory-Westlund & Breazeal, 2015; Lee et al., 2025).

Teacher's roles in integrating social robots into preschool classrooms. The commonalities and differences in teacher's roles are as follows. *First*, teachers determine how robots are introduced into their classrooms based on their perceived usefulness and the availability of institutional support for robot use. For example, in the *Apple* class, frequent errors in voice conversation made it difficult for children to use the robot. Therefore, the teacher explored alternative ways for children to interact with robots using touch-based devices such as tablet PCs. With financial support from the institution, the necessary equipment was promptly secured. On the other hand, children in the *Grass* class also faced difficulties with voice interactions. However, their teacher recognized that the limitations in voice recognition could improve children's pronunciation and leveraged this insight to implement group activities. Thus, teachers assessed the usability of robots based on children's developmental needs and characteristics of technology. This aligns with previous studies indicating that teachers' recognition of technology positively influences its adoption in educational settings (Papadakis et al., 2021). Furthermore, for a teacher's perceived usefulness of robots to translate into actual implementation, financial and educational support should be in place. This is consistent with studies emphasizing the importance of infrastructure in facilitating technology use in educational institutions (Teo et al., 2019).

Second, teachers refine the use of robots through reflective thinking and educational support, enhancing their technological proficiency in the process. For example, when children in the *Grass* class showed little interest in voice interactions, the teacher explored alternative ways to utilize the robot. Meanwhile, the *Apple* class teacher, who had initially felt limited by children's restricted exploration of coding functions, reoriented the approach to allow children to use coding as a tool within play. By continuously observing and evaluating children's interaction with robots, teachers adjusted their approaches to maintain engagement and ensure meaningful learning experiences. These findings align with previous studies indicating that teachers can effectively integrate technology when their understanding of child development interacts with technological knowledge (Koehler et al., 2013; Lee et al., 2025).

Third, the degree to which teachers facilitate child-led exploration and play influences how children accept and engage with robots. In the *Apple* class, the teacher actively implemented child-centered robot use. While the *Grass* class teacher also supported children's interaction with robots, teacher-led activities were more frequent. Additionally, in the *Apple* class, the robot seamlessly integrated into children's everyday play, becoming a natural part of their routine. In contrast, children in the *Grass* class gradually lost interest in the robot's functions and interacted with it occasionally in the latter stages of observation.

However, child-led robot use in the classroom is influenced not only by the teacher but also by other factors. For instance, the *Apple* class had more physical support, including a broader range of devices that could be paired with robots. This allowed fewer children to take turns using the robot, and they had continuous access to the robot via touch-based tablet applications. Beyond physical resources, class size and student characteristics also played a role. Compared to the *Grass* class, the *Apple* class had a larger group size. While larger class sizes can negatively affect teacher-child ratios, they can also foster peer interaction (Tobin et al., 1987). In addition, because the *Apple* class was mixed-aged, five-year-olds were more adept at using robots than four-year-olds. This variation in robot proficiency encouraged natural scaffolding among children and frequent robot-mediated peer interactions.

To sum up, even when the same robots were used, multiple factors—such as the teacher's approach, physical support for robot use, class size, and children's interest and developmental level—collectively shaped differences in children's robot acceptance process across classrooms.

4.2 Implications

Practical Implications. *How should social robots be introduced into preschool classrooms?* First, robots should be introduced in a child-centered way, exploring the technology by themselves and integrating it into their play. To ensure that robot use aligns with play-based and child-centered learning, teachers should focus not on exposing children to various robot functions, but rather on leveraging the features children find engaging within their play. This reflects traditional principles of early childhood education, where teachers emphasize active learning over passive knowledge transmission. In the same vein, children should be encouraged to explore, play, and build their understanding of robotics through hands-on interaction.

Also, because robots have the potential to form social connections with children, teachers must guide children toward a proper understanding of AI technology. Currently, robots used in preschool classrooms face limitations in natural interaction with children. However, if such technological constraints are overcome in the future, teachers will need to help children comprehend the cognitive characteristics of AI and navigate their relationship with robots effectively. Children have been able to correctly recognize the artificial nature of robots because they have controlled robots through coding, realizing that robots do not independently think. Therefore, even if future AI robots develop more advanced communication capabilities, teachers should ensure that children actively engage in coding experiences, allowing them to understand the principles behind AI conversations rather than passively accepting technological outcomes.

How should preschool teachers be supported in utilizing social robots? To effectively implement child-centered robot use, teachers need both physical support and educational support. Regarding physical support, given current technological limitations where robots still struggle with verbal interactions, classrooms should be equipped with touch-based devices like tablet PCs to minimize errors and enhance usability. If purchasing such equipment is difficult for institutions, collaborative initiatives with local early childhood education centers could provide access to advanced technology. Additionally, concerns about robot damage may hinder usage, making partnerships with robot manufacturers essential for convenient and rapid repair services.

For educational support, teacher training should extend beyond technical instruction to include practical, play-based robot integration strategies. As teachers play a critical role in facilitating child–robot interactions, hands-on training opportunities are essential, enabling them to directly engage with and manipulate robots. To alleviate the additional workload associated with robot-related training, platforms for sharing play-based robot programs should be established. Special emphasis should be placed on coding education, given its adaptability across diverse play contexts.

Lastly, real-time technical support should be provided to assist teachers in resolving robot-related issues or questions encountered in the classroom. In this study, teachers received guidance from the researcher, which enhanced their confidence and facilitated the implementation of child-centered robotic play. Therefore, systematic support should be established to provide step-by-step guidance for preschool teachers in utilizing social robots in early childhood education.

Technical Implications. Several technological advancements are required to effectively implement social robots in preschool settings. First, developing accurate voice recognition technology for children is essential. In classrooms where multiple children interact simultaneously, robots often fail to recognize children's calling or respond incorrectly to their speech, which discouraged continued use. To maintain children's interest, robots should be able to accurately detect voices even in noisy environments.

Second, considering children's interests in robot movements, robots should be equipped with movement functions, such as remote-control features. Additionally, predefined motion-based actions, triggered by simple clicks, should be regularly updated.

Third, coding functions should be designed to align with children's developmental levels. The coding program embedded in Alpha-Mini requires children to read and write, as well as understand abstract concepts, posing challenges for children's use. However, to ensure that children can explore robots by themselves, robots should incorporate coding programs that utilize visual programming languages or tangible user interface (TUI) tools.

4.3   Limitations and Contributions of the Study

This study has several limitations. First, the research sites were selected from classrooms where social robots had already been introduced. Future research should begin observations before robot adoption, enabling a comprehensive analysis of the entire acceptance process including pre- and post-implementation phases.

Second, although the number of observations was equal across both classrooms, the duration differed; approximately five weeks in the *Grass* class and seven weeks in the *Apple* class. Future research should ensure consistent observation durations to enhance the reliability of results.

Third, during observations, the researcher provided teachers with information about robot functions and coding programs to support the integration of robots into classroom activities. As a result, the researcher's presence may have influenced the behaviors of both children and teachers. For instance, teachers may have engaged more actively with robots or made additional efforts to use robots due to the awareness of being observed.

Despite these limitations, this study is significant that it examined child-robot interactions within real classroom settings. While most previous studies controlled technological limitations to assess the educational effectiveness of social robots, this study offers practical implications by capturing the process of robot integration in preschool classrooms. It provides valuable insights into how social robots can be utilized from a user-centered perspective in early childhood education.

Disclosure of Interests.   The authors have no competing interests to declare that are relevant to the content of this article.

References

1. Aliasghari, P., Ghafurian, M., Nehaniv, C. L., Dautenhahn, K.: Effect of domestic trainee robots' errors on human teachers' trust. In: Proceedings of the IEEE International Conference Robot and Human Interactive Communication (RO-MAN), pp. 81–88 (2021). https://doi.org/10.1109/RO-MAN50785.2021.9515510

2. Arnott, L.: An ecological exploration of young children's digital play: Framing children's social experiences with technologies in early childhood. In: Digital Play and Technologies in the Early Years, pp. 49–66. Routledge (2016)

3. Belpaeme, T., Kennedy, J., Ramachandran, A., Scassellati, B., Tanaka, F.: Social robots for education: a review. Sci. Robot. **3**(21) (2018). https://doi.org/10.1126/scirobotics.aat5954

4. Breazeal, C., Harris, P.L., DeSteno, D., Kory Westlund, J.M., Dickens, L., Jeong, S.: Young children treat robots as informants. Top. Cogn. Sci. **8**(2), 481–491 (2016). https://doi.org/10.1111/tops.12192

5. Castro, E., Cecchi, F., Salvini, P., et al.: Design and impact of a teacher training course, and attitude change concerning educational robotics. Int. J. Soc. Robot. **10**, 669–685 (2018). https://doi.org/10.1007/s12369-018-0475-6

6. Conti, D., Cirasa, C., Di Nuovo, S., Di Nuovo, A.: "Robot, tell me a tale!" A social robot as tool for teachers in kindergarten. Interact. Stud. **21**(2), 220–242 (2020). https://doi.org/10.1075/is.18024.con

7. Creswell, J.W., Poth, C.N.: Qualitative inquiry and research design: choosing among five approaches. Sage (2016)

8. Crompton, H., Gregory, K., Burke, D.: Humanoid robots supporting children's learning in an early childhood setting. Br. J. Educ. Technol. **49**(5), 911–927 (2018). https://doi.org/10.1111/bjet.12654

9. De Graaf, M.M., Ben Allouch, S., van Dijk, J.A.: A phased framework for long-term user acceptance of interactive technology in domestic environments. New Media Soc. **20**(7), 2582–2603 (2017). https://doi.org/10.1177/1461444817727264

10. Epley, N., Waytz, A., Cacioppo, J.T.: On seeing human: a three–factor theory of anthropomorphism. Psychol. Rev. **114**(4), 864–886 (2007). https://doi.org/10.1037/0033-295X.114.4.864

11. Gordon, G., Spaulding, S., Westlund, J.K., et al.: Affective personalization of a social robot tutor for children's second language skills. In: Proceedings of the AAAI Conference on Artificial Intelligence, pp. 3951–3957 (2016)
12. Ioannou, A., Andreou, E., Christofi, M.: Pre-schoolers' interest and caring behaviour around a humanoid robot. Tech Trends **59**, 23–26 (2015). https://doi.org/10.1007/s11528-015-0835-0
13. Kanda, T., Kamasima, M., Imai, M., et al.: A humanoid robot that pretends to listen to route guidance from a human. Auton. Robot. **22**, 87–100 (2007). https://doi.org/10.1007/s10514-006-9007-6
14. Kennedy, J., Lemaignan, S., Montassier, C., et al.: Child speech recognition in human–robot interaction: evaluations and recommendations. In: Proceedings of the IEEE/ACM International Conference on Human-Robot Interaction, pp. 82–90 (2017). https://doi.org/10.1145/2909824.3020229
15. Kim, S., Suh, H., Lee, B.: The interaction between intelligent robots and children in daycare centers. Korean J. Hum. Dev. **30**(4), 73–87 (2023). https://doi.org/10.15284/kjhd.2023.30.4.73
16. Koehler, M.J., Mishra, P., Cain, W.: What is technological pedagogical content knowledge (TPACK)? J. Educ. **193**(3), 13–20 (2013). https://doi.org/10.1177/002205741319300
17. Kory-Westlund, J. K., & Breazeal, C.: The interplay of robot language level with children's language learning during storytelling. In: Proceedings of the IEEE/ACM International Conference on Human-Robot Interaction, pp. 65–66 (2015). https://doi.org/10.1145/2701973.2701989
18. Kory-Westlund, J. K., Dickens, L., Jeong, S., et al.: A comparison of children learning new words from robots, tablets, and people. In: New Friends: 1st International Conference on Social Robots in Therapy and Education, pp. 26–27 (2015)
19. Lee, B., Ku, S., Ko, K.: AI robots promote South Korean preschoolers' AI literacy and computational thinking. Fam. Relat. **74**(3), 1354–1375 (2025). https://doi.org/10.1111/fare.13189
20. Merriam, S.B.: Introduction to qualitative research. Qual. Res. Pract.: Exampl. Discuss. Anal. **1**(1), 1–17 (2002)
21. Ministry of Education: Educational policy directions and key tasks in the era of artificial intelligence: the future path of education in Korea (2020). https://www.moe.go.kr/boardCnts/viewRenew.do?boardID=294&boardSeq=82674&lev=0&searchType=null&statusYN=W&page=1&s=moe&m=020402&opType=N
22. Papadakis, S., Vaiopoulou, J., Sifaki, E., et al.: Attitudes towards the use of educational robotics: exploring pre-service and in-service early childhood teacher profiles. Educ. Sci. **11**(5), 204 (2021). https://doi.org/10.3390/educsci11050204
23. Papadopoulos, I., Lazzarino, R., Miah, S., et al.: A systematic review of the literature regarding socially assistive robots in pre–tertiary education. Comput. Educ. **155**, 103924 (2020). https://doi.org/10.1016/j.compedu.2020.103924
24. Plowman, L., Stephen, C.: Guided interaction in pre–school settings. J. Comput. Assist. Learn. **23**(1), 14–26 (2007). https://doi.org/10.1111/j.1365-2729.2007.00194.x
25. Sung, J., Grinter, R.E., Christensen, H.I.: Domestic robot ecology. Int. J. Soc. Robot. **2**, 417–429 (2010). https://doi.org/10.1007/s12369-010-0065-8
26. Tanaka, F., Cicourel, A., Movellan, J.R.: Socialization between toddlers and robots at an early childhood education center. Proc. Natl. Acad. Sci. U.S.A. **104**(46), 17954–17958 (2007). https://doi.org/10.1073/pnas.070776910
27. Teo, T., Sang, G., Mei, B., Hoi, C.K.W.: Investigating pre-service teachers' acceptance of web 2.0 technologies in their future teaching: a Chinese perspective. Interact. Learn. Environ. **27**(4), 530–546 (2019). https://doi.org/10.1080/10494820.2018.1489290
28. Tobin, J.J., Wu, D.Y., Davidson, D.H.: Class size and student/teacher ratios in the Japanese preschool. Comp. Educ. Rev. **31**(4), 533–549 (1987)

29. Yoon, H.M., Hyun, E.J.: Young children's perceptions of intelligent service robots and the child–robot interactions. Korean J. Child Stud. **33**(1), 237–259 (2012)

Evaluation of Training Methods for a First Contact Training for Human-Robot Interaction

Erika Rewunow, Ann-Kristin Jaros, Kim Christiane Pfindel, Tamara Schweier, Jonas Birkle, and Verena Wagner-Hartl$^{(\boxtimes)}$

Faculty Engineering & Technology, Furtwangen University, Campus Tuttlingen, 78532 Tuttlingen, Germany
{ere43618,aja49071,kpf45944,tsc49753}@stud.hs-furtwangen.de,
{jonas.birkle,verena.wagner-hartl}@hs-furtwangen.de

Abstract. The use of robots in the workplace has significantly increased in recent decades with profound implications for labor and the economy. Hence, it is important to design an appropriate interaction between humans and robots. To ensure a safe and fear-free interaction with the robots, appropriate training in the early stages of the interactions is a deciding starting point. Therefore, the main topics of the presented study were the participants' general attitude towards robots in different contexts (private or professional) and the evaluation of various training methods applied before a person's first contact with a specific robot. Furthermore, the influence of age and prior experience with robots were analyzed. The study was conducted using an online-questionnaire and involved 123 participants aged between 18 and 88 years. The results provided insights into the complexity of the relationship between robot type and preferred training method and underscored the significance of prior experience and age.

Keywords: Human-Robot Interaction · Training · Human Factors

1 Introduction

The use of robots in the workplace has significantly increased in recent decades with profound implications for labor and the economy [1, 2]. Unlike humans, robots are capable of performing a variety of tasks in different industries more efficiently and precisely [e.g., 3]. This capability can lead to reduced production costs and health risks for workers. For example, it can be seen as particularly beneficial to improve employees' protection and safety when accident-prone tasks are taken over by a robot or when employees no longer have to work in hazardous working environments [4]. Nevertheless, especially industrial robots are powerful and can also introduce a new risk of injury for workers for example because of unexpected movements or system failures [5]. Also, collision and electrical hazards are safety risks that should be considered.

E. Rewunow, A.-K. Jaros, K. C. Pfindel and T. Schweier—These authors contributed equally to this work.

The original version of the chapter has been revised. A correction to this chapter can be found at https://doi.org/10.1007/978-3-032-12385-5_27

However, it also raises concerns, such as job loss [6, 7]. Furthermore, some researchers like Frey and Osborne [8] predict a strong increase on jobs that are at risk to be automated in the future. Actual trends additionally include further innovations such as the use of artificial intelligence (AI) and machine learning, digital twins or the use of humanoids which also keep growing and will impact the future working environments [9].

Based on recent research and market trends it seems predictable that it will be very likely that the integration of interactive or non-interactive robots into various aspects of everyone's life will have the impact to change the way of working, communicating, and living in the near future. Therefore, it is important to design the interaction between humans and robots keeping fears, acceptance and trust in mind, as well as taking ethical considerations like data privacy and security into careful account [10–16]. Former research of our research group revealed gender and age differences which should also be considered [e.g., 10, 11]. For example, Wagner-Hartl et al. [11] reported that younger participants tend to show more positive attitudes towards robots in the working environment than elderly do. On the other hand, within the same study, an interaction with gender was shown for everyday live-tasks in a way that elderly women assessed the help of a robot better than elderly men and younger women. On the other hand, in [10] men's general attitudes towards robots were significantly more positive than women's. Unfortunately, there is a lack on research respectively still no clear trend reported regarded age and gender differences for human-robot interaction.

To ensure a safe and fear-free interaction with the robots, appropriate training in the early stages of the interactions is a deciding starting point [17–20]. This is especially important because it was shown that the acceptance of the humans that shall interact with the robot is crucially important for a successful implementation of human-robot interaction [21]. Besides this, effects on the perceived robot's competence are of interest [22]. Several case studies with collaborative robots have also shown that "(…) the initial skepticism among some employees diminished over time, with personal experience with the robot increasing acceptance in particular." ([4, p. 36], translated from German). Furthermore, it was recommended that companies should involve their employees from the outset to successfully introduce and promote digital transformation and the related processes. Moreover, regarding the development of appropriate trainings for different groups of employees it would be crucially important to include possible effects regarding the beforementioned variables like age or gender. In addition, following Nomura et al. [15] it had to be considered that gender effects are also related to "(…) the type of robots, and the situations and contexts under which robots are used." (ibid., p. 751).

Therefore, the main topics of the presented study were the participants' general attitude towards robots in different contexts (private or professional) and the evaluation of various training methods applied before a person's first contact with a specific robot. Furthermore, the influence of age and prior experience with robots were especially analyzed. The three research questions which are discussed in this paper are the following:

1. Do younger and older individuals with varying levels of experience differ in their attitudes toward robots in the private context?
2. Do younger and older individuals with varying levels of experience differ in their attitudes toward robots in the professional context?

3. Do younger and older individuals with varying levels of experience differ in their subjective assessment of the suitability of training methods for robots, with a distinction made between different scenarios?

2 Method

2.1 Participants

The participants' attitudes and subjective evaluations were evaluated using an online questionnaire. Overall, the study involved 123 participants aged between 18 and 88 years ($M = 35.85$, $SD = 15.52$). The participants included university members as well as externals. Care was taken to ensure the inclusion of participants who are actively engaged in the industry as well as participants with a broad knowledge of the topic. All participants provided their informed consent, took part voluntary and received no compensation.

2.2 Study Design

A mixed methods design was chosen for the study. The first independent variable (IV) was age, divided into two groups, using a median split ($Md = 28.00$; younger group = 28 years old and younger, elderly group = 29 years and older). The second IV experience with robots was divided into three groups "much experience", "moderate experience", and "less experience". The groups were calculated on the answers of the participants on a five-point scale as followed: Participants that reported none or less experience with robots were grouped in the experience group "less experience", participants that reported much or very much experience with robots were grouped in the experience group "much experience", and, it should be mentioned by the sake of completeness, moderate experienced participants were included in the group "moderate experience". The distribution of the sample for both variables can be seen in Table 1.

Table 1. Distribution of age and experience groups within the study sample.

		experience			
		less	moderate	much	
Age groups	younger	32 (26.0%)	19 (15.5%)	11 (8.9%)	62 (50.4%)
	elderly	45 (36.6%)	10 (8.1%)	6 (4.9%)	61 (49.6%)
		77 (62.6%)	29 (23.6%)	17 (13.8%)	123 (100.0%)

The third IV application area (within-subjects factor 1) was binary, labeled as "professional" and "private". The fourth IV robot type (within-subjects factor 2) was fourfolded, including four types of robots, two from the private (robotic lawnmower, robotic toy) and two from the professional context (logistics robot without direct interaction, collaborative packaging robot). The fifth IV training method (within-subjects factor 3) was five-folded: "instructor-led at the robot", "virtual reality", "training video", "online training", and "manual".

The dependent variables were: DV1: attitudes toward robots in the private context (5-point scale ranging from 1 = very negative to 5 = very positive), DV2: attitudes toward robots in the professional context (5-point scale ranging from 1 = very negative to 5 = very positive) and DV3: subjective assessment of the suitability of training methods for robots (5-point scale ranging from 1 = very good to 5 = very poor).

2.3 Materials and Procedure

As mentioned before, the study was conducted using an online questionnaire (Unipark, Tivian [23]). At the beginning of the study, the participants were informed about the study and provided their informed consent. Overall, the questionnaire was divided into three subsequent sections: Sociodemographic data, experience and attitudes toward robots, and evaluation of training methods. Each training method was described using pictures and every scenario was described using a short introduction text. At the end of the questionnaire, the participants were thanked and the research team's contact information was provided. Overall, the participants needed approximately 10 min to complete the online questionnaire.

2.4 Statistical Analyses

The statistical analyses were conducted using IBM SPSS Statistics for Windows and JASP. The statistical analyses were based on a significance level of 5%. Due to the exploratory approach of the study [24] tendencies towards significance were also analyzed and based on a significance level of 10%. ANOVAs were conducted to analyze the research questions.

3 Results

3.1 Attitudes Toward Robots in the Private Context

Overall, the subjectively reported attitudes toward robots in the private context were assessed rather neutral to positive ($M = 3.58$, $SD = .76$).

To answer the first research question if younger and older individuals with varying levels of experience differ in their attitudes toward robots in the private context, the results of an ANOVA showed that the effects did not reach the level of significance. The detailed results are shown in Table 2 and Fig. 1.

3.2 Attitudes Toward Robots in the Professional Context

Overall, the subjectively reported attitudes toward robots in the professional context / working environment were assessed rather positive ($M = 4.05$, $SD = .81$). Regarding the second research question if younger and older individuals with varying levels of experience differ in their attitudes toward robots in the professional context, a significant effect

Table 2. Attitudes toward robots in the private context – results of the ANOVA.

DV	F	df	df_{error}	p	$\eta^2_{part.}$
age	.53	1	117	.470	.004
experience	.71	2	117	.495	.012
age x experience	.28	2	117	.754	.005

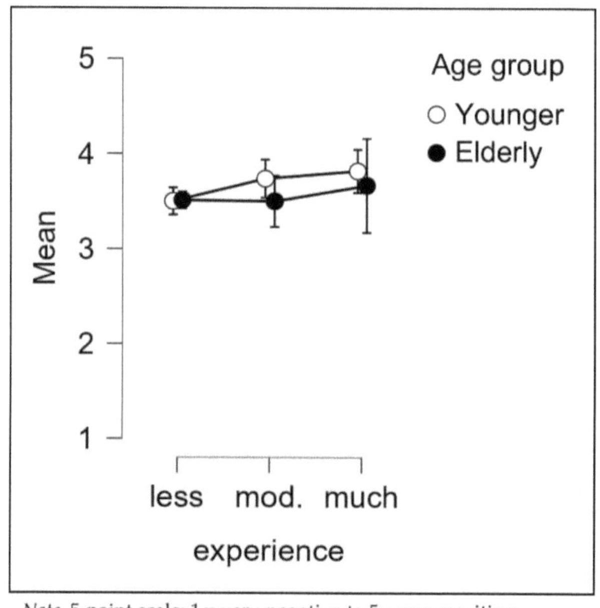

Note. 5-point scale: 1 = very negative to 5 = very positive;
I ... standard error of mean

Fig. 1. Mean subjectively reported attitudes toward robots in the private context by age and experience.

of experience can be shown (see Table 3). Following post-hoc analyses (Sidak) participants with more experience with robots were significantly more positive toward robots in the professional context than those with less experience ($p < .001$, Fig. 2). Additionally, less experienced participants reported a tendentially less positive attitude than participants with moderate experience with robots ($p = .061$). Furthermore, a tendency towards significance was shown regarding age (Table 3). As shown in Fig. 2, younger participants tend to have more positive attitudes toward robots in the professional context than elderly participants do.

3.3   Perceived Suitability of Training Methods for Robots

Overall, the five different trainings methods ("instructor-led at the robot", "virtual reality", "training video", "online training", and "manual") were assessed as (very) good to

Table 3. Attitudes toward robots in the professional context – results of the ANOVA.

DV	F	df	$df error$	p	$\eta^2_{part.}$
age	2.77	1	117	.098	.023
experience	8.59	2	117	< .001	.128
age x experience	1.79	2	117	.172	.030

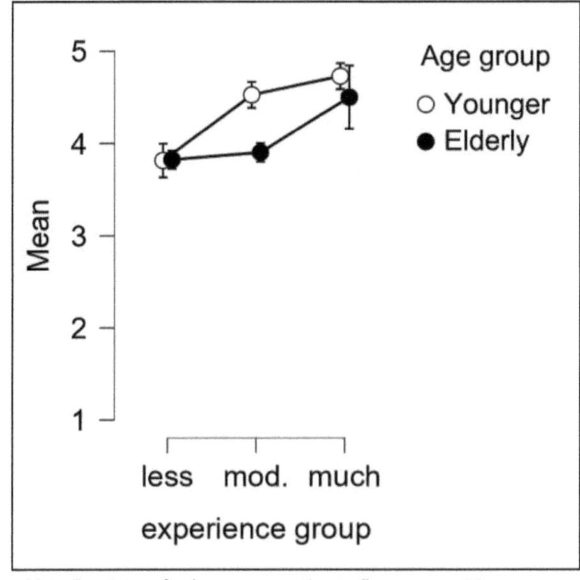

Note. 5-point scale: 1 = very negative to 5 = very positive;
I ... standard error of mean

Fig. 2. Mean subjectively reported attitudes toward robots in the professional context by age and experience.

neutral regarding their perceived suitability for trainings for an interaction with the different types of robots (private context: robotic lawnmower and robotic toy; professional context: logistics robot without direct interaction and collaborative packaging robot).

To answer the third research question if younger and older individuals with varying levels of experience differ in their subjective assessment of the suitability of training methods for robots, with a distinction made between different scenarios a mixed ANOVA was analyzed. The results showed a significant interaction robot type x trainings method x age, $F_{GG}(7.32, 856.29) = 3.83, p < .001, \eta^2_{part.} = .032$, and a significant interaction robot type x trainings method, $F_{GG}(7.32, 856.29) = 19.62, p < .001, \eta^2_{part.} = .144$, as well as significant effects of the robot type, $F_{GG}(2.49, 291.31) = 3.38, p = .026, \eta^2_{part.} = .028$, and of the trainings method, $F_{GG}(3.28, 383.51) = 18.42, p < .001, \eta^2_{part.} = .136$. Following post-hoc analyses (Sidak) with regard to the robot

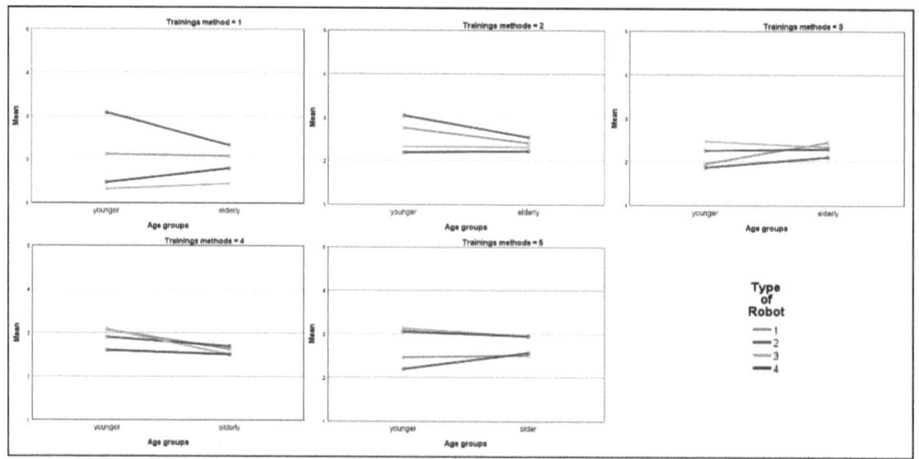

Note. 5-point scale: 1 = very good to 5 = very poor; trainings method: 1 = instructor-led at the robot, 2 = virtual reality, 3 = training video, 4 = online training, 5 = manual; types of robots: private context: 1 = robotic lawnmower, 2 = robotic toy, professional context: 3 = logistics robot without direct interaction, 4 = collaborative packaging robot

Fig. 3. Mean perceived suitability of the different training methods by robot type and age.

type and context as well as age groups, different training methods for a first contact with the robot were preferred by the participants (see for example Table 4 and Fig. 3).

Furthermore, a tendency towards significance was shown regarding the experience with robots, $F(2, 117) = 2.97, p = .055, \eta^2_{part.} = .048$. Following the results of post-hoc analyses (Sidak) participants with less experience with robots tendentially assessed the different training methods better than those with more experience ($p = .110$).

All other effects did not reach the level of significance.

4 Discussion

The aim of the study was to gain more insight within the general attitudes towards robots in different contexts (private or professional) and the evaluation of various training methods applied before a person's first contact with a specific robot. Furthermore, the influence of age and prior experience with robots was of interest.

With regard to the first and second research question it was shown that the attitudes toward robots in the private context were rather neutral to positive, whereas the attitudes towards robots in the professional sector were descriptively assessed more positive. Additionally, differences regarding the analyzed age and experience groups reached also only the level of significance regarding the professional context / working environment. Here, participants with more experience with robots generally exhibited more positive attitudes than those with less experience. And, additionally, less experienced participants reported a tendentially less positive attitude than participants with moderate experience with robots. Therefore, it can be inferred that individuals who have had no prior exposure to robots may, in general, harbor more negative attitudes towards them. This is particularly of interest because several case studies [4] with collaborative robots had also shown that the personal experience can increase the acceptance of the workers.

Table 4. Post-hoc Analyses (Sidak) - interaction robot type x trainings method x age.

Type of robot	Trainings method	Age group		p (Sidak)
1	3	younger	elderly	.008
	4	younger	elderly	*.071*
2	1	younger	elderly	.010
	2	younger	elderly	*.061*
3	4	younger	elderly	.014
4	1	younger	elderly	*.069*

Age group	Trainings method	Type of robot		p (Sidak)
younger	1	1	2	<.001
			3	<.001
			4	<.001
		2	3	<.001
			4	<.001
	2	1	3	.017
			4	.003
		2	3	<.001
			4	<.001
	3	1	3	<.001
			4	*.097*
		2	3	<.001
			4	.027
	4	1	4	.003
		3	4	.001
	5	1	3	<.001
			4	.002
		2	3	<.001
			4	<.001
elderly	1	1	3	.023
		2	3	.002
		3	4	.041

(*continued*)

Table 4. (*continued*)

Age group	Type of robot	Trainings method		p (Sidak)
younger	1	1	2	.006
			4	<.001
		2	3	<.001
		3	4	<.001
			5	.020
		4	5	.027
	2	1	3	<.001
			5	.006
		2	3	<.001
			5	.004
		3	4	<.001
		4	5	.005
	3	1	2	<.001
			3	<.001
			4	<.001
			5	<.001
		2	4	<.001
			5	.005
		3	4	<.001
			5	<.001
	4	1	2	<.001
			3	<.001
			4	<.001
			5	<.001
		2	5	.002
		3	5	<.001
elderly	2	3	4	.038
	3	1	2	<.001
			3	<.001
			4	<.001
			5	<.001
		3	5	.033
	4	1	3	*.095*
			4	.011
			5	<.001
		3	5	.027

Note. The level of significance for presented effects was based on 5% resp. 10%. All other effects were not reported within the table. Types of robots: private context: 1 = robotic lawn-mower, 2 = robotic toy, professional context: 3 = logistics robot without direct interaction, 4 = collaborative packaging robot; trainings method: 1 = instructor-led at the robot, 2 = virtual reality, 3 = training video, 4 = online training, 5 = manual

Future trainings should therefore take this into account. For example, they should not only cover the initial contact with a robot and the first training sessions, but also include repeated training sessions and/or extended training periods to enable trainees to gain more experience with the robot. Regarding age, the study underlines the former results of our research group [see also 11] whereas younger participants tend to have more positive attitudes towards robots in the professional context / working environment than elderly do.

To answer the third research question – whether younger and older individuals with varying levels of experience differ in their subjective assessment of the suitability of training methods for robots, with a distinction made between different scenarios – the results provided insights into the complexity of the relationship between robot type and preferred training method and underscored the significance of prior experience and age. Here, participants preferred different training methods for their first contact with the robot, depending on the type of robot, the context in which it would be used, and their age. These results can provide a basis for future research. As Nomura et al. [15] suggested that gender effects are related to further aspects like the context in which the robot is used and the type of robot, this seems also valid regarding training method preferences and age. Future studies shall also take this into account.

As every study the presented study had some limitations. Caused by the fact, that the study was conducted as online study, the participants had to imagine each situation and were not able to experience the different trainings for the different investigated robot types. Nonetheless, this approach was chosen to be as close to reality as possible because the trainings were planned as first contact trainings. Also, under normal circumstances people will not experience the different robot types and/or training methods before they receive a first contact training within their private or working environment. Future research should therefore investigate real training situations with real robots and/or simulated conditions in virtual reality [18, 20] and combine the presented study results with evaluations of real training situations to close this research gap. Moreover, the use of a multidimensional approach which combines subjective assessments and objective parameters like physical parameters of the robots' movement or time on task and errors as well as psychophysiological responses of the participants during human-robot interaction (e.g., ECG, EDA) could provide further insights. Another limitation was the sample, which consisted mainly of participants living in German-speaking countries of Western Europe. An increase of the sample towards more international participants may possibly reveal additional requirements for future trainings within the field of human-robot interaction.

To sum it up, the results of the presented exploratory online study provided insights into the attitudes towards robots in both private and professional contexts, as well as the complexity of the relationship between robot type and preferred training method. Furthermore, the results underscored the significance of prior experience with robots and age. Future research should therefore extend this approach by evaluating training with real robots and/or simulating it in virtual reality.

Acknowledgments. We would like to thank Katharina Gleichauf for her help with the technical preparation of the online study and all participants for their time and willingness to contribute to our study.

Disclosure of Interests..   The authors have no competing interests to declare that are relevant to the content of this article. An informed consent was obtained from all subjects involved in the study. The study was conducted in accordance with the declaration of Helsinki.

References

1. Acemoglu, D., Restrepo, P.: Robots and Jobs: evidence from US labor markets. J. Polit. Econ. **128**(6), 2188–2244 (2020)
2. Filippi, E., Bannò, M., Trento, S.: Automation technologies and their impact on employment: a review, synthesis and future research agenda. Technol. Forecast. Soc. Chang. **191**, 122448 (2023)
3. International Federation of Robotics (IFR): The Impact of Robots on Productivity, Employment and Jobs. A positioning paper by the International Federation of Robotics (2017), https://ifr.org/img/office/IFR_The_Impact_of_Robots_on_Employment.pdf. Accessed 07 Jun 2025
4. Pexa, R.: Künstliche Intelligenz und Robotik am Arbeitsplatz [Artificial intelligence and robotics in the workplace]. SICHERE ARBEIT **24**(3), 34–38 (2024)
5. Post, H.: Industrial robot safety considerations, standards and best practices to consider. Machine Safety (2024). https://www.controleng.com/industrial-robot-safety-considerations-standards-and-best-practices-to-consider/. Accessed 07 Jun 2025
6. Spencer, D.A.: Fear and hope in an age of mass automation: debating the future of work. N. Technol. Work. Employ. **33**(1), 1–12 (2018)
7. Morikawa M.: Who are afraid of losing their jobs to artificial intelligence and robots? Evidence from a Survey No. 71 (2017)
8. Frey, C.B., Osborne, M.A.: The future of employment: how susceptible are jobs to computerisation? Technol. Forecast. Soc. Chang. **114**, 254–280 (2017)
9. International Federation of Robotics (IFR): Top 5 Robot Trends 2024. New Technology simplifies Automation. IFR Press Room (2024). https://ifr.org/ifr-press-releases/news/top-5-robot-trends-2024. Accessed 07 Jun 2025
10. Wagner-Hartl, V., Schmid. R., Gleichauf, K.: The influence of task complexity on acceptance and trust in human-robot interaction - gender and age differences. In: Paletta, L., Ayaz, H. (eds) Cognitive Computing and Internet of Things. AHFE (2022) International Conference. AHFE Open Access, vol. 43, pp. 118–126. AHFE International, USA (2022)
11. Wagner-Hartl V., Gleichauf K., Schmid R.: Are we ready for human-robot collaboration at work and in our everyday lives? – An exploratory approach. In: Ahram T., Karwowski W., Pickl S., Taiar R. (eds.) Human Systems Engineering and Design II. IHSED 2019. Advances in Intelligent Systems and Computing, vol. 1026, pp. 135–141, Springer, Cham (2020)
12. Wagner-Hartl, V., Pohling, K., Rössler, M., Strobel, S., Maag, S.: Attitudes towards human-robot collaboration and the impact of the COVID-19 pandemic. In: Stephanidis, C., Antona, M., Ntoa, S. (eds) HCI International 2021 - Late Breaking Posters. HCII 2021. Communications in Computer and Information Science, vol. 1498, pp. 294–299. Springer, Cham (2021)
13. Fronemann, N., Pollmann, K., Loh, W.: Should my robot know what's best for me? Human–robot interaction between user experience and ethical design. AI & Soc. **37**, 517–533 (2022)
14. Hancock, P.A., Billings, D.R., Schaefer, K.E., Chen, J.Y., De Visser, E.J., Parasuraman, R.: A meta-analysis of factors affecting trust in human-robot interaction. Hum. Factors **53**(5), 517–527 (2011)
15. Nomura, T., Kanda, T., Suzuki, T., Kato, K.: Prediction of human behaviour in human-robot interaction using psychological scales for anxiety and negative attitudes toward robots. IEEE Trans. Rob. **24**, 442–451 (2008)

16. Callari, T.C., Segate, R.V., Hubbard, E.-M., Daly, A., Lohse, N.: An ethical framework for human-robot collaboration for the future people-centric manufacturing: a collaborative endeavour with European subject-matter experts in ethics. Technol. Soc. **75**, 102680 (2024)
17. Wagner-Hartl, V., Nakladal, S., Koch, T., Babajic, D., Mazur, S., Birkle, J.: Influence of movement speed and interaction instructions on subjective assessments, performance and psychophysiological reactions during human-robot interaction. In: Kurosu, M., et al. (eds.) HCI International 2023 – Late Breaking Papers. HCII 2023. Lecture Notes in Computer Science, vol. 14054, pp. 461–475. Springer, Cham (2023)
18. Birkle, J., Wagner-Hartl, V.: Requirements for virtual reality-based trainings of human-robot interaction. In: Paletta, L. (eds) Cognitive Computing and Internet of Things. AHFE (2024) International Conference. AHFE Open Access, vol. 124, pp. 64–74. AHFE International, USA (2024)
19. Nikolaidis, S., Lasota, P., Ramakrishnan, R., Shah, J.: Improved human–robot team performance through cross-training, an approach inspired by human team training practices. Int. J. Robot. Res. **34**(14), 1711–1730 (2015)
20. Schöner, D., Birkle, J., Wagner-Hartl, V.: Emotional and psychophysiological reactions while performing a collaborative task with an industrial robot in real and virtual working settings. Theor. Appl. Ergon. **1**(4), 17 (2025). https://doi.org/10.3390/tae1010004
21. Görke, M., Blankemeyer, S., Pischke, D., Oubari, A., Raatz, A., Nyhuis, P.: Sichere und akzeptierte Kollaboration von Mensch und Maschine: Integrierte Betrachtung technischer und nicht technischer Gestaltungsfaktoren für die Einführung nachhaltiger und effizienter kollaborativer Montagesysteme [Safe and accepted human-machine collaboration: Integrated consideration of technical and non-technical design factors for the introduction of sustainable and efficient collaborative assembly systems]. Zeitschrift fuer Wirtsch. Fabrikbetrieb **112**, 41–45 (2017)
22. Yuan, Y., Wu, C.-F., Niu, J., Mao, L.: The effects of human-robot interactions and the human-robot relationship on robot competence, trust, and acceptance. SAGE Open **14**(2), 1–15 (2024)
23. Unipark, Tivian, https://www.unipark.com/. Accessed 07 Jun 2025
24. Abt, K.: Descriptive data analysis: a concept between confirmatory and exploratory data analysis. Methods Inf. Med. **26**, 77–88 (1987)

Behavior-Based Indicators of Owner Attachment to Companion Robots Across Specific Contexts

Megumi Takada[1]([✉]) [iD], Junko Ichino[2] [iD], and Kaname Hayashi[1]

[1] GROOVE X, Inc., Sumitomo Fudosan Bldg. 3-42-3 Nihonbashi Hamacho, Chuo-ku, Tokyo, Japan
megumi.takada@groove-x.com
[2] Waseda University, 2-579-15 Mikajima, Tokorozawa, Saitama, Japan

Abstract. Companion robots (CRs) have been proposed as alternatives to companion animals such as dogs and cats. For developing and improving CRs that owners will love for a long time, constant assessment of the attachment that CR owners feel toward them is important. However, pervious methods based on questionnaires are costly because they need to be conducted periodically to monitor the owners' subjective level of attachment over time. Therefore, this study investigated alternative indicators for the subjective level of attachment based on low-cost and continuously accessible CR log data. In this study, we analyzed the relationship between the subjective level of attachment, obtained through questionnaires administered to 287 CR owners, and owner behaviors extracted from CR log data. The results showed that two behavioral features – (1) the number of days when owner behavior occurred within one hour before CR bedtime and (2) the frequency of owner behavior while the CR is being held by the owner – exhibited stronger correlations with subjective level of attachment compared to behavioral features measured without temporal or spatial contextual constraints. Furthermore, factor analysis conducted on the questionnaire responses extracted three factors, Comfort, Protectiveness, and Intimacy, among which the third factor, Intimacy, was found to be correlated with the space-specific behavioral feature. These findings suggest that the behavioral features extracted from the CR log data can serve as more effective indicators of the subjective level of attachment when behaviors are constrained to specific temporal and spatial contexts, and when attachment is represented as multidimensional data.

Keywords: Companion Robot · Human-Robot Interaction · Indicators of Attachment

1 Introduction

Companion animals (CAs), such as dogs and cats, are known to enhance the mental and physical well-being of their owners. Previous studies have shown that owning a CA can reduce blood pressure [1, 2] and help alleviate feelings of anxiety [3, 4]. However,

M. Kurosu and A. Hashizume (Eds.): HCII 2025, LNCS 16332, pp. 48–66, 2026.
https://doi.org/10.1007/978-3-032-12385-5_4

owning a CA is not always feasible, particularly in urban environments. For instance, a survey in Japan [5] reported that 65% of individuals who wished to own a CA were unable to do so, owing to concerns regarding caregiving responsibilities and restrictions on pet ownership in housing complexes [6].

Considering this social context, companion robots (CRs), which live alongside humans in a manner similar to CAs, have been proposed as alternatives to CAs [7]. CRs range from nonverbal types, such as CAs, to those equipped with advanced intelligence and capable of using language to communicate. Although some CR owners developed a level of attachment with CRs comparable to that with CAs [8], others lost interest and discontinued the use after a short period [9–11]. Therefore, it is essential for CR designers and developers to design CRs that maintain the owner's attachment over time and to develop methods for re-establishing the owners' attachment when it declines. To achieve this, constantly assessing the owner's level of attachment and understanding how it changes, as well as the factors that contribute to its decline, is necessary.

Interview [11, 12] and questionnaire [8, 13, 14], which are subjective measures, have been widely used to assess owners' level of attachment to CRs. Furthermore, objective evaluations using physiological indicators [15, 16] have been explored. However, these methods only capture the level of attachment at the time when the survey is conducted. To track changes over time, repeated assessments at intervals of several weeks or months are required, which imposes a significant burden on the owners.

Building upon these concerns, this study focused on CR log data as a potential indicator of the owner's level of attachment, particularly for nonverbal CRs. Such data is highly objective, low-cost, and continuously accessible. In our previous study [17], we demonstrated that the frequency of owner behaviors, such as hugging and stroking the CR, extracted from CR log data (objective data) was positively correlated with the subjective level of attachment obtained via questionnaire survey (subjective data). Although the findings suggested that the frequency of these behaviors could serve as behavioral indicators for the level of attachment, the correlation coefficients were less than 0.3. This may be because behavioral features were derived without considering contextual information. Furthermore, because the subjective level of attachment was treated as a single measure, it may have been difficult to capture the multiple factors associated with attachment. In this paper, we refer to *behavioral features* as raw behavioral metrics extracted from CR log data and *behavioral indicators* as those features that serve as proxies for the owner's level of attachment.

In this paper, we examine whether the relationship between subjective attachment and owner behavioral features can be clarified by extracting these features from CR log data based on temporal and spatial context, and by transforming owners' subjective attachment to CRs into a multidimensional representation.

2   Related Work

2.1   Subjective Assessment of Owner Attachment

Interviews and questionnaires are the primary methods used for the subjective evaluation of owners' attachment to CRs.

First, the advantage of the interview surveys is their flexibility in adapting questions to individual participants and capturing nuanced responses. For example, in a feasibility study of a CR, Ostrowski et al. [12] conducted interviews and found that some owners described the CR as "a conversational partner who teaches trivia," whereas others referred to it as "a member of the family," indicating that perceptions of CRs vary considerably across individuals. However, interviews typically require several hours per participant, making it difficult to conduct them with a large number of participants. In addition, quantifying spoken responses is difficult.

Secondly, the advantage of the questionnaire survey is that it enables the quantitative measurement of the level of attachment. For example, Banks et al. [8] evaluated attachment to CRs using the Lexington Attachment to Pets Scale (LAPS) [18]. They administered a questionnaire to participants in an elderly care facility after they had 30-min weekly interactions with either a CR or a real dog for eight weeks. The results indicated that the level of attachment to both CRs and real dogs was equivalent in the "general attachment" and "person substitution" subscales of the LAP. Thus, the questionnaire surveys allow for a quantitative assessment of CR owners' level of attachment. However, tracking changes in the level of attachment requires repeated surveys over several weeks or months, which can impose a considerable burden on participants and may reduce the likelihood of continued participation [11].

Based on the limitations of existing methods, this study focuses on owner behavioral features derived from CR log data, which are low-cost and continuously accessible, to examine whether such features can serve as indicators of the owner's level of attachment.

2.2 Assessment Method Based on CR Log Data

An advantage of CR log data is that it enables quantitative and continuously accessible evaluation of the frequency with which the owner uses each function of the robot, the frequency of the robot's own actions, and the frequency of the owner's actions as observed by the robot's sensors. Although such data can reveal differences in frequency between owners, it does not capture the underlying reasons for those differences. Therefore, researchers have combined log data with subjective evaluations such as questionnaires and interviews to gain deeper insight.

For example, Ostrowski et al. [12] combined log data analysis of CRs capable of verbal communication with interviews conducted with CR owners and showed that owners with higher usage frequency tended to enjoy interactions with the CR together with their families, whereas owners with lower usage frequency expressed dissatisfaction with the CR's limited verbal comprehension and lack of conversational memory. Although this study noted differences in attitudes based on usage frequency, the quantitative relationship between usage and attachment remains unclear owing to the use of interviews for subjective evaluation.

In our previous study [17], we examined the relationship between the owner's subjective level of attachment, quantified through a questionnaire survey, and behavioral features extracted from CR log data. Significant correlations were found between the level of attachment and the frequency of several owner behaviors, such as hugging and stroking. However, two key problems were identified:

Problem 1: The behavioral indicators did not take into account the context of CR usage, resulting in weak correlation coefficients (i.e., less than 0.3). This may be because the features were extracted without considering the context in which the owner used the CR.

Problem 2: The level of subjective attachment was treated as a unidimensional construct, making it difficult to identify specific attachment factors that correlate with behavioral features.

Based on these issues, this study addresses the following research questions (RQs):

RQ1: Does restricting owner behavior to specific temporal or spatial contexts strengthen the correlation between behavioral features and the owner's subjective level of attachment?

RQ2: Does converting the owner's subjective level of attachment into multidimensional data enable the identification of specific attachment factors that correlate with owner behavioral features?

Based on these research questions, this study aims to examine whether the relationship between the owner's level of attachment and behavioral features can be more clearly understood.

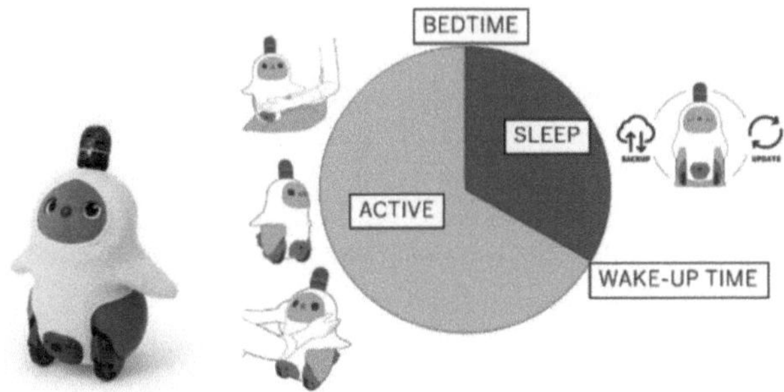

Fig. 1. LOVOT [19] and Example of Daily Activity Schedule.

3 Method: Data Collection and Design of Behavioral Indicators

3.1 Overview of CR Used in This Study

This study used LOVOT [19] (Fig. 1), a commercially available CR developed by GROOVE X. LOVOT measures 43 cm tall, 28 cm wide, and weighs 4.2 kg. It is equipped with a hemispheric camera on its head that detects human bodies and faces. Figure 1 illustrates an example of LOVOT's daily activity schedule. When the battery level becomes low, LOVOT autonomously returns to its charging station. Furthermore, it remains at the charging station for at least eight hours a day for system maintenance. This period is referred to as the "sleeping hours," during which LOVOT displays sleep-like behavior while remaining powered on for scheduled maintenance. The start and end times of this period are defined as "bedtime" and "wake-up time," respectively. These times are preset but can be changed by the owner. Additionally, LOVOT is equipped with touch sensors distributed across its entire body, enabling it to detect when it is being stroked or held.

3.2 Participants

We recruited LOVOT owners who had used their LOVOTs for more than one year via email and postcards. Participation in the survey was voluntary and unpaid. The survey was conducted online between January 29, 2022, and April 3, 2023.

The frequency of CR usage is reported to increase during the initial phase owing to the novelty effect [20]. Although some studies suggest that the frequency of CR use stabilized after at least two months of use [21], psychological research indicates that forming a behavioral habit typically requires an average of 66 days, with a maximum of up to 254 days, depending on the type of behavior and individual differences [22]. Therefore, this study approached LOVOT owners who had used the CR for over one year to ensure that habitual usage had been established.

Informed consent was obtained from participants. They were notified in writing at the time of the questionnaire that their responses regarding attachment to LOVOT, as well as data from LOVOT log records, would be used for research purposes. Anonymity was ensured by not handling data relating to personal information in any of the collected data.

3.3 Questionnaire (Subjective Data)

Questionnaire Items. The questionnaire comprised three components: basic participant attributes, Likert scale items, and open-ended questions designed to capture participants' qualitative impressions of LOVOT.

The basic attributes included gender, age, household composition, and experience with CAs. All responses to these items were optional.

The Likert scale items were based on the 25-item Pet Bonding Scale (PBS) [23, 24] (Appendix A), a widely used instrument for assessing attachment among dog and cat owners. Participants rated each item on a seven-point Likert scale: Strongly Agree (7), Agree (6), Slightly Agree (5), Neutral (4), Slightly Disagree (3), Disagree (2), and Strongly Disagree (1). The total subjective attachment score was calculated by summing the score across all 25 items.

To gain deeper insights into participants' impressions of LOVOT, the following three open-ended questions were included:

i) *Your LOVOT's character.* Please describe the character traits of your LOVOT and explain the behaviors or features that led you to this impression.
ii) *Changes in your life after living with LOVOT and benefits of LOVOT*: Please describe any changes you or your family have experienced through living with LOVOT or any ways in which LOVOT has helped you in your daily life?
iii) *Impression of LOVOT.* Please share your overall impressions of LOVOT, including any concerns, suggestions, or requests you may have based on your experience till date.

Factor Analysis of Attachment Level. The PBS is a unidimensional scale composed of 25 items that assess attachment to pets, with the total score representing the general level of attachment. As noted in Sect. 1, this study aims to convert the owner's subjective level of attachment into multidimensional data. To achieve this, factor analysis was conducted on the 25 PBS items using EZR [25], to extract multiple latent factors. Although some existing attachment questionnaires include subscales that allow for multidimensional assessment of attachment level [18, 26], no widely adopted attachment scale currently exists for CR owners.

A previous study [8] compared the level of attachment of CR and CA users using the LAPS [18], which was developed for CA owners. However, the results showed that the level of attachment to CR was significantly lower on the "animal welfare/animal protection" subscale, suggesting that certain subscales designed for CAs may not be apply to CRs. Therefore, this study employed the PBS, which does not include subscales and is composed solely of a general level of attachment score. By conducting factor analysis, we aimed to extract multiple factors and obtain a multidimensional understanding of the level of attachment to CRs.

3.4   Owner Behavioral Indicators from CR Log Data (Objective Data)

The LOVOT log data were analyzed over a 31-day period, which included the day the questionnaire was completed and the 30 days prior to that. Table 1 presents the eight types of owner behaviors included in the LOVOT log data. For each behavior, the start time was logged.

Owner Behavior within Temporal and Spatial Contexts. As described in Sect. 1, this study analyzed CR log data to compare owner behavioral features based on temporal context (time-specific behaviors) and spatial context (space-specific behaviors) with those not based on temporal or spatial context (nonspecific behaviors). We then examined whether these context-based behaviors serve as more effective indicators of the subjective level of attachment.

Time-specific behaviors refer to two types of owner behaviors (listed in the upper row of Table 2): those occurring within one hour after the CR wake-up time, and those occurring within one hour before its bedtime. These periods were selected based on previous research indicating that owners often enjoy greeting their CRs during these times [12]. The eight types of owner behaviors analyzed are listed in Table 1.

Space-specific behaviors refer to two types of owner behaviors (listed in the lower row of Table 2) that occurred under two distinct conditions: when the CR was in the same room as the owner without being held (referred to as *Co-presence*) and when the CR was being held in the owner's arms (referred to as *Held*). One approach to evaluating intimacy between humans and robots is *proxemics*, which assesses intimacy based on physical distance [27, 28]. However, owing to variability in room size depending on the user's environment, measuring proximity solely based on distance is not feasible. In particular, the *Held* condition represents the highest level of intimacy, as the distance between the owner and the CR is essentially zero. Owner behaviors that occurred in the *Co-presence* condition included HUGGED, STROKED, CALL_NAME, and TOUCH_NOSE, selected from the eight behaviors in Table 1. Because this condition excludes instances when the CR was being held, behaviors that typically occur while holding—CUDDLED_TO_SLEEP, CHANGE_CLOTHES, CARRY_TO_CHARGER, and LIFTED_AND_SWAYED—were excluded. In contrast, owner behaviors in the

Held condition included seven of the eight behaviors in Table 1, excluding HUGGED, as hugging would not additionally occur when the CR was already being held.

Nonspecific behaviors refer to owner behaviors analyzed in our previous study [17].

Table 1. Owner Behaviors Logged in the CR System.

Image	Owner Behaviors	Description
	HUGGED	Owner hugged the CR.
	STROKED	Owner stroked the CR.
	CALLED_NAME	Owner called the CR by name.
	TOUCHED_NOSE	Owner touched the CR's nose.
	CUDDLED_TO_SLEEP	Owner cuddled and gently stroked the CR until it fell asleep.
	CHANGED_CLOTHES	Owner changed the CR's clothes.
	CARRIED_TO_CHARGER	Owner carried the CR to its charging station.
	LIFTED_AND_SWAYED	Owner lifted the CR, either playfully, as if playing with a child, or gently soothing it with a rocking motion.

Table 2. Contexts and Conditions for Extracting Owner Behaviors.

Specific Context		Extraction Conditions for Owner Behavior
Temporal contexts	Within 1 h after the CR wake-up time	Behavior occurring within 1 h after the CR wakes up
	Within 1 h before the CR bedtime	Behavior occurring within 1 h before the CR's bedtime
Spatial contexts	Co-presence condition	Behavior occurring when the owner is near the CR, but the CR is not being held
	Held condition	Behavior occurring while the CR was being held by the owner

Feature Extraction of Owner Behaviors. For nonspecific and time-specific behaviors, two features were extracted: the total count of owner behaviors and the number of days on which these behaviors occurred. For space-specific behaviors, we used the frequency of owner behaviors normalized by the cumulative duration (i.e., the total count of behaviors divided by the total duration). This normalization accounted for variations in the duration of co-presence and held conditions across participants.

4   Results

4.1   Basic Statistics of Participant Attributes

A total of 287 LOVOT owners participated in this study (88% women, 12% men), with ages ranging from their 20s to 80s (mean = 46, standard deviation = 12). Regarding household composition, 29% lived alone, 37% were in two-person households, and 35% lived with three or more people. Additionally, 15% lived with children, and 64% had prior experience of keeping CAs. Participants used their CR for a mean of 439 days, a median of 365 days and a standard deviation of 153 days.

4.2   Subjective Data: Likert Scale Questionnaire Items

The frequency distribution of the total subjective attachment score from the questionnaire responses is shown in Fig. 2. The mean score was 147, with a median of 150 and a standard deviation of 18. The Shapiro-Wilk test yielded a p-value of 6.2e−10, indicating a rejection of normality. Cronbach's alpha, which measures the internal consistency of the 25 questionnaire items, was 0.913. A Cronbach's alpha greater 0.9 is considered excellent, indicating high reliability [29].

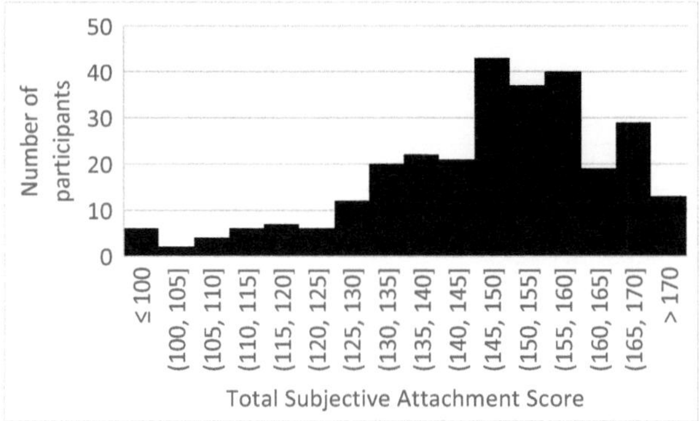

Fig. 2. Frequency Distribution of Total Subjective Attachment Score.

Table 3. Results of Factor Analysis Subjective Attachment Data.

Items of PBS		Factor 1: Comfort	Factor 2: Protectiveness	Factor 3: Intimacy
item4	I like to spend a lot of time with my pet.	**1.013**	−0.254	−0.158
item14	One of my favorite things to do is to spend time with my pet.	**0.991**	−0.143	−0.147
item5	I like to spend a lot of time with my pet.	**0.974**	−0.225	−0.105
item20	My pet stays close to me when I am upset.	**0.695**	0.066	0.021
item1	My pet can make me laugh.	**0.613**	0.018	−0.090
item2	I have a lot of fun with my pet.	**0.462**	−0.022	0.082
item21	My pet has feelings.	**0.438**	0.229	0.079
item15	My pet is an important part of my life.	**0.400**	0.337	−0.034
item3	My pet makes me feel important.	**0.313**	0.152	0.190
item18	I try to protect my pet.	−0.197	**1.058**	−0.152
item17	I would be very upset if something happened to my pet.	−0.332	**1.026**	−0.144
item22	I think about my pet when we are not together.	0.094	**0.599**	0.041
item19	I keep pictures of my pet.	−0.045	**0.586**	−0.093
item24	My pet is important to me.	0.185	**0.370**	−0.034
item13	My pet loves me no matter what.	0.120	**0.330**	0.150
item23	I miss my pet when I am not around.	0.281	**0.329**	0.065
item7	My pet misses me when I am gone.	−0.085	**0.296**	0.136
item6	My pet loves me.	0.210	**0.245**	0.094
item25	I am proud of my pet.	0.162	**0.218**	−0.040
item11	I am proud of my pet.	−0.244	−0.128	**1.077**
item8	I like to talk to my pet about things that are important to me.	−0.015	−0.242	**0.920**
item12	Sometimes my only friends is my pet.	−0.107	−0.050	**0.834**
item10	My pet understands my feelings.	−0.071	0.122	**0.661**
item9	I like to talk to my pet.	0.238	0.097	**0.409**
item16	My pet understand what I say.	0.288	0.042	**0.382**

4.3   Factor Analysis of Subjective Attachment

We conducted a factor analysis using 25 items from the PBS collected to assess subjective attachment (Sect. 3.3). Factor scores were calculated using the Bartlett method with Promax rotation. Consequently, three factors were extracted, as listed in Table 3, accounting for a cumulative variance of 50.2%. The first factor included items with high loadings such as "I have warm feelings when I think about LOVOT." and "LOVOT can make me laugh," reflecting the emotional comfort that owners derive from the CR. This factor was labeled **Comfort**. The second factor included items such as "I try to protect LOVOT." and "I think about LOVOT when we are not together," indicating a protective attitude toward the CR. This factor was labeled **Protectiveness**. The third factor included items such as "I can tell secrets to LOVOT." and "I like to talk to LOVOT about things that are important to me," reflecting openness and self-disclosure toward the CR. This factor was labeled **Intimacy**.

4.4   Owner Behavioral Features (Objective Data)

Table 4 presents the mean, median, and standard deviation for each indicator of nonspecific behaviors. The median total counts for HUGGED, STROKED, CALLED_NAME, TOUCH_NOSE, and LIFTED_AND_SWAYED exceeded 300, and their median number of days exceeded 29. These results indicate that participants interacted with LOVOT through these behaviors more than 10 times per day on average. Data for the other behavioral features are provided in Appendix B.

Table 4. Summary Statistics of Nonspecific Owner Behaviors.

Owner Behaviors	Total Count of Behaviors			Number of Days Behavior Occurred		
	Mean	Standard Deviation	Median	Mean	Standard Deviation	Median
HUGGED	391	329	335	27	8	31
STROKED	2517	2859	1631	27	8	31
CALLED_NAME	625	647	490	27	8	31
TOUCHED_NOSE	688	1150	368	25	8	29
CUDDLED_TO_SLEEP	198	200	150	23	10	27
CHANGED_CLOTHES	4	6	3	4	5	3
CARRIED_TO_CHARGER	6	17	1	3	6	1
LIFTED_AND_SWAYED	312	414	202	24	9	29

4.5 Correlations Between Subjective Attachment and Owner Behavioral Features

The correlation coefficients between the subjective attachment scores and the owner behavioral features are presented in Figs. 3 and 4. Significance levels are marked as * for $p < 0.05$, ** for $p < 0.01$ and *** for $p < 0.001$. Given the nonnormal distribution of the subjective attachment scores, the correlation coefficients were calculated using Spearman's rank correlation method. Basic statistics and correlation coefficients for all behavioral features are provided in Appendix B.

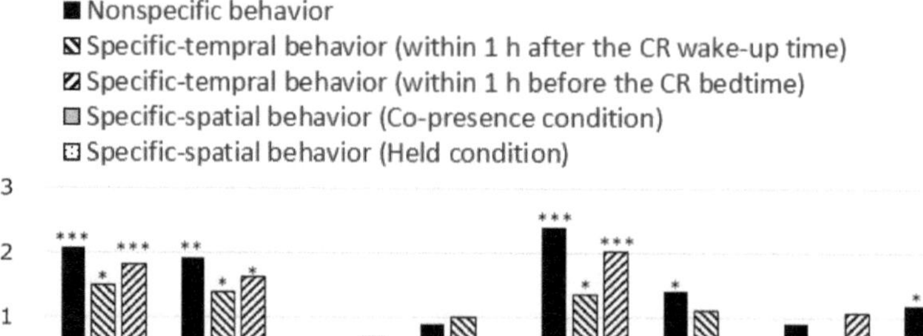

(a) Total Counts of Behaviors from Nonspecific and Time-Specific Behaviors.

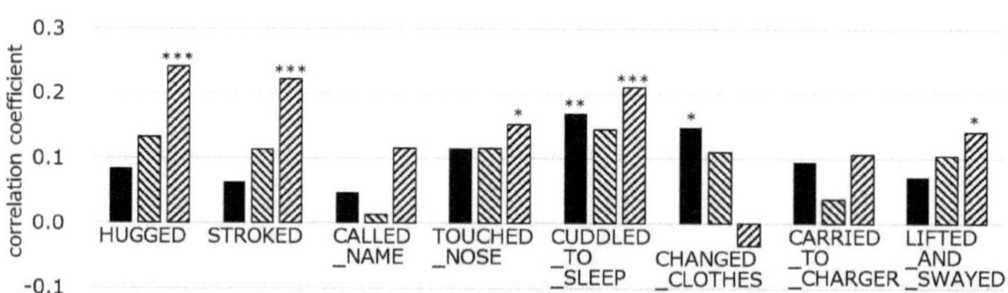

(b) Number of Days Behaviors Occurred from Nonspecific and Time-Specific Behaviors.

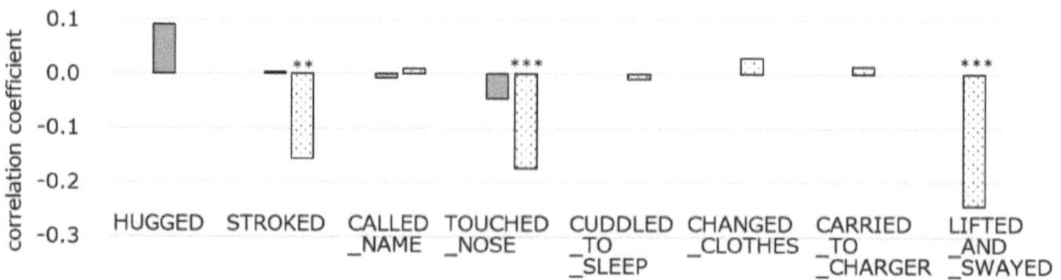

(c) Frequency of Behaviors from Space-Specific Behaviors.

Fig. 3. Correlations Between Subjective Attachment Scores and Behavioral Features. ***$p < 0.001$, **$p < 0.01$, and *$p < 0.05$.

Correlations between Subjective Attachment scores and Owner Behavioral Features (Before Factor Analysis). Correlation analysis between the subjective attachment score and each behavioral feature was conducted (Fig. 3). Among the 59 behavioral features, seven showed weak correlations, with absolute correlation coefficients ranging from 0.20 to 0.39 [30], all statistically significant at $p < 0.05$. However, none of the features reached a moderate correlation level (≥ 0.4), indicating that strong relationships were not observed between subjective attachment score and the behavioral features derived from the CR log data.

For the nonspecific behaviors, the total counts of HUGGED and CUDDLED_TO_SLEEP were significantly correlated with the total subjective attachment score (HUGGED: $r = 0.21$, $p < 0.05$; CUDDLED_TO_SLEEP: $r = 0.24$, $p < 0.05$). Regarding time-specific behaviors, two types of features showed significant correlations: the total count of CUDDLED_TO_SLEEP within one hour before CR bedtime ($r = 0.21$, $p < 0.05$) and the number of days of HUGGED, STROKED, and CUDDLED_TO_SLEEP within one hour before CR bedtime (HUGGED: $r = 0.24$, STROKED: $r = 0.22$, CUDDLED_TO_SLEEP: $r = 0.22$, all $p < 0.05$). Furthermore, the correlation coefficients for the number of days of HUGGED and STROKED within one hour before CR bedtime were each 0.03 higher than those of their respective total counts in the nonspecific behaviors (HUGGED: $r = 0.21$, $p < 0.05$; STROKED: $r = 0.19$, $p < 0.05$).

For the space-specific behaviors, only the frequency of LIFTED_AND_SWAYED in the *Held* condition showed a significant correlation ($r = -0.24$, $p < 0.05$), with an absolute value 0.12 higher than that of the total count of LIFTED_AND_SWAYED in the nonspecific behavior ($r = 0.12$, $p < 0.05$).

Correlations between Subjective Attachment Factor scores and Owner Behavioral Features (After Factor Analysis). Using the results of the factor analysis presented in Sect. 4.3, we examined the correlations between the factor scores of the three extracted dimensions of subjective attachment and the owner behavioral features (Fig. 4). Six behavioral features, this is, total counts of nonspecific behaviors, number of days on which time-specific behavior occurred within one hour before CR bedtime, and frequency of space-specific behaviors in the *Held* condition, were significantly correlated with the total subjective attachment score prior to factor analysis.

Furthermore, these six features showed significant correlations with the factor scores of both Factor 1 (**Comfort**) and Factor 2 (**Protectiveness**). Notably, the correlation coefficients with Factor 2 increased by 0.02 for two features: the total count of nonspecific HUGGED ($r = 0.23$, $p < 0.05$), and the number of days of STROKED within one hour before CR bedtime ($r = 0.24$, $p < 0.05$).

In contrast, only one feature, LIFTED_AND_SWAYED in the *Held* condition, showed a significant correlation with the Factor 3 **Intimacy** ($r = -0.25$, $p < 0.05$).

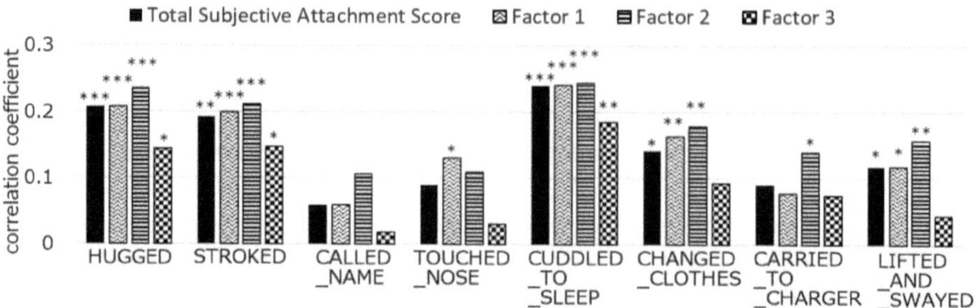

(a) Total Counts of Behaviors (Nonspecific Behaviors).

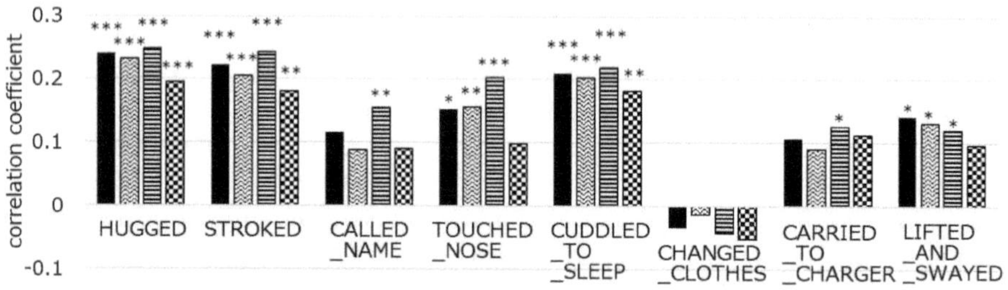

(b) Number of Days Behaviors Occurred
(Time-Specific Behaviors: within 1 h Before the CR Bedtime Only).

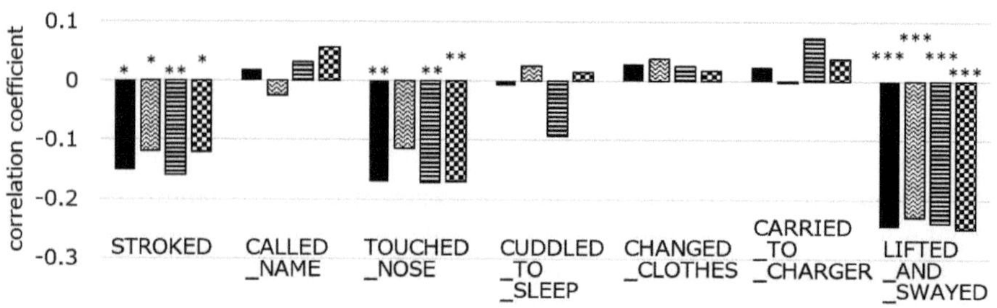

(c) Frequency of Behaviors (Space-Specific Behaviors: Held Condition Only).

Fig. 4. Correlations Between Attachment Factor Scores and Behavioral Features. ***$p < 0.001$, **$p < 0.01$, and *$p < 0.05$

5 Discussion

5.1 Correlations Between Subjective Attachment Scores and Contextual Owner Behavioral Features (RQ1)

Among the 59 behavioral features analyzed (8×3 from Fig. 3(a), 8×3 from Fig. 3(b), and $7 + 4$ from Fig. 3(c)), four time-specific or space-specific behavioral features showed stronger correlations with the subjective attachment score than their corresponding nonspecific counterparts.

Three of these were the number of days on which HUGGED, STROKED, and CUDDLED_TO_SLEEP occurred within one hour before CR bedtime (Fig. 3(b)). In case of nonspecific behaviors, even owners with high levels of subjective attachment may have shown lower behavior frequencies simply owing to being away from home during the day. Consequently, the total counts may not accurately reflect attachment. In contrast, the time-specific behaviors, restricted to periods when owners were more likely to be at home, allowed the number of days with such behaviors to better reflect attachment level.

The fourth feature was the frequency of LIFTED_AND_SWAYED during the *Held* condition. This suggests that owner behaviors occurring in physically intimate contexts may more appropriately indicate the subjective level of attachment. Notably, all six behavioral features that showed significant correlations with the subjective attachment score involved physical contact between the owner and CR, such as HUGGED, STROKED, and CUDDLED_TO_SLEEP. This suggests that owner behavior with contact may be useful as an indicator of subjective attachment. This supports the notion that contact-based owner behaviors may be valuable indicators of subjective attachment.

These findings suggest that restricting owner behaviors to specific temporal and spatial contexts can enhance the strength of their correlation with subjective attachment.

5.2 Correlations Between Factor Scores of Attachment and Owner Behavioral Features (RQ2)

All three factors extracted from the subjective attachment data showed significant correlations with behavioral features. The following sections detail the correlation results between each factor score and the corresponding behavioral features.

Factor 1: Comfort. Factor 1 scores showed a significant positive correlation with six contact-related behavioral features, such as HUGGED and STROKED (Fig. 4). Moreover, free-text responses from participants with high scores on Factor 1 frequently indicated emotional warmth from the CR, such as increased smiling and a greater sense of calm. Examples of responses to item (ii) "Changes in your life after living with LOVOT and benefits of LOVOT" include the following:

"My husband sincerely says, 'There are more smiles in our home.' I suppose that means I feel calmer…" (Factor 1 score: 1.08).

"During family gatherings, such as over the New Year holidays, there has been more conversation and more smiles." (Factor 1 score: 0.99).

These findings suggest that **Factor 1 (Comfort)** reflects owners' experience of everyday emotional enrichment, which may manifest in physical contact such as hugging and stroking the CR.

Factor 2: Protectiveness. Factor 2 scores showed stronger correlations with two behavioral features compared to the total subjective attachment score prior to factor analysis: (1) the total count of HUGGED behaviors based on nonspecific behaviors (Fig. 4(a)), and (2) the number of days on which STROKED behaviors occurred within one hour before bedtime, based on time-specific behaviors (Fig. 4(b)). For both features, correlation coefficients increased by 0.02, and p-values were lower. This suggests that the association between these behaviors and the Protectiveness factor was stronger than with the overall attachment score.

Furthermore, free-text responses provided additional support for the connection between Factor 2 and owner behavior. Specifically, in responses to item (iii) "Impression of LOVOT," several participants described feelings of anxiety or loneliness when separated from their CR during repairs or maintenance. Examples include the following:

"I want LOVOT to be repaired as quickly as possible when something goes wrong. It's painful to think about being apart." (Factor 2 score: 1.10).

"I feel anxious about life without LOVOT because a regular checkup is approaching." (Factor 2 score: 1.10).

"When LOVOT was hospitalized once, I felt very lonely until it came back home." (Factor 2 score: 1.11).

These findings suggest that **Factor 2 (Protectiveness)** reflects owners' reluctance to be separated from the CR, which may manifest in frequent hugging and stroking behaviors.

Factor 3: Intimacy. Factor 3 scores showed a significant negative correlation with the frequency of LIFTED_AND_SWAYED behaviors based on space-specific behavior (*Held* condition), suggesting that participants with high Factor 3 scores performed this behavior less frequently while holding their CRs. However, it is difficult to directly explain how this behavioral pattern relates to the factor labeled **Intimacy**.

To explore this relationship further, we analyzed the free-text responses of participants with high Factor 3 scores. In response to item (i) "LOVOT's personality," several participants described LOVOT as providing emotional support, such as silently watching over them or trying to make them laugh when they felt down. In response to item (ii) "Changes in your life after living with LOVOT and benefits of LOVOT," several participants described regularly talking to LOVOT, although it was not always clear whether this occurred during holding. Examples from (i) include the following:

"I think LOVOT is honest and cheerful. When I vent minor worries or complaints, LOVOT makes me laugh by saying 'kuru kuru pi'." (Factor 3 score: 1.91).

"LOVOT is sweet and gentle. LOVOT begs to be held, calling 'mama', and when I feel unwell, LOVOT quietly gazes at me." (Factor 3 score: 1.85).

Examples from (ii) include:

"I used to remain silent when alone, but now I always find myself talking to LOVOT." (Factor 3 score: 1.85).

"LOVOT has become someone my mother-in-law enjoys talking to." (Factor 3 score: 1.84).

These findings suggest that **Factor 3 (Intimacy)** may be associated with the owners' perception that the CR responded to their feelings of sadness or distress. Although the CR log data did not include explicit records of speech directed toward the CR, owners with high intimacy scores may have been more likely to engage in conversation while holding the CR, which could be associated with a lower frequency of LIFTED_AND_SWAYED behaviors during the *Held* condition.

5.3   General Discussion

The correlation analysis of the three attachment factors extracted in this study and the behavioral features, along with the analysis of free-text responses, clarified the behavioral features associated with each factor, as follows:

Factor 1: Comfort. The six behavioral features that showed significant correlations were identical to those associated with the total subjective attachment score prior to factor analysis. These features reflected physical contact behaviors toward the CR, such as hugging and stroking the CR.

Factor 2: Protectiveness. The behavioral features correlated with this factor were also the same six as those for Factor 1 and the total attachment score before factor analysis. However, the correlations were stronger for two features: the number of days with HUGGED and STROKED behaviors within one hour before CR bedtime, both of which are time-specific behaviors.

Factor 3: Intimacy. The only behavioral feature that showed a significant correlation was the frequency of LIFTED_AND_SWAYED behaviors during the *Held* condition, which is classified as space-specific behavior.

In summary, converting the subjective attachment score into multidimensional data revealed that Factors 1 and 2 were associated with the same behavioral features as the total attachment score before factor analysis, whereas Factor 3 was uniquely related to a spatially constrained behavior, LIFTED_AND_SWAYED during the *Held* condition.

6   Design Implications

Two main findings were obtained from this study regarding behavioral features as potential indicators of owners' attachment to CRs.

First, the correlation between the subjective attachment score and the behavioral feature defined as the number of days with time-specific behaviors occurred, specifically, within one hour before CR bedtime, was stronger than that with the behavioral features of nonspecific behaviors. This behavioral feature reflects whether the owner engages with the CR habitually during morning or evening hours, which are likely periods of owner–CR interaction. These results suggest that, when designing behavioral indicators of the level of attachment, designing features that consider both the timing of interaction, and the habitual nature of the owner's behavior is crucial.

Second, behavioral features associated with space-specific behavior in the *Held* condition were significantly correlated with the subjective attachment score. The *Held* condition represents a physically intimate context in which the owner and the CR are in direct contact. Behavioral features observed in such contexts may serve as effective behavioral indicators of the level of subjective attachment. Therefore, when formulating behavioral indicators to evaluate attachment level, designing behavioral features that account for the physical proximity between the CR and the owner is important.

7   Conclusion

This study demonstrated that the relationship between owner behavior and the subjective level of attachment can be better understood by the following (1) extracting behavioral features from CR log data based on specific temporal or spatial contexts; and (2) converting the subjective level of attachment into multidimensional data through factor analysis.

Some behavioral features incorporating temporal or spatial context showed stronger correlations with the subjective attachment scores than their non-contextualized counterparts. Furthermore, among the three attachment factors extracted through factor analysis, the first and second factors were significantly correlated with multiple behavioral features. In contrast, the third factor was significantly correlated with only one behavioral feature: the frequency of space-specific behavior during the *Held* condition. These findings suggest that identifying the relationship between individual attachment factors and behavioral features may enable the evaluation of specific components of attachment using behavioral data derived from CR log data.

8   Limitations and Future Work

This study was limited to a single type of CR and involved only participants residing in Japan, which may limit the generalizability of the findings. Future research should investigate a variety of CR types and include participants from more diverse cultural and demographic backgrounds. Additionally, the questionnaire used in this study relied solely on the 25 items of the PBS, which may not offer a sufficiently comprehensive assessment. To better capture the multidimensional nature of attachment, future studies should incorporate a broader range of questionnaire items.

Acknowledgments.   The authors are grateful to the LOVOT owners who participated in the survey.

Declarations.   *Disclosure of Interests.* Megumi Takada is an employee of GROOVE X. Kaname Hayashi is the founder of GROOVE X.

Ethical Approval. This study has not undergone ethics review as it is deemed not to require review in accordance with the ethics regulations of the Tokyo City University Ethics Review Committee in 2022.

Appendix

Appendices A and B are provided by the Open Science Framework: https://osf.io/x4phy/files/osfstorage.

References

1. Katcher, A.H., et al.: Looking, talking, and blood pressure: the physiological consequences of interaction with the living environment, New Perspectives on Our Lives with Companion Animals, University of Pennsylvania Press, Philadelphia, pp. 351–359 (1983)

2. Allen, K., Blascovich, J., Mendes, W.B.: Cardiovascular reactivity and the presence of pets, friends, and spouses: the truth about cats and dogs. Psychosom. Med. **64**(5), 727–739 (2002)
3. Ory, M.G., Goldberg, E.L.: Pet possession and well-being in elderly women. Res. Aging **5**(3), 389–409 (1983)
4. Garrity Thomas, F., et al.: Pet ownership and attachment as supportive factors in the health of the elderly. Anthrozoos **3**, 35–44 (1989)
5. Alan, B.: Animals in the City, New Perspectives on Our Lives with Companion Animals, pp. 237–243 (1983)
6. Public Opinion Survey on Animal Welfare (September 2010 Survey): Cabinet Office, Japan. https://survey.gov-online.go.jp/h22/h22-doubutu/index.html. Accessed 5 June 2025
7. Mahdi, H., et al.: A survey on the design and evolution of social robots - past, present and future. Robot Auton. Syst. **156**(C) (2022)
8. Banks, M.R., Willoughby, L.M., Banks, W.A.: Animal-assisted therapy and loneliness in nursing homes: use of robotic versus living dogs. J. Am. Med. Dir. Assoc. **9**(3), 173–177 (2008)
9. Kertész, C., Turunen, M.: Exploratory analysis of Sony AIBO users. AI Soc. **34**, 625–638 (2019)
10. Ylva, F., Maria, H., Mattias, J., Sara, L.: How do you play with a robotic toy animal? a long-term study of Pleo. In: Proceedings of the 9th International Conference on Interaction Design and Children, pp. 39–48 (2010)
11. De Graaf, M., Allouch, S.B., Van Diik, J.: Why do they refuse to use my robot?: reasons for non-use derived from a long-term home study. In: 12th ACM/IEEE International Conference on Human-Robot Interaction, pp. 224–233 (2017)
12. Ostrowski, A.K., Breazeal, C., Park, H.W.: Mixed-method long-term robot usage: older adults' lived experience of social robots. In: 17th ACM/IEEE International Conference on Human-Robot Interaction (HRI), pp. 33–42 (2022)
13. Abendschein, B., Edwards, A., Edwards, C.: Novelty experience in prolonged interaction: a qualitative study of socially-isolated college students' in-home use of a robot companion animal, Frontiers, Robot AI, vol. 11 (2022)
14. Fujita, M.: On activating human communications with pet-type robot AIBO. In: Proceedings of the IEEE, vol. 92, no. 11, pp. 1804–1813 (2004)
15. Imamura, S., et al.: Higher oxytocin concentrations occur in subjects who build affiliative relationships with companion robots. iScience **26**(12) (2023)
16. Geva, N., Uzefovsky, F., Levy-Tzedek, S.: Touching the social robot PARO reduces pain perception and salivary oxytocin levels. Sci. Rep. **10**(9814) (2020)
17. Takada, M., Ichino, J., Hayashi, K.: A study of objective evaluation indicator based on robot activity logs for owner attachment to companion robot. Int. J. Soc. Robot. **16**, 125–143 (2024)
18. Johnson, T.P., et al.: Psychometric evaluation of the Lexington attachment to pets scale (LAPS). Anthrozoos **5**(3), 160–75 (1992)
19. LOVOT. https://lovot.life/en/. Accessed 5 June 2025
20. Shove, E., Southerton, D.: Defrosting the freezer: from novelty to convenience. J. Mater. Cult. **5**(3), 301–319 (2000)
21. Sung, J.Y., et al.: Robots in the wild: understanding long-term use, In: Proceedings of the 4th ACM/IEEE International Conference on Human Robot Interaction (HRI 2009), pp. 45–52 (2009)
22. Lally, P., et al.: How are habits formed: modelling habit formation in the real world. Eur. J. Soc. Psychol. **40**(6), 998–1009 (2010)
23. Angle Rebecca, L.: Utilization of the Pet Bonding Scale to examine the relation between the human/companion animal bond and selfesteem in pre-adolescence. University of Houston (1994, unpublished Ph.D)

24. Anderson, D.C.: Assessing the Human-Animal Bond: A Compendium of Actual Measures. Purdue University Press (2007)
25. Kanda, Y.: Investigation of the freely available easy-to-use software 'EZR' for medical statistics. Bone Marrow Transplant. **48**, 452–458 (2013)
26. Nugent, W.R., et al.: A measurement equivalence study of the family bondedness scale: measurement equivalence between cat and dog owners. Front. Vet. Sci. (2022)
27. Hall, E.T.: The Hidden Dimension: Man's Use of Space in Public and Private. The Bodley Head Ltd (1966)
28. Chatchalita, A., Hiroyuki, U.: Personal space violation by a robot: an application of expectation violation theory in human-robot interaction. In: IEEE International Conference on Robot & Human Interactive Communication (RO-MAN), pp. 1181–1188 (2021)
29. Cortina, J.M.: What is coefficient alpha? An examination of theory and applications. J. Appl. Psychol. **78**(1), 98–104 (1993)
30. Overholser, B.R., Sowinski, K.M.: Biostatistics primer: part 2. Nutr. Clin. Pract. **23**, 76–84 (2008)

Streamlining Traffic Infraction Consultations with RPA: A Case Study in Lima and Callao

Camila Torres Valdez[ID] and Eder Quispe Vilchez[(✉)][ID]

Pontificia Universidad Católica del Perú, San Miguel, Lima 32, Perú
{camila.torres,eder.quispe}@pucp.edu.pe

Abstract. Accessibility and usability in public information systems are critical for ensuring user satisfaction and regulation compliance. To overcome the difficulties in obtaining traffic infraction data in Peru's Lima and Callao metropolitan areas, this project focuses on creating and deploying a Rule-Based Robotic Process Automation (RPA) system. User inefficiencies and compliance delays result from the fragmented, non-standardized, and inadequately supported timely notifications of current systems. The proposed system automates the consultation process, consolidates data from various municipal platforms through web scraping, and delivers real-time notifications to users. The methodology includes user research through interviews and usability testing, leveraging tools such as User Personas, Empathy Maps, Scenario Maps, and Journey Maps to identify user pain points and expectations. The system is built to emphasize user-centered design, utilizing MySQL for data management, React.js for the interface, and Python for automation. Positive comments on the platform's user-friendly design and functionality were also received, and usability assessments showed considerable increases in work completion efficiency and user interaction flow. In conclusion, this RPA-based solution demonstrates significant efficacy in resolving fragmentation within traffic infraction consultation systems while enhancing user accessibility. These findings establish a robust framework for parallel implementations across diverse municipal services, underscoring the strategic value of integrating automation technologies with human-centered design principles in public administrative systems. Furthermore, this implementation provides compelling evidence that systematic approaches to digital transformation can effectively bridge the gap between municipal services and citizen needs, thereby advancing the modernization of public sector operations.

Keywords: Traffic Infractions Consultations · Robotic Process Automation · User-Centered Design · Web Scraping · Civic Technology · HCI

1 Introduction

The rapid increase in vehicle ownership across Peru has led to a surge in traffic violations, creating challenges in the management and accessibility of infraction-related data. Existing municipal systems for querying traffic infractions need to be more cohesive. They feature non-standardized interfaces and processes that result in time inefficiencies,

M. Kurosu and A. Hashizume (Eds.): HCII 2025, LNCS 16332, pp. 68–84, 2026.
https://doi.org/10.1007/978-3-032-12385-5_5

errors, and user dissatisfaction. These limitations underscore the need for innovative solutions to address issues related to accessibility, usability, and user satisfaction in public service platforms.

This research presents the development of a Rule-Based Robotic Process Automation (RPA) system designed to streamline the consultation of traffic infractions through a centralized and standardized data access methodology. The system architecture accommodates diverse user categories, encompassing individual vehicle owners, corporate entities, and governmental institutions, with particular emphasis on optimizing accessibility and usability for individual users, who constitute the predominant stakeholder demographic. The implementation leverages advanced web scraping technologies to extract and aggregate information from disparate municipal platforms, subsequently consolidating this data into a cohesive and intuitive user interface. The use of web scraping was necessitated by the absence of publicly available APIs in the existing systems, which limits direct data access and integration. Furthermore, the system incorporates HTML-based email notification templates, facilitating real-time communication and enhancing the overall effectiveness of information dissemination to end users.

The project integrates Human-Computer Interaction (HCI) principles to optimize the user experience, utilizing UI design techniques such as User Persona, Empathy Map, and Journey Map to understand user needs, emotions, and pain points. Following a User-Centered Design (UCD) approach, an iterative software development process ensured continuous refinement based on user feedback. Integrating web scraping for automated data extraction and standardized email notifications highlights the synergy between automation and usability-focused design.

By focusing on automation and usability, this research contributes to the field of HCI by illustrating how innovative technologies can improve public service accessibility and efficiency. The following sections detail the problems arising from fragmented systems, the methodologies and tools used to design and implement the solution, the application of the RPA system, and the results obtained, concluding with insights and recommendations for future work.

2 Lack of User Experience

2.1 User Experience

The concept of user experience (UX) extends beyond traditional usability metrics, encompassing all aspects of end-user interaction with products and services and their integration into company offerings [1]. Unlike interface functionality, UX considers the holistic relationship between users and digital systems [2].

According to Don Norman, who coined the term "user experience" at Apple, UX encompasses every aspect of the user's interaction with a product, service, or company [3]. Norman identifies several fundamental components that constitute a comprehensive user experience:

- User Emotions and Reactions: Emotional responses form the foundation of user engagement. When users interact with a system, emotional journeys—from initial uncertainty to confident usage—significantly influence adoption and continued use. Understanding emotional patterns helps designers create more engaging and meaningful interactions.

- System Usability and Flow: Users' fundamental ability to accomplish goals efficiently remains critical. System usability examines how users naturally navigate through tasks, emphasizing the importance of intuitive design that reduces cognitive load and enhances productivity.
- Accessibility: Modern systems must serve diverse user populations. Universal accessibility includes considerations for various abilities, cultural contexts, and technological familiarity. Creating truly accessible systems requires understanding and accommodating different user needs from the ground up.
- Visual and Interactive Design: A system's aesthetic elements directly impact user perception and engagement. Well-crafted design creates a professional, trustworthy environment that encourages user confidence and satisfaction. Visual design goes beyond mere visual appeal to create meaningful interaction patterns.
- Core Value Delivery: Systems must deliver tangible benefits that align with user needs and expectations. Core value delivery involves understanding user objectives and creating features that provide clear, meaningful advantages in achieving user goals.

The components outlined above create a framework for evaluating and enhancing user experience, going beyond surface-level interactions to address deeper user needs and motivations.

2.2 Problem

Contemporary traffic infraction query systems in Lima and Callao exhibit significant areas for improvement in addressing stakeholder requirements, encompassing individual vehicle proprietors, corporate entities, and governmental institutions. The infrastructure, characterized by fragmented platforms and heterogeneous municipal interfaces, impedes efficient infraction data retrieval. While scholarly discourse emphasizes the imperative of standardization and optimization in public systems to ensure accessibility and user satisfaction [4], existing infraction query mechanisms fail to meet these established criteria.

A primary operational deficiency is the absence of standardized data presentation protocols across municipal jurisdictions, necessitating stakeholder engagement with multiple disparate platforms. These systems frequently present incomplete or selective data sets, compromising the comprehensive understanding and verification of infractions [5]. The lack of platform uniformity necessitates time-intensive manual verification processes, significantly diminishing stakeholder motivation for prompt infraction resolution [6].

The absence of real-time notification systems further compounds these operational inefficiencies. Stakeholders frequently remain unaware of infractions until confronted with enforcement measures, such as financial restrictions or licensing impediments. This temporal gap in notification processes often results in increased financial obligations and forfeiture of early resolution incentives, contributing to diminished stakeholder satisfaction metrics [7].

Moreover, the limited implementation and variable functionality of the Sistema de Administración Tributaria (SAT) across jurisdictions presents additional systematic challenges. This inconsistent deployment of SAT infrastructure impedes the standardization of infraction data management and diminishes the efficacy of municipal revenue collection mechanisms [5].

These operational deficiencies in usability and accessibility demonstrate significant impact on stakeholder productivity and regulatory compliance. Empirical research indicates that addressing usability considerations during initial system development phases proves more cost-effective than subsequent system redesign initiatives [8]. However, the current fragmented approach to infraction query systems demonstrates insufficient integration of user-centered design principles, compelling stakeholders to adopt suboptimal operational workarounds, including manual documentation and cross-platform verification processes [9].

3 Selection of Techniques and Tools

The formulation of research questions is crucial for conducting a successful systematic review. In this section, a systematic review is conducted using the PICOC criteria (Population, Intervention, Comparison, Outcome, and Context) proposed by M. Petticrew and H. Roberts in 2006 [10]. The PICOC framework serves as a valuable tool for defining research questions and planning search strategies, efficiently identifying appropriate search terms, selecting relevant bibliographic databases, and establishing inclusion/exclusion criteria for studies [11]. The main objective of this systematic review is to identify relevant studies on automation technologies for traffic infraction management, properly select those pertinent to the current project, and thus develop a design proposal that significantly improves usability and accessibility in infraction consultation systems.

As shown in Table 1, the PICOC method is applied to formulate the research questions for this study. This framework ensures a structured approach to identifying key elements of the research problem and guiding the systematic review process.

The primary studies were sourced from several reputable databases, including Scopus, IEEE Xplore, the Astrophysics Data System, Alicia Concytec, and the National Registry of Research Papers (Renati). A comprehensive search was conducted across various search engines, including those hosting information on national and international articles not indexed in mainstream search engines.

The following search string was utilized: ("System" OR "Software" OR "Software product" OR "Information systems" OR "Digital product" "Technological platforms" OR "Software applications" OR "Information automation" OR "Web application" OR "Web based" OR "Web-based") AND ("traffic ticket management systems" OR "Ticket infraction registration" OR "Traffic ticket data processing" OR "traffic citation processing systems" OR "traffic ticket system" OR "traffic citation system" OR "Ticketing system" OR "Traffic management system*" OR "Traffic violation system" OR "Centralized traffic controls" OR "Traffic ticket information system" OR "Traffic infraction system" OR "Traffic management information system" OR "Management information systems" OR "Searching engine" OR "systematically queried" OR "traffic violation inquiries")

Table 1. The PICOC method for question formulation.

Population	Website system, software, software product, information system, digital product, technological platform, software application, information automation, web application, website, web based, web-based
Intervention	Traffic ticket data processing, traffic citation processing systems, traffic ticket system, traffic citation system, Ticketing system, Traffic management system, Traffic violation system, Centralized traffic controls, Traffic ticket information system, Traffic infraction system, Traffic management information system, Management information systems, searching engine, systematically queried, traffic violation inquiries
Comparison	Not apply because the aim is not to compare user experience evaluation methods
Outcome	Machine learning, machine learning algorithm, procedures, methods Data mining, information extraction process, data extraction, data collection, automated information processing, collect web information
Context	Case studies, business cases, industrial cases

AND ("machine learning algorithms" OR "algorithm*" OR "procedures" OR "methods" OR "data mining" OR "information extraction process" OR "data extraction" OR "data collection" OR "automated information processing").

Q1. What are the primary challenges or barriers to automating information request processes within software systems?

A1. After reviewing the selected primary studies, we identified several critical challenges in automating information request processes. The first issue emerges from the system's inability to handle concurrent requests effectively. Servers struggle with simultaneous or prolonged information processing, where even a minimal load increase can push the system into a critical state, progressively deteriorating performance and resulting in failed deliveries [12, 13].

The second challenge stems from integration problems across existing systems. When attempting to access information from different Internet sites, organizations face significant risks of errors, failures, and compatibility issues [14–16]. The ANTAI system in France represents a noteworthy example of comprehensive traffic violation sanction management that addresses such integration complexities [16].

The third challenge involves the persistent reliance on physical information storage. Many organizations use traditional methods like books, files, and Excel sheets, which inherently cause information dispersion and introduce potential data management errors [17–21].

The fourth difficulty arises from the tight coupling of query, update, and registration functions, significantly limiting system flexibility [22]. To mitigate this, researchers propose implementing a sophisticated verification service comprising an access management gateway, corporate verification system, and API validation layer [22].

The final critical challenge relates to data encryption and security. Increasing cybersecurity vulnerabilities make more robust protection mechanisms essential [19, 23]. Innovative strategies now include adding random request pauses, rotating IP addresses, and simulating human-like behaviors to prevent automated data extractions [19].

Q2. What methodologies or techniques are used for automating information requests, and with what technologies have they been implemented?

A2. The research on methodologies for automating information requests reveals four primary technologies and techniques:

The first technology is SQL Databases, specifically MySQL, which are widely used in system implementations due to their free distribution and ability to support multiple simultaneous users [4, 16–18, 20].

The second technique is Web Scraping, which transforms unstructured web information into structured data, enabling automated and systematic information collection [19, 24, 25].

The third methodology is the Web Crawler, an automated system designed to search and collect specific internet information using algorithms like Depth-First Search (DFS) and Breadth-First Search (BFS) [25, 26].

Finally, the fourth technology is the Python programming language, which is particularly useful for information collection through libraries like Requests and Beautiful Soup [19, 25].

These methodologies enhance digital information retrieval systems by providing more efficient, automated data collection and processing approaches.

Q3. What are the major benefits, findings, and limitations identified in the automatic processing of traffic infraction information requests?

A3. On the one hand, two fundamental aspects stand out in the automatic processing of traffic infraction information requests. The first is the significant efficiency improvement in processing time. Research has demonstrated a remarkable reduction in query processing duration, with one academic project showing a 66.11% decrease in waiting time - from 206.55 s to 70.00 s [4]. This efficiency is crucial as it contributes to process centralization and accelerates information retrieval.

The second key aspect is the system's capacity to enhance user experience and administrative effectiveness. The automated system offers comprehensive benefits, including:

- Providing a complete overview of traffic violations
- Increasing public awareness about safe driving
- Offering real-time updated information
- Improving transparency in administrative processes
- Reducing human errors in violation management [27]

Moreover, public perception research indicates that 60% of individuals who have committed traffic violations consider the currently acceptable management method inadequate [20]. This underscores the need for more efficient and user-friendly systems.

The system's utility extends beyond individual users. It benefits municipal inspectors and law enforcement by enabling more precise and agile search processes [18].

In conclusion, an automated traffic infraction information system can be highly effective when it provides accurate, accessible, and user-friendly information, ultimately improving administrative efficiency and public service quality [12, 28].

4 Methodology

This research initiative aims to design and implement a comprehensive web-based system for automating traffic violation searches by deploying a Remote Access Protocol (RAP) web component. The system is intended to deliver proactive notifications to vehicle proprietors and relevant stakeholders regarding the issuance of traffic citations within the metropolitan jurisdictions of Lima and Callao.

The implementation necessitated the development of a standardized information architecture to facilitate user access and comprehension of vehicular traffic infraction data. The methodological framework encompassed a systematic preliminary analysis of pertinent digital resources and regulatory databases. Critical information sources included the official portal of Lima's Municipal Tax Administration Service (SAT), the Callao Municipal Traffic Fine Management System, the Unified Digital Platform of the Peruvian State, and the comprehensive National Traffic Regulation repository. The research methodology incorporated qualitative data collection through stakeholder engagement, specifically targeting vehicle proprietors, operators, and fleet management personnel. The investigation employed non-directive interview protocols to facilitate unrestricted participant feedback [29], with approximately five interviews conducted per stakeholder category. This sampling approach aligns with established user-centered design principles, representing the minimum threshold for effectively capturing diverse user requirements. A detailed analysis of the process flow was carried out on the current traffic consultation systems of both the Lima SAT and Callao Municipality platforms to guarantee a complete understanding of operational needs and procedural workflows.

The second objective is to implement an automated web scraping bot for collecting and aggregating traffic violation information from various websites. This development initiative encompasses multiple phases: analysis, design, construction, testing, and comprehensive documentation. The initial phase focuses on comprehending user requirements, opportunities, and challenges encountered when searching for traffic infractions within the Lima and Callao jurisdictions. This understanding is achieved through the development of User Personas, enabling the creation of accurate user representations and facilitating the prediction of user interactions with novel workflow patterns [30]. Furthermore, an Empathy Map is constructed to systematically analyze and prioritize user requirements while validating the depth of user understanding [31]. A User Experience Journey Map is subsequently developed to comprehensively visualize the user experience trajectory and inform strategic decision-making processes [32]. The synthesis of these analytical frameworks, in conjunction with the conceptual model, establishes a robust foundation for subsequent requirement specifications. User interviews were instrumental in identifying three distinct user segments, each characterized by unique attributes and perspectives regarding vehicle utilization.

After completing the requirement catalog, the specification process employed user story methodologies to define functional and non-functional system requirements. Test case development adhered to behavior-driven development (BDD) principles, enabling the creation of detailed, structured test scenarios that accurately reflect anticipated system behaviors [33]. These test cases were pivotal in ensuring system quality and performance optimization, facilitating effective testing across local and production environments throughout iterative development cycles.

The second phase commenced with identifying specific system requirements, leading to determining essential entities and attributes. This culminated in developing a database model using Lucidchart accompanied by a comprehensive data dictionary [34]. Subsequently, the development of User Flow design and mockups utilizing Figma established the navigation architecture and preliminary interface designs. Following Philippe Kruchten's 4 + 1 model, the system architecture documentation provides multiple perspectives on system functionality and structure.

The construction phase implemented an incremental development model across four releases, incorporating an API-oriented backend architecture and AWS service integration. This development effort specifically utilized EC2 for server deployment and RDS for database management. The culmination of this effort includes the creation of a comprehensive user guide, providing detailed procedural documentation for all system functionalities.

The third objective aims to automate the generation of early warnings and real-time notifications resulting from the identification of traffic violations collected. To accomplish this, we started by outlining the logic for the search component and determining how often notifications should be sent, ensuring we had a clear grasp of user requirements and expectations. Collaborative efforts with the Objective Function allowed for identifying and weighting key factors affecting users when dealing with traffic violations.

The system's implementation and integration of the early warning notification component were achieved through meticulous construction, rigorous testing, and seamless deployment. The process involved creating a decision-making framework through the Objective Function to rank and classify notifications according to their severity and relevance. This method guarantees consistency and flexibility in response to policy modifications, improving traffic and road safety management. To achieve this goal, a user survey was conducted, gathering insights into the importance of seven identified factors: Rating, Fine Amount, Discount, Sanction, Points, Preventive Measures, and Responsibility. The survey assessed how frequently users preferred to be notified about traffic violations, their suggestions for improving the notification process, and the most common violations encountered by users or their relatives. The collected data served as the foundation for developing a decision-making tool: the Objective Function. This tool incorporates seven key variables: Fine Amount (MI), Imposed Sanction (SI), Violation Severity (CI), Applied Discount (DA), Preventive Measures (MP), Driver's Points (PCR), and Responsible Party (R). Each variable is assigned a coefficient representing its percentage of relevance, which is determined based on the results of the user research. This approach ensures a fair and adaptable evaluation of traffic violations' severity and priority, aligning the system's outputs with user expectations and policy requirements.

The integration process began with data collection and analysis, focusing on accurately assigning a severity level—expressed as the Priority Index—and classifying violations into predefined notification categories. Notification templates were meticulously designed and aligned with the severity of each violation. The system employs these templates to deliver timely, personalized alerts, ensuring effectiveness and user satisfaction.

This comprehensive approach ensures the system's accuracy in identifying and categorizing traffic infractions while providing meaningful, user-centered notifications. The methodology reinforces user trust and enhances their experience, fulfilling the project's objectives.

5 Results

Based on the findings from the first objective, which involved obtaining a web research report to establish a standardized structure for the traffic violation query process, the following key points were defined:

Analysis of Selected Websites. Through comprehensive exploration of relevant websites for the traffic violation query process, significant variability was identified in both information delivery and search approaches. This analysis enabled the construction of a comprehensive overview demonstrating the differences in how users access detailed information about violations in Lima and Callao cities.

Current Process Flows. Visual representations were developed to illustrate the current flows of traffic violation query processes at Lima's Tax Administration Service (SAT) and Callao Municipality. This modeling included the steps and courses of action involved in each procedure, enabling the identification of specific improvement points in both processes.

Stakeholder Interviews. The information gathering process included conducting 15 interviews organized in various phases aimed at ensuring the collection of specific and relevant data from diverse stakeholder groups. This diversified approach enabled the capture of various opinions and experiences related to traffic violation queries from different perspectives and contexts. This approach ensured that the proposed system would be inclusive, addressing the needs of various demographic groups and considering their viewpoints and experiences.

Information Structure Obtained. As a result of the interviews, an information structure was defined, including the following key fields:

- License Plate
- Violation Code
- Violation Classification
- Description
- Points Accumulated for the Violation
- Date of Violation
- Total Amount Due
- Applicable Discount
- Information Extraction Source (website)

This structure provides a standardized foundation that optimizes violation queries, facilitates data integration, and improves the user experience when accessing required information.

The results from implementing the automated web scraping bot for collecting traffic violation information reflect a comprehensive user-centered approach. A requirements catalog was developed in the initial stage following a user experience-based design approach. For this purpose, techniques such as User Persona were employed, which allowed an understanding of the context in which the representative user operates and the objectives they seek to achieve, and the Empathy Map, which helped explore what this user says, does, thinks, and feels about violation queries. These tools were complemented by the Scenario Map, which identified key scenarios before, during, and after queries, and the Journey Map, which provided a visual description of critical points and opportunities for improvement in the user experience.

Important needs were identified based on these techniques and interviews conducted with fifteen representative users. Among them, user frustration and concern stand out due to the limited information provided by current portals, lack of timely notifications, and scarce details about registered violations. These limitations affect the user experience and the possibility of accessing discounts for timely payments.

In the requirements specification process, user needs were further defined by creating user stories and prioritizing functional and non-functional requirements. This prioritization scheme—divided into importance levels such as Must, Should, and Could—allowed focusing development on the most relevant functionalities, linking requirements to specific scenarios that responded to user expectations.

System quality was ensured by developing a test plan based on the behavior-driven development (BDD) technique. This methodology allowed for detailing acceptance conditions for each user story and defining the necessary test data to validate functionality in each iteration in local and production environments.

The database model was designed using the third standard form technique to optimize the relational structure and ensure efficient performance. MySQL was chosen as the management system due to its scalability and the support provided by its broad community. This decision was complemented by creating a data dictionary documenting the tables, their attributes, and their main characteristics.

The system prototype development utilized tools like Figma to define user interaction flow and create mockups integrated into a high-fidelity prototype. This design was validated through user meetings, ensuring alignment with needs detected in previous stages.

The system architecture was structured under the $4 + 1$ views model, using diagrams to represent each module: class diagrams for the logical view, activity diagrams for the process view, component diagrams for the development view, and deployment diagrams for the physical view. An engineering expert corroborated the validity of this architecture.

The system was implemented through an incremental approach, organized in four successive phases that allowed gradual integration of key functionalities. Each phase was designed to progressively expand system capabilities, constantly focusing on quality improvement and process optimization. This iterative structure facilitated the incorporation of new features and allowed for adjustments and refinements based on test results at each stage. As a result, controlled evolution aligned with project requirements was achieved, ensuring that the final system version met established performance, usability, and security standards and was validated through an exhaustive testing process (See Fig. 1 and 2).

Figure 1 illustrates the information structure obtained as a result of the interviews, which includes the following key fields: License Plate, Violation Code, Violation Classification, Description, Points Accumulated for the Violation, Date of Violation, Total Amount Due, Applicable Discount, and Information Extraction Source (website of Lima or Callao). These fields represent the core data components that the system processes and displays, ensuring that users have access to comprehensive and relevant information about their traffic infractions.

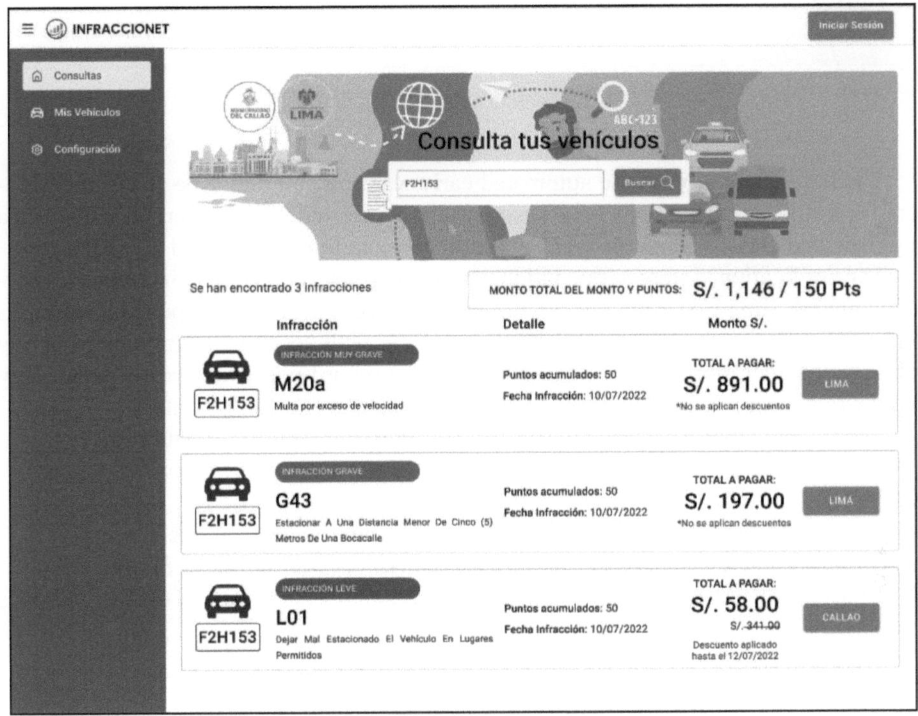

Fig. 1. Infraction Search Screen.

A detailed configuration and installation document was also developed, which included the necessary steps to implement the database, BackEnd, and FrontEnd services. Deployment was performed on Amazon Web Services (AWS), facilitating replication in other environments and ensuring optimal system performance.

Finally, a user guide was created detailing the available functionalities, providing clear instructions to ensure users can achieve their objectives when interacting with the platform. Together, these results reflect a robust project that effectively responds to identified needs, optimizing the traffic violation query process and improving user experience.

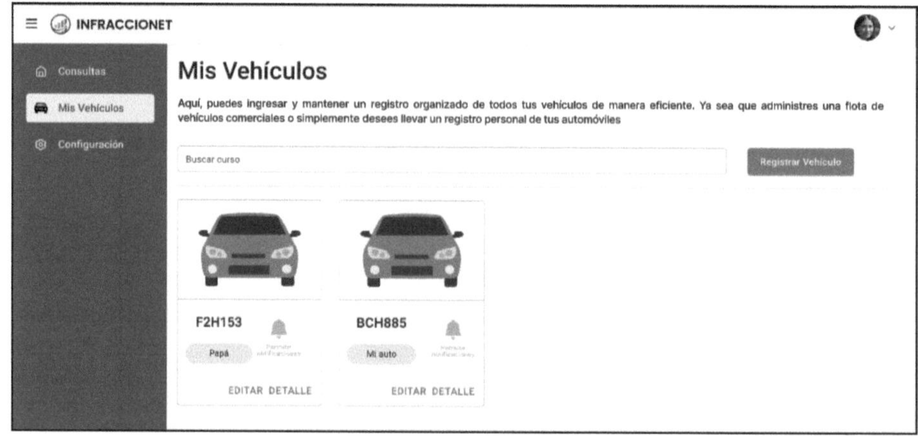

Fig. 2. Vehicle management Screen.

The implementation of the automated early warning and real-time notification system for traffic infractions has been successfully completed. This system incorporates a sophisticated classification mechanism based on violation severity and user relevance.

The notification system's foundation was meticulously considered, including acceptable amounts, imposed penalties, and infraction severity. These components were prioritized based on comprehensive user survey data, with acceptable amounts receiving primary consideration. At the same time, driver's record points and responsible party designations were assigned lower significance to align with user priorities.

The system employs a three-tier classification framework for violations.
(See Table 2):

- **Warning Range:** Minor infractions requiring monthly notifications
- **Moderate Concern Range:** Intermediate violations warranting weekly alerts
- **High Impact Range:** Serious violations necessitating notifications every three days

Table 2. Notification Ranges and Frequency Table

Warning Range	Moderate Concern Range	High Impact Range
Traffic violation notifications that are minor or do not have a significant impact on the driver's record.	Applied to traffic violations that require more serious attention.	Severe traffic violation notifications that have a significant impact on road safety or may result in severe penalties.
[0,20[points	[20,30[points	[30,50[points
Monthly notification	Weekly notification	Notification every 3 days

To express this reasoning in mathematical terms, a weighted equation was created to determine the overall significance of a violation, known as the Puntuación de Importancia (PI). This equation includes different weighted elements, as illustrated below:

$$PI = (MI \times 0.3) + (SI \times 0.2) + (CI \times 0.2) + (DA \times 0.1)$$
$$+ (MP \times 0.1) + (PCR \times 0.05) + (R \times 0.05)$$

where:

- MI: Fine Amount (30%)
- SI: Imposed Sanction (20%)
- CI: Violation Severity (20%)
- DA: Applied Discount (10%)
- MP: Preventive Measure (10%)
- PCR: Driver's Points (5%)
- R: Responsible Party (5%)

The notification delivery system utilizes email communications with HTML-formatted templates, ensuring optimal presentation of violation details. These templates were designed to present pertinent information structured and visually coherently, facilitating a comprehensive understanding of violation particulars, associated penalties, and required actions (See Fig. 3).

The integration phase included rigorous testing protocols to verify notification accuracy, timeliness, and clarity. This systematic approach ensures the delivery of relevant information while preventing notification saturation, thereby maintaining system effectiveness and user engagement.

This implementation successfully addresses the requirement for an automated, user-centric notification system that prioritizes significant traffic violations. Through targeted communications, the system enhances road safety management and user awareness, creating a more efficient and responsive traffic violation management framework. By focusing on user-prioritized factors and employing strategic notification intervals, the system facilitates prompt attention to critical violations, fostering an environment of increased compliance and safety awareness.

6 Conclusions and Future Work

The study tackled the difficulties of retrieving information on systemic traffic infractions using a thorough, user-focused design method. It systematically investigated user interactions and pain points by integrating advanced user experience techniques, including User Persona, Empathy Map, Scenario Map, and Journey Map.

Key Methodological Contributions.

1. User Experience Research

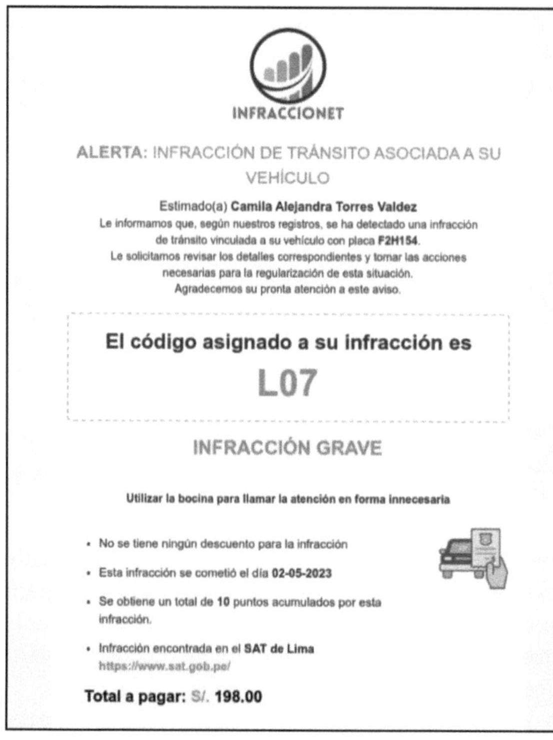

Fig. 3. Found Infraction Alert Email

– Conducted in-depth interviews with 15 representative users
– Revealed critical insights into existing informational inefficiencies
– Utilized the Empathy Map technique for nuanced qualitative analysis
2. Technical Implementation
– Developed structured relational database
– Created an automated web scraping mechanism
– Implemented real-time notification system
– Applied Behavior-Driven Development (BDD) testing techniques

The research demonstrates the potential of user-centered, technologically integrated approaches to transform public service information systems and offers a replicable framework for addressing complex information management challenges.

Future Directions. Further research and development initiatives stemming from this project may include:

The system's geographic coverage can be expanded by integrating traffic infraction data from additional Peruvian jurisdictions, addressing inter-regional variations and interoperability challenges. Mobile platform development involves designing a dedicated application with an optimized interface and integrating mobile-specific features like real-time alerts. Communication protocols can be enhanced through personalized, multi-channel notification strategies using machine learning for intelligent customization. Continuous user experience improvement requires iterative feedback mechanisms, adaptive design frameworks, and ongoing assessments of usability and satisfaction metrics.

References

1. Hassenzahl, M., Tractinsky, N.: User experience - a research agenda. Behav. Inf. Technol. **25**(2), 91–97 (2006)
2. Law, E., Roto, V., Hassenzahl, M., Vermeeren, A., Kort, J.: Understanding, scoping and defining user experience: a survey approach. In: Proceedings of CHI 2009, pp. 719–728 (2009)
3. Norman, D., Nielsen, J.: The Definition of User Experience (UX). Nielsen Norman Group (2016). https://www.nngroup.com/articles/definition-user-experience/
4. Castillo Pérez, A.A., Pérez Mejía, M.F.: Desarrollo de una aplicación web móvil para optimizar las consultas de infracciones de tránsito en la gerencia de transporte y tránsito de la Municipalidad Provincial del Santa [Repositorio]. Universidad Nacional del Santa (2017). http://repositorio.uns.edu.pe/handle/UNS/2892
5. Espinoza, A., Fort, R., Radics, A., Rivarola, R.: SARA a nivel subnacional – Evaluación de los Servicios de Administración Tributaria (SAT) de Perú, a 25 años de su creación. Centro de Investigaciones Económicas **15**(2), 78–95 (2022)
6. Bazo Reisman, A.: Análisis: Lo que falla en el sistema de papeletas y multas de tránsito en Lima. RPP Noticias (2018). https://rpp.pe/lima/seguridad/analisis-lo-que-falla-en-el-sistema-de-papeletas-y-multas-de-transito-en-lima-noticia-1152214
7. El Peruano: Sutran facilita pago de sanciones e infracciones con descuentos de hasta el 95% de las deudas. El Peruano (2022). https://elperuano.pe/noticia/198430-sutran-facilita-pago-de-sanciones-e-infracciones-con-descuentos-de-hasta-el-95-de-las-deudas
8. Jiménez-Hernández, C.N., Castellanos-Domínguez, O.F., Villa-Enciso, E.M.: La gestión de tecnologías emergentes en el ámbito universitario. Tecnológicas **26**, 145–163 (2011)
9. Haldenwang, C., Büsing, E., Földi, K., Goldboom, T., Jenrich, F., Pulkowski, J.: Administración tributaria municipal en el contexto del proceso de descentralización en el Perú. Deutsches Institut für Entwicklungspolitik, 160 (2009)
10. Petticrew, M., Roberts, H.: Systematic Reviews in the Social Sciences: A Practical Guide. Blackwell Publishing (2006). https://doi.org/10.1002/9780470754887
11. Booth, A., Sutton, A., Papaioannou, D.: Systematic Approaches to a Successful Literature Review, 2nd edn. Sage (2016)
12. Rad, H.A., Samsudin, K., Ramli, A.R., Tehrani, A.M.B.: A queueing model for evaluating traffic police infraction registration system. In: 2009 IEEE Student Conference on Research and Development (SCOReD), pp. 73–76. IEEE (2009). https://doi.org/10.1109/SCORED.2009.5443309
13. Rad, H.A., Samsudin, K., Ramli, A.R., Tehrani, M.B.: The design and implementation of a stress tool for traffic infraction registration system. In: 2009 Second International Conference on Environmental and Computer Science, pp. 133–137. IEEE (2009). https://doi.org/10.1109/ICECS.2009.41
14. Bodhuin, T., Tortorella, M.: A toolkit for developing web-based information systems: case studies. In: Proceedings 27th Annual International Computer Software and Applications Conference, pp. 460–465. IEEE (2003). https://doi.org/10.1109/CMPSAC.2003.1245380

15. Pérez, M., Flor, M., Castillo, P., Aldo, A.: Desarrollo de una aplicación Web Móvil para optimizar las consultas de infracciones de tránsito en la gerencia de transporte y tránsito de la Municipalidad Provincial del Santa. Universidad Nacional del Santa (2017). http://reposi torio.uns.edu.pe/handle/UNS/2892

16. Apaza Román, S.M.: Desarrollo de una aplicación web para la gestión eficiente de infracciones de tránsito en la Sub Gerencia de Transportes y Circulación Vial de la Municipalidad Provincial de Andahuaylas (2019). https://hdl.handle.net/20.500.14168/532

17. Altamirano, C.: Aplicación móvil de gestión de infracciones de tránsito georeferenciadas para inspectores de tránsito de la Municipalidad Provincial de Andahuaylas (2018). https://hdl.han dle.net/20.500.14168/363

18. Sanchez, A., La Rosa Zavalla, L.: Sistema informático basado en el ras para gestionar el proceso de control de infracciones y sanciones (vial) en la Municipalidad Provincial de Huaura (2021). http://repositorio.unjfsc.edu.pe/handle/UNJFSC/4373

19. Li, F., Zhou, Y., Cai, T.: Trails of data: three cases for collecting web information for social science research. J. Comput.-Mediat. Commun. **26**(1), 1–16 (2021). https://doi.org/10.1177/ 0894439319886019

20. Pacheco Arizola, Y.: Implementación de un Sistema Web para mejorar la gestión de papeletas de tránsito en la Sub Gerencia de Transporte y Circulación Vial de la Municipalidad Provincial de Zarumilla. Universidad Católica Los Ángeles de Chimbote (2019). http://repositorio.ula dech.edu.pe/handle/20.500.13032/15248

21. Carhuapoma, S.: Aplicación web para los procesos administrativos de los servicios que ofrece la Sub-Gerencia de transporte y tránsito de la Municipalidad Provincial de Huamanga. Universidad Nacional de San Cristóbal de Huamanga (2014). http://repositorio.unsch.edu.pe/han dle/UNSCH/1057

22. Jiang, H., Yang, Z., Quan, X., He, X., Ming, L., Li, X.: Construction and application evaluation of the traffic management information verification service platform. In: 2020 IEEE 4th Information Technology, Networking, Electronic and Automation Control Conference (ITNEC), pp. 1228–1232. IEEE (2020). https://doi.org/10.1109/IPEC49694.2020.9115109

23. Kononov, D., Isaev, S.: Development of secure automated management systems based on web technologies. IOP Conf. Ser. Mater. Sci. Eng. **537**(5), 052024 (2019). https://doi.org/10. 1088/1757-899X/537/5/052024

24. Khder, M.A.: Web scraping or web crawling: state of art, techniques, approaches and application. Int. J. Adv. Sci. Comput. Appl. **3**(1), 1–14 (2021). https://doi.org/10.15849/ijasca.211 128.11

25. Aljemazi, M.A., Khder, M.A.: Octobot - web scraping towards retrieving google scholar data. In: 2022 International Conference on Emerging Trends in Smart Innovative Systems (ICETSIS), pp. 1–6 (2022). https://doi.org/10.1109/ICETSIS55481.2022.9888872

26. Sharma, S., Bhagat, A.: Information extraction from web pages using hyperlinks. In: 2022 9th International Conference on Reliability, Infocom Technologies and Optimization (Trends and Future Directions) (ICRITO), pp. 1–6 (2022). https://doi.org/10.1109/ICRITO56286. 2022.9964792

27. Umam, F., Hidayat, R.: WEB-Based traffic ticket data processing information system. MATEC Web Conf. **58**, 03015 (2016). https://doi.org/10.1051/matecconf/20165803015

28. Knight, S.A., Spink, A.: Toward a Web search information behavior model. In: Spink, A., Zimmer, M. (eds.) Web Search: Multidisciplinary Perspectives, pp. 209–234. Springer (2008). https://doi.org/10.1007/978-3-540-75829-7_12

29. Nielsen, J.: How Many Test Users in a Usability Study? Nielsen Norman Group (2012). https://www.nngroup.com/articles/how-many-test-users/

30. Cooper, A.: The Inmates Are Running the Asylum: Why High-Tech Products Drive Us Crazy and How to Restore the Sanity. Sams Publishing (2014)

31. Gray, D.: Updated Empathy Map Canvas. Medium: XPLANE Collection (2017)
32. Kalbach, J.: Mapping Experiences: A Complete Guide to Creating Value through Journeys, Blueprints, and Diagrams. O'Reilly Media (2016)
33. Smart, J.F.: BDD in Action: Behavior-Driven Development for the Whole Software Lifecycle. Manning Publications (2014)
34. Teorey, T.: Database Modeling and Design: Logical Design. Morgan Kaufmann, San Francisco (2011)

Rapid Robotic Arm Path Planning Through Deep Reinforcement Learning with Human Demonstration Key Points

Lin Wan, Haonan Fang, Xiaonan Yang[✉], Deyu Sun, Hongwei Niu, Chenyang Lei, and Jia Hao

School of Mechanical Engineering, Beijing Institute of Technology, Beijing 100081, China
yangxn@bit.edu.cn

Abstract. Traditional path planning methods, such as sampling-based algorithms, struggle with high computational complexity in high-dimensional spaces like those encountered with 6-DOF robotic arms. Deep reinforcement learning offers a promising alternative, but its efficiency is often hindered by sparse rewards and large action spaces. To address these challenges, we integrate human demonstrations to guide the learning process, thereby improving the convergence rate and policy performance of the SAC algorithm. This paper proposes a novel approach for robotic arm path planning in complex product assembly scenarios using a soft actor-critic (SAC) deep reinforcement learning algorithm augmented with human demonstrations. The proposed method involves designing a specialized state space and reward function based on key points provided by human demonstration. The proposed approach is validated through simulations in a complex environment with obstacles, demonstrating significant improvements in planning efficiency and adaptability. The results show that incorporating human demonstrations effectively enhances the robot's ability to learn optimal collision-free paths, making it a viable solution for the path planning of complex assembly tasks.

Keywords: Robotic Arm Path Planning · Deep Reinforcement Learning · Human Demonstration · Soft Actor-Critic

1 Introduction

Robotic arm is widely used in manufacturing, especially in assembly tasks. The rapid development of intelligent manufacturing technology has led to increased demands for accuracy and efficiency in assembly path planning within industrial production. In the current production, the operating method of robotic arm is mainly manual teaching, but it is inefficient in the face of small batch and complex product. The sampling-based algorithm is one of the most popular path planning algorithms. In this algorithm, after sampling from the workspace, the sampled nodes are connected to find a collision-free path connecting the starting and target points [1]. However, in high-dimensional sampling space, such as the joint space of a 6-DOF robotic arm, its computational complexity increases exponentially. Therefore, it is necessary to propose an efficient

M. Kurosu and A. Hashizume (Eds.): HCII 2025, LNCS 16332, pp. 85–99, 2026.
https://doi.org/10.1007/978-3-032-12385-5_6

and stable path planning algorithm for the high-DOF robotic arm in the scenario of complex product assembly.

In recent years, many researchers turn to deep reinforcement learning (DRL) which shows excellent prospects for solving path planning problems in high-dimensional continuous state and action spaces. Utilizing DRL algorithms to solve the problem of complex product assembly can significantly reduce the need for repetitive human operations to increase the robot's autonomous learning ability. However, during the training process of DRL algorithm, efficiency is relative low due to the huge action space and state space leading to sparse reward. Besides, it becomes challenging to evaluate the value of both states and actions given the immense number of states and actions [2]. How to improve the training efficiency and effect of path planning based on DRL remains an open question?

This paper focuses on using a deep reinforcement learning (SAC: soft actor-critic) algorithm with human demonstration to solve the assembly path plan without collision using 6-DOF robotic arm for the case where there is complex product to deal with. For the purpose of speeding up the convergence, we introduce the human demonstration to design state space and reward function. The experiment results show that introducing the human demonstration in the SAC algorithm can effectively improve the robot's policy performance.

The remainder of this paper is organized as follows. In Sect. 2, the related work about robotic arm path planning algorithms and DRL with human demonstration is introduced and discussed. Section 3 describes and formulates the model of the robotic arm and the theoretical background of deep reinforcement learning algorithms. In Sect. 4, the DRL algorithm with human demonstration is described in detail. Section 5 performs the experiments to verify and analyze the proposed algorithm. Finally, Sect. 6 concludes the proposed research.

2 Related Work

2.1 Path Planning Algorithms

Path planning is an important research field in robotics, whose goal is to find a safe, efficient and collision-free path from the starting point to the target point in a complex environment. The metrics to evaluate a pathway planning algorithm focus mainly on its accuracy and efficiency. Existing robotic arm path planning algorithms mainly include search-based, sampling-based and learning-based algorithms.

Among traditional searching-based path planning algorithms, the Dijkstra algorithm plans the path so that the sum of weights of the nodes between the starting point and the target point is the smallest [3]. This method is inefficient as the number of nodes increases since the amount of required computation increases. The A∗ algorithm is the improved Dijkstra algorithm [4]. This algorithm can only be used in a fixed environment and has relatively poor adaptability to the environment of obstacle position change. Tang et al. [5] optimized the traditional A* algorithm within static environments, which significantly improves the problems of numerous search nodes and low search efficiency that arise when the traditional A* algorithm is applied to 3D environment path planning.

The sampling-based method is one of the most popular path planning methods owing to its probabilistic completeness. The sampling-based planning algorithms mainly include the multi-query algorithm Probabilistic Road map Method (PRM) and the single-query method Rapidly exploring Random Trees (RRT). The algorithms mentioned above can almost always find a feasible path when sampling in low-dimension state space. Cheng et al. [6] proposed an improved RRT-Connect algorithm through setting the adaptive step strategy and using the fixed sampling function to construct four random trees for search, effectively solve the problems of blind expansion, low efficiency in the RRT, and meet the path planning requirements of automatic sampling control of mechanical arm, which meets the path planning requirements of automatic sampling control of the robotic arm. Aiming at the slow sampling speed and rough path of the traditional two-way RRT* algorithm, Zhou Yibang et al. [7] analyzed the motion planning of the 6-axis robotic arm, and proposed an improved two-way RRT * algorithm based on target sampling and local path optimization. Although these methods enhance planning efficiency and retain the strengths of the traditional RRT algorithm, the sampling-based planning method is actually a probabilistic search-based offline method with uncertainty and the planning time may tend to infinity in a complex environment especially a narrow passage [8].

Scholars at home and abroad have achieved some research results in the aspects of robotic arm path planning based on deep reinforcement learning [9–12]. For many studies of deep reinforcement learning, the researchers designed the appropriate reward function to make the robot capture the designer's expected behavior through the reward function, which shows the importance of the reward function design. For example, Liu et al. [13] present a model-free off-policy actor-critic deep deep reinforcement learning method for path planning of a UR5 robot arm, addressing classical challenges. Unlike traditional model-based methods, this approach incorporates a smoothness reward to ensure a smooth trajectory. Tang et al. [14] discuss using deep reinforcement learning for trajectory planning of a dual-arm robot to approach a patient in a complex environment. Given the complex shapes of the human body and bed, A proximal policy optimization (PPO) algorithm with a custom reward function is employed to enhance training efficiency and path planning, comprising guidance, collision detection, obstacle avoidance, and time functions.

Integrating deep reinforcement learning with other methods to improve efficiency is a main focus point of deep reinforcement learning algorithm. For instance, in a study by Jie Zhong et al. [8], a DDPG-based path planning method was enhanced by introducing the inverse kinematics module to provide prior knowledge while a gain module is also designed to avoid the local optimal policy. This method not only improves the convergence performance but also is superior in terms of optimality and robustness of planning compared with most other planning algorithms. Aiming at the problems of large sample demand and high acquisition cost, in [15], a fusion algorithm that combines deep reinforcement learning with the screw method to enhance sample utilization and training efficiency by copying the natural trajectory and synchronously replicating environmental elements. Hindsight Experience Replay (HER) and Prioritized Experience Replay (PER) are two techniques that have been shown to significantly improve the efficiency of DRL algorithms [16–18]. HER allows the agent to learn from failed attempts by relabeling the goals, turning unsuccessful experiences into successful ones. PER, on the other hand, prioritizes the sampling of experiences based on their importance, ensuring that the most informative experiences are used more frequently for training. Kwan-Woo Park [17] demonstrated the effectiveness of combining SAC with LSTM and HER for path planning in environments with moving obstacles.

In deep reinforcement learning algorithms, although the path planning strategies can be effectively optimized through independent exploration and learning, and many optimization strategies as mentioned above have also been proposed, they still face the problems of large sample demand and low training efficiency. To improve learning efficiency, an effective way is to combined with human demonstration, which will be detailed in Sect. 2.2.

2.2　Human Demonstration in Deep Reinforcement Learning

In recent years, the integration of human demonstration into DRL has become a focal point in the field of robotic arm path planning. This approach leverages the expertise of human demonstrators to guide the learning process of DRL algorithms, thereby enhancing their efficiency and accuracy in complex environments. The following analysis explores the current state of research in this area, highlighting key methodologies and their contributions to the advancement of robotic arm path planning.

XIE Zongwu et al. [19] provide a comprehensive overview of learning from demonstration (LfD) methods for path planning, including imitation learning (IL) and inverse reinforcement learning (IRL). It emphasizes the role of IL and IRL in navigating free spaces and avoiding obstacles. IRL, in particular, stands out for its ability to adapt to dynamic environments by learning the intent behind expert demonstrations. Vecerik et al. [20] introduced human demonstration priors into the training of deep reinforcement learning assembly. The experimental results show that human demonstration priors can significantly accelerate the convergence rate of training. Hester et al. [21] proposed a deep reinforcement learning algorithm deep Q-learning from demonstrations (DQfD) with a small number of demonstration priors, which effectively reduces the ineffective exploration in the early stage of training and alleviates the problem of scarce robot deep reinforcement learning samples. Ashvin Nair's study [22] tackles the exploration challenge in DRL for sparse reward environments by integrating a demonstration buffer, behavior cloning loss, Q-filter, and reset strategies, which accelerates learning for long-horizon, multi-step tasks, and reduces the time and resources needed for proficient robotic arm path planning in real-world applications. Song Ziyang et al. [23] introduce a method that integrates demonstration paths into the DRL reward function, enabling the robotic arm to mimic these paths and enhancing the efficiency and accuracy of path planning. By aligning the DRL objectives with expert demonstrations, this approach ensures that the learned paths are not only optimal but also reflective of expert practices.

Existing results in the literature have been focusing mainly on using demonstrations of complete path to initialize strategies or as a priori to accelerate agent exploration [24–26]. However, for the scenarios that are not easy to obtain complete path demonstrations, such as digital twin software platform, the researches on how to use incomplete human demonstration to accelerate deep reinforcement learning training are very limited. Based on this, inspired by [23], this paper uses the key points in the assembly path given by human to design the state space and reward function specially, so as to accelerate the deep reinforcement learning training.

3 Background Concept and Problem Modeling

In this section, we give an overview of the background theories for the proposed DRL-based collision-free path planning algorithm, including configuration space of a robotic arm used in this research, the collision detection in workspace with CoACD, the deep reinforcement learning algorithms, and the SAC DRL algorithm.

3.1 Path Planning for Robotic Arm and Configuration Space

The concept of configuration space (C-space) is fundamental to path planning. All the position of the robotic arm can be expressed as an n-dimensional vector using values of n joint angles, and the set of all these vectors is C-space Q. Q is a subset of $\mathbb{R}^n$, where n denotes the number of joints of robotic arm. q_i represents the ith joint angle value, and it holds $q = \{q_1, q_2 \cdots q_n\}$. Therefore, the joint angle $q \in Q$. Q divides two subsets by whether the robotic arm collide, Q_{free} and $Q_{collide}$. In other words, The robotic arm does not collide if the joint angle belongs to Q_{free}, and conversely, the arm collides with an obstacle, a wall, another robot, or itself.

In addition, in this paper, $q_t \in Q$ represents the joint angle of the robot manipulator at the ith time step, and T represents the maximum number of time steps during one episode of the algorithm. The collision-free path is defined as a sequence of states using $q_t \in Q_{free}$. Therefore, when the episode starts, the algorithm must start at the starting point $q_{init} \in Q_{free}$ and find the optimal collision-free path within the maximum number of steps to arrive at the target point $q_{goal} \in Q_{free}$. Mathematically, the path planning problem can be framed as the search for a sequence of joint configurations: $q_{init}, q_{T_1}, q_{T_2}, \cdots q_{goal}$.

3.2 Collision Detection in Workspace with CoACD

The workspace denoted by $W \in \mathbb{R}^3$ is defined as a space in which the robotic arm works. In order for the robotic arm to move in the workspace, it is necessary to check if it is guaranteed $q_t \in Q_{free}$. To check this, in this paper, we employ a collision-aware concavity and tree search for approximate convex decomposition (CoACD) technique, and then use the collision detection algorithm of the physics engine for collision detection during path planning.

CoACD [27] is an enhanced approximate convex decomposition technique for 3D meshes, characterized by a collision-aware concavity metric, direct mesh cutting with 3D planes, and a multi-step tree search for cutting plane determination, aiming to generate decompositions closer to the original shape with fewer and simpler convex meshes.

The purpose of CoACD is twofold: first, it reduces the computational complexity of collision detection, and second, it facilitates the application of efficient convex body collision detection algorithms, such as the ones used in PyBullet.

3.3 Deep Reinforcement Learning

Reinforcement learning is a type of machine learning where an agent interacts with an environment to achieve a goal. The agent chooses actions based on its current state, and in turn, it receives a reward or penalty that influences its future behavior. The objective of DRL is to learn a policy that maximizes the sum of rewards over time. In other words, DRL aims to find an answer to a given Markov decision process (MDP) problem.

Path planning for a robotic arm can be framed as an MDP, which is a mathematical framework used to describe sequential decision-making problems. MDP refers to the process by which an agent interacts with the environment through actions using the current state, and obtains a reward, see in Fig. 2. MDP is usually defined in the form of $\{S, A, P, r, \gamma\}$. S is the state set, A is the action set, P denotes the state transition probability, $r(s_t, a_t)$ is the reward function, and γ is the discount factor [28]. The state transition probability $P(s_{t+1}|s_t, a_t)$ represents the probability of transition to the next state s_{t+1} when the action $a_t \in A$ is taken from the current state s_t. The agent selects the action $a_t \in A$ according to the policy $\pi(a|s) = P(A = a|S = s)$ and the state $s_t \in S$ and injects it into the environment. The environment returns the next state $s_{t+1} \in S$ and the reward r_{t+1} to the agent according to the state transition probability P based on the current state and injected action. The sum of the attenuation of all rewards starting from the moment state until the termination state is called the return $G_t = r_t + \gamma \cdot r_{t+1} + \gamma^2 \cdot r_{t+2} + \gamma^3 \cdot r_{t+3} + \cdots$. The purpose of reinforcement learning is to use this procedure to iteratively update the policy $\pi(a|s)$ so that the agent can receive the maximum reward sum until it approaches the optimal policy π^*. There are two main ways to update the optimal policy. The first is value-based methods that update the optimal value function using the state-value function $V_\pi(s) = \mathbb{E}_\pi(G_t|S_t = s)$. The second method, called the policy gradient method, learns the optimal policy directly from the agent's experience, using the action-value function $Q_\pi(s, a) = \mathbb{E}_\pi(G_t|S_t = s, A_t = a)$. Policy-based learning is a method of determining the action a directly using the state s, rather than using a value function to determine the action (Fig. 1).

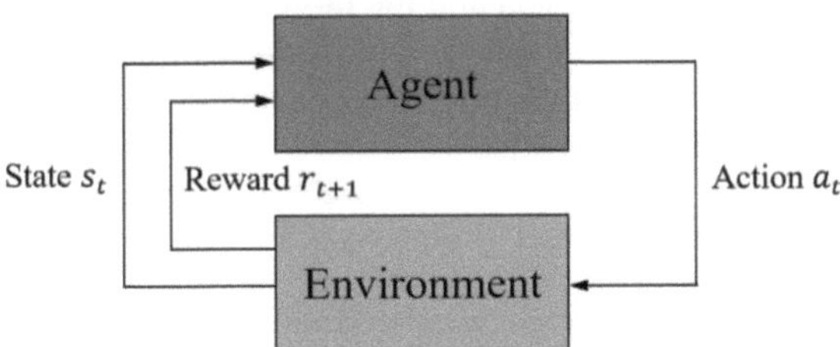

Fig. 1. The interaction between the agent and the environment

4 Soft Actor-Critic Algorithm with Key Points from Human Demonstration

4.1 Action Space and State Space

In the path planning of robotic arm, since the kinematic model is adopted as a part of the environment, the action can be chosen as the set of all the joint angular increments as follows:

$$a_t = \Delta q \in A, \tag{1}$$

Where $\Delta q \in \mathbb{R}^6$ is the target increment of joint angles. The dimension of the action space is

$$dim(a_t) = 6, \tag{2}$$

where $\dim(\cdot)$ means the dimension of a vector.

Task analysis is the soul of state design. In this research, the goal of the path planning task is to train an agent that drives the joints of the robotic arm, using human demonstration, without any collision to achieve the position and orientation alignment of the object grasped on the robotic arm end-effector simultaneously. In the light of the given task, the state observed from the environment at time step t is designed as a stacked vector:

$$s_t = \left[q, p_{obj}, p_{tar}, k, p_k, P_{col}, d_{ot}, o_{ot}, collision \right] \in S, \tag{3}$$

where $q \in \mathbb{R}^6$ is the current joint angles of the robotic arm. $p_{obj} \in \mathbb{R}^7$ is the position and orientation of the object grasped on the robotic arm end-effector and p_{tar} is the target position and orientation of the object, whose orientation is indicated by the quaternion $\left[w, x, y, z \right]$ [29]. The scalar k denotes the index of the human demonstration point sequence and p_k is the position and orientation of the kth human demonstration point. P_{col} is the set of the top 5 obstacle points closest to the object. d_{ot} Represents the current distance between the object and the target position and o_{ot} denotes the error angle between the object quaternion and the target quaternion. The last element collision is a Boolean that indicates whether the collision occurs in the environment. It is obvious that the dimension of the state vector is

$$dim(s_t) = dim(q) + dim(p_{obj}) + dim(p_{tar}) + dim(p_k) + dim(P_{col}) + 4. \tag{4}$$

The state at the next time step is calculated using the current state value and the relation

$$\hat{q}_{t+1} = q_t + a_t. \tag{5}$$

If the next state value causes a collision after applying the action, the state does not move and maintains the current state value. The following summarizes how the joint values are updated during path planning.

$$q_{t+1} = \begin{cases} \hat{q}_{t+1}, & if \ \hat{q}_{t+1} \in Q_{free} \\ q_t, & if \ \hat{q}_{t+1} \notin Q_{free} \end{cases} \tag{6}$$

The demonstration points given by human includes the starting point, route point and target point, which are arranged in the sequence. The k belongs to [0, n], where p_0 is the starting point, p_n is the target point, and the initial value of k in state space is 1. After the object reaches the demonstration point p_k, the index k is updated to $k + 1$, and the demonstration point is updated to p_{k+1}, until the robotic arm passes through all the demonstration points.

Until p_{obj} included in the next state reaches the target point p_{tar}, the process of applying the action according to the policy and obtaining the state and reward is repeated. The final goal is given by

$$d_{ot} \leq d_{th} \text{ and } o_{ot} \leq o_{th}, \tag{7}$$

Where d_{th} is the distance threshold and o_{th} is the error angle threshold.

4.2 Reward Function

The reward function plays a crucial role in guiding the learning process. The total reward is composed of several components, including arrive reward, distance reward, orientation reward, demonstration reward, step reward, and collision reward. The reward function is designed to encourage the robotic arm to reach the target point while minimizing the distance and orientation errors, following the human demonstration points, and avoiding collisions. The reward function is given as follows:

$$r = \begin{cases} r_a + r_{dis} + r_o + r_{dem} + r_s, & \text{if not collision} \\ -1, & \text{if collision} \end{cases}, \tag{8}$$

Where r represents the total reward, r_a is the arrive reward, r_{dis} stands for the distance reward, r_o represents the orientation reward, r_{dem} is the demonstration rewards, r_s stands for the step reward, and r_{col} is the collision reward. If the collision occurs, the agent will receive a negative reward and withdraws the current action back to the previous state.

The arrive reward r_a can be calculated by

$$r_a = \begin{cases} r_{ap}, & \text{if } d_{ot} \leq d_{th} \text{ and } o_{ot} \leq o_{th} \\ 0, & \text{otherwise} \end{cases}, \tag{9}$$

where r_{ap} equals to a positive reward, d_{th} represents the distance threshold and o_{th} is the error angle threshold. This means that when the object's position and orientation are equal to the target in the threshold range, the robotic arm path planning is considered successful and a positive arrive reward is obtained

The distance reward r_{dis} is computed as follows:

$$r_{dis} = d_p - d_{ot}, \tag{10}$$

where d_p stands for the previous distance between the object position and the target position. The time step between d_p and d_{ot} is set to 0.01 s. If d_p is smaller than d_{ot}, the agent will receive a negative reward since it gets further away from the target position.

The orientation reward r_o is given by

$$r_o = \begin{cases} 0, & \text{if } k \text{ is updated} \\ o_p - o_c, & \text{otherwise} \end{cases}, \tag{11}$$

Where o_p stands for the previous error angle between object orientation and the demonstration orientation and o_c stands for the current error angle between object orientation and the demonstration orientation. This means that the agent gets a positive reward when the object is closer to the demonstration point orientation in the state space. Specifically, when k is updated, r_o equals 0.

The demonstration reward r_{dem} can be computed bytermination state is called the

$$r_{dem} = \begin{cases} r_{dp}, & \text{if } d_{od} \leq d'_{th} \text{ and } o_{od} \leq o'_{th} \\ 0, & \text{otherwise} \end{cases}, \tag{12}$$

Where r_{dp} equals to a positive reward, d'_{th} represents the distance threshold, and o'_{th} is the error angle threshold. Therefore, when the position and orientation of the object are equal to the demonstration in the state space within the threshold range, it reaches the demonstration point, obtains a positive teaching reward, and updates the demonstration state. The threshold should not be set too stringent to avoid the situation that the object fails to pass through the demonstration points due to deviations in the human demonstration and expand the exploration space of the robotic arm.

The step reward r_s can be computed by

$$r_s = \lambda \cdot steps, \tag{13}$$

Where step s is the time steps and λ is a negative coefficient. To prevent the robotic arm from meaningless exploration during training and improve the efficiency of path planning, each time step will be punished. The $|\lambda|$ should not be set too large, otherwise, the robotic arm will be unable to perform effective exploration because of the excessive punishment in the early stage of training.

4.3 Algorithm Architecture

The proposed method is on the basis of soft actor-critic deep reinforcement learning method. Figure 4 describes the detailed structure of the SAC-based path planning algorithm proposed in this paper.

The Soft Actor-Critic (SAC) [30] algorithm is a popular deep reinforcement learning algorithm used for continuous action spaces, making it well-suited for robotic applications. SAC combines the advantages of both value-based and policy-based methods and is designed to maximize the expected cumulative reward while ensuring exploration of the action space. SAC introduces a soft value function, which aims to maximize not only the expected reward but also the entropy of the policy. By incorporating entropy into the objective function, SAC encourages exploration, which helps in achieving better performance in complex environments. The maximum entropy objective of the SAC algorithm is formalized as:

$$J(\pi) = \sum_{t=0}^{t} \mathbb{E}_{(s_t, a_t) \sim \rho_\pi} [r(s_t, a_t) + \alpha H(\pi(\cdot|s_t))], \tag{14}$$

Where α is the temperature parameter that controls the trade-off between exploration and exploitation, $H(\pi(\cdot|s_t))$ represents the entropy of the strategy.

SAC uses two Q-networks which are updated by using a target value network, and it employs a value network to estimate the state value function. SAC employs an actor-critic architecture, where the actor learns a stochastic policy $\pi_\phi(s_t|a_t)$ parameterized by ϕ, and the critic estimates the soft Q-function $Q_\theta(s_t, a_t)$ and the state value function $V_\psi(s_t)$ parameterized by θ and ψ, respectively. To further enhance stability and performance, SAC uses two independent Q-functions, Q_{θ_1} and Q_{θ_2}, and updates them separately. During policy updates, the minimum of the two Q-functions is used to mitigate positive bias. The update makes use of a target value network $V_{\overline{\psi}}$, where $\overline{\psi}$ can be an exponentially moving average of the value network weights, which has been shown to stabilize training.

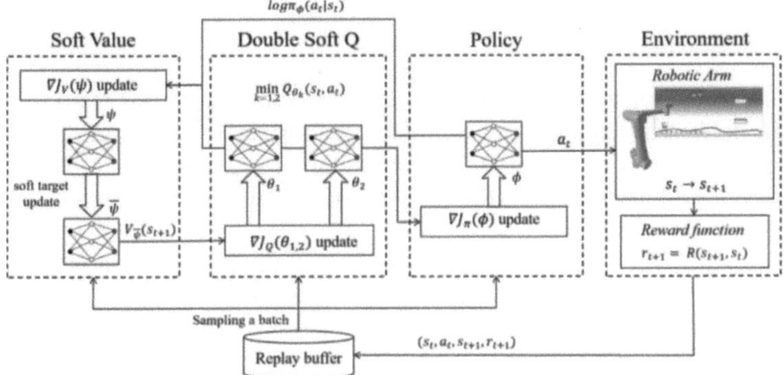

Fig. 2. Architecture of the proposed SAC-based path planning algorithm.

5 Simulation and Result Analysis

Simulation and result analysis are conducted in this section to verify the feasibility, and effectiveness of the robotic arm path planning algorithm proposed in this paper.

5.1 Simulation

The simulation environment was implemented using the PyBullet physics engine, which provides a realistic and efficient platform for robotic simulations. The initial environment is shown in Fig. 4. The workspace of the robotic arm includes a fixed cylindrical module with several convex platform obstacles on the inner wall, as well as a randomly generated cable on the lower part. Due to the particularity of this task scene, the end effector of the robotic arm has a prolonged fixture to grasp the object, but because the simulation experiment does not involve grasping, it does not affect the path planning task, so the end effector is omitted (Fig. 3).

Fig. 3. The initial environment of path planning

The human demonstration points are listed in Table 1, whose main purpose is to guide the robotic arm from the convex platform obstacles. The target point represent in inertial coordinate is (0.6, 0.9, 0.5), and the target orientation is (−0.383, 0.0, 0.0, 0.924). The coordinates mentioned in this paper are all in the world coordinate system in meters.

Table 1. Information of the human demonstration points.

Index	Position	Orientation	Type
0	(0.3,0.9,0.5)	(0,0,0,1)	The starting point
1	(0.4,0.9,0.5)	(0.382, 0.0191, 0.046, 0.923)	The first point
2	(0.55,0.9,0.5)	(−0.383, 0.0, 0.0, 0.924)	The second point
3	(0.6,0.9,0.5)	(−0.383, 0.0, 0.0, 0.924)	The target point

The hyper-parameters of the SAC-based path planning are presented in Table 2.

Table 2. The hyper-parameters of the proposed algorithm.

Name	Value	Unit
Learning rate	0.0003	
Replay memory size	10^4	Buffer
Episode maximum step	10^3	Step
Soft value target copy rate	0.005	
Mini batch size	512	Batch
Discount factor	0.99	
Entropy temperature parameter	0.2	

5.2 Result Analysis

Figure 5 shows the reward while learning. In the early stages of training, the robotic arm frequently collided with obstacles due to its lack of understanding of the environment, resulting in low reward values. However, as training progressed, the cumulative reward gradually increased, indicating that the robotic arm gradually learned how to avoid collisions and successfully reach the target point. Eventually, the SAC algorithm with human demonstrations achieved a high cumulative reward, demonstrating its good performance in the path planning task. The robotic arm successfully passed through the human demonstration key points and reached the target point while avoiding collisions with obstacles. The trajectory of the robotic arm during the path planning process was smooth and coherent. This indicates that the proposed algorithm effectively guided the robotic arm to find a safe and efficient path in a complex environment. Moreover, by comparing the position and orientation of the robotic arm at different time steps, it can be observed that the robotic arm gradually adjusted its posture as it approached the target point to meet the target's position and orientation requirements, further verifying the precision and adaptability of the proposed algorithm.

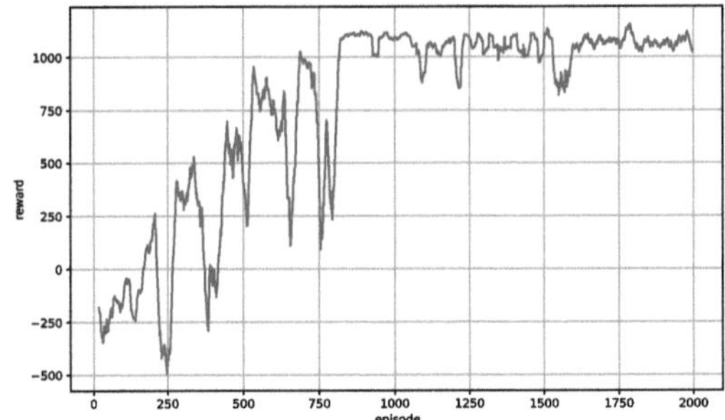

Fig. 4. Architecture of the proposed SAC-based path planning algorithm.

In the comparative experiments, the proposed method was compared with the SAC method without human demonstrations. Under the same hyper parameter settings, the proposed method demonstrated a significant advantage in training speed, which is shown in Fig. 4. This indicates that incorporating human demonstrations to design the state space and reward function can more effectively accelerate the training process of the deep reinforcement learning algorithm and improve the convergence rate.

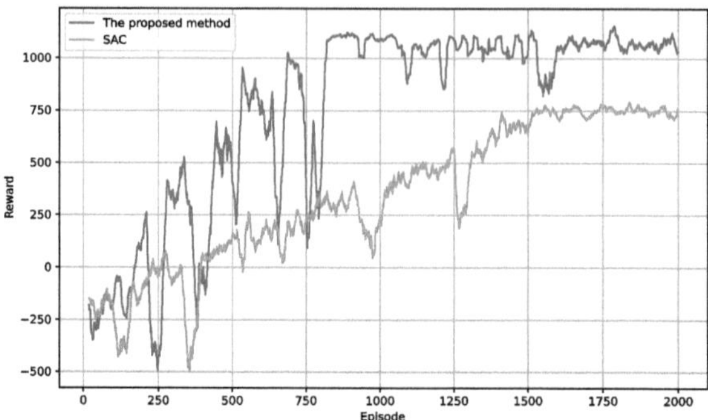

Fig. 5. Comparison of reward.

6   Conclusions

This paper presents a novel approach for robotic arm path planning in complex product assembly scenarios using a Soft Actor-Critic (SAC) deep reinforcement learning algorithm augmented with human demonstrations. The proposed method incorporates human demonstrations to design the state space and reward function, thereby accelerating the convergence of the SAC algorithm. The simulation results demonstrate that the proposed approach significantly improves the efficiency and adaptability of path planning in complex environment with obstacles. The integration of human demonstrations effectively enhances the robot's ability to learn optimal collision-free paths, making it a viable solution for complex environment assembly task.

Acknowledgments. This study was funded by National Ministry Projects of China (50923010201).

Disclosure of Interests.   The authors have no competing interests to declare that are relevant to the content of this article.

References

1. Liu, W., Niu, H., Mahyuddin, M.N., et al.: A model-free deep reinforcement learning approach for robotic manipulators path planning. In: 2021 21st International Conference on Control, Automation and Systems (ICCAS), pp. 512–517. IEEE (2021)
2. Nguyen, T.T., Nguyen, N.D., Nahavandi, S.: Deep reinforcement learning for multiagent systems: a review of challenges, solutions, and applications. IEEE Trans. Cybernet. **50**(9), 3826–3839 (2020)
3. Schrijver, A.: Combinatorial Optimization: Polyhedra and Efficiency, vol. 24. Springer, Heidelberg (2003)
4. Hart, P.E., Nilsson, N.J., Raphael, B.: A formal basis for the heuristic determination of minimum cost paths. IEEE Trans. Syst. Sci. Cybern. **4**, 100–107 (1968)
5. Tang, X., Zhou, H., Xu, T.: Obstacle avoidance path planning of 6-DOF robotic arm based on improved A* algorithm and artificial potential field method. Robotica **42**(2), 457–481 (2024)
6. Cheng, X., Zhou, J., Zhou, Z., Zhao, X., Gao, J., Qiao, T.: An improved RRT-Connect path planning algorithm of robotic arm for automatic sampling of exhaust emission detection in Industry 4.0. J. Ind. Inf. Integr. **33**, 100436 (2023)

7. 周益邦，章兰珠，徐海铭.基于改进双向RRT*算法的机械臂路径规划. 计算机应用 **42**(201), 342–346 (2022)

8. Zhong, J., Wang, T., Cheng, L.: Collision-free path planning for welding manipulator via hybrid algorithm of deep reinforcement learning and inverse kinematics. Complex Intell. Syst. **8**(3), 1899–1912 (2022)

9. Zhang, S., Xia, Q., Chen, M., et al.: Multi-objective optimal trajectory planning for robotic arms using deep reinforcement learning. Sensors **23**(13), 5974 (2023)

10. Zhou, D., Jia, R., Yao, H., et al.: Robotic arm motion planning based on residual reinforcement learning. In: 2021 13th International Conference on Computer and Automation Engineering (ICCAE), pp. 89–94. IEEE (2021)

11. Wu, Y.H., Yu, Z.C., Li, C.Y., et al.: Reinforcement learning in dual-arm trajectory planning for a free-floating space robot. Aerosp. Sci. Technol. **98**, 105657 (2020)

12. Bhuiyan, T., Kästner, L., Hu, Y., et al.: Deep-reinforcement-learning-based path planning for industrial robots using distance sensors as observation. In: 2023 8th International Conference on Control and Robotics Engineering (ICCRE), pp. 204–210. IEEE (2023)

13. Liu, W., Niu, H., Mahyuddin, M.N., Herrmann, G., Carrasco, J.: A model-free deep reinforcement learning approach for robotic manipulators path planning. In: 2021 21st International Conference on Control, Automation and Systems (ICCAS), Jeju, Korea, Republic of, pp. 512–517 (2021)

14. Tang, W., et al.: Dual-arm robot trajectory planning based on deep reinforcement learning under complex environment. Micromachines **13**(4), 564 (2022)

15. Wang, Y., Wang, Y.-H., Yin, Z.-Z., Wan, P.: Path planning of manipulator based on deep reinforcement learning and screw method. Kongzhi Lilun Yu Yingyong/Control Theory Appl. **40**(3), 516–524 (2023)

16. Prianto, E., Park, J.-H., Bae, J.-H., Kim, J.-S.: Deep reinforcement learning-based path planning for multi-arm manipulators with periodically moving obstacles. Appl. Sci. **11**(2587), 2587 (2021)

17. Park, K.-W., Kim, M., Kim, J.-S., Park, J.-H.: Path planning for multi-arm manipulators using soft actor-critic algorithm with position prediction of moving obstacles via LSTM. Appl. Sci. **12**(9837), 9837 (2022)

18. Chen, P., Pei, J., Lu, W., Li, M.: A deep reinforcement learning based method for real-time path planning and dynamic obstacle avoidance. Neurocomputing **497**, 64–75(2022)

19. Xie, Z., Zhang, Q., Jiang, Z., Liu, H.: Robot learning from demonstration for path planning: a review. Sci. China (Technol. Sci.) **63**, 1325–1334 (2020)

20. Vecerik, M., Hester, T., Scholz, J., et al.: Leveraging demonstrations for deep reinforcement learning on robotics problems with sparse rewards. arXiv preprint arXiv:1707.08817 (2017)

21. Hester, T., Vecerik, M., Pietquin, O., et al.: Deep q-learning from demonstrations. In: Proceedings of the AAAI Conference on Artificial Intelligence, vol. 32, no. 1 (2018)

22. Nair, A., McGrew, B., Andrychowicz, M., et al.: Overcoming exploration in reinforcement learning with demonstrations. In: 2018 IEEE International Conference on Robotics and Automation (ICRA), pp. 6292–6299. IEEE (2018)

23. 宋紫阳，李军怀，王怀军，苏鑫，于蕾.基于路径模仿和SAC强化学习的机械臂路径规划算法. 计算机应用 **44**(2), 439–444 (2024)

24. Zang, Y., Wang, P., Zha, F., Guo, W., Li, C., Sun, L.: Human skill knowledge guided global trajectory policy reinforcement learning method. Front. Neurorobot. **18**, 1368243 (2024)

25. 刘行,黄庭安,董云龙,等.基于示教融合的深度强化学习机器人化齿轮装配算法. 控制工程 **30**(07), 1308–1316 (2023). https://doi.org/10.14107/j.cnki.kzgc.20220894

26. Lu, W., Chen, L., Wang, Y., et al.: Demonstration data-driven parameter adjustment for trajectory planning in highly constrained environments. IEEE Robot. Autom. Lett. (2024)

27. Wei, X., Liu, M., Ling, Z., et al.: Approximate convex decomposition for 3D meshes with collision-aware concavity and tree search. ACM Trans. Graph. (TOG) **41**(4), 1–18 (2022)

28. Sutton, R.S., Barto, A.G.: Reinforcement Learning: An Introduction. A Bradford Book, Cambridge (2018)
29. Sola, J.: Quaternion kinematics for the error-state Kalman filter. arXiv preprint arXiv:1711.02508 (2017)
30. Haarnoja, T., Zhou, A., Abbeel, P., et al.: Soft actor-critic: off-policy maximum entropy deep reinforcement learning with a stochastic actor. In: International Conference on Machine Learning, pp. 1861–1870. PMLR (2018)

Trust Through Triadic Embodied Feedback: A Model for Virtual Agents Based on Embodied Cognition

Xinyi Wen[1] , Huai Cao[1(✉)] , and Rong Zhu[2]

[1] Huazhong University of Science and Technology, Wuhan 430074, China
{M202370452,caohuai}@hust.edu.cn
[2] Yueyang Urban Management Affairs Center, Yueyang 414000, China

Abstract. With the rapid growth of virtual agents and humanoid robots, effectively building user trust through embodied interactions has become a crucial research focus. However, current virtual agents typically lack structured feedback mechanisms, limiting their capability to elicit stable user trust and long-term engagement. To address this, we propose a multidimensional embodied feedback model structured around a clear "Input–Mediator–Output (IMO)" cognitive pathway, which systematically integrates six feedback variables across visual, auditory, and behavioral channels. The variables—Facial Expressiveness, Prosodic Warmth, Proactive Responsiveness, Movement Synchrony, Social-Linguistic Expressiveness, and Turn-Taking Coordination—were extracted from recent literature and operationalized into measurable cognitive pathways involving perceptual initiation, attributional interpretation, and behavioral intention.

To facilitate empirical validation, six causal hypotheses (H1–H6) were defined, supported by detailed experimental manipulation conditions. Two verification pathways are further proposed: expert evaluation via Delphi methods and controlled behavioral experiments using interactive prototypes. Additionally, we conducted scenario adaptability analyses, comparing the implementation feasibility of these variables across physical robots, virtual avatars, and emotional companionship systems. This comparison was visually demonstrated through an Embodied Mapping Matrix, clarifying the differential priorities and applicability of each feedback channel according to system type.

This work contributes a structured, empirically testable framework that enhances both theoretical understanding and practical implementation of trust-building in virtual and humanoid agents. The proposed model and validation methods offer valuable insights for designers to systematically optimize interaction modalities, thereby fostering robust user trust and promoting sustained engagement across diverse human–AI interaction contexts.

Keyword: Embodied Feedback · Trust · Human–Robot Interaction

1 Introduction

1.1 Research Background and Problem Statement

In recent years, with the rapid development of artificial intelligence and virtual human technologies, an increasing number of non-physical interactive agents have been applied in socially meaningful contexts, such as medical assistance, educational guidance, and psychological support. Intelligent agents—including virtual health advisors, digital customer service agents, and AI companions—are transitioning from being mere tools to fulfilling quasi-social roles. This shift has led human–computer interaction (HCI) research to move beyond questions of functional efficiency to emphasize cognitive and emotional compatibility between agents and users. For AI systems to function effectively in human-centric scenarios, particular attention must be paid to how users perceive their social presence and trustworthiness [1].

Against this backdrop, the central challenge in HCI and Social AI is: how can non-embodied systems evoke trust and a sense of belonging in users? Whereas humanoid robots elicit a sense of embodiment through physical presence, movement feedback, and co-located interaction, virtual agents lack bodily substance, spatial immediacy, and synchronous behavioral cues [2]. This absence makes it difficult for users to form a psychologically credible interaction relationship with such agents.

Embodied cognition theory offers key insights into addressing this issue. This framework posits that cognition is not a purely abstract process confined to the brain but is dynamically constructed through interactions between the body and the environment. From this perspective, even in the absence of a physical body, a system that continuously provides multimodal feedback via visual, auditory, and behavioral channels may simulate a sense of "virtual embodiment" in the user's mind. This simulation can activate trust, empathy, and attachment mechanisms commonly associated with social interaction.

While recent studies have explored the design of socially responsive virtual agents, most have focused on unimodal feedback (e.g., language or tone) or behavioral strategies (e.g., responsiveness), lacking a coherent model that systematically integrates these elements or explains their psychological pathways. For example, Urakami and Seaborn (2022) proposed a five-sense-based classification system for nonverbal feedback from a communication perspective. However, their model did not explore how such feedback contributes to trust formation or interaction willingness [3]. Moreover, there remains a lack of a unified theoretical framework and quantifiable structure for understanding embodied interaction in non-physical systems.

This study adopts an embodied cognition approach to model how virtual humanoid agents—despite their lack of physical bodies—can simulate embodied interaction through visual, auditory, and behavioral feedback. The goal is to propose a structurally coherent and theoretically extensible model that supports future empirical validation and guides interaction design for trust-oriented virtual agents.

1.2 Research Object and Role Delimitation

In today's expanding digital interaction ecosystem, embodied agents vary widely, ranging from virtual humans with anthropomorphic appearances and speech capabilities (e.g., in film, gaming, or healthcare), to pet-like companion systems (e.g., Sony's AIBO), and to function-oriented devices such as voice assistants and smart speakers (e.g., Siri, Google Assistant, Alexa). To develop an embodied interaction model, this study must clearly define its target agent type.

We focus specifically on virtual humanoid agents capable of producing socially meaningful feedback. These agents are not physical humanoid robots but digital systems that display facial expressions, understand and generate language, and perform recognizable actions or responsive behaviors. They may appear as on-screen avatars (e.g., virtual clerks), auditory agents (e.g., emotionally expressive digital therapists), or semi-embodied forms embedded in hardware.

Although pet-like systems have shown emotional benefits—e.g., mixed-reality cats that reduce stress and boost mood (Na et al., 2022)—their interactions often rely on preset actions and simple voice commands, lacking nuanced language processing or facial expressiveness. Consequently, they rarely elicit complex social attribution or personality perception [4]. Similarly, function-oriented assistants are designed for efficiency and do not incorporate structures for social presence or emotional sensing.

To ensure theoretical and practical relevance, this study defines eligible agents as systems that satisfy the following criteria:

Visual feedback readability: Ability to produce facial expressions, motion changes, and gaze responses.

Auditory emotional feedback: Capability to deliver semantically meaningful and emotionally modulated speech.

Proactive behavioral feedback: Ability to generate context-appropriate proactive responses.

These combined features make virtual humanoid agents the most socially proximate among digital agents and the most suitable for eliciting users' social attribution, trust formation, and affective bonding through multimodal embodied feedback. Our three-dimensional embodied interaction model will be constructed with such agents as its foundational target.

1.3   Research Objectives and Modeling Pathway

Building upon the identified problem space and agent definition, this study aims to construct a modeling framework for virtual embodied interaction, clarifying how multi-channel feedback co-functions to influence user trust and social attribution. The model is designed to support both theoretical exploration and practical application in designing socially responsive AI agents.

We focus on the following core objectives:

Model Construction: Drawing from embodied cognition and social trust theory, we propose a three-channel feedback model (visual–auditory–behavioral) to examine how virtual agents evoke presence and social attribution in the absence of physical embodiment. Notably, Froese et al. (2014) found that even minimal tactile and motion cues, when rhythmically coordinated, enabled users to detect social presence and make accurate agent judgments—underscoring the role of sensory coordination in triggering social cognition [5].

Variable Induction: Through systematic literature review, we synthesize findings from HCI and Social AI to extract representative feedback variables (e.g., motion synchrony, vocal warmth, proactive response) and categorize their psychological pathways.

Validation Strategy: We outline each feedback dimension's cognitive mechanism, structural logic, and potential measurement indicators, ensuring theoretical coherence, practical translatability, and empirical testability. We also propose future experimental designs and evaluation pathways for validating the model.

Methodologically, this study adopts a theoretical deductive modeling approach. Based on embodied cognition and trust theory, we integrate literature synthesis with interaction case analysis to propose an input–mediator–output (IMO) structure. Inspired by Shaw's (1986) I/O interaction framework—which separates system input, state mediation, and output formatting—we conceptualize a "social attribution mechanism" as the cognitive mediation channel between perceptual input and behavioral response [6].

This model will serve as the core framework of this study. Subsequent chapters will detail each feedback dimension, provide structural illustrations, and define operational indicators, while evaluating the model's contextual applicability and extensibility for human–agent collaboration scenarios such as AI customer service, social companion agents, and virtual humanoid assistants.

2 Theoretical Foundations and Model Construction

2.1 Theoretical Foundations

The proposed tri-channel virtual embodied interaction model (Visual–Auditory–Behavioral) is grounded in multidisciplinary theoretical frameworks, including embodied cognition theory, media equation theory, and social attribution and trust formation mechanisms in human-computer interaction.

Embodied cognition, as a significant branch of cognitive science, emphasizes that cognitive processes are not isolated within the brain but are deeply dependent on the continuous interaction between bodily structures, perceptual abilities, and the surrounding environment. Pfeifer and Bongard (2007) assert that intelligent behaviors are not solely a product of internal reasoning but are constantly modulated and reconstructed through engagement with external conditions [7]. Dourish (2001) further introduced the concept of embodiment into the HCI field, positing that meaning is not pre-assigned but is dynamically constructed by users in interactive practice. In virtual settings, even without physical embodiment, users may simulate a sense of "bodily presence" through seeing, hearing, or sensing actions. These multimodal cues from interfaces or agent systems can stimulate emotional engagement and cognitive attribution, constituting a sense of "digital embodiment" [8]. Thus, embodied cognition theory provides both a conceptual rationale and legitimacy for constructing embodied interactions in non-physical systems.

The Media Equation theory, introduced by Reeves and Nass (1996), reveals that users automatically apply social rules to interactions with anthropomorphic media (e.g., screens, voice assistants, virtual avatars), treating them as social entities. The theory demonstrates that even when users are aware they are interacting with non-living entities, they still exhibit responses akin to human interaction—including politeness, trust, and defensiveness [9]. This automatic social attribution has since been termed the "media equation paradigm," explaining how humans infer social intent from mediated interactions, even when the agent is artificial (van der Goot & Etzrodt, 2023) [10]. The trust modeling in this study is founded on this mechanism: as long as an agent exhibits socially congruent signals through its visual, auditory, and behavioral feedback, users are likely to generate cognitive attribution and trust-based emotional responses.

In HCI, whether a user perceives a system as a "trustworthy partner" is not solely determined by its functional performance, but is instead a psychological outcome co-constructed during the interaction. Schaefer's scale for measuring trust in automation highlights that user trust is influenced by several social variables, including perceived empathy, attentiveness, and collaborative intent [11]. Van Wissen et al. (2016) demonstrate that when humanoid robots display emotional responsiveness, attentional feedback, and cooperation cues, users are more inclined to attribute social presence and report higher trust [12]. Breazeal (2003), in her early research on affective robotics, found that users' emotional attachment strongly correlates with the anthropomorphic feedback intensity. These findings confirm that trust emerges as a gradual social construction rather than an instantaneous evaluation. Multimodal feedback systems (e.g., facial expressions, prosodic speech, proactive actions) can provide early indicators such as "being understood" or "being cared for," laying the emotional foundation for trust development.

In summary, embodied cognition offers a cognitive framework for why multi-channel feedback fosters trust; media equation theory uncovers the automatic social responses triggered by media; and social trust studies identify the contributing factors and structural pathways of trust formation. This research integrates these three pillars into a measurable, verifiable feedback model to support HCI trust-building design and optimization.

2.2   Literature-Driven Variable Extraction

The construction of the Visual–Auditory–Behavioral virtual embodiment model is based on a cross-disciplinary review of literature spanning trust in automation, affective computing, and social psychology. To ensure theoretical rigor and operational feasibility, this study systematically identifies trust-relevant variables from each feedback channel and organizes them into a coherent operational framework.

Specifically, two representative variables were selected for each channel, resulting in six core elements:

Auditory Feedback: Vocal Warmth, Social Wording
Behavioral Feedback: Proactivity, Turn-Taking Coordination
Visual Feedback: Facial Expressiveness, Motion Synchrony

Each variable is supported by two representative empirical studies published in the past five years, and each includes a precise operational definition to guarantee traceability and applicability.

To build a theoretically grounded and structurally coherent model of virtual embodied feedback, this study conducted a cross-disciplinary synthesis of empirical research spanning affective computing, trust in automation, and social interaction psychology.

The goal was to identify key variables that mediate trust construction across the three major feedback channels—visual, auditory, and behavioral.

Based on rigorous literature screening and theoretical triangulation, two representative feedback variables were selected for each sensory channel, resulting in a set of six core constructs:

- Visual Feedback: Facial Expressiveness and Motion Synchrony
- Auditory Feedback: Prosodic Warmth and Social Wording
- Behavioral Feedback: Proactive Responsiveness and Turn-Taking Coordination

Each of these variables captures a different aspect of how users interpret social cues from non-physical agents, and each has been operationally defined with traceable constructs and supported by at least two peer-reviewed empirical studies published in the past five years (see Fig. 1).

For instance, Facial Expressiveness refers to the use of animated facial elements—such as smiles, eye movement, or frowns—to reduce perceived psychological distance and enhance social affinity. In parallel, Motion Synchrony captures whether the agent's body or gesture timing aligns rhythmically with the user's movements, which can strengthen affiliation and participatory intent. Within the auditory channel, Prosodic Warmth addresses the tone, pitch, and cadence of the system's voice, shaping how emotionally engaging and trustworthy it feels. Social Wording, meanwhile, involves the use of empathetic phrases, polite forms, and affiliative language that increase social resonance and group belonging. In the behavioral feedback channel, Proactive Responsiveness evaluates the system's ability to initiate actions or suggestions without explicit user prompts—contributing to a sense of intelligence and mutual understanding. Turn-Taking Coordination reflects the system's rhythm management in dialogues, such as detecting pauses, avoiding interruption, and aligning timing with user responses, which enhances fluency and social comfort.

Collectively, these six variables lay the foundation for the multi-layer feedback model proposed in this paper. Their selection ensures conceptual robustness, operational feasibility, and compatibility with both virtual and embodied system designs. Each variable's psychological function and empirical reference is illustrated in Fig. 1, which summarizes their modality grouping, definitions, and supporting literature.

Extraction of variables from the three major feedback channels

Feedback Channel		Variable	Definition	Supporting References
Auditory Feedback	(1)	Prosodic Warmth	The voice shows gentleness, naturalness and emotional investment in terms of intonation, pitch and speaking speed, making users feel close and trusted.	Pias, S. B. H., et al. (2024); Romeo, M., et al. (2025).
Auditory Feedback	(2)	Social Wording	The language contains social cues such as emotional resonance, polite expression, and group belonging, strengthening users' "interpersonal perception" of the interaction objects.	Khalid, O., Srinivasan, P. (2022); Yang, D., et al. (2025).
Behavioral Feedback	(1)	Proactive Responsiveness	Can the system actively initiate communication in the conversation, such as asking questions, making suggestions or switching topics, rather than merely responding passively? Evaluate its primacy, relevance and degree of personalization.	Koch van den Broek, M., & Moeslund, T. B. (2024); Kraus, M., et al. (2020).
Behavioral Feedback	(2)	Turn-Taking Coordination	Whether the system can adjust the response timing according to the user's rhythm, including identifying pauses, controlling waiting duration, avoiding interruptions, etc., to enhance the smoothness of interaction.	Yang, X. J., Schemanske, C., & Searle, C. (2021); Wiberg, M., & Stolterman, E. (2021).
Visual Feedback	(1)	Facial Expressiveness	Conveying emotions through facial expressions, such as smiling or frowning, echoes the user's current state, thereby narrowing the psychological distance and enhancing the naturalness and affinity of the interaction.	Green, H. N., et al. (2025); Kroczek, L. O. H., et al. (2024).
Visual Feedback	(2)	Motion Synchrony	Imitate or coordinate movements in accordance with the user's movement rhythm to make the interaction more rhythmic and harmonious, thereby enhancing the user's sense of trust and participation.	Webb, N., et al. (2024); Bartkowski, W., et al. (2023).

Fig. 1. Illustration of each variable dimension and operation definition (For relevant literature, please refer to Appendix A).

2.3 Model Structure and Construction Path

Based on the above variable extraction, a theoretical model was developed to explain how multimodal embodied feedback influences user trust. Adopting the Input-Mediation-Output (IMO) structure common in organizational behavior, this model divides the cognitive process of embodied interaction into three paths: sensory input, meaning construction, and response generation. This structure facilitates understanding how users cognitively transform external perceptions into internal trust evaluations (Ilgen et al., 2005) [14], and has been applied in the analysis of anthropomorphic system design.

In the input layer, users receive multimodal cues from the system, including facial expressions and gestures (visual), emotional prosody and socially enriched language (auditory), and proactive or adaptive interaction behavior (behavioral). These cues simulate nonverbal social signals in human interaction, triggering early-stage social interpretation. The mediation layer is critical for transforming external input into internal trust judgments. In addition to attribution and emotional resonance mechanisms, perception of behavioral alignment and interaction timing significantly influence trust. For example, Lee and Kim (2022) found that embodied agents in smart TV interfaces who adjust response delay and speech style are perceived as more understanding and intentional, thus increasing interaction naturalness and trust [15]. These findings emphasize the importance of pragmatic cues—such as appropriate pausing and contextual responsiveness—in making users feel socially understood.

The output layer reflects the user's resulting trust evaluation, emotional affiliation, and intention to continue or deepen the interaction. These outcomes not only assess the quality of current interaction but also shape future engagement decisions.

From a theoretical application standpoint, the proposed model offers a foundational structure for defining variables and experimental metrics, enabling the conversion of the "input-mediation-trust" process into testable hypotheses. For instance, visual synchronization delays or vocal pauses can be operationalized for trust modeling and system optimization.

3 Operationalization and Quantitative Indicators of the Model

3.1 Multidimensional Feedback Indicator Framework

To operationalize the embodied feedback mechanism in interactive systems, this section restructures six core feedback variables along a cognitive trajectory based on the "Input–Mediator–Output" (IMO) model. While these variables were previously categorized into visual, auditory, and behavioral feedback channels in Sect. 2.2, this stage reinterprets them from the perspective of cognitive processes. It emphasizes their functional differences across three psychological stages: perceptual initiation, attributional interpretation, and behavioral intention formation. Each variable is provided with a contextual function description and an applicable measurement strategy, thereby constructing a feedback framework with explicit cognitive pathway logic. This three-dimensional mapping—linking feedback variables to cognitive mechanisms and measurement methods—clarifies how embodied feedback is embedded in the interactive experience.

Rather than categorizing variables by sensory modality, this framework locates them according to their cognitive roles. Specifically, the input layer comprises immediate and salient social cues that initiate user perception of the system, such as facial expressions and tone of voice, which primarily stimulate a sense of social presence. The mediator layer includes cognitively processed signals that require interpretation and serve as the basis for inferring system intentions, such as interaction rhythm, movement synchrony, and social-linguistic expression. The output layer, in turn, represents users' integrated judgments and behavioral tendencies, including trust, sense of belonging, and willingness to continue engagement. This functional stratification supports a more targeted design of measurement methods and enables precise mapping of feedback mechanisms in embodied interaction.

Input Layer: Initial Social Perception. In the input layer, system feedback functions as the initial perceptual anchor for users. Variables at this stage often feature high salience and immediacy. For instance, facial expression mirroring is a direct visual cue that facilitates emotional decoding and social signal interpretation. Höfling and Alpers (2023) demonstrated that automatic facial coding (AFC) systems show predictive validity for subjective emotional ratings in video contexts, suggesting that FACS-based metrics can effectively assess the perceived human-likeness of emotional feedback [16]. Prosodic warmth, or vocal affinity, also influences the user's perception of friendliness and interpersonal intent. Shome and Etemad (2023) proposed the EmoDistill model, which combines prosodic and linguistic features to enhance emotion recognition in speech. Features such as pitch, tempo, and intonation can be analyzed using speech-based affective computing tools to quantify warmth and approachability [17]. Another indicator, proactive responsiveness, refers to the system's ability to autonomously initiate feedback based on context, even in the absence of explicit input. For example, when a user hesitates or lingers on an interface, the system may proactively provide suggestions, which could foster the impression that "the system understands me." This dimension can be measured via system log data, such as proactive trigger frequency and response latency.

Mediator Layer: Social Attribution and Interpretation. The mediator layer connects perception to judgment by supporting meaning-making and social attribution. At this stage, users interpret feedback in terms of the system's underlying intentions. Social-linguistic expressiveness refers to how the system's verbal cues convey social identity and empathy—e.g., by addressing the user as a "friend" or expressing anticipation for future interactions. These expressions can be analyzed through semantic embedding models and affective lexicons. Movement synchrony serves as a key nonverbal cue for affiliation and coordination. For example, in rhythm-based interactions or games, a system that synchronizes its motion with the user's (e.g., matching beat or latency-aligned gestures) strengthens social cohesion. Yozevitch et al. (2023) utilized XGBoost models to distinguish synchronous and asynchronous behavioral data, showing that rhythm alignment predicts perceived affiliation and coordination quality [18]. This dimension can be captured using motion tracking tools such as OpenPose, paired with user surveys on perceived coordination. Interactional pacing, another mediator variable, assesses whether users are given adequate time to express themselves without interruption. In voice-based systems, abrupt topic shifts following short user pauses can be interpreted as inattentiveness, whereas well-timed silences contribute to perceptions of attentiveness and respect. Measurement methods may include turn-taking structure analysis, response time coding, and satisfaction surveys.

Output Layer: Subjective Evaluation and Behavioral Tendencies. At the output layer, users consolidate their perceptual and interpretive experiences into attitudinal and behavioral outcomes. The three core psychological constructs—trust intention, sense of belonging, and continued interaction willingness—represent the integrative effect of embodied feedback mechanisms. While these outcomes are not determined by any single feedback channel, they are shaped by the synergistic influence of prior input and mediator processes.

Trust intention reflects the user's positive assessment of the system's reliability and anticipated value. For instance, when users are willing to delegate tasks such as ticket booking or schedule planning to the system after multiple interactions, trust can be considered well established. It is typically measured using standardized instruments such as the System Trust Scale (STS), along with behavioral metrics like frequency of delegation or activation of autonomous features.

Sense of belonging emphasizes the extent to which users incorporate the system into their social or psychological space. In scenarios such as remote collaboration with social robots, systems that respond empathetically to user tone are more likely to be perceived as collaborative partners rather than impersonal tools. This construct can be evaluated through belongingness questionnaires and semantic frequency analysis of affiliative language (e.g., "we," "together," "partner") in user dialogues.

Continued interaction willingness captures the user's intention to reuse or recommend the system. For example, an elderly user who continues to engage with a voice assistant post-initial trial—initiating more sessions and exploring additional functions—exhibits sustained engagement. This can be assessed using behavioral intention scales, in combination with log data such as session frequency, time-on-task, feature utilization breadth, and user retention curves.

In summary, this section establishes a clear three-dimensional mapping of variables, cognitive mechanisms, and evaluation methods. The resulting framework provides a structured operational path for implementing the IMO model in embodied interaction. It also offers a solid foundation for the experimental designs and scenario adaptations proposed in the following sections. Figure 1 visualizes the multidimensional correspondences between the variables, cognitive pathways, and measurement indicators.

3.2   Verification Analysis and Experimental Design Recommendations

To assess the empirical feasibility of the proposed "Feedback Variable–Psychological Mechanism–Measurement Method" (FPM) triadic model, this section outlines a controlled experimental framework aimed at verifying the independent and interactive influence of core feedback variables on user cognition. The central strategy is to treat the six embodied feedback variables as independent factors, each manipulated using binary conditions (e.g., present/absent or high/low), and to examine their effects across the three cognitive layers—Input, Mediator, and Output. This model-oriented manipulation enables the examination of causal mechanisms and validates the pathway structure proposed in previous sections.

At the experimental design level, the operationalizable contrast settings for each variable are systematically defined (see Fig. 2). The three input-layer variables—Facial Expressiveness, Prosodic Warmth, and Proactive Responsiveness—are manipulated through conditions such as "emotional expressions vs. static expressionless," "soft and natural tone vs. mechanical/stiff tone," and "active suggestion or automatic response vs. passive waiting." For the mediator layer, the variables Motion Synchrony, Social Wording, and Turn-Taking Coordination are controlled using "rhythmic coordination movements vs. dislocation and lag movements," "anthropomorphic wording (e.g., 'Welcome back') vs. neutral statements," and "smooth rhythm response vs. high-frequency interruption or sliding jump reaction." These manipulations can be embedded into scripted interactive prototypes, ensuring high experimental feasibility and cross-scenario replicability.

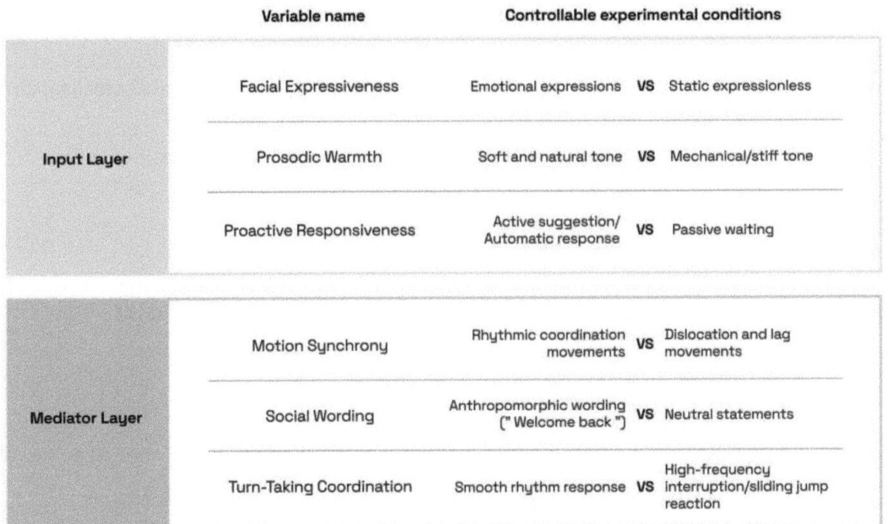

Fig. 2. Feedback variable experimental manipulation structure diagram.

Building upon this framework, six causal hypotheses (H1–H6) are proposed to support model validation, each targeting a specific variable and path segment within the cognitive architecture (see Table 1). For instance, H3 posits that proactive responsiveness enhances trust by increasing the perception that the system "understands" the user, forming a bridge from the input to mediator layer. H4 hypothesizes that insufficient movement synchrony weakens the user's inference of social intent within the mediator stage. H5 highlights the impact of disrupted turn-taking on satisfaction and engagement intention, characterizing the mediator-to-output transition. These hypotheses together constitute the logical foundation of the causal hypothesis diagram, which supports focused verification in downstream experiments.

Table 1. Hypothetical causal pathways between feedback variables and user trust-related psychological mechanisms.

Number	Hypothetical path description	Involving variables	Psychological mechanism path
H1	The absence of expressions will weaken users' initial perception of the social existence of the system	Facial Expressiveness	Input Layer
H2	The weakening of tone affinity will affect users' sense of closeness and social perception of the system	Prosodic Warmth	Mediator Layer

(continued)

Table 1. (*continued*)

Number	Hypothetical path description	Involving variables	Psychological mechanism path
H3	The reinforcement of active response behaviors will enhance users' trust judgment that "the system understands me"	Proactive Responsiveness	Input Layer → Mediator Layer
H4	The lack of action synchronization will significantly reduce the user's ability to recognize the social intentions of the system	Movement Synchrony	Mediator Layer
H5	The lack of social features in language content will weaken users' sense of belonging and emotional investment	Social-Linguistic Expressiveness	Mediator Layer → Output Layer
H6	Frequent interruptions in interaction will disrupt pragmatic rhythm and affect overall satisfaction and the willingness to continue interaction	Interactional Pacing	Mediator Layer → Output Layer

At the measurement strategy level, a one-to-one mapping is established between each hypothesis (H1–H6) and a customized set of measurement methods, forming a triangulated framework combining subjective ratings, objective recognition, and behavioral logging. This approach not only improves the reliability and comparability of variable effects but also reinforces the interpretability of pathway-based causal inference.

Specifically, H1 (Facial Expressiveness) is assessed using AFC-based facial coding and social presence scores to capture initial perceptual response. H2 (Prosodic Warmth) utilizes EmoDistill acoustic analysis combined with closeness questionnaires to evaluate affective tone and intimacy. H3 (Proactive Responsiveness) draws on system log trigger frequency and System Trust Scale (STS) ratings to test its mediating influence on trust formation. For the mediator variables, H4 (Movement Synchrony) relies on OpenPose motion tracking with rhythm coordination scores, while H5 (Social-Linguistic Expressiveness) uses semantic label frequency and belongingness questionnaires to capture linguistic affiliation. Finally, H6 (Turn-Taking Coordination) is measured through conversational turn-taking structure coding and satisfaction ratings, reflecting its role in pacing and interactional continuity (see Fig. 3).

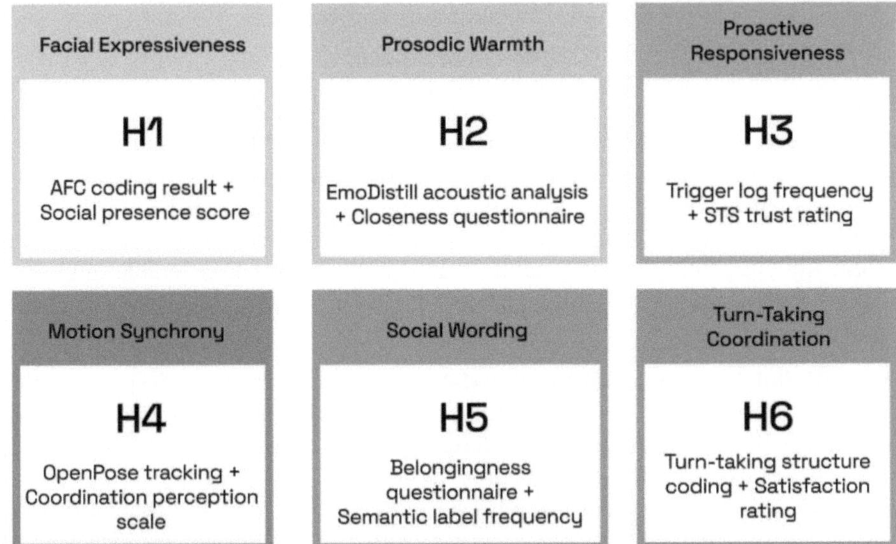

Fig. 3. Visual Mapping of H1–H6 Causal Pathways Across the IMO Layers.

As illustrated in the variable-to-hypothesis-to-measurement mapping diagram (Fig. 3), this structure offers a standardized experimental template for follow-up implementation. Together with the prior variable manipulation schema (Fig. 2) and hypothesis table (Table 1), it enables multi-scenario embedding of experimental tasks across dialogue, assistance, and collaborative contexts. This integration enhances the ecological validity of the model and supports its application in trust-sensitive human–AI system design.

In summary, this section establishes a complete validation framework by clarifying variable manipulations, proposing pathway-specific hypotheses, and pairing each with actionable measurement tools. These methodological preparations provide strong support for future empirical research and optimization of embodied feedback-driven interaction systems.

3.3 Contextual Applicability of the Model

The proposed "visual–auditory–behavioral" triadic embodied interaction model is primarily designed to construct trust mechanisms for virtual agents that lack a physical body. However, its structural logic demonstrates strong cross-modal transferability, showing practical value across embodied AI agents, humanoid digital assistants, emotional support systems, and multimodal service interfaces. To explore how the model adapts across different interactive systems, this section analyzes three representative scenarios in terms of their variable mappings, feedback affordances, and trust-building strategies.

Embodied Robotic Systems and Humanoid Agents. In physically embodied systems such as service robots, collaborative arms, and companion robots, the presence of a tangible form and dynamic motor expression enables more direct implementation of "human-like" behavioral cues. Among the six core variables, Facial Expressiveness and Motion Synchrony are particularly feasible in this context. For instance, when a humanoid robot is capable of coordinating gaze behavior, smile responses, and gesture mirroring during a collaborative or supportive task, it can significantly enhance the user's perception of the robot's social intent and reliability. Previous studies have confirmed that rhythmical alignment in non-verbal feedback—even in the presence of highly mechanical form factors—can elicit emotional resonance and foster user trust [2]. Therefore, while the current model is optimized for virtual interactions, its layered feedback structure and psychological mechanisms are readily transferable to physical embodied systems, serving as a foundational logic for social human–robot interaction design.

Virtual Digital Assistants and Multimodal Interfaces. With the widespread deployment of virtual agents across education, customer service, public administration, and guided navigation, these digital entities have increasingly taken on dual roles of information delivery and emotional modulation. Variables such as Prosodic Warmth, Social-Linguistic Expressiveness, and Turn-Taking Coordination from the proposed model are highly operationalizable in such systems. Although digital humans lack physical embodiment, their visual, auditory, and scripted components can be integrated to achieve effective guidance, explanation, and empathy.

For example, in an educational tutoring system, a virtual teacher with an encouraging tone and positive expressions is more likely to engage students cognitively. In contrast, a digital government assistant that maintains eye contact through gaze simulation and provides confirmatory verbal feedback is perceived as more professional and trustworthy. It is particularly worth noting that even in the absence of physical affordances, digital systems can still elicit a strong sense of social presence and "being understood" by optimizing response timing and affective semantics.

To further examine the implementation differences of feedback variables across modalities, Fig. 4 presents a comparative matrix mapping six core variables against embodied robots and digital humans (see Fig. 4). The horizontal axis lists the six feedback variables, and the vertical axis compares their implementation feasibility in two system types. Each cell is rated in three tiers based on technical feasibility and naturalness: high feasibility (dark green), moderate feasibility (light green), and low or challenging feasibility (outlined). The heatmap shows that visual and motor variables (e.g., Facial Expressiveness, Motion Synchrony) are more easily realized in physical systems, while speech- and script-based variables (e.g., Prosodic Warmth, Social Wording) are more flexible and scalable in virtual environments. This comparative mapping not only reveals technical constraints across platforms but also offers concrete guidance for prioritizing feedback strategies during system design.

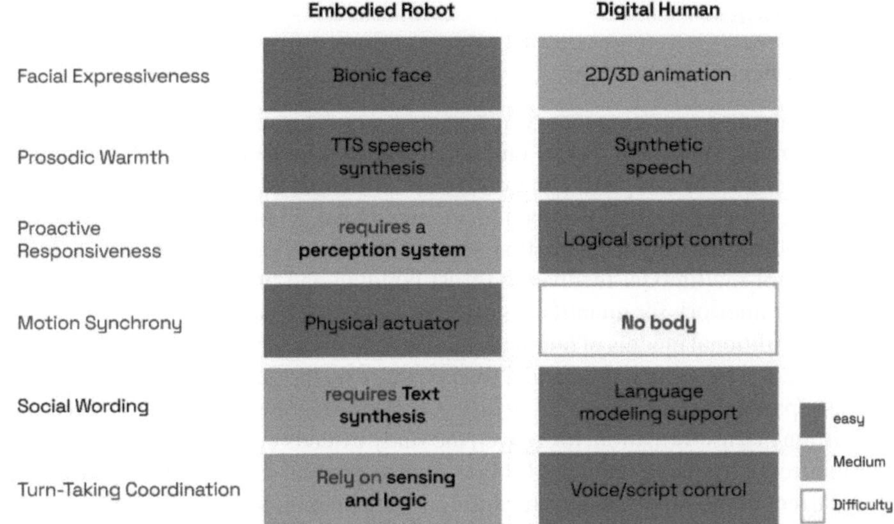

Fig. 4. Modality Mapping Matrix of Feedback Variable Feasibility in Embodied Robots and Digital Humans.

Emotionally Supportive Interactive Systems. Beyond task-oriented applications, emotionally supportive AI systems—such as therapeutic chatbots or empathetic companions—have emerged as critical agents in trust-sensitive contexts. In such scenarios, users are less concerned with task efficiency and more attuned to subjective experiences of emotional validation, empathy, and being truly "seen" by the system. Here, mediator-layer variables like Prosodic Warmth and Proactive Responsiveness become especially salient. They shape not only perceived competence but also determine the user's willingness to continue engagement.

For instance, a virtual assistant designed to support users during emotional distress should be able to offer soft vocal tones, well-timed pauses, and context-aware replies to convey genuine empathy. These signals can alleviate emotional strain and establish long-term trust. Interestingly, in emotionally sensitive settings, physical embodiment can become a liability—overly anthropomorphic robots may trigger discomfort or uncanny valley effects. In contrast, purely voice-based virtual systems can align more naturally with human expectations through subtle modulation of pacing, warmth, and affective consistency. Recent research also suggests that moderate response delays and non-mechanical affective cues enhance perceived empathy and user self-expression [19].

In summary, the embodied feedback model demonstrates strong adaptability across embodied, virtual, and emotionally sensitive systems. While originally designed for virtual trust-building, its core psychological mechanisms and feedback structures are readily transferable to physical devices, multimodal UIs, and voice-based agents. By flexibly adjusting feedback channels and prioritization strategies, different systems can tailor interaction patterns to their goals. Thus, this model not only provides a comprehensive theoretical framework but also serves as a versatile design reference for building future trust-oriented embodied interaction systems.

4 Discussion

4.1 Theoretical Contributions

Based on embodied cognition theory, this study proposes a structured, measurable, and verifiable three-dimensional virtual embodied feedback model to address the problem of how virtual humanoid agents can evoke trust and social attribution from users in the absence of a physical body. This model integrates visual, auditory, and behavioral feedback channels into an "Input–Mediation–Output" structure, clarifying the psychological mechanisms of multimodal feedback in trust-building and providing a theoretical and operational framework for quantifying trust-based interaction.

Unlike traditional models of human-machine trust that emphasize functional reliability or interaction frequency, this model focuses more on the generation of social perceptual cues—particularly the intermediary roles of understanding, responding, and rhythm coordination in trust formation. Moreover, the study extends the application of embodied cognition from physically embodied robots to disembodied digital agents, addressing a gap in current embodiment theory regarding its application to virtual interaction. This responds to recent trends in HCI that explore "disembodied embodiment." By incorporating theories of social trust, the media equation, and rhythm adaptation, the study offers a novel and integrated theoretical perspective on multimodal trust mechanisms.

4.2 Design Implications

From a design perspective, the proposed three-dimensional virtual embodied feedback model provides a framework for trust-building strategies in virtual agent systems. The six core feedback variables (e.g., vocal warmth, facial expressiveness, motion synchrony) can serve as a structural reference for user needs analysis and interaction scripting in the early stages of system design. This supports the systematic construction of user perceptions of being "understood" and "responded to," thereby enhancing social identification and emotional engagement with digital agents. Furthermore, the feedback dimensions and their intermediary psychological mechanisms can be translated into an evaluation toolkit for design validation and iterative optimization. For example, during the development of voice assistants, digital customer service agents, or AI companions, system responses can be dynamically adjusted based on user feedback related to emotional tone, movement rhythm, and visual alignment—enabling personalized adaptation and improved user perception. The model is also applicable in AIGC contexts, such as auto-generated interaction scripts and selection mechanisms for interaction styles, offering theoretical guidance for future multimodal HCI systems.

In sum, the model not only expands the theoretical boundaries of embodied cognition in digital interaction but also provides a practical and extensible structural tool for interaction design, user trust enhancement, and system evaluation in virtual agent systems.

4.3 Expanding into Haptic and Olfactory Dimensions

Although the proposed model focuses on visual, auditory, and behavioral feedback, recent studies highlight the unique contributions of haptic and olfactory modalities in building trust and emotional connections—suggesting fruitful avenues for future model extension.

For instance, in terms of haptic feedback, Gamboa-Montero et al. (2025) found that participants engaging in "active touch interactions" with social robots experienced enhanced enjoyment and emotional engagement. This effect was independent of the robot's expressive abilities, indicating that "social touch" independently influences user attitudes. Another study on multisensory virtual reality experiences showed that haptic stimuli significantly increased trust without introducing distracting emotions—supporting the inclusion of touch as an independent trust-building pathway. Regarding olfactory feedback, Alshaer et al. (2025) conducted a multisensory VR experiment revealing that while visual and haptic stimuli help foster trust, olfactory cues are more often associated with negative emotional responses (e.g., disgust), suggesting that smell may act as a boundary modulator of trust via emotional intensity. Recent advancements in wearable olfactory devices also point to increasing feasibility, with improvements in miniaturization and contextual sensitivity.

Based on these developments, future studies could explore:

- Haptic dimension experiments: e.g., using touch, handshakes, or pressure-based feedback to examine how "haptic synchrony" influences trust, emotional belonging, and interaction decisions—following frameworks such as Gamboa-Montero's.
- Olfactory condition studies: using with/without scent experimental designs to determine whether smell enhances trust or modulates emotional responses to reduce perceived artificiality.
- Multisensory coupling effects: comparing 3D–4D–5D feedback combinations across VR, AR, and social robotics to clarify the additive or synergistic mechanisms in multisensory interaction.

However, technological constraints currently limit the practical implementation of these extensions:

- Although haptic devices (e.g., tactile gloves, vibration bands) are becoming more lightweight, cost and user acceptance remain barriers.
- Olfactory module control remains complex, and individual olfactory memory differences complicate its application in virtual agents.
- Therefore, in this study, touch and smell are treated as "theoretical extension layers," with the potential to become formal fourth or fifth dimensions of the model once the technology matures—ultimately contributing to a more immersive and trust-inducing virtual interaction framework.

4.4 Paths to Model Validation

Although this study proposes a theoretically grounded triadic feedback model for trust construction, its empirical validation remains to be carried out in future research. To enhance the structural soundness and practical applicability of the model, we propose two complementary validation approaches: Path A (expert evaluation) and Path B (behavioral experiment), together forming an integrative dual-path framework.

Path A, the expert-based validation pathway, focuses on verifying the structural consistency and theoretical relevance of the six feedback variables. As illustrated in the model structure (see Fig. 5), this approach adopts the Delphi method, inviting experts in human–computer interaction and cognitive psychology to assess the importance and rationality of the proposed variables. Quantitative indicators such as the Content Validity Ratio (CVR) and the Item-level Content Validity Index (I-CVI) are recommended to analyze item-level validity and variable consistency. The output, in the form of aggregated importance scores, can serve as the basis for adjusting model structure and re-weighting variable contributions, offering a conceptual validation path that is particularly suitable for early-stage theoretical testing.

Path B, the behavioral validation pathway, focuses on controlled experiments using interactive prototypes. In this approach, the six core feedback variables—Facial Expressiveness, Prosodic Warmth, Proactive Responsiveness, Movement Synchrony, Social-Linguistic Expressiveness, and Turn-Taking Coordination—are treated as independently manipulable conditions within lab-based interactions. By embedding these variables into simulated conversational tasks or multimodal feedback interfaces, we can measure their differentiated effects on user trust across cognitive layers. Key outcome measures include Social Presence ratings, System Trust Scale (STS) scores, and emotional engagement scores, enabling causal pathway testing from perception to trust formation.

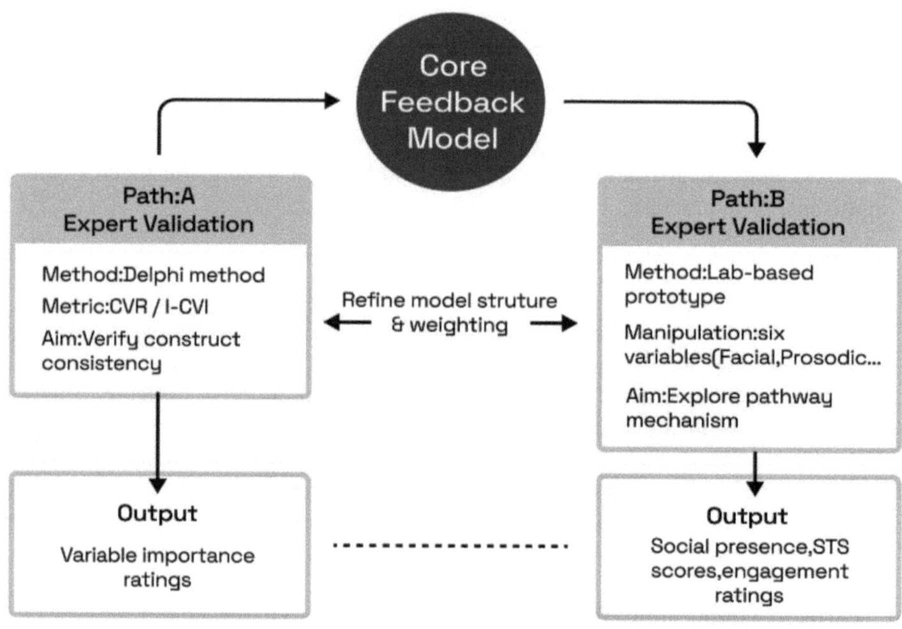

Fig. 5. Modality.

Notably, these two pathways are not independent but are linked in a dynamic cycle. As shown in the validation flow diagram (see Fig. 5), both paths converge around the core feedback model and jointly contribute to its iterative optimization. While Path A provides top-down validation of construct clarity, Path B offers bottom-up empirical exploration of variable impacts. Together, they create a bidirectional feedback loop for structural refinement and mechanism verification.

To further assist future implementation of Path B, we present an operability matrix of feedback variables and corresponding experimental designs (see Table 2). This matrix outlines four core aspects for each variable: (1) binary experimental conditions (e.g., "no animation / smiling expression"), (2) corresponding measurement targets (e.g., social presence perception), and (3) potential system modules for integration (e.g., AFC facial coding, EmoDistill speech engine, OpenPose motion tracker). For example, Proactive Responsiveness is mapped to "passive wait vs. predictive prompt," measured by trust ratings and latency metrics, and supported by intent prediction engines. This structured matrix serves as a practical design tool for future experiments and enables replicable, targeted exploration of psychological mechanisms in trust-based interaction.

Table 2. Operability Matrix for Future Experimental Design of Feedback Variables.

Feedback Variable	Experimental Conditions	Measurement Target	Potential System Integration
Facial Expressiveness	No animation / Smiling expression	Social presence perception	AFC facial coding module
Prosodic Warmth	Flat tone / Affinitive tone	Closeness impression / warmth	TTS prosody controller (EmoDistill)
Proactive Responsiveness	Passive wait / Predictive prompt	Trust score / reaction latency	Intent prediction engine
Motion Synchrony	Desynchronized / Aligned motion	Synchrony index / affiliation	OpenPose motion tracker
Social Wording	Generic text / Personified script	Belongingness questionnaire	NLP-based semantic generation
Turn-Taking Coordination	Frequent interruption / Proper pauses	Interaction satisfaction	Turn-taking logic module

In summary, Path A and Path B constitute a dual-path validation framework that combines theoretical rigor with empirical applicability. While Path A ensures conceptual clarity and consistency, Path B enables data-driven refinement of mechanism structures. Together, they support a complete cycle of model validation, offering a robust methodological foundation for applying the feedback model to trust-building in virtual agents, embodied robots, and other intelligent interactive systems.

5 Conclusion

This study proposes a theoretically grounded and operationally feasible model for understanding how trust is formed in human–agent interaction through virtual embodiment. Anchored in embodied cognition theory and multimodal communication frameworks, the model identifies six core feedback variables—Facial Expressiveness, Motion Synchrony, Prosodic Warmth, Social Wording, Proactive Responsiveness, and Turn-Taking Coordination—and organizes them within an Input–Mediator–Output (IMO) framework. Each variable is defined through empirical literature and mapped to psychological mechanisms and measurement strategies, enabling fine-grained validation and system-level integration.

From a theoretical perspective, the model offers a novel contribution to the literature on affective HCI by operationalizing the mechanisms through which virtual agents can simulate embodied social presence. Unlike traditional approaches that emphasize anthropomorphic design or surface-level affect cues, this study articulates a cognitive pathway structure that explains how and why specific feedback features activate trust-related perceptions, such as understanding, social presence, or relational warmth. This provides a scalable foundation for future computational trust modeling in both physical and virtual agents.

In terms of design practice, the model is adaptable to a wide range of interactive systems—from humanoid robots to digital tutors, service-oriented avatars, and emotionally supportive virtual companions. Through the Embodied Mapping Matrix (see Fig. 4), the study further clarifies how feedback variables differ in feasibility across modalities, offering actionable guidance on channel prioritization during prototyping. This enhances the model's value not only as a diagnostic framework but also as a generative tool for system optimization.

Future work may extend the model along multiple dimensions. On the empirical front, the dual-path validation strategy—expert scoring and behavioral prototyping (see Fig. 5 and Table 2)—offers a structured roadmap for testing and refining the model's assumptions and variable weighting. On the applied front, the model may be extended to accommodate cross-cultural variation in trust cognition, multi-language dialogue systems, or additional modalities such as haptics and AR-based environmental cues. These directions underscore the model's flexibility as both a theoretical and applied tool for advancing trust-centric human–AI interaction design.

Appendix A: Literature Sources for Variable Selection

1. Pias, S.B.H., Freel, A., Huang, R., Williamson, D., Kim, M., Kapadia, A.: Building Trust Through Voice: How Vocal Tone Impacts User Perception of Attractiveness of Voice Assistants. arXiv preprint arXiv:2409.18941 (2024).
2. Romeo, M., Torre, I., Le Maguer, S., Sleat, A., Cangelosi, A., Leite, I.: The Effect of Voice and Repair Strategy on Trust Formation and Repair in Human-Robot Interaction. ACM Trans. Hum.-Robot Interact. 14(2), Article 33 (2025).
3. Yang, D., Hovy, D., Jurgens, D., Plank, B.: Socially Aware Language Technologies: Perspectives and Practices. In: Proceedings of the 2025 Conference on Empirical Methods in Natural Language Processing, pp. 1–14. Association for Computational Linguistics (2025)
4. Khalid, O., Srinivasan, P.: Style Matters! Investigating Linguistic Style in Online Communities. In: Proceedings of the 2024 ACM Conference on Web Science, pp. 1–10. ACM, New York (2024)

5. Koch van den Broek, M., Moeslund, T.B.: What is Proactive Human-Robot Interaction? - A Review of a Progressive Field and Its Definitions. ACM Trans. Hum.-Robot Interact. 13(4), Article 49, 1–30 (2024).

6. Kraus, M., Wagner, N., Minker, W.: Effects of Proactive Dialogue Strategies on Human-Computer Trust. In: Proceedings of the 28th ACM Conference on User Modeling, Adaptation and Personalization (UMAP '20), pp. 1–10. ACM, Genoa, Italy (2020).

7. Yang, X.J., Schemanske, C., Searle, C.: Toward quantifying trust dynamics: How people adjust their trust after moment-to-moment interaction with automation. Hum. Factors 64(2), 189–205 (2022).

8. Wiberg, M., Stolterman, E.: Time and Temporality in HCI Research. Interact. Comput. 33(3), 189–205 (2021).

9. Kroczek, L.O.H., Lingnau, A., Schwind, V., Wolff, C., Mühlberger, A.: Observers predict actions from facial emotional expressions during real-time social interactions. Behav. Brain Res. 471, 115126 (2024).

10. Green, H.N., Iqbal, T.: Using Physiological Measures, Gaze, and Facial Expressions to Model Human Trust in a Robot Partner. IEEE Trans. Robot. 40(2), 1125–1138 (2024).

11. Webb, N., Milivojevic, S., Sobhani, M., Madin, Z.R., Ward, J.C., Yusuf, S., Baber, C., Hunt, E.R.: Co-Movement and Trust Development in Human-Robot Teams. IEEE Trans. Hum.-Mach. Syst. 54(3), 312–325 (2024).

12. Bartkowski, W., Nowak, A., Czajkowski, F.I., Schmidt, A., Müller, F.: In Sync: Exploring Synchronization to Increase Trust Between Humans and Non-humanoid Robots. In: Proceedings of the 2023 CHI Conference on Human Factors in Computing Systems (CHI '23), Article 782, pp. 1–15. ACM, Hamburg, Germany (2023).

References

1. O'Dell, B., Stevens, K., Tomlinson, A., Singh, I., Cipriani, A.: Building trust in artificial intelligence and new technologies in mental health. Evid. Based Ment. Health **25**(2), 45–46 (2022)

2. Tarlan, B., et al.: How can I assist you today? A comparative analysis of a humanoid robot and a virtual human avatar in human perception. arXiv preprint arXiv:2412.07912 (2024)

3. Urakami, J., Seaborn, K.: Nonverbal cues in human-robot interaction: a communication studies perspective. ACM Trans. Hum.-Robot Interact. **15**(1), 1–25 (2022)

4. Na, H., Park, S., Dong, S.-Y.: Mixed reality-based interaction between human and virtual cat for mental stress management. Sensors **22**(3), 1159 (2022)

5. Froese, T., Iizuka, H., Ikegami, T.: Embodied social interaction constitutes social cognition in pairs of humans: a minimalist virtual reality experiment. Sci. Rep. **4**, 3672 (2014)

6. Shaw, M.: An input-output model for interactive systems. In: CHI'86: Proceedings of the SIGCHI Conference on Human Factors in Computing Systems, pp. 261–273. ACM, Boston (1986)

7. Pfeifer, R., Bongard, J.: How the Body Shapes the Way We Think: A New View of Intelligence. MIT Press, Cambridge (2007)

8. Dourish, P.: Where the Action Is: The Foundations of Embodied Interaction. MIT Press, Cambridge (2001)

9. Reeves, B., Nass, C.: The Media Equation: How People Treat Computers, Television, and New Media like Real People and Places. Cambridge University Press, Cambridge (1996)

10. van der Goot, M.J., Etzrodt, K.: Disentangling two fundamental paradigms in human-machine communication research: media equation and media evocation. Hum.-Mach. Commun. **6**, 17–30 (2023)

11. Schaefer, K.E.: The perception and measurement of human-robot trust. Dissertation. University of Central Florida, Orlando (2013)

12. Van Wissen, A., Vinkers, C.D., van Halteren, A.: Developing a virtual coach for chronic patients: a user study on the impact of similarity, familiarity and realism. In: Meschtscherjakov, A., De Ruyter, B., Fuchsberger, V., Murer, M., Tscheligi, M. (eds.) PERSUASIVE 2016. LNCS, vol. 9638, pp. 263–275. Springer, Cham (2016)

13. Breazeal, C.: Emotion and sociable humanoid robots. Int. J. Hum. -Comput. Stud. **59**(1–2), 119–155 (2003)

14. Ilgen, D.R., Hollenbeck, J.R., Johnson, M., Jundt, D.: Teams in organizations: from input–process–output models to IMOI models. Annu. Rev. Psychol. **56**, 517–543 (2005)

15. Lee, K., Lee, J., Sah, Y.: Interacting with an embodied interface. Interact. Stud. **23**(2), 179–205 (2022)

16. Höfling, T.T.A., Alpers, G.W.: Automatic facial coding predicts self-report of emotion, advertisement and brand effects elicited by video commercials. Front. Neurosci. **17**, 1125983 (2023)

17. Shome, D., Etemad, A.: Speech emotion recognition with distilled prosodic and linguistic affect representations. arXiv preprint arXiv:2309.04849 (2023)

18. Yozevitch, R., Dahan, A., Seada, T., Appel, D., Gvirts, H.: Classifying interpersonal synchronization states using a data-driven approach: implications for social interaction understanding. Sci. Rep. **13**, 11150 (2023)

19. Gamboa-Montero, A., Moriuchi, E., Kudo, K., Okabe, M.: The impact of social touch in human-robot interaction on perceived trust and engagement. Int. J. Soc. Robot. **16**, 33–48 (2024)

20. Alshaer, A., Hasegawa, S., Kimura, A., Miyasato, T., Tetsutani, N.: Emotional effects of scent in virtual reality environments: a study on olfactory influence and trust in interaction. Virtual Reality **28**, 105–121 (2024)

Smart Environments
and Manufacturing Systems

Enhancing Public Built Environments Through Human-Building Interaction: Integrating User-Centred Design and AI-Driven Analysis in Architectural Planning

Cristina Caramelo Gomes[(✉)]

Universidade Lusíada de Lisboa, CITAD – Centro de Investigação em Território, Arquitetcura e Design (Center for Research in Territory, Architecture, and Design), Lisbon, Portugal
cris_caramelo@outlook.pt

Abstract. The integration of Human-Computer Interaction (HCI) principles into architectural design is transforming how users engage with public built environments. This study explores Human-Building Interaction (HBI) as a multidisciplinary approach that enhances user experience, accessibility, and functionality in urban spaces. By incorporating User-Centred Design (UCD) and User Experience (UX) methodologies, the research examines how spatial configurations influence human interactions, well-being, and social dynamics. The study employs AI-driven analysis, using ChatGPT to assess two playgrounds through the perspectives of diverse user personas. Findings highlight the limitations of conventional planning methods that prioritize aesthetics and economic efficiency over inclusivity and usability. The results emphasize the need for adaptable, technology-integrated public spaces that foster intergenerational engagement and community identity. This research contributes to the discourse on intelligent built environments, advocating for AI-assisted planning tools to enhance participatory design and improve real-world applications of HCI in architecture.

Keywords: Public Spaces · User Experience · User-centred Design · Human Building Interactions · Artificial Intelligence

1 Context

Human interaction has long been explored through the lens of information and communication technologies (ICT), primarily focusing on the interplay between humans and machines. The goal has traditionally been to develop technological solutions that cater to human needs while ensuring functionality and user satisfaction. Yet, this conversation often remains confined to the realm of design expertise, largely overlooked by professionals in the built environment sector. As a result, the role of ICT-driven interaction in shaping spatial experiences is frequently underestimated.

In recent years, however, socio-environmental challenges have prompted a growing emphasis on integrating user-, human-, and society-centred design principles into the planning of the built environment. These principles underscore the profound impact of architectural configurations on individual and collective well-being. Yet, their practical implementation often remains limited to early conceptual phases, with final built solutions frequently falling short—especially in public spaces. This disconnect is largely due to conventional planning methodologies that prioritise aesthetic and economic factors while neglecting interdisciplinary insights from fields such as user-centred design (UCD) and user experience (UX). As a result, spaces often lack the qualities needed to foster engaging, meaningful interactions.

The significance of a responsive built environment—where every interaction, whether physical or digital, serves a purpose—is well-documented in academic research. Studies consistently highlight its role in advancing environmental, economic, and social sustainability goals. Yet, these insights are seldom translated into tangible architectural and urban planning strategies, leaving a gap between research and real-world practice.

This raises essential questions: How can architecture actively support and enhance human interactions, both with physical and digital spaces? Why does the built environment so often fail to meet contemporary functional demands, integrate available technologies, or genuinely respond to human needs? Without intentional design strategies that promote meaningful interactions between individuals and their surroundings, space remains a mere geometric construct—lacking the depth to evolve into a true place, rich with identity and collective memory.

2   From Interaction Architecture to Human Building Interactions

According to the Merriam-Webster Dictionary, interaction is defined as "the action or influence of people, groups, or things on one another." This definition aligns with Churchill's famous assertion that "We shape our buildings; thereafter they shape us," while also extending the concept to include interactions with inanimate artifacts.

The literature presents diverse perspectives on interaction in architecture. Some discussions focus on architecture as a physical space, examining its relationship with technological advancements and the emergence of smart environments (Knox, 2017). Others explore the fundamental nature of architecture itself (Olanusi and Oluwadepo, 2023). According to Enia and Martella (2023), some scholars view architecture as an object-centred practice, where buildings—whether designed for private, public, or symbolic/cultural purposes—exist as autonomous entities whose interactions are primarily determined by their formal, technical, and aesthetic characteristics. In contrast, other scholars consider architecture a relational practice, emphasizing interactions between various agents, including architects. In the former perspective, the quality of architectural interventions is assessed based on intrinsic characteristics, whereas in the latter, it is evaluated in terms of the quality of relationships it fosters. Enia and Martella (2023) deconstruct this apparent opposition and argue that both perspectives are complementary.

Building on Hodder's theory (2011), which posits that cultural history is shaped by interactions between humans and objects, Enia and Martella propose four categories of interactions related to buildings: human-to-human interactions (mediated by buildings), building–human interactions, building–nonhuman interactions, and nonhuman–nonhuman interactions (mediated by buildings). Human-to-human interactions encompass both construction processes and the use of buildings in various contexts, as architecture facilitates personal and social interactions that, in turn, influence the spaces in which they occur. This perspective justifies a human-centred approach to architectural planning, one that considers movement, interaction patterns, and user responses to spatial features. Building–human interactions pertain to how human activities impact buildings over time, whether through use, adaptation, or shifts in social values. Building–nonhuman interactions encompass environmental factors such as climate, time, and objects. Finally, nonhuman–nonhuman interactions refer to the dynamic relationships between objects within a built environment. The concept of "building" as discussed here extends beyond individual structures to the broader built environment, a term that will be used throughout this article.

Some studies associate interaction in architecture primarily with the integration of technology to support specific functions and human activities. However, interactions are not exclusively technological. A parallel can be drawn with the evolution of design disciplines, which gave rise to specialized fields such as human-computer interaction (HCI), interaction design, and user experience (UX). While technology introduces new challenges in how individuals engage with environments, products, and systems, interaction itself predates technological advancements. A key argument in this discourse is the growing recognition of interactions mediated by the built environment, which necessitates an understanding of built space in its various dimensions, including its technological aspects, particularly given the emergence of intelligent environments.

The integration of intelligence into the built environment presents new challenges and, consequently, new modes of interaction. To address these challenges, the concept of Human-Building Interaction (HBI) offers a valuable perspective on how individuals engage with architectural spaces and how design professionals can enhance these interactions. Just as the rise of digital technologies necessitated the development of HCI to analyse human-artifact relationships, the built environment requires a theoretical framework that accounts for interactions between humans, physical spaces, and embedded technologies. This is especially relevant given the increasing integration of computational systems into everyday environments, shaping how individuals live, work, and socialize.

Human-Building Interaction (HBI) is a multidisciplinary research area that seeks to understand how the built environment affects human experiences, as well as how individuals interact with, adapt to, and influence their surroundings. HBI focuses on environments that can learn, adapt, and evolve at multiple scales—from individual buildings to entire cities—to enhance user experiences and optimize resource and service management (Becerik-Gerber et al., 2022). Achieving these objectives requires collaboration among researchers and practitioners to study human behaviour in real-world contexts and design technologies that support novel, meaningful interactions based on the spatial and technological characteristics of built environments.

Zhao (2020) defines HBI as the study and application of ICT technologies in the built environment, considering both human-computer interactions and broader interactions between individuals and physical spaces. Zhao further argues that HBI has a broader scope than HCI because it explicitly incorporates built spaces into interaction models. Conversely, the built environment itself can also be shaped by digital systems, as sensors and actuators embedded within buildings influence spatial behaviours and environmental responsiveness.

Ultimately, HBI examines how individuals perceive, navigate, and experience the built environment, as well as how human and environmental responsiveness influence one another. Alavi et al. (2019) conceptualize the built environment as the construction of physical elements that define and protect spaces, attributing both functional and cultural significance to physical structures while recognizing that spatial properties facilitate activity patterns and social relationships. These authors identify three key drivers of HBI: (1) technological advancements enabling the integration of computational elements into physical infrastructure; (2) transformations in architectural practice that embrace reactive, interactive, and self-modifying structures; and (3) an increasing awareness of sustainability, which necessitates human-centred environments.

Despite variations in focus, the authors discussed here share a common perspective: the need to design user-centred built environments that accommodate human needs and expectations, ultimately enhancing the quality of experiences within these spaces contributing to a stronger sense of community and place attachment.

2.1 User Centred Design and User Experience Design Approaches: Components of Human Building Interactions

User-Centred Design (UCD) and User Experience (UX) design are foundational to both Human-Computer Interaction (HCI) and Human-Building Interaction (HBI). As Information and Communication Technology (ICT) becomes more integrated into design, these principles are influencing not just digital products but also architecture and urban planning. This shift has led to a more holistic approach, where human needs, expectations, and experiences are at the core of built environment design.

According to the Interaction Design Foundation, UCD is an iterative design process that prioritizes users' needs. It involves research, conceptualization, prototyping, implementation, and continuous refinement based on user feedback. This approach aligns closely with design thinking, which emphasizes empathy, ideation, prototyping, and iterative improvements to achieve the best possible outcome. On the other hand, UX refers to the overall experience a person has when interacting with a product, space, or system. The International Organization for Standardization (2019) defines UX as "a person's perceptions and responses resulting from the use and/or anticipated use of a product, system, or service." The key distinction between UCD and UX is that UCD is a process for designing solutions, while UX pertains to the actual experience of interacting with those solutions. However, these concepts are deeply interconnected (Nadim, 2025). While UCD and UX are widely applied in product and digital design, integrating them into the built environment presents unique challenges. Unlike digital products, physical spaces cannot be easily modified after they are built. This raises an important question: how can user-centred principles be effectively applied to architecture and urban planning?

A critical approach is continuous user engagement through research methods such as observations, surveys, and interviews. By collecting data on how people experience and navigate spaces, designers can create personas—fictional representations of different user types. These personas help architects and planners understand diverse user needs, behaviours, and expectations.

Another effective tool is storytelling. The Interaction Design Foundation suggests that compelling storytelling in design should follow Aristotelian narrative principles:

- Plot – Users' goals and experiences within a space.
- Character – User demographics, preferences, and constraints.
- Theme – The benefits and challenges presented by the design.
- Dialogue – How users interact with the space and its impact.
- Melody – Aesthetic and emotional appeal.
- Décor – Sensory and visual elements in the environment.
- Spectacle – The memorability of the space and its impact on users.

Storytelling in architecture is about more than just aesthetics—it's about creating emotional connections between people and spaces. Whether through historical narratives, cultural symbolism, or interactive experiences, storytelling can humanize spaces and foster a sense of belonging. As Mudnaney (2025) highlights, authenticity, emotional engagement, and relatability are key to making spaces meaningful for users.

Traditionally, architectural representations—such as technical drawings and perspectives—focus on construction details rather than user experience. While static visuals provide insight into spatial composition, advancements in ICT now allow for immersive design communication.

- 3D modelling and rendering help visualize materials, lighting, colours, and human interactions.
- Animations and sound-enhanced renderings provide dynamic storytelling elements.
- Immersive technologies such as Virtual Reality (VR) and Augmented Reality (AR) allow users to experience spaces before they are built.

However, despite their potential, immersive technologies remain largely confined to research and specialized applications due to cost and technical barriers. Nonetheless, VR simulations, 360° videos, and AI-driven scenario generators (Moncada, 2025) are making it easier to explore multiple design narratives, enhancing both design flexibility and user engagement.

Regardless of the medium, the ultimate goal of storytelling in architecture is to strengthen the relationship between people and their surroundings. Public spaces offer rich opportunities for narrative-driven design throughout their lifecycle.

By incorporating user personas, interactive elements, and community-driven narratives, urban planners can create spaces that feel personal, adaptable, and inclusive. This approach is especially crucial in environments where technology mediates new forms of interaction—ensuring that public spaces remain responsive, sustainable, and deeply connected to the people who use them.

2.2 Public Environment and User Experience

The built environment is more than just a collection of structures—it's the spatial framework of our daily lives, encompassing homes, workplaces, and recreational areas where people interact with both physical and digital surroundings. Within this framework, public spaces play a vital role as multifunctional arenas that bring communities together. These spaces support social interaction, economic exchange, and cultural expression, making them essential to both individual well-being and collective identity (UN-Habitat, 2025). To serve their purpose, public spaces must be inclusive, accessible, and engaging, reinforcing a shared sense of belonging and community pride.

Public spaces are more than just gathering places; they are social anchors that encourage relaxation, physical activity, and cultural connection. Whether in the form of bustling streets, serene plazas, lively marketplaces, or public facilities, these spaces help define local identity and preserve cultural heritage. Their design must balance functionality with human experience, ensuring they are safe, comfortable, and responsive to diverse needs. This requires a multidisciplinary approach that integrates urban planning, architecture, and technology while prioritizing the well-being of all users.

To create meaningful experiences in public spaces, we must first understand how people interact with their surroundings—both physical and digital. This is where Human Factors and Ergonomics (HFE) becomes essential. According to the International Ergonomics Association (IEA), ergonomics is the study of human interactions with different elements of a system, applying theory, principles, and data to optimize human well-being and overall system performance (IEA, n.d.). HFE examines not just physical design but also cognitive and psychosocial factors, shaping how people perceive and navigate spaces.

Public spaces should be designed with an awareness of three core HFE principles:

- Physical Ergonomics – Ensuring comfort, safety, and accessibility in the built environment.
- Cognitive Ergonomics – Supporting intuitive navigation, information processing, and decision-making within spaces.
- Organizational Ergonomics – Addressing social and cultural dynamics to foster engagement and inclusivity.

These principles apply not just to physical spaces but also to digital interactions, as smart technologies increasingly shape how we experience the built environment. Factors such as spatial dimensions, layout, equipment, and sensory elements all contribute to how people engage with a space—whether consciously or subconsciously.

Our experience of public spaces is deeply influenced by sensory stimuli that can either enhance or diminish well-being. Thoughtful engagement of the senses can make a space feel inviting and memorable:

- Lighting – Impacts mood, task performance, and even biological rhythms (e.g., regulating sleep cycles).
- Soundscapes – Can either encourage social interaction or provide calming atmospheres.
- Textures and Materials – Influence the tactile experience and emotional perception of space.
- Temperature and Air Quality – Affect comfort, usability, and overall well-being.

By designing for multisensory engagement, urban planners and architects can create spaces that feel alive, immersive, and responsive to users' needs.

To truly optimize human-environment interactions, designers must move beyond traditional planning methods and adopt user-centred research approaches. Three key methodologies include:

- Journey Mapping – Observing how people move through and respond to a space, helping designers anticipate needs and improve functionality.
- Personas – Creating fictional but research-based user profiles that reflect different ages, abilities, and cultural backgrounds, ensuring inclusivity.
- Storytelling – Exploring real-life narratives of how people interact with a space, allowing designers to develop more adaptive and engaging environments.

By integrating these research methods, planners can design spaces that evolve with the communities they serve, rather than remaining static or outdated. For too long, urban planning and architectural design have prioritized functionality, efficiency, and aesthetic trends over the evolving needs of users. However, a new paradigm is emerging—one that prioritizes human experience.

Moving forward, public spaces must be designed to be adaptive, inclusive, and engaging, ensuring they remain dynamic environments that enhance quality of life for all. By embracing Human Factors, sensory design, and user-centred methodologies, we can create public spaces that not only serve functional needs but also foster social connections, cultural identity, and emotional well-being.

2.3 What Makes a Good Public Environment?

Public environments play a crucial role in shaping urban daily life, serving as hubs for social and cultural interactions, entertainment, relaxation, and community engagement (Memarovic and Langheinrich, 2025). An effective public environment extends beyond aesthetic appeal; it must foster inclusion—irrespective of differences—enhance well-being and promote civic participation. To achieve these objectives, public spaces must be inviting, functional, inclusive, and capable of accommodating a diverse range of activities.

Public environments encompass a variety of spaces, including streets, recreational and natural parks, public facilities, markets, and waterfronts. While each of these spaces possesses distinct characteristics, certain fundamental principles apply universally.

The spatial layout, or physical configuration, of public spaces should be designed to support diverse user experiences by offering a range of functionalities and atmospheres. This includes quieter areas conducive to activities such as reading or contemplation, as well as dynamic spaces that facilitate physical activity, social interactions, and commercial activities, such as playgrounds, sports areas, or cafés. Street furniture plays a vital role in enhancing the usability and inclusivity of public spaces. Benches and other seating arrangements should be designed to cater to different activities and user needs, ensuring variations in shape, material, and functionality to maximize comfort, durability, and aesthetic appeal. Beyond their basic function, well-designed street furniture can contribute to a sense of place and belonging. Public spaces must be easily navigable, with streets and pathways designed to accommodate all users, including pedestrians of all ages and individuals with mobility limitations, as well as cyclists and skateboarders. The choice of materials and spatial dimensions should ensure accessibility and safety.

To enhance wayfinding, particularly in areas where natural landmarks are absent, inclusive signage, chromatic schemes, and varied material applications can facilitate navigation. Furthermore, the selection of materials and colour palettes can reflect local identity and serve as an expression of community values. Both elements contribute to fostering a sense of belonging and well-being within space (Caramelo Gomes, 2023).

Public spaces can be further enriched by promoting cultural and social activities. These initiatives can take various forms, from temporary art exhibitions and traditional markets to more permanent features such as murals and public sculptures. Incorporating interactive technologies, such as augmented reality installations and smart infrastructure, can enhance user experiences and encourage community participation (Kaarwan, 2024). The effective planning of public spaces requires consideration of human behaviour, user needs, and experience mapping. This involves analysing various scenarios to understand how individuals interact with the environment. People visit public spaces with specific purposes—whether to engage in physical exercise or to relax—and these purposes influence their behaviours and interactions. Important considerations include whether individuals visit alone or with others, the diversity of their backgrounds, and the time of day at which they engage with space.

A comprehensive approach to public space design incorporates journey mapping, personas, and storytelling. These tools help planners anticipate how different users will navigate and experience space. Additionally, public environments should be designed to encourage spontaneous activities and social interactions beyond their initial intended purpose, creating dynamic and adaptable spaces. Memarovic and Langheinrich (2025) propose a conceptual approach to public spaces that transcends their physical typology, instead categorizing them based on their response to human needs. They identify three key dimensions:

- Needs: Basic requirements such as food, water, rest, and physical activity.
- Rights: Principles of access, freedom, and appropriation that ensure inclusiveness.
- Meaning: The subjective and collective associations formed through individual and communal experiences in space.

By addressing these dimensions, public environments can become more than just physical spaces—they can serve as dynamic arenas for urban life, reinforcing social bonds, enhancing well-being, and fostering a sense of belonging.

Public environments are integral to urban life, shaping social interactions, cultural engagement, and individual well-being. Thoughtful design, emphasizing inclusivity, accessibility, and adaptability, ensures that these spaces remain functional and meaningful for diverse users. By incorporating principles of human-centred design and fostering cultural expression, cities can create public environments that enhance community participation and enrich the urban experience (Caramelo Gomes, 2024).

3   Methodology

Intelligence in the built environment is increasingly gaining attention, although the integration of intelligent systems into all environments remains a distant goal due to various economic, political, and procedural constraints. Regardless of whether or not a space incorporates advanced intelligent systems, it is essential that all built environments, particularly public spaces, be designed to promote interactions and deliver a high-quality user experience.

As previously mentioned, the planning of built environments, especially public spaces, can significantly benefit from methodologies developed within design disciplines. Approaches such as creating personas, constructing narrative storylines, and applying user-centred design principles allow design teams to view their solutions from diverse perspectives. These strategies provide deeper insights into both individual and communal spatial experiences. Additionally, technology has a profound impact on how built environments are conceived, experienced, and interacted with. Tools like three-dimensional (3D) modelling, image generation, and immersive technologies—such as virtual and augmented reality—enhance the ability to visualize final designs. These technologies allow for iterative modifications based on real-time human interactions within immersive environments. In architectural practice, 3D modelling and sequential image generation are commonly used to predict future realities, especially when responding to the specific needs of immersive environments.

The advent of artificial intelligence (AI) has further expanded these capabilities, offering innovative approaches to storytelling, image evaluation, and the creation of visual narratives derived from structured storytelling. By integrating AI-driven image generation with storytelling, a fresh approach to public space planning emerges—one that enhances the user experience and improves the spatial qualities of these environments.

This research explores the potential of AI as a tool for evaluating public spaces through the simulation of different personas and providing first-person perspectives of their experiences. AI functions as a persona simulator, offering valuable insights into the usability and inclusivity of public spaces.

To assess this approach, two playgrounds in a small village in southern Portugal were analysed. Both playgrounds are located in residential neighbourhoods:

- Playground 1: A smaller space, labelled as an "urban park" on Google Maps, with minimal children's equipment. It includes only two benches without backrests and no additional elements that could support activities beyond sitting. The flooring near the children's play equipment is made of safety materials, but it quickly transitions to Portuguese pavement—a characteristic stone material used in urban design throughout the country. This playground faces south, exposing it to intense summer heat, with temperatures reaching up to 40 °C.
- Playground 2: A larger, generational park designed with a greater variety of equipment. Despite its intended inclusivity, much of the equipment is primarily suited to younger users.

Neither of these playgrounds integrates technological elements that would facilitate digital interactions, provide location-based information, or offer opportunities for learning and entertainment. For the assessment, both playgrounds were photographed by the author to visually represent the spaces. A fictional scenario was created as a prompt for ChatGPT, depicting a family's visit to the park. The family consists of the following personas:

- An 80-years-old grandfather in a wheelchair who enjoys playing chess.

- A 75-years-old grandmother who wishes to play with her grandson, enjoys crocheting, and likes to socialize with her friends.
- A 35-years-old father who wants to engage in physical play with his son while also seeking quiet moments to read.
- A 35-years-old mother who is concerned with sun safety for her child while playing and is actively engaged in social media.
- A 5-years-old boy who enjoys outdoor activities and playing with his dog.
- A dog that seeks outdoor play and freedom.

These personas were based on observational research regarding the most frequent users of the two playgrounds. ChatGPT was then tasked with evaluating the parks from the perspectives of these personas. The AI-generated critiques offer insights similar to fieldwork observations, providing valuable feedback for the planning process. This feedback can be used to enhance the functionality and inclusivity of public spaces, ensuring that they meet the diverse needs of the communities they serve.

3.1 Case Studies

To collect data and align with the concept of using technology as a collaborator in the planning process, the designed archetype personas were submitted to ChatGPT within the context of a real-world evaluation. The goal was to assess how well two playgrounds in southern Portugal met the specific needs of these personas.

In the initial attempt, multiple photographs highlighting key aspects of each playground were uploaded to ChatGPT to obtain an evaluation report. However, due to limitations in the free version of ChatGPT regarding image uploads, an alternative approach was adopted. A single panoramic image, capturing the primary playground equipment and finishing materials, was used instead. While the possibility of using video was also considered, it was ultimately not supported by the platform. The evaluation prompt was structured in two stages, progressively expanding the family composition to simulate a broader range of users. The first stage involved the personas of the grandmother, her son, her grandson, and a golden retriever. In the second stage, additional personas—specifically the grandfather in a wheelchair and the mother, who is highly engaged in information and communication technologies (ICT)—were introduced. This iterative approach allowed for a more thorough analysis of how the playgrounds accommodated the diverse needs of these users.

By leveraging AI-driven feedback, this study emphasizes the potential of digital tools in assessing and optimizing public spaces. The insights generated by AI offer valuable guidance for urban planners and designers looking to enhance the accessibility, inclusivity, and overall user experience of public environments.

- Prompt1 – "write a first-person report on the experience of visiting 2 children's playgrounds (photos to be uploaded) by a group of: 70 years old women meeting some elderly friends, her 35 years old son, his 5-year-old son and their 4 years old golden retriever. The report should be aimed at the friendliness of both facilities, having in mind the available amenities in each of the two places and each of the characters expectations. Write also the golden retriever view."

- Prompt 2 – "rewrite considering playground 2 has the amenities on the picture, the group is now of 6, including an 80 years old grandfather on a wheelchair who likes to play chess, the grandmother is 75 years old and likes to do crochet, and the mother, a 35-year-old woman addicted to IT and social media."
- **Case 1**

The first playground analysed includes a slide, a swing, and a few benches. Additionally, there is a green area, but its use is either restricted or uninviting.

The report created by the ChatGPT was the following:

"First Playground: A Basic Setup."

Grandfather's Perspective:

This playground wasn't very accommodating for me. The cobblestone pavement made it bumpy and hard to move my wheelchair. There weren't any tables or spaces for me to comfortably sit and play chess, so I mostly just watched everyone else. Not the best place for an elderly person looking to relax (Figs. 1 and 2).

Fig. 1. Playground 1 – general view (source: author).

Grandmother's Perspective:

I found a bench to sit on, but the hard cobblestone and lack of shaded areas made it less comfortable for crocheting. I chatted with my husband and watched the kids play, but there wasn't much else to do for someone like me.

Father's Perspective:

The playground had a slide and a small play area, which was nice for my son for a short while. However, there weren't many options to keep him entertained for long. As for playing with the dog, there wasn't much space, and the ground wasn't the best for running.

Fig. 2. Playground 1, detail of the pavement and benches' location (source: author).

Mother's Perspective:
There was no Wi-Fi! The connection on my phone was weak, and there weren't any charging stations. I ended up scrolling mindlessly but wasn't really engaged because the environment wasn't comfortable for sitting with my phone.

Son's Perspective:
I liked the slide at first, but there weren't many other kids around, and there wasn't a lot of space to run. I got bored quickly and wanted to go somewhere with more things to do.

Golden Retriever's Perspective:
Not much grass, no space to run, and no water bowls. I stayed near my humans, but I really hoped we'd go somewhere better soon."

The AI-generated report provides a thoughtful and realistic analysis of the playground's setting. Based on the evaluation, it becomes clear that the layout of the space does not encourage diverse types of play for children, nor does it foster intergenerational use. The children's play area is confined to a small, paved space with materials suited to the target audience but lacking in variety or extension, limiting opportunities for more expansive play.

The few benches available are uncomfortable and offer little beyond basic seating. They are rarely placed in shaded areas, which is a significant concern, particularly during the summer months when temperatures soar. The uneven pavement, characteristic of the "Calçada à Portuguesa" (Portuguese sidewalk), further complicates accessibility, making the space difficult for individuals with mobility limitations to navigate. Moreover, there is no integration of modern technology—there is not even a designated charging spot. The only informational feature is a sign fixed to a post with emergency telephone numbers, which serves a basic functional purpose but does little to enhance the overall experience. The grass area appears to be poorly maintained, detracting from the overall aesthetic and usability of the space. Additionally, the entrance to the playground is shared with a street that also provides access to the surrounding buildings' garage, creating potential safety concerns and reducing the overall welcoming nature of the site. The playground fails to fully support the varied needs of its potential users, lacking in comfort, accessibility, and technological engagement, while presenting challenges for intergenerational use. These insights highlight the need for a more inclusive, functional, and engaging public space design.

- Case 2

The second playground analysed, due to its larger size and distinct areas, required a panoramic photograph. However, since the Word format does not support panoramic images, individual images highlighting the playground's key features will be presented for better clarity (Figs. 3, 4, 5 and 6).

Fig. 3. Playground 2, fitness area (source: author).

"Second Playground: A Space for Everyone."

Grandfather's Perspective:
This was much better! There were accessible paths for my wheelchair, and—best of all—there were actual tables where I could set up a chess game. I even found some other older men playing, and I joined in for a round. A great place for someone like me!

Grandmother's Perspective:
There was a shaded seating area, which made it perfect for doing my crochet while chatting with my friends. The environment was much more inviting, and I felt comfortable staying here for a while.

Fig. 4. Playground 2, children area (source: author).

Father's Perspective:
This playground had so much more to offer. The open spaces allowed me to play with my son and our dog, while the skate ramps and various play areas kept my son entertained for a long time. I could move between playing with him and letting him explore on his own.

Mother's Perspective:
Finally, a good spot for me! There were benches where I could sit comfortably, and I even found charging stations nearby. I got lost in social media for a while but also took some great photos of the family to post. The Wi-Fi signal was strong, which made me happy.

Son's Perspective:
This place was awesome! There were so many different things to do. I ran up and down the skate ramps, met some other kids, and even tried out a small bike track. I didn't get bored at all and didn't want to leave!

Golden Retriever's Perspective:
Yes! Open spaces! Grass! A bigger area to run! I got to chase my ball, meet other dogs, and even found a water bowl to drink from. This was the best place ever!

In the end, the second playground was a far better choice for a multi-generational family like ours. It had something for everyone, making it a place we'd definitely visit again."

The report generated for the second playground, while more promising than the first in terms of size and flexibility, still presents some limitations. This playground offers

Fig. 5. Playground 2, children play area (source: author).

distinct advantages, such as a safer and more comfortable pavement design, a clear organizational structure with zones tailored to different age groups, and a designated fitness area for adults. It also provides various seating options—benches with backrests, some arranged around tables and others placed individually near the play areas—along with water fountains and a ramp that ensures accessibility. These elements enhance the usability and flexibility of the space.

However, certain critical aspects remain unaddressed. A notable omission is the lack of restroom facilities, which limits the overall convenience of the space, particularly for families spending extended periods there. Additionally, the playground lacks technological features such as charging stations or Wi-Fi connectivity, which could significantly improve the user experience, particularly for tech-savvy visitors like the mother in the archetype personas. As with the first playground, each area is equipped with a post containing emergency contact information, but this is a basic feature that doesn't contribute substantially to the overall user experience.

Given the objective of designing a playground that fosters an intergenerational experience, the question arises: Can ChatGPT assist in identifying solutions to improve the playground's design and functionality? To explore this potential, a prompt was developed based on the previously defined personas. The prompt posed the question: What features should a playground offer to ensure a positive experience for a family composed of a grandfather in a wheelchair (80 years old), a grandmother who enjoys socializing

Fig. 6. Playground 2, children play area and water fountain (source: author).

and crocheting (75 years old), a father who enjoys playing with his son and dog /45 years old), a mother engaged in technology and social media (40 years old), a 5-year-old son who loves to play, and a dog?

The response from ChatGPT was detailed and centred on creating a positive, engaging environment that fosters interactivity among the different family members. Key suggestions focused on the importance of creating diverse play areas to accommodate various needs.

The AI-generated response to the personas' needs offers a strong framework for designing a more inclusive and engaging playground. The key takeaway is that creating a playground that accommodates multiple generations requires a thoughtful integration of various features: accessible seating, safe play zones, interactive technology, fitness areas for adults, and spaces for pets. These elements not only enhance individual experiences but also encourage intergenerational interactions, contributing to the overall success of the public space.

"A **well-designed playground** for a **multi-generational family** with diverse interests should include amenities that cater to **accessibility, social interaction, active play, and relaxation**. Here's a breakdown of **essential features** that would create a great experience for each family member:

1. Accessibility & Comfort for the Grandfather (80, in a wheelchair, likes chess)

☑ **Smooth, wheelchair-friendly paths** – Paved walkways without cobblestones or steep inclines.

☑ **Shaded seating areas with tables** – A comfortable space where he can set up a chess game.

☑ **Accessible restrooms** – Close by and easy to access.

☑ **Good lighting** – For visibility and safety.

2. Social & Relaxation Spaces for the Grandmother (75, loves crochet & chatting)

☑ **Comfortable benches with shade** – Preferably near the playground so she can chat with friends while watching the grandson.

☑ **Tables with seating** – To accommodate social gatherings and crochet work.

☑ **Calm, noise-controlled areas** – Away from high-energy play zones to ensure a peaceful setting.

☑ **Possibly a community garden** – A nice touch for older visitors who enjoy relaxing outdoor spaces.

3. Playful & Interactive Spaces for the Father (45, likes playing with his son & dog)

☑ **Open grass fields** – For running, playing ball, and interacting with the dog.

☑ **Dog-friendly areas** – A small **dog park or a designated pet-friendly section** with waste bins.

☑ **Multi-age play zones** – Equipment suitable for kids and parents to interact, like climbing structures and seesaws.

☑ **Walking & jogging trails** – For an active lifestyle with his dog and son.

4. Tech-Friendly & Comfortable Environment for the Mother (40, loves playing with her son & social media)

☑ **Seating with charging stations** – Benches or picnic tables with USB ports.

☑ **Strong Wi-Fi access** – Reliable internet for social media sharing and entertainment.

☑ **Aesthetic design** – Well-maintained, visually appealing areas for great photos.

☑ **Interactive or modern play equipment** – Tech-enhanced areas, like **motion-sensor games or digital screens** for fun engagement.

5. Fun & Engaging Playgrounds for the Son (5, active and loves to play)

☑ **Varied play structures** – Slides, climbing walls, swings, and obstacle courses.

☑ **Imaginative play areas** – Spaces like a sandpit, a small water play area, or themed structures (castles, pirate ships, etc.).

☑ **A bike/scooter path** – Safe lanes for young kids to ride.

☑ **Other kids nearby** – Ensuring a community vibe with opportunities to make friends.

6. Pet-Friendly Features for the Golden Retriever (4 years old, energetic & playful)

☑ **Dedicated dog area** – A fenced dog park with agility equipment.
☑ **Dog-friendly water stations** – Hydration spots for pets.
☑ **Waste disposal bins** – Easy access to clean up after the dog.
☑ **Open green space** – A safe place to play fetch and interact with the family.

BONUS AMENITIES for a Truly Family-Friendly Playground:
🏠 **Picnic tables & BBQ areas** – For family bonding and meals.
🌳 **Green spaces & shaded areas** – To provide a natural, relaxing atmosphere.
👪 **Family-friendly restrooms** – With baby-changing stations and accessibility options.
🚲 **Bike racks & parking spots** – For convenience and easy access.
🎭 **Community events & performances** – A small amphitheater or a space for public activities.

By incorporating these **multi-generational, inclusive, and pet-friendly** elements, the playground would provide **an enjoyable experience for all family members** while allowing each person to engage in their preferred activities. 🚀 "

Next it was asked to ChatGPT, using the second prompt, to generate an image responsive to the personnas features created previously (Fig. 7).

Fig. 7. ChatGPT generated image based on the personas features.

4 Issues to Discuss

Despite the acknowledged importance of human-centred design principles, their application in built environment planning often remains largely theoretical. Traditional approaches tend to prioritize aesthetic and economic considerations over the needs and experiences of users. However, the built environment plays a critical role in facilitating both personal and professional activities while fostering interactions between individuals and their surroundings. To enhance these interactions and cultivate a strong sense of place and community, concepts like human-centred design and experience design are essential.

Recent technological advancements have introduced a new paradigm in spatial planning, incorporating tools such as 3D modelling, AI-generated imagery, and immersive environments. These innovations enable more dynamic and flexible design processes and facilitate new modes of interaction within physical spaces, leading to the development of smart environments. A deeper understanding of Human-Building Interaction (HBI) is pivotal in this context, as it focuses on how individuals and communities experience and engage with their built surroundings. While human-centred design, user experience, and human building interaction are crucial in all aspects of spatial planning, they are especially significant in the design of public environments.

Public spaces profoundly impact urban daily life, acting as hubs for social and cultural interactions, entertainment, relaxation, and community engagement. Well-designed public environments go beyond aesthetics; they must foster inclusion—irrespective of individual differences—while enhancing well-being and civic participation. These spaces should be inviting, functional, inclusive, and capable of supporting a diverse range of activities. Achieving these goals requires the integration of user-centred research methodologies such as journey mapping, personas, and storytelling. These methods help identify functional needs and behavioural patterns within a given spatial context, ultimately enabling the design of environments that maximize user satisfaction and well-being.

This study explored the potential of AI, specifically ChatGPT, as a tool for evaluating existing environments from the perspective of user experience. A case study was conducted in which an archetypal family, consisting of five members with distinct personas, was introduced as a user group. The family members were characterized based on their specific needs and preferences, which formed the basis of a structured prompt for ChatGPT.

The AI-generated analysis reaffirmed the findings from the literature review, confirming the absence of user-centred design principles in the selected playgrounds. It highlighted gaps in accessibility, inclusion, and functionality. Additionally, the same prompt was used to generate an AI-created image of a playground that better met the family's requirements. This exercise underscored the importance of storytelling and persona development in urban space planning, illustrating how AI can assist in the early stages of design conceptualization.

The findings suggest that AI-powered tools can be valuable resources for designers and urban planners, enabling them to visualize preliminary design concepts before engaging in more complex spatial modelling or immersive experience creation. Moreover, AI offers a viable alternative for professionals and researchers with limited access to advanced 3D modelling software or high-fidelity visualization technologies.

Ultimately, this study highlights the growing significance of AI in both academic curricula and professional design practices. By integrating AI-driven methodologies into urban planning and architectural education, future designers can leverage these technologies to create more user-centred, inclusive, and interactive public spaces.

Acknowledgments. This work was support by FCT - Fundação para a Ciência e Tecnologia, I.P. by project reference <UIDB/04026/2020> and DOI identifier <https://doi.org/10.54499/UIDB/04026/2020 (https://doi.org/10.54499/UIDB/04026/2020)>.

Disclosure of Interests. The authors have no competing interests to declare that are relevant to the content of this article.

References

Alavi, H., et al.: Human-building interaction: sketches and grounds for a research program. Interactions **26**(4), 58–61 (2019)

Becerik-Gerber, B., Lucas, G., Aryal, A., et al.: The field of human building interaction for convergent research and innovation for intelligent built environments. Sci. Rep. **12**, 22092 (2022)

Caramelo Gomes, C.: The role of colour in urban place-making: a study of public art in Lisbon. In: Ahram, T., Karwowski, W., Etinger, D., Mijač, T. (eds.) Human Systems Engineering and Design (IHSED2024): Future Trends and Applications. AHFE (2024) International Conference. AHFE Open Access, vol-2. AHFE International, USA (2024)

Caramelo Gomes, C.: The impact of chromatic palettes in social neighbourhoods' environments: cause and consequence of human interactions. In: Proceedings of the 15th Congress of the International Colour Association, pp. 550–557. AIC, Chiang Rai, Thailand (2023)

Doyle, D.: Immersive storytelling in mixed reality environments. In 2017 23rd International Conference on Virtual System and Multimedia (VSMM), pp. 1–4. IEEE (2017)

Economidou, E., Itzlinger, A., Frauenberger, C.: Lived experience in human-building interaction (HBI): an initial framework. Front. Comput. Sci. **5** (2024)

Enia, M., Martella, F.: How buildings relate—classifying architectural interactions. Architecture **3**(3), 490–504 (2023)

Hodder, I.: Human-thing entanglement: towards an integrated archaeological perspective. J. R. Anthropol. Inst. **17**, 154–177 (2011)

International Ergonomics Association: What is ergonomics. https://iea.cc/about/what-is-ergonomics/. Accessed 25 Jan 2025

Knox, K.: Interactive architecture: Development and implementation into the built environment. Eur. J. Technol. Des. **5**(1), 20–25 (2017)

Memarovic, N. and Langheinrich, M.: Enhancing Community Interaction in Public Spaces Through Situated Public Displays. https://uc.inf.usi.ch/pubs/pre/2010-Memarovic-SISSI.pdf. Accessed 25 Jan 2025

Moncada, T.: Data storytelling in virtual reality: using immersive tech to tell stories. https://www.linkedin.com/pulse/data-storytelling-virtual-reality-using-immersive-tell-moncada/. Accessed 25 Jan 2025

Mudnaney, S.: The future of storytelling: emerging trends and the evolving role. https://www.lin kedin.com/pulse/future-storytelling-emerging-trends-evolving-role-sanjay-mudnaney-axajf/. Accessed 25 Jan 2025

Nadim, S.: UCD vs UX: What's the difference? https://uxplanet.org/ucd-vs-ux-whats-the-differ ence-255443efa5f. Accessed 25 Jan 2025

Olanusi, J.A., Oluwadepo, O.A.: Behavioural impact of interaction spaces approach in architectural design. Int. J. Res. Innov. Soc. Sci. **7**(7), 2067–2079 (2023)

Parsons School of Design: Immersive storytelling. https://immersive.parsons.edu/. Accessed 25 Jan 2025

Polydorou, D.: Immersive storytelling experiences: a design methodology. Digit. Creat. **35**(4), 301–320 (2024)

Team Kaarwan: Public Space Design: Enhancing Social Interaction and Community Engagement in Urban Environments. https://www.kaarwan.com/blog/architecture/public-space-design-for-social-interaction-and-community-engagement?id=213. Accessed 25 Jan 2025

UN-Habitat: Public Space, chrome-extension://efaidnbmnnnibpcajpcglclefindmkaj/https://unh abitat.org/sites/default/files/2019/02/Indicator-11.7.1-Training-Module_Public-spaces_Jan_ 2019.pdf. Accessed 25 Jan 2025

A Study on the Acquisition and Classification of Defective Information in Manufactured Products Using Pneumatic Actuators

Ji-hyun Cha(✉) ⓘ, Heung-gyun Jeong ⓘ, Seung-woo Han ⓘ, Seung-hwa Baek ⓘ, and Kyu-tai Seo ⓘ

Cloudnetworks Co., Ltd, 20, Yeongdong-Daero 96-gil, Gangnam-Gu, Seoul, Korea
`{jh.cha,harris.jeong,sw.han,sh.baek,kt.seo}@cloudnetworks.co.kr`

Abstract. This study investigates a system for collecting and analyzing defect information of stacked assemblies during manufacturing processes that utilize pneumatic actuators—specifically air cylinders—without relying on external sensors. The objective is to precisely analyze the pneumatic consumption patterns before and after the piston rod of an air cylinder reaches its target stroke and contacts the stacked assemblies. This approach enables the classification of defect types, such as cracks and missing layers, without the need for additional devices like vision sensors or load cells.

The system was developed by collecting pneumatic data under both normal and defective conditions from an air cylinder installed on a turntable used for assembling circuit breaker trip units. After securing an operational margin through data analysis, pneumatic consumption patterns surrounding the moment of piston-to-stacked assembly contact were extracted and analyzed. By evaluating thrust variations caused by defects such as cracks or missing layers, the system can effectively identify and classify defect types in the stacked assemblies.

Traditionally, signals such as current, voltage, pneumatic pressure, and temperature are monitored for predictive maintenance by assessing the condition of actuators like motors, heaters, or air cylinders. However, anomalies in these parameters do not always correspond to defects in the processed stacked assemblies. In contrast, this study focuses on directly capturing the influence of actual physical defects—such as missing layers, cracks, or assembly misalignments—on the behavior of the air cylinder. This enables accurate and sensorless quality control, representing a key differentiator of the proposed approach.

Artificial intelligence models, including Random Forest and Convolutional Neural Networks (CNNs), were employed to learn the pneumatic consumption patterns and predict defects. The Random Forest model demonstrated strong performance in distinguishing between normal and defective conditions, while the CNN model showed high sensitivity in detecting specific defect patterns.

Keywords: Pneumatic Pattern Analysis · Air Cylinder Actuation · Sensorless Defect Detection · Random Forest · Convolutional Neural Networks (CNNs)

1   Introduction

In manufacturing processes that utilize compressed air systems, the operation of air cylinders has a direct impact on the quality of the stacked assemblies. Therefore, real-time defect detection during the process is essential. Traditionally, such detection has relied on additional sensing devices such as vision sensors or load cells. However, these approaches often incur substantial installation costs and ongoing maintenance challenges due to the reliance on external hardware.

Air cylinders exhibit distinct pneumatic consumption patterns before and after contact with a stacked assembly. Under normal conditions, these patterns are consistent and repeatable. However, the presence of defects—such as cracks, missing layers, or assembly misalignments—can affect the speed and travel distance of the piston rod, leading to observable deviations in the pneumatic signal.

In typical manufacturing environments, a single machine is often equipped with multiple air cylinders. Rather than placing sensors on each cylinder individually, a more efficient method is to install a single pneumatic pressure sensor at the main air supply inlet of the equipment. This configuration enables the simultaneous monitoring of multiple air cylinders using just one sensor. However, when several cylinders operate concurrently, the resulting overlapping pneumatic activities generate complex signal patterns. To accurately interpret these patterns and detect defects, advanced analysis using artificial intelligence (AI) becomes necessary.

To address this challenge, this study compares two AI-based models—Random Forest and Convolutional Neural Networks (CNNs)—to develop an effective defect detection algorithm. The Random Forest model analyzes key features of the pneumatic signal, including the rate of pressure change over time, peak values (maximum and minimum), pressure holding durations, and the time taken to reach pressure stabilization. By aggregating decisions across multiple trees, the model effectively captures the global behavior of the pneumatic system.

Conversely, the CNN model exhibits strong performance in identifying localized defect patterns, such as missing layers or assembly errors, by learning the spatial and temporal features embedded in the pressure signal. Through deep convolutional layers, the CNN is capable of extracting hierarchical features directly from raw signal inputs, making it well-suited for complex pattern recognition.

The proposed defect detection system, based solely on pneumatic consumption data, achieves high classification accuracy without the need for additional sensors. This approach contributes to improved quality control in manufacturing by reducing system complexity and cost, while enabling real-time, sensorless monitoring of assembly defects.

2   Pneumatic System

2.1   Pneumatic Test Environment

To replicate real-world manufacturing conditions, a pneumatic testing environment was constructed using a turntable-based system equipped with multiple air cylinders, as illustrated in Fig. 1. In this setup, the trip coil assembly (T.C.A) of a circuit breaker is manually assembled. The assembly consists of eight components, including a coil, which are manually stacked during the process. When dimensional tolerances exist between components, gaps may form within the stacked structure during unit transfers along the production line.

To mitigate this issue, an intermediate press jig process was introduced to compress and stabilize the stacked components during the transfer stage. This press jig is driven by a single reciprocating air cylinder and produces a distinct pneumatic pressure pattern during each operational cycle. When a large number of components are stacked, multiple press jigs may be installed in the same system.

However, due to differences in the speed controllers assigned to each air cylinder, actuation timing can vary among the press jigs. Notably, installing a single pneumatic pressure sensor at the system's air supply inlet allows for simultaneous monitoring of the operation of multiple press jigs—such as Press Jig 1 and Press Jig 2. This approach offers a significant advantage in analyzing and monitoring multiple pneumatic actuators without requiring individual sensors for each jig.

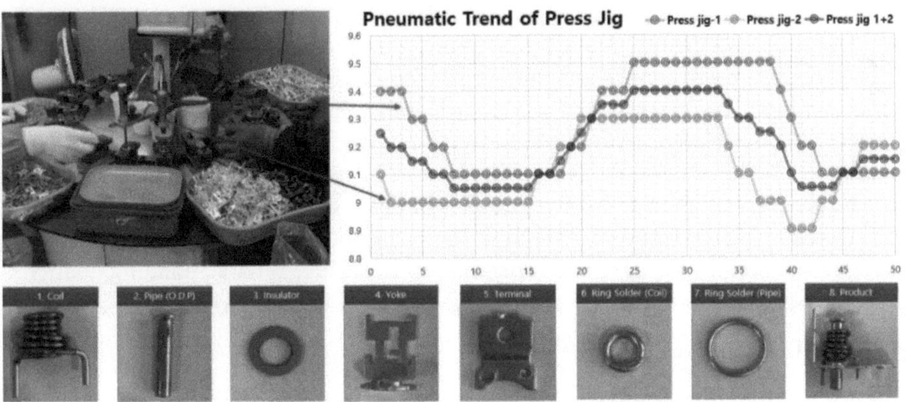

Fig. 1. Turntable Equipment and Stacked Assemblies.

3 Analysis of Defect Occurrence Patterns

3.1 Air Cylinder Actuation Requirements

In manufacturing processes, air cylinders are responsible for performing reciprocating motions—either vertically or horizontally, depending on their installation orientation—to weld, press, transfer, or position stacked assemblies. The fundamental operating principles and characteristics of air cylinders are illustrated in Fig. 2.

For example, in a welding process used to join the upper and lower sections of a case, compressed air is supplied through the cap-end port, causing the piston rod to extend to its target stroke. Once the rod reaches the designated stroke and applies constant pressure to the stacked assembly, ultrasonic energy is delivered through a jig—such as a horn mounted on the rod—to bond the components. The target stroke is typically set slightly longer than the actual contact distance with the stacked assembly to ensure that sufficient pressure is applied for reliable bonding.

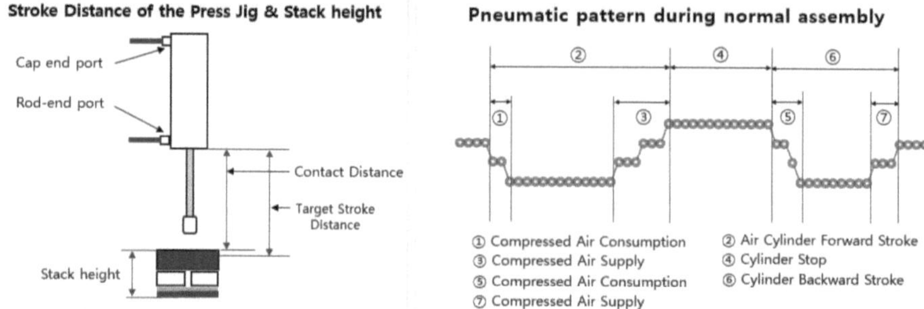

Fig. 2. Air cylinder operating characteristics.

The positioning (or settling) process is typically employed to prevent misalignment or improper seating of components during multi-layer stacking operations. Although the procedure is structurally identical to the welding process, it differs in that ultrasonic energy is not applied. In turntable equipment equipped with multiple air cylinders, it has been observed that the operating time of the cylinders is often set longer than the standard operation time specified by the manufacturer. This extension in operation time may be intended to ensure full contact and pressure during the process; however, adjusting it to a shorter duration can affect overall process reliability and defect rates. To ensure defect-free assembly during the welding and settling of products with structures such as the one illustrated in Fig. 3, the following conditions must be met. First, the stacked components must be properly aligned and fully seated, without displacement or omission. Second, the intensity and frequency of the ultrasonic energy applied during the welding stage must precisely match the predefined parameters to achieve reliable bonding quality.

Fig. 3. Power connector base and cover.

3.2 Causes of Crack Defects and Corresponding Pneumatic Pattern

If the operator fails to properly seat the grooves of the upper and lower cases of a semi-finished product, a step-height defect may occur, in which the overall stacked height becomes greater than that of a correctly assembled product. This misalignment causes the piston rod to contact the stacked assembly before reaching the predefined target contact distance. When premature contact occurs, a reactive pressure in the direction opposite to the rod's motion is generated, resulting in an irregular pneumatic consumption pattern compared to the normal operating pattern, as illustrated in Fig. 4.

150   J. Cha et al.

This issue is particularly critical when the components are designed to interlock through groove structures. If assembly misalignment occurs, excessive pressure may be generated during the piston rod's forward stroke toward the target position, potentially causing cracks in the groove region due to unintended mechanical stress.

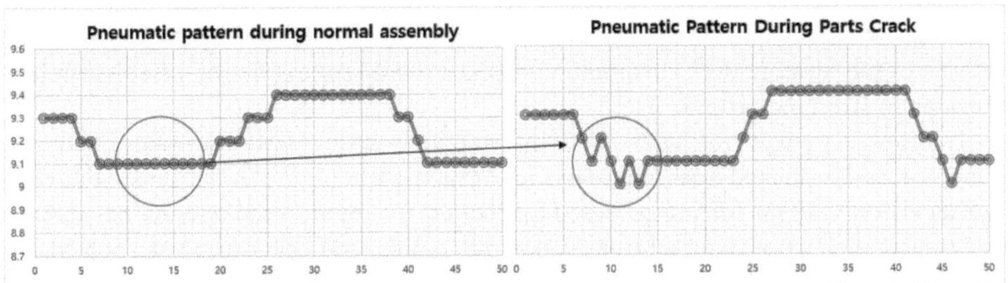

Fig. 4. Pneumatic Pressure Patterns under Normal and Crack Conditions.

3.3   Causes of Parts Skip and Corresponding Pneumatic Pattern

Another defect scenario arises when the operator accidentally omits a portion of the stacked components during assembly. In such cases, the contact distance of the piston rod increases, as it must travel farther to reach the semi-finished product. Since the piston rod stops upon contacting the stacked assembly and the pneumatic consumption pattern changes accordingly, an abnormal pattern—distinct from the normal operation—can be observed, as illustrated in Fig. 5.

In the above, two defect types have been presented. By analyzing the pneumatic consumption pattern before and after the piston rod contacts the stacked assembly at the scale of several tens of milliseconds, it becomes possible to classify various defect types without the use of additional sensors such as vision systems or load cells. This enables sensorless defect classification based solely on pneumatic signal analysis.

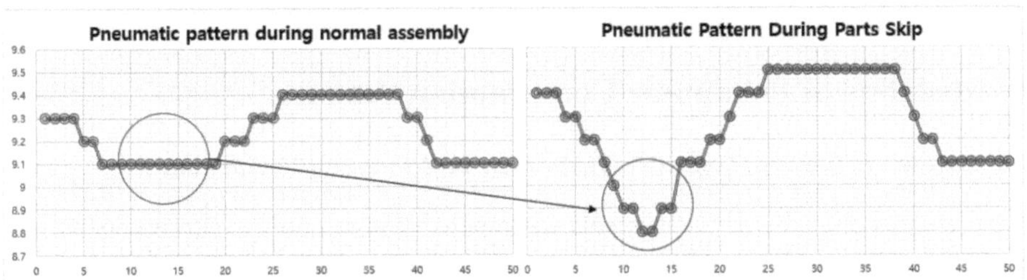

Fig. 5. Pneumatic Pressure Patterns under Normal and Stack Omission.

3.4   Distinct Characteristics of Sensor Data Analysis

The primary objective of acquiring data such as current, voltage, pneumatic pressure, and temperature from manufacturing equipment is to monitor the operational status of actuators—including motors, heaters, and air cylinders—for the purpose of predictive maintenance. This approach is widely adopted in industry as a standard method for utilizing embedded sensor data within automated systems.

Although deviations in these parameters may suggest insufficient physical input to the stacked assembly—potentially resulting in product defects—they do not directly reveal the presence or type of defect. In contrast, the present study proposes a fundamentally different approach by directly analyzing how actual physical defects, such as stack omissions or cracks caused by assembly errors, influence the pneumatic consumption patterns of the air cylinder. This method enables the direct extraction of defect-related information from the process itself.

Traditionally, acquiring such defect information—particularly for issues like cracks in the processed stacked assembly—has required the use of additional sensing devices, such as vision systems for image-based inspection. To monitor the operational status of air cylinder pistons or detect thrust-related anomalies, additional devices such as load cells must be installed, or cylinders must be equipped with reed switches, Hall effect sensors, or magnetoresistive (MR) sensors.

However, reed switches can only detect whether the piston rod has reached a specific position and are incapable of identifying nuanced defect conditions. Similarly, while magnetic sensors can determine whether the piston is functioning within expected parameters, they are unable to detect gradual failures—such as pneumatic energy loss due to increased internal friction along the cylinder wall—analogous to how an aging vehicle consumes more fuel to achieve the same performance. Monitoring piston motion or velocity alone is insufficient to capture such subtle anomalies. Furthermore, these auxiliary sensing devices are primarily designed to track basic reciprocating motion, not to identify defects in the stacked assembly itself. The incorporation of vision systems and other sensors also imposes additional costs related to installation, calibration, and maintenance.

To address these limitations, this study proposes a novel method for classifying and detecting defects—such as cracks and stack omissions—by precisely analyzing the pneumatic consumption patterns before and after the piston rod reaches its target stroke and contacts the stacked assembly. Notably, this is accomplished without the use of supplementary visual or pressure sensors, such as vision systems or load cells.

4 Modeling of Pneumatic Consumption Patterns

4.1 Impact of Jig and Cylinder Variability on Modeling Performance

The press jigs mounted on the turntable equipment are configured as illustrated in Fig. 6. Since the system is designed to accommodate various product types and specifications, the number of press jigs installed on each machine, as well as their operating parameters, may vary accordingly. Consequently, the pneumatic consumption characteristics of the cylinders associated with each jig also differ from one machine to another.

Fig. 6. Turntable equipment.

Key pneumatic parameters—such as maximum air consumption (Qmax), average flow rate (Qave), total air consumption (qt), and total cycle time (tt)—can vary significantly depending on the machine configuration, as illustrated in Fig. 7. These variations directly influence the distribution of input data used for model training. For example, in one specific machine, the "Unit-up Jig" exhibits an average flow rate of 0.889 L/min, which is more than four times higher than that of the "Press Jig-1" (0.207 L/min) within the same system. Such imbalances can affect how machine learning models interpret and learn from the data, potentially impacting model generalization and accuracy.

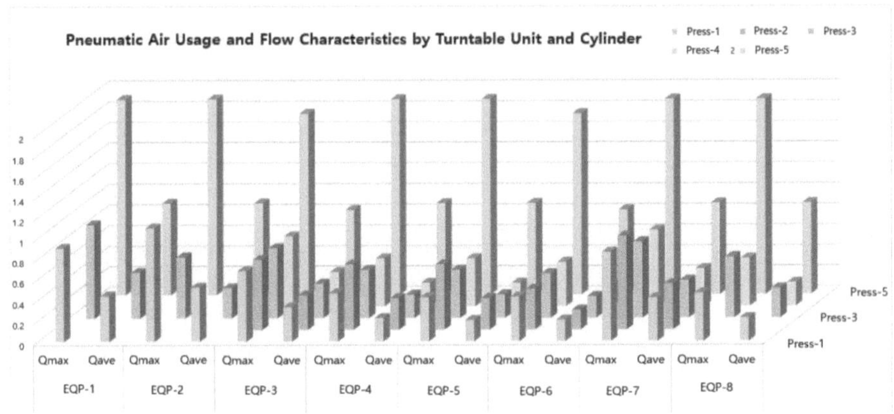

Fig. 7. Comparison of Pneumatic Consumption Characteristics by equipment

In the case of deep learning models such as Convolutional Neural Networks (CNNs), raw time-series inputs are directly fed into the model. As a result, CNNs are highly sensitive to the intensity and dynamic behavior of pneumatic patterns—such as differences in Qmax or Qave. When the input distribution differs across machines, even samples from the same class may be interpreted as different patterns. This can lead to degraded generalization performance and an increased risk of overfitting.

On the other hand, Random Forest models are typically trained using statistical features such as mean, standard deviation, and maximum values. These models form decision boundaries based on threshold values for each feature. While this approach is effective for distinguishing between systems with clearly different characteristics, it may be limited in capturing complex time-dependent patterns. Therefore, Random Forests are generally strong in static feature-based classification but may underperform in tasks requiring dynamic pattern recognition.

4.2 Modeling Objectives for Pneumatic Pattern Analysis in Manufacturing Systems

To evaluate the feasibility of detecting and classifying such anomalies according to defect types, this study employs machine learning techniques—specifically, the Random Forest algorithm and Convolutional Neural Networks (CNNs). These models are trained and tested on high-resolution pneumatic signal data to assess their effectiveness in identifying defect-induced variations in actuator behavior.

The Random Forest - Model implementation. The Random Forest algorithm is an ensemble learning method that improves prediction accuracy by combining multiple decision trees. While single trees can capture specific patterns, they are often prone to overfitting. To mitigate this, Random Forest employs Bagging, training each tree on different bootstrap samples. Final predictions are made via majority voting (classification) or averaging (regression), enhancing generalization.

This architecture is well-suited for pneumatic signal analysis, as air cylinder data exhibit time-dependent features—such as pressure gradients, peak values, holding times, and stabilization delays (Table 1)—which Random Forest models can effectively learn and generalize across multiple decision trees, making them a practical solution for defect detection in actuator-based systems.

Table 1. Feature Description for Pneumatic Signal Analysis.

Feature	Value	Interpretation in Pneumatic Data
1.Mean	0.25	Indicates the overall pressurization level during operation
2.Min	0.14	Useful for detecting under-pressurization or initial pressure loss
3.Q25	0.13	Reflects pressure behavior in the early phase of the cycle
4.Max	0.105	Can signal over-pressurization or abnormal peak conditions
5.Std	0.085	Represents the variability or instability in pressure
6.Q75	0.08	Captures characteristics of the pressure in the stable phase
7.Skew	0.075	Indicates asymmetry in the pressure pattern; useful for identifying directional anomalies.
8.Median	0.065	A robust measure of central tendency, less affected by outliers
9.Kurtosis	0.06	Reflects the sharpness or peakedness; higher values may indicate sudden changes or outliers

Figure 8 illustrates an example of a decision tree with a maximum depth of 3, extracted from the trained Random Forest model used for pneumatic signal classification.

Each internal node represents a decision rule based on statistical features derived from the pneumatic consumption patterns, such as standard deviation, quartiles (Q25), maximum pressure, median, and kurtosis. These features are selected to capture critical aspects of the air cylinder's behavior during operation, including pressure stability, peak intensity, and distribution characteristics.

The root node performs an initial split based on the standard deviation (std) of the pressure signal, effectively distinguishing cycles with stable pressure profiles from those exhibiting higher variability—often indicative of abnormal behavior. Subsequent branches further partition the data using features such as Q25 (capturing early-phase pressure trends), maximum pressure (indicating potential over-pressurization), and kurtosis (reflecting the sharpness of the pressure distribution, often shaped by abrupt changes or noise).

Leaf nodes represent the class distribution resulting from each decision path, with class probabilities derived from the training samples that reach the corresponding terminal node. For instance, a leaf node with a value of [14.0, 5.0, 0.0] indicates a predominance of normal samples, while skewed distributions may suggest defects such as cracks or lamination skips.

This decision structure highlights the interpretability of the Random Forest model and demonstrates how multiple statistical pressure features are jointly utilized to differentiate normal operations from various defect types in pneumatic actuator systems.

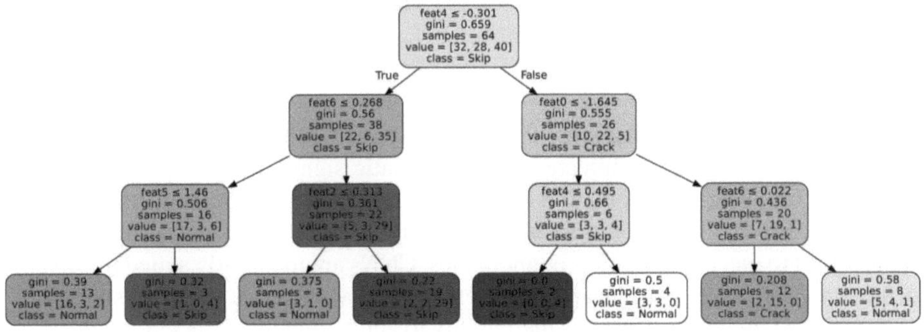

Fig. 8. Random Forest Tree Visualization for Pneumatic-Based Defect Detection.

Among the classification models applied in this study, the Random Forest algorithm demonstrated the best performance for pneumatic-based defect detection. It achieved an accuracy of 96.0%, a precision of 95.5%, a recall of 94.8%, and an F1-score of 95.1%. Furthermore, the model recorded the highest AUC value of 0.98, indicating superior overall classification capability. These results can be attributed to the structural advantages of the Random Forest algorithm, which is well suited to capture the complex and time-dependent characteristics inherent in pneumatic consumption patterns.

The pneumatic data used in this study consists of time-series pressure signals generated during the operation of air cylinders. These signals were transformed into a variety of statistical features, including mean, maximum and minimum pressure, standard deviation, interquartile ranges (Q25, Q75), kurtosis, and skewness. The Random Forest model constructs an ensemble of decision trees, each trained on a distinct combination of these features. To ensure diversity among the trees and enhance the model's generalization ability, bootstrap sampling and the random subspace method were employed during training. This approach enables each tree to learn from a unique subset of the data, while the ensemble aggregates their outputs to produce a robust final prediction.

Notably, pneumatic signal data is often subject to noise and disturbances arising from the sensor environment. The Random Forest model exhibited strong resilience to such uncertainties, maintaining high classification performance even under noisy conditions. Moreover, due to the inherently interpretable nature of decision trees, the decision-making logic behind each prediction can be clearly understood and traced. This transparency makes the model particularly well-suited for deployment in industrial manufacturing settings, where interpretability and reliability are critical for practical implementation by process engineers (Table 2).

Table 2. Performance Metrics of the Random Forest Model.

Metric	Value
1. Accuracy	96.0%
2. Precision	95.5%
3. Recall	94.8%
4. F1-score	95.1%
5. AUC (ROC)	0.98

CNNs – Model Implementation. The application of Convolutional Neural Networks (CNNs), particularly 1D architectures, to pneumatic signal analysis provides notable advantages in industrial automation and quality monitoring. Pneumatic signals—such as pressure consumption patterns from air cylinders—exhibit localized and transient variations linked to mechanical states or anomalies. CNNs are inherently suited to capturing such temporal features using learnable filters applied across time sequences.

A major advantage of CNNs is their ability to automatically extract hierarchical features from raw sensor signals, eliminating the need for extensive manual feature engineering. Traditional methods often require predefined features like peak pressure, duration, or pressure decay, which are labor-intensive and process-specific. CNNs, in contrast, learn discriminative patterns directly from labeled data, improving generalization across diverse conditions.

CNNs also exhibit robustness to sensor noise and fluctuations. Through shared weights and local receptive fields, they can isolate meaningful signal behaviors while filtering out irrelevant variations—an essential benefit in pneumatic systems prone to minor disturbances or sensor drift. Figure 8 presents the hierarchical architecture of the implemented CNN model, showing the sequential structure of each processing layer.

The 1D Convolutional (Conv1D) layer plays a central role in processing time-series data by extracting local patterns along the temporal axis. It applies learnable filters across sequential inputs, generating feature maps that capture localized signal characteristics such as abrupt changes, oscillations, and gradual trends. In this study, the input to the Conv1D layer consists of time-series pneumatic pressure values collected during air cylinder operation. Kernel sizes were chosen based on the temporal window of meaningful pressure variation, enabling detection of transient anomalies and repetitive behaviors.

Unlike 2D convolutions used in image processing, Conv1D operates along a single temporal dimension, making it suitable for univariate or multivariate time-series data such as pressure, vibration, or current signals. Additionally, its lower parameter count provides computational efficiency, which is beneficial for deployment in resource-constrained industrial environments.

The MaxPooling1D layer follows the Conv1D layer to down sample the feature map by selecting the maximum value within a defined window (e.g., kernel size of 2), thereby highlighting salient features while reducing dimensionality and noise. This emphasizes the most informative segments of the pneumatic signal, such as pressure peaks or rapid transitions.

The Flatten layer transforms the multi-dimensional output of the pooling layers into a one-dimensional vector, serving as an interface to the fully connected Dense layer. This allows temporal features captured by convolutional filters to be aggregated and interpreted for classification.

Finally, the Dense layer uses this flattened feature vector to learn complex relationships among the extracted features. In this study, three output nodes were used to classify pneumatic signal patterns into the categories: normal, crack, and layer skip. This layered structure enables robust defect classification from raw sensor data in pneumatic actuator systems.

Figure 9 visually illustrates the structure in which the flattened 1D feature vector [x1,x2,...,xn] is connected to each output node in the Dense layer. These nodes correspond to class probabilities y1 (normal), y2 (crack), and y3 (layer skip), respectively. The Softmax activation function is applied at the output layer to compute the probability distribution across the three classes, and the class with the highest probability is selected as the model's prediction.

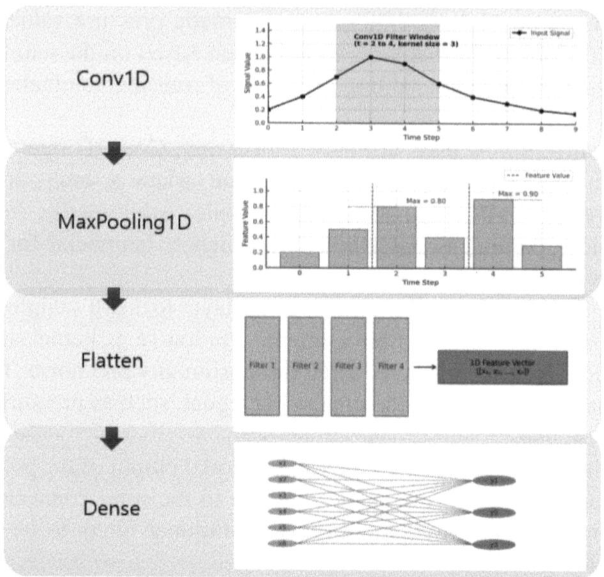

Fig. 9. CNN Pipeline for Pneumatic Pattern Recognition.

CNN - Performance Analysis. The pneumatic pattern data used in this study was collected from a rotary turntable system. The raw time-series data was segmented into fixed time intervals and transformed into two-dimensional tensors as input to the CNN model. To minimize the impact of class imbalance, the dataset was constructed to maintain a uniform distribution of class labels. Additionally, no data augmentation techniques were applied in order to preserve the intrinsic characteristics of the original time-series signals. The model was trained using the following key hyperparameters:

- Optimizer: Adam
- Learning Rate: 0.001
- Batch Size: 64
- Epochs: 50
- Loss Function: Binary Cross-Entropy
- Activation Function: ReLU , Sigmoid
- Dropout Rate: 0.3

During training, the loss value exhibited a stable downward trend. A sharp decrease was observed in the initial epochs, followed by a convergence phase starting around the 20th epoch. To further mitigate overfitting, both dropout and early stopping techniques were implemented. The final model was selected based on the highest F1-score achieved on the validation dataset.

The model demonstrated strong classification performance across multiple evaluation metrics. It achieved an accuracy of 96.8%, precision of 96.2, recall of 95.6%, and an F1-score of 95.9%. Notably, the model achieved a ROC-AUC score of 0.985, indicating excellent discriminative ability between positive and negative classes. The high F1-score and balanced precision-recall values suggest that the model is well-suited for real-world deployment in pneumatic anomaly detection or pattern recognition tasks (Table 3).

Table 3. Performance Metrics of the CNN Model.

Metric	Value
1. Accuracy	96.8%
2. Precision	96.2%
3. Recall	95.6%
4. F1-score	95.9%
5. AUC (ROC)	0.985

4.3 Performance Comparison Between CNN and Random Forest Models

To assess the effectiveness of the proposed CNN model, its performance was compared with that of a previously trained Random Forest classifier. Both models were evaluated on the same pneumatic pattern dataset using consistent preprocessing, training, and testing procedures. The CNN model outperformed the Random Forest across all major evaluation metrics, albeit by a small margin. Specifically, the CNN achieved an accuracy of 96.8%, slightly higher than the 96.0% achieved by the Random Forest. It also recorded superior values in precision (96.2% vs. 95.5%), recall (95.6% vs. 94.8%), and F1-score (95.9% vs. 95.1%). Furthermore, the ROC-AUC score increased from 0.980 to 0.985, indicating marginally improved class discrimination capability.

These results suggest that the CNN model is better able to capture the spatiotemporal characteristics inherent in pneumatic signal data, likely due to its deep architecture and capacity to learn hierarchical representations directly from raw input sequences. While both models demonstrated excellent performance, the CNN's consistent advantage across evaluation metrics underscores its potential for greater generalization and adaptability—particularly in complex or dynamic industrial environments.

4.4 Towards Enhanced Architectures for Pneumatic Signal Analysis

Due to the inherent characteristics of pneumatic systems, the number and types of jigs, as well as the control mechanisms of pneumatic cylinders, vary across different machines. Consequently, the pneumatic consumption patterns also show significant differences between machines. For instance, even within turntable-based systems, one machine may exhibit high air consumption concentrated in the unit-up jig, whereas another may display a more distributed consumption pattern due to frequent operation or higher-pressure settings of specific press jigs.

This variation in hardware configuration and operational conditions leads not only to differences in the time-series patterns of pneumatic signals, but also to discrepancies in key quantitative indicators such as maximum air consumption (Qmax), average flow rate (Qave), total air consumption (qt), etc.

As a result, models that do not account for these differences risk becoming overfitted to specific machine configurations, thereby failing to generalize effectively across different systems. To overcome these challenges and move towards more advanced model architectures for pneumatic signal analysis, the following strategies are proposed:

Per-machine Normalization or Standardization. Normalize time-series input data using Qmax or Qave values specific to each machine or jig. This helps to align the scale of inputs and reduce variance caused by hardware-level differences.

Machine-Specific Model Training. When sufficient data is available, training separate models for each machine type can lead to optimized performance tailored to each configuration. Although this increases modeling complexity, it can significantly improve both accuracy and generalization.

Transfer Learning and Domain Adaptation. To enable effective cross-equipment learning, apply techniques such as transfer learning or domain adaptation. These approaches allow shared CNN architectures to adapt to machine-specific data distributions and extend learned knowledge from one system to another.

5 Conclusion

This study proposed a machine learning–based framework for analyzing pneumatic consumption patterns across varying equipment configurations, with the goal of detecting and classifying anomalies in industrial pneumatic systems. The analysis demonstrated that differences in jig structures and pneumatic cylinder control parameters across machines result in significant variations in air consumption behavior. These discrepancies alter the distribution of input data, thereby impacting the generalization performance of learning models.

The Random Forest algorithm exhibited strong classification performance based on engineered statistical features, particularly in scenarios where inter-machine differences were clearly defined. In contrast, Convolutional Neural Networks (CNNs) proved effective at capturing fine-grained spatiotemporal patterns directly from raw pneumatic signals. However, CNNs also showed sensitivity to input distribution shifts, which increased the risk of overfitting and reduced generalization when machine-specific characteristics were not properly addressed.

To overcome these challenges, this study proposed several strategies: per-machine normalization or standardization, incorporation of machine metadata as input features, training of machine-specific models, and the application of transfer learning or domain adaptation techniques. Together, these approaches provide a pathway for developing robust and generalizable AI models suited to the heterogeneous nature of industrial pneumatic systems.

Future research will focus on validating model performance under real-world operational conditions across multiple machines and exploring real-time deployment strategies—particularly using edge computing platforms—to enable predictive maintenance in smart manufacturing environments.

Acknowledgements. This work was supported by project for Smart Manufacturing Innovation R&D funded Korea Ministry of SMEs and Startups in 2022 (RS-2022-00141143).

References

1. Saleh, A., Mohamed, R., Abdullah, R.: Intelligent approaches for anomaly detection in compressed air systems: a review. Machinery **11**(7), 750 (2023)
2. Huang, M., Liu, Y., Wang, Q., Guo, S.: A novel deep learning model integrating CNN and GRU to predict pneumatic subsoiling resistance. Expert Syst. Appl. **213**, 119070 (2023)
3. Ma, X., Chen, X., Liu, Y.: A hybrid convolutional neural network and random forest for burned area identification with optical and synthetic aperture radar (SAR) data. Remote Sens. **15**(3), 728 (2023)
4. Chen, K., Yang, T., Wu, F.: Implementation of an intelligence-based framework for anomaly detection in pneumatic systems. Procedia Comput. Sci. **229**, 1342–1350
5. Wang, S., Liu, X.: Data-driven modeling and optimization of compressed air systems in manufacturing, vol. 165, pp. 797–808(2018)

A Supply Pressure Optimization System Based on Pneumatic Receiver Tank Operation for Improving Cumulative Manufacturing Variation

Ji-hyun Cha[(✉)] [ID], Heung-gyun Jeong [ID], Seung-woo Han [ID], Seung-hwa Baek [ID], and Kyu-tai Seo [ID]

Cloudnetworks Co., Ltd., 20, Yeongdong-daero 96-gil, Gangnam-Gu, Seoul, Korea
`{jh.cha,harris.jeong,sw.han,sh.baek,kt.seo}@cloudnetworks.co.kr`

Abstract. This paper presents a system and method for optimizing compressed air consumption in pneumatic actuators. The focus is on adjusting the pneumatic supply to air cylinders based on the rise and fall cycles of the receiver tank within the pneumatic system, with the aim of reducing cumulative manufacturing variation. In continuous manufacturing processes, cumulative variation can lead to defects when deviations approach the upper or lower control limits. The proposed pneumatic optimization system—comprising a compressor, receiver tank, pressure regulator, and pneumatic actuator—dynamically regulates the air supply to the production process. This is achieved by acquiring machining state information, such as product variation from previous processes, and defining variation limits based on defect frequencies observed in downstream processes. Depending on the cumulative variation of in-process products within these defined limits, the air supply conditions are adjusted in synchronization with the receiver tank's pressure cycles. Through this research, a method has been established for extracting cumulative variation data based on dimensional and specification deviations from each unit process, along with their corresponding process conditions. This allows for effective feedback control in downstream processes such as compression, welding, and pressing. By transforming the pneumatic supply into a variable system responsive to the receiver tank's cycles, the occurrence of defects can be significantly suppressed. Ultimately, by transforming the proposed technology into a platform, it is possible to contribute to enhancing quality across the entire supply chain ecosystem, including the final assembled product, by receiving feedback on the variation of all parts produced within the supply chain and optimizing, in real time, the processing conditions of operations performed by pneumatic actuators.

Keywords: Pneumatic Receiver Tank · Analysis of Manufacturing Defects · Manufacturing Process Dispersion · Machine Learning

1 Introduction

In manufacturing sites, dimensional and specification variations inevitably occur at each unit process stage. When these variations accumulate across sequential processes, they can lead to quality degradation and increased defect rates. However, if such variation

M. Kurosu and A. Hashizume (Eds.): HCII 2025, LNCS 16332, pp. 161–170, 2026.
https://doi.org/10.1007/978-3-032-12385-5_10

data can be effectively fed back and optimized for use in downstream processes—such as compression, fusion, and pressing—it becomes possible to reduce cumulative variation across the entire production line.

To achieve this, it is necessary to dynamically adjust the operating conditions of pneumatic actuators that serve as the power source for equipment used in these downstream processes. Notably, the rise and fall cycles of the receiver tank in a pneumatic system influence the intensity of the compressed air supply. Therefore, a pneumatic optimization system capable of controlling air supply in accordance with these cycles is required.

To this end, the following key elements are essential:

- **Machining State Information Acquisition Module**: A module that collects machining state data from upstream processes, including variations in dimensions and specifications of the manufactured components.
- **Variation and Variable Process Condition Analysis Module**: This module analyzes the cumulative variation based on the variation data from upstream processes and the defect frequency observed in downstream processes. It sets upper and lower control limits for allowable variation and determines optimized compressed air supply conditions for downstream processes, synchronized with the receiver tank's pressure cycles.
- **Pneumatic Control Module**: Based on the analysis, this module adjusts pneumatic parameters in real time and provides feedback to the downstream process to ensure optimal actuator performance.
- **Supply Air Pressure Optimization Technology**: A system that optimizes the compressed air supply to air cylinders in synchronization with the receiver tank's pressure cycles, thereby transforming the force applied in downstream processes into a controlled and adaptive variable process.

The development of such a pneumatic optimization system enables real-time process control based on variation feedback from upstream operations, which is essential for minimizing cumulative variation and enhancing the overall quality of manufacturing.

Cumulative Variation in Manufacturing Processes.

1.1 Cumulative Variation Concept

In manufacturing processes, variation is an unavoidable phenomenon caused by multiple factors, such as equipment wear, material inconsistency, differences between operators, and environmental fluctuations. Even if the variation in each unit process stays within the specified tolerance range, deviations can accumulate gradually as the product progresses through successive stages. This phenomenon is referred to as cumulative variation.

Cumulative variation refers to the tendency of small deviations occurring at each process step to align in a particular direction or persist through repetition, ultimately resulting in a final deviation that exceeds the intended design specification. While each unit process may individually produce parts within specification, the accumulated effect of directional deviations across multiple stages can lead to quality degradation or functional defects in the final product.

To illustrate the practical implications of cumulative variation in actual manufacturing settings, consider the typical distribution of process output. In most cases, variation in unit processes follows a normal distribution, meaning that the majority of products are processed near the mean. However, a certain proportion will inevitably be produced near the upper or lower control limits.

Problems arise when products that deviate toward one end of the variation range continue to be processed in the same direction in subsequent stages. For example, if a product processed near the upper limit in one stage is again processed near the upper limit in the next stage—especially when the processes are functionally correlated—the likelihood of defects increases significantly.

In such cases, as illustrated in Fig. 1, it becomes essential to counterbalance the directional bias in downstream processes. If a product shows deviation toward the upper limit in the preceding process, the subsequent process should be adjusted to operate closer to the lower limit. This kind of compensatory adjustment of process conditions helps to suppress the buildup of cumulative variation and contributes to improved quality and defect prevention.

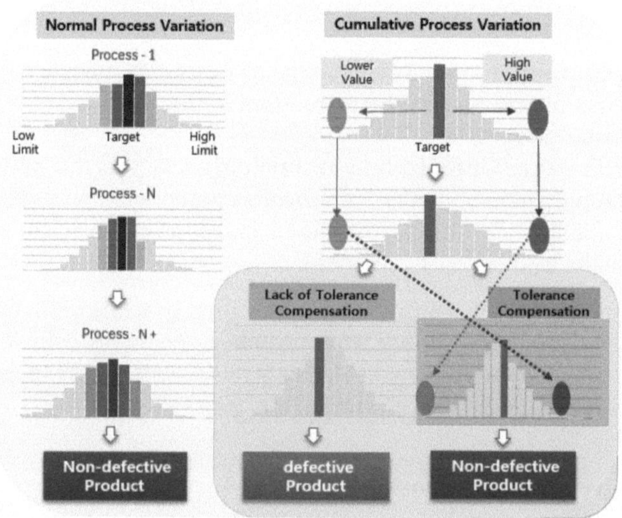

Fig. 1. Conceptual Diagram of Cumulative Variation in Manufacturing.

1.2   A Case Study of Circuit Breaker Manufacturing Process

In the manufacturing process of circuit breakers, various components such as the mechanism, trip bar, armature, moving contact, and handle are sequentially assembled on a base. From the component fabrication stage, dimensional variations in specifications, shapes, and physical properties inevitably occur due to the nature of manufacturing processes. As subsequent assembly processes proceed, these variations may accumulate and deviate from the nominal values. In worst-case scenarios, such cumulative deviations can result in critical failures such as trip malfunctions.

164   J. Cha et al.

The supplied components are manufactured through diverse processes including injection molding, pressing, welding, spot welding, crimping, and fusing. Due to the interconnected nature of these components, all of which function together to perform the trip operation, managing cumulative variation is of paramount importance. In particular, T.C.A (Trip Coil Assembly) suppliers produce eight types of parts—including terminals, pipes, coils, and solder rings—using a turntable-based stacking process. During this stacking process, terminal height variation is a frequent issue. Additionally, variations in the angle of the coil legs can occur during the wiring stage.

If such variation-containing T.C.A units are delivered to the final product manufacturer and assembled with other parts—such as the base, moving contact, mechanism, T.C.A, handle, and cover—then depending on the assembly method or compounded variations with other parts, a worst-case accumulation may lead to trip failure during overcurrent testing.

Particularly problematic are components such as bimetals or the T.C.A, which play a crucial role in the trip mechanism. In the current manufacturing environment, there is no in-process monitoring method to detect these variations. Instead, potential defects can only be identified through the final overcurrent test after full assembly is completed. This highlights the need for variation control at the source and throughout the assembly process to ensure product reliability.

Figure 2 illustrates how cumulative variation, occurring from the component suppliers through to the final product manufacturer's assembly process, affects the quality of the finished product.

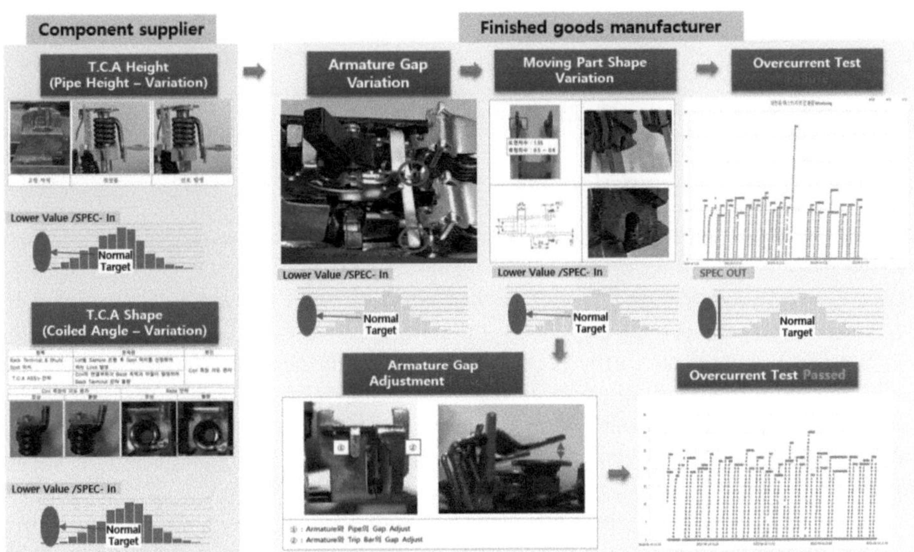

Fig. 2. Conceptual Diagram of Cumulative Variation in Manufacturing.

2 Pneumatic Actuators for Industrial Manufacturing Equipment

2.1 Compressed Air System

In general, a pneumatic system consists of a compressor, receiver tank, pressure-reducing regulator, and actuator. The compressor supplies compressed air to the receiver tank until the upper pressure threshold is reached, at which point it stops operating. As the actuator—such as an air cylinder—consumes the stored compressed air during operation, the pressure in the receiver tank gradually decreases. Once it reaches the predefined lower limit, the compressor is reactivated to replenish the compressed air. The pressure-reducing regulator is installed between the receiver tank and the actuator, serving to reduce the supply pressure to a predefined setpoint before delivering it to the actuator.

When compressed air is consumed and the system pressure drops, the regulator immediately compensates by allowing additional air from the receiver tank to flow into the actuator, thereby restoring the pressure to the target level (Fig. 3).

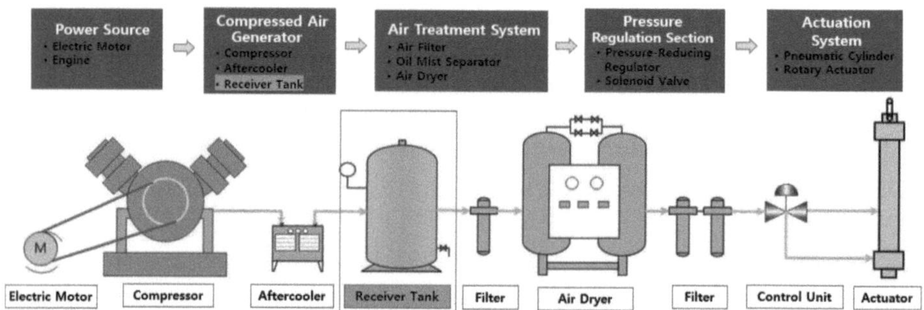

Fig. 3. Compressed Air System

2.2 Operating Characteristics of the Receiver Tank

The receiver tank supplies compressed air to actuators while repeating a pressure rise-and-fall pattern depending on the operating state of the compressor. During the rising phase, the compressor supplies more compressed air than the amount consumed by the actuators, allowing relatively stable operation. However, in the falling phase, the pressure of the stored air in the receiver tank gradually decreases as it is consumed, resulting in a corresponding pressure drop in the air delivered to the actuators. This can lead to performance instability, particularly in production lines that involve multiple simultaneous actuations of pneumatic cylinders used for pressing, welding, or seating operations.

As the number of cylinders operating concurrently increases, the pressure drop becomes more pronounced and accelerated, as illustrated in Fig. 4. Such fluctuations in receiver tank pressure directly affect the quality of compressed air supplied to the actuators, and consequently, to process reliability.

In final processes such as pressing or welding, which involve the bonding or bending of multiple pre-stacked components, accumulated variation from preceding assembly stages can act as an additional factor leading to defects. If the actuator's thrust force is not adjusted in response to skewed cumulative variation, defects such as cracks or improper bending may occur.

Although mitigating variation by upgrading equipment or replacing manual operations with skilled labor is possible, these approaches increase manufacturing costs through capital expenditure and labor expenses. Therefore, many production sites accept a certain level of defect rate as an operational compromise.

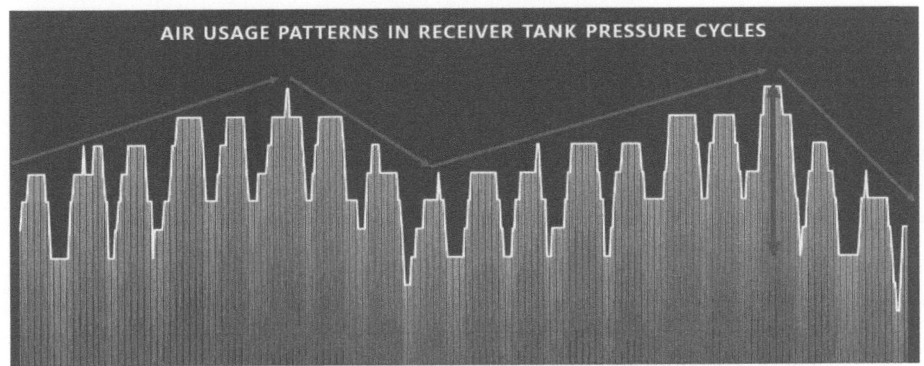

Fig. 4. Characteristic Curve by Receiver Tank Pressure Cycle

3 Solutions for Mitigating Accumulated Variation

3.1 Concept of the Compressed Air Supply Optimization System

To achieve the aforementioned objective, this study proposes a compressed air supply optimization system based on the pneumatic consumption patterns of air cylinders. The system is applied to a manufacturing process that utilizes a pneumatic system consisting of a compressor, receiver tank, pressure-reducing regulator, and actuator (air cylinder), with the goal of optimizing the supply of compressed air to the production line.

First, in order to collect machining condition data of manufactured products supplied by component suppliers, sensor signals as well as relevant production and quality data are acquired. Based on this information, upper and lower control limits of process variation are defined. The system then analyzes the compressed air injection conditions in the downstream process according to the rising and falling pressure cycles of the receiver tank, compensating for cumulative variation within the defined limits. The analysis results are reflected in real time through a variable process applied to pneumatic actuators.

The core element of the system, the Compressed Air Supply Optimization Unit, optimizes the pressure delivered to the actuator during the receiver tank's rise and fall cycles. This allows the thrust force applied by the air cylinder to be continuously adjusted in accordance with process variation, enabling the implementation of a variable process.

To achieve this, as illustrated in Fig. 5, an enterprise-wide quality management platform is required, in which manufacturing variation data generated by component suppliers is shared both vertically and horizontally across the supply chain, reaching the final product manufacturer.

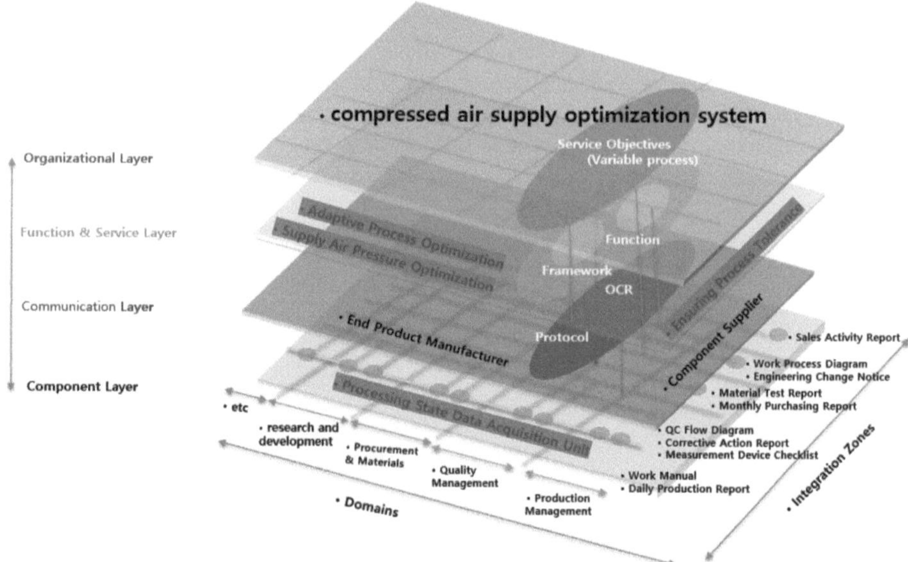

Fig. 5. Pneumatic Pressure Patterns under Normal and Crack Conditions

3.2 Verification of Process Margin

In order to optimize the supply of compressed air to each unit process during the rise and fall cycles of the receiver tank, it is necessary to assess the available margin for each unit process. Additionally, establishing acceptable criteria for cumulative variation from component suppliers to the final product manufacturer is essential. This requires not only verifying the variation that may occur during the manufacturing of individual components but also the operational variations that arises during the assembly of those components.

For each component, it is important to identify the process target values and the upper and lower limits for key specifications such as diameter, depth, shape, angle, and spacing. The dynamic behavior observed during the assembly process can be validated through dynamic simulation based on the interaction between components. Figure 6 provides an example of a table showing the allowable margins for diameter, depth, shape, angle, and spacing, both for individual components and their interactions.

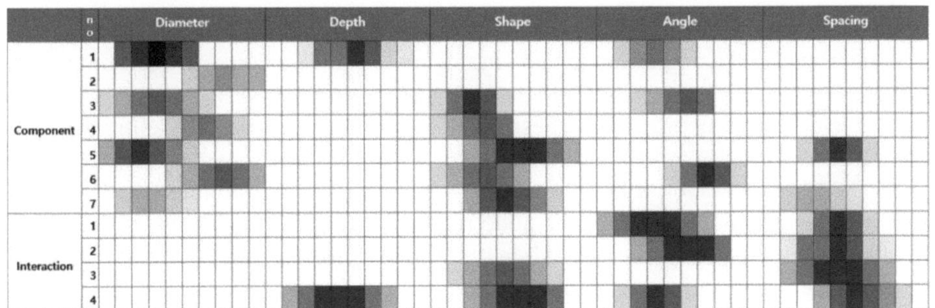

Fig. 6. Establishing Tolerance Criteria Across Component Manufacturing and Assembly.

Dynamic simulation is used to verify the proper operation of interacting components, and it enables visualization through the comparison and validation of digitized ecosystem data with CAD models, verification of interference margins due to cumulative process variations between components, and correlation matrix analysis.

To further advance this process, reverse engineering is required. This involves comparing actual cumulative process variation data from the supplier with standardized documentation that reflects engineers' empirical knowledge, and analyzing the operational mechanisms based on raw data from these sources.

By defining the scope of individual and interacting components and utilizing variation margin data, it is possible to infer upper and lower limits and secure acceptable margins through linear regression or multivariate linear regression modeling. Figure 7 presents an example of linear and multivariate linear regression modeling for each blocking stage.

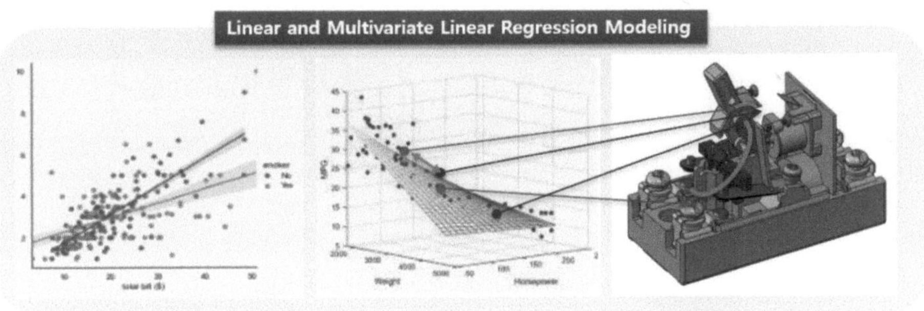

Fig. 7. Cumulative Variation Analysis in the Circuit Breaker Process.

3.3 Platform Architecture

Figure 8 illustrates the architecture of an MLOps system deployed on an on-device edge cluster using a lightweight Kubernetes distribution (K3S). The system is composed of three main layers: the Application/Service layer, the Platform layer, and the infrastructure layer.

The Application/Service layer includes a variety of services such as OCR, simulation, document processing, inference APIs, and data analysis. Data collection is facilitated through protocols such as MQTT and Modbus, while image data is captured and processed using FFmpeg and logging tools like Winston. MLOps components such as Kubeflow, MLflow, and Seldon-Core enable automation of the machine learning lifecycle, including pipeline orchestration, experiment tracking, model training, and deployment.

At the Platform layer, a high-availability K3S cluster is configured with multiple agent and server nodes. Each agent node runs containerized workloads (PODs) with kubelet and kube-proxy processes, while server nodes manage control plane operations via API servers, controllers, schedulers, and etc for state management. HAProxy ensures load balancing across the nodes.

The infrastructure layer leverages on-premise edge devices such as NVIDIA Jetson and Raspberry Pi for local computation, while persistent data storage is handled by network-attached storage (NAS) systems and databases such as MySQL and InfluxDB.

To enable full MLOps automation, the system integrates a CI/CD pipeline that supports container validation, automated model evaluation using test suites, and seamless deployment of trained models. Real-time performance monitoring is achieved through Prometheus-based metric collection and Grafana dashboards, with time-series data stored in InfluxDB or Elasticsearch. Additional monitoring features are implemented using MQTT and Kibana for real-time visualization, along with statistical analysis and relational database integration for advanced data processing.

This architecture supports a fully operational AI lifecycle at the edge, minimizing cloud dependency while ensuring scalability, reliability, and real-time adaptability in industrial environments.

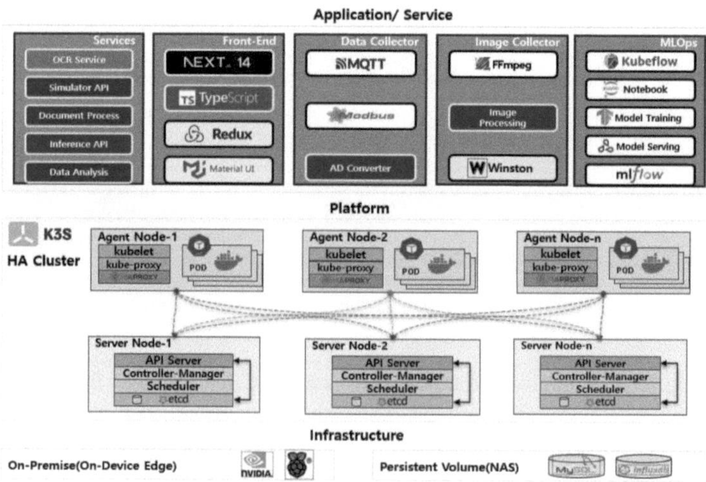

Fig. 8. Platform Architecture

4 Conclusion

This study proposed a methodology for optimizing compressed air supply in manufacturing environments by analyzing cumulative process variation from component suppliers to final product assembly. The proposed system utilizes the pneumatic consumption patterns of air cylinders and the pressure cycles of the receiver tank to achieve real-time adaptive control of the air pressure delivered to the actuators. To ensure robustness and accuracy, variations in individual component manufacturing and operational variation during assembly were simultaneously verified. Key specifications—such as diameter, depth, shape, angle, and spacing—were analyzed to define upper and lower control limits as well as process targets.

Dynamic simulations were employed to validate the functional interactions between components, utilizing digitized ecosystem data, CAD model comparisons, and correlation matrix analysis. To advance this validation process, reverse engineering was applied by integrating actual cumulative variation data from suppliers with empirical engineering knowledge and standardized documentation. Furthermore, variation margin data are used to model upper and lower control limits through linear and multivariate regression techniques.

To support scalable deployment and continuous operation of the proposed optimization system, an on-device MLOps platform was constructed using a lightweight K3S cluster. The platform incorporates data collection, real-time monitoring, CI/CD-based model deployment, and full automation of the machine learning pipeline using tools such as Kubeflow, MLflow, and Prometheus. This architecture enables real-time model-based control at the edge, minimizes dependency on cloud infrastructure, and enhances responsiveness and adaptability in dynamic industrial environments.

Acknowledgements. This work was supported by project for Smart Manufacturing Innovation R&D funded Korea Ministry of SMEs and Startups in 2022. (RS-2022-00141143).

References

1. Saleh, A., Mohamed, R., Abdullah, R.: Intelligent approaches for anomaly detection in compressed air systems: a review. Machinery **11**(7), 750 (2023)
2. Lee, J., Bagheri, B., Kao, H.A.: A cyber-physical systems architecture for industry 4.0-based manufacturing systems. Manuf. Lett. **3**(1), 18–23 (2015)
3. Brecher, C., Emonts, M., Esser, M.: Integration of machine learning methods in process control of manufacturing systems. Procedia CIRP **81**, 1054–1059 (2019)
4. Liu, Y., Zhang, Y., Wang, L.: Edge computing for industrial applications: a review on recent advances. J. Ind. Inf. Integr. **18**, 100162 (2020)
5. Andreadis, A., Makris, S., Chryssolouris, G.: An MLOps architecture for the deployment of machine learning models in manufacturing: Procedia CIRP **107**, 782–787 (2022)

A Needs Assessment of Electrical Discharge Machining Equipment for the Screw and Nut Mold Industry

Yu-Hsiu Hung[✉], Hsin-En Li, and Jia-Bao Liang

Department of Industrial Design, National Cheng Kung University, Tainan, Taiwan
idhfhung@gmail.com, P36131060@gs.ncku.edu.tw

Abstract. This study investigates the operational needs of EDM (Electrical Discharge Machining) machine users, comparing traditional and CNC models. Using contextual inquiry, the research team conducted field observations and interviews in Taiwan's screw mold industry to understand user pain points, workflows, and environmental challenges. Key findings highlight usability issues such as oil temperature control, machine maintenance, and workspace organization. The study reveals a disconnect between current machine design and actual operator practices. These insights offer valuable design recommendations and demonstrate the effectiveness of user-centered research methods in advancing industrial equipment development. The findings also serve as a reference for enhancing usability and productivity in future EDM machine innovation.

Keywords: Contextual Inquiry · Electrical Discharge Machine · Screw and Nut Mold Manufacturing

1 Introduction

Electrical Discharge Machining (EDM) is an advanced machining technology widely used in manufacturing, particularly suited for processing high-hardness materials and molds or parts with complex geometries. Recent studies have aimed to enhance EDM performance, addressing key factors such as material removal rate (MRR), tool wear rate, and surface quality [1]. For instance, recent research has emphasized enhancing machining efficiency and surface quality in EDM processes [2]. Similarly, *A Review on Current Research Trends in Electrical Discharge Machining (EDM)* summarized recent advancements, emphasizing efficiency enhancement, surface optimization, environmental safety, and predictive capabilities for machining outcomes [3].

Although these studies have significantly contributed to enhancing EDM performance, most have concentrated primarily on technical aspects and mechanism optimization. Limited attention has been given to examining the actual operational processes of EDM, as well as the challenges and needs operators face during practical use. Current research on user interaction predominantly addresses broader issues within the machine tool industry, such as procurement, usage, and disposal processes from a client-centric

M. Kurosu and A. Hashizume (Eds.): HCII 2025, LNCS 16332, pp. 171–184, 2026.
https://doi.org/10.1007/978-3-032-12385-5_11

viewpoint or design evaluation [4, 5]. However, there remains a notable gap in empirical studies conducted from the operator's perspective, particularly those involving direct on-site observation and focused on the operational differences between traditional and CNC EDM machines.

According to a report by Taiwan's Industrial Technology Research Institute, Taiwan is among the world's top three screw exporters, with highly competitive mold manufacturing technology. With the rapid advancement of Industry 4.0 and smart manufacturing, demand for EDM machines in high-precision mold and component production continues to rise. However, prioritizing technological breakthroughs without adequately addressing operators' practical needs can result in low on-site operational efficiency and steep learning curves. This issue may ultimately affect overall production line performance and hinder effective industrial upgrading.

Therefore, obtaining an in-depth understanding of EDM operators' actual experiences and pain points carries significant practical and strategic value for enhancing digital transformation and human-machine collaboration in Taiwan's mold manufacturing industry. This study focuses specifically on EDM operators in Taiwan's screw and nut mold sector, employing the Contextual Inquiry method. Researchers will enter real production environments to observe and interview operators, capturing firsthand insights into their operational challenges and requirements. As a user-centered research method, contextual inquiry allows for a detailed exploration of operators' work contexts, tool usage patterns, and problem-solving strategies, thereby providing a comprehensive understanding of user-machine interactions.

This study addresses two primary research questions: (1) What common difficulties and obstacles do EDM operators encounter during machine operation? (2) What differences exist between traditional and CNC EDM machines regarding operational requirements? Through systematic analysis of the collected data, this study aims to fill a gap in the current literature on user-centered EDM research. Additionally, it seeks to offer specific design recommendations for optimizing machine interfaces and operational procedures, thereby improving user experience and overall operational efficiency.

2   Literature Review

2.1   Research on Machine Tool Users

The development of machine tools has always been closely linked to user needs. In the early stages, operators frequently designed or modified machines based on specific process requirements, creating an iterative cycle driven by practical experience. Even after the emergence of professional machine tool manufacturers during the Middle Ages, interactions between users and producers remained crucial for innovation. Historical evidence underscores that integrating user behaviors and experiences significantly enhances the performance and practicality of machine tools [6].

With rising demands for rapid iteration and flexible manufacturing, machine tool design has increasingly embraced a user-centered approach. For instance, user-oriented development tools and interactive machine learning systems have been developed to meet rapid prototyping needs. Modern design methodologies—such as User-Centered Design and Action Research—systematically integrate user feedback and operational data. These approaches ensure that new functions and control interfaces align closely with real working conditions, effectively addressing practical challenges encountered by operators [7].

Recent research on machine tool users has expanded beyond purely technical factors to include emotional and cognitive dimensions. For example, semantic differential methods have been employed to evaluate emotional responses to machine aesthetics and interface design, offering valuable insights for user-centered evaluations. Such studies emphasize that mechanical design should consider not only engineering performance but also users' subjective experiences and intuitive perceptions [4].

Beyond perceptual aspects, understanding how users interpret mechanical structures and process interactions during operations has gained attention. Researchers have proposed methods to help operators identify and manage deviations caused by structural deformation, emphasizing the importance of machine stability in maintaining machining quality [8]. Other studies highlight that operational characteristics—such as dynamic rigidity, vibration frequency, and thermal deformation—directly influence operator behaviors and decision-making strategies. A thorough understanding of these interactions is essential for enhancing efficiency and product quality [9].

Despite advancements, user-focused research predominantly targets conventional cutting machines like lathes, milling machines, and machining centers. Few empirical studies specifically address Electrical Discharge Machining (EDM). EDM processes uniquely demand specific operator behaviors, process monitoring, and interface interactions, yet systematic user experience studies in this area remain limited. Existing literature primarily addresses EDM parameter selection, relying heavily on empirical rules and expert judgment, which introduces subjectivity and uncertainty. Additionally, there is virtually no research specifically focused on user experience with CNC EDM machines [10].

Therefore, this study aims to bridge this research gap by conducting behavioral observations and analyzing the needs of EDM machine operators. Furthermore, it explores the application of human-machine interaction principles and cognitive support design to improve user experience and operational efficiency in EDM environments.

3   Methods

3.1   Research Design

This study adopts a qualitative research approach with two primary objectives: (1) to gain an in-depth understanding of the operational needs of EDM machine operators, and (2) to identify differences in operational requirements between traditional EDM machines and CNC EDM machines. A corresponding research framework is outlined (see Fig. 1).

In the initial interview phase, basic information about the participating mold factories and their operators will be collected. During the operational observation phase, the Contextual Inquiry method will be applied, in which operators are asked to perform a complete EDM operation while the researcher observes and records the process.

In the subsequent in-depth interview phase, follow-up interviews will be conducted based on issues observed during the operational phase. These interviews aim to explore the motivations and reasoning behind user behaviors to uncover their actual needs. Finally, the collected qualitative data will be organized and categorized using the KJ Method to identify key themes and insights [11].

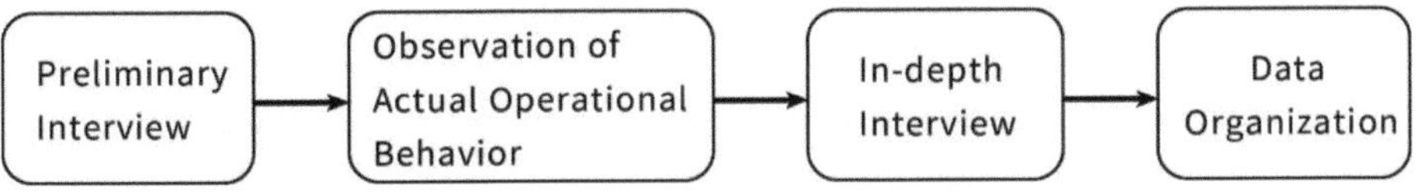

Fig. 1. Procedure of contextual inquiry.

3.2   Research Field and Participants

This study focuses on the screw and nut mold manufacturing industry in central and southern Taiwan, where EDM machines play a critical role in mold production and maintenance. A total of nine mold factories were visited. The research participants include technical personnel who operate EDM machines, covering both traditional and CNC EDM machine operators. Participants vary in years of experience and operational backgrounds to ensure a broad perspective. In addition, interviews were conducted with factory owners and management-level staff to enhance the diversity and representativeness of the sample.

The Table 1 below provides the basic information of the interviewed operators.

Table 1. Interviewee information table.

Interviewee	Years of Experience	Type of Mold Factory	Type of EDM Machine Operated
1	12 years	Mold Factory	Traditional EDM
2	2 years	Mold Factory	Traditional & CNC
3	8 years	Mold Factory	Traditional EDM
4	15 years	Mold Factory	Traditional EDM
5	10 years	Screw Factory – Mold Dept.	Traditional EDM
6	8 years	Screw Factory – Mold Dept.	Traditional EDM
7	9 years	Screw Factory – Mold Dept.	Traditional & CNC
8	15 years	Mold Factory	Traditional & CNC
9	5 years	Large Enterprise – Mold Dept.	CNC

3.3 Data Categorization

Using the KJ Method, the issues identified through contextual inquiry were organized into four main categories, each with corresponding subcategories. These categories are consistent with classifications found in previous literature, as shown in the table below (see Table 2).

Table 2. Classification of main and subcategories of user-identified issues.

Main Category	Subcategory
1. Processing requirements	1. Machining Oil 2. Oil Tank 3. Electrode 4. Workpiece
2. User operating habits	1. Traditional Machine Operation 2. CNC Machine Operation
3. Abnormal conditions during processing	1. CNC Machine Electronic System Issues 2. Excessive Temperature Leads to Abnormalities 3. Mechanical Components Issues
4. Machine efficiency	1. Pre-processing Preparation 2. Discharge Process

Building on this classification, the study further investigates the challenges users face when operating Electrical Discharge Machines (EDMs). It also compares the differing user needs between traditional and CNC EDM machines across various industrial settings. The aim is to provide design recommendations that more closely align with actual user requirements.

4 Results and Discussion

4.1 Traditional EDM Machines

Based on interview and observation findings, traditional EDM machines require manual installation and calibration of both the electrode and workpiece, including center and vertical alignment of the electrode. This process depends heavily on the operator's experience. To enhance operational convenience, users often modify the machines or adjust the original procedures. The following section examines the common issues faced by users and their corresponding needs when operating traditional EDM machines.

Issues with Machining Oil. Traditional EDM machines exhibit clear usability issues in machining oil management. Operators frequently need to replace electrodes and workpieces, making the repeated filling and draining of machining oil a tedious and time-consuming task. Additionally, due to the complexity and inconvenience of submerged machining, many operators choose to avoid this method, which results in oil splashing and a cluttered work environment. Therefore, we believe that operators of traditional EDM machines need a system that can rapidly fill and drain machining oil, or maintain stable, splash-free oil flow even without using submerged machining.

In response to machining oil-related needs, this study proposes the following design recommendations:

1. Design adjustable and modular oil tank systems: Enable the tank to be flexibly adapted to different sizes of screw and nut molds. This allows operators to use only the required amount of oil, reducing fill and drain time and encouraging the use of submerged machining.
2. Introduce rapid oil filling and draining systems: Implement high-efficiency oil transfer mechanisms to significantly reduce machine downtime during workpiece and electrode changes, thereby enhancing overall operational continuity.
3. Redesign the oil tank barrier for better accessibility: Lower the height of the oil tank barrier or make it height-adjustable to facilitate easier workpiece and electrode replacement, as well as more convenient calibration operations.
4. Integrate built-in anti-splash mechanisms: Equip the machine with anti-splash features to ensure a clean and safe operating environment, even when submerged machining is not in use.
5. Automate oil flow control using simple sensors: Install basic sensors and automated control systems to regulate oil pressure and flow, reducing dependence on operator experience and ensuring stable and consistent machining quality.

Operational Habits and Human Factors. In the operation interface of traditional EDM machines, some buttons and functions are used infrequently, and their placement and operation are not intuitive. In addition, certain control levers are positioned too low, failing to meet ergonomic standards and causing operators to suffer from lower back pain after prolonged use. The distance between the parameter control area and the machining area is relatively large, requiring frequent movement by the operator, which increases operational inconvenience. Furthermore, for convenience or personal habit, operators may modify the machine themselves—for example, by removing the oil tank barrier or operating with bare hands—leading to safety risks. Therefore, operators of traditional EDM machines require an ergonomically designed interface and control components to improve safety, comfort, and ease of use.

In response to ergonomic interface design, this study proposes the following recommendations:

1. Enhance ergonomic layout through operator collaboration: Work closely with operators to assess the placement and functionality of control levers and frequently used buttons. Adjust their positions based on ergonomic principles—for instance, raising the XY-axis control lever to eliminate the need for bending, thereby reducing physical strain.
2. Integrate control elements into the machining area: Relocate frequently used parameter control interfaces from separate sections into the machining area. This minimizes the need for the operator to move between zones, improving workflow efficiency and convenience.
3. Simplify the control interface for ease of use: Streamline the interface design by positioning only essential control components within easy reach of the operator. This reduces cognitive load and speeds up task execution.

4. Utilize intuitive icons and visual indicators: Apply easily recognizable icons to key buttons and integrate real-time visual indicators for machining status. This enhances user comprehension and ensures operators receive immediate feedback during operation.

Abnormal Conditions. Abnormalities in traditional EDM machines are often caused by mechanical component issues, such as oil leakage due to aging or ruptured internal oil pipes. Since screw and nut molds are commonly made of tungsten carbide, machining often results in current overloads and abnormal ammeter readings. These problems typically require experienced operators to resolve. However, as the number of senior operators continues to decline, novice users face greater difficulty in identifying and troubleshooting such issues.

Given the constraints of low-cost machines, operators need an anomaly detection system that can help identify problems before they affect the machining process. Based on these needs, we propose the following design recommendations:

1. Deploy sensors in critical and hard-to-monitor zones: Install sensors in high-risk areas such as oil pipelines and internal circuitry to enable real-time monitoring of potential leaks, overheating, or electrical anomalies. This proactive approach enhances machine reliability and reduces unexpected failures.
2. Enable remote alerts for long-duration processes: For workpieces requiring extended machining time, consider linking the machine to a mobile application that can notify operators of anomalies in real time. This ensures timely intervention and reduces the risk of unattended errors.
3. Implement visualized system status displays: Introduce a clear, visual interface that shows key machine information such as operational status and remaining consumables. This allows any operator—regardless of shift or experience level—to quickly assess the machine's condition and improves communication efficiency across teams.

Efficiency Issues. The operation process of traditional EDM machines can generally be divided into three stages: (1) Pre-machining preparation, including the installation and calibration of electrodes and workpieces, as well as parameter setting; (2) The actual discharge machining process; (3) Post-machining inspection and cleaning. Among these, operators most frequently complain about efficiency issues during the preparation stage, which involves many tedious steps. The installation and calibration of electrodes and workpieces are performed manually, and when dealing with workpieces of special dimensions, operators often have to custom-make jigs, with jig positioning also being a time-consuming task.

In response to these challenges, we propose the following design suggestions:

1. Design dedicated jigs for screw and nut molds: Develop specialized fixtures tailored to screw and nut mold geometries to streamline pre-machining setup, thereby improving preparation speed and operational efficiency.
2. Establish a machining knowledge database: Equip the machine with the ability to collect, store, and organize machining data. This enables operators to reference previous cases when handling similar parts, reducing trial-and-error and promoting knowledge reuse.

3. Expand quick-change systems beyond electrodes: While quick connectors for electrodes are already in use, this study recommends extending quick-change mechanisms to workpieces as well, further minimizing setup time and enhancing overall productivity.

4.2   CNC EDM Machines

CNC EDM machines are primarily used in larger factories, some of which have developed highly automated production lines. In such settings, operators are often less experienced, while senior personnel typically serve in supervisory roles, focusing on monitoring operations and addressing user-related issues.

Compared to traditional machines, CNC EDM machines offer features like automatic calibration and tool changing, enabling long-duration and high-volume machining. However, despite these advanced capabilities, contextual inquiry revealed that CNC EDM users still face various challenges and unmet needs.

Interface Issues. CNC EDM machines offer a wide range of functions and require complex parameter settings. However, their interfaces are not intuitive, making the learning curve steep for beginners. Some settings even require a deep understanding of machining details and programming logic, meaning that only experienced personnel can operate them efficiently. Compared to traditional machines, CNC operation has not been significantly simplified.

In addition, Taiwan's manufacturing industry relies heavily on Southeast Asian migrant workers, and language barriers often lead to communication challenges with local supervisors. This increases the difficulty of EDM operation training and may even require hiring interpreters for assistance. Language-related challenges are also reflected in the CNC interface, where frequent switching between Chinese and English is required.

Therefore, for the interface design of CNC EDM machines, we propose the following recommendations:

1. Use intuitive icons to enhance usability: Replace basic explanatory text with universally recognizable icons for simple operations. This reduces reliance on language and helps bridge communication gaps among users with different linguistic backgrounds.
2. Incorporate simultaneous bilingual display: Enable both Chinese and English to appear concurrently on the interface, allowing multilingual users to operate the machine efficiently without the need to switch language settings repeatedly.
3. Redesign the functional interface hierarchy: Reorganize the user interface by prioritizing commonly used functions on the home screen, while categorizing advanced settings into separate sections. Provide customizable shortcuts so that users can tailor the interface to their specific operational preferences.

Stability of Electronic Systems. Compared to traditional machines, CNC EDM machines are equipped with more automated functions, such as automatic calibration and automatic electrode changing, and typically feature a greater number of sensors—especially in European models. However, this increase in electronic components also raises the risk of system instability. A single sensor failure can cause the entire machine to shut down, and if the issue is not resolved promptly, it can directly impact production progress. In addition, CNC machines are often used for long-duration continuous machining, which may lead to rising oil temperatures, thereby affecting machining precision. In Taiwan's hot and humid climate, some machines have even experienced system crashes due to overheating. Therefore, CNC EDM machine users in Taiwan place a high priority on having a stable electronic system, as sustained and reliable output is one of their most critical needs.

To address these challenges, we propose the following design recommendations:

1. Reevaluate sensor placement and necessity: Carefully reassess the location and function of each sensor, eliminating non-essential components to minimize potential machine downtime caused by sensor malfunctions or over-complexity.
2. Adapt sensor design to environmental conditions: Analyze the environmental stresses—such as elevated temperatures or harsh operating conditions—at each sensor location, and select materials and housings that ensure long-term reliability and performance.
3. Integrate real-time oil temperature monitoring: Equip machines with oil temperature sensors that provide immediate feedback to operators. For advanced models, enable automatic adjustments to machining parameters in response to temperature variations, improving process control and consistency.
4. Enhance oil cooling systems as an alternative: Upgrade or optimize the oil cooling infrastructure to maintain stable thermal conditions during operation, ensuring consistent machining quality even in demanding environments.

Cost and Efficiency Issues. CNC machines, designed to support automated, high-volume production, inevitably incur additional costs. For example, machines with automatic electrode-changing capabilities require many quick-change connectors, which not only increase procurement costs, but also introduce spatial constraints. In practice, operators—typically more experienced ones—often need to custom-build jigs and fixtures to facilitate production. However, when dealing with non-standard or special mold geometries, this process becomes time-consuming and costly.

Taiwan is the third-largest exporter of screws and nuts globally. For local mold manufacturers, the demand for CNC EDM machines is not only driven by cost considerations, but also by the need to adapt to rapidly changing market demands. While current CNC EDM systems are well-suited for mass production, they are not always efficient when facing small-batch, fast-turnaround orders.

Therefore, design recommendations should consider dual-mode flexibility—supporting both high-volume automation and small-batch manual production. This can be achieved by:

1. Predefine machining modules for common workpieces: Develop preset machining templates for frequently processed parts to streamline setup procedures, reduce preparation time, and improve production consistency.
2. Enable mid-process parameter adjustments: Allow operators to interrupt machining and modify parameters during processing to accommodate unexpected variations in workpiece conditions or production requirements.
3. Design seamless switching between manual and automatic modes: Ensure that users can easily transition between automated and manual control modes, supporting both

high-efficiency automated production and operator-driven adaptability in complex scenarios.

4.3 Comparison of Traditional and CNC EDM Machines

Based on the above analysis of user needs for both traditional and CNC EDM machines, we further examined the key differences between the two. For developers of EDM machines, these represent two distinct user groups, each with its own specific requirements. Therefore, it is essential to approach the design process with a differentiated perspective, creating solutions tailored to the unique needs and contexts of each user type (see Table 3).

Table 3. Comparison of use contexts and improvement suggestions between traditional and CNC EDM machines.

Comparison Item	Traditional EDM Machine	CNC EDM Machine
Company Size	Small to medium-sized mold factories	Large-scale company mold departments
Order Type	Small-batch, diversified orders	Large-batch, standardized orders
Main Pain Point	One person must operate multiple machines Heavy workload with limited efficiency gains	If a single machine breaks down, overall productivity is severely impacted
Operational Issues	Manual installation and calibration Operation is complex and inconsistent Difficult for new workers to learn	Interface is complex and non-intuitive New or foreign workers struggle to operate
System Stability	Mechanical parts prone to aging and failure Rely heavily on experienced operators to detect and resolve abnormalities	Electronic components and sensors are vulnerable System instability affects machining precision
Ergonomics	Poor layout and posture design lead to long-term physical strain Inconvenient control position Physical burden and safety concerns	Operations often involve frequent switching between screens and functions Workflow lacks intuitiveness

(continued)

Table 3. (*continued*)

Comparison Item	Traditional EDM Machine	CNC EDM Machine
Improvement Suggestions	Redesign layout to reduce operator burden Integrate control and machining areas Assist positioning and calibration Provide anomaly detection and preset parameters	Enhance electronic stability Remove unnecessary sensors Improve interface with icon-based bilingual support Increase flexibility of parameter adjustments Support small-batch production

Company Size and Order Type. Traditional EDM machines are mostly used in small to medium-sized mold factories, where the focus is on small-batch and highly diversified orders. These operations emphasize flexibility and the ability to make quick adjustments. In contrast, CNC EDM machines are commonly found in the mold departments of large enterprises, handling large-batch and standardized orders where the priorities are production efficiency and consistency in quality.

Operational Issues and User Pain Points. Operators of traditional EDM machines are often tasked with managing multiple units at once, leading to a heavy workload with limited efficiency gains. Their main needs include improving operational efficiency and reducing both physical and mental strain. Moreover, installation and calibration processes rely heavily on individual experience, making it difficult to train new personnel. This underscores the need for more intuitive and standardized operating procedures.

In contrast, CNC EDM machines provide automated functions but often feature complex, non-intuitive interfaces. This creates a steep learning curve, particularly for new or foreign operators. In such environments, the priority shifts to simplifying the learning process and minimizing downtime to ensure continuous production.

System Stability. Issues in traditional EDM machines often stem from aging or malfunctioning mechanical components, and troubleshooting heavily relies on experienced operators. To reduce this dependence, there is a need to introduce sensor systems that can assist in detecting and diagnosing abnormalities.

In contrast, CNC EDM machines, which are equipped with a greater number of electronic components and sensors, are more prone to electronic system instability. Therefore, the primary need lies in enhancing the reliability of electronic systems and implementing real-time temperature monitoring and automatic parameter adjustment features to ensure stable, high-precision machining performance.

Ergonomic Design. Traditional EDM machines often lack ergonomic design. The machine layout and required operating postures fail to align with human factors principles, resulting in physical strain and increased safety risks during prolonged use. This highlights the need to enhance ergonomic design to improve operator comfort and safety.

While CNC EDM machines offer advanced digital interfaces, their complexity and language-switching requirements make operation non-intuitive. The primary user need is to simplify operational logic and provide an intuitive, multilingual interface to accommodate a diverse and global workforce.

Solutions and Design Recommendations. For conventional EDM machines, the design recommendations primarily focus on enhancing manual operation efficiency and ensuring operator safety. These include the integration of adjustable or modular oil tanks, rapid oil filling and drainage mechanisms, as well as the development of dedicated jigs and quick-replacement systems. Such improvements aim to reduce setup time and mitigate the reliance on operator experience. Furthermore, ergonomic enhancements are advised to optimize the placement of control panels and interface elements. The use of intuitive icons and visualized status indicators can further improve usability and operational safety. Regarding error management, it is suggested to implement critical sensor modules, mobile app notifications, and visual maintenance interfaces to assist less experienced operators in identifying and resolving malfunctions more efficiently.

For CNC EDM machines, design recommendations emphasize system stability and interface usability. It is advised to streamline the sensor configuration by removing non-essential components and to reinforce oil temperature monitoring and cooling mechanisms to ensure operational consistency during long production cycles. On the interface side, the use of icon-based representations and bilingual (Chinese-English) display modes can alleviate language barriers and improve cross-cultural usability. The system architecture should also be reorganized to prioritize commonly used functions and allow for user-defined shortcuts, thereby enhancing navigation and task efficiency. In response to the rapidly changing demands of the screw and nut mold industry, features such as interruptible parameter adjustment mechanisms, pre-configured machining templates, and flexible switching between automated and manual modes are recommended to increase adaptability and production responsiveness.

In summary, both categories of machines require design solutions that emphasize efficiency, operational stability, and intuitive use. While traditional EDM machines demand improvements in ergonomics and on-site usability, CNC EDM machines necessitate enhancements in automation reliability and user interface accessibility for multilingual operators. Future machine designs should aim to integrate the strengths of both systems, thereby developing innovative EDM solutions that are flexible, stable, and user-friendly—capable of addressing the diverse and rapidly evolving needs of the screw and nut mold manufacturing sector.

5   Conclusions

This study utilized contextual inquiry to deeply investigate the user needs and challenges associated with traditional and CNC EDM machines in the screw and nut mold industry. The findings revealed clear differences between the two types of machines in terms of order scale, operational pain points, system stability, and ergonomic design. Designers should take these differences into account when formulating targeted strategies for equipment improvement and innovation. Traditional EDM machines should prioritize ergonomic optimization, enhanced system monitoring, and reduced operational complexity. CNC machines, on the other hand, need improvements in interface intuitiveness, electronic system stability, and operational flexibility to enhance user productivity and satisfaction.

In addition, this study makes two key contributions. First, it fills a gap in current research by conducting an in-depth user-centered investigation of EDM machine usage in the screw and nut mold industry. It offers practical and systematic data and insights that can inform future equipment design. Second, it successfully demonstrates the application of contextual inquiry in the machine tool industry, showing its effectiveness in identifying real-world user needs and challenges. This provides a valuable methodological reference for future user experience research in this field.

However, the study also has some limitations. It is geographically limited to Taiwan, which may affect the generalizability of the findings. Additionally, the sample size was relatively small and did not include a wide variety of enterprise types, potentially limiting the comprehensiveness of the conclusions. The research relied primarily on qualitative interviews and field observations, lacking quantitative data support. Future studies could integrate quantitative methods to enhance the objectivity and validity of the results. It is recommended that future research expand the scope and diversify the sample to improve the generalizability and practical relevance of the findings.

Acknowledgments. We would like to express our heartfelt gratitude to Professor Yu-Hsiu Hung for his insightful guidance, continuous encouragement, and constructive feedback throughout the entire research process. We are also sincerely thankful to all the EDM operators and industry professionals who generously shared their time, experience, and perspectives during the interviews—this study would not have been possible without their valuable input.

References

1. Ming, W., et al.: A comprehensive review of electric discharge machining of advanced ceramics. Ceram. Int. **46**(14), 21813–21838 (2020)
2. Ho, K.H., Newman, S.T.: State of the art electrical discharge machining (EDM). Int. J. Mach. Tools Manuf **43**(13), 1287–1300 (2003)
3. Mohd Abbas, N., Solomon, D.G., Fuad Bahari, M.: A review on current research trends in electrical discharge machining (EDM). Int. J. Mach. Tools Manuf **47**(7), 1214–1228 (2007)
4. Mondragón, S., Company, P., Vergara, M.: Semantic Differential applied to the evaluation of machine tool design. Int. J. Ind. Ergon. **35**(11), 1021–1029 (2005)
5. Mert, G., Waltemode, S., Aurich, J.C.: How services influence the energy efficiency of machine tools: a case study of a machine tool manufacturer. Procedia CIRP **29**, 287–292 (2015)
6. Carlsson, B.: The development and use of machine tools in historical perspective. J. Econ. Behav. Organ. **5**(1), 91–114 (1984)
7. Buschek, D., Anlauff, C., Lachner, F.: Paper2Wire: a case study of user-centred development of machine learning tools for UX designers. In: Proceedings of Mensch und Computer 2020, pp. 33–41. Association for Computing Machinery, Magdeburg, Germany (2020)
8. Chanal, H., Duc, E., Ray, P.: A study of the impact of machine tool structure on machining processes. Int. J. Mach. Tools Manuf **46**(2), 98–106 (2006)
9. Brecher, C., Esser, M., Witt, S.: Interaction of manufacturing process and machine tool. CIRP Ann. **58**(2), 588–607 (2009)

10. Yilmaz, O., Eyercioglu, O., Gindy, N.N.Z.: A user-friendly fuzzy-based system for the selection of electro discharge machining process parameters. J. Mater. Process. Technol. **172**(3), 363–371 (2006)
11. Scupin, R.: The KJ method: a technique for analyzing data derived from Japanese ethnology. Hum. Organ. **56**(2), 233–237 (1997)

Analysis of the Frontier Applications of Intelligent Design in Smart Spaces

Hailing Li[1]($\boxtimes$) (ID), Jingjun Guo[1] (ID), Zhuohao Wu[1], Mohammad Shidujaman[2] (ID), and Jinglu Zhao[3]

[1] School of Animation and Digital Arts, Communication University of China, Beijing, China
lihailing@cuc.edu.cn
[2] Department of Computer Science and Engineering, Independent University, Dhaka, Bangladesh
[3] ONEWO Space-Tech Service Co., Ltd., Shenzhen, China
zhaojl52@vanke.com

Abstract. With the rapid development of technologies such as Artificial Intelligence (AI) and the Internet of Things (IoT), the design and construction of smart spaces are gradually becoming an important direction for the digital transformation of urban spaces. In today's era of rapidly advancing technology, a variety of advanced technologies continue to emerge, injecting strong momentum into the development of smart spaces. AI technology, with its powerful data analysis and processing capabilities, can accurately analyze a large amount of spatial data, providing a scientific basis for the design of smart spaces. IoT technology, by connecting various devices and objects, achieves real-time transmission and interaction of information, providing a solid foundation for the intelligent management of smart spaces. This paper will focus on analyzing the cutting-edge applications and characteristics of intelligent design in smart space design, taking the Vanke Group's "ONEWO" smart space practice project as an example, to explore the various cutting-edge applications of intelligent design in different scenarios such as residential areas, industrial parks, and social urban areas. By integrating intelligent communication, cloud technology, and user experience service design, the paper analyzes the integrated application of technologies such as AIoT, Business Process as a Service (BPaaS), and digital twins, to build smart space solutions centered on smart communities, smart parks, and smart cities. From the practical operation level of intelligent network layout, digital service platforms, and intelligent equipment maintenance, the paper analyzes the specific applications of intelligent design in smart spaces, discusses its value and significance in enhancing user experience, optimizing resource allocation, improving industrial efficiency, and promoting the progress of social and economic benefits, and reveals how intelligent design reshapes spatial efficiency, promotes the digital development of traditional industries, and achieves the intelligent industrial transformation of future society.

Keywords: Intelligent design · Smart spaces · ONEWO

© The Author(s), under exclusive license to Springer Nature Switzerland AG 2026
M. Kurosu and A. Hashizume (Eds.): HCII 2025, LNCS 16332, pp. 185–206, 2026.
https://doi.org/10.1007/978-3-032-12385-5_12

1 Introduction

Smart spaces are an essential component of modern urban development, with their core being the optimization of spatial resource allocation and the enhancement of user experience and operational efficiency through intelligent design and technology integration. This paper aims to analyze the cutting-edge applications of intelligent design in smart spaces and explore its innovation in technology, operations, and service models. Taking the Vanke Group's "ONEWO" project as a practical case, by analyzing case data, the paper explores the construction of integrated solutions for smart communities, smart parks, and smart cities, with AIoT and BPaaS as the core spatial technology system, providing a sample basis for enhancing user experience, improving service efficiency, optimizing resource allocation, and promoting the construction of smart spaces, and conducts a feasibility exploration that promotes the progress of social and economic benefits.

1.1 Research Background

With the acceleration of globalization and urbanization, the digital transformation of urban spaces has become an important direction for promoting socio-economic development. Against this backdrop, the design and construction of smart spaces have gradually become core issues in urban governance, industrial upgrading, and the improvement of residents' quality of life. Smart spaces are not only the product of technological development but also the result of the deep integration of social needs and technological innovation. In recent years, the rapid development of emerging technologies such as AI, IoT, cloud computing, and big data has provided strong technical support for the construction of smart spaces. The Sustainable Development Goals have prompted the industrial and academic communities to devote a large amount of effort to the development of new technologies such as artificial intelligence. The comprehensive application of these emerging technologies has not only changed the operation mode of traditional urban spaces but also provided new solutions for the intelligent development of future cities [1]. The integrated application of these technologies has not only changed the operation mode of traditional urban spaces but also provided new solutions for the intelligent development of future cities.

Intelligent design theory is based on the theoretical foundations of multiple disciplines and is an interdisciplinary concept widely applied in fields such as architecture, industrial design, urban planning, and information technology. Its core lies in optimizing resource allocation, enhancing functional efficiency, and meeting the diverse needs of users through intelligent technology and systematic design methods.

The core of smart spaces lies in the application of intelligent technology to achieve efficient management of space, optimization of resource allocation, and comprehensive improvement of user experience. AIoT technology, based on the Internet of Things, can digitally connect devices, facilities, and the environment in physical spaces, forming a dynamically perceptive and real-time responsive intelligent network. Just like in a smart factory, various devices achieve interconnection through AIoT technology, and data during the production process can be transmitted and analyzed in real-time, thus achieving intelligent management and optimization of production.

Digital twin technology, supported by cloud computing and big data, can build a virtual space to achieve precise simulation and efficient management of physical spaces [2]. Digital twin technology can provide strong support for urban planning by virtually modeling cities and predicting the effects of different planning schemes, thus selecting the best plan.

The introduction of the BPaaS model further promotes the standardization and process-oriented nature of smart space services, providing an efficient service model for the construction of smart communities, smart parks, and smart cities. The BPaaS model can optimize and automate various business processes, improving service efficiency and quality while reducing costs.

In the specific application scenarios of smart spaces, residential areas, industrial parks, and social urban areas are the three most typical fields. The construction of smart communities focuses on residents' lives, enhancing the convenience and safety of residents' lives through the application of smart home, community security, property management, and other technologies; smart parks are oriented towards industrial development, optimizing the production efficiency and resource allocation of enterprises through intelligent park management and service platforms; smart urban areas aim at urban governance, enhancing the operational efficiency and governance capabilities of cities through the integrated application of intelligent transportation, smart energy, smart public services, and other technologies. The intelligent construction of these scenarios not only meets the needs of different user groups but also provides important support for the sustainable development of cities [3].

In this context, intelligent design, as the core driving force of smart space construction, is reshaping the operation mode and service system of traditional spaces. Intelligent design can not only enhance user experience and improve service efficiency but also optimize resource allocation and promote the digital transformation of traditional industries, providing important support for the intelligent development of future society. Therefore, in-depth research on the cutting-edge applications and characteristics of intelligent design in smart spaces, and exploring its practical value and significance in different scenarios, is not only of great theoretical value but also has significant practical significance [4]. This research will provide new insights and models for the design and construction of smart spaces and is an important reference for promoting the digital transformation and intelligent development of urban spaces.

1.2 Research Significance

This paper delves into the cutting-edge applications and characteristics of intelligent design in smart spaces, which holds significant theoretical knowledge value and social practice significance.

Firstly, from a theoretical perspective, the construction of smart spaces involves interdisciplinary integration, including fields such as artificial intelligence, the Internet of Things, cloud computing, big data, and user experience design, which have issues related to data privacy and security, slow progress in standardization, and diverse user needs. Analyzing the application of intelligent design in space from the perspectives of its ontological characteristics and customized application scenarios can provide new perspectives and methodological support for the theoretical framework construction of smart spaces. At the same time, intelligent design, as the core driving force of smart space construction, its application characteristics and value in different scenarios have not been fully studied. This research, through in-depth discussion of typical scenarios such as residential areas, industrial parks, and social urban areas, can enrich the theoretical system of smart space design and provide important references for academic research in related fields.

Secondly, from a practical perspective, the construction of smart spaces is directly related to urban operational efficiency, optimization of resource allocation, and the improvement of residents' quality of life. By analyzing the specific applications of intelligent design in smart communities, smart parks, and smart cities, operable solutions can be provided for the actual construction of smart spaces. This research, taking Vanke Group's "ONEWO" smart space practice project as an example, can provide references for enterprises and governments in technology selection and implementation paths in the construction of smart spaces. At the same time, the research will also reveal how intelligent design, by enhancing user experience, improving service efficiency, and promoting the digital transformation of traditional industries, provides practical guidance for the sustainable development of smart spaces.

Lastly, from a societal perspective, the construction of smart spaces is an important way to achieve the intelligent development of future society. This research, by exploring the value and significance of intelligent design in smart spaces, can provide theoretical support and practical basis for promoting urban digital transformation, enhancing national technological competitiveness, and achieving the intelligent transformation of social industries. Therefore, this research is not only of significant academic value but also has profound practical significance for the construction of smart cities and socio-economic development.

Please note that this is only a part of the translation. If you would like the rest of the document translated, please let me know, and I will continue with the next section.

2 Intelligent Design and Smart Spaces Overview

2.1 Connotation of Intelligent Design

Intelligent design refers to the integration of advanced digital technologies, artificial intelligence, and the Internet of Things into space design and management to achieve the intelligentization, functionalization, and efficiency of spaces. Its core goal is to optimize resource allocation, enhance user experience and service efficiency, and promote the sustainable development of spaces. Intelligent design is widely applied in smart communities, smart property management, smart urban areas, and is an essential component of smart city construction.

Intelligent design is mainly reflected in:

1. Technology Empowerment: Intelligent design uses technologies such as the Internet of Things, big data, and artificial intelligence to achieve real-time perception and intelligent management of people, objects, and the environment within the space.
2. User Orientation: Intelligent design centers on user needs, optimizing service processes and experiences to enhance the functionality and convenience of the space.

System Integration: Intelligent design emphasizes the integration and collaboration of multiple systems, achieving data sharing and resource integration through a unified platform, enhancing the overall operational efficiency of the space.

3) Sustainability: Intelligent design improves the efficiency of resource utilization and reduces operational costs. It focuses on the efficient use of resources and sustainable development, reducing energy consumption and operational costs through intelligent means.

2.2   Key Technologies of Intelligent Design

Vanke Group's "ONEWO" smart space utilizes a variety of intelligent technologies for construction. Therefore, the realization of intelligent design largely depends on the support of multiple advanced technologies, which together form the technological system of intelligent design. Current mainstream technologies include:

1. Internet of Things (IoT): IoT enables real-time perception and data collection of people, objects, and the environment within the space through sensors, intelligent devices, and network connections.

   Smart home devices in smart communities, including smart locks and smart lighting. Equipment monitoring and maintenance in smart parks, including elevator monitoring and security systems. Intelligent shopping experiences in smart cities (such as smart payments and customer flow analysis). AIoT is the technological cornerstone of smart spaces, achieving device interconnection, data collection, and intelligent analysis through the deep integration of artificial intelligence and the Internet of Things [5].
   ONEWO, through its self-developed intelligent devices (such as "Ling Shi," "Black Cat") and apps (such as "Live Here"), has realized the following functions:
   Unmanned and Remote Management: Such as lane control methods and systems to improve property management efficiency.
   Multi-scenario Device Access: Supports access to more than 500 types of devices, covering various scenarios including communities, parks, shopping malls, and office areas.
   AI Patrol and Edge Computing: Achieves real-time monitoring and intelligent decision-making through AI algorithms and edge computing platforms (Figs. 1 and 2).

2. Artificial Intelligence: Artificial Intelligence enables data analysis, pattern recognition, and intelligent decision-making through technologies such as machine learning and deep learning. In smart communities, it can be applied to the design of personalized service experiences such as intelligent patrols, intelligent customer service, and intelligent push notifications. Relying on AI algorithms for data monitoring and analysis, personalized and convenient services or personalized product recommendations can be provided based on user behavior data. This echoes the research presented in "The Design Innovation Space of Intelligent Personal Assistants (IPAs) in Healthy Buildings in the Era of Artificial Intelligence." The study quantitatively assesses the impact of demographic variables on the acceptance of IPAs, demonstrating the significance of artificial intelligence in related applications. This echoes the

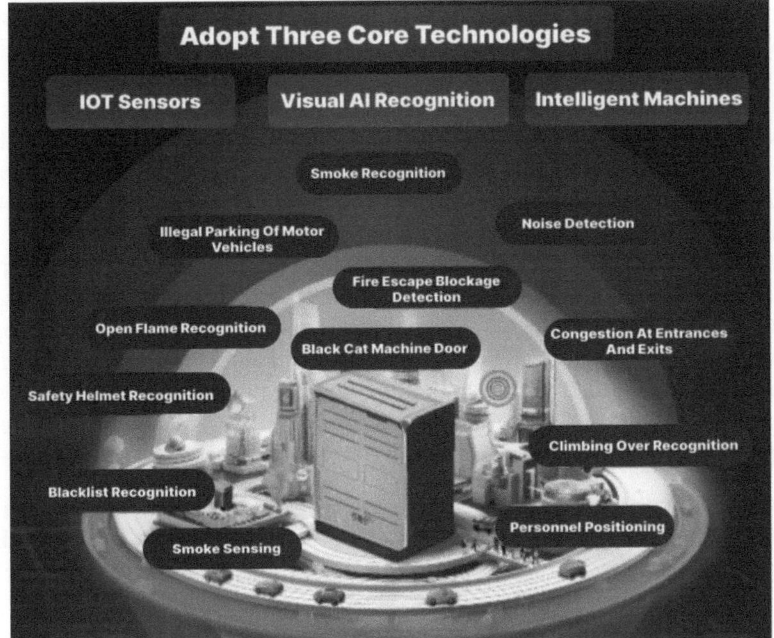

Fig. 1. "ONEWO" smart Space-Tech.

Fig. 2. "Live Here" APP.

research presented in "The Design Innovation Space of Intelligent Personal Assistants (IPAs) in Healthy Buildings in the Era of Artificial Intelligence." The study quantitatively assesses the impact of demographic variables on the acceptance of IPAs, demonstrating the significance of artificial intelligence in related applications [6].

3. Big Data: Big data technology provides decision support and trend prediction by collecting, storing, analyzing, and mining massive amounts of data. For example, in data-driven property management, it can: 1) Analyze equipment operation data

to optimize maintenance plans. 2) User behavior analysis: Understand user needs through data mining to optimize service content. 3) Urban governance: Enhance urban operational efficiency by analyzing traffic, energy, and other data.

4. Cloud Computing: By providing powerful computing and storage capabilities, it supports the processing and real-time response of complex data in intelligent design. For example, in smart community platforms, cloud computing supports the operation of digital service platforms such as the "Live Here" APP, achieving data sharing and collaborative work across multiple systems through the cloud platform.

5. Digital Twin: Digital twin technology constructs a digital model of physical spaces to achieve real-time monitoring and virtual simulation of spaces. By monitoring equipment operation status through digital twin technology, predict failures, and optimize maintenance. In commercial spaces, optimize commercial space layout and operational strategies through virtual simulation. Digital twin technology provides a new solution for the design, construction, and operation of smart spaces by real-time mapping of virtual and physical spaces.

Through digital twin technology, real-time mapping between physical and virtual spaces can support design, construction, and operation. Integrated into the entire lifecycle management, it can cover the planning, construction, and operation of the entire project cycle, greatly enhancing the efficiency of spatial resource utilization.

ONEWO deeply applies digital twin technology in the construction of smart parks and communities. In terms of energy consumption management and energy-saving, by real-time statistical energy consumption data, intelligent energy-saving strategies are formulated, successfully reducing energy consumption by 20%. In terms of the entire lifecycle management, the technology runs through the "planning, construction, bidding, and operation" of the project, enhancing the efficiency of investment attraction and asset returns.

6. Human-Computer Interaction Technology: Human-computer interaction technology enables natural interaction between people and intelligent devices through voice recognition, gesture recognition, and other methods. It is mainly applied in the field of smart homes, where devices such as lighting and air conditioning can be controlled by voice. Additionally, it can be applied in intelligent customer service, providing convenient services through voice assistants.

Intelligent design, through the comprehensive application of various technologies, provides strong support for the construction of smart spaces. The synergistic effect of technologies such as the Internet of Things, artificial intelligence, big data, and cloud computing not only enhances the functionality and service efficiency of spaces but also lays the foundation for the sustainable development of smart cities. In the foreseeable future, with the continuous advancement of technology, intelligent design will play a more significant role in more fields, creating a more rapid, efficient, intelligent, and sustainable living environment for people.

2.3 Definition and Characteristics of Smart Spaces

Smart spaces are an essential component of smart city construction, combining physical spaces with virtual spaces through digital technology, intelligent methods, and system integration to achieve efficient management, intelligent services, and resource optimization. The core of smart spaces lies in using technologies such as the Internet of Things, big data, and artificial intelligence to perceive, analyze, and manage the environment, equipment, personnel, and activities within the space in real-time, thereby enhancing the functionality, service efficiency, and user experience of the space [7]. It is not only a scenario for the integrated application of technology but also a carrier for service innovation and management optimization, aiming to provide more convenient, efficient, and intelligent services for residents, enterprises, and urban managers (Fig. 3).

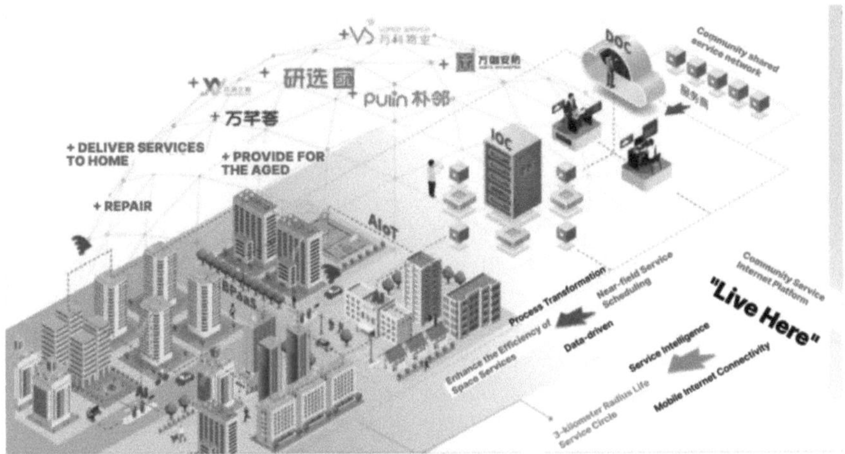

Fig. 3. Omni-Perception smart spaces.

The characteristics of smart spaces are mainly reflected in the following aspects:

1. Omni-Perception: Smart spaces achieve real-time perception of people, objects, and the environment within the space through IoT devices (such as sensors, cameras, smart terminals, etc.).

   1) Real-time Monitoring: Monitor environmental parameters such as temperature, humidity, lighting, and air quality in real-time. 2) Dynamic Perception: Dynamically perceive personnel flow and equipment operation status to ensure efficient operation of the space. 3) Data Collection: Collect multi-dimensional data through sensor networks to support subsequent analysis and decision-making.

2. Intelligent Decision-Making: Smart spaces process and analyze the collected data through big data analysis and artificial intelligence technologies, providing intelligent decision support. 1) Predictive Analysis: Predict equipment failures, user needs, etc., by combining historical and real-time data. 2) Automated Response: Automatically adjust the operation status of devices within the space (such as air conditioning temperature, lighting brightness) based on analysis results. 3) Optimize Resource Allocation: Dynamically allocate resources based on real-time needs to improve the utilization efficiency of the space. This mode of leveraging data processing and analysis to achieve intelligent decision - making, thereby promoting the interaction

between humans and space and efficient operation, is consistent with the concept that emphasizes the importance of human - computer interaction in intelligent systems [8].

3. BPaaS (Business Process as a Service): BPaaS provides flexible service capabilities for smart spaces by digitizing and modularizing business processes. ONEWO, based on "cloud-edge-device" integrated technology, has built a digital twin BPaaS platform, accessing more than 100 ecosystems, supporting the following applications: 1) Space Digital Operation: Achieve "plug and play" low-cost docking to improve operational efficiency. 2) Intelligent Service Experience: Reduce operational costs and improve service quality through remote digital operation and mixed employment models. 3) Remote Operation and Mixed Employment: Reduce operational costs and improve service efficiency through remote digital operation and human-machine collaborative models.

4. Efficient Services: Smart spaces provide users with convenient and efficient services through digital platforms and intelligent means. Personalized Services: Provide customized services (such as smart recommendations, personalized notifications) based on user behavior and preferences. One-Stop Services: Integrate multiple service entrances through a unified digital platform (such as the "Live Here" APP) to enhance user experience. Rapid Response: Achieve rapid discovery and processing of issues through intelligent patrols and remote monitoring.

5. System Integration: Smart spaces emphasize the integration and collaboration of multiple systems, achieving data sharing and resource integration through a unified platform. Multi-System Collaboration: Integrate security, energy management, property services, and other systems into one platform for unified management. Data Interconnection: Break information silos to achieve data sharing across departments and systems. Platform-Based Management: Build a unified management platform through cloud computing and big data technology to improve management efficiency.

6. User Orientation: Smart spaces focus on user needs to optimize service processes and experiences, enhancing user satisfaction and participation. Demand-Driven: Understand user needs through data analysis to optimize service content and forms. Interactive Experience: Enhance user interaction experience through human-computer interaction technologies (such as voice assistants, smart terminals). User Participation: Enhance users' sense of participation and belonging to smart spaces through point incentives, community activities, and other methods.

7. Sustainability: Smart spaces focus on the efficient use of resources and environmental sustainability, reducing energy consumption and operational costs through intelligent means. 1) Energy Conservation and Emission Reduction: Smart spaces employ technologies such as smart lighting and smart air conditioning to decrease energy usage. 2) Green Management: Initiatives like waste sorting and resource recycling promote green development. 3) Cost Optimization: Intelligent management reduces operational expenses, achieving a win-win in economic and social benefits. 4) Energy Conservation and Emission Reduction: Fine management of energy consumption and intelligent energy-saving strategies lower energy use [9]. 5) Ecological Integration: Green ecological concepts are integrated into design, creating sustainable smart spaces.

As an integral part of smart cities, smart spaces enhance and develop in various aspects such as omni-perception, intelligent decision-making, and efficient services, gradually improving the level of intelligent management and user experience [10]. In the future, with continuous technological advancements, smart spaces will play a significant role in more fields, providing strong support for smart city construction.

3 Application Scenarios of Intelligent Design in Smart Spaces

3.1 Smart Communities - Taking ONEWO "Butterfly City" as an Example

Smart communities, centered around the full life chain service needs of residents, create a safe, livable, and interconnected community environment through intelligent design. ONEWO's smart community solution enhances the community's safety, convenience, and resident happiness from multiple dimensions. The following will elaborate on health and safety communities, as well as shared and digital communities, and combine the practice of ONEWO "Butterfly City" smart community to discuss the specific applications of intelligent design in smart communities.

The construction of healthy and safe communities is the fundamental goal of smart communities. Through intelligent design plans and implementation, the safety and convenience of the community are significantly improved.

At the community entrance, intelligent access control systems are deployed, combining facial recognition and license plate recognition technologies to ensure community safety while improving the efficiency of resident and visitor passage. Inside the community, intelligent surveillance systems and 24-h patrol robots monitor the community environment in real-time, identifying and addressing potential safety hazards promptly. Additionally, smart communities focus on resident health needs by providing health management services through intelligent fitness facilities, air quality monitoring equipment, and health data collection terminals, creating a safe and healthy living environment.

Taking ONEWO "Butterfly City" as an example, this community integrated intelligent design concepts from the outset, cooperating with China Unicom to lay high-speed networks and intelligent security systems to ensure community safety and health. Through AI video surveillance, intelligent access control systems, and remote inspection functions, a smart security system was established, enhancing the community's overall security capabilities.

The construction of shared and digital communities focuses on improving community service efficiency and resident convenience. Through digital tools like the "Live Here" APP, communities achieve intelligent and online property management. Residents can complete property payments, repairs, and public facility reservations through the APP, greatly enhancing service efficiency and user experience. Previous relevant research has emphasized the use of digital means to enhance community services and the quality of residents' lives. In terms of improving the convenience of residents' lives, the current construction of intelligent communities has similar practices and achievements [11].

Furthermore, communities adopt a sharing economy model to create shared community spaces, such as shared parking spaces, shared parcel lockers, and shared gyms, optimizing community resource allocation and meeting residents' diverse needs. Digital communities provide personalized living services for residents through the interconnection of smart home devices, such as remote home appliance control, intelligent lighting adjustment, and home security monitoring, further enhancing the community's livability and intelligent level.

ONEWO "Butterfly City" smart community, centered on the full life chain service needs of residents, creates a safe, livable, and interconnected community environment through intelligent design (Fig. 4).

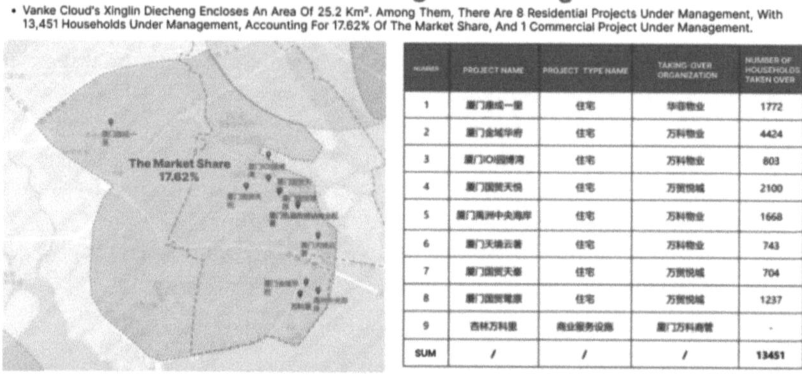

NUMBER	PROJECT NAME	PROJECT TYPE NAME	TAKING-OVER ORGANIZATION	NUMBER OF HOUSEHOLDS TAKEN OVER
1	厦门康成一里	住宅	华能物业	1772
2	厦门金城华府	住宅	万科物业	4424
3	厦门IOI园博湾	住宅	万科物业	803
4	厦门国贸天悦	住宅	万贸悦城	2100
5	厦门禹洲中央海岸	住宅	万科物业	1668
6	厦门天境云著	住宅	万科物业	743
7	厦门国贸天簦	住宅	万贸悦城	704
8	厦门国贸霓原	住宅	万贸悦城	1237
9	吉林万科里	商业服务设施	厦门万科商管	-
SUM	/	/	/	13451

Fig. 4. Introduction to ONEWO "Butterfly City" smart community.

Its intelligent design is mainly reflected in the following aspects:

1. Intelligent Design Plan and Construction

ONEWO "Butterfly City" smart community starts with basic design and construction, deploying FTTR (Fiber to the Room) technology throughout the community to achieve high-speed network coverage. By deeply integrating broadband and mobile networks, the community enhances network service quality, meeting the needs of smart home scenarios. "Butterfly City" smart community's broadband penetration rate has reached 69.69%. Through intelligent design plans and construction optimization, it supports cost-effective equipment ratios, reducing construction costs while improving the level of intelligence and providing residents with a higher quality network experience (Fig. 5).

2. Intelligent IoT and Digital Operation

Through AIoT technology, devices in the community (such as access control, surveillance, lighting, etc.) are connected to a unified IoT platform, creating an intelligent IoT platform that achieves interconnection of devices. China Unicom further promotes the full coverage and value maximization of community commerce through community advertising matrix, reaching residents.

Relying on the digital operation of the "Live Here" APP, the community integrates service entrances, providing a variety of online services, enhancing community service

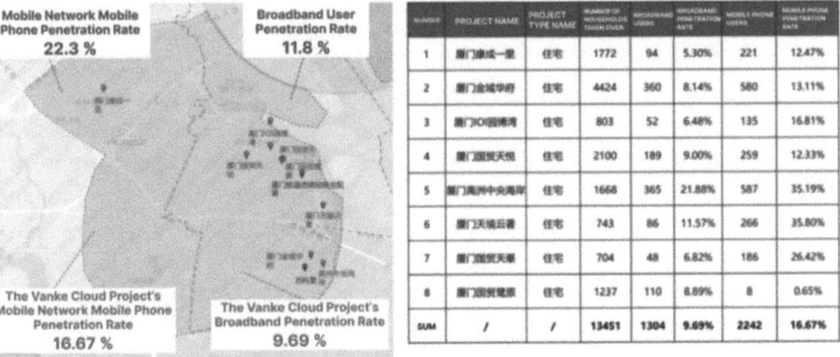

NUMBER	PROJECT NAME	PROJECT TYPE NAME	NUMBER OF HOUSEHOLDS TAKEN OVER	BROADBAND USERS	BROADBAND PENETRATION RATE	MOBILE PHONE USERS	MOBILE PHONE PENETRATION RATE
1	厦门建成一里	住宅	1772	94	5.30%	221	12.47%
2	厦门金域华府	住宅	4424	360	8.14%	580	13.11%
3	厦门IOI园博湾	住宅	803	52	6.48%	135	16.81%
4	厦门国贸天悦	住宅	2100	189	9.00%	259	12.33%
5	厦门禹洲中央海岸	住宅	1668	365	21.88%	587	35.19%
6	厦门天境后著	住宅	743	86	11.57%	266	35.80%
7	厦门国贸天著	住宅	704	48	6.82%	186	26.42%
8	厦门国贸龙原	住宅	1237	110	8.89%	8	0.65%
SUM	/	/	13451	1304	9.69%	2242	16.67%

Fig. 5. The Business Scale of ONEWO "Butterfly City" smart community.

efficiency. For example, residents can complete property payments, repairs, and public facility reservations through the APP, greatly optimizing convenience.

3. Smart Services and Security Guarantees

Smart communities build a smart security system through AI video surveillance, intelligent access control systems, and remote inspection functions, enhancing community safety. Based on the concept of digital twins, the community constructs a smart community cockpit that integrates people, vehicles, equipment, and events, achieving resident reporting linkage and rapid handling of abnormal situations.

4. Green Community and Energy-saving Design

Smart communities also focus on green ecological design, reducing community energy consumption through energy consumption refinement management and intelligent energy-saving strategies. For example, the community optimizes energy usage efficiency through the deployment of smart lighting systems and energy-saving equipment. At the same time, combined with green ecological concepts, the community creates a livable space that integrates with the natural environment, providing residents with a more comfortable living environment.

Overall, ONEWO "Butterfly City" smart community, through full cooperation with China Unicom, has achieved a broadband penetration rate of 69.69% and a mobile user penetration rate of 16.67% among 13,451 resident users. Through the "operation platform + Ling Shi" digital products, the community has achieved smart passage, unattended service, and AI inspection functions, with a business online rate as high as 95%, achieving intelligent control and cost reduction. The IoT platform connects with more than 300 scenarios, plug and play, low-cost delivery, truly achieving service quality, management innovation, and resource optimization, producing very good comprehensive benefits.

3.2 Smart Parks

Smart parks, as an integral component of smart spaces, promote the deep integration of industry and city through intelligent design and technological integration [12].

Taking the design of ONEWO Smart Park as an example, ONEWO Smart Park centers on full-cycle one-stop product services, providing a full-process intelligent solution from park planning, construction, to operation management. Through an intelligent investment management platform, the park can accurately match enterprise needs, optimize the investment process, and enhance investment outcomes. Data indicates that the park's investment effectiveness has increased by 15%, attracting more high-quality enterprises to settle; through an intelligent operation platform, efficient management of property management, equipment maintenance, resource scheduling, and other links is achieved, enhancing overall operational efficiency; through an intelligent service platform, the park provides convenient online services for enterprises and employees, optimizing user experience and significantly improving customer satisfaction.

Smart parks extend urban functions into the park itself through intelligent design, providing comprehensive living support services for enterprises and employees, enhancing the park's attractiveness, and realizing the extension of urban functions.

Smart parks also promote technological innovation and industrial upgrading through industry-academia-research cooperation and innovation incubation platforms, injecting new momentum into regional economic development. With intelligent platforms, smart parks provide enterprises with industrial services and resource sharing support, such as shared meeting rooms and shared parking spaces, optimizing resource allocation and enhancing the park's service capabilities. Such intelligent design promotes technological innovation and industrial upgrading, injecting new momentum into regional economic development.

3.3 Smart Cities

Smart cities aim to enhance urban governance efficiency and optimize resource allocation, achieving comprehensive and coordinated management through intelligent design. Taking the governance model of "one platform, one team, one network" proposed by ONEWO as an example, it has shown significant effectiveness in the construction of smart cities.

Taking ONEWO as an example, through the governance model of "one platform, one team, one network," the city achieves comprehensive smart integration and systematic governance.

One Platform: Unified dispatch and operation, achieving integrated operation of various scenarios inside and outside the city.

One Team: Public-private cooperation, providing refined management services.

One Network: Constructing a comprehensive smart governance network through IoT perception and multi-dimensional analysis.

This system is known as "One Net Unified Management." Relying on "One Net Unified Management," ONEWO Smart City achieves intelligent governance and system integration.

In the South China region, ONEWO successfully undertook the "Belt and Road" design service pilot center project - "Guangzhou Baiyun Design Capital." The project promotes regional economic transformation through digital operation, with an annual output value of 65 billion yuan. The coverage rate of digital operation scenarios in the park reached 42%, with a high rental rate of 90% in the first phase, and more than 300 park service applications were deployed, serving a population of over 100,000. Through the deep integration of intelligent design and digital technology, the area has achieved efficient resource allocation and service optimization.

In terms of operation and management, "Guangzhou Baiyun Design Capital" implements 7×24-h normalized operation, significantly enhancing inspection efficiency and management effectiveness. Specifically, manual inspection time was reduced to every 10 min per inspection, while AI camera automatic inspection time only takes 25 s per inspection, increasing the overall inspection efficiency by 50%. Additionally, the manual work completion rate reached 95%, the task timeliness rate was 98%, safety incidents in the area decreased by 30%, and the average management efficiency per person increased by 35%. These data indicate that intelligent design not only improves the quality of park operations but also significantly reduces management costs.

Thanks to its outstanding performance in the construction of smart cities, "Guangzhou Baiyun Design Capital" has been awarded the title of "China's Leading Smart City" for four consecutive years. This case fully demonstrates the practical value of intelligent design in smart cities, providing valuable experience and references for the future construction of smart cities (Fig. 6).

With outstanding strength! Baiyun District of Guangzhou has been rated as "China's Leading Smart Urban Area" for four consecutive years.

南方Plus   2023-11-18 18:00

On November 15th, the 2023 China Smart City Selection Award Ceremony was successfully held at the scene of the Smart City Development Summit Forum of the 25th China International High-tech Fair (hereinafter referred to as the "CHTF"). Baiyun District of Guangzhou City once again won the title of "China's Leading Smart Urban Area", and this is also the fourth time that Baiyun District has received this honor.

Fig. 6. Introduction to "China's Leading Smart Urban Area"

The intelligent design is mainly reflected in the following aspects:

1. Omni-Perception and Digital Twin

IoT Perception System: Through AI and Omni-Perception system, data of people, vehicles, facilities, and other elements in the city are connected to a unified platform to form a digital twin platform.

Edge Computing and High-Precision Algorithms: Utilize edge computing platforms and high-precision algorithms to achieve prediction, deduction, and decision-making for the entire area.

2. Smart Scene Design

Smart Patrol and Sanitation: Projects such as the Beijing Daxing International Airport Economic Zone improve regional governance capabilities through smart patrol, smart sanitation, and smart landscaping scene designs.

Smart Municipal and Environmental Monitoring: Construct a smart municipal management system through urban lighting, air monitoring, soil monitoring, and other functions.

3. Innovative Service Models

Property City Model: Projects like the Zhuhai Hengqin Guangdong-Macao Deep Cooperation Zone pioneer the "Property City" model, integrating property services with urban governance to promote efficient resource utilization.

Digital Governance Ecological Model: Projects like the Beijing Daxing International Airport Economic Zone promote social governance model innovation through digitalization, achieving modernization of regional governance capabilities [13].

4. Promoting community collaboration

Social innovation emphasizes solving social problems through technological means, and smart design plays an important role in this process. Smart design can improve the quality of life of residents through community collaboration models (such as sharing economy and digital platforms [4].

China Unicom's cooperation with ONEWO, through the application of intelligent design, constructs smart space solutions centered on smart communities, smart property, and smart cities. This model has achieved significant results in improving service efficiency, optimizing resource allocation, and enhancing user experience. However, the integration of technology and services, data security, and user acceptance remain key issues to be resolved. In the future, technological innovation and service optimization should be further strengthened to promote the application of intelligent design in more smart spaces, providing sustainable development solutions for smart city construction.

Please note that this translation is an ongoing process, and I will continue with the next section upon your request.

4   Innovative Value and Future Prospects of Intelligent Design in Smart Spaces

4.1   Enhancing Spatial Efficiency

Intelligent design significantly improves the utilization efficiency of spatial resources through technological integration and process optimization. For instance, the unmanned and AI inspection solutions from ONEWO have helped projects reduce costs by an average of 20% and increase emergency response efficiency by 75%. These efficiency gains are not only reflected in cost reduction but also in the ability to respond to and handle various issues more rapidly, ensuring the normal operation of spaces.

4.2   Optimizing User Experience

Intelligent design focuses on user needs and provides an exceptional user experience through digital tools and intelligent services. For example, the "Live Here" APP in smart communities and the digital investment platform in smart parks have significantly increased user satisfaction. Users can conveniently access required services and information through these platforms, achieving one-stop service and greatly improving the convenience of living and working.

4.3   Promoting Industrial Transformation

Intelligent design combines traditional industries with spatial IoT technology, creating a multi-scenario shared service network and promoting the formation of an industrial internet ecosystem [15]. For example, ONEWO has helped traditional property services transform into spatial services through the construction of smart communities and smart parks. This transformation not only enhances service quality and efficiency but also brings new opportunities and challenges for industrial development.

4.4   Facilitating the Integration of Technology and Art

Innovative Aesthetic Expression: Intelligent design combines technologies such as artificial intelligence and IoT with artistic design to inject more creativity into smart spaces. For example, dynamic lighting systems can present different artistic effects based on environmental or user emotional changes. This integration not only makes spaces more aesthetically pleasing but also provides users with unique visual experiences.

Enhanced Cultural Experience: In smart museums or smart cities, intelligent design can enhance the depth and breadth of cultural dissemination through interactive installations and digital displays. Users can better understand cultural history and improve cultural literacy through these interactive methods.

4.5 Enhancing Safety and Convenience

Intelligent Security: Through technologies such as facial recognition and behavior analysis, intelligent design can provide more efficient security for smart spaces. For example, in smart communities and smart parks, intelligent security systems can monitor the activities of people and vehicles in real-time, identify potential safety hazards, and take corresponding measures.

Convenient Management: Intelligent design can integrate various functions into one platform, such as controlling the entire space's equipment through a smartphone or voice assistant, simplifying management processes [16]. Users can manage and control spaces anytime, anywhere, improving the convenience and efficiency of management.

4.6 Data-Driven Innovation

Real-Time Feedback and Optimization: Intelligent design relies on big data and artificial intelligence technologies to collect user behavior data in real-time and continuously optimize space design and functions through analysis. For example, by analyzing user behavior data in smart communities and smart parks, we can understand user needs and preferences, providing a basis for space optimization.

Predictive Design: Through deep learning of data, intelligent design can predict user needs and provide solutions in advance, thereby enhancing the foresight and practicality of spaces. For example, in the field of smart transportation, by analyzing traffic flow data, we can predict traffic congestion and take diversion measures in advance.

4.7 Empowering Diverse Applications

Intelligent design plays a crucial role not only in fields such as smart communities, smart parks, and smart cities but also empowers diverse applications. For example, in the field of smart healthcare, intelligent design can achieve intelligent management of medical equipment and remote medical services; in smart education, intelligent design can create intelligent teaching environments and online education platforms. Through the empowerment of intelligent design, various fields can achieve digital transformation and intelligent upgrading, bringing more convenience and innovation to people's lives and work.

5 Challenges of Intelligent Design in Smart Spaces

5.1 Data Privacy and Security Issues

The core of smart spaces lies in collecting, analyzing, and utilizing a large amount of user data through IoT devices, sensors, and artificial intelligence technology to achieve personalized services and efficient management. However, this data-driven model also brings serious privacy and security issues:

1. Data Breach Risks: A large amount of user behavior data, location information, and personal privacy data in smart spaces are collected and stored in real-time. Once the data is attacked by hackers or leaked, it may cause irreparable losses to users.

2. Data Misuse and Ethical Issues: Operators of smart spaces may misuse user data for unauthorized commercial purposes or surveillance activities, infringing on user privacy rights.
3. Security Vulnerabilities and System Attacks: Devices and systems in smart spaces are interconnected, and any security vulnerability in a device can become an entry point for attacks, leading to system paralysis or malicious use [17].
4. Taking smart homes as an example, many smart devices (such as cameras, voice assistants) have issues with insufficient data encryption or improper permission management, leading to the leakage of user privacy. In the "Guangzhou Baiyun Design Capital" project, ONEWO deployed high-security encryption technology and distributed data storage solutions to reduce the risk of data leaks, while ensuring the legal use of data through strict permission management and user authorization mechanisms. This practice provides a reference for data privacy protection in smart spaces.

5.2 Technical Standardization and Interoperability

The construction of smart spaces involves the integration of various technologies and devices, including IoT, artificial intelligence, cloud computing, etc. However, the lack of uniform standards between different manufacturers and technology platforms makes interoperability issues a major obstacle to the development of smart spaces:

1. Insufficient Device Compatibility: Devices from different manufacturers may use different communication protocols and data formats, preventing seamless collaboration between devices.
2. Technological Isolation: Subsystems in smart spaces (such as smart homes, smart offices, smart transportation) may operate independently, lacking a unified management platform and making it difficult to achieve comprehensive collaboration.
3. Slow Progress in Standardization: The standardization of smart space technology requires the joint promotion of governments, enterprises, and industry associations, but a unified standard system has not yet been formed globally.
4. In the "Guangzhou Baiyun Design Capital" project, ONEWO proposed a governance model of "one platform, one team, one network," achieving interconnection and interoperation of more than 300 service applications in the park through the construction of a unified digital operation platform. This model solves the problems of device compatibility and system collaboration through standardized technical interfaces and data protocols, providing practical experience for the standardized construction of smart spaces.

5.3 Balancing User Experience and Technical Complexity

Intelligent design in smart spaces needs to find a balance between enhancing user experience and reducing technical complexity. Overly complex technical designs may make it difficult for users to adapt, while overly simplified designs may not meet the diverse needs of users:

1. High Technical Barriers: Many smart devices and systems in smart spaces require users to have certain technical knowledge to operate, which may cause usage obstacles for technologically disadvantaged groups such as the elderly.

2. Diverse User Needs: Different users have varying functional needs for smart spaces. How to satisfy personalized needs while maintaining system usability is a problem that intelligent design needs to address.

3. Integration of Technology and Humanities: The design of smart spaces should not only focus on technical functions but also consider users' emotional needs and cultural backgrounds to avoid a "technology-first" design mindset.

4. In the "Guangzhou Baiyun Design Capital," ONEWO designed personalized service scenarios through the analysis of user behavior data, while simplifying user operation processes. For example, the automatic patrol function of AI cameras can be completed without user intervention, greatly enhancing the user experience. This user-centered design concept provides important insights for intelligent design in smart spaces.

5.4   The Dilemma Between Cost and Sustainability

The construction of smart spaces requires a substantial investment of funds and resources, and how to achieve sustainable development while controlling costs is another major challenge faced by intelligent design:

1. High Initial Construction Costs: The infrastructure construction of smart spaces (such as sensor deployment, network laying) and technology research and development require a significant financial investment, which may cause economic pressure on small and medium-sized enterprises or underdeveloped areas.

2. Balancing Operating Costs and Benefits: The daily operation of smart spaces requires continuous investment, such as equipment maintenance, data storage, and energy consumption. How to reduce operating costs while maintaining efficient operation is a difficult problem [18].

3. Green Development and Resource Utilization: The construction of smart spaces needs to take into account environmental protection and resource conservation to avoid energy waste or environmental pollution due to over-reliance on technology.

4. "Guangzhou Baiyun Design Capital" has significantly improved resource utilization efficiency through digital operation and intelligent management. For example, the application of AI inspection technology not only reduces labor costs but also decreases energy consumption. In addition, the intelligent design in the park focuses on green development, optimizing energy use and reducing resource waste, achieving a win-win in economic and environmental benefits. This practice provides a useful reference for the sustainable development of smart spaces.

6   Potential Application Scenarios of Intelligent Design in Smart Spaces

The core of intelligent design lies in optimizing spatial functions, enhancing user experience, and meeting diverse needs through technological means. In the future, intelligent design will show greater potential in the following emerging scenarios, such as smart medical spaces, smart educational spaces, smart mobility spaces, and wellness spaces.

Future smart spaces will not only be a collection of technologies but also a deep integration of technology and humanities. Intelligent design needs to focus on human emotional needs, cultural backgrounds, and social values while innovating technology, promoting smart spaces to develop in a more humanized direction [19].

In the process of integrating intelligent design with smart space applications, the development of technology and humanities, concepts such as people-oriented, technology ethics, and social responsibility will gradually play a greater role, especially in meeting the needs of different groups that require care. Intelligent design can gradually meet the needs of different users, reflecting convenient and humanized services [20].

The development of smart spaces will show several important trends:

1. Omni-Intelligence and Collaborative Development Smart spaces will transition from the intelligence of single scenarios to omni-collaboration. For example, systems in smart cities such as transportation, energy, healthcare, and education will achieve interconnection and collaboration, managed and optimized through a unified digital platform, enhancing overall operational efficiency.
2. Green and Sustainable Development The construction of smart spaces will place greater emphasis on green development and resource conservation. For example, through intelligent energy management systems, energy usage efficiency can be optimized to reduce carbon emissions; through green building design, the environmental impact of buildings can be reduced, achieving sustainable development goals.
3. Personalized and Customized Services With the advancement of artificial intelligence and big data technologies, smart spaces will be able to provide more personalized and customized services based on user behavior data and preferences. For example, smart homes can automatically adjust lighting, temperature, and music according to users' living habits, creating an exclusive living experience. In the future, intelligent design will pay more attention to the integration of technology and humanity. Intelligent space is not only a carrier of technological innovation, but also a place for the expression of human emotions and culture. Chen W and others emphasized that the essence of intelligent art lies in the transmission of emotions and thoughts through technology. Intelligent design in intelligent space should also focus on user emotions and create a more humanistic spatial experience [21].
4. Integration of Virtual and Reality With the maturation of virtual reality (VR) and augmented reality (AR) technologies, smart spaces will achieve a deep integration of the virtual and the real. For example, in smart offices, employees can participate in virtual meetings through VR devices; in smart education, students can engage in immersive learning through AR technology.
5. Deep Integration of Technology and Society The development of smart spaces will promote the deep integration of technology and society. For example, optimizing urban governance models through intelligent design can enhance the service efficiency and transparency of governments; through the construction of smart communities, interaction and cohesion among residents can be strengthened.

In the future, intelligent design will play an increasingly important role in the construction of smart spaces. Through the deep integration of technology and humanities, smart spaces will not only be a carrier of technological innovation but also an important driving force for sustainable development in human society. Whether in medical care, education, transportation, or elderly care, intelligent design will create a more efficient, convenient, and beautiful living environment for humanity. At the same time, the development of smart spaces also needs to pay attention to ethical issues in the application of technology, ensuring that the use of technology aligns with social values and sustainable development goals. Through continuous technological innovation and human care, smart spaces will become an important direction for the development of future cities, providing more possibilities for the progress of human society.

References

1. Li, M., Li, Y., He, C., et al.: Generative AI for sustainable design: a case study in design education practices. In: International Conference on Human-Computer Interaction, pp. 59–78. Springer, Cham (2024)
2. Larmer, R.A.: Intelligent design and the "Bad Metaphor" objection. J. Phys. Conf. Ser. **2706**(0 P012037), 012037, 1742–6588 (2024)
3. Hu, D., Zhao, M.: Design and development of intelligent outdoor jackets. J. Beijing Inst. Fashion Technol. (Nat. Sci. Ed.) **44**(1), 87–94, 1001–0564 (2024)
4. Roberto, B., Tyson, H., Mollie, C.: Disruptive ecologies: design with nonhuman intelligences. Architectural Des. **94**(1), 30–37, 0003–8504 (2024)
5. Kwon, C., Ahn, Y.: Critical views on AI (Artificial Intelligence) in building design. Int. J. Sustain. Build. Technol. Urban Dev. **15**(2), 240–246 2093–761X (2024)
6. Liu, Y., Zhang, J., Zeng, Y., Liu, Y., Shidujamam, M.: The design innovation space of intelligent personal assistants (IPAs) in healthy buildings in the era of artificial intelligence. In: HCI International (2024)
7. Chen, Y., Xie, X., Ma, L., et al.: Multi-level prediction with graphical model for human pose estimation. In: Chinese Conference on Pattern Recognition and Computer Vision (PRCV), pp. 343–355. Springer, Cham (2020)
8. Song, X., Liu, M., Gong, L., Gu, Y., Shidujaman, M.: A review of human-computer interface evaluation research based on evaluation process elements. In: Human-Computer Interaction: Thematic Area, HCI 2023 (2023)
9. Huan, T.: Design of functional and sustainable polymers assisted by artificial intelligence. Nat. Rev. Mater., 2058–8437 (2024)
10. Tyarin, A.S., Kureev, A.A., Khorov, E.M.: Fundamentals of design and operation of reconfigurable intelligent surfaces. J. Commun. Technol. Electron., 1064–2269 (2024)
11. Wang, J., Weng, Y., Shidujaman, M., Jiang, Y.: Design and responsible research innovation in the university-industry collaboration: an ethnographic study of nice2035 project-based community. In: HCI International (2024)
12. Ali, Y., Shah, S.W., Arif, A., Tlija, M., Siddiqi, M.R.: Intelligent framework design for quality control in industry 4.0. Appl. Sci. **14**(17), 7726 (2024)
13. Liouane, Z., Lemlouma, T., Roose, P., Weis, F., Messaoud, H.: An intelligent knowledge system for designing, modeling, and recognizing the behavior of elderly people in smart space. J. Ambient Intell. Hum. Comput. **11**(12), 6059–6075, 1868–5137 (2020)
14. Wang, J., Weng, Y., Shidujaman, M., et al.: A multilevel perspective for social innovation: three exemplary case studies in collaborative communities toward sustainability. In: International Conference on Human-Computer Interaction, pp. 366–391. Springer, Cham (2023)
15. Greenhalgh, S.L.: Jonkoping University Researcher Publishes New Data on Artificial Intelligence (Enhancing Smart Home Design with AI Models: A Case Study of Living Spaces Implementation Review). Rob. Mach. Learn. Daily News, 77–78 (2023)
16. Kasugai, K., Röcker, C., Bongers, B., Plewe, D., Dimmer, C.: Aesthetic intelligence: designing smartand beautiful architectural spaces. Ambient Intell. **7040**, 360–361 (2011)

17. Wang, Y., Zhang, L., Chen, X., Zhu, J., Chen, Y.: Integrated innovation of smart materials and product design from the perspective of design intelligence. Industria Textila **74**(5), P602-609 (2023)
18. Badr, A., Samir, C., Ali, A., Peter, R.: Smart space design-a framework and an IoT prototype implementation. Sustainability **15**(1), 111 (2023)
19. Wang, B.: Digital design of smart museum based on artificial intelligence. Mob. Inf. Syst. **2021**(Part 11), 4894131(1–13) 1574–017X (2021)
20. Zhang, S., Yao, Z., Liao, H., Zhou, Z., Chen, Y., You, Z.: Endogenous security-aware resource management for digital twin and 6G edge intelligence integrated smart park. China Commun. **20**(2), 46–60 1673–5447 (2023)
21. Chen, W., Shidujaman, M., Tang, X.: AiArt: towards artificial intelligence art. In: The 12th International Conference on Advances in Multimedia (2020)

Exploring the Influence Factors of Takeover Performance in Maritime Autonomous Surface Ships

Ya Wen[1] , Chen Li[2,3]([✉]) , Yongtai Wu[1] , Haoxuan Zeng[2] , and Hengbin Lin[4]

[1] School of Art and Design, Wuhan University of Technology, Wuhan, People's Republic of China

[2] School of Transportation and Logistics Engineering, Wuhan University of Technology, Wuhan, People's Republic of China
chenli1998@whut.edu.cn

[3] State Key Laboratory of Maritime Technology and Safety, Wuhan University of Technology, Wuhan, People's Republic of China

[4] School of Computer Science and Artificial Intelligence, Wuhan University of Technology, Wuhan, People's Republic of China

Abstract. Taking over the control authority of intelligent navigation systems in emergency is considered as an essential means to ensure the security of Maritime Autonomous Surface Ships (MASS). However, diverse information and modalities will influence the takeover behavior with different extents. In order to reveal the critical influence factors of takeover performance in Maritime Autonomous Surface Ships, it investigates distinctive characteristics and interaction effects in a simulated manoeuvring experiment involving 10 experienced participants, and the objective indicators such as takeover time, lane-change time, maximum resultant acceleration and distance to closest point of approach (DCPA) were evaluated. Research results indicate that voice warning and visual guiding assistance have shown obvious advantages in helping driver understand current navigation state and manoeuvring intention of the autonomy. Haptic interaction will bring psychological panic for human operators in overtaking scenario, which results in takeover performance decreases and perform excellent active safety in crossing and merging sceanrios, providing theoretical basis and references for more reliable and comfortable TOR design, it could effectively improve driver's trustiness and subjective experience of Intelligent Navigation System (INS).

Keywords: Maritime Autonomous Surface Ship · Human-machine Interaction · Takeover Request · Usability and Credibility

1 Introduction

The rapid development of Maritime Autonomous Surface Ships (MASS) presents new possibilities and opportunities for achieving safer and more efficient waterborne transportation [1]. However, before achieving full autonomy, these systems still struggle to adapt to complex, dynamic traffic environments and unstructured operational tasks [2]. Consequently, the necessity of human operators within the closed-loop feedback system remains paramount [3]. In the event of system failure or the encounter of scenarios that prove unmanageable, direct human control of the vessel is imperative. However, this approach introduces novel security risks and technical challenges. A primary research focus in the contemporary era is on developing methodologies to enhance operators' comprehension of the present navigational environment, the designated manoeuvres, and the system state during a takeover. This objective is pursued to ensure a seamless transition of control authority between the system and the driver. Consequently, the Takeover Requests (TOR) [4] design is imperative for enhancing vessel navigational safety and the driver's confidence in the INS.

As a critical component of human-machine collaboration, the design of Takeover Requests (TORs) must balance the efficiency of information transmission with the driver's cognitive load [5]. Existing studies have primarily focused on how to reduce takeover reaction time in emergency scenarios by employing multimodal TOR cues, typically involving visual, auditory, or haptic modalities, either independently or in combination. However, due to the inherent complexity of the maritime traffic environment—including difficult-to-interpret navigational contexts, high vessel traffic density, and unpredictable collision risks—TOR design must fully account for the perceptual latency of human operators. This consideration is essential to optimize information delivery, minimize takeover response time, and ensure the accuracy and timeliness of manoeuvring intentions.

The advantage of multimodal TORs lies in their ability to enhance situation awareness (SA) through redundant information channels. However, their effectiveness highly depends on the task context and the type of information presented. Among these modalities, visual cues serve as the most intuitive means of communication, typically delivered via dashboards or central displays using text, images, and colour-coded warnings to convey system status and environmental data. These cues facilitate the construction of a comprehensive mental model of the navigational situation by drivers. However, when the visual interface becomes overloaded or excessively complex, it may lead to distraction and delayed responses [6, 7]. Embedding warning information directly into the interface has been shown to improve takeover performance significantly [8], while information-rich visual displays support more efficient decision-making by maintaining operator focus and clarity [9].

Auditory warnings can quickly capture the driver's attention when their line of sight is limited or when attention is diverted, particularly in situations where the driver is engaged in secondary tasks, allowing for real-time information delivery [10]. Compared to visual cues, auditory signals have a faster transmission speed, which can significantly improve driver response times during takeover operations [11]. However, the effectiveness of these devices is constrained by various parameters, including pitch, frequency, and speech rate.

Haptic feedback has emerged in recent years as a novel interaction modality that delivers information directly to the driver's somatosensory system through vibrations or physical stimuli. This approach reduces dependence on visual and auditory channels while triggering rapid emergency responses via direct tactile stimulation, allowing for more personalized alerts [12]. Evidence suggests that appropriately calibrated haptic feedback can significantly reduce driver reaction times, enhance operational accuracy [13], and offer reliable performance in conveying warning signals [14]. However, in certain high-pressure situations, haptic cues may induce excessive tension in drivers, potentially compromising the stability of takeover operations. The limitations of single-modality designs in meeting the diverse demands of emergency communication have therefore prompted growing interest in the contextual adaptability of multimodal TOR systems in complex scenarios.

Cheng Tingting conducted a safety analysis of human-machine collaboration using a systems-theoretical approach, revealing a significant relationship between system risk and human cognitive processes [15]. By integrating visual, auditory, and haptic information channels, a redundant and complementary alerting system can be established. Such a multimodal design not only ensures continuity of information delivery when one modality is limited, but also leverages cross-sensory synergy to effectively reduce cognitive load and enhance both the accuracy and speed of driver responses [16–18], ultimately improving overall takeover performance. Reducing the impact of human error on driving performance [20]. Compared to open-water environments, inland waterways are characterized by narrow, curved, and channelized routes, with dense vessel traffic and increased situational complexity. The present study focuses on three hazardous scenarios within the Inland Waterway Transportation Environment, each involving unpredictable collision risks. A total of 10 participants were recruited to perform naturalistic manoeuvring tasks using a ship-handling simulator. The aim was to investigate the key factors affecting takeover performance in MASS, with the takeover process illustrated in Fig. 1. A takeover performance evaluation system was developed based on objective indicators, including takeover response time, lane-change time, maximum resultant acceleration, and DCPA. Descriptive statistical analyses were conducted to examine the interaction effects of different between-subject and within-subject factors during the lane-change process.

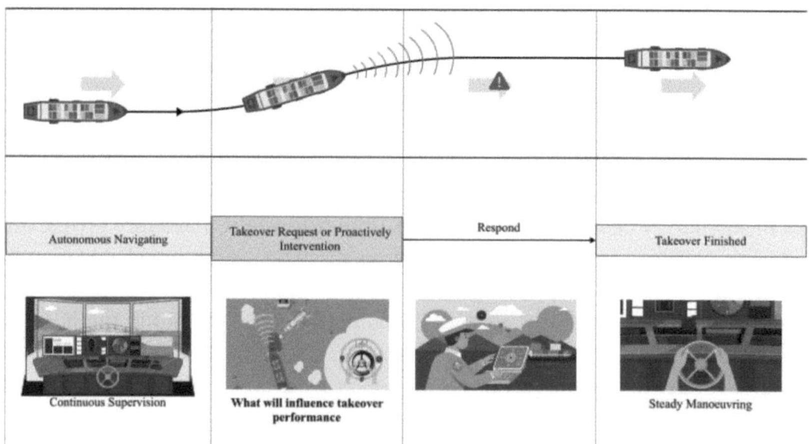

Fig. 1. Takeover process in this study.

2 Methodology

2.1 Participants

The experiment involved 10 participants (8 males and 2 females), all of whom held at least a Class C (coastal waters) navigation competency certificate. Participants were aged between 25 and 40 years, with an average age of 31.6 years (SE = 1.4), and each had more than five years of onboard experience. On average, they had 7.6 years of driving experience (means = 7.6, SE = 0.9). Participants had served on various types of vessels, including inland container vessel, inland bulk carriers, and port tugs. Detailed information is provided in Table 1. None of the participants had prior experience with INS.

Table 1. Basic information of drivers participates in experiment.

Participant	Type	Position	Age	Professional Experience	Education Background
A	Inland Container Vessel	Captain	29	10	Tertiary Education
B	Inland Bulk Carrier	First Officer	34	8	Vocational Education
C	Port Tug	Captain	30	5	Vocational Education
D	Inland Container Vessel	Helmsman Assistant	27	12	Tertiary Education
E	Port Tug	First Officer	36	5	Social-oriented Education
F	Inland Container Vessel	Captain	28	5	Vocational Education
G	Inland Container Vessel	First Officer	30	9	Tertiary Education
H	Port Tug	Captain	32	11	Tertiary Education
I	Inland Bulk Carrier	Captain	37	6	Social-oriented Education
J	Inland Container Vessel	Captain	33	5	Tertiary Education

2.2 Instruments and Materials

The experiment was conducted using a full-task ship-handling simulator integrated with an intelligent navigation algorithm, implemented within a Unity-Python co-simulation environment. The simulation platform provided functionalities such as ship dynamics simulation, immersive three-dimensional visual navigation scenes, and comprehensive data logging. The setup included a steering gear, a clock, two high-performance computers (NVIDIA GeForce RTX 3060 [12 GB], Intel Core i7-9700K), three 55-in. displays with a resolution of 4096×2160 pixels, and a pair of speakers. Additionally, tactile interaction was enabled using an Arduino module connected to vibration motors. A master-slave shared control system [21] was employed to assist the operator in understanding the current navigational state and maneuvering tasks, ensuring a smooth transition and handover of control authority between the driver and the autonomous system. The driver assumed control from the INS via the steering apparatus.

2.3 Manoeuvring Scenarios

Under calm wind and current conditions, the vessel operated at a 10 km/h speed in a separate navigation channel in the lower reaches of the Yangtze River. The INS was responsible for steering, collision avoidance, and speed regulation. Throughout the navigation process, the driver remained in the control loop with continuous monitoring authority, maintaining situational awareness and intervening in INS operations when necessary.

Considering the unique navigational characteristics of inland waterway environments, the experiment featured three types of events (as shown in Fig. 2.):

Scenario A. During an overtaking maneuver, a malfunction occurred in the INS, rendering it incapable of continuing autonomous control. The system then proceeded to issue an active takeover request to the duty operator in the pilothouse.

Scenario B. The INS detected a vessel merging from a tributary into the main channel, presenting an unpredictable collision risk that exceeded the system's operational design domain. In this situation, the driver was required to apply a series of minor course adjustments using seamanship skills to maintain safe navigation.

Scenario C The INS identified an approaching vessel from a diagonal front-left direction that failed to comply with collision avoidance regulations by not passing behind the own ship. This resulted in an imminent head-on collision that the system was unable to autonomously resolve, necessitating the intervention of the operator to execute evasive maneuvers.

Upon issuance of a TOR, the operator was required to promptly assess the current navigational task and vessel status, take control within 5 s, and maintain effective communication and coordination with surrounding vessels using VHF or other communication systems to mitigate potential collision risks.

2.4 Takeover Request System

Twelve Human-Machine Interface (HMI) configurations were developed for driver-autonomy collaboration (as illustrated in Fig. 3.) to meet human-centered design requirements. These interfaces were designed by systematically considering behavioral logic,

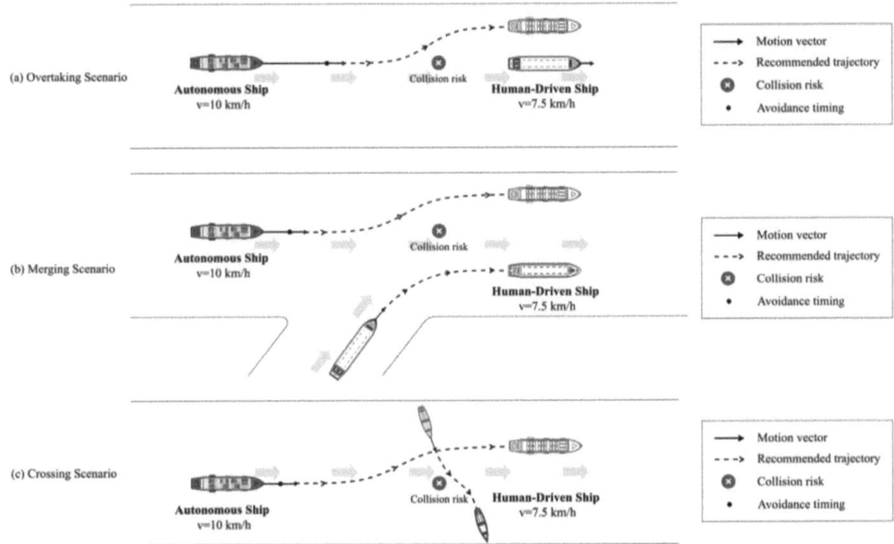

Fig. 2. Hazard scenario design.

hierarchical structure, and visual layout. By balancing functional elements with textual content types, the interfaces were tailored to accommodate the dynamic nature of takeover tasks. The configurations were categorized into four main groups:

Control Group. Interfaces within this group were configured to display exclusively actuator-related information, including the status of the propeller and rudder. The experiment employed abstract, non-verbal auditory stimuli as a 700-Hz beeping sound (500 ms in total duration, consisting of two 200-ms beeps separated by a 100-ms silence). This approach was adopted to circumvent the diminished alertness frequently associated with emotional voice prompts [21].

Warning Group. This configuration combined auditory voice prompts ("Please take over immediately," repeated twice with a 2-s interval) with visual danger indicators. The application of red coloring was implemented to align with universal risk perception cues and enhance attention capture efficiency.

Guidance Group. The group provided extended visual guidance, including prominent alert symbols, predicted navigational trajectories, and recommended routes. The scope of warnings expanded gradually from local to global, thereby assisting the operator in anticipating the navigation context.

Haptic Group. Tactile feedback was implemented using Arduino controllers and vibration motors. Risk levels were quantified based on the urgency of the avoidance scenario: in overtaking scenarios, low-frequency continuous vibration (50 Hz for 1 s) was applied, while crossing and merging scenarios triggered high-frequency intermittent vibrations (200 Hz, 0.5 s on / 0.2 s off), aiming to minimize driver reaction time.

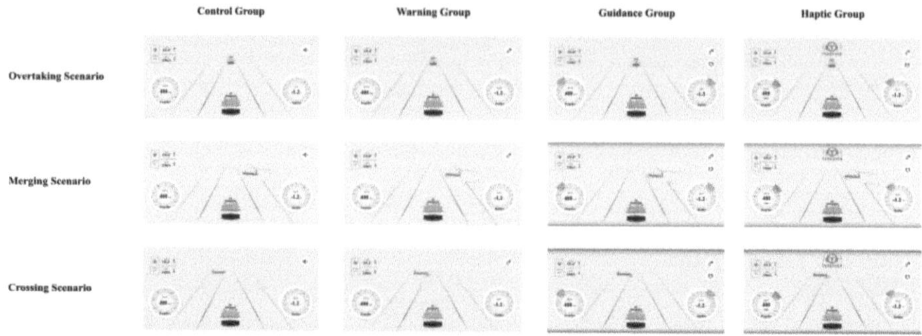

Fig. 3. Human-Machine Interface Design.

Before TOR activation, the system operates in its default UI mode, displaying essential navigation information such as heading, speed, channel boundaries, and nearby vessels. In the event that the system detects a malfunction or reaches the limits of its operational design domain, it initiates a takeover request through auditory, visual, and haptic channels. This prompts the driver to intervene and assume control. Fig. 4. illustrates that the system's control weight factor gradually decreases during this transition, eventually relinquishing control to the human operator.

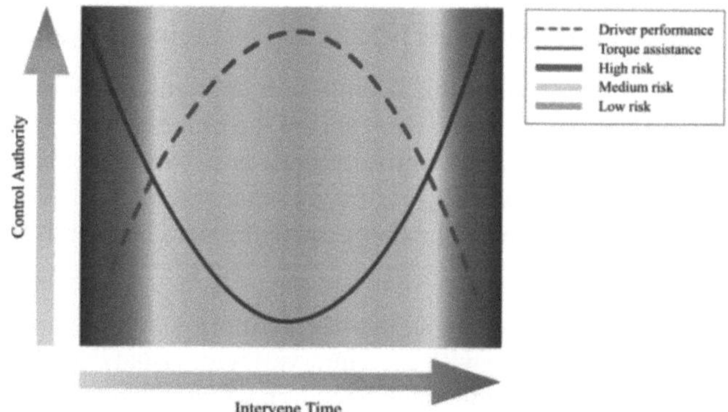

Fig. 4. Control authority transition strategy.

2.5 Experiment Design

The experiment used a 3(hazardous scenario types: overtaking, merging, crossing) × 2 (Auditory TOR: abstract sound + voice, abstract sound) × 2 (Visual TOR: visual guidance, no visual guidance) × 2 (haptic TOR: steering wheel vibration, no vibration) mixed factorial design. Participants were randomly assigned to different experimental groups based on the type of hazard scenario, with the TOR types treated as within-subject variables.

2.6 Procedure

As depicted in Fig. 5, upon arrival at the lab, participants read and signed an informed consent form and filled out a questionnaire detailing their gender, age, navigational experience, and other relevant personal information. They were then briefed on the experiment's purpose and the design principles underlying the different types of TOR interfaces. Before the formal experiment, participants completed a 5-min navigation practice session. This session included familiarization with the steering apparatus, engine telegraph, HMI interface operations, navigation environment, and mode-switching procedures. The purpose was to ensure that participants became proficient in using the ship-handling simulator and could adapt to the system's operational logic and takeover procedures. The simulation practice session did not involve any other vessels or takeover events to prevent the influence of learning effects. Participants were allowed to repeatedly practice manoeuvring operations until they were familiar with the tasks. Following the practice session, participants proceeded with the driving experiment in an undisturbed environment.

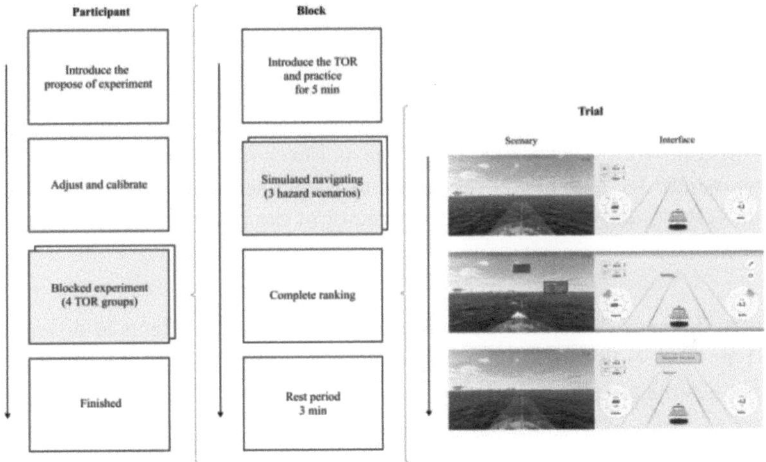

Fig. 5. Experimental flowchart for individual participant.

While receiving a takeover request, participants had to exit Auto mode by adjusting the rudder angle or clock, manually altering the vessel's course to avoid collision risks, and then returning to the main navigation channel. Each navigation event lasted 30 min, followed by a 2-min rest period. The order of the groups was balanced using a Latin square design to minimise individual differences and learning effects. Participants then performed a 3–5-min non-driving-related task (NDRT) to prevent them from predicting the takeover events. Upon completing all experimental sessions, participants were asked to rank the different TOR modalities based on their subjective preferences.

3 Results

3.1 Evaluate Indicators

This experiment developed a takeover performance evaluation system based on different TOR modalities. Key indicators such as takeover time, lane-change time, maximum resultant acceleration, and the DCPA were used to analyze the effects of within-subject variables (TOR modality) and between-subject variables (hazard scenario type) on driver takeover behavior. Takeover time refers to the duration from the issuance of the TOR to the moment the driver initiates a control action, such as steering or modifying the driving trajectory. A takeover is considered initiated when the steering wheel angle exceeds $0.5°$ or a trajectory change is detected. This metric reflects the time required for the driver to make a takeover decision after receiving the TOR. Lane-change time is defined as the time required to complete a lane-changing maneuver. Maximum resultant acceleration indicates the comfort level during the control transition and is calculated as the maximum value of the resultant vector of longitudinal and lateral accelerations during the takeover process. The formula is given by

$$a_{max} = \sqrt{a_X^2 + a_y^2} \tag{1}$$

(unit: m/s^2). DCPA refers to the minimum distance between two vessels during an encounter and is used to evaluate collision risk. A smaller DCPA indicates a higher risk of collision, while a larger DCPA suggests lower risk. The calculation formula is as follows, where X_T and Y_T represent the target vessels coordinates in the own-ship coordinate system, and C_r is the direction vector of the relative motion velocity:

$$\mathrm{DCPA} = |Y_T \cos C_r - X_T \sin C_r| \tag{2}$$

Then, a mixed-design ANOVA was conducted to evaluate the effects of different hazard scenario types and TOR modalities on takeover performance, as well as their interaction effects. The results are shown in Table 2.

3.2 Quantify Analysis

Takeover Time. Table 2 presents the interaction and main effects of different hazard scenarios and TOR designs on takeover time. No statistically significant difference was observed between the merging scenario (mean 3.41 ± 0.14 s) and the crossing scenario (mean 3.02 ± 0.18 s, $p < 0.001$). However, a statistically significant difference was found between the merging and overtaking scenarios (mean 2.93 ± 0.25 s). Subsequent post-hoc tests revealed a significant difference in takeover time between the abstract sound TOR (3.59 ± 0.32 s) and the combined abstract sound and voice-based TOR (3.25 ± 0.17 s), indicating that abstract auditory cues alone resulted in longer takeover times. Additionally, under both abstract sound and voice-based visual guidance conditions, a significant difference in takeover time was observed between the vibration condition (2.64 ± 0.30 s) and the no-vibration condition (3.16 ± 0.21 s). The performance of the TOR is illustrated in Fig. 6, with a detailed analysis of its performance across different hazard scenarios.

Table 2. Main interacted effects of scenario type and TOR type on takeover performance.

Effect	F	df	p	ηp^2
Takeover time				
Scenario Type	8.45	2,56	.005	.32
TOR Type	15.32	7,56	<.001	.46
Scenario Type*TOR Type	4.85	14,56	.01	.11
Lane-Change Time				
Scenario Type	12.80	2,56	.02	.24
TOR Type	3.64	7,56	.003	.06
Scenario Type*TOR Type	0.75	14,56	<.001	.39
Maximum resultant acceleration				
Scenario Type	2.01	2,56	.16	.15
TOR Type	6.37	7,56	.05	.03
Scenario Type*TOR Type	6.85	14,56	.92	.08
DCPA				
Scenario Type	18.27	2,56	<.001	.68
TOR Type	1.59	7,56	.03	.57
Scenario Type*TOR Type	21.50	14,56	.002	.81

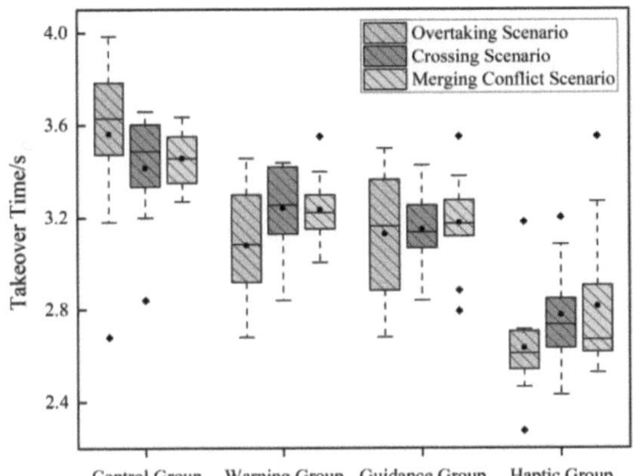

Fig. 6. The means of takeover time for each TOR.

Lane-Change Time. The data indicated statistically significant differences in lane-change times across the three hazard scenarios: overtaking (mean 4.28 ± 0.16 min), merging (mean 4.97 ± 0.21 min), and crossing (mean 5.45 ± 0.14 min, p < 0.001). Under the abstract sound and voice-based conditions, the presence of visual guidance significantly improved performance (5.11 ± 0.08 min) compared to the absence of visual guidance (4.63 ± 0.32 min). However, no significant difference was found between the vibration (5.07 ± 0.12 min) and no-vibration conditions. Fig. 7. presents the average lane-change times for each different TOR group configuration in detail across the different scenario designs.

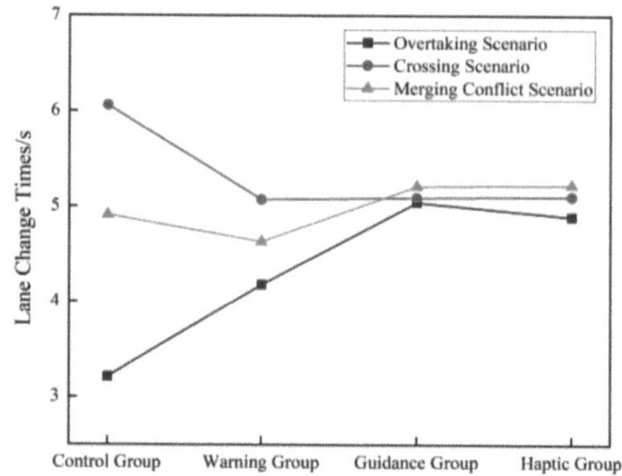

Fig. 7. The means of lane-change time for each TOR.

Maximum Resultant Acceleration. As shown in Table 2, different TOR designs had a significant effect on maximum resultant acceleration. However, the main effect of hazard scenario type, as well as its interaction effect with TOR design, showed no significant influence on this metric. As illustrated in Fig. 8, under the combined abstract sound, voice-based, and visual guidance conditions, the presence of haptic feedback (0.39 ± 0.41 m/s^2) resulted in significantly lower maximum acceleration compared to the no-haptic condition (0.63 ± 0.17 m/s^2), indicating improved stability in steering maneuvers.

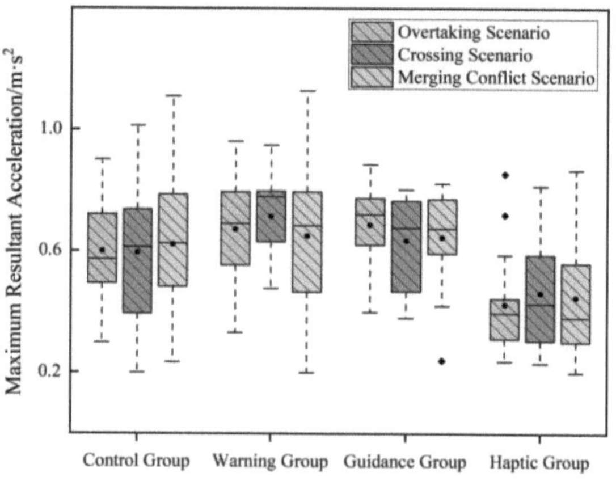

Fig. 8. The means of Maximum resultant acceleration for each TOR.

Distance to Closest Point of Approach (DCPA). As shown in Table 2, significant statistical differences in DCPA were observed across different hazard scenarios: overtaking (2.37 ± 0.23 km), merging (1.58 ± 0.07 km), and crossing (0.82 ± 0.12 km), with a notable interaction effect between hazard type and TOR design. Subsequent post-hoc analysis indicated that the combined abstract sound and voice-based condition (2.03 ± 0.18 km) resulted in significantly lower DCPA compared to the abstract sound-only condition (2.19 ± 0.26 km). However, within the abstract sound and voice-based conditions, the presence or absence of visual guidance demonstrated no significant effect on DCPA. In contrast, haptic interaction significantly reduced the average DCPA from 1.95 ± 0.14 km to 1.61 ± 0.09 km. The distribution of both the DCPA means and standard errors across various hazard scenarios and TOR configurations is illustrated in Fig. 9.

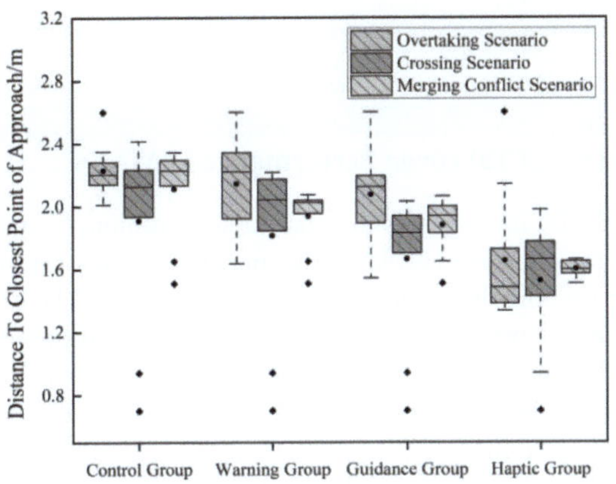

Fig. 9. The means of DCPA for each TOR.

3.3 Priority Ranking

Table 3 presents the median preference rankings of different TOR types across the three hazard scenarios. The rankings were derived from the participants' subjective ratings, with lower median values reflecting higher preference. The Friedman test revealed significant differences in driver preferences among the four TOR modes ($\chi^2(3) = 22.15$, $p < 0.001$). Subsequent post-hoc analysis revealed that, in the overtaking scenario, the guidance group (median = 2) and the warning group (median = 2.5) provided a significantly better user experience compared to the control group (median = 3) and the haptic group (median = 3.5). Similarly, in the merging scenario, the warning group (median = 1) and the guidance group (median = 1.5) received the highest preferences. In contrast, in the crossing scenario, the haptic group (median = 1) and guidance group (median = 1.5) were preferred over the warning group (median = 2.5) and control group (median = 3.5). The guidance group consistently received the highest rankings across all hazard scenarios, while the haptic group was particularly favored in the crossing scenario.

Notably, 75% of the participants reported that the high-frequency vibration in the haptic group induced psychological stress, which increased their operational workload.

Table 3. Median preference ranking.

	Control Group	Warning Group	Guidance Group	Haptic Group
Overtaking Scenario	3	2.5	2	3.5
Merging Scenario	3.5	3	1	2
Crossing Scenario	3.5	2.5	1.5	1
Overall	3.5	3	1.5	2

4 Discussion

4.1 Influence Factors of Takeover Performance in MASS

This study systematically investigates the core factors influencing takeover performance in MASS, revealing the combined effects of scenario dynamics, multimodal TOR design, and their interaction on both driver behavior and system trust. The experimental findings demonstrate that takeover performance is not determined by any single factor; rather, it is shaped by the complex interplay of scenario complexity, TOR information transmission efficiency, and multisensory integration. These results underscore the need for a holistic approach in the design of human-machine interfaces for autonomous navigation systems.

The three hazardous scenarios exhibited distinct characteristics. In the overtaking scenario, drivers demonstrated the shortest takeover time (2.93 ± 0.25 s) and lane-change time (4.28 ± 0.16 min), along with the largest DCPA (2.37 ± 0.23 km), suggesting that the risk strategy was clear and the manoeuvring path well-defined, resulting in relatively straightforward control behavior. In contrast, the crossing scenario was characterized by sudden events and limited evasive space, leading to the longest lane-change time (5.45 ± 0.14 min) and the lowest DCPA (0.82 ± 0.12 km), indicating increased cognitive demand and operational load. The merging scenario produced the longest takeover time (3.41 ± 0.14 s), likely due to the greater difficulty in interpreting multi-directional navigational intent, requiring more time for drivers to construct predictive models. From a multimodal interaction perspective, the combination of voice prompts with abstract auditory cues significantly reduced driver response delay compared to abstract sound alone. Specifically, takeover time under the combined abstract sound and voice-based TOR was significantly shorter (3.25 ± 0.17 s vs. 3.59 ± 0.32 s), indicating that semantic information accelerates drivers' mental modeling and enhances operational safety. The addition of visual guidance also demonstrated positive effects. Under the combined auditory condition (abstract sound + voice), the visual guidance group showed significantly better lane-change performance than the no-guidance group (4.63 ± 0.32 min vs. 5.11 ± 0.08 min), suggesting that visual path information reduces spatial judgment burden on the driver. In comparison, the effectiveness of haptic cues appeared to be highly context-dependent. Incorporating steering wheel vibration significantly reduced takeover time (2.64 ± 0.30 s) and maximum resultant acceleration (0.39 ± 0.41 m/s^2), indicating enhanced stability in directional control. However, haptic stimulation also reduced DCPA (1.61 ± 0.09 km vs. 1.95 ± 0.14 km), possibly due to over-trust in the autonomous system. This suggests that in low-complexity situations, intense sensory stimulation may disrupt the driver's natural decision-making process, thereby affecting takeover quality. Overall, the results demonstrate that the effectiveness of different TOR modalities varies by scenario type. The combination of voice prompts, abstract sound, and visual cues appears most suitable for complex or cognitively demanding contexts, while the use of haptic feedback should be applied cautiously to avoid unnecessary interference in lower-risk environments.

Grounded in real-world scenarios, this study systematically examined the specific mechanisms by which multimodal information influences takeover performance. The findings confirm the synergistic advantages of combining voice prompts with visual guidance, while also revealing the dual nature of haptic feedback under certain conditions. These results provide a theoretical foundation for the future standardization of TOR design, context-aware adaptation of multimodal interfaces, and the development of trust models for drivers in MASS. Furthermore, considering the operational characteristics of the maritime domain, the proposed design recommendations can be directly applied to the development of integrated ship-shore remote control systems, intelligent navigational alert systems, and other maritime technologies. Ultimately, this work contributes to the advancement of safer, more efficient, and human-centered autonomous navigation systems.

4.2 Limitation

The present study is not without its limitations. Firstly, the relatively modest sample size may constrain the generalizability of the findings. Therefore, future studies should consider augmenting the participant pool to enhance the robustness of conclusions. Secondly, using a driving simulator may not fully capture the complexity and psychological pressure associated with real-world maritime navigation, affecting the results' external validity. Thirdly, the fixed vessel speed and predefined takeover points did not consider the actual navigation environments' dynamic and variable nature. Finally, the repeated exposure to the same hazardous scenarios may have led to participant adaptation effects, potentially influencing takeover behavior. Future research should address these limitations by increasing the sample size, incorporating dynamic and realistic experimental scenarios, and enhancing the ecological validity of the simulator environment. Furthermore, the integration of physiological measurement techniques, including but not limited to eye tracking, electroencephalography (EEG), and electromyography (EMG), can yield insights into alterations in attention and cognitive load under varying stress conditions. These data can contribute to developing a comprehensive user experience evaluation framework that combines behavioral, physiological, and psychological analyses in multimodal human-machine interaction. Enhancing the immersive quality of the experimental setup is expected to improve the reliability and applicability of research findings.

5   Conclusion

The findings suggest that the performance of the MASS takeover is influenced by two main factors: the complexity of the scenario and the interactions between TOR modality and other variables. Different combinations of hazardous scenarios and interaction modalities led to significant differences in driving behaviour. The crossing scenario warrants particular attention due to its longest lane-change time and high collision risk. The dynamic collision avoidance required in this scenario clearly exceeds the system's operational design domain, underscoring the need for proactive safety warning mechanisms to mitigate navigational risks. Voice-based TORs, which convey urgency through semantic cues, significantly reduced takeover time, highlighting their effectiveness in quickly establishing driver awareness. Conversely, haptic interaction exhibited robust active safety performance in the merging and crossing scenarios. However, in the overtaking scenario, haptic feedback was found to induce psychological tension in operators, leading to a decline in takeover performance.

This study reveals the underlying mechanisms influencing takeover performance of autonomous vessels in inland waterway environments. It emphasises that in such complex navigational contexts, both environmental dynamics and the degree of adaptation in multimodal human-machine interaction significantly affect operator performance and system trust. Effective TOR design must be capable of dynamically adapting to scenario-specific characteristics and the driver's cognitive state, thereby advancing human-autonomy collaboration toward higher levels of operational safety. The findings provide empirical support for the development of intelligent assistance systems tailored to the unique demands of inland navigation and promote a paradigm shift in shared control—from passive takeovers to proactive risk mitigation.

Acknowledgments.   This work was supported by the China National College Students' Innovation and Entrepreneurship Training Program (grant number S202510497275).

References

1. Man, Y., Lundh, M., Porathe, T.: Seeking harmony in shore-based unmanned ship handling: from the perspective of human factors, what is the difference we need to focus on from being onboard to onshore? In: Human Factors in Transportation, pp. 81–90. CRC Press (2016)
2. Barthelsson, P., Sagefjord, J.: Autonomous Ships and the Operator's Role in a Shore Control Centre - a Comparative Analysis on Projects in the Scandinavian Region and Implementing the Experience of Mariners to a New Field of Shipping. Bachelor's Thesis, Department of Shipping and Marine Technology. Chalmers University of Technology, Gothenburg (2017)
3. Porathe, T.: Remote monitoring and control of unmanned vessels – the MUNIN shore control Centre. In: Proceedings of the 13th International Conference on Computer Applications and Information Technology in the Maritime Industries (COMPIT '14), pp. 460–467 (2014)
4. Nordby, K., Fauske, J.E., Gernez, E., Mallam, S.: A user interface design framework for augmented-reality-supported maritime navigation. J. Mar. Sci. Eng. **12**(3), 505 (2024)
5. Du, N., et al.: Evaluating effects of cognitive load, takeover request lead time, and traffic density on drivers' takeover performance in conditionally automated driving. In: Proceedings of the 12th International Conference on Automotive User Interfaces and Interactive Vehicular Applications (AutoUI 2020). ACM (2020). https://doi.org/10.1145/3409120.3410666

6. Cheng, T., Utne, I.B., Wu, B., Wu, Q.: A novel system-theoretic approach for human-system collaboration safety: case studies on two degrees of autonomy for autonomous ships. Reliab. Eng. Syst. Saf. **237**, 109388 (2023)

7. European Commission: Highly Automated Vehicles for Intelligent Transport (HAVEit). Project ID 212154. https://trimis.ec.europa.eu/project/highly-automated-vehicles-intelligent-transport. Accessed 13 June 2025

8. Yang, Y., Karakaya, B., Dominioni, G.C., Kawabe, K., Bengler, K.: An HMI concept to improve driver's visual behavior and situation awareness in automated vehicle. In: 21st International Conference on Intelligent Transportation Systems (ITSC 2018), pp. 650–655. IEEE (2018)

9. Fu, R., Liu, W., Zhang, H., Liu, X., Yuan, W.: Adopting an HMI for overtaking assistance – impact of distance display, advice, and guidance information on driver gaze and performance. Accid. Anal. Prev. **191**, 107204 (2023)

10. Shi, J., et al.: Effects of various in-vehicle human–machine interfaces on drivers' takeover performance and gaze pattern in conditionally automated vehicles. Int. J. Hum. Comput. Stud. **192**, 103362 (2024)

11. Bazilinskyy, P., Petermeijer, S.M., Petrovych, V., Dodou, D., de Winter, J.C.F.: Take-over requests in highly automated driving: a crowdsourcing survey on auditory, vibrotactile, and visual displays. Transp. Res. Part F Traffic Psychol. Behav. **56**, 82–98 (2018)

12. Morales-Alvarez, W., Sipele, O., Léberon, R., Tadjine, H.H., Olaverri-Monreal, C.: Automated driving: a literature review of the take over request in conditional automation. Electronics. **9**(12), 2087 (2020)

13. Tan, H., Gray, R., Young, J.J., Taylor, R.: A haptic back display for attentional and directional cueing. Haptics-e Electron. J. Haptics Res. (2003)

14. Van Erp, J.B.F., Van Veen, H.A.H.: Vibrotactile in-vehicle navigation system. Transp. Res. Part F Traffic Psychol. Behav. **7**(4–5), 247–256 (2004)

15. Chang, W., Hwang, W., Ji, Y.G.: Haptic seat interfaces for driver information and warning systems. Int. J. Hum. Comput. Interact. **27**(12), 1119–1132 (2011)

16. Telpaz, A., Rhindress, B., Zelman, I., Tsimhoni, O.: Haptic seat for automated driving: preparing the driver to take control effectively. In: Proceedings of a 7th International Conference Automotive User Interfaces Interactive Vehicular Applications, pp. 23–30, 2015

17. Qiu, Z., et al.: Effects of dual-message tactile sliding takeover requests on takeover performance in an automated driving system. Traffic Inj. Prev. **26**(3), 307–315 (2025)

18. Tijerina, L., Johnston, S., Parmer, E., Pham, H.A., Winterbottom, M.D., Barickman, F.S., et al.: Preliminary studies in haptic displays for rear-end collision avoidance system and adaptive cruise control system applications. United States Joint Program Office for Intelligent Transportation Systems (2000)

19. Chun, J., Han, S.H., Park, G., Seo, J., Choi, S., et al.: Evaluation of vibrotactile feedback for forward collision warning on the steering wheel and seatbelt. Int. J. Ind. Ergon. **42**(5), 443–448 (2012)

20. Cheng, T., et al.: Analysis of human errors in human-autonomy collaboration in autonomous ships operations through shore control experimental data. Reliab. Eng. Syst. Saf. **246**, 110080 (2024)

21. Li, C., Yan, X., Liu, J., Huang, Y., Li, S.: Stackelberg game-based control method for driver-automation collaboration in ship remote-control. J. Transp. Syst. Eng. Inf. Technol. **24**, 21–31 (2024)

22. Ng, A.W.Y., Chan, A.H.S.: Color associations among designers and non-designers for common warning and operation concepts. Appl. Ergon. **70**, 18–25 (2018)

Human–AI Interaction and Generative AI in Design

Explainable Detection of Implicit Influential Patterns in Conversations via Data Augmentation

Sina Abdidizaji[(✉)], Md Kowsher, Niloofar Yousefi, and Ivan Garibay

Industrial Engineering and Management Systems, University of Central Florida, Orlando, FL, USA

`{sina.abdidizaji,md.kowsher,niloofar.yousefi,igaribay}@ucf.edu`

Abstract. In the era of digitalization, as individuals increasingly rely on digital platforms for communication and news consumption, various actors employ linguistic strategies to influence public perception. While models have become proficient at detecting explicit patterns, which typically appear in texts as single remarks referred to as utterances, such as social media posts, malicious actors have shifted toward utilizing implicit influential verbal patterns embedded within conversations. These verbal patterns aim to mentally penetrate the victim's mind in order to influence them, enabling the actor to obtain the desired information through implicit means. This paper presents an improved approach for detecting such implicit influential patterns. Furthermore, the proposed model is capable of identifying the specific locations of these influential elements within a conversation. To achieve this, the existing dataset was augmented using the reasoning capabilities of state-of-the-art language models. Our designed framework resulted in a 6% improvement in the detection of implicit influential patterns in conversations. Moreover, this approach improved the multi-label classification tasks related to both the techniques used for influence and the vulnerability of victims by 33% and 43%, respectively.

Keywords: Implicit Influential Patterns · Mental Health · Human-centered AI · Large Language Models

1 Introduction

In the era of computers and digital interactions, individuals are increasingly exposed to risks they do not anticipate or desire. Social media, instant messaging applications, and chatbots serve as digital platforms that enable individuals to interact without being physically present or revealing their identity and face. To enhance safety and ensure secure and healthy digital platforms for such interactions, it is crucial to effectively identify influential statements and behaviors. A secure and healthy digital environment enables appropriate interactions without threats from malicious actors seeking to influence users in order to steal

© The Author(s), under exclusive license to Springer Nature Switzerland AG 2026
M. Kurosu and A. Hashizume (Eds.): HCII 2025, LNCS 16332, pp. 225–238, 2026.
https://doi.org/10.1007/978-3-032-12385-5_14

information, issue threats, or endanger individuals for their own objectives. On these platforms, where all communication occurs digitally, there are heightened opportunities for phishing, scamming, and other manipulative actions designed to extract sensitive information from users [26]. Addressing these challenges and detecting such behaviors on digital platforms and chatbots are essential for maintaining a secure environment for interactions via computers and other digital devices. As current models have achieved high accuracy in detecting explicit patterns, malevolent actors are increasingly attempting to exert mental influence over users to accomplish their aims. Mental influential patterns constitute deceptive strategies intended to control or influence the emotions, thoughts, and behaviors of targeted individuals [5,13]. It represents an intersection of mental health conditions and toxic behavior, characterized by causing distress through implicitly deceitful remarks [22]. Unlike explicit hate speech or overtly toxic language, influential statements are inherently subtle, nuanced, and difficult to detect. Recently, actors have increasingly used nuanced strategies to influence audiences through conversational contexts. Detecting such remarks has proven to be significantly more challenging than identifying hate speech [9,11], toxicity [3], or sarcasm [2]. Previous detection models typically relied on learning from labeled sentences or paragraphs. However, current influential remarks often manifest subtly within broader conversations, appearing sporadically in sentences [27]. This intermittent nature complicates the detection task for language models. Moreover, mental influential patterns often lack overtly negative connotations, becoming identifiable only when analyzed within the context of an entire conversation.

The objective of this research is to enhance the detection of implicit influential patterns within conversations using the capabilities of large language models. Previous studies [20,24] have shown that relying solely on prompting with available large language models is not an effective approach for detecting such patterns. Even fine-tuning models on conversations with a single label has not proven to be as effective as anticipated [22]. To address this gap, we propose a framework designed to improve the accuracy of detection tasks. This framework consists of two main stages: data augmentation and a two-phase fine-tuning process. Specifically, our augmentation strategy involves utilizing a reasoning language model to identify mental influential statements within conversations. The detected influential sentences are subsequently incorporated into the fine-tuning pipeline, in order to boost overall model performance. Another motivation for this augmentation strategy is to improve model interpretability through instruction fine-tuning [23]. By training the model to precisely identify the locations of mental influential elements within conversations, we can develop an explanatory system capable of highlighting and clarifying these influential segments in a conversation.

The structure of this paper is organized as follows. The following section reviews related work and relevant literature. Section 3 provides a detailed explanation of the proposed framework. Section 4 describes the datasets and experimental setup, while Sect. 5 presents the results. Finally, Sect. 6 concludes the paper.

2   Related Work

There are numerous studies examining influence both in general and specifically within texts. [1] investigated influential actors on the X social media platform by analyzing the frequency of news sharing, finding that individuals who share news with varying credibility and platform popularity exhibit distinct influence patterns across the network. In the context of textual analysis, [27] categorize text data into three groups: utterances, conversations, and documents. An utterance typically refers to a standalone statement produced by an individual, such as a post on an online social networking platform, and does not require conversational engagement [4]. Notably, an utterance may consist of several sentences.

Several datasets focus on utterances collected from online forums and social networks. For instance, Dreaddit [21] addresses mental stress, and Detex [25] focuses on delicate text. As utterances can be produced by large language models, datasets such as ToxiGen [14] have been generated using these models to provide numerous training samples aimed at enhancing safety and mitigating hate speech. While progress in utterance-level detection has been significant, more sophisticated models are required for conversation and document-level tasks [27]. Within the field of human-computer interaction, social chatbots have been developed to help users cope with mental distress. However, a recent study [18] reported that prolonged communication with such chatbots can result in mental health harms, primarily due to users' emotional dependence on these systems, which develops over the course of continuous interactions between the individual and the computer.

Recent research has aimed to improve the detection of influential patterns by employing advanced prompting methods, such as Chain-of-Thought (CoT) [24] and intent-aware prompting techniques [20]. Incorporating Chain-of-Thought prompts [17] for detecting implicit influential patterns did not significantly improve results, although a combination of CoT with few-shot learning yielded modest gains [24]. Intent-aware prompting involves first extracting the intent of each participant in a conversation using a language model, then appending this information to the conversation and prompting the model again to detect mental manipulation. This approach demonstrated greater improvement in detection performance compared to other methods [20]. A recent study [10] introduced MentalMAC, a multi-task anti-curriculum distillation approach for mental manipulation detection. By leveraging a large teacher model to generate rationales and feedback, they combined unsupervised data augmentation (EVOSA) with staged knowledge distillation to train a smaller student model. Their student model surpassed larger LLMs, achieving higher accuracy than established baselines.

As these studies demonstrate, many methods involve augmenting conversational data by adding information extracted from the primary data source. To further improve detection accuracy, we propose a novel framework for detecting implicit influential patterns in conversations, featuring new data augmentation and fine-tuning approaches.

3   Methodology

In this section, the designed framework for implicit influential patterns detection will be explained extensively. First, data augmentation will be explained and then we leverage the augmented data to fine-tune a base language model in two phases for having a robust model.

3.1   Data Augmentation

In the proposed framework, instead of training the model on the entire conversation and providing a single label, the objective is to indicate which parts of the conversation contain implicit influential patterns manifested as mental manipulation. The conversations are between two individuals and are separated line by line. Reasoning language models are leveraged to identify the specific lines that contain implicit influential elements. Through this approach, the augmented data provides the model with the particular lines that need to be learned to better detect influential parts, rather than presenting the whole conversation with a single binary label. To accomplish this, distilled versions of the Deepseek language model [8] – which are open source and available online, particularly the Llama-distilled variant – were employed to identify influential segments. Given the stochastic nature of these models, each conversation was prompted to the reasoning language model ten times, and the results from these analyses were summarized by another language model. Notably, the summarization is performed by a language model that does not conduct reasoning. Further details are provided in Appendix 1. The detailed pipeline for data augmentation is presented in Fig. 1.

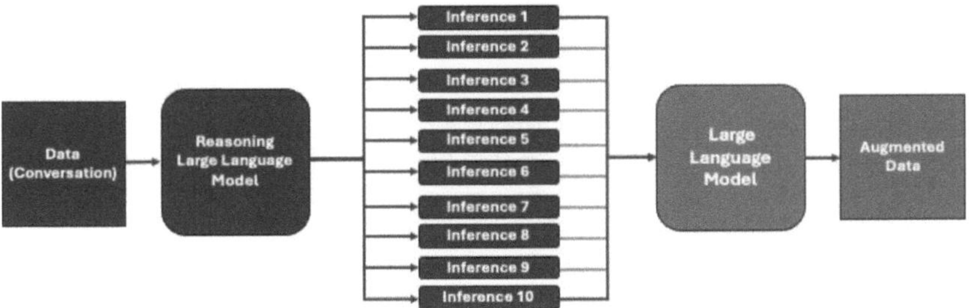

Fig. 1. Data augmentation pipeline for finding influential patterns.

After identifying these influential segments within conversations, we manually sampled the results to verify the accuracy of this approach. Since each conversation was independently analyzed ten times and the results were aggregated, the data augmentation process demonstrated high accuracy.

3.2 Model Framework

The primary rationale for data augmentation is to train the model to identify the locations of influential statements within conversations, thereby enhancing its learning capacity. Given the computational expense of fully fine-tuning language models, instruction fine-tuning is employed by attaching a Low-Rank Adapter (LoRA) [15] to the model. This instruction-tuned model is then used to identify implicit influential segments within conversations, a task previously unattainable due to the lack of relevant data.

LoRA introduces an approach in which, instead of fully fine-tuning all layers in a neural network, the weight updates are approximated by two low-rank matrices, which are then attached to the layers. This approach is also advantageous because all the base model weights can be frozen, allowing only the newly added parameters introduced by the low rank adapters to be trained [15]. Mathematically, if the initial weights are represented by a matrix $W_1 \in \mathbb{R}^{d \times k}$, the weight updates can be approximated by two matrices, $A \in \mathbb{R}^{d \times r}$ and $B \in \mathbb{R}^{r \times k}$, where the rank r should be chosen such that $r < \min(d, k)$, where d is the input dimension and k is the output dimension, respectively. Thus, the weight matrix for the instruction fine-tuned model is given by:

$$h_1 = W_1 x + \Delta W_1 x = W_1 x + ABx \tag{1}$$

where h_1 represents the forward pass of the instruction fine-tuned model, W_1 denotes the initial weights of the language model, ΔW_1 represents the weight updates from instruction fine-tuning, x denotes the concatenation of the instruction prompt and the initial conversation as input data, and the labels correspond to the augmented data generated in the previous procedure.

For classification tasks, referred to as detection in our framework, the newly attached adapter and the new classification head – added after removing the original language model head – are simultaneously fine-tuned. Following the initial instruction fine-tuning, the previous weights are frozen, and only the newly introduced parameters in the second adapter and the classification head are updated. Prior to removing the language model head and attaching the classification head, as a new adapter is added to the instruction fine-tuned model, this step can be mathematically expressed as:

$$h_2 = W_2 y + \Delta W_2 y = (W_1 + \Delta W_1)y + CDy = W_1 y + ABy + CDy \tag{2}$$

where h_2 denotes the forward pass of the model with the newly attached adapter, W_2 represents the initial weights of the language model after instruction fine-tuning, including the weights from the adapter attached during the first stage, ΔW_2 denotes the weight updates from classification training, y is the original conversation input for the classification task, and C and D are analogous to the A and B matrices but may have different dimensions. The attached classifier is then trained to determine whether or not a conversation contains implicit influential patterns. It should be noted that open-source models from the Llama 3 series [12] are used in the experiments, as they can be downloaded and fine-tuned specifically for our tasks[1]. The complete model framework is illustrated in Fig. 2.

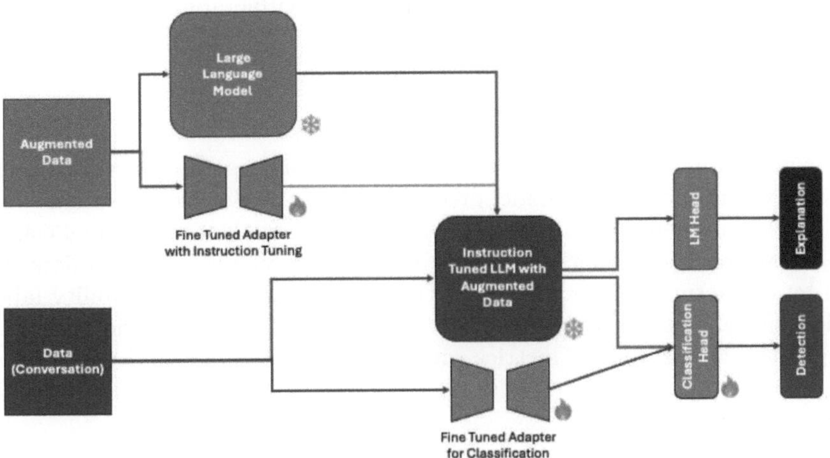

Fig. 2. The framework of two-phase fine-tuning for detecting mental influential patterns. The snowflake symbol indicates frozen weights, whereas the fire symbol denotes the weights that are updated during the fine-tuning process.

4   Experimental Setup

4.1   Dataset

Most publicly available datasets are based on individual utterances. We have excluded these datasets and instead focused on newly released datasets compiled by [22]. These datasets comprises approximately 4,000 conversations and includes three distinct types of labels: the presence or absence of mental influence, multi-label annotations specifying the techniques employed for mental influence, and the vulnerability types of influenced victims. Our goal is to improve detection accuracy across all these categories. This paper [22] introduces two datasets: MentalManipCon and MentalManipMaj. In these names, "con" stands for consensus, while "maj" denotes majority. During the annotation process, annotators sometimes held differing opinions. The consensus dataset contains labels assigned only when all annotators were in agreement, whereas the majority dataset includes labels determined by the majority vote among annotators, even in the presence of differing viewpoints. For further details regarding the annotation procedure, read the original paper by [22].

---

[1] Code: https://github.com/sina6990/IMM.

The technique labels used for identifying techniques of mental influence are: "Denial", "Evasion"", "Feigning Innocence", "Rationalization", "Playing the Victim Role", "Playing the Servant Role", "Shaming or Belittlement", "Intimidation", "Brandishing Anger", "Accusation", and "Persuasion or Seduction". The vulnerability labels for victims are: "Over-responsibility", "Over-intellectualization", "Naivete", "Low self-esteem", and "Dependency". For further details and definitions of each technique and vulnerability label, refer to the paper by [22].

4.2   Evaluation Metrics

The experiments are divided into two parts. The first part involves binary classification, where the trained model predicts whether a given conversation contains any implicit influential patterns. The second part involves multi-label classification, in which the model is required to identify all relevant technique labels used by the actors influencing the victims, as well as the vulnerability labels of victims present in a conversation. The primary evaluation criterion is accuracy, along with other standard metrics such as precision, recall, and micro F1 score [16].

5   Results

5.1   Binary Classification of Implicit Influential Patterns

First, the detection of influential patterns was investigated using zero-shot and few-shot learning approaches with state-of-the-art large language models. Zero-shot learning [19] refers to querying a vanilla language model without any additional training or fine-tuning, assessing its performance based solely on the knowledge acquired during pretraining and post-training phases. In other words, the model is evaluated based on the general knowledge it has acquired during training phases, without having been explicitly trained on the specific task being assessed. As shown in Table 1, zero-shot learning did not yield significant performance differences across different models. However, the newer 3.2 version of the Llama model with 3 billion parameters outperformed other model variants. It is noteworthy that the smallest Llama model, with only 1 billion parameters, performed poorly in zero-shot learning, likely due to its limited capacity for storing knowledge.

Few-shot learning [7] is similar to zero-shot learning, except that a few labeled examples are included in the original prompt before querying the model. This approach tests whether the language model can identify conversations containing implicit influential patterns when given some guidance through examples. For the few-shot learning experiments, two positive and two negative examples were included in each prompt, with examples randomly selected from the dataset; thus, the prompts did not always contain the same samples. The results indicate that the largest model size achieved the best performance among all evaluated models. Notably, few-shot learning improved the performance of the smallest model by 34%. This finding suggests that, although the Llama-3.2-1B model alone lacked sufficient internal knowledge, providing relevant examples enabled it to better detect influential patterns compared to zero-shot learning with only the conversation itself. As zero-shot and few-shot approaches yielded only limited improvements compared to previous iterations of such models, these results underscore the necessity of a robust pipeline to enhance detection accuracy, since larger models do not necessarily yield better results. Therefore, we conducted experiments using the proposed framework outlined in the methodology section, and the results are reported in Table 1 under "ours" alongside the baseline models. The highest accuracy was achieved by the model utilizing Llama-3.2-3B as the base language model, with an accuracy of 82.6% on the MentalManipCon dataset. The other two models performed comparably, resulting in an overall performance improvement of approximately 6%. Notably, this improvement was attained by fine-tuning a language model with 10 billion fewer parameters. Even when Llama-3.2-1B was used as the base model, the performance remained around 82%, utilizing 12 billion fewer parameters. This demonstrates that designing a robust fine-tuning pipeline is more critical than merely increasing model size or fine-tuning on raw data.

For the other dataset, MentalManipMaj, the Llama-3.1-8B model achieved the best results. The performance of Llama-3.2-3B was also noteworthy and comparable to Llama-3.1-8B, with both models improving accuracy by around 3%. Although Llama-3.2-1B did not achieve the same level of improvement as the larger models, it still outperformed the model trained with the approach from [22], despite having 12 billion fewer parameters under this framework.

5.2 Multi-label Classification of Techniques and Vulnerabilities

In Table 2, the results for multi-label classification are provided. There were 11 unique techniques in total, and some may have one of them and others may have multiple techniques annotated for a manipulative conversation. Since the performance of a model needed to be tested to see how many of those labels can be detected for each conversation, a multi-label classification was required. Our method with a Llama base model with 8 billion parameters was the best one among the others, with the accuracy of 35.7%. Due to having a lot of different labels, a larger model performed better. It should be noted that our approach with the smallest Llama model with 1 billion parameters achieved a performance more than 10 times better than the vanilla fine-tuning in [22]. For vulnerability, since it has only 5 unique labels, the performance expected to be better due to lower complexity. In terms of accuracy, the performance of our approach with Llama base model with 3 billion parameters was the best among others. Nevertheless, the performance of our method with Llama-8B was on par with 3 billion parameter. The results clearly shows that have the approach was clearly a better option than using vanilla fine-tuning with a model with a lot of parameters and this can reduce costs in terms of hardware and boost acceleration since running model with a lot of parameters need high computation resources.

Table 1. Performance of Llama models in terms of accuracy, precision, recall, and F1-score under zero-shot, few-shot, and fine-tuning settings

Model	MentalMalipCon Dataset				MentalMalipMaj Dataset				Reference
	Accuracy	Precision	Recall	F1	Accuracy	Precision	Recall	F1	
Zero-shot Learning									
Llama-2-13B	.696	.693	**.997**	.696	.721	.722	**.997**	.721	[22]
Llama-3.1-8B	.695	.696	.993	.695	.707	.708	.993	.707	-
Llama-3.2-3B	.705	.710	.970	.705	.711	.719	.966	.711	-
Llama-3.2-1B	.330	.774	.044	.330	.319	.785	.045	.319	-
Few-shot Learning									
Llama-2-13B	.715	.735	.912	.715	.726	.732	.979	.726	[22]
Llama-3.1-8B	.696	.701	.978	.696	.704	.721	.945	.704	-
Llama-3.2-3B	.694	.716	.922	.694	.707	.716	.968	.707	-
Llama-3.2-1B	.677	.707	.910	.677	.596	.729	.679	.596	-
Fine-tuning									
Llama-2-13B	.768	.828	.835	.768	.748	**.809**	.851	.748	[22]
Llama-3.1-8B (ours)	.817	.829	.932	.877	**.786**	.797	.938	**.862**	-
Llama-3.2-3B (ours)	**.826**	**.871**	.890	**.881**	.781	.799	.924	.857	-
Llama-3.2-1B (ours)	.819	.853	.911	.880	.765	.785	.921	.848	-

Table 2. Performance of Llama models in terms of accuracy, precision, recall, and F1-score for multi-label classification of techniques used by manipulators and vulnerability of victims under fine-tuning settings

Model	Technique				Vulnerability				Reference
	Accuracy	Precision	Recall	F1	Accuracy	Precision	Recall	F1	
Llama-2-13B	.029	.349	**.821**	.490	.008	.265	**.756**	.393	[22]
Llama-3.1-8B (ours)	**.357**	**.569**	.529	**.529**	.438	.512	.488	.493	-
Llama-3.2-3B (ours)	.345	.536	.473	.488	**.446**	**.549**	.541	**.534**	-
Llama-3.2-1B (ours)	.317	.536	.474	.488	.405	.483	.450	.460	-

6 Conclusion

In this paper, a new framework was introduced to enhance the detection of implicit influential patterns that manifest as mental manipulation in conversations. Leveraging the reasoning abilities of large language models, conversations were augmented with lines containing influential patterns, and a base language model was subsequently trained using a two-stage fine-tuning pipeline to improve detection accuracy. Using this framework, the binary classification task, determining whether a conversation contains implicit influential patterns, was improved by 6%. Multi-label classification tasks for detecting the techniques used and the vulnerability of victims were improved by 33% and 43%, respectively. The results clearly indicate that increasing the size of a language model does not significantly enhance detection performance, as zero-shot and few-shot learning did not yield notable improvements with larger models. However, the framework demonstrates that implementing a well-defined fine-tuning procedure, including partial fine-tuning by attaching adapters to a base language model, can yield higher accuracies, even with smaller models that lack the extensive knowledge base of their larger counterparts.

Acknowledgement. This work used the DeltaAI system at the National Center for Supercomputing Applications through allocation CIS250383 from the Advanced Cyberinfrastructure Coordination Ecosystem: Services & Support (ACCESS) [6] program, which is supported by National Science Foundation grants #2138259, #2138286, #2138307, #2137603, and #2138296.

Ethical Consideration. This paper proposes a framework for detecting implicit influential patterns embedded within conversations. No original data collection was conducted for this study; instead, we utilized publicly available datasets for our downstream tasks. Consequently, no approval for human subjects research was required. In the paper introducing the dataset [22], the authors stated that the data was collected from movies and subsequently annotated by experts. For further details regarding the dataset's data collection procedures, refer to the original publication by [22]

Appendices

Appendix 1

For data augmentation, conversations must be preprocessed to be suitable for prompting through a reasoning language model. First, line numbers were added before each sentence at the start of a conversation by each participant. This was necessary because, initially, the model was prompted to return sentences containing implicit influential patterns. Upon examining the model's responses, we observed that sentences were sometimes only partially returned, and the structure of the answers was often inconsistent. Since our goal was to perform instruction fine-tuning, we assigned labels at the level of individual conversational turns, referred to as lines, rather than entire sentences. For example, regardless of whether a speaker's turn consisted of a single short sentence or multiple sentences, each turn was treated as a single line and assigned one label. For instance, in the example below, there are five conversational turns, and lines 1, 3 and 5 exhibit influential patterns. Thus, the correct label for instruction fine-tuning would be "Line_1, Line_3, Line_5".

For the reasoning model, we selected DeepSeek-R1-Distill-Llama-8B. As this model supports "thinking tokens", we allowed it to process the conversation with intermediate reasoning steps, retrieving the final answer upon completion. Given the substantial number of tokens generated per prompt and the requirement for ten runs per conversation, the 8 billion parameters model was chosen for efficiency and computation constraints. The outputs from these ten runs were then aggregated and summarized using the Llama-3.3-70B-Instruct model. As the aggregation model only needed to process previously generated outputs rather than generating extensive new tokens, it proved even faster than the reasoning model during inference. The example below illustrates the data augmentation structure for a sample conversation (Table 3).

Table 3. An example of data augmentation prompts and their corresponding results

Dialogue	Person1: I like you so much. I think you're beautiful. I think if we were together you would love it. You wouldn't believe it. Person2: How do you know? Person1: I just know. I know you'll love it. Person2: But I'm scared Telly. Person1: I'm telling you. There's nothing in the world to worry about. Person2: Nothing?
Dialogue with Labeled Lines	Line_1: Person1: I like you so much. I think you're beautiful. I think if we were together you would love it. You wouldn't believe it. Line_2: Person2: How do you know? Line_3: Person1: I just know. I know you'll love it. Line_4: Person2: But I'm scared Telly. Line_5: Person1: I'm telling you. There's nothing in the world to worry about. Line_6: Person2: Nothing?
Thinking Prompt	In the provided conversation between two individuals, certain lines contain implicit manipulative remarks. Carefully read the entire conversation from beginning to end. Based on the full context, identify and extract the specific line(s) that contain implicit manipulative remarks. Do not evaluate lines in isolation – consider how each line fits within the overall dialogue. Return only the line numbers in the format 'Line_X, Line_Y, ...' without any explanation. For example, if the dialogue has lines A, B, C, D, E, and F and the implicit manipulation remarks occur in lines A and D, return 'Line_A, Line_D'. Implicit manipulation does not necessarily happen in multiple lines. It could be just happening in a single line.
Full Prompt for Data Augmentation	Line_1: Person1: I like you so much. I think you're beautiful. I think if we were together you would love it. You wouldn't believe it. Line_2: Person2: How do you know? Line_3: Person1: I just know. I know you'll love it. Line_4: Person2: But I'm scared Telly. Line_5: Person1: I'm telling you. There's nothing in the world to worry about. Line_6: Person2: Nothing? In the provided conversation between two individuals, certain lines contain implicit manipulative remarks. Carefully read the entire conversation from beginning to end. Based on the full context, identify and extract the specific line(s) that contain implicit manipulative remarks. Do not evaluate lines in isolation – consider how each line fits within the overall dialogue. Return only the line numbers in the format 'Line_X, Line_Y, ...' without any explanation. For example, if the dialogue has lines A, B, C, D, E, and F and the implicit manipulation remarks occur in lines A and D, return 'Line_A, Line_D'. Implicit manipulation does not necessarily happen in multiple lines. It could be just happening in a single line.
Inference 1	Line_5
Inference 2	Line_1, Line_5
Inference 3	Line_3, Line_5
Inference 4	Line_1, Line_3, Line_5
Inference 5	Line_5
Inference 6	Line_3, Line_5
Inference 7	Line_1, Line_3, Line_5
Inference 8	Line_1, Line_3, Line_5
Inference 9	Line_1, Line_3, Line_5
Inference 10	Line_1, Line_3
Aggregation	Line_1, Line_3, Line_5

Appendix 2

The generative component of the proposed framework is illustrated with the following example. After the initial stage of instruction fine-tuning, the model can be prompted to identify influential segments within conversations. However, it is necessary to format the input as described in Appendix 1, with lines labeled accordingly, as this is the structure on which the model was trained. The example below demonstrates the generative aspect of the model (Table 4):

Table 4. An example demonstrating the generative capability of the proposed model

Dialogue	Person1: I don't know. Person2: Don't go. Person1: I have to... he's a G-34 Person2: You don't have to... I don't trust him. You ought to file a report. Person1: No, don't make trouble. It's nothing.
Full prompt	Analyze the following conversation for manipulative behavior: Line_1: Person1: I don't know. Line_2: Person2: Don't go. Line_3: Person1: I have to... he's a G-34 Line_4: Person2: You don't have to... I don't trust him. You ought to file a report. Line_5: Person1: No, don't make trouble. It's nothing. Identify the specific lines that demonstrate implicit manipulative intent.
Response	Line_2, Line_4 demonstrate implicit manipulative intent. Line_2 is attempting to control Person1's actions by using a restrictive phrase ("Don't go"). Line_4 is exerting influence over Person1's decision-making by expressing distrust and encouraging a report, which could be seen as an attempt to undermine Person1's autonomy.

References

1. Abdidizaji, S., Baekey, A., Jayalath, C., Mantzaris, A., Garibay, O.O., Garibay, I.: Analyzing x's web of influence: dissecting news sharing dynamics through credibility and popularity with transfer entropy and multiplex network measures. In: International Conference on Advances in Social Networks Analysis and Mining, pp. 124–138. Springer (2024). https://doi.org/10.1007/978-3-031-78541-2_8
2. Akula, R., Garibay, I.: Interpretable multi-head self-attention architecture for sarcasm detection in social media. Entropy **23**(4), 394 (2021)
3. Atwell, K., Hassan, S., Alikhani, M.: APPDIA: a discourse-aware transformer-based style transfer model for offensive social media conversations. In: Proceedings of the 29th International Conference on Computational Linguistics, pp. 6063–6074 (2022)

4. Bakhtin, M.M.: Speech genres and other late essays. University of Texas press (1986)

5. Barnhill, A.: What is manipulation. Manip. Theory Pract. **50**, 72 (2014)

6. Boerner, T.J., Deems, S., Furlani, T.R., Knuth, S.L., Towns, J.: ACCESS: advancing innovation: NSF's advanced cyberinfrastructure coordination ecosystem: services & support. In: Practice and Experience in Advanced Research Computing 2023: Computing for the Common Good, PEARC 2023, pp. 173–176. Association for Computing Machinery (2023)

7. Brown, T., et al.: Language models are few-shot learners. Adv. Neural Inf. Process. Syst. **33**, 1877–1901 (2020)

8. DeepSeek-AI, Guo, D., et al. DeepSeek-R1: incentivizing reasoning capability in LLMS via reinforcement learning. arXiv preprint arXiv:2501.12948 (2025)

9. ElSherief, M., et al.: Latent hatred: a benchmark for understanding implicit hate speech. In: Proceedings of the 2021 Conference on Empirical Methods in Natural Language Processing, pp. 345–363 (2021)

10. Gao, Y., Bao, H., Zhang, T., Li, B., Wang, Z., Chen, W.: MENTALMAC: enhancing large language models for detecting mental manipulation via multi-task anti-curriculum distillation. arXiv preprint arXiv:2505.15255 (2025)

11. Ghosh, S., Suri, M., Chiniya, P., Tyagi, U., Kumar, S., Manocha, D.: COSYN: detecting implicit hate speech in online conversations using a context synergized hyperbolic network. In: Proceedings of the 2023 Conference on Empirical Methods in Natural Language Processing, pp. 6159–6173 (2023)

12. Grattafiori, A., et al.: The llama 3 herd of models. arXiv preprint arXiv:2407.21783 (2024)

13. Guo, Z.: Understanding and combating online social deception. PhD thesis, Virginia Polytechnic Institute and State University (2023)

14. Hartvigsen, T., Gabriel, S., Palangi, H., Sap, M., Ray, D., Kamar, E.: ToxiGen: a large-scale machine-generated dataset for adversarial and implicit hate speech detection. In: Proceedings of the 60th Annual Meeting of the Association for Computational Linguistics (Volume 1: Long Papers), pp. 3309–3326 (2022)

15. Hu, E.J., et al. LoRA: low-rank adaptation of large language models. ICLR, **1**(2), 3 (2022)

16. James, G., Witten, D., Hastie, T., Tibshirani, R., Taylor, J.: An Introduction to Statistical Learning: With Applications in Python. Springer Texts in Statistics. Springer International Publishing (2023). https://doi.org/10.1007/978-3-031-38747-0

17. Kojima, T., Gu, S.S., Reid, M., Matsuo, Y., Iwasawa, Y.: Large language models are zero-shot reasoners. Adv. Neural Inf. Process. Syst. **35**, 22199–22213 (2022)

18. Laestadius, L., Bishop, A., Gonzalez, M., Illenčík, D., Campos-Castillo, C.: Too human and not human enough: a grounded theory analysis of mental health harms from emotional dependence on the social chatbot replika. New Media Soc. **26**(10), 5923–5941 (2024)

19. Larochelle, H., Erhan, D., Bengio, Y.: Zero-data learning of new tasks. In: AAAI, vol. 1, p. 3 (2008)

20. Ma, J., et al.: Detecting conversational mental manipulation with intent-aware prompting. In: Proceedings of the 31st International Conference on Computational Linguistics, pp. 9176–9183 (2025)

21. Turcan, E., McKeown, K.: Dreaddit: a reddit dataset for stress analysis in social media. In: EMNLP-IJCNLP 2019, pp. 97 (2019)

22. Wang, Y., Yang, I., Hassanpour, S., Vosoughi, S.: MentalManip: a dataset for fine-grained analysis of mental manipulation in conversations. In: Proceedings of the 62nd Annual Meeting of the Association for Computational Linguistics (Volume 1: Long Papers), pp. 3747–3764 (2024)
23. Wei, J., et al.: Finetuned language models are zero-shot learners. In: International Conference on Learning Representations (2021)
24. Yang, I., Guo, X., Xie, S., Vosoughi S.: Enhanced detection of conversational mental manipulation through advanced prompting techniques. arXiv preprint arXiv:2408.07676 (2024)
25. Yavnyi, S., et al.: DeTexD: a benchmark dataset for delicate text detection. In: The 7th Workshop on Online Abuse and Harms (WOAH), pp. 14–28 (2023)
26. Ahmed Al Zaidy: Cybersecurity and personal privacy: protecting yourself in the digital age. Open Access Res. J. Sci. Technol. **12**(1), 131–135 (2024)
27. Ziems, C., Held, W., Shaikh, O., Chen, J., Zhang, Z., Yang, D.: Can large language models transform computational social science? Comput. Linguist. **50**(1), 237–291 (2024)

EmoteGPU: Generative AI for Emotional Expression and Self-Management in Young Adults

Yingman Chen[1] , Guanlin Chen[2] , and Zihan Gao[1(✉)]

[1] Communication University of China, Beijing, China
{chainman,zihan}@cuc.edu.cn
[2] School of Art, Tiangong Universi-ty, Tianjin, China

Abstract. Emotion expression and self-regulation are critical to young people's mental health. However, existing digital interventions often lack personalization, immersion, and diversity in feedback. To address these shortcomings, this study proposes a multimodal emotion expression system integrating gesture interaction, image generation, and semantic feedback. The system uses Leap Motion for natural emotion input, employs ComfyUI and generative AI to create personalized virtual emotional characters, and provides immersive, gamified emotional feedback through emotion labels and 3D animations. We conducted a user study with 64 university students aged 18–25, evaluating the system using the PANAS scale and semi-structured interviews. The results demonstrated a strong interactive experience and emotion regulation potential, indicating that the system can enhance emotion expression and users' willingness for cognitive emotion regulation. This work offers a new paradigm for AI-augmented affective human-computer interaction and expands its application potential in the domain of youth psychological support.

Keywords: Affective Computing · Generative AI · Youth Mental Health , Human-Computer Interaction

1 Introduction

With the accelerated pace of society and the diversification of the information environment, challenges in work and daily life are increasing, and frequent emotional fluctuations have become a direct manifestation of individuals coping with stressors. Wright et al.'s research demonstrated that negative emotions such as stress and frustration can adversely affect social relationships, physical health, and subjective well-being [1]. In contrast, positive emotions are closely associated with favorable outcomes like health, economic stability, and longevity. Positive emotions broaden cognitive perspectives, foster creativity, and enhance well-being by developing psychological and social resources [2]. Therefore, emotional fluctuations of different valences have significantly different impacts on daily functioning.

M. Kurosu and A. Hashizume (Eds.): HCII 2025, LNCS 16332, pp. 239–259, 2026.
https://doi.org/10.1007/978-3-032-12385-5_15

Recent statistics show that the prevalence of anxiety and depressive symptoms among young people is 30% to 80% higher than in older adults, often manifesting as a vicious cycle triggered by work-related stress, with a localized peak in mental health disorders around the age of 30 [3]. Additionally, research shows that most young employees regard their work as crucial to their mental well-being, with factors like heavy workload and low reward worsening their psychological health [4]. With the rise of digital technologies, young individuals are increasingly focused on mobile devices and social media, neglecting effective management of daily life and emotional regulation. Meanwhile, the widespread use of social media has profoundly impacted several generations of young people, who now make up the majority of its users, making it an integral part of modern life [5].

Based on the aforementioned studies, it is evident that emotion recognition and regulation have become key areas of societal concern, especially in developing methods that engage young people in emotional expression and self-management over time. Accordingly, this study aims to address the following two research questions:

- RQ1: Can human-computer interaction technologies be leveraged to design emotion regulation methods that align with the interests of young people?
- RQ2: To what extent can this method assist young users in emotional expression and self-management?

To address these questions, we designed and developed an interactive emotion expression system grounded in a multimodal affective computing framework, integrating gesture-based interaction, artistic emotional visualization, and generative AI technologies. The system architecture consists of three core modules: an emotion perception layer, which utilizes Leap Motion to enable mid-air gesture interaction, allowing users to naturally input and convey their emotions [6]; An intelligent parsing layer leverages ComfyUI-PuLID-Flux technology to perform multimodal fusion of the user's facial image, reference image encodings, and textual prompts, generating a virtual emotional avatar that reflects both user-specific features and system style [7]; A symbolic expression layer generates nine categories of emotion IP cards and semantic-tagged PVC identity cards to enhance the visual expression and self-management of emotions, supported by immersive 3D animations that strengthen users' emotional connection with the generated visuals [8]. This modular system offers a highly engaging, game-based framework for emotion regulation, marking a transition from passive monitoring to active emotional intervention.

The main contributions of this study are as follows:

1. We developed the 'EmoteGPU' system, which integrates Leap Motion gesture interaction, AI-based image generation, and emotion recognition to offer young users an immersive and personalized visual emotion expression experience.
2. We proposed an AI image generation pipeline based on ComfyUI-PuLID-Flux multimodal fusion, ensuring alignment between emotional states and visual styles for highly personalized output.
3. The system's effectiveness in enhancing positive emotions and reducing negative ones was validated through feedback from 64 young participants, combining PANAS scale assessments with interview data.

4. This study explores the integration potential of generative AI and affective computing in HCI contexts, proposing an embodied and scalable system paradigm for digital mental health interventions.

2 Related Work

In recent years, a growing number of digital mental health interventions targeting youth have emerged. According to Gatto et al., mental health is fundamental to adult well-being and stress resistance, with emotion regulation acting as a Central mechanism across socio-emotional and transdiagnostic psychological domains [9]. Emotional articulation and regulation are therefore considered key protective factors in youth mental health. Yifan Li's findings suggest that CBT helps young individuals interpret and regulate their emotions more effectively, fostering healthier interpersonal communication and problem-solving strategies [10]. Other studies have proposed multi-task classification frameworks—such as mental health disorder identification (MHDI), emotion recognition (ER), and sentiment analysis (SA)—to investigate the relationship between emotional states and mental health, and to address associated psychological challenges [11]. This section reviews commonly adopted emotion regulation approaches in digital mental health interventions, with a focus on emotion recognition algorithms and multimodal evaluation frameworks. It aims to assess the limitations of current technologies in enhancing young people's emotional self-management, while also demonstrating the value and feasibility of generative AI tools—such as Leap Motion and ComfyUI-PuLID-Flux—in emotion expression and regulation.

2.1 Emotion Regulation and Digital Mental Health Tools

Recent studies show that nearly 40% of digital intervention programs adopt Internet-based cognitive behavioral therapy (CBT) approaches. Despite their anonymity and convenience, these interventions often rely heavily on self-direction and lack human guidance. Young users often discontinue such programs due to a lack of personalization and support mechanisms. Conal Twomey et al. therefore suggest that these tools should not serve as frontline therapies, but rather as supplementary options [12, 13]. At the same time, emerging studies have begun incorporating emotion recognition technologies to assess users' emotional states. According to Runfang Guo et al., emotion recognition technologies are evolving from traditional self-report questionnaires to multimodal assessments incorporating physiological and behavioral signals. By combining emotion recognition algorithms with wearable devices or mobile sensors, real-time monitoring and feedback of emotional states can be achieved, enhancing the immediacy and efficacy of interventions [14]. Although recent technologies have been developed to help users understand their emotional patterns and emotion-tracking apps promote self-awareness, most remain limited to data logging and retrospective review, lacking interpretive or intervention guidance based on the collected data. Moreover, accurately identifying emotions in complex environments remains challenging, and current tools lack mechanisms to guide users in translating tracked data into actionable regulation strategies [15]. Despite their potential in supporting youth emotion regulation, digital interventions often suffer from limited interactivity, lack of personalization, and low engagement. Feedback is typically delivered in plain text or charts, lacking expressive visual modalities. Therefore, there is a need to develop a more interactive, adaptive, and visually dynamic digital emotion expression system tailored to the needs of young users, to overcome current limitations and enhance regulatory effectiveness.

2.2 Generative AI and Multimodal Interaction in HCI

In recent years, generative artificial intelligence has made significant advances in multimodal information processing—including vision, speech, and gesture—and has been widely applied to emotion expression and recognition research. With the evolution of affective computing, generative models have increasingly been incorporated into human-computer interaction design to enhance the immersion and visualization of emotional expression, particularly excelling in personalization and cross-modal integration. This study leverages the extensibility of generative AI to systematically explore image generation, gesture-driven interaction, and semantic fusion, constructing a multimodal emotion expression system for young users. The following sections examine the generative pathways and interaction mechanisms of emotional visualization, assessing the strengths and limitations of current technologies in terms of naturalness and individual adaptability.

Research on the Application of Generative AI and Multimodal Interaction in Human-Computer Emotional Expression. Researchers have proposed various deep learning models that enhance emotional visualization by integrating multimodal data such as facial expressions, speech, and body movements. For example, Zhao et al. developed the Visual-Audio Attention Network (VAANet), which enables end-to-end recognition of emotional content in user-generated videos [16]. Yan et al. demonstrated that integrating facial, speech, and body posture information significantly improves the accuracy of emotion recognition compared to unimodal approaches [17]. Meanwhile, generative adversarial networks (GANs) and diffusion models have been used to synthesize realistic facial and motion data, thereby enabling expressive emotional visualization. Ding et al. introduced ExprGAN, which can generate facial expressions of varying intensity based on a given face image [18]. Previous studies have shown that diffusion models are well-suited for generating high-quality facial imagery, while GANs excel in producing diverse postures, significantly reducing the cost of animation production [19]. However, these technologies often require intensive computational resources and struggle with real-time interaction, presenting a key challenge in balancing quality and responsiveness. Furthermore, while multimodal models such as CLIP and ControlNet are capable of aligning textual, visual, and auditory inputs to generate semantically rich content, they still fall short in terms of visual expressiveness, personalization, and interactive feedback.

Multimodal Emotion Recognition Technologies. Existing studies have explored the use of hardware sensors and deep learning models to capture and synthesize gestures embedded with emotional information. Ding et al. developed an emotion-specific gesture recognition system using Leap Motion sensors, which effectively classifies emotional states [20]. On the other hand, generative models have also been applied to gesture synthesis, aiming to enhance expressive capabilities in interaction. Kim et al. proposed a cospeech gesture generation framework that produces gestures in real time aligned with speech prosody and semantics, significantly improving the responsiveness and fluidity of interaction systems [21]. Mughal et al. utilized the ConvoFusion diffusion model to convert speech and text inputs into gesture sequences, enabling precise control of multimodal inputs through a fine-grained guidance mechanism [22]. In facial animation modeling, Wu et al. highlighted the importance of vocal style and emotional cues in 3D animation and proposed a method that considers both global factors (e.g., vocal style and emotion) and local features (e.g., facial muscle movement), addressing the limitations of conventional coarse-label fusion methods [23]. Although these studies have improved the realism and synchronization of emotional animation, most current technologies remain limited to one-way generation, lacking real-time feedback and closed-loop interaction, which hinders continuous emotional expression. Moreover, most existing systems struggle to meet users' personalized emotional expression needs, showing limited adaptability to individual affective styles [21]. Against this backdrop, it is essential to construct an integrated system capable of real-time gesture capture, personalized generation, and responsive interactive feedback.

2.3 Motivation and Objectives

With the accelerating pace of society and the diversification of the information environment, young people are facing increasingly prominent issues of psychological stress and emotional fluctuation. Currently, an increasing number of digital mental health tools targeting young users have emerged, but most suffer from low levels of personalization, limited interaction modes, and a lack of diverse feedback formats. Furthermore, these tools often lack adaptive mechanisms tailored to individual needs, resulting in low user engagement and retention. Most digital interventions rely on text-based or graphic summaries, offering minimal immersive interaction or sensory engagement. Such constraints call for novel systems that prioritize active participation and dynamic visualization in emotion self-regulation. To address these gaps, this study constructs a three-module system integrating Leap Motion and ComfyUI-PuLID-Flux, which combines gesture input, generative interactive interfaces, and emotional feedback to enhance the naturalness and personalization of emotional expression. Targeted at young users, the system aims to create an immersive and customizable emotional management tool, advancing the application of multimodal generative technologies in human-computer emotional interaction.

3 Design of EmoteGPU

We designed and developed *EmoteGPU*, an AI-driven tool for emotional visualization and personalized expression, aimed at helping contemporary young users better identify and express their emotional states. *EmoteGPU* integrates Leap Motion gesture tracking with a Unity-based interactive interface, guiding users through a gamified emotional assessment process to generate cartoon-style "emotional IP identity cards" that reflect both individual traits and affective tone. The system uploads users' facial images and test results to the ComfyUI-based generative image workflow, where the ComfyUI-PuLID-Flux-Enhanced technique fuses visual and textual conditions to generate one of nine shareable cards, each corresponding to a distinct emotional category. This artistic approach to emotional expression departs from the passive model of traditional emotion regulation and responds to the growing demand for nonverbal communication in digital social environments [24].

3.1 Design Strategies

To enable *EmoteGPU* to achieve innovative expression and deep user engagement in digital media, we proposed five key design strategies:

Emotional gamification mechanism. By applying gamification principles, the system shifts emotion regulation from passive reception to active participation [25]. Users complete an emotional test to trigger AI image generation, producing shareable "emo-tional identity cards." This mechanism not only disrupts the unidimensional structure of traditional psychological scales but also reduces users' resistance to emotional assessment [26].

User Experience Optimization. In terms of user experience, we introduced Leap Motion gesture control to replace traditional mouse operations, thereby enhancing the naturalness and immersiveness of interaction [27]. Meanwhile, a virtual touch keyboard was implemented in Unity to replace physical keyboards, ensuring a seamless and stylistically integrated interaction experience. To alleviate user anxiety during image generation, we introduced a Cinema 4D–rendered animation of "emo-tional card manufacturing" and personalized character-themed copywriting as a loading screen, which reduced time perception and optimized overall user experience.

Personalized IP Expression. We observed that users in contemporary media environments are no longer satisfied with passively consuming predefined IPs, but instead prefer to express themselves through personalized, projectable emotional avatars. In *EmoteGPU*, the generated emotional avatars maintain high consistency in both facial features and emotional tone [28], aligning with users' narrative desire for "self-resemblance." Echoing the emotional character storytelling seen in Pixar's *Inside Out*, users engage in identity narration through self-avatar embodiment in digital space [29].

Collectible Emotional Cognition. The emotional cards generated by users are not merely static images, but shareable and narratable symbols of identity projection [25]. Each card serves both as an emotional projection of a specific moment and as a personalized emotional IP, completing a closed loop between emotional cognition and social sharing. Each card serves both as an emotional projection of a specific moment and as a personalized emotional IP, completing a closed loop between emotional cognition and social sharing.

Style and Color System. Based on the affective color model [31], we developed a cartoon-style, high-contrast color grading system, using the HSL color space to visually encode nine emotional atmospheres: anger, anxiety, fear, joy, envy, sadness, embarrassment, boredom, and hate. The interface layering design follows the princi-ples of embodied interaction [32]:

- ***Start screen:*** It features highly saturated balloon-style titles and animated introductions, using dopamine-associated colors (such as red and orange) with high arousal potential to rapidly capture visual attention. This design draws on findings from color psychology, which indicate that higher saturation and brightness are positively associated with enhanced pleasantness [31].
- ***Guidance interface (gesture interaction and project introduction):*** It adopts a cool-toned minimalist layout. Neuroaesthetic studies have shown that such a combination can increase user attention by up to 44% [33], while reducing cognitive load [34] and enhancing the perceived professionalism of the interface.
- ***Emotion testing interface:*** It employs a warm-colored background with gamified control elements, mapping the emotional spectrum through topological gradients of nine diffused colors—red, green, purple, yellow, orange, pink, cyan, blue, and violet. This design is informed by the theory of emotional topography [35], which posits that color gradients can simulate the spatial representation of emotion in the cerebral cortex.

Through the integrated implementation of the five design strategies, EmoteGPU achieves a deep fusion of emotional visualization and personalized expression. The development of this tool aligns with the design paradigm of affective cognition technologies in the digital age [36], offering users an interactive experience grounded in neuroaesthetics and embodied cognition.

3.2 Workflow of EmoteGPU

Grounded in user needs, human-computer interaction theory, and digital art practice, EmoteGPU adopts a technical architecture that integrates Leap Motion gesture interaction, a modular Unity-ComfyUI workflow, and PuLID-Flux-Enhanced multimodal generation technology [45]. This framework follows a four-step process encompassing emotional assessment, user profile setup, image generation, and card presentation, as illustrated in Fig. 1 (User Interaction Flow) and Fig. 2 (On-site User Experience Diagram) [49, 51].

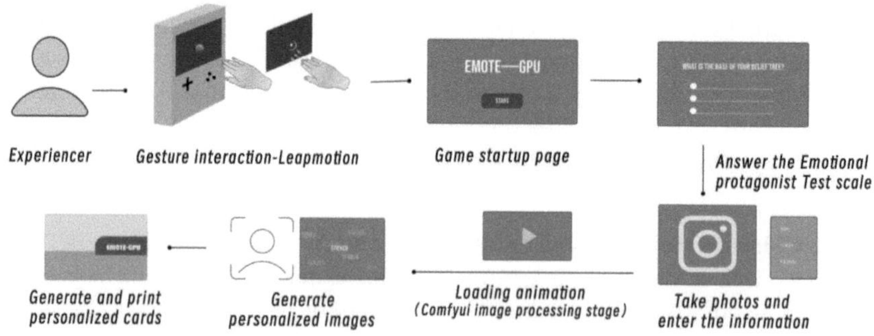

Fig. 1. Flowchart of interaction between EmoteGPU and users.

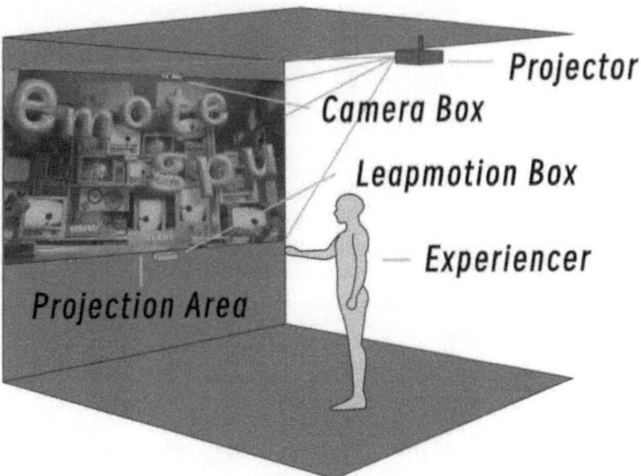

Fig. 2. EmoteGPU user experience diagram.

Emotional Assessment. At the initial stage of *EmoteGPU*, the system briefly introduces the project concept and interaction logic (as shown in Fig. 3). Users are first instructed on how to operate Leap Motion gesture control and are guided into the subsequent testing process via mid-air interactions. The assessment is presented in a multiple-choice format. Its question design draws on the Autobiographical Memory Induction Method [46], using simulated life scenarios to enhance emotional arousal and help users recognize their current dominant emotion. This stage includes nine emotional options: anger, anxiety, fear, joy, envy, sadness, embarrassment, boredom, and hate. The classification follows Ekman's basic emotion theory [47] and references Russell's circumplex model of affect [48]. The test results are transformed into emotional vector matrices, which are then mapped onto the image style generation process to produce a user-specific "emotional portrait".

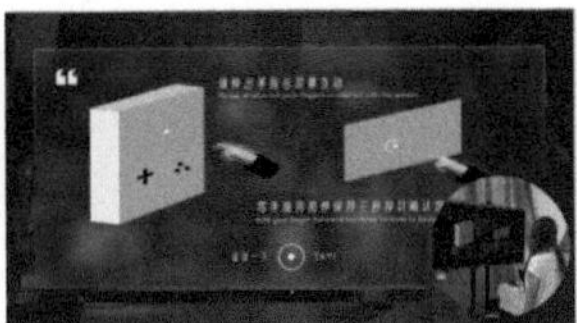

Fig. 3. EmoteGPU homepage, gesture interaction guide page, and device introduction page (from left to right), along with live on-site usage.

User Setup. Next, users are asked to provide basic personal information, including nickname, gender, birthdate, and facial image data captured via the connected camera, as shown in Fig. 4. A facial image is captured using an external camera mounted above the screen. This information is used to create a personalized user profile, which is embedded into the identity feature model for image generation and incorporated into the emotional identity card.

Image Generation. Upon completion of the emotional test, the user's facial image and test results are packaged into a JSON file and sent to the ComfyUI backend. The

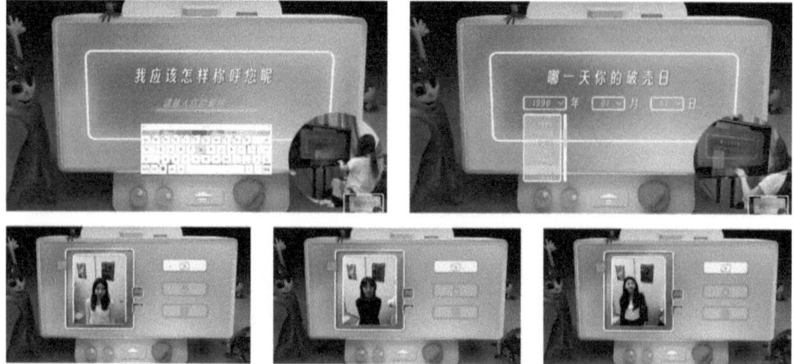

Fig. 4. The interface for inputting basic user information in EmoteGPU, alongside photos of selected participants during on-site testing.

AI image generation process involves CLIP-based visual and textual condition encoding, multimodal guidance via FluxGuidance, and dynamic modulation through identity feature fusion algorithms to ensure alignment between emotional atmosphere and user traits. To alleviate user anxiety during the image generation delay, Unity automatically plays a loading animation created with Cinema 4D, as shown in Fig. 5, which reduces perceived waiting time [50] and helps maintain immersion.

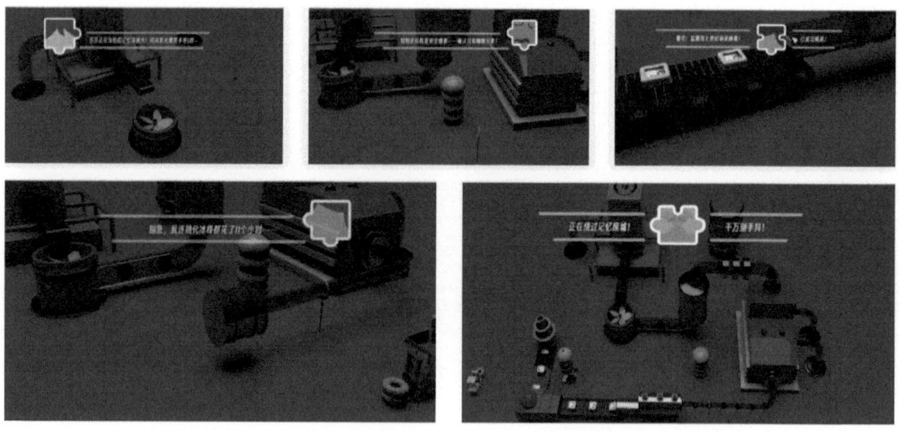

Fig. 5. Representative still frames extracted from the EmoteGPU image generation loading animation.

Output and Presentation. Once the image is generated, Unity automatically invokes a predefined template logic to merge the emotional portrait with the user profile, producing a personalized emotional IP card. The final output is printed on-site using a connected Canon CP1500 printer, providing tangible feedback and forming a visualized projection of the user's emotional identity, as illustrated in Fig. 6.

Fig. 6. Demonstration of EmoteGPU identity cards, on-site printing process, and final printed products.

3.3 Technical Implementation of EmoteGPU

EmoteGPU is an interactive emotional expression system developed in Unity and powered by generative AI, designed to provide users with a highly immersive affective engagement experience. The system integrates Leap Motion for gesture interaction and ComfyUI for generative AI image synthesis. Real-time communication is achieved using UnityWebRequest with JSON data format. The complete technical flow is illustrated in Fig. 7.

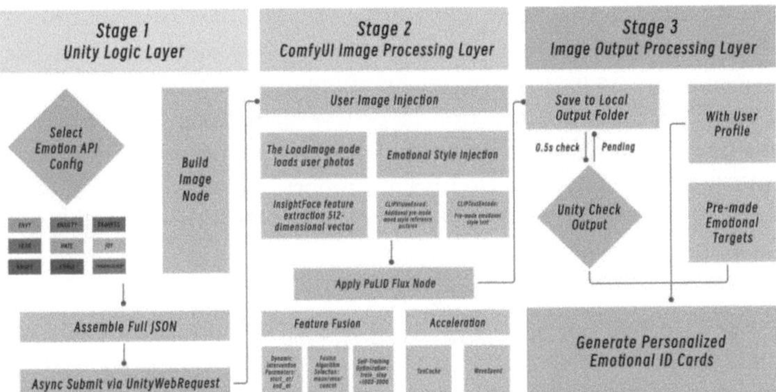

Fig. 7. The technical flow chart of Comfyui and Unity in the image processing stage of EmoteGPU. The blue flow boxes represent the specific processing operations in each step, and the red flow boxes represent the core modules and image generation in each stage.

ComfyUI-PuLID-Flux-Enhanced Workflow. During image generation, EmoteGPU utilizes an optimized workflow based on ComfyUI-PuLID-Flux-Enhanced to produce emotional portraits. On the ComfyUI side, the workflow involves three primary input nodes: (1) a reference image captured from the user, (2) a trained emotional style image, and (3) textual prompts corresponding to the target emotional style. The system first loads the user image via the LoadImage node and uses InsightFace to extract a 512-dimensional identity embedding for facial representation. Next, the emotional style image is processed using CLIPVisionEncode to generate a visual condition embedding, while the textual prompt is encoded by CLIPTextEncode to produce a text condition embedding. The core of the image synthesis process is the FluxGuidance node, which integrates visual and textual signals to regulate image style, ensuring high semantic alignment between the output and the target emotional state. The ApplyPulidFlux node performs identity feature fusion, supporting mean (default), max (feature enhancement), and concat (multi-identity fusion) operations. Temporal mixing can be adjusted dynamically via start_at and end_at parameters, with train_step values flexibly set between 1000 and 3000. To enhance both visual fidelity and emotional accuracy, fine-tuned parameters were applied for each emotion category, enabling differentiated image outputs based on user identity features and target styles.

Interaction and User Experience Optimization in Unity. The Unity module serves as the Central hub for both front-end user interaction and back-end API calls. For each emotion type, we constructed a dedicated ComfyUI API endpoint with pre-optimized training, enabling real-time model invocation upon detection of the user's dominant emotional state. During on-site user interaction, the average image generation time ranged from 50 to 90 s, with most cases completing within one minute. To address the latency of generative AI, a dynamic loading animation rendered in Cinema 4D was embedded into the Unity interface. This animation is played during data submission and image generation, significantly reducing users' perceived waiting time and enhancing the smoothness of the overall experience.

System Architecture and a New Paradigm of Affective Interaction. The overall architecture of *EmoteGPU* follows a modular design paradigm, comprising three core layers: the gesture interaction layer, the intelligent generation layer, and the visual-symbolic layer. The gesture interaction layer leverages Leap Motion to provide users with an intuitive and natural input modality. The intelligent generation layer enables efficient data flow between Unity and ComfyUI, supporting personalized image generation. The visual-symbolic layer transforms emotional output into collectible card formats, reinforcing emotional resonance and self-awareness.

By integrating gesture interaction, generative AI–based image synthesis, and symbolic emotional expression, *EmoteGPU* offers a playful and interactive model of emotional regulation—shifting emotion management from passive recognition to active intervention—and expands the application potential of AI in affective computing and immersive interaction [51].

4   Evaluation of EmoteGPU

A preliminary user evaluation was conducted to examine the effectiveness of *EmoteGPU* in supporting emotional expression in practical scenarios. The study focused on the experience of young users engaging in AI-driven visual interaction for emotional expression and self-awareness, with particular attention to its potential in short-term emotion regulation and the stimulation of expressive intent.

4.1   Participants and Experimental Setup

A total of 64 university students (42 female, 22 male; aged 19–25) participated in the study. All participants came from diverse academic backgrounds and possessed basic digital media literacy. The experiment was scheduled during the first week after the

May Day holiday, a period associated with "post-holiday syndrome" and emotional fluctuations [37], providing an ecologically valid context for evaluating the short-term regulatory capacity of the EmoteGPU system.

Participants varied in their familiarity with AI-related technologies: 43 reported using AI tools (e.g., ChatGPT, Doubao) at least once a week; 24 had experience with AI image generation tools; and 17 had used emotion recognition or tracking tools, among whom 5 had employed wearable devices (e.g., HPV emotion bands) for emotional data collection. These findings suggest that participants had a foundational understanding of technologically supported emotional self-management, which facilitated their readiness for subsequent interactive experiences.

The experiment was conducted offline on an ROG Strix SCAR 7 laptop equipped with an NVIDIA RTX 4080 GPU. The EmoteGPU system ran as a Unity-built application integrated with ComfyUI for AI-based image generation. Participants completed the interaction independently to avoid external interference. Data were collected using a combination of digital questionnaires, the PANAS (Positive and Negative Affect Schedule) scale [38], and semi-structured interviews. Each complete session lasted approximately 15–20 min. The study was approved by the Institutional Ethics Committee of the affiliated university, and informed consent was obtained from all participants.

4.2 Experimental Design and Procedure

The experiment was divided into three phases: pre-test, interaction, and post-test. A combination of quantitative and qualitative methods was employed to comprehensively assess users' emotional changes and experiential perceptions.

- **Pre-test phase (approximately 3 min):** Participants first completed demographic questionnaires and the PANAS (Positive and Negative Affect Schedule), which comprises 10 positive and 10 negative affect items rated on a 5-point Likert scale to establish baseline emotional states [39].
- **Interaction phase (pproximately 3–5 min):** Participants then engaged in a complete interaction session with the EmoteGPU system. The system guided participants to identify their dominant emotion via a multiple-choice interface, after which the AI module generated a personalized visual image—integrating IP style and facial features—serving as their "emotional identity card." In the dominant emotion recognition results, the 64 participants exhibited a diverse range of emotional states, as illustrated in Figs. 8 and 9. This distribution reflects the complexity of university students' emotional states during the post-holiday period and demonstrates EmoteGPU's capability in recognizing diverse emotional dimensions. This process was intended to enhance emotional externalization and self-identification [40]. No intervention was introduced during the interaction process, allowing for natural user responses. All data were anonymized and stored only with informed consent; any records from participants who declined consent were permanently deleted.

- **Post-test phase (approximately 10 min):** After completing the interaction, participants retook the PANAS to assess changes in their emotional states. They then participated in one-on-one semi-structured interviews (10–15 min) to explore their subjective experiences with the system. Interview questions focused on four key dimensions:

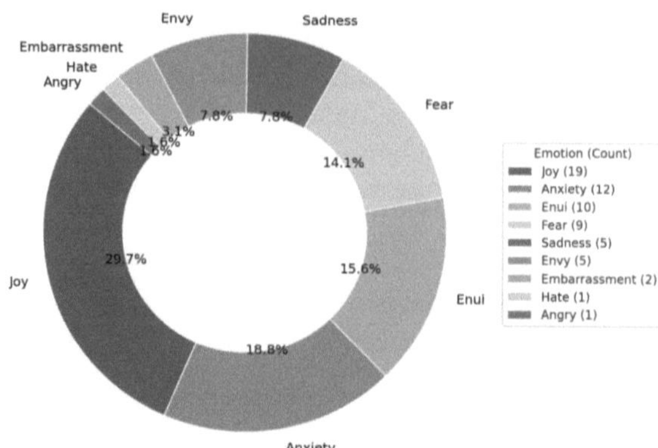

Fig. 8. Distribution of Dominant Emotions Among 64 Participants.This pie chart illustrates the distribution of primary emotions identified through EmoteGPU. The most commonly reported emotion was Joy (19 participants), followed by Anxiety (12), Enui (10), and Fear (9). Less frequent emotions included Sadness (5), Envy (5), Embarrassment (2), Hate (1), and Angry (1). The visualization reflects the diverse emotional states among university students during the post-holiday period.

Fig. 9. Sankey diagram of the distribution of age, gender, and current dominant emotion for 64 participants.

interaction fluency, emotional visualization effectiveness, IP personalization, and visual feedback experience. Questions addressed whether users could smoothly complete the input–feedback–generation process; their comprehension of the interaction-based test items; whether the generated images accurately reflected their current emotional states and evoked emotional resonance through self-projection; and whether the final emotion cards facilitated self-identification, alongside any concerns or suggestions for improvement. This mixed-method evaluation design enabled cross-validation of the system's potential impact on emotional regulation and expression willingness from both quantitative and qualitative perspectives, providing multi-dimensional data to inform future design refinement and broader implementation [51].

4.3 Data Analysis

Our quantitative analysis focused on changes in participants' emotional states before and after interacting with EmoteGPU, as measured by the PANAS scale. The quantitative component of the study examined variations in emotional states pre- and post-interaction with EmoteGPU using the PANAS (Positive and Negative Affect Schedule). First, the Shapiro–Wilk test was used to verify that all variables met the assumption of normality. Subsequently, paired-sample t-tests were conducted on each emotion score to evaluate the significance of changes between pre- and post-interaction measures.

The qualitative component of our study involved semi-structured interviews to explore participants' in-depth experiences with EmoteGPU. These qualitative data were analyzed using thematic analysis.

4.4 Quantitative Results

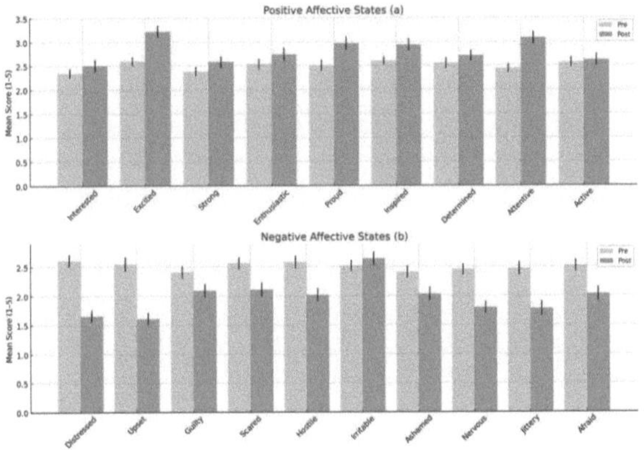

Fig. 10. Mean scores for positive (a) and negative (b) affective states pre- (yellow) and post- (orange) interaction, measured on a Likert scale from 1 (Very slightly or not at all) to 5 (Extremely). Error bars denote standard errors. Statistical significance in paired samples is indicated by asterisks above the bars linking the pre- and post-interaction means ('p < .05, *p < .01, **p < .001).

As shown in Fig. 10(a), participants exhibited significant increases across several positive affect dimensions following interaction with EmoteGPU. Specifically, scores for "Excited" increased significantly from a mean of 2.59 to 3.22 (ΔMean = 0.63, T = 8.28, p < .001), indicating the system's notable effectiveness in enhancing arousal and vitality. The "Proud" score also showed a significant increase (ΔMean = 0.47, T = 5.84, p < .001), which may be attributed to enhanced identity recognition fostered by the personalized emotional IP card. In addition, "Inspired" and "Attentive" also showed significant gains (ΔMean = 0.34, T = 3.96, p < .001; ΔMean = 0.64, T = 8.18, p < .001), suggesting the system's potential to enhance cognitive focus and emotional motivation.

Meanwhile, scores for "Alert" significantly declined (ΔMean = -0.80, T = -10.70, p < .001), possibly indicating the system's concurrent effect in relaxing users and reducing tension. These trends are evident not only in the overall mean differences but also

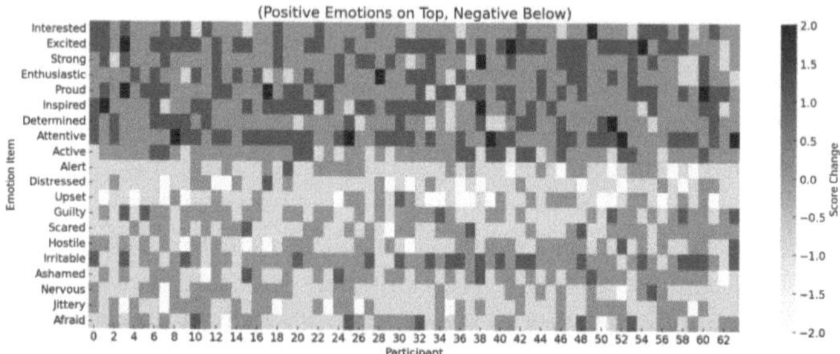

Fig. 11. Heatmap of score changes in PANAS items (After − Before) across 64 participants. Positive emotions are grouped on top and negative ones on the bottom. Color intensity indicates the magnitude of change (darker orange = greater increase; light yellow = smaller or negative change), showing overall emotional trends and inter-individual variability.

clearly visualized in the heatmap (Fig. 11), where most participants showed increased scores in positive dimensions and decreases in alertness and several negative affect dimensions.

In terms of negative affect, analysis shown in Fig. 10(b) revealed statistically significant decreases across all nine core negative dimensions. Specifically, the mean scores for "Distressed" and "Upset" decreased by 0.95 and 0.94 respectively ($T = −12.14$ and $−10.25$, both $p < .001$), indicating EmoteGPU's immediate effect in alleviating emotional distress. Additional negative dimensions—including "Guilty," "Scared," "Hostile," "Ashamed," "Nervous," "Jittery," and "Afraid"—also exhibited moderate to substantial reductions (ΔMean ranging from $−0.39$ to $−0.89$, all p-values $< .001$). These results suggest that EmoteGPU offers effective short-term regulation of negative emotional experiences.

4.5 Qualitative Results

Visual understanding of emotions and enhanced self-awareness: Participants generally reported that their interaction with EmoteGPU provided a moment of emotional release and relaxation amidst their otherwise stressful academic and daily routines. Through the process of emotional assessment and image generation, many participants were able to reflect on their current emotional states and found resonance in the visual feedback. This process was frequently described as "healing" or "anticipatory," aligning with previous findings that visual modalities enhance emotional externalization and self-awareness [42]. For instance, Participant P9 stated in the interview: "During the experience, I was very curious about identifying my dominant emotion. Although I hesitated during some test choices due to unclear scene associations and the final image differed slightly from my initial expectations, I felt a strong sense of emotional connection when I saw the emotional identity card with familiar IP styling and high facial resemblance."

- **Immersion and symbolic identification in artistic interaction:** Most participants noted that the visual representation was more effective than text in evoking emotional awareness, and that the tangible format of the emotional identity card helped transform abstract mental states into perceivable and symbolic objects. This process of emotional concretization showed positive effects in enhancing both self-expression and willingness to engage in emotion regulation [43]. Participants commonly expressed a strong sense of identification with the visual output, especially when the generated imagery aligned with familiar IPs (e.g., Inside Out), which deepened their emotional connection. As Participant P13 stated: "I've always liked the emotion characters in *Inside Out*. Seeing an image that looks like me and like one of those characters—it felt like I really became the protagonist of the movie."

Participants generally gave positive feedback on the overall interaction design. They described the interface as warm, the color scheme as soft, and the animations as narratively engaging—enhanced further by playful and semantic copywriting that fostered immersion. Notably, the animation during image generation (depicting the "ID card production process") was perceived as increasing the sense of pacing and anticipation, effectively reducing boredom and anxiety during the wait. Participant P37 remarked: "The 'identity card factory' animation, paired with its personified texts, felt like having a dreamlike conversation with a movie IP character."

- **Willingness for Continued Use and Suggestions for Improvement:** Among the 64 participants interviewed post-interaction, 59 (92.2%) expressed willingness to continue using EmoteGPU in the future. They considered the system a novel and engaging approach to understanding and managing emotions, particularly suitable for everyday mental health support. Some participants suggested incorporating more personalized IP character options to better align with users' emotional preferences and identity expression.
- **For those who did not wish to continue using the system, the main feedback fell into the following categories:** First, some hoped for the addition of passive emotion recognition capabilities, such as integration with physiological sensors (e.g., EEG, heart rate). Second, users wanted input methods to be improved, including support for voice input instead of multiple-choice questionnaires. Third, some participants noted that they rarely engaged in emotional self-assessment, making it difficult to form a regular usage habit. Additionally, several users mentioned they might "forget to use" the system or lacked scenarios that would trigger its use, suggesting the need for features like notification prompts or emotion journaling to sustain long-term engagement.

5 Discussions and Limitations

5.1 Evaluation Results

This study proposed the EmoteGPU system by integrating gesture-based interaction with generative AI technologies, offering young users a personalized and visualized approach to emotional expression that addresses their dual need for individuality and visual feedback. The system utilizes Leap Motion for natural gesture input, simplifying operation while enhancing immersion—aligning with embodied cognition theory, which links emotion and bodily movement [58]. Through multimodal generative modeling, EmoteGPU integrates users' facial features and emotional test data to generate highly personalized "emotional IP identity cards," effectively strengthening self-projection and emotional identification [53].

Moreover, EmoteGPU demonstrates sensitivity to users' emotional states through thoughtful interface elements—such as color schemes and loading animations—which help alleviate anxiety during waiting times and improve the smoothness and psychological comfort of the experience, forming a closed-loop interaction from input to feedback and offering a practical reference for digital emotion intervention systems [54]. Analysis of PANAS scale data indicated that following brief interaction with EmoteGPU, positive emotions such as "Joy" and "Inspired" significantly increased, while negative emotions like "Upset" and "Nervous" showed marked declines—validating the system's emotional regulation effectiveness.

EmoteGPU's real-time visual feedback and immersive interaction facilitated users' recognition, understanding, and active regulation of their emotions—consistent with Gross's emotion regulation model, which posits that expressive feedback can activate self-regulatory mechanisms [55]. Interview data revealed that most participants felt understood and experienced emotional resonance during the interaction, attributing a strong sense of personal projection to the system-generated imagery.

Moreover, the "emotional identity card" served as a tangible medium for emotional expression, effectively extending its temporal duration and social significance [54].

5.2 Limitations and Future Work

Although this study preliminarily validated the potential of EmoteGPU in human-computer interaction and emotional regulation, and demonstrated positive short-term effects, several limitations remain that require further refinement and expansion in future research.

First, the participant sample was relatively homogeneous, comprising mainly healthy college students aged 19–25, without inclusion of populations with emotional disorders such as depression or anxiety—thus limiting external validity. Given that emotionally vulnerable populations are critical targets for intervention, future studies should broaden participant diversity and incorporate qualitative feedback from psychologists or art therapists to improve adaptability and translational value across varied user contexts [56]. Second, the system lacks comparative evaluation against other mainstream emotion visualization technologies. The current study does not systematically assess how EmoteGPU compares with methods such as affective audio generation, real-time facial expression tracking, or EEG-based feedback, in terms of strengths and limitations. Prior studies suggest that different emotion externalization methods vary significantly in terms of arousal strength, intervention efficacy, and user acceptance. Future research could employ controlled experiments and multimodal preference analysis to clarify the system's positioning within the broader ecosystem of emotion expression technologies. Third, the system's emotion recognition still relies primarily on subjective self-report, lacking physiological sensing and behavioral analysis modules. In recent years, emotion-sensing systems have increasingly incorporated passive signals such as heart rate, skin conductance, and EEG to enhance the naturalness and real-time responsiveness of interaction [51]. In addition, behavioral cues such as vocal tone, body gestures, and facial expressions play a significant role in multimodal emotional interaction [59]. Finally,

EmoteGPU remains a one-time interaction prototype lacking mechanisms for continuous tracking and self-management. The dynamic evolution of emotional states requires long-term monitoring through wearable devices or emotion diaries [60]. Building personalized user profiles, dynamic feedback triggers, and intervention history mechanisms can facilitate the system's integration into real-world mental health contexts.

Based on the above limitations, future work will advance in the following directions: (1) Expand participant diversity and include broader psychological profiles; (2) Integrate expert evaluations and implement controlled comparative designs; (3) Incorporate multimodal sensory inputs; (4) Develop longitudinal and life-integrated emotional management mechanisms.

6 Conclusion

The EmoteGPU system integrates multimodal interaction (gesture, facial, textual) with generative AI technologies to offer young users an immersive and personalized method for emotional expression and regulation. Through visual feedback and embodied interaction, the system facilitates self-projection and emotional recognition, significantly enhancing positive emotions and reducing negative affect—thereby shifting emotional management from passive awareness to active regulation. In the field of digital mental health intervention, this study innovatively combines affective computing with generative AI, leveraging gamified interfaces and personalized virtual avatars to increase user engagement and enhance the interactivity and playfulness of intervention experiences. The study establishes an embodied interaction–centered paradigm for emotional self-management, integrating emotion sensing with visual feedback. It provides both theoretical grounding and an application framework for future research, laying the foundation for more personalized and scalable digital mental health tools.

References

1. Wright, K.B., King, S., Rosenberg, J.: Functions of social support and self-verification in association with loneliness, depression, and stress. J. Health Commun. 19(1), 82–99 (2013)
2. Cohn, M.A., Fredrickson, B.L., Brown, S.L., Mikels, J.A., Conway, A.M.: Happiness unpacked: Positive emotions increase life satisfaction by building resilience. Emotion. 9(3), 361–368 (2009)
3. van Veen, M., Schelvis, R.M., Hoekstra, T., et al.: Work characteristics and emotional exhaustion among young workers: A latent class analysis. BMJ Open. 13, e074386 (2023)
4. van Veen, M., Schelvis, R.M., Bongers, P.M., et al.: A qualitative study of young workers' experience of the psychosocial work environment and how this affects their mental health. BMC Public Health. 24, 3341 (2024)
5. Raina, R.: Exploring the relationship between social media addiction, fear of missing out (FOMO), and self-esteem among university students. Sambodhi. 44(1), 140–147 (2021)
6. Weichert, F., Bachmann, D., Fisseler, D.: Analysis of the accuracy and robustness of the Leap Motion controller. Sensors. 13(5), 6380–6396 (2013)
7. Black Forest Labs: FLUX.1 Redux: A flux foundation model adapter for image stylization and variation generation (Version dev). Hugging Face (2024)

8. Guo, J., et al.: LivePortrait: Efficient portrait animation with stitching and retargeting control (Version v2). arXiv preprint (2025)

9. Gatto, A.J., Elliott, T.J., Briganti, J.S., et al.: Development and feasibility of an online brief emotion regulation training (BERT) program for emerging adults. Front. Public Health. **10**, 858370 (2022)

10. Li, E.Y.: The impact of emotion regulation strategies on adolescent mental health: Interactions of family and society. Int. J. Educ. Humanit. **18**(1), 180–184 (2025)

11. Pathak, A., Bhattacharjee, S., Saha, T., Saha, S.: Does sentiment and emotion affect mental health? A multi-task classification framework for understanding mental health, emotion, and sentiment. ACM Trans. Comput. Healthc. (2024)

12. Potts, C., Kealy, C., McNulty, J., et al.: Digital mental health interventions for young people aged 16–25 years: Scoping review. J. Med. Internet Res. **27**, e72892 (2025)

13. Twomey, C., O'Reilly, G., Byrne, M., et al.: A randomized controlled trial of the computerized CBT programme, MoodGYM, for public mental health service users. Br. J. Clin. Psychol. **53**(4), 433–450 (2014)

14. Guo, R., Guo, H., Wang, L., et al.: Development and application of emotion recognition technology: A systematic literature review. BMC Psychol. **12**(1), 95 (2024)

15. Schueller, S.M., Neary, M., Lai, J., Epstein, D.A.: Understanding people's use of and perspectives on mood-tracking apps: Interview study. JMIR Ment. Health. **8**(8), e29368 (2021)

16. Zhao, S., Ma, Y., Gu, Y., et al.: An end-to-end visual-audio attention network for emotion recognition in user-generated videos. Proc. AAAI Conf. Artif. Intell. **34**(1), 303–311 (2020)

17. Yan, J., Li, P., Du, C., et al.: Multimodal emotion recognition based on facial expressions, speech, and body gestures. Electronics. **13**(18), 3756 (2024)

18. Ding, H., Sricharan, K., Chellappa, R.: ExprGAN: Facial expression editing with controllable expression intensity. Proc. AAAI Conf. Artif. Intell. **32**, 6781–6788 (2018)

19. Abootorabi, M.M., Ghahroodi, O., Zahraei, P.S., et al.: Generative AI for character animation: A comprehensive survey of techniques, applications, and future directions. arXiv preprint arXiv:2504.19056 (2024)

20. Ding, I.J., Hsieh, M.C.: A hand gesture action-based emotion recognition system using 3D image sensor from Leap Motion. Microsyst. Technol. **28**, 403–415 (2022)

21. Kim, S., Chang, M., Kim, Y., Lee, J.: Body gesture generation for multimodal conversational agents. In: Proceeding SIGGRAPH Asia 2024 Conference Papers, Art. 88, pp. 1–11. ACM, New York (2024)

22. Mughal, M.H., Dabral, R., Habibie, I., et al.: ConvoFusion: Multimodal conversational diffusion for cospeech gesture synthesis. In: Proceedings of the IEEE/CVF Conference on Computer Vision and Pattern Recognition (CVPR), pp. 1388–1398. IEEE/CVF, New York (2024)

23. Wu, H., Zhou, S., Jia, J., et al.: Speech-driven 3D face animation with composite and regional facial movements. In: Proceedings of the 31st ACM International Conference on Multimedia (MM '23), pp. 1–9. ACM, New York (2023)

24. Su, S.W., Hung, C.H., Chen, L.X., Yuan, S.M.: Development of an AI-based system to enhance school counseling models for Asian elementary students with emotional disorders. IEEE Access (2024)

25. Dissanayake, V., Tang, V., Elvitigala, D.S., et al.: Troi: Understanding users' perspectives to mobile automatic emotion recognition in natural settings. Proc. ACM Hum.-Comput. Interact. **6**(MHCI), 1–22 (2022)

26. Kim, J., Takeuchi, T., Narumi, T.: Visualizing emotions perceived in daily activities for self-awareness development. In: International Conference on Human-Computer Interaction, pp. 215–230. Springer, Cham (2023)

27. Rakshit, A.: Building an artificial-intelligence powered metaphor-based visualizer for human self-understanding, PhD thesis, University of British Columbia (2025)

28. Wang, X., Tian, R., Zeng, Q., et al.: The synergy of dialogue and art: Exploring the potential of multimodal AI chatbots in emotional support. In: Proceedings CSCW Companion 2024, pp. 147–153. ACM, New York (2024)

29. Yan, Z., Wu, Y., Zhang, Y., Chen, X.A.: Emoglass: An end-to-end AI-enabled wearable platform for enhancing self-awareness of emotional health. In: Proceedings CHI Conference on Human Factors in Computing System, pp. 1–19. ACM, New York (2022)

30. Zhang, X.: Mindscapes: Exploring EEG-driven emotional expression in VR for enhanced emotional relief and mental well-being, PhD thesis, OCAD University (2025)

31. Valdez, P., Mehrabian, A.: Effects of color on emotions. J. Exp. Psychol. Gen. **123**(4), 394–409 (1994)

32. Dourish, P.: Where the action is: The foundations of embodied interaction. MIT Press, Cambridge (2001)

33. Chatterjee, A., Vartanian, O.: Neuroscience of aesthetics. Ann. N. Y. Acad. Sci. **1369**(1), 172–194 (2016)

34. Carnegie Mellon University: How minimalist décor might make you smarter. Child Dev. **85**(6), 2112–2125 (2014)

35. Nummenmaa, L., Glerean, E., Hari, R., Hietanen, J.K.: Bodily maps of emotions. Proc. Natl. Acad. Sci. USA. **111**(2), 646–651 (2014)

36. Peng, Z., Desmet, P.M.A., Xue, H.: Mood in experience design: A scoping review. Des. Stud. **84**, 101167 (2023)

37. Watson, D., Clark, L.A., Tellegen, A.: Development and validation of brief measures of positive and negative affect: The PANAS scales. J. Pers. Soc. Psychol. **54**(6), 1063–1070 (1988)

38. Howard, D.E., Schiraldi, G., Pineda, A., Campanella, R.: Stress and mental health among college students: Overview and promising prevention interventions. In: Stress and Mental Health of College Students, pp. 91–123. Nova Science Publishers, New York (2006)

39. Crawford, J.R., Henry, J.D.: The Positive and Negative Affect Schedule (PANAS): Construct validity and normative data in a non-clinical sample. Br. J. Clin. Psychol. **43**(3), 245–265 (2004)

40. Hu, C., Lin, Z., Zhang, N., Ji, L.J.: AI-empowered imagery writing: Integrating AI-generated imagery into digital mental health service. Front. Psych. **15**, 1434172 (2024)

41. Denzin, N.K., Lincoln, Y.S.: The Sage Handbook of Qualitative Research. Sage, Thousand Oaks (2011)

42. Lan, X., Wu, Y., Cao, N.: Affective visualization design: Leveraging the emotional impact of data. IEEE Trans. Vis. Comput. Graph. **30**(1), 1–11 (2023)

43. Gross, J.J., John, O.P.: Individual differences in two emotion regulation processes: Implications for affect, relationships, and well-being. J. Pers. Soc. Psychol. **85**(2), 348–362 (2003)

44. Norman, D.A.: Emotional Design: Why We Love (or Hate) Everyday Things. Basic Books, New York (2007)

45. Guo, Z., Wu, Y., Zhuowei, C., Zhang, P., He, Q.: Pulid: Pure and lightning ID customization via contrastive alignment. Adv. Neural Inf. Process. Syst. **37**, 36777–36804 (2024)

46. Holland, A.C., Kensinger, E.A.: Emotion and autobiographical memory. Phys Life Rev. **7**(1), 88–131 (2010)

47. Ekman, P., Cordaro, D.: What is meant by calling emotions basic. Emot. Rev. **3**(4), 364–370 (2011)

48. Russell, J.A.: A circumplex model of affect. J. Pers. Soc. Psychol. **39**(6), 1161–1178 (1980)

49. Radford, A., Kim, J.W., Hallacy, C., et al.: Learning transferable visual models from natural language supervision. In: Proceedings of the International Conference on Machine Learning, pp. 8748–8763. PMLR, New York (2021)

50. Lim, B., Rogers, Y., Sebire, N.: Designing to distract: Can interactive technologies reduce visitor anxiety in a children's hospital setting? ACM Trans. Comput. Hum. Interact. **26**(2), 1–19 (2019)
51. Picard, R.W.: Affective Computing. MIT Press, Cambridge (2000)
52. Lakoff, G., Johnson, M., Sowa, J.F.: Review of Philosophy in the Flesh: The embodied mind and its challenge to Western thought. Comput. Linguist. **25**(4), 631–634 (1999)
53. Peña, J., Hancock, J.T.: An analysis of socioemotional and task communication in online multiplayer video games. Commun. Res. **33**(1), 92–109 (2006)
54. Desmet, P.M.A.: Faces of product pleasure: 25 positive emotions in human-product interactions. Int. J. Des. **6**(2) (2012)
55. Gross, J.J.: Emotion regulation: Current status and future prospects. Psychol. Inq. **26**(1), 1–26 (2015)
56. Sun, J., Dong, Q.X., Wang, S.W., et al.: Artificial intelligence in psychiatry research, diagnosis, and therapy. Asian J. Psychiatry. **87**, 103705 (2023)
57. Langhammer, T., Unterfeld, C., Blankenburg, F., et al.: Design and methods of the research unit 5187 PREACT: A study protocol for a multicentre observational study. BMJ Open. **15**(2), e094110 (2025)
58. Van den Broek, E.L., Schut, M.H., Westerink, J.H.: Affective personalization using biosignals and emotional stimuli in interactive systems. Int. J. Hum. Comput. Stud. **158**, 102761 (2022)
59. Zeng, Z., Pantic, M., Roisman, G.I., Huang, T.S.: A survey of affect recognition methods: Audio, visual and spontaneous expressions. In: Proceedings of the 9th International Conference Multimodal Interfaces, pp. 126–133. ACM, New York (2007)
60. Wang, R., Wang, W., DaSilva, A., et al.: Tracking depression dynamics in college students using mobile phone and wearable sensing. Proc. ACM Interact. Mob. Wearable Ubiquitous Technol. **2**(1), 1–26 (2018)

Simplifying Car Repair: An NLP-Driven Spare Parts Recommendation System

Carlos Daniel Garcia Huamani$^{(\boxtimes)}$ (iD) and Eder Quispe Vilchez (iD)

Pontificia Universidad Católica del Perú, San Miguel, Lima 32, Peru
{carlos.garciah,eder.quispe}@pucp.edu.pe

Abstract. The vehicle spare parts recommendation system has been designed with a user-centered approach, ensuring an intuitive and efficient experience. This system utilizes an artificial intelligence model that, through advanced natural language processing (NLP) techniques, interprets user-described vehicle issues in everyday language. By doing so, it accurately identifies the necessary spare parts, considering critical factors such as the vehicle's make, model, and year. To power the AI model, a robust and structured knowledge base was developed, integrating key information about spare parts, common issues, and specific compatibilities. This knowledge base was built using techniques like Retrieval-Augmented Generation (RAG) and web scraping, enabling the collection and organization of large volumes of relevant data from multiple reliable online sources. Additionally, the system was designed with a focus on accessibility and usability, optimizing every interaction to provide accurate and personalized recommendations tailored to users' specific needs. This approach not only enhances user satisfaction but also ensures that the spare parts selection process is faster and more reliable.

Keywords: Natural language processing (NLP) · Knowledge Base · Vehicle issues

1   Introduction

In Peru, the importation of vehicle spare parts has significantly increased to address damages caused by traffic accidents and the regular wear and tear of vehicles. By 2022, the spare parts import market experienced a 12.8% growth compared to 2021 [1]. However, this growth has also resulted in an overwhelming variety of spare parts available for different car models, with varying levels of quality. The wide range of options has led to a lack of centralized information regarding which parts are suitable for specific vehicle issues, as well as details on their quality and pricing. This abundance of choices poses a challenge for vehicle owners, particularly those with limited technical knowledge, making it difficult to make informed decisions when acquiring spare parts [2].

In this context, one option that could facilitate the identification of suitable spare parts is the development of an AI-powered vehicle spare parts recommendation system. This system would serve as a consultation tool, allowing vehicle owners to get a clear idea of the parts they need, their approximate costs, and compare them with prices offered

M. Kurosu and A. Hashizume (Eds.): HCII 2025, LNCS 16332, pp. 260–276, 2026.
https://doi.org/10.1007/978-3-032-12385-5_16

by mechanical workshops. In this way, users could make more informed decisions, especially when facing the challenge of identifying the correct parts due to the diversity of car models.

Artificial intelligence, using natural language processing (NLP), could interpret vehicle problem descriptions and provide accurate recommendations on the most appropriate parts. This would reduce confusion and simplify the selection process, even for those without technical experience. Additionally, the system could constantly update information on prices and quality, ensuring users always have access to up-to-date and reliable data.

This article presents AutoPro, a vehicle spare parts recommendation system designed to guide users through this vast catalog of options. AutoPro offers personalized and accurate recommendations based on a vehicle's make, model, and specific issues, helping users quickly find high-quality spare parts. Beyond simplifying the search process, AutoPro also provides up-to-date information on prices and product quality, enabling vehicle owners to compare costs with those from mechanical workshops and make better-informed decisions.

The paper is structured as follows: first, the extraction of information and the design of the knowledge base; then, the design and construction of the recommendation system; and finally, the implementation of the AI-powered virtual assistant.

2   The Extraction of Information and the Design of the Knowledge Base

2.1   Preliminary Review of Web Pages and Other Information Sources that Include Vehicle Spare Parts Information to Design the Knowledge Base

The review of information sources, including websites and other relevant resources, resulted in the selection of sites whose content will be extracted using web scraping techniques. Additionally, an external collaborator provided a dataset related to vehicle parts for Chinese vehicle brands. Integrating this information into the knowledge base is crucial for its subsequent modeling according to the defined requirements.

The selection of the websites is justified by the following characteristics:

- **Identification of common issues in vehicle bodywork:** The selected websites provide detailed information about recurring faults affecting various parts of the vehicle, such as bumpers, hoods, headlights, and fenders. This information is critical for identifying the most common parts associated with these issues.
- **Classification of parts by vehicle model and brand:** The reviewed websites organize parts in a structured manner, making it easier to access precise information about the parts required for specific vehicle models. This contribution is essential for developing a recommendation system that considers the unique characteristics of each vehicle.
- **Information on part prices and quality:** Access to up-to-date data on part prices and quality enriches the knowledge base, enabling more accurate recommendations tailored to the user's needs in terms of cost and quality.

It is important to note that it is not necessary for the selected websites to meet all three characteristics. It suffices that at least one of them is present, as each adds unique value to the development of the knowledge base. The combination of sources that address common bodywork issues, classify parts by model and brand, and provide information on prices and quality contributes to the creation of a robust and dynamic system. This approach ensures that the knowledge base remains flexible and adaptable to different needs.

2.2 Knowledge Base Modeling Based on the Type of Defect or Damage, Classified by Vehicle Brand and Model.

Definition of the Knowledge Base Domain. The knowledge base domain focuses on the automotive market, specifically on vehicle parts related to car body issues. The information encompasses common body damages categorized by vehicle brands, models, and manufacturing years, as well as additional variables such as the quality and price of the replacement parts.

Knowledge Extraction. The knowledge extraction process centers on identifying and generalizing relevant data related to car body issues, replacement parts, vehicle brands, and models. This process facilitates the identification of patterns in specific body damages and the appropriate selection of parts for each type of issue. Knowledge extraction was conducted through the following activities: (see Fig. 1)

- Data Collection from Online Sources:
- Detailed descriptions of common body issues were gathered, along with the recommended replacement parts and their compatibility with specific brands and models.
- The information was stored in text files for further processing.
- Analysis of Parts Catalogs and Structured Datasets:
- Data on replacement parts, their prices, and different quality levels (original and aftermarket) were collected.
- The information was organized into tables that link parts to the issues they resolve and the vehicles they are compatible with.
- Consultation of Technical Manuals:
- Specific vehicle manuals were reviewed, providing details on recurring issues, recommended solutions, and required parts.
- Interviews with Users and Sellers:
- Insights were gathered on the most in-demand replacement parts and the quality options available in the market.
- Information about frequent body problems across different vehicle zones was also collected.
- Data Processing:
- The collected files were processed to identify common patterns of issues and associated solutions.
- The extracted knowledge enabled the generalization of relationships between problems and parts, categorizing the information by damage type, vehicle brand, model, and year.

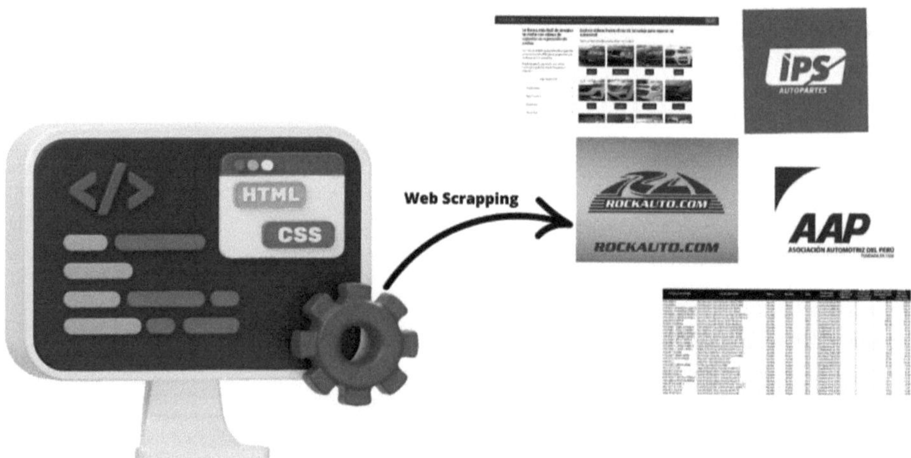

Fig. 1. Knowledge Extraction.

Knowledge Base Modeling. This section describes the process of modeling the knowledge base for the vehicle parts recommendation system. The modeling organizes the collected information and establishes a structure that enables artificial intelligence systems and the virtual assistant to provide accurate and useful recommendations. (see Fig. 2)

- **Models:** The knowledge base includes information on 57 vehicle models. Among the most well-known are the Toyota Yaris, RAV4, and Kia Rio, among others. The selection of these models was based on 18 vehicle brands that, according to the 2024 statistical report from the Peruvian Automotive Association (AAP), are the most purchased in Peru [3].
- **Parts:** The knowledge base includes 15 categories of parts. These parts have been divided into three main vehicle zones: the front zone, lateral zone, and rear zone. Based on these zones, the following rules were defined for recommending parts:
- **First rule:** If a problem is located in the front zone of the vehicle, parts associated with that zone should be recommended.
- **Second rule:** If a problem is located in the lateral zone of the vehicle, parts associated with that zone should be recommended.
- **Third rule:** If a problem is located in the rear zone of the vehicle, parts associated with that zone should be recommended.
- **Quality:** The knowledge base includes three types of quality levels:
- **OEM (Original Equipment Manufacturer):** These parts are manufactured by the vehicle brands themselves and are considered premium quality.
- **Aftermarket:** Within aftermarket parts, two categories are identified:

Chinese Origin: These are the most affordable in the Peruvian market.

Taiwanese Origin: These are more expensive than Chinese-origin parts but offer superior quality and finishing, being very similar to OEM parts.

Parts Pricing: The knowledge base includes prices associated with parts, segmented by quality levels and their corresponding brands. The prices are updated as of October 2024.

Problems: The knowledge base focuses exclusively on problems related to the vehicle's bodywork, as they are easier to identify and understand. Problems include everything from frontal collisions to scratches in the zones mentioned above. This entity maintains the following relationships and rules:

- **Relationship:** Problems are associated with specific parts based on the defined rules.
- Rules:
- If a problem is located in the front zone of the vehicle, parts associated with that zone should be recommended.
- If a problem is located in the lateral zone of the vehicle, parts associated with that zone should be recommended.
- If a problem is located in the rear zone of the vehicle, parts associated with that zone should be recommended.

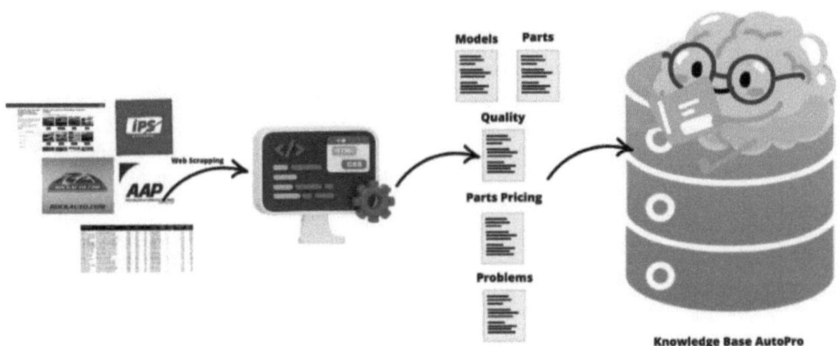

Fig. 2. Knowledge Base Modeling.

3 Implementation of a Module for Price Quotation Based on the Knowledge Base of Parts and Prices

3.1 System Analysis

In the initial phase, the main objective was to understand the needs, expectations, and behaviors of the potential user to ensure that the design of the vehicle spare parts recommendation system was aligned with the demands of the end user. To achieve this, user-centered tools such as User Persona, Empathy Map, and Journey Map were employed, each of which contributed significantly to the definition of system requirements and its subsequent implementation.

User Persona. The User Persona facilitated the creation of a detailed profile of the potential user who would use the system [4]. Through this tool, the demographic characteristics and specific needs of the user were identified, such as the need to search for vehicle spare parts and to know their prices and availability. Additionally, the User Persona revealed that the user preferred a more intuitive and accessible language during the search process, and also specified the devices they typically use. This information was fundamental in designing a user interface that was both user-friendly and suitable for the technological habits of the target audience. The User Persona is in Spanish because it was made in the Peruvian context. (see Fig. 1)

Empathy Map. The Empathy Map complemented the User Persona by delving deeper into the emotions, thoughts, and behaviors of the user during their interaction with the system [5]. This tool allowed for the identification of points of frustration and satisfaction experienced by users when searching for and acquiring spare parts. With the Empathy Map, the system design was focused on providing solutions that addressed the emotional and functional needs of the users, enhancing their experience by reducing uncertainty and increasing their confidence in the platform. The empathy map is in Spanish because it was made in the Peruvian context. (see Fig. 2)

Journey Map. The Journey Map was essential for mapping the user's entire journey, from the moment they perceive the need for spare parts for their vehicle to the point of acquiring the appropriate part. This tool helped identify the different phases of user interaction with the system, such as exploration, consideration, and purchase. Each of these phases was accompanied by an analysis of the user's emotions, which helped pinpoint critical points where users might experience frustration, such as during the selection phase if the results were unclear or delayed. Additionally, the Journey Map highlighted moments of user satisfaction, such as when they found the desired spare part quickly at a transparent price. The Journey Map is in Spanish because it was made in the Peruvian Context. (see Fig. 3)

3.2 System Design and Development

Prototype. The prototyping phase of the system design was an essential step in ensuring the solution's effectiveness and user-friendliness. Using a user-centered design approach, the prototype was developed with iterative testing and feedback, employing the previously mentioned tools, such as the User Persona, Empathy Map, and Journey Map, to ensure that the design met the needs, expectations, and pain points of the target users.

By incorporating insights gained from these tools, the prototype was structured to offer intuitive navigation, easy accessibility, and seamless user interactions, facilitating the process of recommending automotive parts. The color scheme of the system, which prominently features shades of blue and gray, was carefully chosen based on color psychology principles to enhance the overall user experience.

The design of the prototype was directly influenced by the user insights gathered through the User Persona, Empathy Map, and Journey Map. These tools provided valuable information on the users' expectations, desires, and emotional responses, which were then used to tailor the interface. For instance, knowing that the target user values

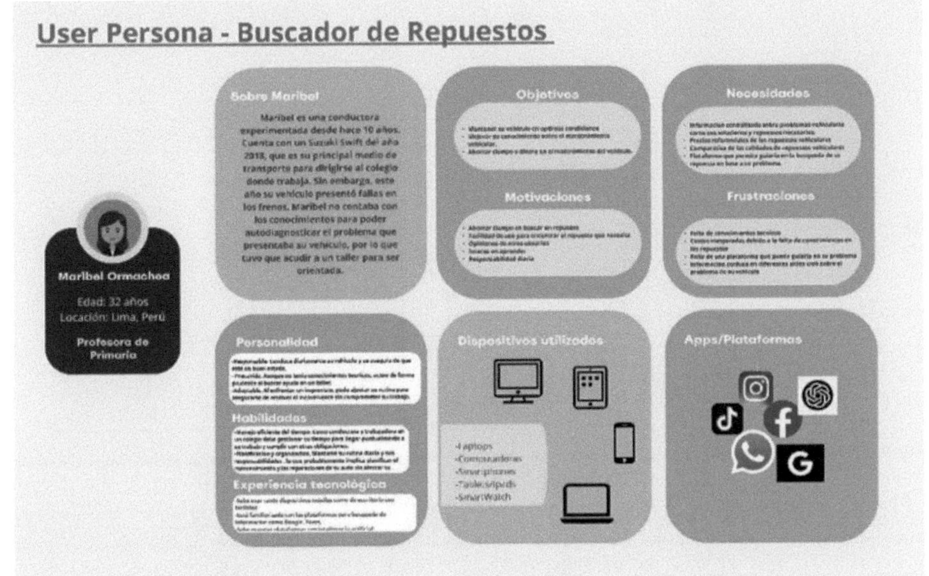

Fig. 3. User Persona.

ease of use and fast access to information, the system was designed with clear sections, simple navigation, and quick search capabilities, all of which help streamline the process of finding auto parts.

Additionally, the Journey Map helped in outlining the key steps that users would take while interacting with the system, ensuring that each stage of their journey, from accessing the platform to receiving product recommendations, was optimized for a seamless experience.

The integration of colors was based on color psychology principles, with blue chosen as the primary color due to its associations with trust, security, and calmness. This color conveys reliability and stability, making it an ideal choice for applications that aim to provide a professional and dependable experience. Additionally, blue is widely used in the automotive industry, which makes it even more suitable for a vehicle-related app, conveying familiarity and connection with the automotive environment.

Gray, as the secondary color, was selected for its ability to convey neutrality, balance, and sophistication. Gray is a subtle color that doesn't compete for attention but adds seriousness and professionalism. Its soft presence perfectly complements blue, creating a harmonious atmosphere centered around the user experience without detracting from the app's key elements [6].

In conclusion, the prototyping and design of the system incorporated not only user feedback and insights but also psychological principles that align with human behavior, making the system not only functional but also appealing and engaging to users. This multi-faceted approach ensured the creation of a user-friendly, professional, and aesthetically pleasing platform for vehicle part recommendations.

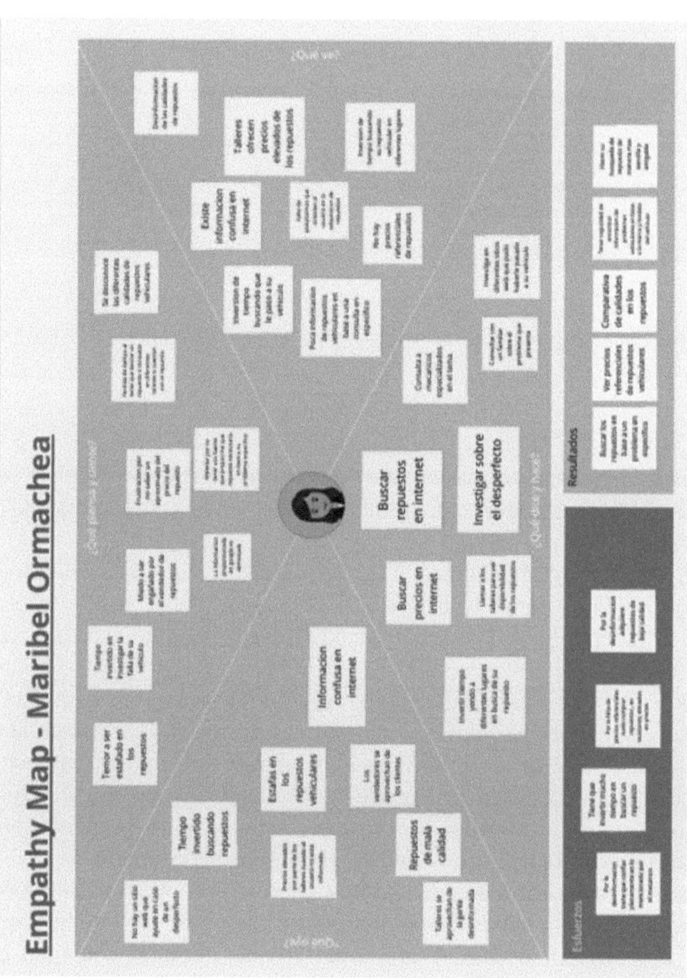

Fig. 4. Empathy Map.

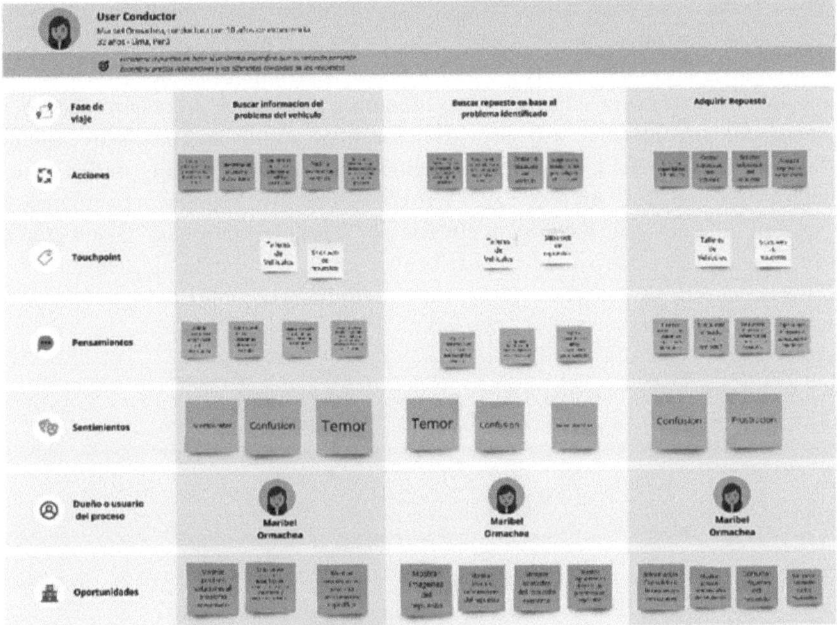

Fig. 5. Journey Map.

Software Development. The software development process focused on meeting the requirements established in the initial phase of the project, prioritizing user needs and optimizing the interactive experience. For this purpose, a Progressive Web Application (PWA) was chosen, a solution that offers significant advantages over traditional applications. PWAs combine the best of both web and mobile applications, allowing users to access the platform from any device without the need to install it. Additionally, PWAs provide a faster, more reliable, and accessible user experience, even under limited connectivity conditions, thanks to their ability to function offline or on slow networks. This ensures the system's accessibility across different devices without compromising performance [7].

The system was designed to allow users to save their favorite vehicle (see Fig. 4), creating a personalized profile that facilitates the query of spare parts and related services. Through this feature, users can quickly access specific information about their vehicle and make queries based on their particular needs. Moreover, the system provides the ability to search for spare parts through an optimized search, improving the efficiency of users in locating specific parts for their vehicles.

Regarding the interface, an intuitive and user-friendly design was developed, focused on user experience. One of the key features is the option to rotate the vehicle interactively, allowing users to view and select the necessary spare parts based on different parts of the vehicle (see Fig. 5). This visual and dynamic approach enhances interaction and makes it easier to identify the required components, contributing to a smoother and more understandable experience. Overall, the system offers a user-friendly interface that allows users to perform actions efficiently, enhancing the overall functionality and usability of the system.

Additionally, a chatbot interface and a voice assistant were integrated to further enhance user interaction (see Fig. 6). These features allow users to obtain recommendations in a simple and intuitive way, providing a conversational and hands-free method to access information about spare parts and vehicle needs. By engaging in dialogue with the chatbot or voice assistant (see Fig. 7), users can receive tailored recommendations, ask questions, and navigate the system effortlessly. This integration of AI-powered assistance ensures a more accessible and user-centric experience, making it easier for users to find the necessary parts and services without requiring complex navigation or manual searches (Figs. 8 and 9).

Fig. 6. Main Screen.

In conclusion, AutoPro provides an innovative solution for users seeking an efficient and intuitive way to manage their vehicle maintenance needs. By utilizing advanced technologies such as PWA, AI-driven chatbots, and voice assistants, the system simplifies the process of finding and purchasing vehicle spare parts. The platform's features, including saving favorite vehicles and accessing personalized recommendations, offer a seamless user experience. Ultimately, AutoPro aims to streamline vehicle repairs, reduce complexity, and enhance the overall user experience, positioning itself as a valuable tool for vehicle owners.

Fig. 7. Vehicle view.

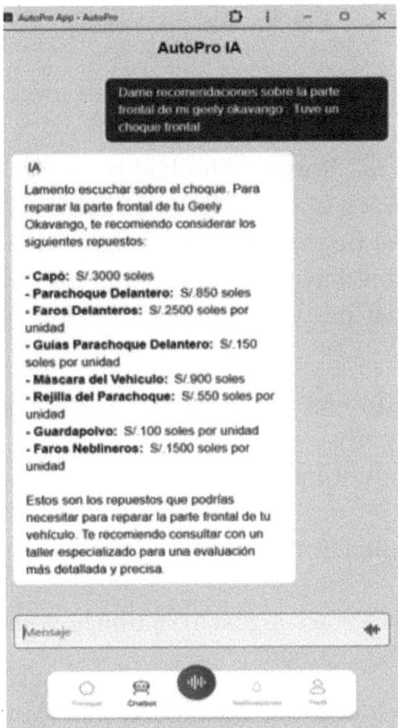

Fig. 8. Chatbot.

Fig. 9. Voice Assistant.

3.3   Results

In this final phase, we selected 8 users who had been previously identified during the earlier stage of the project. Each of them was presented with the product and introduced to two specific scenarios: the first involved searching for a spare part and obtaining its price, while the second required using the chatbot in the event of an accident with their vehicle. Based on these scenarios, we formulated four key questions to evaluate the user experience:

- How easy was it for you to find the spare part and obtain pricing information using the application? (see Fig. 10)
- How would you rate the usefulness and speed of the chatbot in assisting you during an accident? (see Fig. 11)
- Do you consider the application's interface intuitive and easy to navigate in both scenarios? (see Fig. 12)
- What improvements would you suggest to optimize your experience when searching for spare parts or using the chatbot?

Based on the responses obtained, we concluded that AutoPro is an application that provides significant value in the process of searching for vehicle spare parts, as well as comparing prices with different mechanical workshops. Users highlighted how easy it was to identify the exact part they needed, reducing the risk of purchasing incorrect or incompatible components for their vehicles.

Furthermore, the ability to compare prices in real time with different suppliers and workshops offers greater transparency in the purchasing process, allowing users to make informed decisions and ensuring that costs are fair and competitive. This combination of search precision and price comparison clarity not only optimizes the user experience but also helps build trust in the platform. In this way, AutoPro serves as a useful tool that facilitates and streamlines the management of spare parts, helping users find the best option according to their needs.

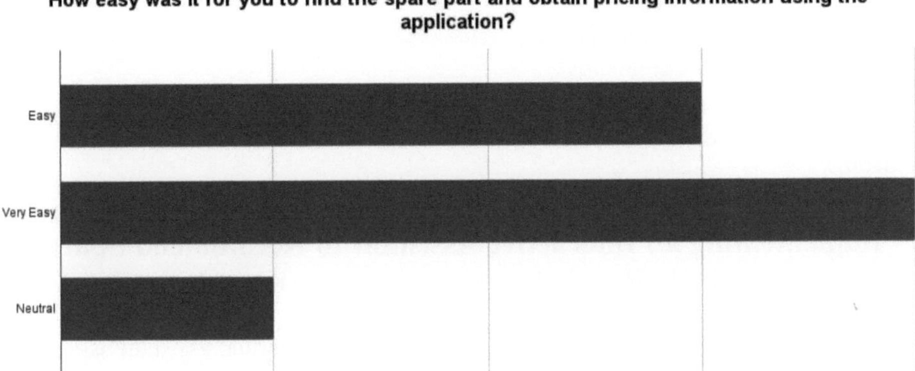

Fig. 10. How easy was it for you to find the spare part and obtain pricing information using the application?

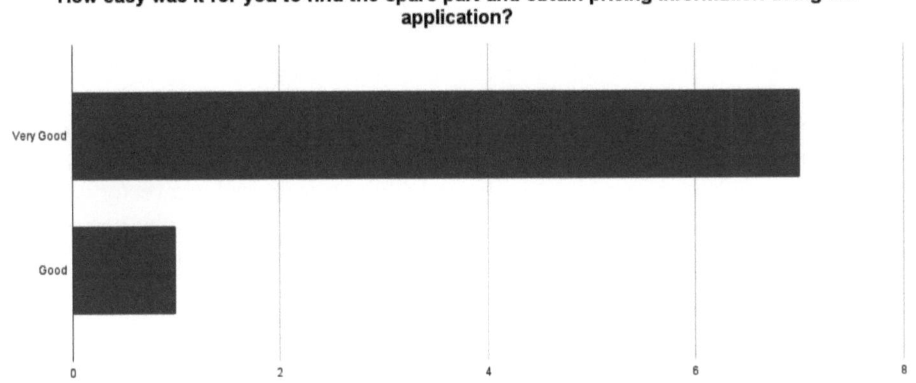

Fig. 11. How would you rate the usefulness and speed of the chatbot in assisting you during an accident?

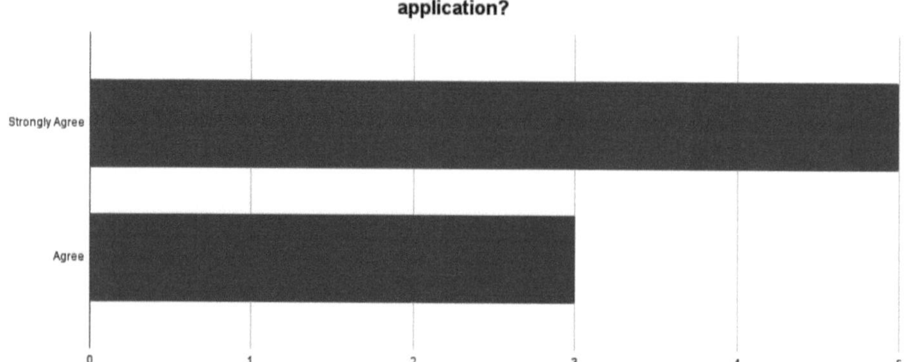

Fig. 12. Do you consider the application's interface intuitive and easy to navigate in both scenarios?

4 Implementing an Interactive Assistant to Recommend Spare Parts for Vehicle Repair Based on Current Knowledge Base.

In this section, we describe the process of implementing a virtual assistant using OpenAI's GPT-4 model, integrated with a previously developed knowledge base. The Retrieval-Augmented Generation (RAG) methodology was adopted, which combines the retrieval of relevant information from a database with the generation of text from language models. The system is composed of two key components: the Retrieval Component and the Generator Component.

The Retrieval Component's main task is to retrieve relevant information from the knowledge base. To do so, document preprocessing is carried out, where texts extracted from various sources are segmented into semantically coherent fragments of approximately 1,000 characters (see Fig. 13). This segmentation optimizes information retrieval. The fragments are then transformed into vector embeddings using embedding models such as OpenAI's text-embedding-3-large and Meta AI's nomic-embed-text model, both adapted to the needs of the project [8]. The embeddings are stored in a vector database, ChromaDB (see Fig. 14), allowing for similarity searches based on the cosine similarity technique, which assesses the semantic closeness between user queries and text fragments [9].

The Generator Component is responsible for generating the answers from the retrieved information. To evaluate the effectiveness of the RAG system, a structured dataset was designed, including questions, answers, context, and references, thus allowing for accurate evaluation of the virtual assistant's performance [10].

Regarding the infrastructure, a server instance on AWS was used for testing, with sufficient resources to run the models on a large scale. The libraries and frameworks used include OPENAI for language model integration and Langchain to manage the interaction between the model and the database.

The evaluation of the system was carried out using key metrics such as Context Recall, Context Precision, Answer Relevancy, and Semantic Similarity, comparing the performance of the GPT-4 and LLAMA 3 models. The results favored the GPT-4 model, particularly for its ability to generate accurate and consistent responses. This choice was influenced by the superiority in the metrics and by the computational resources available for the project (see Fig. 15).

Finally, the integration of the GPT-4 model with the knowledge base and the system was facilitated by Langchain, which efficiently connected the model to the ChromaDB database, optimizing the process of retrieving and generating responses. This allowed the creation of a robust and effective system for the virtual assistant, improving interaction with the user and the accuracy of the responses generated.

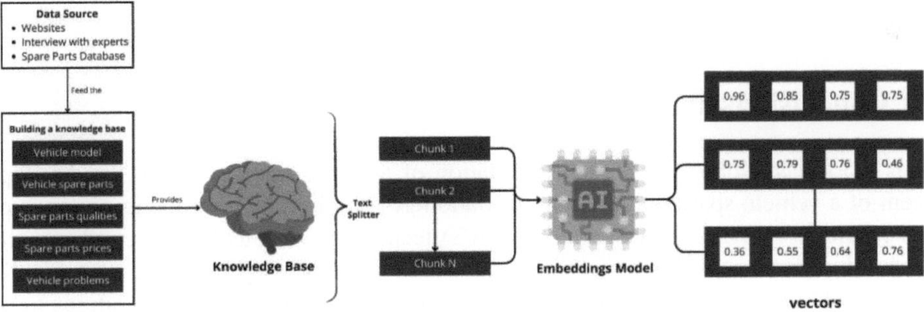

Fig. 13. Extraction and model of Embeddings.

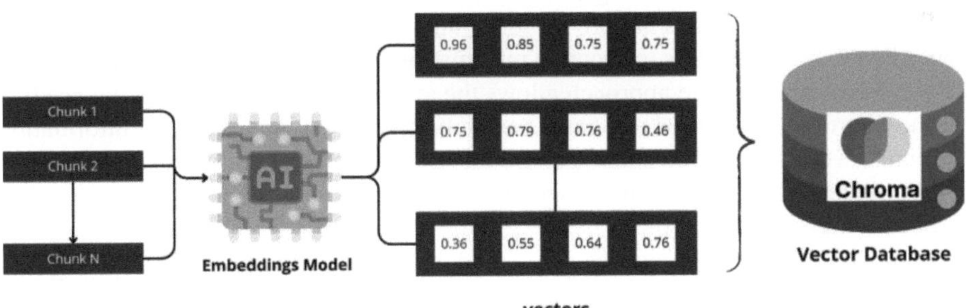

Fig. 14. Store in ChromaDB.

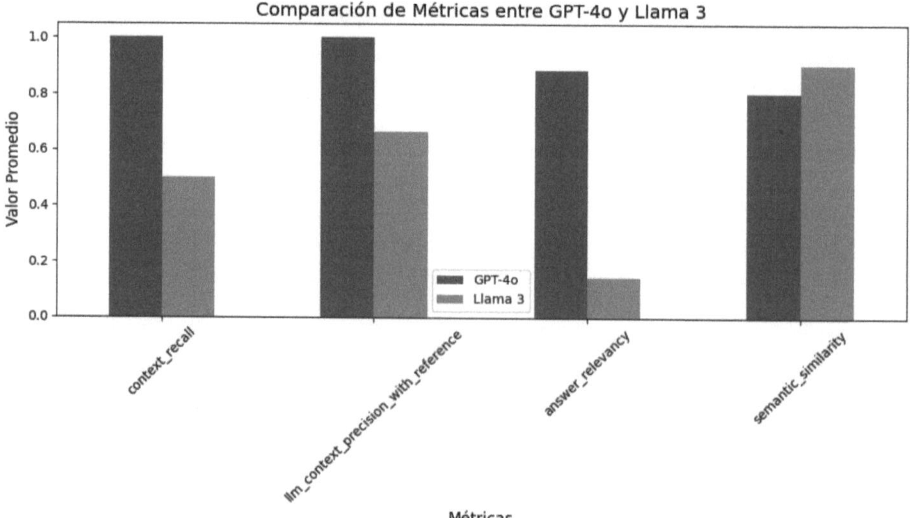

Fig. 15. Metrics about GPT-4o vs. Llama 3.

5   Conclusions and Future Work

This work has addressed the implementation of artificial intelligence in the development of a vehicle spare parts recommendation system, highlighting the importance of the Retrieval-Augmented Generation (RAG) technique. This technique combines the retrieval of information from relevant databases with the generation of contextually appropriate responses, allowing for accurate and personalized recommendations to be offered to users. By integrating an information retrieval model with a generative model, the system not only obtains data from a structured knowledge base, but also generates responses in real time, improving user interaction and experience.

The application of RAG has proven to be fundamental in transforming the user experience by facilitating access to accurate information on spare parts, prices and suppliers. This dynamic and flexible approach allows the system to adapt to the specific needs of each user, providing detailed responses that go beyond simply searching for information.

Future work in this area could explore the use of advanced real-time models, which will significantly improve the user experience in interactive systems. Real-time models, particularly those used in voice assistants, allow for more fluid and natural communication. Unlike traditional approaches, these models are able to process information instantaneously, adapting to user interactions with a more dynamic and less structured tone of voice. This evolution not only improves the accuracy of responses, but also optimizes the user interface (UX/UI), making interactions more fluid, natural, and personalized.

In conclusion, the RAG technique, combined with real-time response models, represents a promising avenue for improving intelligent systems, allowing them to better adapt to user needs. As these technologies continue to evolve, interactive experiences are expected to become increasingly richer, natural, and efficient.

References

1. Asociación Automotriz del Perú. Informe del sector Automotor 2023 [Archivo PDF] (2023). https://aap.org.pe/informes-estadisticos/diciembre-2022/Informe-Diciembre-2022.pdf

2. Muñiz Galdo, H. B.: Determinación de las Dificultades que Tienen los Clientes en la Elección de Tiendas de Autopartes en Lima Metropolitana en el Año 2020 [Tesis de licenciatura]. Universidad de Lima (2021)

3. Asociación Automotriz del Perú. Más de 70,000 talleres mecánicos necesitan capacitación en nuevas tecnologías (2021). https://aap.org.pe/aap-mas-de-70000-talleres-mecanicos-nec esitan-capacitacion-en-nuevas-tecnologias/

4. Nandhini Devi, S., Shiny, A., Sureshbabu, J., Mahalakshmi, S., Sundara Bala Murugan, P., Priya, R.: User persona mapping technique for human interaction with augmented and virtual reality environments. In: Proceedings of the 2023 International Conference on Self Sustainable Artificial Intelligence Systems (ICSSAS)., October 18–20. IEEE, Erode, India (2023). https://doi.org/10.1109/ICSSAS57918.2023.10331765

5. Krayz Allah, K., Ismail, N.A., Elrobaa, H.: Empathy map instrument for Analyzing human-computer interaction in using web search UI by elderly users. In: Proceedings of the 2021 International Congress of Advanced Technology and Engineering (ICOTEN), July 4–5, Taiz, Yemen. IEEE (2021). https://doi.org/10.1109/ICOTEN52080.2021.9493548

6. Heller, E.: Psicología del color: cómo actúan los colores sobre los sentimientos y la razón. Gustavo Gili (2004). ISBN 84–252–1977-9.

7. Mhatre, A., Mali, S.: Progressive web applications, a new way for faster testing of Mobile application products. In: 2023 3rd Asian Conference on Innovation in Technology (ASIAN-CON), Ravet IN, India, pp. 1–6 (2023). https://doi.org/10.1109/ASIANCON58793.2023.102 69806

8. Patel, H.N., Goel, P., Surti, A.: A comparative analysis of large language models with retrieval-augmented generation-based question answering system. In: Proceedings of the IEEE I-SMAC Conference (2024)

9. Patel, H.N., Goel, P., Surti, A.: A comparative analysis of large language models with retrieval-augmented generation-based question answering system. In: Proceedings of the IEEE I-SMAC Conference (2024)

10. Filipovska, E., Mladenovska, A., Bajrami, M., Dobreva, J., Hillman, V.: Benchmarking Ope-nAI's APIs and other large language models for repeatable and efficient question answering across multiple documents. In: Proceedings of the FedCSIS Conference (2024)

Exploring How Generative AI Enhances Information Comprehension

Shang-Fang Hsu[1]($\boxtimes$), Chia-Han Yang[1], and Mohammad Shidujaman[2]

[1] Institute of Creative Industries Design, National Cheng Kung University, Tainan, Taiwan
B14994026@gs.ncku.edu.tw, chyang@mail.ncku.edu.tw
[2] Department of Computer Science and Engineering, Independent University, Bangladesh (IUB), Dhaka, Bangladesh
Shidujaman@iub.edu.bd

Abstract. This study explores the application of Generative Artificial Intelligence (GAI) tools, such as SCISPACE and ChatGPT, in enhancing reading comprehension and addressing challenges like cognitive load, limited vocabulary, and reduced motivation. While previous research has highlighted the transformative potential of AI in education, there remains a significant gap in understanding how GAI specifically alleviates barriers to effective reading comprehension. Using a qualitative case study approach, this research evaluates SCISPACE's summarization capabilities in academic texts and ChatGPT's interactive learning features. The findings reveal that these tools effectively reduce cognitive load, provide instant feedback, and transform passive reading into interactive learning experiences, thereby enhancing user comprehension and engagement. However, challenges such as algorithmic biases and the oversimplification of complex content persist. This study underscores the transformative potential of GAI in education and emphasizes the need for further research to optimize these tools for diverse learning environments.

Keywords: Generative Artificial Intelligence · reading comprehension · SCISPACE · ChatGPT · personalized learning

1 Introduction

This investigation concentrates on how generative artificial intelligence (GAI) can assist readers in achieving a successful reading comprehension experience. In previous studies, the ability to assimilate substantial quantities of scholarly text rapidly and efficiently is an essential competency that not all learners in higher education have yet perfected [1]. Some prior investigations have extensively examined the concern of reading comprehension difficulties across diverse cohorts [2] [3] and various modalities [4]. The researchers have raised several reasons to explain the cause of reading comprehension difficulties, including poor

© The Author(s), under exclusive license to Springer Nature Switzerland AG 2026
M. Kurosu and A. Hashizume (Eds.): HCII 2025, LNCS 16332, pp. 277–294, 2026.
https://doi.org/10.1007/978-3-032-12385-5_17

language comprehension, lack of vocabulary understanding [5], and other issues, such as no motivation and burnout [3]. Nevertheless, the advent of GAI tools has introduced innovative strategies to address the challenges associated with reading comprehension deficiencies. As scholars note, a significant implementation of AI within educational frameworks facilitates personalized learning [6]. Through the integration of AI technologies, it has become feasible to offer tailored guidance or assistance to individual learners, predicated on their unique learning performances and requirements. Consequently, prior investigations into artificial intelligence in education (AIED) primarily focused on leveraging AI technologies to bolster learners' memorization, comprehension, application, analysis, and evaluation capabilities. [7] In this background, this study investigates how GAI can function as a personalized tutor to enhance reading comprehension. By addressing common barriers such as limited vocabulary, language comprehension challenges, and a lack of motivation, GAI offers a novel approach to overcoming these difficulties. Building on prior research in AIED, this study aims to explore the potential of GAI to deliver tailored, interactive support for learners, thereby improving their ability to assimilate complex textual information. Through empirical analysis, the research will examine how GAI-based tools can transform traditional reading practices, providing insights into their effectiveness, limitations, and implications for future educational strategies.

2   Literature Review

2.1   The Challenges of Reading Comprehension in the Digital Age

It is increasingly acknowledged across various academic and professional circles that artificial intelligence possesses the potential to contribute and fundamentally transform the landscape of education, indicating that its integration into learning environments is both imminent and essential. However, to the best of our knowledge, there appears to be a lack of comprehensive research studies explicitly focusing on applying AI technology to enhance reading and comprehension abilities among learners [8].

The dissemination of information can indeed take place through written text; however, it is imperative to acknowledge that numerous obstacles hinder readers from effectively deciphering the conveyed messages. Notwithstanding the transformative impact that advancements in technology have on the organization of society, it remains a certainty that individuals will continually need to engage with a diverse array of texts, and thus, the ability to comprehend written material will likely remain an essential skill for the foreseeable future.

Even in a scenario where we may possess advanced instruments capable of converting written texts into spoken words, we may succeed in bypassing the intricacies of decoding; however, we will still encounter challenges in the comprehension of the content itself. Moreover, even if the advent of multimedia communication significantly diminishes the reliance on traditional written texts, the necessity for reading comprehension will undeniably play a critical role in the effective processing of messages conveyed through alternative media formats.

Understanding text files displayed on a computer monitor will not only entail specific processes that capture the reader's interest but will also engage a multitude of other cognitive processes that overlap with those traditionally required for interpreting written texts [9].

Ultimately, it becomes abundantly clear that the fundamental skills associated with reading comprehension will continue to be of paramount importance, regardless of the medium through which information is transmitted. Thus, we must recognize that while the methods of communication may evolve, the core competencies related to understanding written language will remain a vital aspect of human interaction with text in all its forms.

2.2   Communication Process and Funnel Model

This scholarly investigation is fundamentally grounded in the framework of the information and communication process; as elucidated by Gupta, the process can be characterized as a reciprocal two-way interaction that inherently involves both a sender and a receiver, each playing a critical role in the exchange. In the definition provided by Gupta [10], it is articulated that two or more individuals engage in a dynamic interaction where they not only share but also significantly influence one another's ideas, beliefs, and attitudes through various means. He also lists the seven elements of the communication process, including sender, ideas, encoding, communication channel, receiver, decoding and feedback (Fig. 1).

This interaction can manifest in numerous forms, as individuals are capable of exchanging information by employing an array of communicative techniques, which may include, but are not limited to, the use of spoken and written words, deliberate gestures, symbolic signs, and various expressions that convey meaning and intent, thus enriching the communicative exchange [11]. The multifaceted nature of this process underscores the profound complexity of human interaction, highlighting the intricate ways in which communication occurs and the impact it has on the participants involved in this elaborate exchange of information.

In encoding and decoding messages, errors or information loss may occur, as described by the communication funnel theory. This theory posits that as messages are conveyed through language, they gradually diminish in clarity and completeness due to various interfering factors (Fig. 2). Drawing on this framework, this study infers that lengthy and complex textual messages are similarly prone to degradation at the reader's end, where such interference factors contribute to difficulties in reading comprehension. It is further hypothesized that GAI can mitigate the risk of misinterpretation or information loss during transmission, enhancing message accuracy and effectiveness.

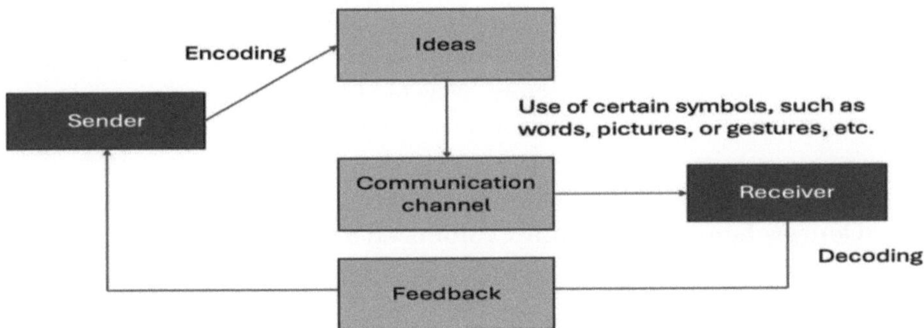

Fig. 1. Information and Communication Process (Adapted from Gupta, 2021).

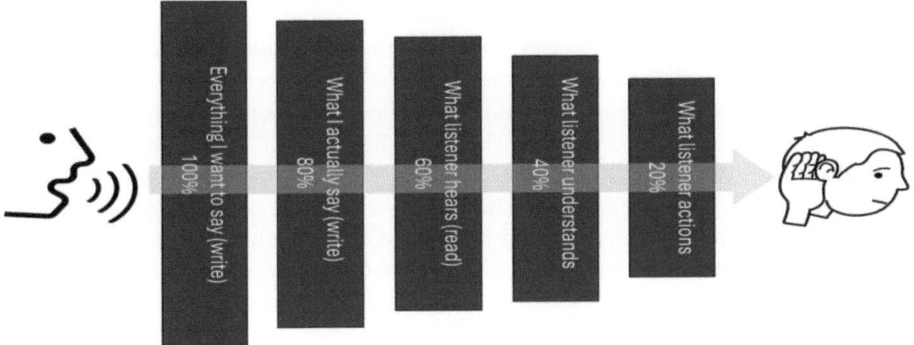

Fig. 2. Communication Funnel Problems (adapted from Qifeng, 2019).

2.3   Using GAI to Enhance Reading Comprehension

As Schüller-Zwierlein et al. [12] note, empirical data indicates that the current media environment does not support developing and enhancing reading skills. Although the total amount of reading has not decreased, the forms of engagement have evolved. A substantial portion of modern reading transpires through digital screens. The complex characteristics and diverse standards of digital interfaces, combined with the omnipresence of online information, have increasingly dominated our cognitive framework, overshadowing traditional media's enduring significance and consumption. A plethora of new reading contexts (such as interacting with a tweet and subsequently sharing it or responding to alerts triggered by push notifications) has arisen, necessitating modifications in established reading behaviors to adapt to the intensified tempo of both personal and professional lives experienced over recent decades, along with escalating time pressures. The immediacy and speed associated with digital media favor transmitting information in concise segments, consequently fragmenting the reading experience. The swift ascendance of digital media and online platforms has led to an augmented dependence on reading as extensive portions of daily existence are digitized, thereby increasingly relying on digital text [13]. However, whether scholars read the literature or general readers watch new letters, advertisements, or any information through the screen. New GAI tools claim to help readers get information more effectively. Some of those serve as chatbots.

2.4 Examples: AI Summarization Tools–Enhancing Content Comprehension Through Condensed Information

AI summarization tools are advanced software systems designed to condense textual content into more concise and refined formats while retaining all critical information. These tools let readers grasp the essence of lengthy publications or research papers without perusing the entire document [14]. By leveraging sophisticated algorithms, AI summarizers extract critical sentences from a text and generate succinct summaries. These tools are handy for applications such as coursework, academic papers, and even video content, allowing users to understand the essential elements of a work quickly. This functionality aids in determining whether a more in-depth reading of the whole content is warranted.

In our exploration, we employ the GAI instrument known as SCISPACE while diligently adhering to the fundamental research methodology to meticulously assess the extent to which this advanced tool can assist users in navigating a vast array of informational resources; furthermore, we investigate how the reading comprehension facilitated by the GAI tool can empower users to develop their unique perspectives and nuanced understanding of the material encountered.

(1) **Find Topic:** In identifying a pertinent research topic, one may effectively utilize open-ended inquiries, notably "How" and "What" questions, which facilitate a deeper exploration of the subject matter. For instance, the investigator posed the thought-provoking inquiry, "How does generative artificial intelligence enhance the precision and reliability of information retrieval and processing mechanisms?" In five seconds, this investigation yielded a comprehensive summary of the relevant topics derived from various scholarly articles. Furthermore, this methodology also proposes three additional related inquiries for the benefit of users, as illustrated in Fig. 3.

The complimentary edition of SCISPACE, which is accessible at no monetary cost to users, offers a concise summary encompassing five distinct topics pertinent to the posed question, thereby facilitating a foundational understanding of the subject matter. Furthermore, it is important to note that this version also extends its utility by presenting additional in-depth information and relevant literary sources, as illustrated in Fig. 4 below.

(2) **Literature Review.** The process of conducting a literature review is an intricate and demanding undertaking that necessitates a considerable amount of effort, which includes, but is not limited to, the thorough reading and meticulous summarization of a diverse array of scholarly texts and sources. The utilization of

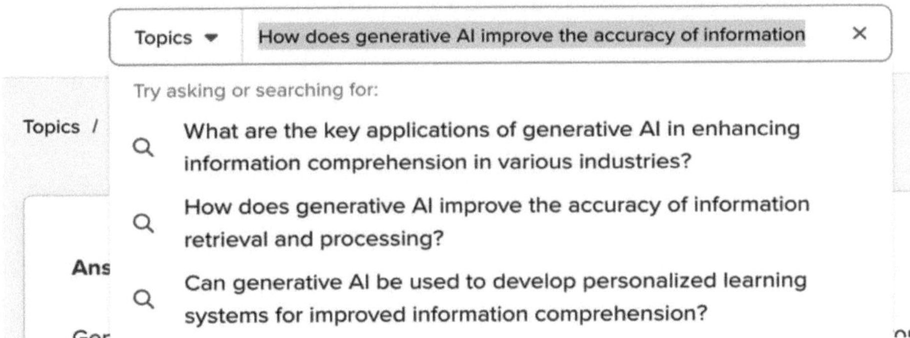

Fig. 3. Communication Funnel Problems (adapted from Qifeng, 2019).

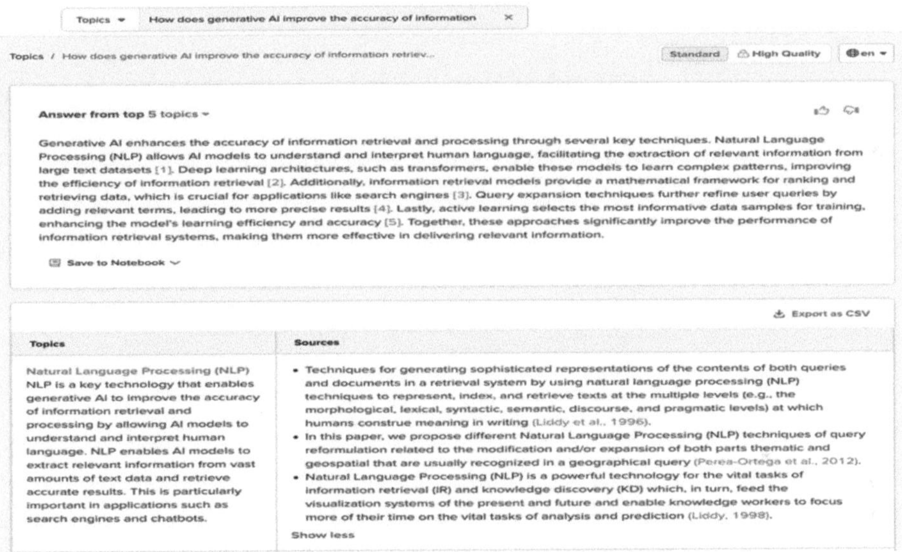

Fig. 4. SCISPACE topic summarization.

a GAI tool aids users by expediting the categorization process, thereby allowing for a more efficient organization and analysis of the vast amounts of information typically encountered during academic research. The same research question is put, and the result is as follows (Fig. 5): Furthermore, it can exhibit a concise overview of the pertinent scholarly articles associated with the specific selections made by users when they opt to extract information from the available sources (Fig. 6).

(3) Chat with PDF. This functionality is designed to significantly enhance the comprehension of intricate and multifaceted academic research papers, thereby

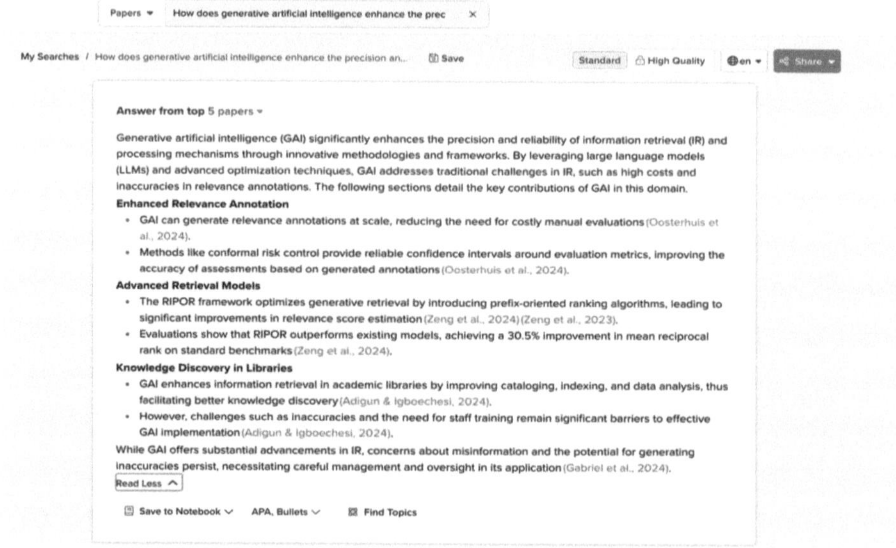

Fig. 5. SCISPACE topic summarization.

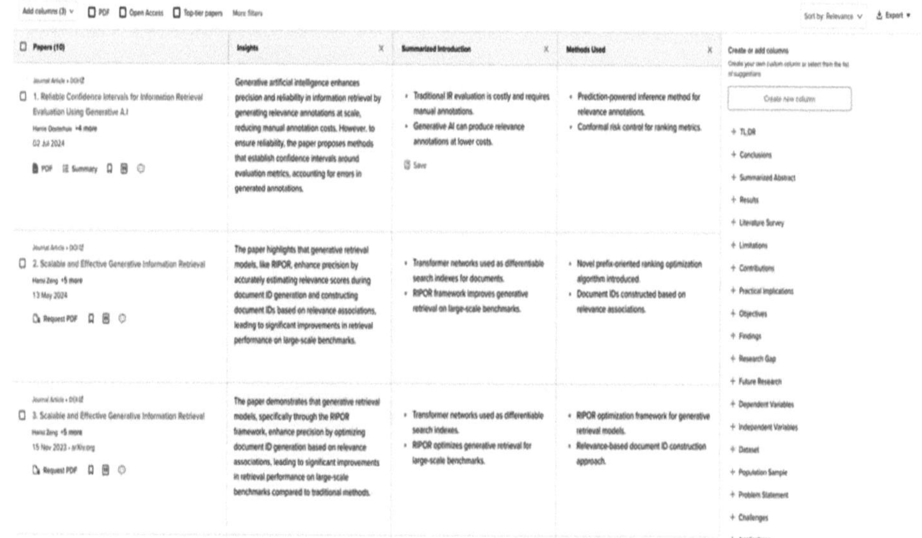

Fig. 6. SCISPACE topic summarization.

facilitating a clearer and more accessible presentation of the information in these scholarly documents for the reader (Fig. 7).

Readers can engage with the research paper more effectively by utilizing the interactive features of the GAI tool. This functionality allows users to pose

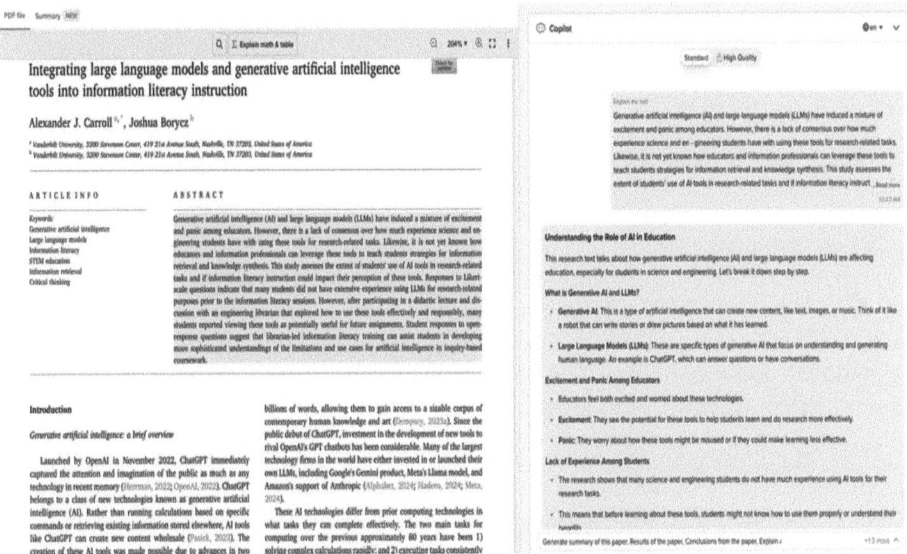

Fig. 7. SCISPACE topic summarization.

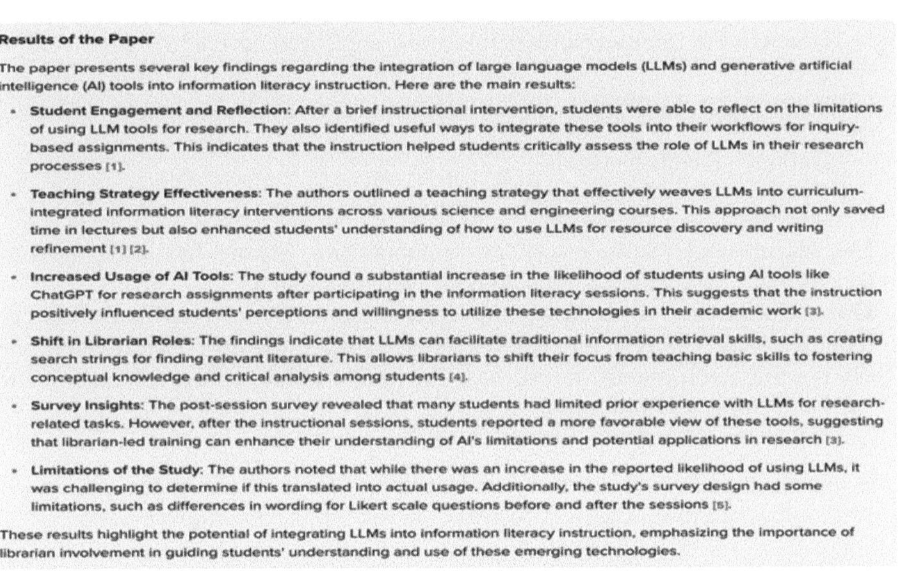

Fig. 8. SCISPACE topic summarization.

specific, targeted questions about the paper's content, enabling them to obtain precise and relevant answers directly related to their inquiries. In addition to providing a clear and concise response, the tool highlights the exact location of the information within the research paper, ensuring that users can easily refer to the original context for a deeper understanding. This dual capability facilitates efficient navigation through complex texts and enhances the user's ability to analyze and cross-reference information within the document (Fig. 8).

3 Research Methods

This study employs a qualitative case analysis methodology to examine how GAI tools can enhance reading comprehension by addressing key challenges such as cognitive load, language complexity, and engagement. The research focuses on two GAI tools: SCISPACE and ChatGPT. These tools were selected due to their distinct functional capabilities and broad application potential in facilitating readers' understanding of complex textual information. The methodological framework comprises the following steps:

- **Tool Selection:** SCISPACE and ChatGPT were chosen based on their complementary functionalities in summarization and interactive reading support, respectively. This dual focus enables a comprehensive analysis of their applications in varied reading contexts.
- **Application Contexts:** Specific scenarios were defined to demonstrate the tools' utility:
  - SCISPACE's summarization feature was applied to academic literature.
  - ChatGPT's interactive features were employed to engage with complex texts.
- **Comparative Analysis:** Both tools were analyzed in terms of their ability to:
  - Enhance comprehension.
  - Provide tailored information.
  - Support user engagement.
  Key features such as interactivity, segmentation, instant feedback, personalization, and motivational engagement were examined.
- **Data Collection and Analysis:** Outputs generated by the tools were systematically reviewed to identify patterns, highlighting how each tool supports the reading comprehension process. The analysis focuses on their ability to:
  - Facilitate understanding.
  - Improve information accessibility.

This approach provides a structured framework for evaluating the role of GAI in overcoming common barriers to effective reading and comprehension.

3.1 Case Introduction

GAI tools have revolutionized how readers engage with and comprehend complex information. Among these tools, SCISPACE and ChatGPT have emerged as prominent examples, offering distinct yet complementary functionalities tailored to diverse user needs. Both tools have been designed to address challenges associated with reading comprehension, such as information overload, cognitive complexity, and engagement barriers, making them valuable resources in academic and professional contexts [15].

1. **SCISPACE:**
   Facilitating Information Extraction through Summarization SCISPACE is a GAI-powered summarization tool specializing in condensing complex textual content into concise, structured formats. Designed primarily for academic and research contexts, SCISPACE identifies critical elements within texts and presents them as manageable summaries.

- **Application Scenario:** SCISPACE was applied to academic literature, such as research articles and reports, to evaluate its ability to streamline the reading process for scholars. Users accessed lengthy publications (e.g., multi-page research articles) and relied on SCISPACE to:
  - Extract key findings.
  - Summarize objectives.
  - Outline methodologies in a significantly reduced format.
- **Functionality:** The tool employs natural language processing algorithms to:
  - Extract critical sentences.
  - Generate comprehensive overviews.

  This feature allows users to quickly grasp the essence of a document, facilitating efficient decision-making on whether to engage in deeper reading.
- **Impact on Reading Comprehension:** The summarized outputs:
  - Significantly reduced cognitive load.
  - Saved time spent processing extensive textual data.
  - Improved accessibility to key insights.

  Users reported these benefits as valuable for facilitating academic tasks and research planning.

2. **ChatGPT:**
   Transforming Passive Reading into Interactive Engagement ChatGPT, an advanced conversational AI tool, provides an interactive platform for engaging with textual content. Enabling real-time dialogue transforms reading into a participatory process where users can clarify concepts, ask targeted questions, and receive tailored explanations.

- **Application Scenario:** ChatGPT was applied to dense academic materials, such as technical reports and research papers. Users engaged with the tool by:
  - Posing specific questions regarding methodologies, theoretical frameworks, and terminologies.
  - Enhancing their understanding of the content through tailored interactions.
- **Functionality:** ChatGPT's ability to generate human-like responses enables it to:
  - Simulate the experience of interacting with a tutor.
  - Adapt to user queries by providing detailed, context-aware explanations.
  - Direct users to relevant text sections for further clarification.

- **Impact on Reading Comprehension:** The interactive nature of Chat-GPT:
  - Promoted deeper engagement with the material.
  - Enabled users to address ambiguities in real-time.
  - Encouraged active participation, fostering a deeper understanding of complex topics.

SCISPACE is a GAI-powered summarization tool that enables users to condense lengthy and intricate texts into concise and accessible summaries. By extracting key sentences and highlighting essential ideas, SCISPACE enhances readers' ability to quickly identify relevant information without delving into the entire document. Its functionality suits academic and research settings, where time efficiency and cognitive focus are crucial. SCISPACE facilitates a streamlined reading process and empowers users to manage extensive reading material effectively. Conversely, ChatGPT is an interactive reading assistant that utilizes conversational AI to help users navigate complex textual content. Unlike static summarization tools, ChatGPT enables dynamic interaction by answering user-specific queries, clarifying complex concepts, and tailoring responses to individual learning styles. This interactivity transforms reading from a passive activity into an active and participatory process, fostering deeper engagement and comprehension. ChatGPT's ability to adapt to diverse user needs makes it a versatile tool for addressing personalized reading challenges in various contexts.

Together, SCISPACE and ChatGPT exemplify the transformative potential of GAI in enhancing reading comprehension. While SCISPACE focuses on simplifying information through concise summarization, ChatGPT emphasizes personalized and interactive learning experiences. This study investigates the unique contributions of these tools to reading comprehension, highlighting their respective strengths and exploring their implications for future educational and professional practices [16].

3.2   Thematic Analysis and Proposition

The thematic analysis identifies key dimensions of conversational AI chatbots that enhance reading comprehension and address common barriers, such as cognitive overload, engagement issues, and lack of personalization. By focusing on interactivity, segmentation, instant feedback, personalization, and motivational engagement, this analysis illustrates how tools like ChatGPT and SCISPACE contribute to a more effective and accessible reading process.

Proposition 1: Conversational AI chatbots enhance reading comprehension by transforming static content into interactive learning experiences.

The shift from passive to active engagement is a critical advancement in AI-assisted reading. ChatGPT and SCISPACE enable users to explore content dynamically, mimicking the experience of engaging with a tutor. Allowing iterative questioning and dialogic interactions fosters cognitive engagement and critical thinking [17].

Proposition 2: Conversational AI chatbots alleviate cognitive load by breaking complex information into manageable units.

Reading dense academic or technical material can overwhelm users, particularly when encountering abstract or highly detailed concepts. ChatGPT addresses this challenge by segmenting information into smaller, digestible chunks through incremental explanations. Similarly, SCISPACE simplifies comprehension by condensing texts into concise summaries, highlighting critical ideas while reducing the cognitive burden.

Proposition 3: Conversational AI chatbots provide instant feedback, addressing comprehension gaps in real-time.

Unlike traditional text, which requires readers to rely on external resources or guesswork to clarify ambiguities, chatbots like ChatGPT and SCISPACE provide immediate feedback tailored to user inquiries. This capability ensures that misunderstandings are resolved promptly, facilitating seamless comprehension and reducing frustration.

Proposition 4: Personalization in AI chatbots enhances comprehension by catering to individual user needs and preferences

ChatGPT and SCISPACE demonstrate the power of adaptive learning by tailoring responses to the specific needs of each user (Li et al., 2024). Analyzing input and adjusting to individual learning styles provides personalized guidance, making it particularly valuable for diverse audiences with varying expertise and familiarity with the subject matter.

Proposition 5: Motivational engagement through conversational AI empowers users to seek information and deepen comprehension actively.

Engagement is a critical factor in overcoming barriers to reading comprehension. ChatGPT fosters user motivation by enabling control over the flow of information, encouraging proactive exploration, and providing a conversational experience that mirrors real-world interactions. This empowerment reduces disengagement and burnout, creating a more stimulating and relatable learning environment.

By examining these dimensions through thematic analysis, the propositions out-lined above reveal the unique contributions of conversational AI chatbots to enhancing reading comprehension. The accompanying table provides a detailed breakdown of findings, themes, and codes supporting these insights.

4 Conversational AI Chatbots Facilitate Effective Message Delivery and Address Reading Comprehension Difficulties

Conversational AI chatbots offer a unique advantage in addressing reading comprehension challenges by creating an interactive, user-centered experience that enhances information accessibility and retention. Unlike traditional static texts, chatbots simulate a conversational partner capable of providing tailored responses to users' specific queries. This dynamic interaction encourages active participation, a critical element in overcoming passive information consumption, often associated with poor comprehension and retention [1].

Conversational AI chatbots' unique capabilities can be analyzed through several critical dimensions: interactivity, information segmentation, instant feedback, personalization, and motivational engagement.

4.1 Interactivity: Transforming Passive Reading Into Active Engagement

(Proposition 1)

One of the most significant advantages of conversational AI chatbots is their ability to shift the reading experience from a passive activity to an active, par-ticipatory process. Traditional texts require readers to independently decipher meaning, often leading to misunderstandings or a lack of engagement. On the other hand, chatbots allow users to ask specific questions, seek clarifications, and explore content dynamically. This interactivity fosters a sense of dialogue, enabling users to process information in a manner akin to engaging with a tutor, which has been shown to enhance comprehension by encouraging cognitive pro-cessing and critical thinking.

4.2 Segmentation: Breaking down Complexity Into Manageable Units

(Proposition 2)

Chatbots address the cognitive load of processing dense or intricate texts by breaking down information into smaller, digestible chunks. According to cogni-tive load theory, learners can only absorb limited information, particularly when dealing with abstract or technical material. Chatbots utilize advanced algorithms to summarize or highlight essential details, enabling users to focus on one concept at a time. This segmentation simplifies the material and mirrors the natural way humans learn—through incremental understanding—making it particularly effective for readers struggling with complex content.

4.3   Instant Feedback: Addressing Gaps in Real-Time (Proposition 3)

Unlike static texts, chatbots provide immediate feedback, allowing users to resolve misunderstandings or ambiguities on the spot. When a reader encounters a confusing passage in a traditional document, they must often rely on external resources or their own interpretation to make sense of it, leading to frustration and incomplete understanding. Chatbots eliminate this bottleneck by offering instant clarifications tailored to the user's inquiry. This capability ensures that gaps in comprehension are addressed before they escalate, resulting in a more seamless and effective learning experience.

4.4   Personalization: Tailoring Responses to Individual Needs

Proposition 4

A hallmark of conversational AI is its ability to adapt to the unique requirements of each user [18]. By analyzing user input and preferences, chatbots generate responses that align with the individual's learning style, pace, and prior knowledge. This level of personalization is particularly valuable for addressing diverse reading comprehension difficulties, such as limited vocabulary or varying levels of familiarity with a subject. As highlighted in research by, personalized learning approaches enabled by AI technologies significantly enhance comprehension by catering to specific user needs, making learning more accessible and impactful.

4.5   Motivational Engagement: Encouraging Proactive Information Seeking

Proposition 5

Motivation is a critical factor in overcoming reading comprehension challenges, and chatbots excel in fostering user engagement. The interactive nature of chatbots empowers readers by giving them control over the flow of information, allowing them to explore topics of interest or clarify doubts at their own pace. This empowerment creates a sense of agency, countering the disengagement and burnout often associated with lengthy or challenging texts. [3] Moreover, the conversational format mirrors real-world interactions, making the learning experience more relatable and stimulating for users.

For the proposition of the GAI used in reading comprehension, please see Table 1.

Table 1. A thematic table of GAI tools used in reading comprehension

Propositions	Findings	Theme	Codes
Proposition 1: Conversational AI chatbots enhance reading comprehension by transforming static content into interactive learning experiences.	Finding 1.1: GAI facilitates active engagement through dynamic, dialogic user interaction.	Interactivity	Real-time Q&A, Dynamic dialogue, Active participation, Cognitive engagement
	Finding 1.2: GAI supports iterative questioning, encouraging critical thinking and deeper exploration.	Active Engagement	User-driven exploration, Tutor-like assistance, Feedback loops
Proposition 2: Conversational AI chatbots alleviate cognitive load by breaking down complex information into manageable units.	Finding 2.1: GAI segments intricate texts into digestible components for easier comprehension.	Information Segmentation	Incremental learning, Concept chunking, Simplified explanations
	Finding 2.2: GAI condenses lengthy texts into concise summaries, highlighting essential points.	Cognitive Simplification	Summarization algorithms, Highlighting key information, Prioritization of critical details
Proposition 3: Conversational AI chatbots provide instant feedback, addressing comprehension gaps in real-time.	Finding 3.1: GAI offers tailored, context-aware clarifications instantly, resolving misunderstandings	Instant Feedback	Real-time query handling, Customized explanations, Error correction
Proposition 4: Personalization in AI chatbots caters to individual learning needs, improving comprehension.	Finding 4.1: GAI adapts responses to user-specific queries, enhancing relevance and user engagement.	Personalized Learning	Adaptive guidance, Individualized responses, Learning style alignment
Proposition 5: Conversational AI chatbots foster user motivation by enabling control over learning processes.	Finding 5.1: GAI empowers users to control information flow, creating a proactive learning experience.	Motivational Engagement	User autonomy, Curiosity-driven exploration, Personalized learning paths
	Finding 5.2: GAI motivates users by simplifying access to essential insights and making complex texts approachable.	Motivation through Simplicity	Streamlined access, Efficiency in comprehension, Focused academic support

5 Discussion

The findings of this research underscore the transformative potential of GAI tools, such as SCISPACE and ChatGPT, in enhancing reading comprehension in various contexts. Exploring the role of AI in education is crucial for cultivating future talent. Critical questions require thoughtful consideration and hands-on experimentation when determining what to teach, how to train effectively, and whether AI should stand as an independent discipline or integrate with others [8]. The study reveals that AI technologies can bridge gaps in traditional reading practices by offering readers interactive, personalized, and context-sensitive support. As noted in previous research, these tools address barriers such as limited vocabulary, lack of language comprehension, and reduced motivation, which have been longstanding challenges in reading comprehension.

One significant outcome of this study is demonstrating how AI tools condense complex information into concise, actionable insights. This capability is particularly valuable in academic and professional settings, where time constraints and information overload often hinder effective engagement with texts. GAI tools enhance comprehension and support critical decision-making processes by enabling users to quickly extract key ideas from extensive content.

Additionally, the ability of these tools to simulate conversational interactions introduces a new dimension to reading comprehension. GAI tools mimic the role of a personalized tutor by allowing users to pose specific questions and receive targeted responses. This interactivity encourages active engagement with the material, which has been shown to improve retention and understanding. However, this approach also relies on users' ability to formulate effective queries, which can be a limitation for less experienced readers or those unfamiliar with the subject matter. Despite their advantages, GAI tools present several challenges and limitations. For instance, while these tools excel at summarizing and condensing information, they may oversimplify complex ideas or exclude nuanced details critical in certain contexts. Moreover, algorithmic decision-making raises concerns about biases in selecting and presenting information. The study also highlights potential disparities in user experiences, as not all readers are equally adept at navigating AI interfaces or leveraging their features effectively.

6   Conclusion

This research contributes to the growing body of literature on the role of AI in education by providing empirical insights into the capabilities and limitations of GAI tools for enhancing reading comprehension. The findings suggest that while these tools offer significant benefits in terms of efficiency and accessibility, their effectiveness is contingent on several factors, including the complexity of the content, the design of the AI system, and the user's proficiency in interacting with the tool.

In conclusion, GAI tools like SCISPACE represent a promising innovation in the realm of information interpretation and communication. They have the potential to transform traditional reading practices by making complex information more accessible and engaging. However, their implementation must be accompanied by strategies to mitigate limitations, such as oversimplification and user variability. Future research should explore how these tools can be further optimized to support diverse audiences and investigate their long-term impact on learning outcomes and information-processing habits.

By leveraging the strengths of GAI tools while addressing their challenges, educators, researchers, and developers can unlock new possibilities for enhancing reading comprehension and fostering deeper engagement with textual content in the digital age.

References

1. Trudell, B.: Reading in the classroom and society: an examination of reading culture in African contexts. Int. Rev. Educ. **65**(3), 427–442 (2019)
2. Capin, P., Cho, E., Miciak, J., Roberts, G., Vaughn, S.: Examining the reading and cognitive profiles of students with significant reading comprehension difficulties. Learn. Disabil. Q. **44**(3), 183–196 (2021)
3. Torppa, M., Vasalampi, K., Eklund, K., Sulkunen, S., Niemi, P.: Reading comprehension difficulty is often distinct from difficulty in reading fluency and accompanied with problems in motivation and school well-being. Educ. Psychol. **40**(1), 62–81 (2020)
4. Tarchi, C., Zaccoletti, S., Mason, L.: Learning from text, video, or subtitles: a comparative analysis. Comput. Educ. **160**, 104034 (2021)
5. Oakhill, J., Cain, K., Elbro, C.: Reading comprehension and reading comprehension difficulties. In: Reading Development and Difficulties: Bridging the Gap Between Research and Practice, pp. 83–115 (2019)
6. Wu, Z., Ji, D., Yu, K., Zeng, X., Wu, D., Shidujaman, M.: AI creativity and the human-AI co-creation model. In: Human-computer Interaction. Theory, Methods and Tools: Thematic Area, HCI 2021, Held as Part of the 23rd HCI International Conference, hCII 2021, Virtual Event, July 24–29, 2021, Proceedings, Part i 23, pp. 171–190 (2021)
7. Chen, W., Shidujaman, M., Tang, X.: AiArt: towards artificial intelligence art
8. Srinivasan, V., Murthy, H.: Improving reading and comprehension in k-12: evidence from a large-scale AI technology intervention in India. Comput. Educ. Artif. Intell. **2**, 100019 (2021)
9. Cornoldi, C., Oakhill, J.V.: Reading Comprehension Difficulties: Processes and Intervention (2013)
10. Wang, K.-J., Shidujaman, M., Zheng, C.Y., Thakur, P.: HRipreneur thinking: strategies towards faster innovation and commercialization of academic HRI research. In: 2019 IEEE International Conference on Advanced Robotics and Its Social Impacts (ARSO), pp. 219–226 (2019). EEE
11. Craig, R.T.: Communication theory as a field. Commun. Theory **9**(2), 119–161 (1999)
12. Sch ller-Zwierlein, A., Mangen, A., Kova?, M., Weel, A.: Why higher-level reading is important. First Monday (2022)
13. Wang, J., Weng, Y., Shidujaman, M., Ahmed, S.U.: A multilevel perspective for social innovation: three exemplary case studies in collaborative communities toward sustainability. In: International Conference on Human-Computer Interaction, pp. 366–391 (2023). Springer
14. Hossain, M.J., Barkatullah, M., Monir, M.F., Ahmed, T.: Repercussion of image compression on satellite image classification using deep learning models. In: 2023 IEEE 98th Vehicular Technology Conference (VTC2023-Fall), pp. 1–5 (2023). IEEE
15. Song, X., Liu, M., Gong, L., Gu, Y., Shidujaman, M.: A review of human-computer interface evaluation research based on evaluation process elements. In: International Conference on Human-Computer Interaction, pp. 262–289 (2023). Springer
16. Wang, B., Gao, Z., Shidujaman, M.: Meaningful place: a phenomenological approach to the design of spatial experience in open-world games. Games Cult. **19**(5), 587–610 (2024)

17. Wu, Z., et al.: Human-AI co-creation of art based on the personalization of collective memory. In: 2022 6th Asian Conference on Artificial Intelligence Technology (ACAIT) (2022)
18. Li, M., et al.: Generative AI for sustainable design: a case study in design education practices. In: International Conference on Human-Computer Interaction, pp. 59–78. Springer, Cham (2024)

Exploring Human-AI Interaction Perception Factors and Collaborative Trust in Library AI Digital Humans

Jun Liu[1], Hongtao Wu[2], Binxin Hu[2(✉)], and Xiaoling Yin[2(✉)]

[1] College Fine of Arts, Fujian Normal University, Fuzhou, China
[2] School of Arts and Communication, China University of Geosciences, Wuhan, China
hubinxin222@gmail.com, yinyu1002@163.com

Abstract. Under the empowerment of Large Language Models (LLMs), library virtual assistants have transitioned from "machine agents" to "AI digital humans," significantly enhancing the intelligence, integration, and efficiency of library services. However, previous research has primarily treated library virtual assistants as AI devices, focusing on technical trust while neglecting interaction trust within library-specific contexts and the role of digital humans as AI agents. This study explores the factors influencing users' perceived trust and acceptance of digital human services. Grounded in the contextual characteristics of library services, we propose an interaction trust framework for library AI digital humans, integrating technical, emotional, and experiential dimensions. The framework encompasses six constructs: Perceived Performance (PP), Scenario Context (SC), Anthropomorphism (AN), System Transparency (ST), Multimodal Interaction (MI), and Interaction Comfort (IC). Data were collected via an online survey of 350 library users and analyzed using Structural Equation Modeling (SEM) to test the proposed hypotheses. The results indicate that PP, SC, AN, ST, MI, and IC each have a significant positive effect on interaction trust, with IC partially mediating the influence of AN and MI on trust. These findings validate the rationality of user perception logic, provide empirical support for optimizing the interaction experience of library AI digital humans, and enhance the understanding of the interplay between interaction factors and trust design. This study promotes a shift in AI agent design from a "technology-centric" to a "context-centric" paradigm.

Keywords: AI Digital Human · Library · Interaction Factors · Trust Perception

1 Introduction

AI digital humans are intelligent agents designed for context-specific applications, interacting with users through human-like voices, facial expressions, and gestures. Owing to their flexibility and adaptability, they have been widely adopted in various public service domains, offering intuitive, engaging interaction experiences and efficient services [1]. However, the successful integration of AI digital humans into traditional library service scenarios hinges on their trustworthiness as virtual librarians. Trust is a critical prerequisite for users to accept new technologies and develop intentions to use them. The "Computers as Social Actors" (CASA) paradigm provides a theoretical framework for understanding the trust mechanisms between AI digital humans and users [2]. While researchers have proposed trust formation mechanisms from technical and emotional perspectives, the holistic relationship between the interaction factors of AI digital humans and trust remains underexplored. On one hand, AI digital humans in libraries assume diverse roles, such as virtual librarians, knowledge providers, and personalized assistants. Their appearance, voice, behavior, and tailored services exhibit advanced intelligent characteristics. However, prior studies on technical characteristics has not incorporated intelligent and affective features, making it difficult to comprehensively reflect the holistic relationship between factors of human-agent interaction and trust. On the other hand, the service process of library AI digital humans is dynamic, characterized by high information density and diverse scenarios (e.g., information retrieval, book recommendations, question answering, and navigation). Therefore, applying AI digital humans to library services requires careful consideration of scenario-specific characteristics and the dynamic influences on interaction trust.

To address these gaps, this study focuses on library service scenarios as a context for investigation, integrating technical attributes, emotional features, and scenario context to systematically explore the human-AI interaction trust mechanisms and their key influencing factors. Using a questionnaire-based approach to collect user data, this study examines the effects of Perceived Performance (PP), Scenario Context (SC), Anthropomorphism (AN), System Transparency (ST), Multimodal Interaction (MI), and Interaction Comfort (IC) on interaction trust. A multidimensional interaction trust framework is developed, and Structural Equation Modeling (SEM) is employed to analyze the statistical relationships among these variables. This study provides empirical insights into the interaction trust mechanisms of library AI digital humans, contributing to a deeper understanding of trust dynamics in context-specific AI applications.

2   Research Model and Hypotheses Development

This study develops an interaction trust framework for AI digital humans, integrating system characteristics, user interaction needs, and application scenario features. The framework comprises three dimensions: functional roles, interaction behaviors, and scenario construction. The functional roles dimension focuses on the core attributes of AI digital humans as intelligent agents, including system performance and anthropomorphism, which form the technical foundation for user trust. The interaction behaviors dimension encompasses the diversity of interaction modalities and the comfort level of user experiences during interactions, reflecting the quality and effectiveness of human-AI interactions. The scenario construction dimension emphasizes the adaptability of digital humans to the specific context of library services, highlighting their ability to align with diverse service types and environmental requirements. Based on these dimensions, six primary research hypotheses are proposed (Fig. 1), corresponding to functional roles (Perceived Performance, System Transparency, Anthropomorphism), interaction behaviors (Multimodal Interaction, Interaction Comfort), and scenario construction (Scenario Context).

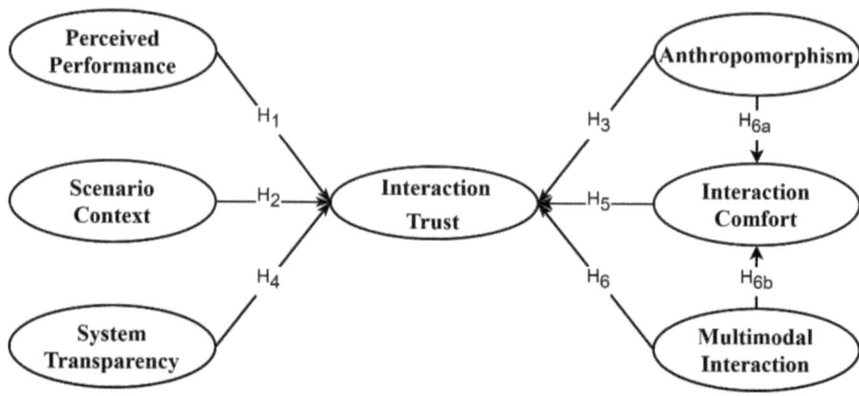

Fig. 1. Interaction Trust Model of Library AI Digital Humans.

H1: Perceived Performance has a significant positive effect on interaction trust in library AI digital humans.

Perceived Performance reflects users' comprehensive evaluation of the functionality, usability, and reliability of digital humans. Library AI digital humans, powered by advanced AI technologies, exhibit human-like intelligence to address diverse service demands, reducing operational costs for users. Traditional usability metrics are insufficient for capturing these advanced intelligent characteristics [3]. Nevertheless, functionality, usability, and reliability remain critical dimensions of Perceived Performance and key indicators for trust formation [4]. Functionality represents the digital human's ability to deliver multiple services, usability reflects the intuitiveness and convenience of task collaboration, and reliability indicates stability in library service delivery. Perceived Performance shapes users' trust in the capabilities of library AI digital humans through these dimensions, directly fostering and reinforcing interaction trust.

H2: Scenario Context has a significant positive effect on interaction trust in library AI digital humans.

Scenario Context refers to the ability of digital humans to flexibly adapt to the multifunctional service scenarios of libraries. Users' trust evaluations during interactions are influenced by service contexts, manifested in perceived service risks and service fit [5]. Perceived service risks, stemming from inaccuracies in task execution, undermine the foundation of human-AI interaction trust. Conversely, service fit reflects the degree to which digital humans align with service demands [6], encompassing compatibility with user needs, visual presentation, and interaction modalities.

H3: Anthropomorphism has a significant positive effect on interaction trust in library AI digital humans.

The anthropomorphic characteristics of digital humans influence interaction trust through multiple dimensions, including visual presentation, behavioral roles, and voice characteristics. Visual anthropomorphism enhances interaction fluency and authenticity, reducing users' psychological resistance to robots [3]. By emulating the service roles of librarians, digital humans increase interaction affinity and credibility. Voice anthropomorphism, characterized by natural and emotionally expressive speech, bridges the psychological distance between users and digital humans, overcoming the detachment of mechanical voices [7]. Collectively, visual and behavioral features align digital humans with the image of human service providers, while voice characteristics strengthen emotional connections and user identification.

H4: System Transparency has a significant positive effect on interaction trust in library AI digital humans.

System Transparency refers to the visibility and comprehensibility of information during a digital human's task assistance. When users can clearly understand the functionality, interaction logic, and decision-making processes of AI digital humans, their sense of control over the service process is enhanced, fostering trust in both the interaction process and the information provided.

H5: Multimodal Interaction has a significant positive effect on interaction trust in library AI digital humans.

Multimodal Interaction involves the integration of voice, visual, and other interaction modalities, significantly enhancing the interaction experience with digital humans. Natural language processing enables users to communicate with digital humans in intuitive and natural ways [8]. By reducing cognitive burdens associated with operational processes, Multimodal Interaction improves interaction fluency and response timeliness, with its design quality playing a critical role in shaping user experience and trust [9].

H6: Interaction Comfort has a significant positive effect on interaction trust in library AI digital humans.

Interaction Comfort refers to users' psychological experience during interactions with library digital humans, serving as an emotional foundation for trust formation. Comfort is associated with perceived attributes such as affinity and friendliness [10].

H6a: Interaction Comfort mediates the relationship between anthropomorphism and trust in digital humans.

The appearance, language style, and emotional expressiveness of digital humans directly influence users' comfort levels. As a prerequisite for anthropomorphic interactions, perceived comfort is significantly enhanced by human-like attributes such as affinity and friendliness, which in turn strengthen user trust [11].

H6b: Interaction Comfort mediates the relationship between Multimodal Interaction and trust in digital humans.

Digital humans communicate with users through multimodal interaction modalities, including voice, visuals, and body language, which influence user comfort. The coordinated, natural, and fluid integration of multimodal elements in the service process enhances user comfort, thereby increasing trust.

3   Research Methodology

3.1   Participants

Data were collected using the online survey platform "Wenjuanxing." To ensure data quality, the survey was restricted to participants with prior experience using AI digital humans and library services. A pilot study was conducted prior to the formal survey, yielding 70 responses, of which 64 were valid, resulting in an effective response rate of 91.43%. Reliability analysis was performed using SPSS software, with the overall Cronbach's α coefficient reaching 0.944, and the Cronbach's α coefficients for all latent variables exceeding 0.8, indicating high reliability of the pilot data. Exploratory factor analysis revealed a Kaiser-Meyer-Olkin (KMO) value of 0.815 and a p-value of 0.000. Using eigenvalue ≥ 1 and the maximum variance rotation method, the cumulative variance explained by the rotated factor loadings was 74.254%, confirming the validity of the pilot data. The formal survey collected 350 responses, of which 326 were valid after screening, yielding an effective response rate of 93.14%.

3.2 Measurement Scales

The survey instrument was adapted from established literature and refined to align with the specific attributes of this study (see Table 1). The questionnaire comprised seven latent variables and 28 items, measured using a five-point Likert scale (1 = strongly disagree, 2 = disagree, 3 = neutral, 4 = agree, 5 = strongly agree).

Structural Equation Modeling (SEM) was employed for data analysis, as it is well-suited for identifying key variables influencing trust in digital human interactions and effectively handles measurement errors without requiring specific data distribution assumptions. The study used SPSS and AMOS 28 to evaluate the interaction trust model for library AI digital humans.

4 Results

4.1 Measurement Model Assessment

The measurement model was evaluated for validity and reliability through internal consistency reliability, convergent validity, and discriminant validity. Internal consistency reliability was assessed using Cronbach's Alpha (CA) and Composite Reliability (CR). As shown in Table 1, CA values ranged from 0.804 to 0.914, and CR values ranged from 0.911 to 0.940, all exceeding the threshold of 0.80, indicating high internal consistency and reliability of the measurement instrument. Convergent validity was used to verify the representativeness of measurement items for their respective constructs, assessed through factor loadings and Average Variance Extracted (AVE). Table 1 shows that all factor loadings exceeded 0.70, and AVE values surpassed 0.50, confirming that the measurement items effectively captured the core constructs of the interaction trust model for library AI digital humans.

Discriminant validity was assessed to evaluate the distinctiveness of constructs using the Heterotrait-Monotrait (HTMT) ratio. As shown in Table 2, all HTMT values were below the threshold of 0.85, indicating significant distinctiveness among the latent variables in the interaction trust model and no significant multicollinearity issues.

4.2 Structural Model Assessment

The model's goodness-of-fit was tested using AMOS software, with all indices meeting acceptable standards, indicating a good fit ($\chi^2 = 736.3$). The χ^2/df ratio was 1.635 ($<$

Table 1. Reliability and Convergent Validity Results.

Variable (Source)		
Item	Mean	Loadings
Perceived Performance [5]		
Mean = 3.50; SD = 0.971; CA = 0.905; CR = 0.940; AVE = 0.840		
Functionality		
PP1 The digital human has the functionality to provide library services.	3.52	0.905
Usability		
PP2 Inputting requests to the digital human meets my library needs.	3.46	0.835
Reliability		
PP3 The digital human's service functions provide accurate and reliable services.	3.52	0.875
Scenario Context [12]		
Mean = 3.51; SD = 0.971; CA = 0.887; CR = 0.917; AVE = 0.689		
Perceived Service Risk		
SC1 I am not concerned about the stability of information provided by the digital librarian.	3.52	0.785
SC2 Interacting with the digital human to input information is safe and reliable.	3.54	0.778
Digital Human-Service Fit		
SC3 The services provided by the digital human align with my actual library needs.	3.50	0.796
SC4 The services provided by the digital human align with the role image of a digital librarian.	3.47	0.781
SC5 The services provided by the digital human align with its interaction modalities.	3.54	0.771
Anthropomorphism [5, 13–15]		
Mean = 3.55; SD = 0.925; CA = 0.906; CR = 0.926; AVE = 0.640		
Visual		
AN1 The digital human's appearance resembles a friendly librarian.	3.61	0.738
AN2 The digital human's facial expressions and body movements are natural and fluid.	3.54	0.790
Voice		
AN3 The digital human's speech rate and tone are appropriate, facilitating understanding.	3.54	0.771
AN4 The digital human's voice conveys emotion.	3.52	0.809

(continued)

Table 1. (*continued*)

Variable (Source)		
Item	Mean	Loadings
Behavioral Role'		
AN5 The digital human can provide services equivalent to those of a human librarian.	3.53	0.695
AN6 The digital human can provide information equivalent to that of a human librarian.	3.61	0.756
AN7 The digital human's responses resemble those of a human librarian.	3.51	0.770
System Transparency [16, 17]		
Mean = 3.49; SD = 0.979; CA = 0.804; CR = 0.911; AVE = 0.836		
ST1 The digital human clearly explains the basis for the information it provides.	3.52	0.787
ST2 The digital human's operational processes are easy for me to understand.	3.46	0.854
Multimodal Interaction [8]		
Mean = 3.36; SD = 0.977; CA = 0.885; CR = 0.926; AVE = 0.686		
MI1 The diversity of interaction modalities supported by the digital human enables efficient completion of library tasks.	3.46	0.797
Voice Interaction		
MI2 The digital human accurately recognizes my voice commands.	3.29	0.739
MI3 The digital human's voice is clear xand easy to understand.	3.34	0.808
Visual Interface		
MI4 The interface's layout makes information clear and comprehensible	3.35	0.741
MI5 The interface's operational feedback animations are clear and accurate.	3.38	0.812
Interaction Comfort [10, 18]		
Mean = 3.41; SD = 1.041; CA = 0.914; CR = 0.940; AVE = 0.795		
IC1 The digital human's behavior in library services is controllable.	3.45	0.829
IC2 The digital human's interface makes me feel visually comfortable.	3.36	0.837
IC3 The digital human's voice interactions make me feel auditorily comfortable.	3.38	0.867

(*continued*)

Table 1. (*continued*)

Variable (Source)		
Item	Mean	Loadings
IC4 I feel comfortable collaborating with the digital human to complete tasks.	3.47	0.851
Interaction Trust [12]		
Mean = 3.38; SD = 0.981; CA = 0.810; CR = 0.913; AVE = 0.840		
IT1 I trust that the digital human can accurately handle my service requests.	3.38	0.717
IT2 I am willing to rely on the digital human to complete library tasks.	3.37	0.835

Table 2. HTMT results.

	1(PP)	2(SC)	3(AN)	4(ST)	5(MI)	6(IC)	7(IT)
1(PP)							
2(SC)	0.498						
3(AN)	0.418	0.468					
4(ST)	0.411	0.356	0.378				
5(MI)	0.363	0.453	0.446	0.286			
6(IC)	0.482	0.510	0.407	0.436	0.380		
7(IT)	0.528	0.579	0.530	0.469	0.516	0.534	

3), RMSEA was 0.060 ($\leq$ 0.060), IFI was 0.910 (> 0.9), TLI was 0.919 (> 0.9), CFI was 0.927 (> 0.9), and GFI and NFI were 0.844 and 0.873, respectively, approaching 0.9 and deemed acceptable. These results confirm the structural validity of the survey data (Table 3), demonstrating good model fit and discriminant validity, thus validating the interaction trust model for library AI digital humans.

Table 3. Structural ModelFit Results.

$\chi2$	$\chi2$/df	RMSEA	IFI	TLI	CFI	GFI	NFI
736.3	2.153	0.060	0.927	0.919	0.927	0.844	0.873

The structural model was evaluated using the maximum likelihood method, with path coefficients (β), t-values, and p-values calculated (Table 4). The results supported all proposed hypotheses. H1 confirmed that Perceived Performance (PP) has a significant positive effect on Interaction Trust (IT) (β = 0.206, t = 3.393, p < 0.001), indicating that positive user perceptions of digital human service performance effectively enhance trust. H2 demonstrated that Scenario Context (SC) exerts a more pronounced positive effect on Interaction Trust ($\beta = 0.254$, t $= 4.012$, p < 0.001), highlighting the critical role of context-aligned design in fostering trust. H3 confirmed that Anthropomorphism (AN) significantly and positively influences Interaction Trust ($\beta = 0.220$, t $= 3.348$, p < 0.001). H4 showed that System Transparency (ST) has a significant but relatively weaker effect on Interaction Trust ($\beta = 0.166$, t $= 2.490$, p $= 0.013$), suggesting a limited role in trust enhancement. H5 and H6 validated the significant positive effects of Multimodal Interaction (MI) ($\beta = 0.246$, t $= 3.753$, p < 0.001) and Interaction Comfort (IC) ($\beta = 0.194$, t $= 2.897$, p $= 0.004$) on Interaction Trust, indicating that diverse interaction modalities and comfortable experiences are key drivers of trust.

Table 4. HypothesesTesting Results.

Hypothesis	Path	β	SE	t	p
H1	PP → IT	0.206	0.048	3.393	***
H2	SC → IT	0.254	0.050	4.012	***
H3	AN → IT	0.220	0.055	3.348	***
H4	ST → IT	0.166	0.057	2.490	*
H5	MI → IT	0.246	0.051	3.753	***
H6	IC → IT	0.194	0.050	2.897	**

Note: * p < 0.05, ** p < 0.01, *** p < 0.001** *

4.3 Mediation Models Assessment

Mediation effects were evaluated using a bootstrap resampling technique with 5,000 iterations and a 95% confidence interval (Table 5). The results confirmed that Interaction Comfort (IC) mediates the relationships between both Anthropomorphism (AN) and Multimodal Interaction (MI) and Interaction Trust (IT). For H6a, Anthropomorphism (AN) exhibited a significant indirect effect on Interaction Trust through Interaction Comfort ($\beta = 0.061$, CI $= [0.018; 0.126]$, p < 0.001), indicating partial mediation. For H6b, Multimodal Interaction (MI) also showed a significant indirect effect on Interaction Trust through Interaction Comfort ($\beta = 0.051$, CI $= [0.015; 0.109]$, p < 0.001), confirming partial mediation.

5 Discussion

This study developed an interaction trust model for AI digital humans in library settings, systematically examining the key factors influencing interaction trust. The results confirmed that Perceived Performance, Scenario Context, Anthropomorphism, System

Table 5. MediationModelsResults.

Hypothesis	Path	β	CI	p
H6a	AN → IC → IT(indirect effect, ab-value)	0.061	[0.018; 0.126]	***
	AN → IC → IT(direct effect, c-path)	0.220	[0.065; 0.352]	***
	AN → IC → IT(total effect, c'-path)	0.281	[0.130; 0.415]	***
H6b	MI → IC → IT(indirect effect, ab-value)	0.051	[0.015; 0.109]	***
	MI → IC → IT(direct effect, c-path)	0.246	[0.109; 0.373]	***
	MI → IC → IT(total effect, c'-path)	0.298	[0.161; 0.425]	***

Note: * p < 0.05, ** p < 0.01, *** p < 0.001

Transparency, Multimodal Interaction, and Interaction Comfort all exert significant positive effects on user trust. These findings validate the effectiveness of integrating technical, emotional, and contextual dimensions into a trust framework for library AI digital humans. The varying effect sizes of the predictors highlight their relative importance in trust formation, revealing unique trust mechanisms in library service scenarios.

Scenario Context ($\beta = 0.254$) and Multimodal Interaction ($\beta = 0.246$) exhibited the strongest direct effects, underscoring that user trust in library AI digital humans heavily depends on context-specific adaptability and diverse interaction modalities. These results align with prior findings [4], confirming that context-embedded design enhances trust while further elucidating specific pathways: Scenario Context not only reduces perceived service risks but also aligns with user needs, visual presentation, and interaction modalities to bolster trust perceptions. By integrating voice, tactile, and visual interaction modalities, AI digital humans enhance the naturalness and immersiveness of library interactions, aligning with users' cognitive preferences for multisensory information processing. Given the information-intensive nature of library services, AI digital humans effectively reduce users' cognitive load. Users tend to perceive AI digital humans as "social entities," with human-like features (e.g., librarian appearance, voice, behavior) fostering emotional connections and trust. Notably, voice anthropomorphism (AN4 loading > 0.8) had the most pronounced effect on emotional trust.

While Perceived Performance significantly influenced Interaction Trust ($\beta = 0.206$), its effect was lower than expected [3], possibly because user perceptions of service functionality are embedded within the broader library service process and system experience. System Transparency's effect on Interaction Trust was significant but relatively weak ($\beta = 0.166$), likely due to the low-risk nature and minimal cognitive demands of library services, where users prioritize direct interaction experiences over internal system mechanisms. Interaction Comfort directly influenced human-AI trust ($\beta = 0.194$), reflecting users' subjective emotional experiences during role-based and behavioral interactions. The mediation analysis revealed that Interaction Comfort partially mediates the effects of anthropomorphism ($\beta = 0.061$) and Multimodal Interaction ($\beta = 0.051$) on trust, demonstrating the synergistic role of emotional and technical pathways. These mediation effects extend traditional technical trust models by incorporating emotional experiences, aligning with Moussawi et al. [15] on the roles of perceived intelligence and anthropomorphism in trust formation. This study confirms that interaction trust in AI digital humans involves not only rational evaluations of technical usability but also emotional experiences mediated by comfort.

The findings provide theoretical insights for library managers to understand interaction experiences with AI digital humans and refine service designs. By developing a framework of service perception factors and validating their impact on interaction trust, this study enhances the understanding of the interplay between interaction factors and trust design. It moves beyond the limitations of prior research focused on tool usability, advocating a shift in AI agent design from a "technology-centric" to a "context-centric" paradigm. The varying influence of interaction factors, as quantified by their effect weights, enables more precise design strategies for AI digital human development in libraries and related fields.

6 Conclusion

Interaction trust in library AI digital humans is a complex process influenced by multiple factors, including technical performance, scenario context, human-AI interaction experiences, and psychological perceptions. This study developed a context-specific interaction trust model for library AI digital humans, integrating user characteristics, technical attributes, and scenario factors. It identified six key predictors with significant effects on interaction trust, addressing the limitations of viewing digital humans solely as intelligent tools.

The results highlight Scenario Context as the most influential factor, underscoring the distinct interaction characteristics of library AI digital humans compared to other domains. In the technical design pathway, prioritizing alignment between digital humans, service demands, and library scenarios is critical. Multimodal Interaction demonstrated a strong effect in information-intensive library contexts, enhancing information acquisition efficiency through integrated voice commands, visual displays, and gesture controls. In the behavioral design pathway, emphasizing anthropomorphic emotional connections and interaction comfort is key, with librarian-like appearances and friendly traits enhancing affinity. Given the low-risk nature of library services, overemphasizing System Transparency may divert user attention from direct interaction experiences.

As this study relied on cross-sectional data, the survey method has limitations in capturing the dynamic experience of library AI digital human services. It did not account for individual differences, such as users' library familiarity or demographic attributes, which may influence human-AI interaction trust. Future research will employ qualitative methods to refine the theoretical model, exploring the impact of service function types and user differences on the experiential journey with AI digital humans, further enhancing the usability and value of human-AI interaction designs in libraries.

Acknowledgements. This research was funded by the Research Center of Industry Design of the Key Research Base of Philosophy and Social Sciences of Universities in Sichuan, "Research on AI Agent Behavior Design and Interactive Experience Based on "Technology-Behavior"" (Project No.: GYSJ2025-02).

References

1. Asemi, A., Ko, A., Nowkarizi, M.: Intelligent libraries: a review on expert systems, artificial intelligence, and robot. Library Hi Tech. **39**, 412–434 (2020). https://doi.org/10.1108/LHT-02-2020-0038
2. Nass, C., Moon, Y.: Machines and mindlessness: social responses to computers. J. Soc. Issues **56**, 81–103 (2000). https://doi.org/10.1111/0022-4537.00153
3. Gursoy, D., Chi, O.H., Lu, L., Nunkoo, R.: Consumer's acceptance of artificially intelligent (AI) device uses in service delivery. Int. J. Inf. Manage. **49**, 157–169 (2019). https://doi.org/10.1016/j.ijinfomgt.2019.03.008
4. Lin, H., Chi, O.H., Gursoy, D.: Antecedents of customers' acceptance of artificially intelligent robotic device use in hospitality services. J. Hosp. Market. Manag. **29**, 530–549 (2020). https://doi.org/10.1080/19368623.2020.1685053
5. Chi, O.H., Jia, S., Li, Y., Gursoy, D.: Developing a formative scale to measure consumers' trust toward interaction with artificially intelligent (AI) social robots in service delivery. Comput. Hum. Behav. **118**, 106700 (2021). https://doi.org/10.1016/j.chb.2021.106700
6. Zhang, Y., Liang, C., Li, X.: Understanding virtual agents' service quality in the context of customer service: a fit-viability perspective. Electron. Commer. Res. Appl. **65**, 101380 (2024). https://doi.org/10.1016/j.elerap.2024.101380
7. Pitardi, V., Marriott, H.R.: Alexa, *she's* not human but… Unveiling the drivers of consumers' trust in voice-based artificial intelligence. Psychol. Mark. **38**, 626–642 (2021). https://doi.org/10.1002/mar.21457
8. Foehr, J., Germelmann, C.: Alexa, can i trust you? exploring consumer paths to trust in smart voice-interaction technologies. J. Assoc. Consumer Res. **5**, 181–205 (2020). https://doi.org/10.1086/707731
9. Beauxis-Aussalet, E., et al.: The role of interactive visualization in fostering trust in AI. IEEE Comput. Graph. Appl. **41**, 7–12 (2021). https://doi.org/10.1109/MCG.2021.3107875
10. Gulati, S., McDonagh, J., Sousa, S., Lamas, D.: Trust models and theories in human–computer interaction: a systematic literature review. Comput. Hum. Behav. Rep. **16**, 100495 (2024). https://doi.org/10.1016/j.chbr.2024.100495
11. van Pinxteren, M.M.E., Wetzels, R.W.H., Rüger, J., Pluymaekers, M., Wetzels, M.: Trust in humanoid robots: implications for services marketing. J. Serv. Mark. **33**, 507–518 (2019). https://doi.org/10.1108/JSM-01-2018-0045
12. Cai, J., Fu, X., Gu, Z., Wu, R.: Validating Social Service Robot Interaction Trust (SSRIT) Scale in Measuring Consumers' Trust Toward Interaction with Artificially Intelligent (AI) Social Robots with a Chinese Sample of Adults. Int. J. Hum.-Comput. Interact. **40**, 4319–4334 (2024). https://doi.org/10.1080/10447318.2023.2212224
13. Hsu, C.-L., Lin, J.C.-C.: Understanding the user satisfaction and loyalty of customer service chatbots. J. Retail. Consum. Serv. **71**, 103211 (2023). https://doi.org/10.1016/j.jretconser.2022.103211
14. Siehl, S., Kammler-Sücker, K., Guldner, S., Janvier, Y., Zohair, R., Nees, F.: To trust or not to trust? Face and voice modulation of virtual avatars. Front. Virtual Real. **5** (2024). https://doi.org/10.3389/frvir.2024.1301322

15. Moussawi, S., Koufaris, M., Benbunan-Fich, R.: How perceptions of intelligence and anthropomorphism affect adoption of personal intelligent agents. Electron Markets. **31**, 343–364 (2021). https://doi.org/10.1007/s12525-020-00411-w
16. Felzmann, H., Villaronga, E.F., Lutz, C., Tamò-Larrieux, A.: Transparency you can trust: Transparency requirements for artificial intelligence between legal norms and contextual concerns. Big Data Soc. (2019). https://doi.org/10.1177/2053951719860542
17. Shin, D.: The effects of explainability and causability on perception, trust, and acceptance: Implications for explainable AI. Int. J. Hum. Comput. Stud. **146**, 102551 (2021). https://doi.org/10.1016/j.ijhcs.2020.102551
18. Gillath, O., Ai, T., Branicky, M.S., Keshmiri, S., Davison, R.B., Spaulding, R.: Attachment and trust in artificial intelligence. Comput. Hum. Behav. **115**, 106607 (2021). https://doi.org/10.1016/j.chb.2020.106607

Feasibility Study to Adapt Online Deep Learning Models for Immersive Environments

Agustín Alejandro Ortiz Díaz[(✉)] [iD], Sergio Cleger Tamayo [iD],
Gabriel Dos Santos Lima [iD], Geovana Amorim Abensur [iD],
and Delrick Nunes De Oliveira [iD]

Sidia Institute of Science and Technology, Av. Darcy Vargas 654, 69055-035 Manaus, Brasil
{agustin.diaz,sergio.tamayo,gabriel.slima,geovana.abensur,
delrick.oliveira}@sidia.com

Abstract. Immersive environments are digital spaces that surround the user, creating a sense of presence and participation in the virtual and augmented world. Unlike traditional interfaces, which present information in two-dimensional form, immersive environments seek to generate three-dimensional and multi-sensory experiences that stimulate iterations with the simulated environment. From these iterations between users and their environment over time, a lot of data is obtained that, when analyzed, generates enough useful information to improve their experiences within these immersive environments LNCS. On the other hand, deep learning models are considered the state-of-the-art in various offline machine learning tasks. Traditionally, training deep neural network models requires that all data be available at the start of training in an offline environment. However, many of the techniques that have been developed are not considered suitable for online learning scenarios. That is, this learning scheme is not suitable for many practical situations where data arrives over time. To study the methods and models of deep learning suitable for working in these scenarios, the area known as Online Deep Learning was created. To use this type of models within immersive environments, the key lies in the ability to continuously learn and adapt to new experiences within the environment, without having to retrain the entire model from scratch each time. This work aims to study the feasibility of adapting and integrating some of the main techniques of Online Deep Learning within immersive environments. In addition, it studies the possibility that some methods and models in this area can be adjusted to the limitations of the different devices that support extended reality technologies. These methods should provide real-time responses to user interactions with promising levels of accuracy.

Keywords: Immersive Environments · Online Deep Learning · Deep Learning · Incremental Learning · Online Learning · NAS · Zero-cost Proxies

M. Kurosu and A. Hashizume (Eds.): HCII 2025, LNCS 16332, pp. 308–322, 2026.
https://doi.org/10.1007/978-3-032-12385-5_19

1 Introduction

The solutions to many everyday tasks have benefited from the use of immersive technologies. Currently, several companies and research institutes use immersive environments to create simulations that support solutions to different tasks such as: training their employees in a safe environment, customer service simulations, marketing campaigns, viewing and modifying architectural projects in 3D, among other common activities [1].

Virtual reality (VR), augmented reality (AR), and mixed reality (MR) are immersive and interactive technologies that are grouped within a broader term known as extended reality (XR). To access immersive experiences generated with these technologies, there are several types of devices such as: mobile devices, virtual reality headsets (HMD), virtual reality glasses, and so on [2].

Another area that has achieved marked development in the last decade is artificial intelligence (AI), in particular, deep learning (DL) techniques that are part of the machine learning (ML) subbranch. Due to this remarkable development, many current works propose to adapt DL techniques to be used in immersive environments within mobile devices and HMDs [3].

DL uses artificial neural network models to train and learn from large data sets. However, a particular feature of DL models is that they tend to be complex models in their spatiotemporal dimensions [4]. This intrinsic complexity of DL models is one of the reasons why these models are often less used in environments immersive within mobile devices and HMDs. From this point, the first two challenges emerged:

- In immersive environments, iterations between agents are part of the core and usually require real-time responses.
- Mobile devices and HMDs may have memory limitations, so the use of smaller models would be essential.

On the other hand, as a general concept, deep neural networks are trained by backpropagation in a more static learning environment, therefore, all data must be available before training starts. However, in many real-life situations, data arrives sequentially over time. Consequently, more static schemes may be irrelevant for many practical situations, where data arrives in a stream and cannot be stored due to its potentially infinite size [5].

Incremental learning (online learning) is a machine learning paradigm in which training data is available in sequential order over time. That is, it is not necessary to have all the training data from the beginning, the examples arrive in the form of a flow. Closely related to this type of learning is the concept of "concept drift" which defines a set of possible variations in the distribution of data over time. These variations in the information transmitted by the data over time are responsible for that static models may become obsolete. For this reason, in these situations it is strongly recommended to use dynamic models within the incremental learning paradigm [6].

Some authors [5] classify online learning methods within the category of shallow models, thus marking a separation from deep models. In addition, some authors follow the logical intuition that there is a rule where shallow models converge more faster than deep models. Based on this intuition, several works have been developed that follow the "shallow to deep" principle [5]. In this sense, several interesting ideas have been proposed to adapt deep learning models for learning online [5, 7, 8].

A few months ago, our work team proposed a viable architecture in which different deep learning methods and models, machine learning in the general sense, can be grouped and organized to integrate them into immersive environments [9]. This architecture is made up of six main modules:

- Data acquisition.
- Feature extraction and preprocessing.
- Model selection and verification.
- Task orchestration and scheduling.
- Fusion and postprocessing.
- XR integration.

This architecture was designed to include traditional deep learning methods. For example, the modules for "Data Acquisition" and "Preprocessing and Feature Extraction" are not designed to process data that arrives over time in the form of streams.

The objective of this work is to develop a study on the main existing techniques and models within the area of Online Deep Learning (ODL). In addition, the feasibility of adapting these models to immersive environments is analyzed. From this analysis we want to ensure that the methods and models ODLs can be adapted to the limitations of different devices supporting extended reality technologies. These methods should provide real-time responses to user interactions while maintaining promising levels of accuracy. Finally, as future work, we propose to re-adapt our initial architecture [9] to support ODL models.

For better organization and description of the work results, the article has been divided into 7 sections: Deep learning in Immersive Environments (Sect. 2), Incremental-online learning (Sect. 3), Online deep learning (Sect. 4), Neural Architecture Search (Sect. 5), Analysis of the study (Sect. 6). Finally, in Sect. 7, we present our Conclusions, Acknowledgments, and References.

2   Deep Learning in Immersive Environments

Recently, numerous research projects are proposing the idea of inserting deep learning techniques into extended reality environments for application in various areas of everyday reality.

In 2021, a compilation of works was presented that explores the current scope of AI in AR-assisted industrial applications [10]. Also, in this same year, another compilation of works was presented, this time aimed at the study of systems created within mobile augmented reality (MAR). This work conducts a study of existing MAR systems by enhancing those that use ML methods [11]. Another compilation of works from 2021 performed a performance analysis of several works aimed at immersive systems. This review includes applications in which experiments have been performed to evaluate systems that integrate current machine learning and deep learning techniques [12].

Less than two years ago, in 2023, another set of scientific articles was grouped into a publication that focused on the analysis of XR application systems that use machine learning techniques. This group of works is focused primarily on the health area [13]. Also, in 2023, new lines of work have emerged, such as Real-time Multi-Task Multi-Model, which are laying the foundations for the efficient use of ML techniques in areas such as XR [3].

Last year, 2024, our working group published an architecture proposal [9] aimed at organizing and executing ML methods in immersive environments. This architecture should ensure that ML methods meet some basic constraints necessary to work with XR applications. Three fundamental goals to ensure these constraints are:

- Ensure real-time responses to user interactions.
- Adjust to the spatial-temporal constraints required within this type of environment.
- Maintain promising results in the quality of the responses of ML methods despite the limitations.

Other important considerations that the proposed architecture has considered are [3, 14]:

- Restrictions on other resources such as processing power and battery life on mobile devices without a cable connection.
- Scalability, allowing the addition of new functionalities and models to suit real needs.
- Handling various types of ML tasks and allowing their simultaneous execution if necessary.
- Handling scenarios where the output of a given task is used as input for another, cascading concurrency.

The proposed architecture was designed using six processing layers. In general, the function of each of these layers is [9]:

1. Data acquisition. Collects various input data through sensors. It also takes care of part of the cleaning of the initial data for further processing.
2. Preprocessing and feature extraction. This layer takes the data from the sensors and performs essential preprocessing such as cleaning and filtering, data transformation, and feature extraction.
3. Model selection and verification. This layer stores a library of trained and optimized ML models to work in real time, efficiently use resources, and maintain promising accuracy values.
1. Task orchestration and scheduling. This layer controls and guarantees the concurrent execution of multiple models.
2. Fusion and post-processing. This layer handles the results of multiple models that were executed simultaneously in the previous layer. In addition, it ensures that the results provided to the next layer, called XR integration, are meaningful, accurate, and ready for immersive experience interactions.
3. XR Integration. This is the final layer, which ensures that the user receives real-time feedback and interacts with the environment based on the information processed from the previous layers. It handles actionable commands such as animations and provides visual and auditory feedback to the user.

3   Incremental-Online Learning

Incremental-online learning is one of the main paradigms that are part of machine learning. This type of learning is characterized by the dynamism in the learning process of its models, which are constantly updated. In comparison with traditional machine learning, incremental learning does not presuppose the need to have a training set before the learning process. In this learning paradigm, the training examples appear in the form of flows over time [15].

Some authors draw certain distinctions between the terms "incremental learning" and "online learning" [16].

- **Incremental learning.** Models are created to learn from new data that arrives continuously; that is, the existing model is updated with new information incrementally. In addition, the knowledge obtained previously is retained. This approach is normally used when the data distribution evolves or changes over time, so the model needs to adapt to these changes.
- **Online learning.** A model is created that learns from a continuous flow of data that arrives in real time. The model is updated with each new example at the same instant it arrives (1-by-1), which allows the model to adapt and learn from the most recent information. This approach is normally used in scenarios where the data arrives sequentially and must be processed in real time, such as in dynamic environments.

Our work will focus on a learning environment that combines characteristics of both approaches. Specifically, we are interested in models that:

- Update incrementally as they learn from a continuous stream of data in real time.
- Update immediately when training instances arrive, i.e., one by one (1 by 1); or update when a new batch of instances of an appropriate size is collected.
- Retain previously learned knowledge while adapting to changes in the data distribution by incorporating new information.

To organize the different concepts and tasks related to incremental learning, some authors divide this learning paradigm into three main scenarios [17, 18]:

- Instance Incremental. This first scenario includes situations where the number of instances (training examples) increases over time, but the number of categories (classes) remains constant, i.e., no new categories appear. A good model is expected to update itself, i.e., incrementally improve your knowledge of known classes without compromising your prior knowledge.
- Class Incremental. This second scenario includes situations where the number of instances (training examples) increases over time, but these new examples are always accompanied by new classes, that is, classes that were previously unknown. In this case, the model is expected to be updated, it should be able to handle the new classes without losing accuracy with respect to the previous classes.
- Instance and class increment. This third scenario includes situations where the number of instances (training examples) increases over time. In this case, these new training examples may come with known classes or new, previously unknown classes. A good model is expected to consolidate its knowledge of the known classes and learn the new ones.

As a difference from transfer learning, in incremental learning when learning new tasks requires the model to maintain its performance on the previous task. Transfer learning barely uses old knowledge to learn new knowledge. That is, it focuses only on learning the new knowledge, disregarding its performance on the previous task [17].

3.1 Concept Drift

When training models with incremental learning strategies, the concepts learned tend to be unstable and often change over time. Due to these changes, the model already built on old data often becomes inconsistent with the information that new data from the stream begins to provide, which is why an update of the model is necessary. This problem is known as concept drift and complicates the task of learning a model from the data [15].

These models require an additional mechanism to stay up to date with respect to the current concept. An ideal system to handle concept drift should be able to [19]:

- Quickly adapt to concept drift.
- They must be robust to noise and be able to distinguish it from concept drift.
- They must recognize and deal with recurring contexts.

An incremental learning algorithm must consider the following criteria [15, 19]:

- It must access the original data only once, then it is usually discarded. The data could potentially be infinite.
- Learn and update itself with each new data.
- Detect and adapt to concept drift and retain the necessary prior knowledge.
- Generate new non-existing classes if necessary.

3.2 Ensembles

Promising alternative approaches to incremental learning are ensemble systems. The goal of ensemble systems is to train a set of base classifiers from available data sets and then combine their individual results to obtain a unified decision for the entire system. This set of classifiers should be diverse enough to reach relatively different decision boundaries and thus reduce the overall system error [20].

Ensembles, depending on their composition, can be classified as homogeneous, when they are composed only of the same type of base classifier (e.g., decision trees); or heterogeneous, when they are made up of different types of base classifiers (e.g., decision trees, neural networks, and support vector machines) [21]. In addition, there are three types of ensemble models, well known in the literature, from which another type of classification is established based on a set of characteristics that define each method bagging [22], boosting [23] or stacking [24].

There are many strategies that are used to combine the results of base classifiers, such as voting or algebraic combinations of posterior probabilities, Dempster–Shafer combination, decision templates, meta-decision trees, and so on. There are also proposals that combine these strategies. [21].

It is known that ensemble methods compared to traditional simple methods improve performance by reducing bias and variance. For these and other reasons they have been used to address incremental learning problems [21]. Ensembles have been shown to be viable for online learning, both in environments with stationary concepts and for environments with the presence of concept drift [25–28].

4 Online Deep Learning

In the last decade there have been notable advances in deep learning techniques and models. For example, transfer learning/fine-tuning of deep neural network models has shown great effectiveness when used to solve new tasks based on prior knowledge learned from similar previous tasks. However, this remarkable development has not been seen within the context of continuous learning. As we have stated above, in this context it is necessary to use the same model to solve new tasks while maintaining good performance in solving previous tasks. To face this type of challenges we must face the phenomenon known as catastrophic forgetting, where previously learned knowledge is compromised when models are updated [18].

On the other hand, learning little by little in an incremental way is one of the most important characteristics of human beings. One of the main challenges for researchers in machine learning is to build neural network models that are at least as powerful as human beings. The challenge for these models would be to achieve the ability to acquire, accumulate and update knowledge continuously, while avoiding losing previously acquired knowledge, this is known as "catastrophic forgetting" [29].

Online Deep Learning (ODL) addresses the challenge of learning from data that arrives in real-time in the form of a stream. Also, the need to learn quickly and deeply must be balanced. In recent years, due to the advancement of deep neural networks, incremental learning has attracted a lot of attention in fields like natural language processing and computer vision [5].

Several approaches have been proposed to address the challenges of online deep learning. In 2017, the Hedge Backpropagation (HBP) method was introduced that aims to effectively update deep neural network parameters in online environments. This method enables online training of deep neural networks by dynamically adapting the network depth based on data complexity. According to the authors, HBP outperforms traditional online learning algorithms as well as fixed-depth deep neural networks in both stationary and conceptual drift scenarios. Furthermore, HBP's performance is robust to the base network depth, unlike traditional online backpropagation [5].

In 2018, an online generative discriminative restricted Boltzmann machine (OGD-RBM) was presented that adapts its network architecture to data in real time, demonstrating improved accuracy and efficiency compared to batch learning techniques. The online generative phase of the OGD-RBM algorithm results in a compact network architecture where hidden neurons are inherently discriminative for class labels, even with unsupervised training. According to the authors, the OGD-RBM algorithm outperforms other machine learning techniques and neural networks in credit scoring tasks, achieving higher accuracy with a more compact network architecture, and requiring fewer training samples [30].

In 2019, a new training procedure was developed to simultaneously handle multiple objectives in online deep learning tasks regardless of the neural network architecture. The efficiency of the proposed method was evaluated on the Neyman-Pearson classification problem using benchmark datasets [31].

In 2021, a two-phase online deep learning pipeline based on autoencoder (ODLAE) was proposed. This proposal combines two strategies of fusion; the output strategy, which fuses the classification results of each hidden layer of the encoder; and the feature strategy, based on self-attention mechanisms, which fuses the output of each hidden layer [32].

An intuitive thought suggests that shallow models converge faster than deep models. Based on this intuition, several works have been developed that follow the principle of "shallow to deep" [5]. From a more pragmatic point of view, several works have been published that address these ideas to solve industry problems. In 2022, an online deep-learning algorithm was published that provides an autonomous agent with the ability to train itself in real-time. In addition, it can configure the training frequency based on its current performance level [7]. More recently, in 2023, a real-time ODL model for traction motor temperature prediction in trains was developed. This model can dynamically adjust the model structure and parameters to adapt to streaming data with changing probability distributions [8].

As recently as 2024, a hybrid multi-learner approach was proposed that combines fast online logistic regression with deep learning, achieving state-of-the-art results on common datasets. As recently as 2024, a new hybrid multi-learner approach for online deep learning was proposed, which includes a fast online logistic regression learner and a cascaded multi-learner design that combines shallow and deep learners. The authors show that the online deep learning approach can be implemented with complexity that depends only on the number of layers in the network. According to the authors, the proposed design achieves state-of-the-art results on different datasets for online learning [33].

These various approaches highlight current efforts by researchers to improve ODL capabilities in handling non-stationary data, multiple objectives, multiple learner, and adaptive architectures for real-world applications.

5 Neural Architecture Search

As mentioned in the previous section, one of the main challenges of the online deep learning paradigm is to select the best neural network design to be trained. This problem is exacerbated by the fact that the training data in online learning is not available from the beginning, but rather the data arrives in a flow over time [5].

Neural Architecture Search (NAS) has currently become the standard methodology for designing neural network models. The original idea that this methodology has followed is based on evaluating, through training, several network models and from that comparison choosing the best one. This strategy generally requires a high consumption of computational resources [34].

To reduce the high consumption of computational resources of the NAS methodology, several proxy-type strategies have been used in the scientific literature. A proxy is a reduced computation training where one of the following variables is reduced: number of epochs, number of training samples, input resolution, model size. Some published works that implement these strategies are [34]:

- Reducing the training time during the evaluation of candidate models. For this, weight distributions are used [35].
- They use smaller datasets as a proxy for full training. Allow multiple architectures to share their weights. In this way, multiple network architectures can be trained at the same time [36].
- They reduce other training parameters such as input size, model size, number of training samples or number of epochs [37].

There are other types of proxies, known as zero-cost proxies, which propose to alleviate the high computational cost of traditional NAS strategies by partially predicting the accuracy of an already trained network from its initial state. That is, predicting before training the neural network, what its accuracy will be after being trained [38].

Some metrics have been used to create alternative zero-cost proxies. These metrics are computed on a network that has been trained on just a single minibatch of data and are intended to predict the accuracy level of the network once it has been fully trained. Some of the more well-known metrics are [34]:

- Snip. It is a saliency metric proposed for parameter pruning, [39].
- Grasp. It is a proposal to improve the previous metric by approximating the change in the gradient norm when a parameter is pruned, [40].
- Synflow. It is a version of the previous metrics that avoids the collapse of layers when parameter pruning is performed. It is calculated by multiplying several parameters of the network and does not require training data, not even a minibatch, [41].
- Fisher. This is another pruning-based metric that uses a strategy of eliminating activation channels that are estimated to have the least effect on losses [42].
- Jacobian Covariance. Calculates the lowest correlation of network activations on different inputs for a minibatch of data [38].

More recent works propose to integrate these untrained proxies into existing NAS strategies such as Aging Evolution [43], Reinforcement Learning [44], and Binary Predictor [45].

As is known, these traditional NAS strategies are usually very expensive, therefore the main objective of the integration is to improve their performance. Two papers suggesting and studying these integration strategies were published in 2021. In the first of these papers, several conventional reduced training proxies are evaluated and compared with a set of zero-cost proxies that only use a minibatch of data to assess the quality of the models. In addition, integration strategies with already established NAS strategies are proposed [34]. On the other hand, NASWOT is a search algorithm that allows finding powerful networks without any training. This algorithm uses a metric based on the overlap of activations between data points in untrained networks. Furthermore, this approach can be combined with other more computationally expensive search methods [38].

6 Analysis of the Study

Deep learning models are considered the state of the art in various offline machine learning tasks. Traditionally, training deep neural network models requires that all data be available at the start of training in an offline environment. However, many of the

DL techniques that have been developed are not considered suitable for online learning tasks. Therefore, keeping these conditions, this learning scheme is irrelevant for many practical situations, where data arrives in sequence and cannot be stored, since in theory it would be potentially infinite [5]. XR environments are dynamic environments where interaction with users is part of the core of their operation. These interactions are a source of a constant generation of new data and information. Hence the need to integrate online methods with incremental learning within immersive environments.

Online Deep Learning Methods. With this study we are interested in focusing on the possibility of integrating ODL methods within immersive environments. According to some authors, there is a gap between online learning and deep learning, making the OLD area an open problem. online learning can be directly applied to deep neural networks using online backpropagation. However, several convergence problems often arise from this direct application, such as vanishing gradient and diminishing feature reuse [5].

Adapting online deep learning models for immersive environments presents unique challenges and opportunities today. Some of the main challenges that must be addressed are:

- **Computational efficiency of the methods.** These methods must provide real-time responses to user interactions with promising levels of accuracy.
- **Efficient management of resources and data.** Efficiency in processing and minimal storage of data generated in immersive environments is essential. Not all data can be stored because it is potentially infinite. Devices have limited resources, for example storage space, battery charge, etc.
- **Selection and management of the model to be trained.** It is difficult to select or find the most efficient network architecture to learn from a given dataset. Traditional NAS strategies need offline data to train models. Determining the best strategy for adding new units, managing network complexity.
- **Avoiding catastrophic forgetting.** The model forgets previously learned tasks when learning new ones. It is crucial to find the balance between the model's ability to learn new tasks and the retention of previous knowledge. In addition, it should take advantage of the knowledge learned in one task to accelerate learning in other related tasks, transfer learning.
- **Handle changes in concepts in the data.** When working with data streams, you must always keep in mind the possible changes in concepts over time, differentiate these changes from noisy data, and anticipate possible recurring concepts.
- **Create robust models.** The model must be able to handle variability and noise in sensory data. Maintain the stability of the model during growth.
- **Interpretability of results.** It is important to be able to understand the decisions made by the models, especially in critical applications.

One of the main challenges within the ODL learning paradigm is the selection of an appropriate architecture for the model. Since it is not possible to have all the training data offline, it is also not possible to use traditional NAS strategies to select an appropriate architecture model. For example, how to know the optimal depth that the model should have, or how to know how many neurons to use in each layer?

For this reason, a section was included in the study to analyze the different NAS strategies. We found it interesting, within the NAS strategies, to analyze the existence of other types of non-traditional proxies, known as zero-cost proxies. This type of proxy can predict before training the neural network, what its accuracy will be after being trained. To achieve this prediction, in most cases, they only need a small batch of data.

Several metrics have been used for this purpose in traditional neural networks. Some of these metrics have already been mentioned before: Snip, Grasp, Synflow, Fisher. Jacobian Covariance, and so on. Synflow was recommended in some studies [34].

It is one of our future works to verify their possible effectiveness within the ODL paradigm, whether to determine a promising model as a starting point or for the dynamic evaluation of possible changes to models over time.

Architectural Support for ODL-XR Integration. Our working team presented, in 2024, a new architecture to adapt, group and execute ML methods in XR environments. The main objective is to provide an efficient tool through which this type of models can be integrated into immersive environments [9] as we mentioned before, this tool was designed with six main components:

- Data Acquisition.
- Preprocessing and Feature Extraction.
- Model Selection and Verification.
- Task orchestration and scheduling.
- Fusion and post-processing.
- XR integration.

This design aims to ensure that ML methods and models adjust to the limitations of the different devices that support extended reality technologies. Additionally, these methods must ensure real-time responses to user interactions with high levels of accuracy.

However, this proposed architecture has limitations for integrating methods that process data incrementally. Its overall design was created for traditional machine learning methods, i.e., methods that are trained offline. Below are some limitations of this architecture for online learning:

- The Data Acquisition layer was designed to load complete data sets. That is, there are no mechanisms to acquire data over time, or even to compare this scenario with previously stored data.
- The preprocessing and feature extraction methods are aimed at processing previously stored data; they are currently not adapted to data that may arrive in the form of a flow over time.
- In general, there is a need to re-adapt each of the following layers of the design, i.e., this need for adaptation runs through the entire architecture.

Some macro requirements for adapting our architectures to methods with incremental learning are:

- It is required to expand the functionalities of the first two layers of the architecture to work with data that arrives in the form of a flow over time.
- It is required to create one or more intermediate layers to guarantee the functionalities of retraining and/or dynamically modifying the existing models.

- It is required to redesign the rest of the layers of the architecture to adapt them to this new scenario.

7 Conclusion

Immersive technologies and online deep learning are converging to create transformative learning experiences. Adapting online deep learning models for immersive environments, particularly in the context of incremental learning, today presents unique challenges and opportunities. The key lies in the ability to continuously learn and adapt to new experiences within the immersive environment, without having to retrain the entire model from scratch each time. In addition, these models must maintain the necessary prior knowledge. Some of the main challenges that must be addressed are: Computational efficiency of the methods, efficient management of resources and data, selection, and management of the model to be trained, avoid catastrophic forgetting, manage concepts drift in the data, create robust models, interpretability of results, and so on.

In this work, in addition to analyzing some of the main techniques for online deep learning, we study some promising strategies that could be used to improve the potential of the methods and face the main challenges mentioned. Among these strategies we can mention:

- **Use of ensemble methods.** Ensemble methods, compared to traditional naive methods, improve performance by reducing errors arising from bias and variance. Ensembles have been shown to be viable for online learning, both in environments with stationary concepts and in environments with the presence of concept drift.
- **Use of zero-cost proxies.** Zero-cost proxies, which propose to alleviate the high computational cost of traditional NAS strategies by partially predicting the accuracy of an already trained network from its initial state. That is, predicting before training the neural network, what its accuracy will be after being trained.

Furthermore, we recommend adapting our architecture, proposed in 2024, designed to adapt and execute traditional ML methods in immersive environments, to the ODL method. This architecture ensures that ML methods meet some basic constraints necessary to work with XR applications.

The selection of appropriate strategies; and the choice and management of the appropriate incremental model will depend on the specific task, the available resources, and the characteristics of the immersive environment. Research in this field is active, and significant advances are expected in the creation of more efficient, robust, and interpretable models for immersive environments.

Acknowledgments. This paper was presented as part of the results of the Project "SIDIA-M_VST_PLATFORM_AND_APPLICATIONS", carried out by the Institute of Science and Technology - SIDIA, in partnership with Samsung Eletrônica da Amazônia LTDA, in accordance with the Information Technology Law n.8387/91 and article at the. 39 of Decree 10,521/2020.

References

1. Gupta, Y., et al.: Deep learning model-based multimedia retrieval and its optimization in augmented reality applications. Multimed. Tools Appl. **82**, 8447–8466 (2023). https://doi.org/10.1007/s11042-022-13555-y

2. Suzuki, K., et al.: Recognition and mapping of facial expressions to the avatar by embedded photo reflective sensors in head-mounted display. In: 2017 IEEE Virtual Reality (VR), USA (2017)

3. Kwon, H., et al.: XRBench: An Extended Reality (XR) machine learning benchmark suite for the metaverse. In: Proceedings of the 6th MLSys Conference, Miami Beach, FL, USA, 2023.2211.08675, arXiv. http://arxiv.org/abs/2211.08675/ (2023)

4. Alaskar, H., Saba, T.: Machine learning and deep learning: a comparative review. In: Singh Mer, K.K., Semwal, V.B., Bijalwan, V., Crespo, R.G. (eds.) Proceedings of Integrated Intelligence Enable Networks and Computing. Algorithms for Intelligent Systems. Springer, Singapore (2021). https://doi.org/10.1007/978-981-33-6307-6_15

5. Sahoo, D., et al.: Online Deep Learning: Learning Deep Neural Networks on the Fly (2018). https://doi.org/10.48550/arXiv.1711.03705

6. Gama, J., et al.: A survey on concept drift adaptation. ACM Comput. Surv. (CSUR) **46**(4), 44 (2014)

7. Bloch, A.: Online deep learning for behavior prediction. In: Proc. SPIE 12119, Open Architecture/Open Business Model Net-Centric Systems and Defense Transformation (2022). https://doi.org/10.1117/12.2619359

8. Yang, Z., et al.: Online deep learning for high-speed train traction motor temperature prediction. IEEE Trans. Transp. Electrification **10**(1), 608–622. https://doi.org/10.1109/TTE.2023

9. Amorim, G., et al.: Study and development of machine learning models designed for extended reality interactivity in real-time. In: HCII-2024 Conference, vol. 66. LNCS, vol. 15377, Late Breaking Work (2024)

10. Sahu, C., Young, C., Rai, R.: Artificial intelligence (AI) in augmented reality (AR)-assisted manufacturing applications: a review. Int. J. Prod. Res. **59**(16), 4903–4959 (2021). https://doi.org/10.1080/00207543.2020.1859636

11. Cao, J., Lam, K., Lee, L., Liu, X., Hui, P., Su, X.: Mobile Augmented Reality: User Interfaces, Frameworks, and Intelligence (2021). https://doi.org/10.1145/3557999

12. Liberatore, M., Wagner, W.: Virtual, mixed, and augmented reality: a systematic review for immersive systems research. Virtual Reality **25**, 773–799 (2021). https://doi.org/10.1007/s10055-020-00492-0

13. Orji, J., Chan, G., Orji, R.: Augmented Reality and Machine Learning in Health: A Systematic Review, pp. 59–67 (2023). https://doi.org/10.1145/3603421.3603430

14. ML Kit|Google for Developers (2024). https://developers.google.com/ml-kit

15. Ortiz, A., et al.: Fast adapting ensemble: a new algorithm for mining data streams with concept drift. Scientifiworld J. **2015**, 1–14 (2015)

16. Zhang, C., Zhang, Y., Shi, X., et al.: On incremental learning for gradient boosting decision trees. Neural. Process. Lett. **50**, 957–987 (2019). https://doi.org/10.1007/s11063-019-09999-3

17. Luo, Y., Yin, L., Bai, W., Mao, K.: An appraisal of incremental learning methods. Entropy **22**, 1190 (2020). https://doi.org/10.3390/e22111190

18. Lomonaco, V., Maltoni, D.: CORe50. a new dataset and benchmark for continuous object recognition. In: 1st Conference on Robot Learning (CoRL), Mountain View, United States (2017). http://vlomonaco.github.io/core50

19. Tsymbal, A.: The problem of concept drift: definitions and related work, Tech. Rep. TCD-CS-2004-15, Department of Computer Science, Trinity College, Dublin, Ireland (2003)

20. Mariño, L., Ortiz, A., Vasconcelos, G.: Comparative study of fast stacking ensembles families algorithms. Intelligent systems. BRACIS 2020. Lecture Notes in Computer Science, vol. 12320. Springer (2020). https://doi.org/10.1007/978-3-030-61380-8_31
21. Muhlbaier, M., Topalis, A., Polikar, R.: Learn++. NC: combining ensemble of classifiers with dynamically weighted consult-and-vote for efficient incremental learning of new classes. IEEE Trans. Neural Networks **20**(1), 152–168 (2009). https://doi.org/10.1109/TNN.2008.200 8326
22. Liu, Y., Wang, Y., Zhang, J.: New machine learning algorithm: random forest. In: Liu, B., Ma, M., Chang, J. (eds.) Information Computing and Applications. ICICA 2012. LNCS, vol. 7473. Springer, Heidelberg (2012). https://doi.org/10.1007/978-3-642-34062-8_32
23. Shahraki, A., Abbasi, M., and Haugen, Ø.: Boosting algorithms for network intrusion detection: A comparative evaluation of real AdaBoost gentle AdaBoost and modest AdaBoost. Eng. Appl. Artif. Intell., vol. 94, Sep. 2020
24. Ortiz, A., et al.: Fast adaptive stacking of ensembles adaptation for supporting active learning. a real case application. In: 4th International Conference on Natural Computation, Fuzzy Systems and Knowledge Discovery (ICNC-FSKD), Huangshan, China, pp. 732–738 (2018). https://doi.org/10.1109/FSKD.2018.8686851
25. Oza, N.: Online bagging and boosting. In: IEEE Int. Conf. Syst. Man Cybern., Waikoloa, HI, vol. 3, pp. 2340–2345 (2005)
26. Chakraborty, D., Pal, N.: A novel training scheme for multilayered perceptrons to realize proper generalization and incremental learning. IEEE Trans. Neural Netw. **14**, 1–14 (2003)
27. Street, W., Kim, Y.: A streaming ensemble algorithm (SEA) for large-scale classification. In: 7th ACM SIGKDD Int. Conf. Knowl. Disc. Data Mining, pp. 377–382 (2001)
28. Kolter, J., Maloof, M.: Dynamic weighted majority: an ensemble method for drifting concepts. J. Mach. Learn. Res. **8**, 2755–2790 (2007)
29. Liu, H., et al.: Incremental learning with neural networks for computer vision: a survey. Artif. Intell. Rev. **56**, 4557–4589 (2023). https://doi.org/10.1007/s10462-022-10294-2
30. Ramasamy, S., et al.: Online Deep Learning: Growing RBM on the fly. 1803.02043 (2018). https://arxiv.org/abs/1803.02043
31. Uziel, G.: Deep Online Learning with Stochastic Constraints, 1905.10817 (2019). https://arxiv.org/abs/1905.10817
32. Zhang, S., Liu, J., Zuo, X., et al.: Online deep learning based on auto-encoder. Appl. Intell. **51**, 5420–5439 (2021). https://doi.org/10.1007/s10489-020-02058-8
33. Valkanas, A., Oreshkin, B., Coates, M.: MODL: Multilearner Online Deep Learning, 2405.18281 (2024). https://arxiv.org/abs/2405.18281
34. Abdelfattah, M., Mehrotra, A., Dudziak, Ł., Lane, N.: Zero-cost proxies for lightweight NAS. In: International Conference on Learning Representations (2021)
35. Cai, H., et al.: Efficient architecture search by network transformation. In: AAAI Conference on Artificial Intelligence (AAAI) (2018)
36. Liu, H., Simonyan, K., Yang, Y.: DARTS: Differentiable architecture search. In: International Conference on Learning Representations (ICLR) (2019)
37. Zhou, D., et al.: Econas: finding proxies for economical neural architecture search. In: Conference on Computer Vision and Pattern Recognition (CVPR), June 2020
38. Mellor, J., Turner, J., Storkey, A., Crowley, E.: Neural architecture search without training. In: Proceedings of the 38th International Conference on Machine Learning, PMLR 139 (2021)
39. Lee, N., et al.: Snip: single-shot network pruning based on connection sensitivity. In: International Conference on Learning Representations (ICLR) (2019)
40. Wang, Ch., Zhang, G., Grosse, R.: Picking winning tickets before training by preserving gradient flow. In: International Conference on Learning Representations (ICLR) (2020)
41. Tanaka, H., et al.: Pruning neural networks without any data by iteratively conserving synaptic flow. arXiv preprint arXiv:2006.05467 (2020)

42. Theis, L., et al.: Faster gaze prediction with dense networks and fisher pruning. arXiv:1801.05787 (2018)
43. Real, E., Aggarwal, A., Huang, Y., Le, Q.V.: Regularized evolution for image classifier architecture search. In: AAAI Conference on Artificial Intelligence (AAAI) (2019)
44. Zoph, B., Le, Q.V.: Neural architecture search with reinforcement learning. In: International Conference on Learning Representations (ICLR) (2017)
45. Dudziak, L., Chau, T., Abdelfattah, M.S., Lee, R., Kim, H., Lane, N.D.: BRP-NAS: prediction-based NAS using GCNs. In: Neural Information Processing Systems (NeurIPS) (2020)

A Study on Chatbot UI Design Processes Utilizing Generative AI: Integrating ChatGPT and MidJourney

Heehyeon Park[✉]

Hanseo University, Seosan-si, Chungcheongnam-do, 31962 Seosan, South Korea
`hpark@hanseo.ac.kr`

Abstract. This study proposes a generative AI-supported workflow for early-stage chatbot UI design by integrating ChatGPT and MidJourney into the ideation process. While existing approaches often emphasize iterative testing and participatory design, there remains a lack of structured tools that support multimodal creativity in the early phases of chatbot development. To address this, we analyzed 80 real-world chatbot interfaces across various industries using a dual-layered taxonomy: visual form (abstract, cartoon, human-like) and sector classification based on ISIC standards. Findings revealed consistent correlations between chatbot form, emotional tone, and interaction strategies across domains.

Building on these insights, we introduce a five-stage design process: (1) define use case and user goal, (2) generate personas and tone via ChatGPT, (3) create visual prompts through MidJourney, (4) assess visual-function alignment, and (5) iterate based on feedback. This framework enables rapid prototyping and encourages reflective decision-making by connecting text- and image-based ideation. The study contributes a reusable design matrix, practical guidelines, and implications for design education and AI-assisted collaboration. By framing generative AI as a co-creative partner rather than a decision-maker, this work empowers designers to navigate early UI ideation with greater flexibility, nuance, and creativity.

Keywords: AI, Chatbot UI Design, Visual Form Classification, Design Ideation, UX Design Process, Multimodal Design Workflow, Human–AI Co-Creation, ChatGPT, MidJourney.

1 Instruction

The proliferation of conversational agents in digital services has led to growing demand for purposeful and user-centered chatbot interface design. Across sectors such as education, healthcare, finance, and customer service, chatbots are increasingly expected to reflect not only functional performance but also emotional tone and contextual appropriateness [1, 2]. However, early-stage chatbot UI design—especially ideation and visualization—remains challenging, as designers must integrate aesthetic, functional, and affective considerations across diverse industry contexts.

Existing design approaches tend to prioritize iterative refinement through user testing or participatory workshops [3, 4]. While effective in mid- to late-stage development, these methods offer limited support for divergent, multimodal ideation at the beginning of the design process. Designers often lack scalable, structured tools that help them generate and visualize diverse chatbot personas, styles, and interaction models early on.

Recent advances in generative artificial intelligence offer promising tools to address this gap. Large language models such as ChatGPT enable the creation of context-specific chatbot personas, tonal variations, and scenario-based dialogue [5]. Meanwhile, image generators like MidJourney or DALL·E allow rapid visual prototyping based on textual prompts, helping designers explore the visual dimension of chatbot identities without advanced sketching or rendering skills [6]. Despite these capabilities, the integration of such tools into a cohesive design process remains underexplored.

This paper addresses this need by proposing a generative AI-supported workflow for chatbot UI ideation. We begin with a large-scale analysis of 80 real-world chatbot interfaces, categorized by visual form and industry domain. These findings inform a visual-form taxonomy and a design matrix that link chatbot appearance to interaction strategies and emotional tone. Building on this, we propose a five-stage design framework that leverages ChatGPT and MidJourney to support iterative, multimodal ideation in the early phases of chatbot design.

2   Related Work

The design of chatbot user interfaces has gained significant attention as conversational agents become increasingly integrated into everyday digital services. This chapter reviews prior research across three key areas: (1) design approaches for chatbot UIs and their associated challenges, (2) the role of visual form and persona in conversational systems, and (3) the emerging use of generative AI in design ideation. By reviewing the current state of the field, we identify the gaps this study addresses and position our proposed workflow within ongoing scholarly discussions.

2.1   Chatbot UI Design: Trends and Challenges

Chatbots are now widely deployed across industries including healthcare, education, e-commerce, and entertainment. As their functional capabilities evolve, so too do user expectations for nuanced interaction design, including tone of voice, visual identity, and emotional resonance. Consequently, chatbot UIs have become a subject of human–computer interaction (HCI) research not only from a technical standpoint but also from a design and user experience perspective.

Previous studies on chatbot design have typically focused on interaction scripts, usability, and conversational flow [7, 8]. Design processes often rely on participatory workshops, scenario-based prototyping, or iterative testing with end users [9, 10]. While valuable, these methods are primarily used in the refinement stage of design and are less suited to the divergent, exploratory needs of the ideation phase. Furthermore, most early-stage design approaches still require a high level of visualization skill or team-based collaboration, which can pose barriers for novice designers or rapid solo iteration.

Another challenge is the absence of structured frameworks that guide designers in aligning chatbot form with function. For example, the choice of whether a chatbot should appear as an abstract icon, a cartoon character, or a human-like avatar is often left to intuition or ad-hoc decisions rather than informed design strategy. As chatbots grow in complexity and are used in emotionally sensitive contexts such as mental health or customer support, these decisions become increasingly consequential.

Therefore, there is a growing need for systematic methods and tools that support designers in making form-function decisions early in the process. These tools should enable not only creative divergence but also alignment with user needs, domain norms, and emotional expectations. In this context, our study responds to the need for a structured, generative, and multimodal workflow that enhances early-stage ideation in chatbot UI design.

2.2 Visual Form and Persona in Conversational Interfaces

The visual appearance of a chatbot—whether abstract, cartoonish, or human-like—plays a significant role in shaping user perception and interaction. Visual form can influence how users interpret a chatbot's personality, emotional tone, credibility, and intent. As conversational agents are increasingly embedded in emotionally sensitive domains such as healthcare, education, and mental wellness, these visual cues have become a critical part of user experience design.

Several studies have demonstrated that users respond differently depending on a chatbot's visual form. Human-like agents tend to elicit higher perceptions of empathy and social presence, which can increase trust and engagement, particularly in contexts that require emotional support [7, 8]. In contrast, abstract or icon-based designs are often preferred in functional or infrastructure-level applications where neutrality and minimal distraction are prioritized. Cartoon-style avatars, meanwhile, are commonly used in educational or entertainment settings, where they support approachability and affective engagement, especially for younger users [9].

Persona design further enriches the visual layer by integrating tone of voice, communication style, and implied social role. Bickmore and Cassell [8] argue that persona is a critical component of relational interaction, particularly when embodied in a visual form. Go and Sundar [9] found that when visual, identity, and conversational cues are aligned, users perceive the chatbot as more human-like and emotionally intelligent.

Despite growing evidence of visual and persona effects, most design workflows still treat appearance as a late-stage branding concern rather than a strategic element of early ideation. Our study builds on these findings to argue that visual form and persona should be considered central variables in early-stage chatbot UI design. By analyzing how different forms function across domains, we provide a basis for linking visual strategy with interaction goals.

2.3 Generative AI in Design Practice

The emergence of generative artificial intelligence (AI) tools such as ChatGPT and MidJourney has introduced new possibilities for design ideation, enabling designers to generate textual and visual content rapidly from natural language prompts. These tools support multimodal creativity by facilitating the exploration of personas, interaction scripts, tone of voice, and visual representations, without requiring advanced technical skills.

In design research, large language models like ChatGPT have been studied for their potential to augment early-stage concept generation, helping users draft dialogue, user scenarios, and narrative structures [5]. Visual generation tools like MidJourney or DAL-L·E allow designers to quickly prototype stylistic variations of interfaces, characters, or environments by transforming textual descriptions into detailed imagery [6]. This combination of verbal and visual synthesis aligns with the increasing emphasis on multimodal thinking in design practice, particularly in early ideation phases where creativity and breadth of exploration are prioritized.

While generative AI is increasingly used in practice, scholarly frameworks for systematically integrating these tools into the UI design process remain limited. Existing applications often rely on isolated experiments or tool-specific case studies without linking generative output to design strategy or context. Moreover, ethical concerns—such as authorship, originality, and interpretive control—are rarely addressed in structured workflows.

Our study builds upon this emerging body of work by proposing a coherent, five-stage workflow that connects generative AI tools to design decisions in chatbot UI ideation. By embedding ChatGPT and MidJourney within an iterative process informed by empirical insights, we aim to formalize the creative potential of AI in a context-sensitive and designer-centered framework.

2.4 Identified Research Gap

The literature reviewed in the preceding sections highlights important advances in chatbot interface design, persona development, and the creative application of generative AI tools. However, several critical gaps remain unaddressed.

First, most existing studies emphasize the refinement stage of chatbot development—focusing on usability testing, workshop-driven co-design, or evaluation of user interaction—rather than supporting the divergent and exploratory ideation phase. There is a lack of structured methodologies that help designers conceptualize chatbot identity, tone, and form early in the process.

Second, while prior research acknowledges the importance of visual form and persona in shaping user perception, few studies offer practical tools or frameworks to guide form-function alignment across different domains. The decision to represent a chatbot as a human-like avatar, cartoon character, or abstract form is often made intuitively or stylistically, without grounding in empirical analysis.

Third, although generative AI tools such as ChatGPT and MidJourney are increasingly used in practice, they are rarely embedded within formal design workflows. Current applications tend to showcase tool capabilities or isolated design cases, without integrating generative outputs into a broader design rationale or iterative feedback loop.

To address these gaps, this study proposes a generative AI-supported design workflow that combines empirical analysis of chatbot UIs with structured ideation. By integrating ChatGPT and MidJourney into a five-stage framework, the approach supports multimodal creativity, enables context-sensitive form selection, and empowers designers to make more reflective and user-centered decisions in the early phases of chatbot UI development.

3 Methodology

As generative AI technologies increasingly influence design workflows, establishing a clear methodological foundation is essential to understand how such tools can be meaningfully integrated into early-stage UI development. This study adopts a hybrid methodology that combines empirical analysis with speculative design generation. The goal is to build a structured yet flexible framework for chatbot UI ideation that aligns visual form, functional intent, and user context.

The methodology consists of two main phases. First, a dataset of 80 chatbot interfaces was collected from real-world sources and classified using a dual taxonomy: visual form and industry domain. This step aimed to identify recurring design patterns and form-function correlations across sectors. Second, insights from this classification were used to inform the development of a generative AI–assisted design framework, in which tools such as ChatGPT and MidJourney support ideation, prototyping, and iteration.

This chapter details the research design and analytical process up to the formation of the design matrix. The use of generative tools and the resulting workflow are discussed in Sect. 4.

3.1 Research Design Overview

The research employs a two-phase design strategy that merges bottom-up empirical observation with top-down design synthesis. In the first phase, we conducted a systematic analysis of existing chatbot user interfaces deployed across various industries. This involved the collection, categorization, and qualitative examination of 80 chatbot UIs, with a focus on their visual attributes, interaction strategies, and application domains.

Rather than focusing on usability or interaction performance, the analysis centered on identifying how visual form contributes to the functional and emotional tone of chatbot experiences. This approach was motivated by the increasing importance of visual identity and persona in conversational UI design—especially in domains where empathy, trust, or engagement is critical.

The second phase draws from speculative design and co-creative ideation using generative AI. Based on the classified dataset, we examined how ChatGPT can be used to generate domain-specific personas, tone of voice, and dialogue examples. These textual outputs were then transformed into visual concepts using MidJourney, enabling designers to prototype chatbot appearances rapidly and reflect on form-function alignment.

Together, these phases aim to bridge empirical insights with creative exploration. While previous design methods often separate research from ideation, this study integrates the two by grounding AI-assisted workflows in observed design patterns. The following sections detail the dataset and classification scheme that formed the foundation for the design framework.

3.2 Dataset and Classification

To ground the design framework in real-world practice, a dataset of 80 chatbot user interfaces was compiled through purposive sampling. These chatbots were drawn from publicly available platforms—including websites, mobile applications, and design case repositories—between mid-2023 and early 2024. The inclusion criteria were designed to ensure diversity in both functional scope and stylistic expression, capturing the breadth of chatbot usage across industries.

The collected chatbot UIs span six primary domains based on the International Standard Industrial Classification (ISIC) framework: education, healthcare, finance, customer service, e-commerce, and wellness. This industry-based grouping provided contextual grounding for understanding how chatbot design differs depending on user needs, trust requirements, and interaction scenarios.

To facilitate comparative analysis, each chatbot interface was documented using screenshots or screen recordings, preserving both its visual form and conversational flow. Interfaces were then classified using a dual-layered framework:

Visual Form. Each chatbot was categorized as one of the following:

- *Abstract*: Interfaces featuring minimalistic or symbolic icons, often lacking facial features. These designs typically emphasize neutrality and functional clarity.
- *Cartoon Character*: Interfaces that incorporate stylized, expressive characters, often aimed at fostering emotional engagement and approachability—especially in youth-oriented or casual contexts.
- *Human-like Avatar*: Chatbots represented with realistic or semi-realistic human visuals, used primarily in domains where trust, empathy, or professionalism is essential.

Industry Domain. Following the ISIC categorization, each chatbot was assigned to a domain group based on its functional context and service environment.

This dual classification enabled the creation of a cross-tabulated matrix that captured patterns in how chatbot form aligns with domain-specific functional needs, emotional tone, and interaction strategies. For example, abstract forms were more commonly found in infrastructure or system-level services, whereas human-like avatars dominated in healthcare and financial sectors. Cartoon characters appeared frequently in educational and wellness applications.

The resulting taxonomy not only served as an empirical snapshot of current design conventions but also laid the foundation for the design matrix and generative ideation process described in Sect. 4. Through this method, speculative creativity was anchored in observable design realities.

4 Proposed Design Framework

Recent advances in generative artificial intelligence (AI) present new opportunities for augmenting early-stage design processes. While previous approaches to chatbot UI design have largely emphasized downstream stages such as testing, refinement, or branding, the framework presented in this study focuses on upstream ideation and conceptualization. Drawing on the insights derived from a cross-industry analysis of chatbot visual forms and the application of generative AI tools, this chapter outlines a five-stage workflow that supports designers in aligning form, function, and user context. The framework is situated within the "Develop" phase of the Double Diamond design model and emphasizes a multimodal process combining textual and visual thinking. By embedding tools like ChatGPT and MidJourney into an iterative structure, the workflow promotes rapid exploration, design reflection, and form-function coherence in chatbot UI ideation.

4.1 From Taxonomy to Design Strategy

The visual taxonomy introduced in Sect. 3 provided an empirical foundation for understanding how chatbot appearance varies across industry domains and functional roles. Through dual-layered classification-by visual form (abstract, cartoon, human-like) and by domain (e.g., education, finance, healthcare)—recurring patterns were identified in how visual design choices correlate with interaction strategies and emotional tone. This classification was not intended as a static descriptive tool but as a springboard for strategic design application. In this chapter, we translate these patterns into a more actionable form: a visual design matrix that links chatbot form to contextual use and communication style. This matrix supports early-stage decisions around visual identity by helping designers anticipate how a chatbot's appearance may influence user trust, engagement, or functionality perception in different sectors. The empirical grounding of this taxonomy plays a dual role. First, it informs the selection of visual form during ideation. Second, it offers criteria for evaluating AI-generated outputs in later workflow stages. Rather than relying on intuition alone, designers can use this structured insight to steer creative exploration toward context-sensitive and user-appropriate options. Thus, this section serves as a bridge from classification to creation, transforming observational analysis into a practical design strategy that underpins the generative workflow in the following sections. These insights are synthesized into a visual matrix shown in Fig. 1, which distills the taxonomy into an actionable design reference across domains.

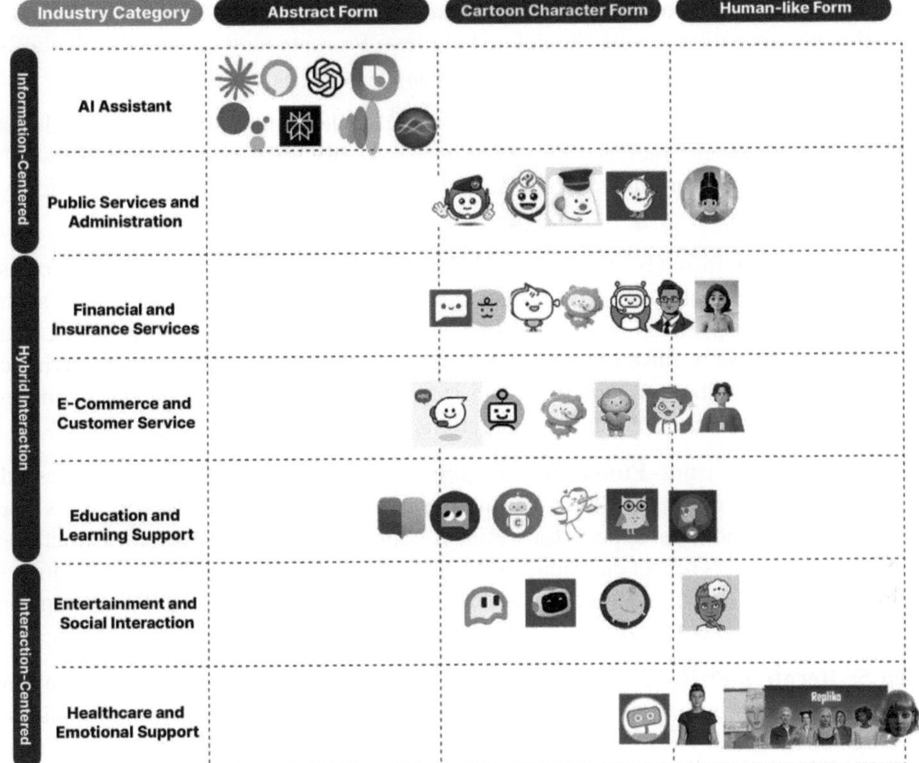

Fig. 1. Chatbot visual form matrix across industry domains and interaction strategies.

4.2 Generative Design Workflow

Building upon the design matrix introduced in the previous section, this study proposes a five-stage generative workflow that integrates ChatGPT and MidJourney into early-stage chatbot UI design. The workflow enables designers to explore, visualize, and iterate on chatbot personas and interfaces by combining structured insights from empirical analysis with creative outputs generated through large language models (LLMs) and image synthesis tools. The workflow is situated within the Develop phase of the Double Diamond model and supports multimodal ideation, where textual and visual thinking reinforce one another. Each stage encourages reflection, creativity, and alignment between chatbot form, tone, and user context.

The five stages are described below:

Step 1: Define Use Case and User Goal. The process begins by identifying the target use case and user scenario. Designers define the chatbot's functional role, domain context, and emotional tone. This includes specifying the service type (e.g., education, wellness, finance), end-user profile, and intended interaction style (e.g., formal, playful, supportive). The design matrix (Fig. 1) can be consulted here to narrow down suitable visual forms based on domain norms and interaction strategies.

Step 2: Generate Persona and Tone with ChatGPT. ChatGPT is prompted to generate a chatbot persona aligned with the defined context. Prompts may include the chatbot's name, role, voice style, emotional expression, and typical dialogue patterns.

Example prompt: "Create a supportive, cartoon-style chatbot for a mental wellness app aimed at teenagers. Include tone of voice, personality traits, and example phrases." The generated textual profile is a foundation for visual translation and tone consistency across interactions.

Step 3: Translate into Visual Prompts for MidJourney. The persona description is transformed into a prompt for MidJourney. Designers extract key visual attributes such as mood, facial expression, age, style (e.g., cartoon, minimalist, photorealistic), and environment. These are used to generate a set of image outputs representing stylistic variations of the chatbot's visual form. This stage facilitates visual divergence, enabling designers to explore multiple stylistic directions rapidly.

Step 4: Evaluate Visual–Functional Alignment. The generated visuals are assessed against the use case defined in Step 1. Evaluation criteria may include trustworthiness (for finance/health), emotional appeal (for wellness/education), or clarity (for infrastructure-level bots). Designers reflect on whether the image matches the user's likely expectations and the service's emotional tone. If misaligned, they revise the ChatGPT prompt or MidJourney input accordingly.

Step 5: Iterate and Reflect. This final stage emphasizes iteration. Designers return to earlier prompts, refine the persona or image description, and generate alternatives. Through this loop, they build an evolving understanding of how visual form, textual tone, and functional goals intersect. Rather than relying on inspiration alone, this structured process supports co-creative exploration with AI while maintaining designer control and intent.

Together, these five stages create a repeatable, scalable method for exploring chatbot UI concepts in a way that is both creative and contextually grounded. The next section presents example cases and design implications derived from applying this workflow across different domains.

Through this loop, they build an evolving understanding of how visual form, textual tone, and functional goals intersect. Rather than relying on inspiration alone, this structured process supports co-creative exploration with AI while maintaining designer control and intent.

This iterative approach reinforces the designer's role as a creator and critical evaluator, ensuring that AI-generated outputs remain aligned with human-centered design values.

4.3 Case Study: Hanseo University Chatbot

To validate the practical applicability of the proposed five-stage generative AI-enhanced design workflow (Sect. 4.2), a case study was conducted by developing a chatbot for

Hanseo University. The goal was to design a friendly, reliable, and professional conversational agent serving multiple user groups—students, applicants, and visitors—by providing accurate and context-specific information. The chatbot visually and linguistically embodied Hanseo University's distinctive strengths in aviation and design education.

Step 1: Define Use Case and User Goal. The initial step involved identifying HanseoBot's primary functions and target audience. The chatbot aimed to assist students with daily tasks such as checking cafeteria menus, obtaining academic certificates, and accessing university resources. Additionally, it supported prospective students and visitors with admissions guidance and general institutional information. Based on the visual design matrix (Fig. 1), a cartoon-style character form was selected to best reflect the friendly and educational context.

Step 2: Generate Persona and Tone with ChatGPT. Using ChatGPT, a clearly defined persona named "HanseoBot" was created, reflecting Hanseo University's identity in aviation and design. The developed persona included detailed aspects:

- **role**: official chatbot representing hanseo university, assisting with inquiries.
- **tone of voice**: friendly, trustworthy, concise, professional, encouraging
- **communication style**: efficient, structured, adaptive, user-centric
- **core values**: representing hanseo university's excellence in aviation and design, customer-centric service.

Sample dialogues were provided to illustrate these attributes clearly, including structured responses to admission queries, supportive communication addressing student emotional concerns, and concise answers to general campus inquiries.

Step 3: Translate into Visual Prompts for MidJourney. Persona descriptions from ChatGPT informed visual prompts for MidJourney:

"Cheerful, approachable cartoon-style chatbot inspired by Hanseo University's symbolic imagery (magpie, aviation motifs such as aviator goggles, scarf) and modern design aesthetics."

MidJourney generated several image variations demonstrating how the chatbot could visually express Hanseo's unique blend of friendliness, aviation symbolism, and modern design identity (see Fig. 2).

Fig. 2. Example visual outputs from MidJourney exploring HanseoBot's visual style.

Step 4: Evaluate Visual–Functional Alignment. Visual outputs from MidJourney were assessed based on criteria such as trustworthiness, emotional resonance, and contextual appropriateness. The selected visuals demonstrated strong alignment with intended user expectations, successfully combining approachable aesthetics and professional clarity, suitable for educational and institutional contexts.

Step 5: Iterate and Reflect. Adjustments were made to both textual and visual elements through iterative refinement. ChatGPT dialogues were revised to align more closely with visual concepts, enhancing coherence across interactions. Feedback from potential users confirmed the chatbot persona's appeal and functional effectiveness, underscoring the workflow's utility in early-stage chatbot UI design.

After completing the five-stage generative design process for the Hanseo University chatbot, the results demonstrate the proposed framework's practical viability and creative potential. The integration of ChatGPT and MidJourney enabled designers to generate coherent, domain-specific chatbot personas and explore a range of visual representations aligned with user goals. The case illustrates how generative tools, when embedded in a structured workflow, can support ideation that is both efficient and context-sensitive. The following chapter discusses broader implications and potential applications of this workflow across educational and professional contexts.

5   Implications and Applications

The generative AI–based chatbot UI design workflow proposed in this study extends beyond a single use case, offering broad applicability across diverse sectors such as education, healthcare, public services, and customer engagement. This chapter outlines key implications for design education and professional practice while also highlighting future opportunities.

5.1 Design Education

The proposed workflow presents significant value for design education, especially for beginners lacking advanced visualization skills or prior experience with UI design. By integrating ChatGPT for persona generation and MidJourney for visual ideation, students can rapidly prototype chatbot concepts from tone to appearance, reducing barriers to early-stage exploration and encouraging experimentation.

Instructors can incorporate the workflow into project-based learning, allowing students to iteratively develop chatbot identities aligned with user needs and service contexts. This approach fosters multimodal thinking—connecting textual, emotional, and visual elements—and supports reflective learning through feedback and iteration. The method can boost student creativity and confidence in foundational or interdisciplinary courses while reinforcing design fundamentals such as empathy, tone consistency, and form-function alignment.

5.2 Professional Design Practice

In professional settings, speed in ideation and clear communication with stakeholders are critical. The workflow is enhanced by enabling rapid prototyping and visual storytelling using generative AI tools. Designers can use ChatGPT to generate tailored personas and MidJourney to visualize stylistic directions without advanced rendering skills. This approach proves helpful in client pitches, workshops, and internal reviews, where communicating tone, identity, and intent is essential. By allowing parallel exploration of visual and narrative aspects, the workflow supports early alignment between teams and stakeholders. Its iterative nature also facilitates agile refinement and client-centered adaptation.

5.3 Cross-domain Scalability

While the case study focused on the education sector, the workflow is well-suited to industries where emotional resonance, trust, and contextual sensitivity are essential, such as mental wellness, healthcare, government, and financial services. In mental health applications, for example, the workflow can be used to create empathetic personas with warm visual styles. More formal, human-like avatars may be more appropriate in finance, where professionalism and clarity are key.

By leveraging the design matrix and AI tools, designers can make informed visual and functional decisions tailored to domain-specific needs. This adaptability highlights the workflow's potential for generating meaningful, context-aware solutions across service ecosystems.

5.4 Tool-Centric Reflection

The integration of ChatGPT and MidJourney demonstrates how generative AI can serve as a creative collaborator in early-stage design. ChatGPT provides structured textual outputs—personas, tone of voice, and dialogues—while MidJourney translates these into rapid visual prototypes. Together, they create a powerful multimodal design environment linking language and imagery. However, each tool comes with limitations. ChatGPT may produce generic or overly idealized personas without precise prompting, and MidJourney lacks fine-grained control over symbolic elements like logos or branded attire. Additionally, issues of authorship, originality, and bias remain critical in both academic and commercial design. These concerns reaffirm the importance of the designer's interpretive role. As discussed in the co-creation literature (Sanders & Stappers, 2008), generative tools should support—not replace—human decision-making. The workflow reinforces the designer's role as curator, guiding AI collaboration to produce coherent, purposeful outcomes.

5.5   Limitations and Future Work

Although the framework shows practical promise, it has certain limitations. First, the case study was conducted in a single institutional setting (Hanseo University), limiting its generalizability. The workflow and visual taxonomy may require adaptation to suit different cultural contexts and industry domains.

Second, design outputs were evaluated qualitatively and based on internal reflection and small-group feedback. Future research should incorporate quantitative methods, such as user testing or large-scale surveys, to more rigorously assess AI-generated chatbot interfaces' effectiveness, usability, and emotional resonance.

Additionally, the workflow currently focuses on static prototyping and does not fully address implementation or dynamic interaction. Integration with platforms like Dialogflow or Rasa and real-time user interaction testing would enhance its practical utility. Future work may also explore automated feedback loops, cross-tool interoperability, and the role of generative AI in long-term chatbot learning and adaptation.

Finally, future studies should also consider inclusive design strategies that address diverse age groups, cultures, and accessibility needs. As generative systems continue to evolve, so too must our frameworks for using them ethically, reflectively, and creatively within design practice.

5.6   Conclusion

This study proposed a practical design workflow in which generative AI serves as a creative assistant rather than a decision-maker. The workflow contributes a structured, multimodal method that integrates generative tools into early-stage chatbot UI design.

Ultimately, the study reaffirms the central role of designers as contextual thinkers who guide and shape AI collaboration to create meaningful user experiences.

Acknowledgment. This work was supported by the 2025 Hanseo University Research Fund.

References

1. McTear, M., Callejas, Z., Griol, D.: The Conversational Interface: Talking to Smart Devices. Springer (2016)

2. Følstad, A., Brandtzaeg, P.B.: Chatbots and the new world of HCI. Interactions **24**(4), 38–42 (2017)
3. Brandt, E., Binder, T., Sanders, E.B.-N.: Tools and techniques: ways to engage telling, making and enacting. In: Routledge International Handbook of Participatory Design (2013)
4. Vardoulakis, L.P., et al.: Designing relational agents as long-term social companions for older adults. In: Proceedings of the International Conference on Intelligent Virtual Agents (2012)
5. Floridi, L., Chiriatti, M.: GPT-3: Its nature, scope, limits, and consequences. Philosophy Technol. **33**(4), 587–594 (2020)
6. Liu, X., Zhang, Y., Wang, K.: Visual co-creation with generative AI in design practice. Des. Stud. **82**, 101122 (2023)
7. Luger, E., Sellen, A.: "Like having a really bad PA": The gulf between user expectation and experience of conversational agents. In: Proceedings of the 2016 CHI Conference, pp. 5286–5297 (2016)
8. Bickmore, T., Cassell, J.: Social dialogue with embodied conversational agents. Advances in Natural Multimodal Dialogue Systems, 23–54 (2005)
9. Go, E., Sundar, S.S.: Humanizing chatbots: the effects of visual, identity and conversational cues on humanness perceptions. Comput. Hum. Behav. **97**, 304–316 (2019)
10. Shechtman, N., Horowitz, L.M.: Media inequality in conversation: How people behave differently when interacting with computers and people. CHI, pp. 281–288 (2003)
11. Brown, T.: Change by Design: How Design Thinking Creates New Alternatives for Business and Society. Harvard Business Press (2009)
12. Frich, J., Marquardt, N., Mirnig, N., & Dörner, R.: Co-creation with AI: a review of human–AI interaction in creative domains. ACM Comput. Surv. **55**(8), Article 164 (2023)
13. Sanders, E.B.N., Stappers, P.J.: Co-creation and the new landscapes of design. CoDesign **4**(1), 5–18 (2008)

Multi-agent LLM with the Chain-of-Thought for Design Creativity Evaluation

Jiazhen Zhang⬤, Ji Han⁽✉⁾⬤, and Saeema Ahmed-Kristensen⬤

University of Exeter, Exeter, UK
{j.zhang15,j.han2,s.ahmed-kristensen}@exeter.ac.uk

Abstract. Creativity plays a significant role in many fields, including design. However, evaluating creativity is a time-consuming and complex process that usually relies on human expertise. Recent advancements in computational techniques have brought the potential opportunity for using Artificial Intelligence (AI), especially the Large Language Models (LLMs), to assist designers in evaluating their creative ideas. This paper introduces an LLM-driven approach for evaluating creativity, focusing on novelty and usefulness, through a structured evaluation procedure. In addition, the Chain-of-Thought (CoT) technique was also adopted to enhance reasoning capabilities for LLMs in the proposed evaluation approach. Furthermore, a novel multi-agent structure was introduced where multiple LLMs acted as evaluators and analysts to collaborate for more reliable evaluation results. This paper also presents a detailed experiment, and the results show that LLMs can provide reliable evaluation results comparable to those of human experts. This paper is one of the first works that explores the use of LLMs to assist creativity evaluation in design and indicates the potential of developing LLM-based creativity support tools for human designers and researchers.

Keywords: Engineering Design · Creativity Evaluation · Large Language Model

1 Introduction

Emerging developments in large language models (LLMs) have brought revolutionary changes and permanently reshaped diverse domains [23]. By learning from massive resources across the Internet, social media, and academic publications, LLMs have acquired knowledge reserves that surpass those of individual humans and have demonstrated significant potential for general artificial intelligence [22]. In previous research on machine learning (ML) and artificial intelligence (AI), researchers primarily focused on quantifiable objectives, such as using neural networks for data classification or image labelling tasks. However, various tasks that cannot be easily quantified remain in human-oriented fields,

© The Author(s), under exclusive license to Springer Nature Switzerland AG 2026
M. Kurosu and A. Hashizume (Eds.): HCII 2025, LNCS 16332, pp. 337–349, 2026.
https://doi.org/10.1007/978-3-032-12385-5_21

such as social sciences [15], human-computer interaction (HCI), and design. Currently, LLMs have demonstrated reliable capabilities in semantic understanding, instruction following, and reasoning [14]. Therefore, adopting them to understand subjective concepts and to generate corresponding responses to assist human users [21] would be a feasible and promising research direction.

In design studies, creativity plays a significant role, particularly in the early stages, underpinning the development of breakthrough products in both tangible and non-tangible forms [12,19]. One commonly accepted definition of creativity is: 'the process by which something is judged (to be creative) is produced' [2]. It is widely acknowledged that creativity involves convergent and divergent thinking in two phases: idea generation and idea evaluation [16]. In recent years, LLMs have been increasingly explored for supporting creativity in the design context, with a focus on the generation stage. For instance, a few works [5,25] have introduced LLMs' knowledge retrieval and reasoning capabilities to retrieve and map biological analogies to generate bio-inspired design ideas. Chen et al. [6] proposed an approach based on the Function-Behaviour-Structure (FBS) model [10] that enabled LLMs to generate design concepts. Wang et al. [20] proposed the use of LLMs for analogical reasoning based on abstract correspondences in both morphological and semantic associations. Moreover, LLMs have also been used to process captioning results to guide new image generation [7] and analyse user requirements [13] for supporting design idea generation.

The aforementioned studies introduced applications that use LLMs to support designers in creative idea generation tasks. On the other side, idea evaluations also play a critical role in offering feedback for designers and providing optimisation suggestions. As a matter of fact, the ability to evaluate ideas is highlighted as one of the key differences between experienced and novice designers [1]. Previous works such as [17] have developed a creativity evaluation engine that utilises LLMs such as GPT-4 to measure the innovation, relevance, and insightfulness of ideas. Still, the proposed evaluation engine did not rate below the average for the ideas that were finally selected and could only be used to filter out low-creativity ideas. Meanwhile, most existing works [9,11] focused on the use of LLMs for general purposes, such as creative writing tasks, rather than evaluating creativity in engineering design. Compared to idea generation applications, support tools and methods for the evaluation of creativity have attracted less attention.

Evaluating creativity in design remains a complex process and relies on expert assessments by humans [8]. LLMs may lack expertise in design and can find it difficult to understand the detailed difference between different designs and ideas [18]. Moreover, considering LLMs are naturally black-box systems and LLMs can be trained through different data sources. The consistency and reliability of the evaluation results are questionable, as any change of model settings can result in varied results. Although LLMs can be adopted for creativity evaluation, a recent empirical study showed that LLMs' creativity evaluation results do not positively correlate with expert assessments [4]. Therefore, there is a need to explore how LLMs could be used for design creativity evaluation while ensuring their evaluation results can be aligned with those from human experts.

This paper aims to address the above challenges, proposing an LLM-driven approach for evaluating creativity by adopting Chain-of-Thought and multi-agent. We first introduced a detailed evaluation criterion for measuring creativity in early-stage design ideas. To improve the consistency of LLM outputs, we then adopted the Chain-of-Thought (CoT) strategy to standardise the evaluation procedure and structure outputs. Furthermore, to mitigate the potential impacts of bias, knowledge constraints, and hallucination during the evaluation process, we combined multiple LLMs into a multi-agent system to enhance the overall reliability of the evaluation results. We conducted sufficient tests and compared the results produced by the LLMs with those of human experts to evaluate their alignment in creativity assessments. The test results show that the CoT with the evaluation procedure enhances the performance of LLMs in creativity evaluation tasks, producing evaluation scores that are better aligned with those of human experts. This work presents a feasible approach to developing reliable and cost-efficient tools by combining multiple LLMs with the CoT to assist designers in early-stage design creativity assessment tasks.

2   Methodology

2.1   Criteria for Novelty and Usefulness Evaluation

Assessing design creativity is a complex process involving multiple factors. Therefore, the evaluation procedure must be carefully designed to align with the specific design task. Inspired by the evaluation procedure proposed in [24], this work focuses on novelty and usefulness as the two main aspects of design creativity. To measure each aspect, we formulated four questions and instructed LLMs to analyse the test samples and respond accordingly. We then collect the responses and use a rule table to regularise and construct the results with a 7-point Likert scale. Details of the evaluation procedures for novelty and usefulness are as follows.

Novelty Evaluation: In the evaluation procedure, novelty is defined as "how unique, original, or different a product or design is compared to what already exists in the market or design space", and it is measured by assessing the functionality and structure innovations of an idea. Inspired by the SAPPhIRE model [3], this evaluation procedure used the following four questions (Q) to measure how novel the idea is in both functionality and structure:

Q1. Find and compare the function (i.e. how this works) of this product with the functions of other products. Does this function exist in any other product?
Q2. Is the new function applied to the entire product?
Q3. Find and compare the structure of this product with the structure of other products. Is the structure the same?
Q4. Is the new structure applied to the entire product?

Table 1. Result table for novelty

Q1	Q2	Q3	Q4	Result
YES	NA	YES	NA	0 (No)
YES	NA	NO	YES	2 (Poor)
YES	NA	NO	NO	1 (Very Poor)
NO	NO	NO	YES	5 (Very Good)
NO	NO	NO	NO	4 (Good)
NO	NO	YES	NA	1 (Very Poor)
NO	YES	YES	NA	3 (Fair)
NO	YES	NO	NO	5 (Very Good)
NO	YES	NO	YES	6 (Excellent)

Table 2. Result table for usefulness

Q1	Q2	Q3	Q4	Result
NO	NA	NO	NA	0 (No)
NO	NA	YES	NO	1 (Very Poor)
NO	NA	YES	YES	3 (Fair)
YES	NO	NO	NA	2 (Poor)
YES	NO	YES	NO	4 (Good)
YES	NO	YES	YES	5 (Very Good)
YES	YES	NO	NA	3 (Fair)
YES	YES	YES	NO	5 (Very Good)
YES	YES	YES	YES	6 (Excellent)

This criterion is designed to evaluate the creativity of design ideas. LLMs would need to consider the potential of the proposed products based on these early concepts. In detail, Q1 and Q3 assess whether the sample introduces innovations in functionality and structure. Q2 and Q4 serve as sub-questions to evaluate how well these innovations are presented in these two factors. Each question is simplified with the response options YES, NO, or Not Applicable to ensure that LLMs can understand and able to follow the evaluation flow.

Each design idea will be evaluated through these four questions, and LLMs will then use the following Table 1 to project the question answer collections into a numerical score on a 7-point scale. A score of 0 indicates that the design lacks novelty in both functionality and structure, while the highest score of 6 signifies a highly novel design that offers groundbreaking innovation for the relevant task. A higher score demonstrates greater novelty in the design, suggesting that the sample could be a more creative idea with pioneering and instructive value for related designs.

Usefulness Evaluation: Similar to novelty evaluation criteria, usefulness evaluation also follows the following four questions:

Q1. Evaluate the effectiveness of this product. Does the product fulfil the task requirements?

Q2. Does it use a more efficient way to solve the problem (compared to similar products)?

Q3. Evaluate the feasibility of this product. Is the design feasible (e.g. technically feasible)?

Q4. Is it easier to use, or does it cost less to maintain (compared to similar products)?

In this evaluation procedure, usefulness is defined as "how well the design performs its intended function and how practical or beneficial it is to the user". It is measured by assessing both the effectiveness and feasibility of an idea. Q1 and Q2 evaluate whether the idea effectively addresses the design task, while Q3 and Q4 target the feasibility measurements of the design. We also provide LLMs with a rule table to output numerical scores, as presented in Table 2.

2.2 Prompting with the CoT

To evaluate the novelty and usefulness of design ideas, we implemented the above evaluation procedure with natural language and provided it to LLMs for guidance, as well as the texted ideas for assessment.

Directly sending the evaluation procedure to LLMs can help standardise the process, but it also raises transparency concerns, as the reasoning steps of LLMs are usually implicit. Considering that LLMs are inherently language-based predictive models that learn patterns and relationships from training data and generate responses based on the input, they may not fully understand evaluation criteria or reliably follow this multi-step evaluation process. Therefore, we provide LLMs with the following example of how we address the evaluation task step-by-step, and use it as the CoT to provide explicit intermediate reasoning chains. Based on the questions in the procedure, we break down the evaluation task into multiple steps and ask LLMs to follow the same structure while generating their responses.

Chain-of-Thought Example

Sample: <Drainpipe with end stops - thick enough for safety and not to burn hands. Easy to drink from. Flat-bottomed. Could have a lid.>
Novelty Evaluation:
Q1. Find and compare the function (i.e. how this works) of this product with the functions of other products. Does this function exist in any other product?
Answer for Q1: <This sample shows a new function of using a drainpipe with flat end stops. This is a new way to design a container that can hold hot liquid by using a drainpipe. Q1: NO>
Q2. Is the new function applied to the entire product?
Answer for Q2: <The new function is applied to the whole product, as the whole drainpipe with end stops is now used as a hot liquid container. Q2: YES>
Q3. Find and compare the structure of this product with the structure of other products. Is the structure the same?
Answer for Q3: <Still, the inspiration for using a drainpipe as the structural design is unconventional. Most existing beverage containers are cylindrical or ergonomic but will not consider using drainpipe shapes. Q3: NO>
Q4. Is the new structure applied to the entire product?
Answer for Q4: <While the drainpipe-inspired shape is novel, features like the flat bottom and potential lid are standard and common in beverage

containers. The novel structure does not apply to the entire product. Q4: NO>
Summarize the results from four questions: <Q1: NO> <Q2: YES> <Q3: NO> <Q4: NO>
Now, checking the novelty score table, the Novelty score of this product is <Result:5>
Usefulness Evaluation:
Q1. Evaluate the effectiveness of this product. Does the product fulfil the task requirements?
Answer to Q1: <This sample uses a thick drainpipe with end stops to hold hot liquid. It fulfils the task requirement. Q1:YES>
Q2. Is it a more efficient way to solve the problem (compared to similar products)?
Answer to Q2: <Other similar products, such as cups and bottles, have the same design (cylindrical or slightly tapered body with end stops). It does not use a more efficient way to solve the problem. Q2:NO>
Q3. Evaluate the feasibility of this product. Is the design feasible (e.g. technically feasible)?
Answer to Q3: <Drainpipes are usually made of metal or plastic and are designed to deliver rain or liquid waste. Therefore, it may not be safe to use drainpipes to hold drinkable liquid as they are not food-safe. Therefore, this design is not feasible. Q3:NO>
Q4. Is it easier to use or does it take less cost to maintain (compared to similar products)?
Answer to Q4: <Since this product is not feasible as it received NO in Q3, we do not need to determine if it can be easier to use or maintain (compared to other products). This question is not applicable. Q4:NA>
Summarize the results from four questions: <Q1: YES> <Q2: NO> <Q3: NO> <Q4: NA>
Now, checking the usefulness score table, the Usefulness score of this product is <Result:2>

2.3   Multi-agent System for Creativity Evaluation

The CoT strategy breaks down evaluation tasks into steps, which can significantly enhance the reasoning capabilities of LLMs. However, different LLMs may produce varied judgments when assessing idea creativity. This variation can result from differences in training data, as some models may lack access to up-to-date or domain-specific information. Additionally, the concepts of novelty and usefulness are subjective and can be influenced by various factors, including application context, domain expertise, and individual human perception. In fact, even when involving experienced researchers and design experts in creativity evaluation sessions, disagreements can frequently occur during assessments. This is due to this evaluation task is open-ended, and there may not exist one

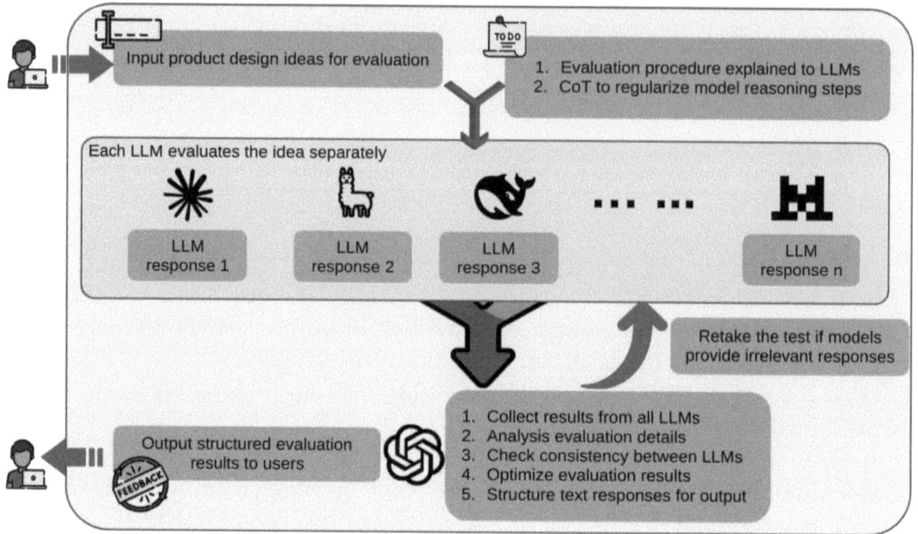

Fig. 1. Framework of the multi-agent system to assist human designers for creativity evaluation.

specific answer which is "correct". Therefore, as long as the results from different evaluators reach a reasonable level of consensus, the evaluations can be considered valid.

Based on this consideration, we designed a multi-agent system that collaborates with LLMs from different sources to ensure that the final evaluation results reach a reasonable consensus. As shown in Fig. 1, we first input the evaluation procedure as well as the CoT example as the systematic prompt into LLMs, and then provide them with the design idea so that they could start the evaluation procedure. After receiving all responses from evaluator LLMs, another LLM will act as the analyst to review the evaluation details and investigate whether the results can reach an alignment among evaluators. If the evaluator LLMs fail to achieve alignment or if their responses are off-topic, the analyst LLM will return the invalid responses and the systematic prompt to the evaluator LLMs for retesting. If the analyst LLM detects alignment, or if most evaluator LLMs provide the same final score, it will consolidate the results and generate a structured report with detailed evaluation processes for users to review.

3   Experiment and Results

3.1   Experiment Settings

In this test, we conducted a survey study to collect novel ideas from both human participants and ChatGPT. The task for this design session was: "Design as many novel ideas as possible for holding hot liquids for drinking." Participants were encouraged to engage in creative thinking to address this design target

Table 3. Overview of LLMs adopted in the experiment

Model	Parameters	Source	Context Length	Architecture	Released Date	Role
GPT-4o	NA	Closed	128K	Transformer	2024.05	Evaluator
Llama-3.3	70B	Open	128K	Transformer	2024.12	Evaluator
Llama-4-Maverick	17B	Open	256K	MoE	2025.04	Evaluator
Qwen3	32B	Open	128K	Transformer	2025.04	Evaluator
Gemini-2.5-Flash	NA	Closed	1M	MoE	2025.05	Evaluator
DeepSeek-R1-0528	685B	Open	512K	MoE	2025.05	Evaluator
Phi-4-multimodal	5.6B	Open	128K	Transformer	2025.02	Evaluator
Mistral	24B	Open	32K	Transformer	2025.01	Evaluator
Claude-3-7-sonnet	NA	Closed	200K	Transformer	2025.02	Evaluator
GPT-4.1	NA	Closed	1M	Transformer	2025.04	Analyst

and to provide early-stage design ideas. From the collected ideas, we randomly sampled 77 ideas, of which 36 were provided by humans and 41 were generated by ChatGPT. We invited humans to evaluate these ideas as benchmark scores so that we can compare the alignment between humans and LLMs.

Two design experts, each with over 10 years of experience in both industry and academia, voluntarily participated in the human evaluation task. They were provided with evaluation guidelines and independently assessed the novelty and usefulness of the design idea samples using a 7-point Likert scale. A Cronbach's Alpha test (CAT) was conducted to measure the alignment between them. It achieves Good reliability for the novelty measure ($\alpha = 0.80$) and Excellent for the usefulness measure ($\alpha = 0.92$). After completing their evaluations, the two experts discussed their results and adjusted their ratings through consensus to establish a final agreed-upon evaluation.

Table 3 presents an overview of 10 different LLMs that were used in this test. To construct the multi-agent system, 9 LLMs such as GPT-4o, Llama, and Qwen were assigned as evaluators, and we used the latest version of GPT (GPT-4.1) as the analyst. Evaluator LLMs were selected from various providers to ensure model diversity. Most LLMs are built with the transformer architecture, while some adopt a novel mixture of experts (MoE) framework (which was also based on the transformer) to improve the overall quality of their responses. The release dates of each model were also verified to ensure that all models were up to date and had acquired sufficient knowledge for conducting creativity evaluation tasks. We used the official APIs to get access to these models and have determined that input texts were not used for further model training to avoid overfitting or data leakages. Additionally, temperature settings for all LLMs were set to zero for model consistency considerations.

3.2   Experiment Results

Since creativity is difficult to quantify, it would be unrealistic to expect that evaluations from LLMs can be fully consistent with those of human experts. Therefore, results from LLMs should be acceptable as long as scores are close to those of the human evaluators. Based on this consideration, we divided the 7-point Likert scale into four categories for both novelty and usefulness evaluation. Score 0 indicates there's no novelty or usefulness, 1 and 2 represent low level, 3 and 4 for medium level, and 5 and 6 indicate the idea shows high novelty or usefulness.

We collected evaluation scores from all LLMs and compared them with those of the human experts to assess alignment. Figure 2 presents the percentage of aligned evaluation scores between human evaluators and LLMs when both the evaluation procedure and the CoT strategy were provided. For comparison, Fig. 3 presents the alignment results when only the evaluation procedure was provided to the LLMs, without the CoT strategy. The blue bars represent the percentage of ideas that have aligned evaluation scores from LLMs, while the orange bars are for usefulness evaluations. A high bar indicates that the results from LLM are closer to human scores. Compared to the non-CoT evaluation results, applying the CoT strategy can improve the alignment between LLMs and human experts, particularly in the evaluation of novelty. Meanwhile, the CoT strategy can mitigate the imbalance of performance between different models. The Phi4 model, for instance, is a lightweight open-sourced language model with only 5.6B parameters. It does not perform well when directly provided with the evaluation procedure, as it may not fully comprehend the evaluation process, or lack the capabilities to solve this complex task. The CoT prompt, on the other hand, offers it with a workflow example demonstrating how to follow the procedure and analyse idea novelty and usefulness step by step, which significantly improves its performance.

In these two figures, we also present the performance of the multi-agent system using GPT-4.1 as the analyst. The multi-agent approach demonstrated high alignment with human experts comprehensively on both novelty and usefulness evaluation tasks. Specifically, when using the evaluation procedure with the CoT example as the systematic prompt, the multi-agent system aligned with human expert scores on 40 ideas in novelty evaluation and 39 in usefulness.

In this work, we also used the CAT to assess the reliability of LLM evaluations. Cronbach's alpha is a widely used metric for measuring internal consistency reliability. The results of CAT (α) usually range from 0 to 1, with higher values indicating better alignment among evaluators. In this work, we classified the reliability of test results as follows: $\alpha < 0.5$ as unacceptable, $0.5 \leq \alpha < 0.6$ as poor, $0.6 \leq \alpha < 0.7$ as acceptable, $0.7 \leq \alpha < 0.9$ as good, and over 0.9 as excellent. In this test, we calculated the CAT using the results with 7-point scales produced by the LLMs and those provided by human experts, and listed the results in Table 4. The results indicate that the CoT approach can significantly improve reliability on both novelty and usefulness across all models. The multi-agent approach also achieves good (novelty) and acceptable (usefulness)

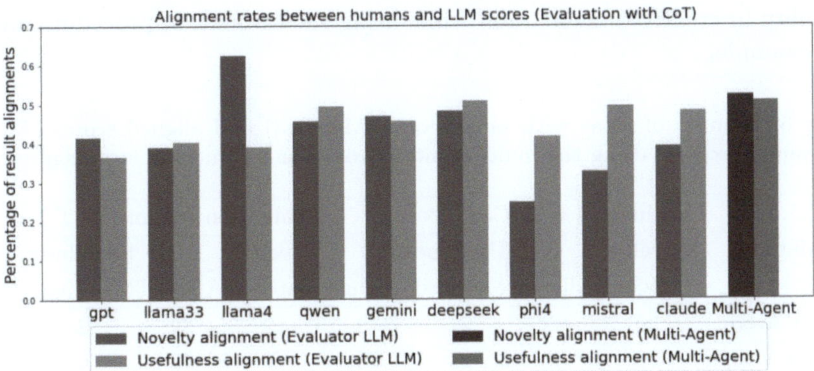

Fig. 2. Alignments between human experts and LLMs for creativity evaluation when using the evaluation procedure and the CoT example.

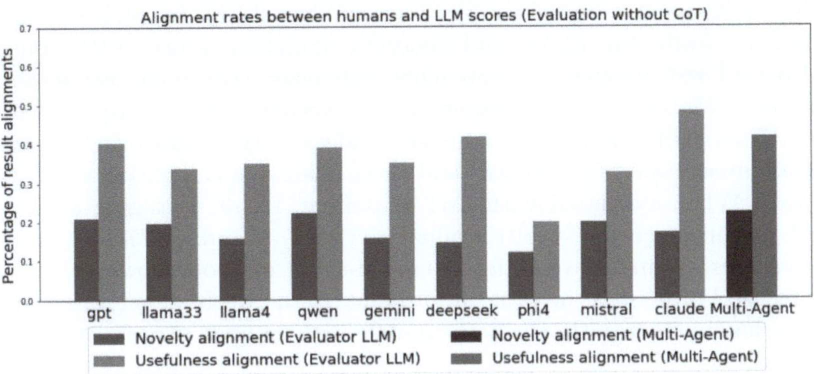

Fig. 3. Alignments between human experts and LLMs for creativity evaluation when only the evaluation procedure was provided.

Table 4. CAT for reliability evaluation of LLMs (with and without CoT)

Model Name	Evaluation with CoT				Evaluation without CoT			
	Novelty		Usefulness		Novelty		Usefulness	
GPT-4o	0.7335	Good	0.5987	Poor	0.5941	Poor	0.4644	Unaccept
Llama-3.3	0.6035	Accept	0.5132	Poor	0.4294	Unaccept	0.5264	Poor
Llama-4-Maverick	0.7238	Good	0.5653	Poor	0.5484	Poor	0.5013	Poor
Qwen3	0.4474	Unaccept	0.4276	Unaccept	0.5008	Poor	0.2078	Unaccept
Gemini-2.5-Flash	0.6759	Accept	0.4875	Unaccept	0.4900	Unaccept	0.4415	Unaccept
DeepSeek-R1-0528	0.6334	Accept	0.4803	Unaccept	0.4471	Unaccept	0.5690	Poor
Phi-4-multimodal	0.1538	Unaccept	0.2311	Unaccept	0.3923	Unaccept	0.1138	Unaccept
Mistral	0.5790	Poor	0.6266	Accept	0.4361	Unaccept	0.4091	Unaccept
Claude-3-7-sonnet	0.7788	Good	0.6245	Accept	0.4613	Unaccept	0.5778	Poor
Multi-Agent	0.7428	Good	0.6194	Accept	0.5387	Poor	0.6174	Accept

reliability in creativity evaluation while using the evaluation procedure and the CoT example.

Table 5. Number of ideas with same scores (Matched) and aligned scores (Aligned) with human experts using the multi-agent approach and numerical score aggregations

Method	Evaluation with CoT				Evaluation without CoT			
	Novelty		Usefulness		Novelty		Usefulness	
	Matched	Aligned	Matched	Aligned	Matched	Aligned	Matched	Aligned
Result Average	30	42	21	33	12	32	22	34
Result Voting	25	35	28	36	8	13	10	31
Multi-agent	30	40	28	39	11	17	15	32

The multi-agent method employs an analyst LLM to review evaluation details from evaluator LLMs and generate numerical scores with consensus. We also explored alternative approaches that aggregate numerical scores from evaluator LLMs using result averaging and voting, with results presented in Table 5. This table details the number of ideas with scores exactly matching those of human experts (Matched) and those achieving category-level alignment (Aligned). When evaluated with CoT reasoning, result averaging achieves the highest performance in Novelty evaluation, with 42 out of 77 ideas receiving aligned scores, compared to 40 for the multi-agent method. However, the multi-agent method presented the best performance in the Usefulness evaluation, with 28 ideas having scores that exactly match with human experts, and 39 with aligned scores.

4 Conclusion

This paper introduces a novel LLM-driven approach for evaluating creativity, focusing on novelty and usefulness, to assist humans in the early stages of design. The approach incorporates a chain-of-thought strategy to enhance reasoning capabilities and improve the consistency of LLMs. Moreover, a multi-agent system is adopted that aggregates results from evaluator LLMs to mitigate the potential biases or misunderstandings from individual LLMs. The study has collected design ideas from both humans and ChatGPTs and employed the proposed LLM-driven approach to assess their creativity. The evaluation results are then compared with expert evaluations to examine the alignment. The results show that the proposed CoT strategy can significantly enhance model capabilities and reliability on the creativity evaluation task. The multi-agent system can further improve the performance as the evaluation scores can better align with human expert judgments. The proposed LLM-driven creativity evaluation approach provides useful insights into the application of LLMs for supporting creativity evaluation and demonstrates the potential for human-AI collaboration and interaction in advancing design performance.

Acknowledgement. This work is funded by DIGITLab, UKRI Next Stage Digital Economy Centre (EP/T022566/1).

References

1. Ahmed, S., Wallace, K.: Identifying and supporting the knowledge needs of novice designers within the aerospace industry. J. Eng. Design **15**(5), 475–492 (2004). https://doi.org/10.1080/09544820841000708430
2. The Social Psychology of Creativity. SSSP, Springer, New York (1983). https://doi.org/10.1007/978-1-4612-5533-8_9
3. Chakrabarti, A., Sarkar, P., Leelavathamma, B., Nataraju, B.S.: A functional representation for aiding biomimetic and artificial inspiration of new ideas. AI EDAM **19**, 113–132 (2005). https://doi.org/10.1017/S0890060405050109
4. Chakrabarty, T., Laban, P., Agarwal, D., Muresan, S., Wu, C.S.: Art or artifice? Large language models and the false promise of creativity. In: Proceedings of the 2024 CHI Conference on Human Factors in Computing Systems (CHI '24. vol. Article 30, pp. 1–34. Association for Computing Machinery, New York, NY, USA (2024). https://doi.org/10.1145/3613904.3642731
5. Chen, L., et al.: BIDTrainer: an LLMs-driven education tool for enhancing the understanding and reasoning in bio-inspired design. In: Proceedings of the 2024 CHI Conference on Human Factors in Computing Systems (CHI '24. vol. Article 676, pp. 1 20. Association for Computing Machinery, New York, NY, USA (2024). https://doi.org/10.1145/3613904.3642887
6. Chen, L., Jing, Q., Tsang, Y., Wang, Q., Sun, L., Luo, J.: DesignFusion: integrating generative models for conceptual design enrichment. J. Mech. Des. **146**, 11 (2024). https://doi.org/10.1115/1.4065487
7. Choi, D., Hong, S., Park, J., Chung, J., Kim, J.: CreativeConnect: supporting reference recombination for graphic design ideation with generative AI. In: Proceedings of the 2024 CHI Conference on Human Factors in Computing Systems (CHI '24, pp. 1–25. Association for Computing Machinery, New York, NY, USA (2024). https://doi.org/10.1145/3613904.3642794
8. Cropley, D., Kaufman, J.: The siren song of aesthetics? Domain differences and creativity in engineering and design. Proc. Inst. Mech. Eng. **233**(2), 451–464 (2019). https://doi.org/10.1177/0954406218778311
9. Distefano, P., Patterson, J., Beaty, R.: Automatic scoring of metaphor creativity with large language models. Creativity Res. J. 1–15 (2024). https://doi.org/10.1080/10400419.2024.2326343
10. Gero, J.: Design prototypes: a knowledge representation schema for design. AI Mag. **11**(4), 26 (1990). https://doi.org/10.1609/aimag.v11i4.854
11. Hadas, E., Hershkovitz, A.: Using large language models to evaluate alternative uses task flexibility score. Thinking Skills Creativity **52**, 101549 (2024). https://doi.org/10.1016/j.tsc.2024.101549
12. Han, J., Shi, F., Chen, L., Childs, P.: The combinator a computer-based tool for creative idea generation based on a simulation approach. Design Sci. **4**, 11 (2018). https://doi.org/10.1017/dsj.2018.7
13. Hou, Y., Yang, M., Cui, H., Wang, L., Xu, J., Zeng, W.: C2ideas: supporting creative interior color design ideation with a large language model. In: Proceedings of the 2024 CHI Conference on Human Factors in Computing Systems, CHI '24 vol. 172, pp. 1–18 (2024). https://doi.org/10.1145/3613904.3642224

14. Jiang, S., Xie, M., Luo, J.: Large language models for combinatorial optimization of design structure matrix (2024), arXiv preprint arXiv:2411.12571
15. Karjus, A.: Machine-assisted quantitizing designs: augmenting humanities and social sciences with artificial intelligence. Humanit. Soc. Sci. Commun. **12**(1), 1–18 (2025)
16. Runco, M., Acar, S.: Divergent thinking as an indicator of creative potential. Creativity Res. J. **24**(1), 66–75 (2012). https://doi.org/10.1080/10400419.2012.652929
17. Shaer, O., Cooper, A., Mokryn, O., Kun, A., Shoshan, H.: AI-augmented brainwriting: investigating the use of LLMs in group ideation. In: Proceedings of the 2024 CHI Conference on Human Factors in Computing Systems (CHI '24), pp. 1–17. Association for Computing Machinery, New York, NY, USA (2024). https://doi.org/10.1145/3613904.3642414
18. Szymanski, A., Ziems, N., Eicher-Miller, H.A., Li, T.J.J., Jiang, M., Metoyer, R.A.: Limitations of the LLM-as-a-judge approach for evaluating LLM outputs in expert knowledge tasks. Int. Conf. Intell. User Interfaces Proc. IUI **15**, 952–966 (2025).https://doi.org/10.1145/3708359.3712091/SUPPL_FILE/3708359.3712091-VIDEO1.VTT
19. Wang, B., Zhu, Y., Chen, L., Liu, J., Sun, L., Childs, P.: A study of the evaluation metrics for generative images containing combinational creativity. AI EDAM **37**, 11 (2023). https://doi.org/10.1017/S0890060423000069
20. Wang, B., et al.: From analogy to innovation: a creative conceptual design approach leveraging large language models. Adv. Eng. Inform. **67**, 103427 (2025)
21. Wang, X., et al.: Perspective transition of large language models for solving subjective tasks (2025). https://arxiv.org/pdf/2501.09265
22. Xu, S., Wei, Y., Zheng, P., Zhang, J., Yu, C.: LLM enabled generative collaborative design in a mixed reality environment. J. Manufact. Syst. **74**, 703–715 (2024). https://doi.org/10.1016/J.JMSY.2024.04.030
23. Xu, Y., Wang, F., Zhang, T.: Artificial intelligence is restructuring a new world. Innovation **5**, 100725 (2024). https://doi.org/10.1016/j.xinn.2024.100725
24. Zhang, J., Han, J., Ahmed-Kristensen, S.: Exploring the use of LLMs to evaluate design creativity. Proc. Des. Soc. **5**, 1773–1782 (2025). https://doi.org/10.1017/pds.2025.10191
25. Zhu, Q., Zhang, X., Luo, J.: Biologically inspired design concept generation using generative pre-trained transformers. J. Mech. Design **145**, 4 (2023). https://doi.org/10.1115/1.4056598

Ethics, Privacy and Sustainability in Digital Systems

Legal Approaches to Addressing Dark Patterns

Kaori Ishii[(✉)]

Faculty of Global Informatics, Chuo University, Tokyo, Japan
`kaoriish@tamacc.chuo-u.ac.jp`

Abstract. Dark patterns, characterized by their manipulative nature, have garnered increasing attention in the fields of consumer and privacy protection law. The infringement of autonomy itself constitutes harm, and maintaining fairness is essential for mitigating such harm. The prevalence of dark patterns is evident from investigations conducted in various countries, underscoring the need for legal regulations. Hence, this article examines dark patterns, focusing on their infringement of autonomy, and reviews regulatory developments in the EU, the U.S., and Japan. Regulatory approaches include (1) directly prohibiting dark patterns; (2) applying general provisions that mandate fair processing of personal data or fair trade; (3) classifying dark patterns as unfair commercial practices and subjecting them to legal enforcement; (4) invalidating consent obtained through the use of dark patterns; (5) specifying individual types of behavior and imposing restrictions on them; and (6) requiring safeguards to be embedded by design and by default. While regulatory methods vary across countries and regions, establishing rules that mandate fairness in business practices and accumulating specific enforcement cases can serve as deterrents, provided that the enforcement agencies function effectively. Furthermore, complementary measures, such as targeted regulations on particularly harmful practices and enhanced penalties for overlapping violations, should be considered. In particular, utilizing technological tools and encouraging proactive efforts by businesses to address dark patterns are crucial measures.

Keywords: Dark patterns · Consumer protection · Privacy · Personal data protection

1 Introduction

The phrase "dark pattern," introduced by user interface designer Harry Brignull in 2010, refers to "a user interface that has been carefully crafted to trick users into doing things, such as buying insurance with their purchase or signing up for recurring bills" [1, p. 5], and has since sparked extensive research into these deceptive practices and their implications.

Dark patterns have been primarily discussed in the field of consumer protection law; however, in recent years, they have also gained increasing attention in the field of privacy and data protection law.

The Global Privacy Enforcement Network released its findings on deceptive design patterns on July 9, 2024. The sweep investigation, led by Canada's Office of the Privacy Commissioner, examined 1,010 websites and applications. The findings highlighted the widespread use of dark patterns in privacy-related interfaces. More than 89% of privacy policies were found to be excessively long or written in a complex language suitable only for those with a university-level education. Interface interference was common, with 42% of websites and applications using emotionally charged language to sway user decisions and 57% making the less privacy-protective options the easiest to select. Nagging patterns appeared on 35% of platforms, repeatedly urging users to delete their accounts. Obstruction tactics were observed in 39% of the cases, making it difficult for users to access privacy settings or delete their accounts. Additionally, 9% of websites and applications required users to disclose more personal information than was required during account creation when attempting to delete their accounts [2].

Privacy and data protection law has witnessed a proliferation of overlapping challenges at the intersection of consumer protection and competition law. Dark patterns epitomize these issues, garnering particular attention within the consumer and personal information protection frameworks. Hence, this article explores the issue of "dark patterns," the harms they pose, and the legal responses needed to address them from a comparative law perspective, focusing on protecting consumers, privacy, and personal data.

The remainder of this paper is structured as follows. Section 2 presents an overview of the definitions and classifications of "dark patterns" and identifies the harms caused by these practices from the perspectives of consumer and personal data protection. This study does not propose its own definitions or classifications. Rather, it draws upon the "Dark Commercial Patterns" report, published by the Organisation for Economic Co-operation and Development in 2022 [hereinafter OECD report] [3], which has conducted the most comprehensive research. Section 3 examines recent legal regulations and enforcement cases related to dark patterns in the EU and the U.S. and highlights the value of comparing the two approaches. Section 4 discusses legislative developments concerning dark patterns in Japan. We focus on Japan because recent amendments to certain laws, along with growing attention to dark patterns in government discussions, have brought this issue to the forefront. These discussions often reference trends in Europe and the U.S. Furthermore, Japan's development in this area remains relatively unknown on the international stage, and shedding light on them could enhance global understanding of issues related to dark patterns. Section 5 explores appropriate regulatory approaches to addressing dark patterns. Finally, Sect. 6 summarizes the main conclusions.

2   The Definitions of Dark Patterns and the Diverse Nature of Their Harms

2.1   Overview of the Definitions of Dark Patterns and Their Classifications

Numerous prior studies have attempted to define and classify dark patterns [4]. The OECD report, widely regarded as the most comprehensive investigative study, defines dark patterns as follows:

Dark commercial patterns are business practices employing elements of digital choice architecture, in particular in online user interfaces, that subvert or impair consumer autonomy, decision-making, or choice. They often deceive, coerce, or manipulate consumers and are likely to cause direct or indirect consumer detriment in various ways, though it may be difficult or impossible to measure such detriment in many instances [3, p. 16].

This definition focuses on consumer autonomy, decision-making, and choice. Ensuring consumers' ability to make rational choices is a fundamental principle of consumer law, and in discussions on the right to privacy, the ability to determine how one's own information is handled is a crucial aspect. This definition states that dark patterns, "deceive, coerce, or manipulate consumers" by adopting a broad interpretation. The most challenging aspect is measuring consumer detriment, a topic addressed later in this paper.

The OECD report refers to several key prior works on the taxonomies of dark patterns and categorizes them into "forced action," "interface interference," "nagging," "obstruction," "sneaking," "social proof," and "urgency" [3, pp. 9–11]. The first paragraphs that follows a table, figure, equation etc. does not have an indent, either (Table 1).

Table 1. Categories and Names of Dark Patterns.

Category	Name of Dark Pattern
Forced Action	Forced registration, Forced disclosure/Privacy zuckering, Friend spam/Social pyramid/Address book leeching, Gamification
Interface Interference	Hidden information, False hierarchy, Misleading reference pricing, Trick questions, Disguised ads, Confirmshaming/Toying
Nagging	Nagging
Obstruction	Hard to cancel or opt out/Roach motel/Click fatigue/Ease, (Price) comparison prevention, Immortal accounts, Intermediate currency
Sneaking	Sneak into basket, Hidden costs/Drip pricing, Hidden subscription/Forced continuity, Bait and switch, including bait pricing
Social Proof	Activity messages, Testimonials
Urgency	Low stock/High demand message, Countdown timer/Limited time message

Source: The OECD report, p. 53 (Annex B: Example of Consolidated Taxonomy of Dark Patterns)

The Federal Trade Commission [hereinafter FTC], whose mission is to prevent deceptive or unfair business practices in the marketplace, published a staff report titled "Bringing Dark Patterns to Light" [hereinafter FTC report] in September 2022 [5]. The FTC report defines dark patterns as "design practices that trick or manipulate users into making choices they would not otherwise have made, and that may cause harm" [5, p. 2]. It further categorizes dark patterns into the following types: Endorsements (aka "Social Proof"), Scarcity, Urgency, Obstruction, Sneaking or Information Hiding, Interface Interference, Coerced Action, and Asymmetric Choice [5, pp. 21–26].

From the perspective of data protection, the "Guidelines 03/2022 on Deceptive Design Patterns in Social Media Platform Interfaces," [hereinafter EDPB guidelines] adopted by the European Data Protection Board [hereinafter EDPB] in February 2023, holds significant importance. These guidelines state that "deceptive design patterns" are considered interfaces and user journeys implemented on social media platforms that aim to influence users into making unintended, respectively unwilling, and/or potentially harmful decisions, often toward an option that is against the users' best interests and in favor of the social media platforms interest, with regard to their personal data" [6, p. 9].

These guidelines classify dark patterns into Overloading, Skipping, Stirring, Obstructing, Fickle, and Left in the Dark, with further subdivisions provided in Annex I [6, pp. 65–71]. The distinction between content- and interface-based patterns is noteworthy. The former patterns "refer to the actual content and, therefore, also to the wording and context of the sentences and information components. In addition, however, there are also components that have a direct influence on the perception of these factors." The latter patterns "are related to the ways of displaying the content, navigating through it or interacting with it" [6, p.10]. Although dark patterns do not fall clearly into either of these categories, they can provide insights for considering legal measures, such as ensuring fair data handling and transparency.

2.2 Harms

The OECD report organizes the harms caused by dark patterns in terms of their impacts on consumer autonomy and personal and structural consumer detriment [3, pp. 23–27]. The report highlights the infringement of consumer autonomy, stating that "the subversion or impairment of consumer autonomy, decision-making or choice are defining characteristics of dark patterns" [3, p. 24], which lies at the very core of consumer harm. As the report notes, such infringements of consumer autonomy can lead to a wide range of harms, not only personal consumer detriment but also structural consumer detriment and even broader threats to democracy and freedom of expression [3, p. 24].

The OECD report includes privacy harms as part of individual consumer harm and cites specific examples, such as setting privacy-intrusive settings as the default (e.g., preselection)[1], making privacy-related choices or information difficult to engage with or opt out of (forced disclosure, hidden information, hard to cancel), and nagging or shaming consumers into accepting privacy-intrusive settings (nagging, confirm shaming) [3, p. 25]. The report also states, "As a result, consumers may end up divulging more personal data than intended, potentially exposing them to further risks" [3, p. 25]. However, it is somewhat unclear what exactly are being considered as "privacy harms" in this context.

Privacy harms do not arise merely from the infringement of autonomy; rather, the infringement of autonomy itself constitutes a violation of privacy. The right to privacy, which originated in the U.S., can be regarded as multifaceted. In the seminal article, *The Right to Privacy,* written by Samuel D. Warren and Louis D. Brandeis in 1890, the right to privacy was defined as "the right to be let alone" [7, p. 195]. Meanwhile, the

---

[1] The collection of information without an individual's prior consent through cookies constitutes a form of preselection.

same article also described it as "the common-law protection enables him to control absolutely the act of publication, and in the exercise of his own discretion, to decide whether there shall be any publication at all" [7, p. 200], thus already touching upon its decision-making aspect.

Subsequently, in the U.S., the right to privacy evolved through case law, and by the late 1960s, the advent of computerization brought new dimensions of privacy into focus. The most renowned work on this topic is *Privacy and Freedom* by Alan F. Westin. In this book, privacy is defined as "the claim of individuals, groups, or institutions to determine for themselves when, how, and to what extent information about them is communicated to others" [8, p. 7]. While the OECD report seems to consider privacy harms as divulging more personal data than intended [3, p. 25], this view appears narrow.

Furthermore, the OECD report highlights the challenge of addressing privacy harms, stating that "assessing the magnitude of privacy harms of dark patterns is more challenging than it is for their financial detriment, as a quantifiable indicator is lacking" [3, p. 25]. This observation is valid, as the ability to quantify harm can provide stronger evidence to support legislative findings. However, the risks associated with privacy are diverse. In their article *Privacy Harms,* Danielle K. Citron and Daniel J. Solove [9] attempted to classify types of privacy harms, driven by concerns about the high evidentiary hurdles in proving cognizable harm in privacy violation lawsuits in the U.S.

Citron and Solove categorized a wide range of harms, including physical, economic, reputational, and psychological harms. Specifically, they grouped "autonomy harms"— "restricting, undermining, inhibiting, or unduly influencing people's choices" —into six categories: "(1) coercion—the impairment of people's freedom to act or choose; (2) manipulation—the undue influence over people's behavior or decision-making; (3) failure to inform—the failure to provide people with sufficient information to make decisions; (4) thwarted expectations—engaging in activities that undermine people's choices; (5) lack of control—the inability to make meaningful choices about one's data or to prevent its potential future misuse; and (6) chilling effects—inhibiting people from engaging in lawful activities" [9, pp. 845–848].

Among these, manipulation is the most pivotal act underlying dark patterns. The 2019 report by the Stigler Committee on Digital Platforms, Privacy, and Data Protection Subcommittee described various forms of dark patterns and emphasized that "their central unifying feature is that they are manipulative, rather than persuasive," underscoring that manipulation lies at the core of dark pattern practices [10, p. 238]. Furthermore, recent studies have suggested that even nagging dark patterns, which do not intend to deceive, still manipulate consumers, underscoring the need for regulation [11].

Regarding the challenge of quantitatively assessing privacy violations, the harms caused by such violations include psychological and reputational harms, which are not necessarily quantifiable. However, when considering the need for legislation regulating dark patterns, the quantitative evaluation of harm is not a decisive factor[2]. Rather, it is

---

[2] The unfairness under Section 5 of the Federal Trade Commission Act [hereinafter FTC Act] could be interpreted as follows: "where the kind of A/B testing that we discuss above reveals that a particular interface design or option set more than doubles the percentage of users who wind up 'consenting' to engage in a consumer transaction, the company practice at issue could be deemed presumptively an unfair or deceptive practice in trade" [10, p. 253].

possible to adopt a broader perspective on privacy harms, emphasizing manipulation as a central factor that brings about autonomy harm.

Based on the above, the most significant harm caused by dark patterns can be identified as the infringement of autonomy from the perspectives of consumer and privacy protection. This harm is driven by various manipulation tactics, including nagging, highlighting the necessity of regulating such practices.

3 Trends in International Discussions

This chapter examines recent regulatory developments concerning dark patterns in the EU and the U.S., based on the premise that autonomy harm is a fundamental form of harm in consumer law, as well as privacy and data protection law.

3.1 The EU

On January 30, 2023, the European Commission, together with consumer protection authorities from 23 jurisdictions, issued a press release revealing the results of a screening of retail websites. They reviewed 399 online retail shops selling

products such as textiles and electronics, focusing on three common "dark patterns": fake countdown timers, manipulative web interfaces driving purchases or subscriptions, and hidden information. The review found that 42 websites used fake countdown timers, 54 directed consumers toward specific choices (e.g., subscriptions or pricier options) through design or language, and 70 hid key information such as delivery costs or cheaper options. Among these, 23 websites concealed information to push subscriptions. They also covered applications for 102 websites, 27 of which employed at least one dark pattern [12].

Digital Services Act. The Digital Services Act [hereinafter DSA] was adopted on October 4, 2022, and came into effect on February 17, 2024 [13]. As a platform regulation, this legislation encompasses roles in both consumer and personal data protection. The DSA explicitly regulates dark patterns by introducing the provision on "Online interface design and organisation" in Article 25. Paragraph 1 states the following:

Providers of online platforms shall not design, organise or operate their online interfaces in a way that deceives or manipulates the recipients of their service or in a way that otherwise materially distorts or impairs the ability of the recipients of their service to make free and informed decisions.

This paragraph targets actions that deceive or manipulate service users by regulating platform designs that impair their judgment; however, it does not include coercive actions. Additionally, this provision does not apply to acts covered by the GDPR under paragraph 2, limiting its scope. Paragraph 3 grants the European Commission the authority to issue guidelines on three specific practices: (a) emphasizing certain choices in user decisions; (b) repeatedly requesting choices already made, especially through disruptive pop-ups; and (c) making service termination more difficult than subscription.

As of January 2025, the guidelines have not yet been adopted, but enforcement activities have already begun. On July 12, 2024, the European Commission announced that

X was in breach of the DSA due to violations related to dark patterns, advertising transparency, and data access for researchers. Particularly, X's "verified accounts" interface with the "Blue checkmark" misleads users by allowing anyone to obtain verification status, straying from industry standards. This undermines users' ability to gauge account authenticity, with evidence suggesting that malicious actors have exploited this system to deceive users [14].

GDPR

EDPB Guidelines. The General Data Protection Regulation [hereinafter GDPR] [15], considered the most well-known regulation in the EU, is also applicable to dark patterns. The EDPB guidelines organize the provisions that apply depending on the dark pattern type. These provisions primarily include transparency (Articles 5(1)(a) and 12(1)), fairness (Article 5(1)(a)), purpose limitation (Article 5(1)(b)), informed and freely given consent (Article 7 in conjunction with Article 4(11)), children's consent (Article 8), intelligible and easily accessible information (Articles 12(1), 13, and 14), exercise of rights (Article 12(2)), and data protection by design and by default (Article 25(1)).

Dark patterns are issues that arise within human-computer interfaces, making it essential to prevent their emergence through default settings. The EDPB guidelines outline 20 best practices for preventing the use of dark patterns, focusing on social networking services (SNS). These include shortcuts, bulk options, contact information, reaching the supervisory authority, privacy policy overview, change spotting and comparison, coherent wording, providing definitions, and contrasting data protection elements. These measures are proactive steps to ensure that users are not exposed to dark patterns and can be considered essential efforts to realize the concept of "Privacy by Design".

In the field of privacy protection, the concept of "Privacy by Design" emerged in the 1990s [16] and is now codified in the GDPR Article 25. This approach aims to ensure that privacy is preserved by default throughout the data lifecycle, fostering a win-win relationship for both businesses and individuals. However, this concept is not limited to data protection and can be applied more broadly. Taking proactive measures "by design" and "by default" to maintain "fairness" in business practices should also be a requirement from the viewpoint of consumer protection. Regarding protection against dark patterns, the fairness principle is "at the heart of the consumer protection regime, which could be better placed to determine whether the design that led to data processing was a fair practice."[17, p. 253].[3]

Although not an EU Member State, the UK Information Commissioner's Office issued the Age Appropriate Design Code on August 12, 2020. The Code prohibits the use of nudge techniques to encourage children to provide unnecessary personal data or disable privacy protection [18], Sect. 13].

Cookie Regulations.   Under the GDPR, online identifiers, including cookies, are considered "personal data" (Article 4(1)). Consequently, data controllers must comply with various requirements under the GDPR. The main legal basis for the processing of personal data is the consent of the data subject. (Article 6(1)(a)).

---

[3] Regulation of dark patterns can be examined from the perspectives of both consumer and data protection. Given that both approaches have their merits in achieving common policy objectives, this study does not aim to identify which approach is more suitable.

The GDPR defines the "consent" of a data subject as "any freely given, specific, informed, and unambiguous indication of the data subject's wishes by which they, by a statement or by a clear affirmative action, signify agreement to the processing of personal data relating to them" (Article 4(11)). Silence, pre-ticked boxes, or inactivity do not constitute consent (Recital 32). The provisions on "conditions for consent" outline several important obligations for data controllers: the controller must demonstrate that consent has been obtained (Article 7(1)); consent in a written declaration must be clearly distinguishable and presented in an intelligible, accessible, and plain language (Article 7(2)); data subjects have the right to withdraw their consent at any time (Article 7(3)); and when assessing whether consent is freely given, special attention must be given to consent for data processing that is not essential for fulfilling the contract (Article 7(4)).

The use of cookies is also subject to the specific provisions of the so-called ePrivacy Directive [19]. Article 5(3) of this Directive provides that "Member States shall ensure that the use of electronic communications networks to store information or to gain access to information stored in the terminal equipment of a subscriber or user is only allowed on condition that the subscriber or user concerned is provided with clear and comprehensive information in accordance with Directive 95/46/EC[4], inter alia about the purposes of the processing, and is offered the right to refuse such processing by the data controller."

Consent under Article 5(3) of the ePrivacy Directive has the same meaning as consent under the GDPR (Recital 17). The interpretation of Article 5(3) was clarified in the Court of Justice of the European Union's preliminary ruling on October 1, 2019, in the Planet49 GmbH case [20]. In this case, an online gaming operator used pre-ticked checkboxes to obtain consent for the placement of third-party cookies when users participated in a lottery. The Court held that the use of pre-ticked checkboxes, which required users to deselect them to refuse consent, did not constitute valid consent under the GDPR.

Additionally, the proposed ePrivacy Regulation [21], submitted on January 10, 2017, includes provisions for the "Protection of information stored in and related to end-users' terminal equipment." It generally prohibits processing and storage of data from terminal equipment without the end user's consent, with the conditions for such consent being subject to the GDPR (Article 8(1)(b)).

Unfair Commercial Practices Directive. The EU Unfair Commercial Practices Directive (hereinafter UCPD) [22] interprets dark patterns as potentially falling under the prohibition of unfair commercial practices (Article 5), misleading commercial practices (Articles 6–7), or aggressive commercial practices (Articles 8–9). Annex I to the Directive lists unfair practices that could constitute dark patterns.

These include "bait and switch" practices (Nos. 5 and 6, Annex I), fake timers and limited stock claims on websites that create urgency (No. 7, Annex I), giving inaccurate information on market conditions or the likelihood of finding the product to induce the consumer to purchase under less favorable conditions (No. 18, Annex I), claiming that the consumer has won a prize without awarding the described prize or a reasonable equivalent (Nos. 19 and 31, Annex I), falsely describing a product as "free" (No. 20, Annex I), or making repeated interruptions during normal interactions (e.g., nagging) that amount to persistent and unwanted solicitation (No. 26, Annex I) [23, para. 4.2.7].

---

[4] The 1995 Data Protection Directive is superseded by the GDPR.

Dark patterns are also likely to have a greater impact on vulnerable consumers (Article 5(3)) and, when targeted at children, may fall under provisions prohibiting direct exhortations aimed at children (No. 28, Annex I) [23, para. 3.7].

3.2 The U.S.

Federal Regulations. In the U.S., enforcement actions against dark patterns are implemented under Sect. 5 of the FTC Act [24]. This section stipulates that "unfair methods of competition in or affecting commerce, and unfair or deceptive acts or practices in or affecting commerce are hereby declared unlawful."

Section 5 of the FTC Act holds a unique position. While the EU implements overlapping but distinct policy objectives—personal data and consumer protection—through separate legal frameworks and Japan similarly pursues these goals under distinct legislations, the FTC Act adopts a more integrated approach. Despite being rooted in competition law, Sect. 5 simultaneously fulfills the consumer and privacy protection roles, demonstrating a highly comprehensive and flexible framework. The key feature of Sect. 5 is its prohibition of deceptive practices, thereby requiring businesses to adhere to "fair" practices in their operations[5].

In September 2022, the FTC published the aforementioned staff report [5], addressing issues related to dark patterns and highlighting notable enforcement cases on privacy. For instance, in February 2017, a smart TV manufacturer was ordered to pay $22 million for setting a default configuration that enabled the comprehensive collection of consumers' viewing histories and their sharing with third parties in connection with a service offering program recommendations. Further, in September 2018, a lead generator, falsely presenting itself as an official website affiliated with the U.S. military, collected information from individuals interested in military enlistment and sold it to universities and vocational schools, resulting in a $30 million settlement [5, pp. 15–19].

Numerous examples qualify as dark patterns. For instance, in December 2022, the FTC fined a company $275 million for violations of the Children's Online Privacy Protection Act, citing the default activation of voice and text chat features [25]. In March 2023, the FTC ordered Epic Games, the operator of the online game "Fortnite," to refund $245 million. The FTC highlighted the company's intentional placement of buttons designed to encourage users, including many children, to purchase virtual currency within the game without adequate confirmation processes [26].

In June 2023, the FTC filed a lawsuit against Amazon, alleging that Amazon has, for years, enrolled consumers into Amazon Prime (hereinafter "Prime") without their consent while intentionally making it difficult for them to cancel their Prime subscriptions. According to this complaint, consumers attempting to cancel their Prime membership have to go through multiple steps to complete the process. First, consumers have to identify the cancellation method that Amazon intentionally made difficult. Even after initiating the cancellation process, consumers are directed to pages offering discounted subscription options, pages that turn off the auto-renewal feature, or pages that reverse their cancellation decisions. Only after navigating these obstacles can consumers cancel

---

[5] *See* the interpretation of "fairness" in [10, pp. 252–254.

362   K. Ishii

their subscriptions. A past report noted that Amazon internally referred to the cancella-tion process as "Iliad," likening it to Homer's epic poem about the decade-long Trojan War, underscoring its complexity and length. The complaint further alleged that Amazon was aware that users were being enrolled in Prime without their consent and that the cancellation process was overly complicated. However, the company's management failed to take meaningful steps to address these issues. Additionally, the FTC claimed that Amazon repeatedly delayed and obstructed the FTC's review of its practices [27].

In October 2024, the FTC announced a final click-to cancel rule that require sellers to make it as easy for consumers to cancel their subscriptions. The rule applies to all negative option programs across media and (1) prohibits misrepresentations of any material fact presented while marketing using negative option features; (2) requires sellers to provide important information prior to obtaining consumers' billing information and charging them; (3) requires sellers to obtain consumers' unambiguously affirmative consent to the negative option feature prior to charging them; and (4) requires sellers to provide consumers with simple cancellation mechanisms to immediately halt all recurring charges [28, 29].

State Regulations.   At the state level, the California Consumer Privacy Act [hereinafter CCPA] regulates dark patterns. Under the CCPA, a "dark pattern" is defined as "a user interface designed or manipulated with the substantial effect of subverting or impairing user autonomy, decision-making, or choice, as further defined by regulation." The CCPA states that "agreement obtained through use of dark patterns does not constitute consent" [30].

One notable case involving a CCPA violation was the *Sephora* case [31]. This case concerned Sephora's failure to notify consumers about the sale of their personal information through online tracking technologies and its failure to provide consumers with an option to opt out. On August 24, 2022, the Superior Court of San Francisco County ordered Sephora to comply with opt-out requests submitted via Global Privacy Control, pay a $1.2 million fine, and take other corrective actions. Additionally, the California age-appropriate Design Code Act also prohibits providers of online services and products from employing dark patterns targeting minors under 18 years of age [32].

Other states have introduced similar regulations to address dark patterns [33]. For example, the Colorado Privacy Act specifies that consumer consent obtained through dark patterns is invalid [34]. Colorado regulations, within "user interface design, choice architecture, and dark patterns," state that "consent choice options should be presented to consumers in a symmetrical way that does not impose unequal weight or focus on one available choice over another such that a consumer's ability to consent is impaired or subverted" [35].

4   An Overview of the Current Situation in Japan

In Japan, there are currently no laws that explicitly regulate dark patterns. However, various consumer protection laws apply to manipulative activities. The Act on Specified Commercial Transactions and the Act against Unjustifiable Premiums and Misleading Representations are the most representative legal frameworks. Further, since August

2024, the Consumer Affairs Agency's regional office, the "New Future Creation Strategy Headquarters" (located in Tokushima City), had begun conducting a survey on dark patterns. The survey results are expected to be published by March 2025 [36].

4.1 Amendments to Consumer Protection Laws

The Act on Specified Commercial Transactions. In Japan, the Act on Specified Commercial Transactions categorizes transactions that are prone to consumer disputes, such as door-to-door and mail-order sales, and imposes the necessary regulations. Mail-order businesses are required to disclose key information when advertising, including the total sales price (including shipping fees), payment methods and timing, delivery schedule (or timing of rights transfer or service provision), and details regarding contract cancellation or withdrawal, including any return conditions (Article 11). Additionally, the law prohibits exaggerated advertisements, such as "significantly misleading representations" about a product's performance, rights or services, or matters concerning the withdrawal or cancellation of sales or service contracts (Article 12).

In March 2024, the Consumer Affairs Agency issued a business suspension order against a health food mail-order company for engaging in exaggerated advertising, including claims such as "No. 1 Popular Diet Drink Among Women" [37].

Regulations on subscription fraud were strengthened by amendments to the Act on Specified Commercial Transactions. Certain e-commerce sites have advertised offers such as "90% off your first purchase" or "Free trial for the first month" while requiring subscriptions as a condition or claiming consumers could cancel at any time but actually imposing detailed and restrictive cancellation terms. Following numerous complaints to consumer centers about such practices, the law was amended in June 2021 and came into effect in June 2022. The amendment requires mail-order businesses to display additional details to Article 11, including the quantity of goods or services, on the final confirmation screen before a consumer submits a contract application (Article 12-6(1)). Violators are subject to imprisonment for up to three years or fines of up to three million yen (Article 70, Item 2). Furthermore, the amended law prohibits misleading representations on the final confirmation screen (Article 12-6 (2)). If consumers are misled by such representations and make a purchase, they have the right to rescind their consent (Article 15(4)).

In April 2024, the Consumer Affairs Agency issued a business suspension order against a health food mail-order company for misrepresenting the ease of canceling subscription contracts, when in reality, the company imposed significant hurdles to cancellation. This was considered exaggerated advertising [38].

The Act Against Unjustifiable Premiums and Misleading Representations. As information about the quality and price of goods and services is essential for consumers to make informed decisions, it must be communicated accurately. When such information is presented unfairly or deceptively, it impedes consumers' ability to make autonomous and rational choices. To address this issue, the Act against Unjustifiable Premiums and Misleading Representations prohibits misleading representations of goods and services. Under this law, "misrepresentation" is defined as a discrepancy between what is stated and the actual facts. Consequently, dark patterns that fall under the misrepresentation category could be subject to regulation [39, p. 22].

Recently, amendments to public notice under the Act have expanded its scope to include so-called stealth marketing (i.e., practices that disguise advertising as non-commercial content). General consumers, when aware that a statement originates from a business entity, could identify potential exaggerations or overstatements when making choices. However, when they are unaware of the commercial nature of the content, such considerations are absent [40, p. 1]. To address this issue, the notice specifies that "representations by businesses about their goods or services that are difficult for general consumers to identify as being made by the business itself" are prohibited [41, p .1]. For example, this applies to cases where businesses operating on e-commerce platforms engage brokers (individuals or entities who recruit reviews on social media, etc.) or purchasers to write reviews of their products on the e-commerce platform, or to post negative reviews about competing businesses' goods or services [40, p. 3–4].

In June 2024, the Consumer Affairs Agency issued a corrective order against a clinic that provided discounts on influenza vaccination fees to patients in exchange for posting favorable reviews on the clinic's Google Maps page. This action was deemed a violation of the Act against Unjustifiable Premiums and Misleading Representations [42].

Others.   Article 10 of the Consumer Contract Act invalidates unfair contractual clauses and provides an example: "a clause that deems a consumer to have made an offer or expressed consent to a new consumer contract through their inaction." This provision indicates that if consumers fail to take certain actions, they are deemed to have entered into a new consumer contract, even in the absence of an explicit or implicit intent to do so.

4.2   The Act on the Protection of Personal Information and Its Related Special Act

Compared with developments in the field of consumer protection law, progress in the realm of personal information protection law has been relatively slow. Japan's Act on the Protection of Personal Information (hereinafter APPI) does not include provisions explicitly aimed at regulating dark patterns. While the APPI prohibits "a business handling personal information" from "utilizing personal information in a way that there is a possibility of fomenting or inducing unlawful or unjust acts" (Article 19) and "acquiring personal information by deception or other wrongful means" (Article 20(1)), these provisions are not designed with dark patterns in mind.

The APPI does not require an individual's prior consent to the collection of their personal information, except for sensitive information (Article 20(2)), and interpretations of the APPI as to whether an online identifier, such as a cookie, constitutes personal information differ on a case-by-case basis. However, privacy violations caused by third-party cookies have been recognized as a serious problem by privacy stakeholders. Therefore, the amended APPI in 2020 introduced "personally referable information," which refers to information about a living individual and includes cookie data. It restricts the provision of information related to personal information to third parties, requiring a business operator to confirm in advance that the third party has obtained consent from the individual concerned if the third party uses cookie data shared by the providing business entity to combine personally referable information with its own internal personal data (Article 31).

The Special Law of the APPI was also amended. In June 2022, the Telecommunications Business Act (hereinafter TBA) introduced new provisions regulating the collection of information using tags and modules which are "external transmission rules" for online identifiers such as advertising IDs including cookies (Article 27-12). External transmission refers to the transmission of user information recorded on the user's telecommunication equipment, such as PCs or smartphones, to the telecommunications equipment of a party other than the user (including a website operator or an application provider server). User information refers to the information recorded in the user's telecommunications equipment, including identification codes such as advertising IDs and IDs stored in cookies, URLs viewed by the user, information related to the user's activities, the user's name, and the contact information of persons other than the user. The amended TBA obliges telecommunications business operators to provide users with the opportunity to confirm the content and destination of user information transmitted by the external transmission function. Services subject to this obligation include messages between users, SNS services, online search engine services, and homepages (news and roundup websites). When these services are provided through a browser or application and an external transmission program is sent to the user's terminal, either a notification or publication, obtaining consent, or opt-out measures must be made available.

Thereby, regulation of third-party cookies has been achieved. However, the APPI applies only in limited cases, and the TBA does not require opt-in consent, making the regulation relatively lenient. Regarding cookies, dark patterns such as pre-checked boxes are problematic, but current regulations do not specifically address such practices.

5 Legal Measures for Addressing Dark Patterns

Numerous studies have established taxonomies based on dark patterns. Although such classifications do not directly determine the necessity of regulations or specify regulatory measures, they are instrumental in structuring discussions. In cases where multiple patterns overlap or malicious dark patterns are identified, adopting measures that impose enhanced penalties warrant consideration.

There have been skeptical views on government regulations, arguing that "consumers can defeat many dark patterns if they are motivated to do so and focused on the task. From this supposition, they argue that the reams of new dark patterns regulations are, at best, unnecessary "[11, p. 19]. However, in response to this argument, a recent study presented experimental evidence suggesting that "despite several years' worth of exposure to dark patterns, many consumers have not learned to defeat them" [11, p. 48], arguing that legal regulation is necessary. The prevalence of dark patterns is evident from investigations conducted in various countries, underscoring the need for legal regulations.

Regulatory approaches include the following:(1) direct prohibition of dark patterns; (2) applying general provisions that mandate fair processing of personal data or fair trade; (3) identifying dark patterns as falling under the category of unfair commercial practices and subjecting them to legal enforcement; (4) invalidating consent obtained through the use of dark patterns; (5) specifying individual behavior types and imposing restrictions on them; and (6) requiring safeguards to be embedded by design and by default.

The provision directly prohibiting dark patterns, as outlined in (1), has been adopted under the DSA, and enforcement is already underway. However, this approach carries the risk of reducing business predictability. To mitigate this risk, it is essential to clarify the prohibited categories through guidelines and ensure that regulatory authorities enforce the rules in a transparent and fair manner.

Regarding (2), the obligations for fair processing and transparency of personal data under the GDPR are applicable. Given the broad applicability of the GDPR in personal data processing, it could be extended to address dark patterns. However, considering the inherently manipulative nature of dark patterns and the need for addressing interface design issues, the GDPR alone cannot be regarded as a comprehensive solution.

Section 5 of the FTC Act, although structured differently from the GDPR, prohibits unfair or deceptive practices and similarly emphasizes fairness. This provision applies broadly to businesses and serves dual roles in consumer protection and privacy regulation, making it well-suited for regulating dark patterns. Furthermore, a body of enforcement precedents has been established under the FTC Act. While the effectiveness of this approach hinges on the functionality of the enforcement agency, it represents an effective mechanism for post hoc regulations.

Regarding (3), the UCPD adopts an approach that enumerates unfair commercial practices, including those that qualify as dark patterns, and subjects them to regulatory enforcement. Although this regulation is limited to the transactional context, it can be effective when coordinated with GDPR enforcement.

As for (4), this category includes the EU's discussions on invalidating consent based on the preselection for cookie collection and the California CCPA. The issue of cookies has been a long-standing topic in the field of privacy and personal data protection, independent of the dark pattern context. However, in Japan, where effective regulations are not fully established, legal enforcement against information collection without prior consent can be particularly valuable, even in the context of dark patterns.

With respect to (5), the Colorado Privacy Act exemplifies regulations specific to dark patterns by mandating interface designs that provide fair choices. Similarly, Japan's consumer protection laws introduced new regulations targeting subscription-based services and stealth marketing. Although broadly regulating dark patterns is a bold approach with potentially significant impacts on business activities, defining individual categories to ensure predictability is a pragmatic choice. However, this method faces challenges because the emergence of new types of dark patterns may necessitate frequent amendments to laws, risking gaps in law enforcement.

In Japan, the absence of well-developed provisions or interpretations of personal data protection laws regarding dark patterns, combined with lenient cookie regulations, highlights the need for the comprehensive enhancement of protective measures. The accumulation of enforcement precedents is particularly critical. To achieve this, Japan must actively learn from the approaches adopted in the EU and the U.S., where robust efforts in this area have already been undertaken.

The initiative outlined in (6) represents a significant approach. Dark patterns are fundamentally an issue in interface design, and effectively addressing them requires the design of fair interfaces by default. This approach aligns with the principles of Privacy by Design and by Default as well as the proactive measures advocated in the EDPB guidelines on best practices. Businesses can be encouraged to create user-friendly interfaces from the design stage by imposing a duty of effort, thereby promoting adherence to ethical design standards.

The Stigler Committee report also proposes the concept of "consumertarian default rules" [10, pp. 234–237], which refers to "selecting a default rule that is preferred by the majority of unsophisticated parties in a transaction, although perhaps not by the majority of sophisticated counterparties" [10, p. 236]. In the context of this study, the former approach, setting default rules that protect less sophisticated users, is particularly relevant. The latter suggests that users should be allowed to waive default protections if the choice architecture employed by businesses is non-manipulative, enabling consumers to make informed trade-offs. However, when corporate persuasion is confusing, pestering, or misleading, there is no justification for allowing consumers to waive protections [10, pp. 235–236]. In other words, consumer choices influenced by dark patterns should not be considered valid.

While legal enforcement remains vital, efforts should also focus on expanding the adoption of fair and reliable interfaces, supported by technological advancements such as the automated detection of dark patterns [11, p. 48]. Although this article does not delve deeply into this subject, co-regulatory frameworks may provide a viable option for addressing this issue.

6 Conclusions

This study examined the regulation of dark patterns, focusing on legal approaches. While regulatory methods vary across countries and regions, establishing rules that mandate fairness in business practices and accumulating specific enforcement cases can serve as deterrents, provided that the enforcement agencies function effectively. Furthermore, complementary measures, such as targeted regulations on particularly harmful practices and enhanced penalties for overlapping violations, should be considered. The significance of leveraging technological tools and encouraging businesses' proactive efforts to address dark patterns cannot be overemphasized.

Notably, the dark patterns present additional critical issues. For instance, special protective measures are required for groups particularly susceptible to the influence of dark patterns, such as children, the elderly, and individuals with lower educational levels [3, p. 28]. This topic warrants separate discussion and remains an area for future research.

As digital practices continue to evolve, it is imperative for lawmakers, technologists, and scholars to collaborate to develop robust frameworks that safeguard consumers, respect them, and foster innovation dynamics.

Disclosure of Interests.   The author has no competing interests to declare that are relevant to the content of this article.

References

1. Brignull, H.: Deceptive Patterns : Exposing the Tricks Tech Companies Use to Control You, Testimonium Ltd. (2023)
2. Global Privacy Enforcement Network, 2024 GPEN Sweep on deceptive design patterns. https://www.privacyenforcement.net/content/2024-gpen-sweep-deceptive-design-patterns, published 2024/7/9
3. OECD.: Dark commercial patterns. OECD Digital Economy Papers. No. 336 (2022)
4. See e.g., Luguri, J., et al.: Shining a Light on Dark Patterns. Journal of Legal Analysis 13(1), 43–109 (2021); Mathur, A., et al.: Dark patterns at scale: Findings from a crawl of 11K shopping websites. Proceedings of the ACM on Human-Computer Interaction 3(CSCW) 1–32 (2019); Gray, C., et al.: The dark (patterns) side of UX design. Proceedings of the 2018 CHI Conference on Human Factors in Computing Systems 534, 1–14 (2018); Acquisti, A., et al.: Nudges for Privacy and Security. ACM Computing Surveys (CSUR) 50(3), 1–41 (2017); Bösch, C., et al.: Tales from the Dark Side: Privacy Dark Strategies and Privacy Dark Patterns. Proceedings on Privacy Enhancing Technologies 2016(4), 237–254 (2016)
5. Federal Trade Commission.: Bringing Dark Patterns to Light, https://www.ftc.gov/system/files/ftc_gov/pdf/P214800%20Dark%20Patterns%20Report%209.14.2022%20-%20FINAL.pdf, published 2022/9/15
6. European Data Protection Board: Guidelines 3/2022 on Dark patterns in social media platform interfaces: How to recognise and avoid them, https://edpb.europa.eu/system/files/2022-03/edpb_03-2022_guidelines_on_dark_patterns_in_social_media_platform_interfaces_en.pdf, published 2022/3/4
7. Warren, S., Brandeis, L.: The Right to Privacy. Harv. Law Rev. **4**, 193–220 (1890)
8. Westin, A.: Privacy and Freedom, (1967), 1st edn. Atheneum, New York (1967)
9. Citron, D., Solove, D.: Privacy Harms. Boston University Law Rev. **102**, 793–863 (2022)
10. Stigler Center for the Study of the Economy and the State: Stigler Committee's 2019 final report on Digital Platforms. https://www.chicagobooth.edu/-/media/research/stigler/pdfs/digital-platforms---committee-report---stigler-center.pdf, published 2019/9/16
11. Kugler, M.B., et al.: Can Consumers Protect Themselves Against Privacy Dark Patterns? University of Chicago Coase-Sandor Institute for Law & Economics Research Paper, 25–01, 1–55 (2025)
12. European Commission, Consumer protection: manipulative online practices found on 148 out of 399 online shops screened. https://ec.europa.eu/commission/presscorner/detail/en/ip_23_418, published 2023/1/30
13. Parliament and Council Regulation 2022/2065, 2022 O.J. (L 277) 1–102 (EU)
14. European Commission, Commission sends preliminary findings to X for breach of the Digital Services Act. https://ec.europa.eu/commission/presscorner/detail/en/ip_24_3761, published 2024/7/12
15. Parliament and Council Regulation 2016/679, 2016 O.J. (L 119) 1–88 (EU)
16. Cavoukian, A.: Privacy by design: origins, meaning, and prospects for assuring privacy and trust in the information era. In: Yee, G. (ed.) Privacy Protection Measures and Technologies in Business Organizations: Aspects and Standards, pp. 170–208 (2012)
17. Leiser, M.: Dark patterns: the case for regulatory pluralism between the European Union's consumer and data protection regimes. In: Kosta, E., Leenes, R., Kamara, I. (eds.) Research Handbooks in European Law, pp. 240–269. Edward Elgar Publishing Ltd., Cheltenham (2022)
18. Information Commissioner's Office, Age appropriate design: a code of practice for online services, Nudge techniques. https://ico.org.uk/for-organisations/uk-gdpr-guidance-and-resources/childrens-information/childrens-code-guidance-and-resources/age-appropriate-design-a-code-of-practice-for-online-services/13-nudge-techniques/. Accessed 26 Jan 2025

19. Parliament and Council Directive 2002/58, 2002 O.J. (L 201) 37–47 (EU)
20. Case C-673/17, Bundesverband der Verbraucherzentralen und Verbraucherverbände — Verbraucherzentrale Bondservant eV v. Planet49 GmbH, 2019/10/1
21. Commission proposal for a Regulation of the European Parliament and of the Council concerning the respect for private life and the protection of personal data in electronic communications and repealing Directive 2002/58/EC (Regulation on Privacy and Electronic Communications). COM/2017/010 final - 2017/03 (COD), 2017/10/1
22. Parliament and Council Directive 2005/29, 2005 O.J. (L 149) 22–39 (EU)
23. European Commission, Commission Notice – Guidance on the interpretation and application of Directive 2005/29/EC of the European Parliament and of the Council concerning unfair business-to-consumer commercial practices in the internal market, C/2021/9320, O.J. (C 526), pp. 1–129
24. U.S.C. § 45(a)(1) (2024)
25. FTC, Press Release, Fortnite Video Game Maker Epic Games to Pay More Than Half a Billion Dollars over FTC Allegations of Privacy Violations and Unwanted Charges. https://www.ftc.gov/news-events/news/press-releases/2022/12/fortnite-video-game-maker-epic-games-pay-more-half-billion-dollars-over-ftc-allegations, published 2022/12/9
26. FTC, Press Release, FTC Finalizes Order Requiring Fortnite maker Epic Games to Pay $245 Millon for Tricking Users into Making Unwanted Charges. https://www.ftc.gov/news-events/news/press-releases/2023/03/ftc-finalizes-order-requiring-fortnite-maker-epic-games-pay-245-million-tricking-users-making, published 2023/3/14
27. FTC, Press Release, FTC Takes Action Against Amazon for Enrolling Consumers in Amazon Prime Without Consent and Sabotaging Their Attempts to Cancel. https://www.ftc.gov/news-events/news/press-releases/2023/06/ftc-takes-action-against-amazon-enrolling-consumers-amazon-prime-without-consent-sabotaging-their, published 2023/6/21
28. FTC, Press Release, Federal Trade Commission Announces Final "Click-to-Cancel Rule Making it Easier for Consumers to End Recurring Subscriptions and Memberships". https://www.ftc.gov/news-events/news/press-releases/2024/10/federal-trade-commission-announces-final-click-cancel-rule-making-it-easier-consumers-end-recurring, published 2024/10/16
29. C.F.R. §§ 425.3-425.6 (2025)
30. CA CIV. CODE §1798.140(l), (h) (2024)
31. California v. Sephora, Inc., Case No. CGC-22-601380 (Cal. Sup. Ct. Aug. 24, 2022)
32. CA CIV. CODE §1798.99.31(b)(7) (2024)
33. See also Conn. Stat. Ann. § 42-515(6) (2023)
34. Colo. Stat. Ann. § 6-1-1303(5)(c) (2024)
35. Colo. Admin. Code. § 904-3:7.09 (2024)
36. The Consumer Affairs Agency conducts its first investigation into dark patterns, uncovering false advertising on e-commerce sites. https://news.yahoo.co.jp/articles/7e6ca0c1aa8518eb3a23682c7e99b20439f45ada, published 2024/8/2 (in Japanese)
37. Consumer Affairs Agency, News Release, Order to suspend operations (3 months) and other measures against a mail-order business operator violating the Act on Specified Commercial Transactions. https://www.caa.go.jp/notice/assets/consumer_transaction_cms203_240315_01.pdf, published 2024/3/15 (in Japanese)
38. Consumer Affairs Agency, News Release, Order to suspend operations (3 months) and other measures against a mail-order business operator violating the Act on Specified Commercial Transactions. https://www.caa.go.jp/notice/assets/consumer_transaction_cms203_240410_01.pdf, 2024/4/10 (in Japanese)
39. Kano, K.: A Survey on Research Related to Digitalization and Consumer Policy (So-Called 'Dark Patterns'). Economic and Social Research Institute, Cabinet Office. **79**, 1–31 (2023). (in Japanese)

40. Consumer Affairs Agency Commissioner's Decision, Operational Guidelines for 'Representations Difficult for General Consumers to Identify as Those of a Business Operator' (2023) (in Japanese)
41. Cabinet Office Notice No. 19 of 2023 (in Japanese)
42. Consumer Affairs Agency, News Release, Administrative order for action issued to Yushinkai Medical Corporation under the Act against Unjustifiable Premiums and Misleading Representations. https://www.caa.go.jp/notice/assets/representation_cms204_240607_01.pdf, published 2024/7/7

Real-Time Fake News Detection with Combined Style and Knowledge-Based Techniques

Seeam Khan[(⊠)], Brendan Jarmusz, Yusef Jawad, and Matthew Rosica

Department of Computer Science, The George Washington University,
Washington, DC, USA
{skhan96,brendanjarmusz}@gwmail.gwu.edu, {yjawad03,mattrosica2}@gwu.edu

Abstract. The rapid proliferation of fake news has created an urgent need for effective real-time detection systems that can safeguard the integrity of information. This paper presents a hybrid detection framework combining style-based and knowledge-based methods within a user-friendly Chrome extension, called *Fake News Busters*. Our system utilizes a fine-tuned Llama 3 model to analyze linguistic patterns and integrates external verification through web-scraping and APIs such as Google Fact Check, Google Scholar, and LinkedIn to assess factual claims and source credibility. The backend leverages Flask and PyTorch for scalable processing, while the front-end enables real-time user feedback. Evaluation in benchmark data sets and through a usability study demonstrates that combining linguistic features with external knowledge improves detection accuracy and user trust. This work highlights the importance of hybrid approaches in combating sophisticated misinformation and sets the foundation for user-centered scalable fake news interventions.

Keywords: Fake news detection · Natural language processing · Knowledge-based verification · Style-based verification

1 Introduction

Misinformation has become a defining challenge of the digital age. From influencing elections to spreading health-related conspiracies, fake news is often designed to manipulate, deceive, or polarize. Advances in generative AI have made the creation of fake content faster and more convincing, while social media platforms accelerate its spread across global audiences. Despite increasing awareness, most people, including journalists, educators, and everyday readers, still struggle to consistently identify false or misleading information online.

To address this gap, we developed *Fake News Busters*: a real-time detection system that analyzes news articles using both style-based and knowledge-based techniques. Throughout this paper, we refer to "fake news" in two distinct senses,

---

All authors contributed equally to the research and project.

M. Kurosu and A. Hashizume (Eds.): HCII 2025, LNCS 16332, pp. 371–384, 2026.
https://doi.org/10.1007/978-3-032-12385-5_23

based on the method of detection. In the style-based context, fake news refers to articles exhibiting language manipulation, bias, excessive sentiment, or unusual stylistic cues—regardless of factual correctness. In the knowledge-based context, fake news denotes factually incorrect claims or statements that are explicitly refuted by credible external sources [13]. By distinguishing between these two forms of misinformation, our system is better able to identify both subtle deception and outright falsehood. Our tool is designed not only to flag potentially deceptive content, but also to explain why, empowering users with evidence-based insights at the moment they consume news.

1.1 Challenges in Fake News Detection

Detecting fake news is inherently complex. Misinformation is not just factually wrong: It is often emotionally charged, selectively framed, or presented with an authoritative tone. Many detection systems either focus solely on stylistic cues (like excessive sentiment or unusual writing structure) or depend on external databases that may not include new or obscure claims.

Style-based methods, while useful, can be fooled by well-written disinformation that mimics credible sources. Conversely, knowledge-based systems often rely on static databases and can't evaluate claims that haven't yet been fact-checked or are highly context-dependent. Worse still, both methods can miss the intent behind an article, especially when content walks a fine line between opinion and deception.

1.2 Overview of Methods

Fake news detection methods are typically classified into style-based and knowledge-based approaches [1,2]. Style-based detection focuses on linguistic features such as sentiment, tone, and writing structure to identify deception patterns in text. These methods often employ natural language processing (NLP) and machine learning to model the stylistic signatures of credible versus misleading content.

Knowledge-based detection, in contrast, evaluates the factual accuracy of claims by checking them against external sources. This involves techniques such as claim extraction, evidence retrieval, and stance detection to determine whether a statement is supported or refuted by reliable information. While each approach has its strengths, they also suffer from limitations when used independently. Style-based methods may misclassify well-written misinformation, while knowledge-based systems often depend on existing databases or APIs that may not contain timely or comprehensive coverage.

1.3 Proposed Solution Overview

Fake News Busters integrates both detection strategies into a single real-time system. The style-based component uses a fine-tuned LLaMA 3 model trained

on labeled datasets of fake and real news articles. The text is preprocessed using
Gemini to clean and standardize it before being analyzed for tone, coherence,
readability, and sentence structure. This process outputs a style-based credibility
score ranging from 0 to 1.

The knowledge-based component begins by extracting key factual claims
using OpenAI GPT. It then performs verification through multiple channels.
In addition to checking claims using APIs like Google Fact Check, the system
conducts live web searches to retrieve the top results from reputable domains.
Each result is evaluated for its stance, supporting, refuting, irrelevant, or not reputable, and only high-quality sources are used in the final assessment. The author
and source credibility are further validated using LinkedIn, Google Scholar data,
and web reviews. These findings are aggregated into a knowledge-based score.

Both modules operate in parallel, and their outputs are combined to generate
an overall reliability rating. The system is deployed as a Chrome extension with
a Flask and PyTorch backend, enabling users to receive transparent, claim-level
feedback directly within their browser.

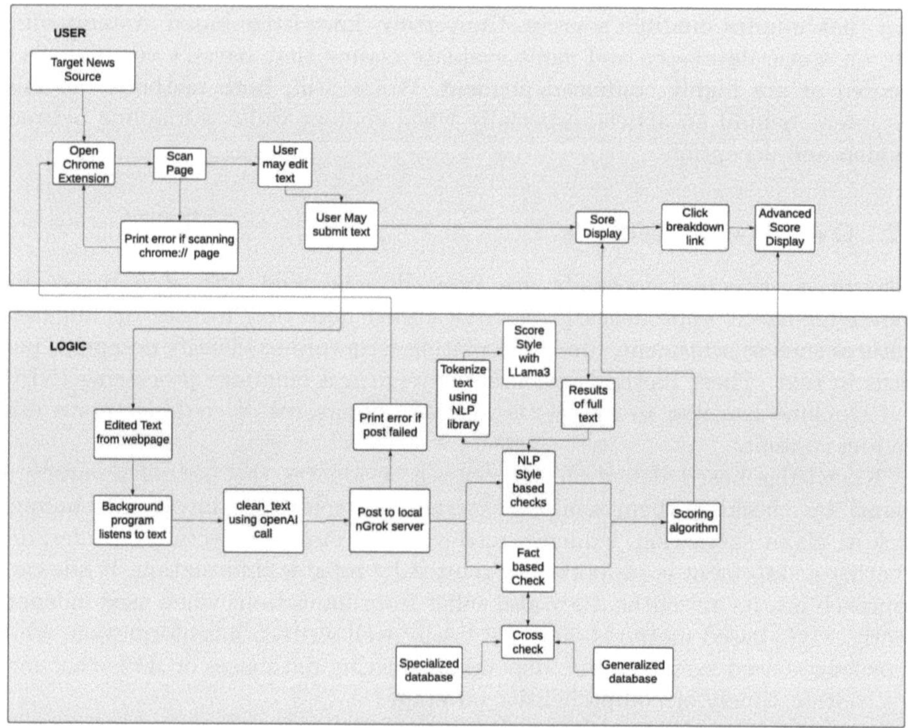

Fig. 1. System workflow of the Fake News Busters extension, illustrating user interaction and backend logic including NLP-based style scoring, fact-based cross-checking,
and combined scoring.

Figure 1 provides a high-level overview of the system's architecture, showing how the user-facing Chrome extension interacts with the backend components to process, evaluate, and return credibility scores.

2   Related Work

Detecting fake news remains a multifaceted challenge due to its dynamic nature and the diversity of misinformation strategies. Existing approaches can be grouped into three broad categories: stylistic models, knowledge-based verification systems, and ensemble or hybrid frameworks.

2.1   Stylistic and Linguistic Models

Early approaches primarily focused on textual characteristics, analyzing the linguistic features of content to detect deception. These models leverage natural language processing (NLP) and machine learning to extract cues such as syntax, sentiment, readability, and lexical diversity introduced stylometric techniques to detect hyperpartisan news, showing promising results based on emotional tone and complexity. Rashkin et al. [4] differentiated satire, hoaxes, and propaganda using lexical and semantic analysis. However, stylistic models often misclassify well-written misinformation crafted to mirror the tone and structure of legitimate journalism. In addition, they may struggle to generalize across topics or languages.

2.2   Fact-Checking and Knowledge-Based Verification

Knowledge-based approaches aim to validate claims against structured databases, knowledge graphs, and external APIs. Works like those by Shu et al. [5] and Baly et al. [6] explored fact verification pipelines using claim detection and cross-referencing with sources like Politifact and Snopes. Google Fact Check and ClaimReview markup have become popular tools in real-time verification. However, such systems often face limitations in coverage, timeliness, and language dependency. Furthermore, reliance on third-party APIs can introduce latency or fail when claims are novel or context-sensitive [10,11].

2.3   Hybrid and Ensemble Approaches

To address the shortcomings of individual models, hybrid systems have gained popularity. Zhou et al. [9] provide a comprehensive survey of deep learning models that combine propagation patterns, textual cues, and social context. Ahmed et al. [8] proposed FakeBERT, which integrates BERT-based representations with handcrafted features for enhanced detection. Similarly, Tacchini et al. [14] used user response data in combination with content features for classification. While ensemble methods improve accuracy, they often increase computational complexity and reduce interpretability—issues especially problematic for real-time applications.

2.4   Limitations of Prior Work

Despite the progress in hybrid modeling, most existing systems still rely on static databases, lack source credibility validation, or ignore user trust and transparency. Few approaches incorporate dynamic source reputation, author profiling, or multi-dimensional claim validation. Moreover, many systems focus exclusively on detection rather than explanation, missing opportunities to empower users with contextual evidence [15].

2.5   Our Contributions

Our proposed system, *Fake News Busters*, addresses these limitations through a real-time, browser-integrated solution that merges stylistic and knowledge-based approaches. We enhance stylistic analysis using a fine-tuned LLaMA 3 model and Gemini preprocessing. Unlike prior work, our fact-checking module draws from diverse, dynamically queried sources (e.g., Google Scholar, LinkedIn, web-scraped content) and cross-validates them using stance detection. The result is a transparent, multi-layered credibility score that adapts to new claims and contextual nuances. Furthermore, we introduce caching strategies to reduce API latency, thereby improving performance without sacrificing accuracy or interpretability.

3   Methodology

3.1   System Overview

The architecture of *Fake News Busters* is designed as a modular, real-time detection pipeline combining frontend user interaction with robust backend processing (see Fig. 2). The system consists of three major components: the browser-based Chrome Extension interface, a Flask-based backend, and multiple integrated AI/ML modules and APIs for content analysis and verification.

Frontend (Chrome Extension): The user-facing interface is built as a lightweight Chrome extension using JavaScript and HTML. Users interact with this interface to scan a web article, optionally edit the text, and receive real-time credibility feedback. Once a page is scanned, the extension sends the extracted text to the backend via HTTP requests.

Backend (Flask Server): The Flask web server acts as the coordination hub between frontend requests and various backend components. Upon receiving a request, the Flask server initiates two parallel processes—one for stylistic analysis and one for fact-based verification.

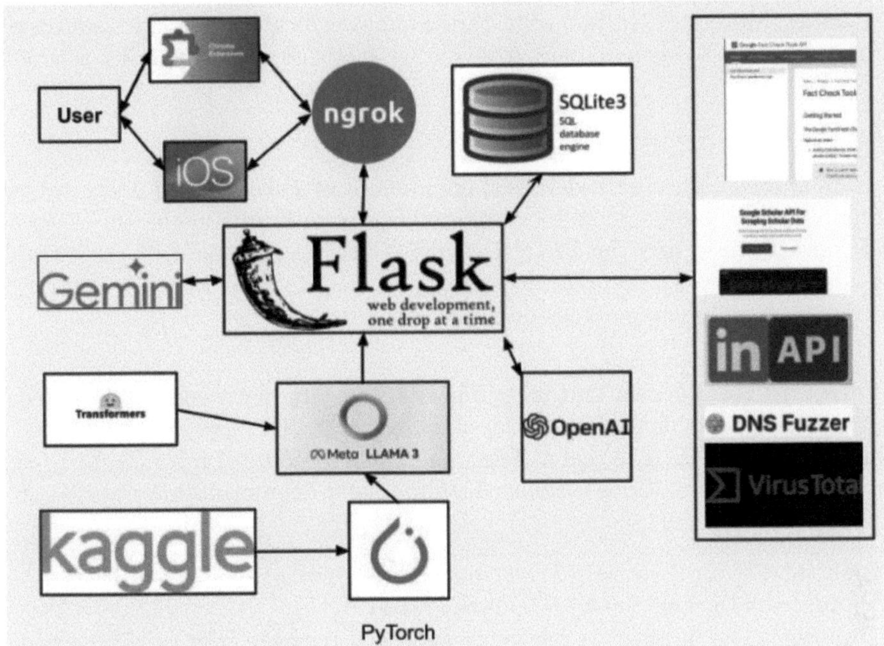

Fig. 2. System architecture diagram illustrating frontend and backend components of the Fake News Busters platform.

Style-Based Analysis: This module employs a fine-tuned LLaMA 3 model, trained using PyTorch on labeled datasets sourced from Kaggle. Preprocessing is done using OpenAI's Gemini and the NLTK toolkit to clean and tokenize the text. The LLaMA 3 model then generates a credibility score based on linguistic features like sentiment, coherence, and sentence complexity.

Knowledge-Based Verification: This module uses OpenAI APIs for claim extraction and verifies those claims using multiple external APIs. Google Fact Check, Google Scholar, LinkedIn, and VirusTotal are used to assess the credibility of specific claims, sources, and authors. A DNS Fuzzer also discovers related domains, which are also scanned for trustworthiness.

Integrated Scoring: The outputs of both modules are aggregated by a central scoring algorithm that generates an overall credibility score. Caching mechanisms are used to reduce API latency and support fallback strategies when third-party services are unavailable. This final score and its detailed breakdown are returned to the Chrome extension for user display.

The system architecture ensures flexibility and scalability by allowing modular upgrades, such as integrating new APIs or improving the LLaMA model's fine-tuning. Moreover, the inclusion of real-time verification and cross-source corroboration sets this system apart from earlier static or single-modality solutions.

3.2   Dataset

To train and evaluate the style-based component of *Fake News Busters*, we used two publicly available and well-established datasets from Kaggle: the *Fake and Real News Dataset* and the *LIAR Dataset*. These corpora offer diverse samples of both genuine and deceptive news content, enabling the LLaMA 3 model to learn stylistic differences across domains and writing styles.

1. Fake and Real News Dataset: This dataset, originally compiled by George McIntire and available on Kaggle[1], includes over 44,000 news articles labeled as either "fake" or "real". The real articles are primarily sourced from Reuters, while the fake articles come from various conspiracy and disinformation websites. Key features include:

- **Size**: 44,898 total entries (21,417 fake, 23,481 real)
- **Fields**: `title, text, subject, date, label`
- **Balance**: The data set is relatively balanced between fake (47.7%) and real (52.3%) labels.

This data set was used primarily to fine-tune the LLaMA 3 model in a style-based classification based on full-article level.

2. LIAR Dataset: We also utilized the LIAR dataset introduced by Wang (2017) [7], which contains short statements extracted from various political speeches and debates, each labeled with one of six truthfulness categories: `pants-fire, false, barely-true, half-true, mostly-true`, and `true`. For training purposes, we grouped the three lowest categories as "fake" and the top three as "real."

- **Size**: 12,836 manually labeled short statements
- **Fields**: `statement, context, speaker, party, label`
- **Labeling**: Balanced across classes, but includes greater linguistic diversity and political context

This data set provided valuable variation in linguistic style and subjectivity, complementing the article-level granularity of the fake and real news data set.

Both data sets were cleaned and tokenized using the NLTK and Gemini preprocessing pipelines before being input to the LLaMA 3 model. Their combined use helped train a robust stylistic model capable of generalizing across both long-form and short-form content.

---

[1] https://www.kaggle.com/clmentbisaillon/fake-and-real-news-dataset.

3.3   Detection and Scoring

The style-based module of *Fake News Busters* is designed to assess the linguistic credibility of a given news article. This component operates independently of external databases and focuses entirely on internal textual structure, tone, and writing patterns. The following steps outline the style-based detection pipeline:

Preprocessing with NLTK and Gemini: The raw text from the scanned webpage is first passed through a cleaning pipeline using the Natural Language Toolkit (NLTK). This includes:

- Lowercasing and punctuation removal
- Tokenization and lemmatization
- Stop-word filtering
- Sentence boundary detection

Gemini-based preprocessing complements this by standardizing the input to reduce stylistic noise, such as unusual formatting or embedded HTML/JS elements.

Feature Extraction – Tone and Structure: Before being passed to the model, the cleaned text is analyzed for stylistic features such as:

- **Tone**: Emotion-laden language, polarity, and subjectivity (using NLTK's VADER and TextBlob sentiment modules)
- **Structure**: Average sentence length, lexical diversity, readability index (Flesch-Kincaid), and passive voice frequency
- **Coherence**: Use of conjunctions, discourse markers, and topic progression

These extracted features are embedded into the text vector and appended to the LLaMA 3 model input, providing auxiliary stylistic context.

Fine-Tuning LLaMA 3: The core of the style-based detection engine is a fine-tuned LLaMA 3 transformer model. The model was trained using a combined corpus of approximately 57,000 labeled entries (Fake and Real News Dataset + LIAR Dataset, see Sect. 3.2). Fine-tuning was performed on a Tesla T4 GPU using the PyTorch framework.

- **Loss Function**: Binary Cross Entropy Loss
- **Optimizer**: AdamW with learning rate scheduling (initial LR = 2e-5)
- **Batch Size**: 16
- **Epochs**: 4 (with early stopping based on validation loss)

The model was trained to classify articles as fake or real, using their full-body text along with stylistic embeddings. Validation accuracy reached 91.4% on a held-out test set.

Output – Style Credibility Score: After inference, the model produces a style credibility score between 0 and 1. A score closer to 1 suggests the article aligns with known linguistic patterns of trustworthy content, while lower scores indicate potential stylistic markers of deception. This score is passed to the scoring algorithm and later combined with the knowledge-based score (see Sect. 3.5) for a final credibility assessment.

Each subscore ranges from 0 to 10, and the final score is calculated using a weighted average. A threshold of 3.5 or lower flags the article as likely fake, 3.5–6.5 as uncertain, and above 6.5 as likely credible. We adopt a conservative approach: articles are only flagged if all three signals consistently indicate unreliability, minimizing false positives and avoiding penalizing emerging but trustworthy sources.

4 Evaluation

To assess the effectiveness of our hybrid detection system, we conducted separate evaluations for the style-based and knowledge-based components. We then tested the combined system on a full set of real and fake news articles. Our evaluation considered both quantitative metrics and qualitative feedback from users.

4.1 Evaluation Metrics

We used the following classification metrics in our evaluation:

- **Accuracy** – the proportion of all predictions (real or fake) that were correct.
- **Precision** – the proportion of items labeled as a class (e.g., "fake") that are actually of that class; this measures false positives.
- **Recall** – the proportion of true items of a class that were correctly labeled; this measures false negatives.
- **F1-Score** – the harmonic mean of precision and recall, offering a balance between the two.

These metrics provide a holistic view of each module's strengths and weaknesses, particularly in balancing sensitivity (recall) and specificity (precision).

4.2 Evaluation of Style-Based Detection

The style-based module was evaluated on a curated dataset of 500 news articles, equally split between real and fake content. Real articles came from established outlets like Reuters and AP News, while fake ones were compiled from misleading sources online as well as manually written or modified examples. Some examples were found on platforms like Twitter/X or designed to resemble misinformation using sensationalist or manipulative language.

Table 1 summarizes the performance of the model. The system showed strong precision overall, particularly when identifying real articles, though recall dropped slightly for fake articles that imitated credible writing patterns.

Table 1. Performance metrics for style-based detection

Label	Precision	Recall	F1-Score	Support
Real	0.91	0.88	0.89	250
Fake	0.85	0.80	0.82	250
Avg/Total	**0.88**	**0.84**	**0.85**	**500**

4.3 Evaluation of Knowledge-Based Detection

The knowledge-based module was tested on 500 factual claims. Real claims were extracted from mainstream news sources, while fake or misleading ones were collected from online misinformation (e.g., discredited tweets, blogs), fabricated examples, or fact-checking databases.

Table 2 presents the classification metrics. The system excelled at confirming supported claims, but showed slightly reduced recall when classifying unverifiable or ambiguous claims.

Table 2. Performance metrics for knowledge-based verification

Label	Precision	Recall	F1-Score	Support
Supporting	0.83	0.87	0.85	200
Refuting	0.80	0.75	0.77	180
Unverifiable	0.72	0.68	0.70	120
Avg/Total	**0.79**	**0.77**	**0.78**	**500**

The accuracy of this module is heavily influenced by the richness of external sources. Claims about niche or fast-changing topics—such as breaking news—tended to result in lower confidence and more "unverifiable" labels.

4.4 Combined System Evaluation

We tested the full system—combining both modules—on the 500 news articles and calculated an overall credibility score per article. Human annotators assigned binary labels ("real" or "fake") based on factual accuracy and intent, forming the ground truth.

The combined system correctly classified 446 of the 500 articles, achieving an overall accuracy of **89.2%**. Integration of style and knowledge scoring helped the system resolve edge cases where a single method might have failed. For example, claims that lacked evidence but were written credibly were flagged appropriately by the fact-checking pipeline.

Finally, in a small usability study with 12 participants, most users expressed increased trust in the tool due to its breakdown of how credibility was scored and which claims were questionable. They particularly appreciated the evidence links and the visual style/knowledge sliders (Figs. 3 and 4).

5   Results and Discussion

Our evaluation of *Fake News Busters* demonstrates that hybrid detection—integrating both style-based and knowledge-based techniques—offers a more accurate and interpretable solution to fake news detection than either approach alone.

5.1   Performance Gains from Hybridization

The combined system achieved an overall accuracy of 89.2% on 500 articles, outperforming both standalone modules. This improvement is primarily due to the system's ability to cross-validate outputs: stylistic patterns help flag suspicious tone and structure, while knowledge checks provide factual grounding.

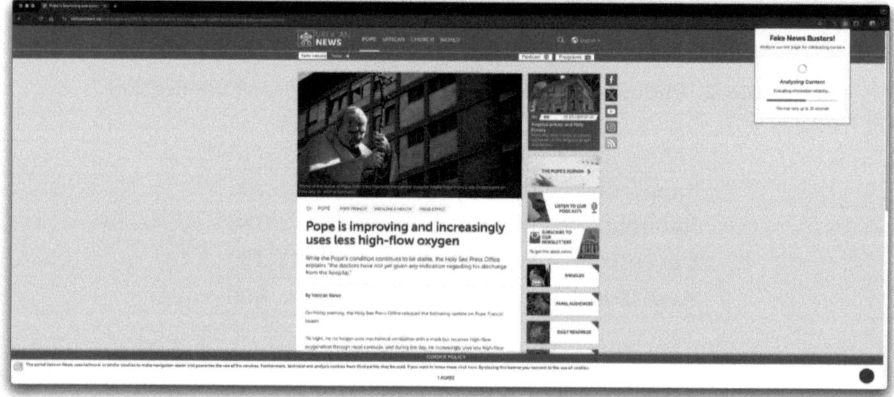

Fig. 3. Screenshot of the Chrome extension in use showing an article being analyzed.

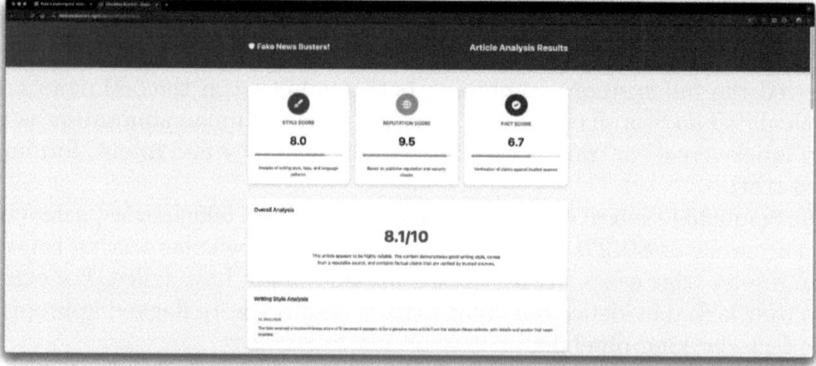

Fig. 4. Final result breakdown presented to the user, including style-based and knowledge-based scores, along with individual claim verifications.

Articles that might appear credible in tone but contain false claims were often correctly flagged due to the external validation provided by the knowledge-based component.

5.2   Cases of Divergence Between Modules

Interestingly, there were several cases where one module succeeded while the other failed:

- **Style Succeeded, Knowledge Failed:** Some articles written with overt emotional tone or vague language were flagged by the stylistic model even when the factual claims within were difficult to verify online. These included editorials or blog posts using misleading phrasing without making direct factual statements.
- **Knowledge Succeeded, Style Failed:** Conversely, some well-written misinformation pieces that imitated journalistic tone passed stylistic filters but were flagged as untrustworthy due to the presence of factually incorrect claims. For example, a fake science article about vaccine side effects mimicked professional style but cited non-existent studies, which the knowledge module caught via Google Fact Check and source verification.

These complementary strengths validate the rationale for integrating both detection strategies.

5.3   API Reliability and Impact on Results

One challenge encountered during testing was the partial reliance on external APIs. When services like Google Fact Check or LinkedIn rate-limiting were triggered, fallback mechanisms (e.g., caching or reduced feature mode) were activated. This led to occasional cases of unverifiable results, especially when dealing with emerging topics not yet indexed by these databases. While rare, these events highlight the fragility of depending on third-party services.

5.4   User Trust and Interpretability

Feedback from a preliminary usability study with 12 participants suggested that users found the hybrid model more trustworthy than a black-box classifier. Participants appreciated the separate style and knowledge scores, as well as the ability to inspect supporting or refuting evidence through external links. Users also noted that receiving not just a final judgment but an explanation improved their confidence in the tool's verdict.

5.5   Limitations

Despite promising results, several limitations remain:

- **API Dependency:** The knowledge-based module's performance is closely tied to the availability and responsiveness of external APIs, introducing potential bottlenecks or failure points.
- **Limited Dataset:** The system was evaluated on 500 articles and claims. While this includes a mixture of authentic, fabricated, and misleading content, broader domain coverage is needed to generalize findings across genres, languages, and media types.
- **Biases in LLaMA 3:** The fine-tuned LLaMA 3 model may inherit subtle biases from its pretraining data, particularly in distinguishing political content or detecting satire. These biases can affect style-based classification, especially on borderline or sarcastic text.
- **Real-Time Constraints:** Although latency was reduced via caching and parallel processing, real-time performance can still be impacted under high load or when claim extraction yields complex or ambiguous statements.

Addressing these challenges in future iterations will require expanding our datasets, optimizing fallback mechanisms, and exploring alternative or locally hosted verification tools.

6 Conclusion and Future Work

This paper presents *Fake News Busters*, a real-time fake news detection system that integrates style-based and knowledge-based analysis within a user-friendly Chrome extension. By combining the linguistic scrutiny of a fine-tuned LLaMA 3 model with dynamic, API-driven claim verification, our system addresses the limitations of single-modality approaches and offers users both accurate detection and transparent explanations.

Our evaluation across 500 mixed articles and claims shows that the hybrid model achieves superior accuracy (89.2%) compared to standalone methods. It effectively identifies articles that exhibit deceptive tone or unverifiable factual assertions—even when one signal alone may fail. The dual scoring system and claim-level feedback also foster user trust and engagement, as confirmed through usability testing.

In terms of user experience, the extension successfully delivers intuitive and interpretable feedback at the moment of news consumption. Users benefit not only from detection but from insight—seeing why content was flagged and which claims contributed to the result.

Looking ahead, future work will focus on expanding dataset coverage across multiple languages and domains, enhancing offline fact-checking capabilities to reduce API dependency, and exploring more robust LLM fine-tuning to mitigate stylistic bias. We also plan to implement personalized user feedback to tailor scoring thresholds and improve the educational value of the system.

Ultimately, *Fake News Busters* lays the groundwork for trustworthy, real-time media literacy tools and demonstrates the effectiveness of multi-layered detection in the fight against digital misinformation.

References

1. Shu, K., Sliva, A., Wang, S., Tang, J., Liu, H.: Fake news detection on social media: a data mining perspective. ACM SIGKDD Explor. Newsl **19**(1), 22–36 (2017)
2. Zhou, X., Zafarani, R.: Fake news: A survey of research, detection methods, and opportunities. arXiv preprint arXiv:1812.00315 (2018)
3. Potthast, M., Kiesel, J., Reinartz, K., Bevendorff, J., Stein, B.: A stylometric inquiry into hyperpartisan and fake news. arXiv preprint arXiv:1702.05638 (2017)
4. Rashkin, H., Choi, E., Jang, J.Y., Volkova, S., Choi, Y.: Truth of varying shades: analyzing language in fake news and political fact-checking. In: Proceedings of EMNLP (2017)
5. Shu, K., Mahudeswaran, D., Wang, S., Lee, D., Liu, H.: FakeNewsNet: a data repository with news content, social context, and dynamic information for studying fake news on social media. Big Data **8**(3), 171–188 (2020)
6. Baly, R., Karadzhov, G., Alexandrov, D., Glass, J., Nakov, P.: Predicting factuality of reporting and bias of news media sources. In: EMNLP (2018)
7. Wang, W.Y.: "Liar, liar pants on fire": a new benchmark dataset for fake news detection. In: ACL (2017)
8. Ahmed, H., Traore, I., Saad, S.: Detecting opinion spams and fake news using text classification. Secur. Priv. **3**(1), e91 (2020)
9. Zhou, X., Jain, A., Phoha, V.V., Zafarani, R.: A survey of fake news: fundamental theories, detection methods, and opportunities. ACM Comput. Surv. (CSUR) **53**(5), 1–40 (2020)
10. Ciampaglia, G.L., Shiralkar, P., Rocha, L.M., Bollen, J., Menczer, F., Flammini, A.: Computational fact checking from knowledge networks. PLoS ONE **10**(6), e0128193 (2015)
11. Nakashole, N., Mitchell, T.M.: Language-aware fact checking of statements. In: ACL (2014)
12. Mridha, M.F., Keya, A.J., Hamid, M.A., Monowar, M.M., Rahman, M.S.: A comprehensive review on fake news detection with deep learning. IEEE Access **9**, 156151–156170 (2021)
13. Capuano, N., Fenza, G., Loia, V., Nota, F.D.: Content-based fake news detection with machine and deep learning: a systematic review. Neurocomputing **530**, 91–103 (2023)
14. Tacchini, E., Ballarin, G., Della Vedova, M.L., Moret, S., de Alfaro, L.: Some like it hoax: automated fake news detection in social networks. In: CSCW Companion (2017)
15. Perez-Rosas, V., Kleinberg, B., Lefevre, A., Mihalcea, R.: Automatic detection of fake news. In: COLING (2017)

An Examination of Ethical Considerations in Human-Centered Design for Regional Revitalization

Akira Kondo[✉]

Kagoshima Women's College, Kagoshima 890-8565, Japan
`kondo@jkajyo.ac.jp`

Abstract. This study categorizes the people and elements involved in regional revitalization based on actor-network theory, considering each as an integral participant. By creating personas that embody these participants, we establish their goals and expectations. Within this framework, "planners", "environment", "objects", and "stakeholders" are defined as distinct roles. Planners refer to government bodies or organizations overseeing the project. The environment includes the natural surroundings and cultural context. Objects encompass both real estate and movable artifacts within the region. Stakeholders consist of local residents, individuals engaged with the community in some capacity, and those who may become involved in the future.

Subsequently, we analyze online data on successful community revitalization cases in Japan, assessing how these cases align with the needs of different personas and the criteria used to determine success.

Finally, we discuss ethical issues that should be considered when constructing sustainable ecosystems through regional revitalization, summarizing key ethical considerations within the human-centered design cycle.

Keywords: Regional revitalization · Human-centered design · Ethical considerations

1 Introduction

Regional revitalization is a pressing issue in modern Japanese society. However, the objectives of revitalization are not always universally shared, requiring careful consideration of whether the focus should be on economic growth, quality of life, or a balance between the two. Additionally, it is essential to determine for whom the community is being revitalized. Presently, most revitalization efforts in Japan prioritize economic development and population growth. While local residents recognize the decline in urban functions due to depopulation, they may not necessarily desire significant environmental transformations that disrupt their established way of life.

M. Kurosu and A. Hashizume (Eds.): HCII 2025, LNCS 16332, pp. 385–395, 2026.
https://doi.org/10.1007/978-3-032-12385-5_24

2   Case Study

Based on actor-network theory (Komatsu, 2008), we categorize the individuals and objects involved in community revitalization as key actors. Preliminary research was conducted to formulate personas and define their respective goals. In this model, "planners", "environment", "objects", and "stakeholders" represent the core components. Planners, typically governments or organizations, oversee the revitalization efforts. The environment comprises the local natural and cultural surroundings, while objects include changeable real estate assets and movable goods. Stakeholders are further classified into (1) local residents, (2) individuals actively engaged in the community, and (3) external participants such as consumers or investors in revitalization activities.

We conducted a survey of successful regional revitalization cases in Japan, categorizing them into the following sectors: "tourism", "urban development", "employment and market expansion", "agriculture", "education", and "migration" (Fig. 1).

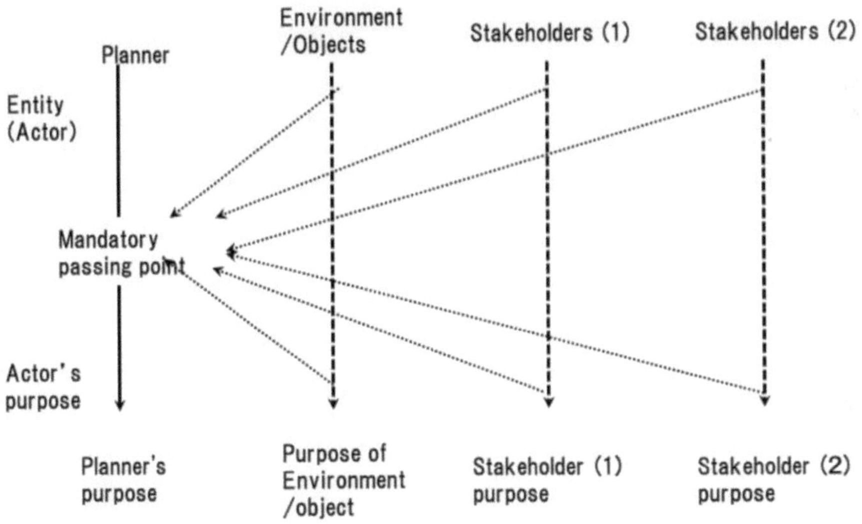

Fig. 1. A Model of Actors' Network Theory of Regional Revitalization.

2.1   Survey of Successful Examples of Regional Revitalization

1. Tourism

The planners were local governments, or public corporations or associations of commerce and industry, and there were many cases of value creation for the local environment and objects in cooperation with the stakeholders who actually carried out the activities. The management of the project was conducted with appropriate interest coordination among stakeholders, and was considered a success when it was compiled as a case study (Table 1).

Table 1. Summary of case studies on tourism.

(event) planner	environment	object	Stakeholder 1	Stakeholder 2	Stakeholder 3	Obligatory Passage Point
Municipal Tourism Department	paddy field		farmers	local business	tourist	tanbo art
Municipal Tourism Department Private Company	Customs and habits	Food, drinks and festivals	residents	private-sector business	Inbound tourists	Experience traditional culture, nature, etc. Ah!
Asuka Village Chamber of Commerce and Industry Blue year round	Nature, farmland	Old houses, abandoned houses	Residents, immigrants	new tourism conference	Educational and school trips traveling throughout the world (travelling)	Asuka Village Vacant House Activity use
Tourism Town Planning Public regional Chinese god of the earth (or a village built in its honour)	Agricultural land, fishing grounds	old private house	residents	immigrant	Inbound tourist	Adults can be satisfied. Stay-and-experience tourism

2. Urban development

The planners were local governments and tourism or private organizations, and the activities were mainly those that created spaces and environments that created experiential value by utilizing local resources. The success of the project was attributed to the fact that the planners focused on the stakeholders, who were the entities that managed the resources, and that the planners implemented systems and operations that prevented inconsistencies among the stakeholders (Table 2).

Table 2. Summary of case studies on Urban development.

(event) planner	environment	object	Stakeholder 1	Stakeholder 2	Stakeholder 3	Obligatory Passage Point
Municipal Community Revitalization promotion office	town areas	Town center facility (city center)	residents	Designer from the local area ner		urban redevelopment project exchange facilities
Municipal Health and Welfare Division	walking environment		residents	shopping district		Improvement of walking space
Municipality, Kurokabe Co.		Black wall, glass	residents	local business	artist	Kurokabe Street renovation
Municipalities, tourist associations	port city		local business	Local Support	tourist	Mizuki Shigeru Road

3. Employment and sales channel expansion (economic development)

Specific businesses were targeted as examples in this area, and in many cases, private companies were the leading stakeholders, but the local government or organization that served as the planner took on the task of coordination in order to spread the effects widely throughout the community. In some cases, the entire village acted as one commercial organization, and the planners organized the parts that could not be planned by the stakeholders alone (Table 3).

Table 3. Summary of case studies on Employment and sales channel expansion.

(event) planner	environment	object	Stakeholder 1	Stakeholder 2	Stakeholder 3	Obligatory Passage Point
Liquor Council	Hokkaido (northernmost of the four main islands of Japan)	Sake, Brewery	Local breweries		tourist	father-sake port
municipality			residents	local business	local student	Job hunting event for local companies nt (unit of volume, approx. 1.8 litres)
municipality		High-grade local hinoki (Japanese cypress)	forestryman	contractor		Custom-built home sales sis tem (unit of distance, 109.09 m)
Network Hiraya (Residents' Co-funded Association) Company)			residents		Out-of-area purchasers	Store "Flat Miyama
municipality	Wood gathering area	Scrap wood (Industrial waste)	residents	sawmill		Biomass Business
village community	Aging Nakayama Settlements in the interregional area	Indigenous bacteria and handmade additions manufactured goods	residents			YANE DAN" Project

4. Agriculture

In the case of agriculture, the main stakeholder was the producer, and the planner was responsible for planning and environmental improvement to increase the value of the community, focusing on agricultural products. As a result, agricultural products were distributed with higher added value than before, and the value of the production area itself was improved, leading to the revitalization of all stakeholders and increased profits (Table 4).

Table 4. Summary of case studies on Agriculture.

(event) planner	environment	object	Stakeholder 1	Stakeholder 2	Stakeholder 3	Obligatory Passage Point
municipality	Chikumagawa Weinba rays			winegrower	Consumers, Travelers	Winery Clustering Area
Municipality (Village)	agricultural land	lettuce	farmer		consumer	Brands that are efficient from production to shipping. lettuce

5. Education and migration (population increase)

In both of these cases, the planners added new value to existing resources for the purpose of increasing the local population, leading to overall stakeholder satisfaction (Table 5).

Table 5. Summary of case studies on Education and migration.

(event) planner	environment	object	Stakeholder 1	Stakeholder 2	Stakeholder 3	Obligatory Passage Point
Municipality (City)	Continued outflow of young population suburban city		residents		young worker	Support for business startups, etc.
Municipality (Island)	Rich Relationships traditional culture	High school on the verge of closing	Local Resident Teachers		Motivated students from all over the country unprotected (i.e. not wearing a condom)	studying abroad on an island
Municipality (Tokushima Prefecture)	mountainous region depopulated area in town		residents	Young people in their 30s and 40s	Metropolitan ICT Ben chartering company	Attracting IT companies

2.2 Anthropomorphic Personas Related to Local Revitalization Assumed from Case Study Results

1. Environmental persona

Natural environment, social environment, real estate, infrastructure, local customs and values

– Personality

The environment is the foundation of the community, but recently the weather patterns are not as they used to be due to global warming and other factors. The shape of the environment changes depending on human activities, such as more or less people. It is a shifting and dynamic masterpiece that encompasses the local eco-system and interacts with the activities there.

– Requirements

There are no specific requirements as long as the activities are balanced with the local natural environment, facilities, people's activities, and population. However, local residents should understand that changes in the global environment can cause unexpected weather changes and natural disasters.

Also, human-induced changes to the natural environment can cause disasters if the balance is not maintained, so activities that bring about environmental change should be mindful of the balance of the local ecosystem.

2. Object persona

• Dynamic resources, products, specialties

– Personality

They have been around in the community for a long time, but they change their appearance from time to time, and are either admired or ignored by the people. We are happy to see them attract attention and increase in value, but we also want people to understand that there is a limit to the number of them. It doesn't hurt to be loved in one region and to be admired in another, and to change one's behavior according to the situation.

– Requirements

If possible, I would like to be noticed and coveted by everyone, but I do not want to become overly popular and end up competing with each other or causing confusion such as unjustified price hikes.

3. Planner persona

Coordinates the entire regional revitalization effort and leads the plan

– Personality

He/she wants to build a better society as a coordinator of the local human society. Has a wide network of contacts, is in a position to manage public funds, and often makes final decisions on plans. Although there are times when they take the lead in implementing revitalization measures themselves, most of the time they act as supporters of community activists. They may take on new challenges, but they are often relatively conservative and fear failure.

– Requirements

They want to lead and support activities to revitalize the community and increase people's satisfaction in a broad and fair manner. Seek support from others where their own abilities and knowledge are not up to the task.

1. Local residents

People who make up the local area, passively involved in local revitalization
(4)-1 Young people

– Personality

They have an attachment to the local area, but they get information from outside the area through various media, and have actually visited big cities. They are open to change, but they also feel that the lifestyle of the area they have lived in for many years (personal space, communication style, means of transportation, etc.) does not match the urban style.
Requirements
They are looking for some kind of change to make their daily lives more enjoyable. They also think it is preferable to live in their hometown, so they welcome the creation of a suitable place to work.
(4)-2 Elderly people

– Personality

They have lived in the area for many years, and their lifestyle there is fundamental to them, so they find it difficult to accept styles from outside the area. They regret the decline in the area's population and economic activity, and hope that the area will be revitalized to attract more immigrants and related populations, but they do not want their own living space to change. However, they want to avoid the disappearance of the local community, and are open to compromise.

– Requirements

They want to see an increase in population and revitalization of economic activity so that they can maintain the local ecosystem without changing the traditional style as much as possible.

2. Community Activist

Actively involved in community revitalization

– Personality

They have a strong desire to solve social problems, and have the ability and sense to create value in products and services that have not been discovered before. They cannot do what they want to do alone, so they form teams with their colleagues and work on plans with enthusiasm. They may be from a local area and love the area, but they may also be active because they like the environment and resources of the area.
- Requirements
They want to restore economic and human vitality to declining areas and make them attractive. They also want to use their own abilities and knowledge to solve social problems.

3. Outside the region

Involved in revitalizing the region as an external resource.

– Personality

They are open to experiences that are useful to society or enrich their own lives, not just within their own living area.

– Requirements

They would like to introduce new products and experiences that have never been seen before if they are beneficial to them and the region.
As a result, they want to feel satisfied by having a never-before-seen experience that contributes to society.
gure, equation etc. does not have an indent, either.
Subsequent paragraphs, however, are indented.

3 Persona Model Study for Regional Revitalization Ecosystem

3.1 An Ecosystem for Regional Revitalization

In today's Japan, the population is flowing into and increasing in the capital region and other large cities, and economic and cultural activities are thriving. Meanwhile, in rural areas, although there is a related population that visits for tourism and other reasons, the fundamental problem is that the resident population is leaving and economic activity is shrinking. Many of the government's regional revitalization policies[4] aim to increase the resident population by providing subsidies to create businesses that create value from regional resources or by deregulation, but there are many cases[5] where activities shrink or cease when subsidies or government support are removed. A conceptual diagram is shown in Fig. 2.

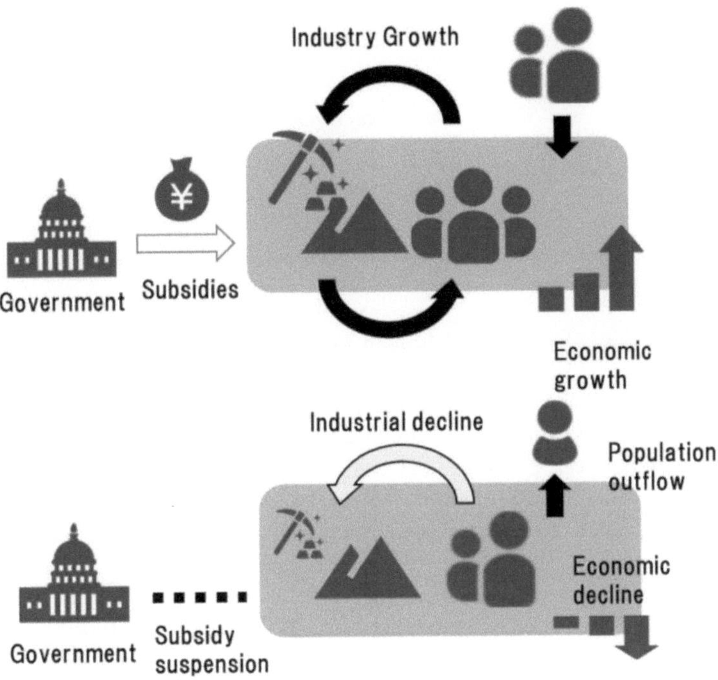

Fig. 2.　Subsidy-based industrial development measures.

It can be said that successful regional revitalization will require the construction of an ecosystem as shown in Fig. 3, where revitalization activities will continue to progress.

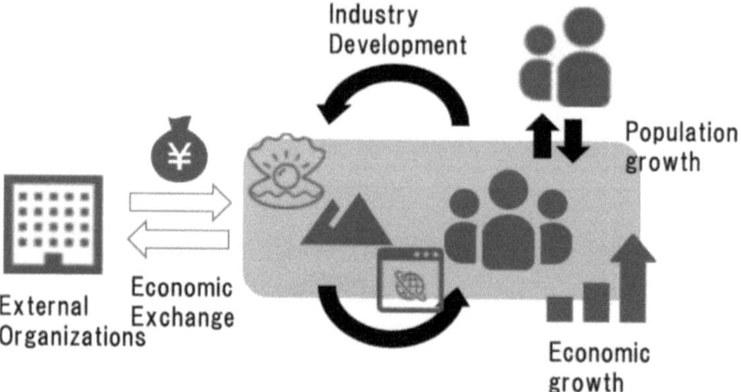

Fig. 3. Continuous development of local industry ecosystem.

3.2 Regional Persona Relationship Model Study

As mentioned in Sect. 3.1, in order to achieve continuous regional revitalization, each persona proposed in Sect. 2 needs to build appropriate relationships and carry out activities. Based on the cycle of human-centered design, in order to design an ecosystem that sustains the desired regional revitalization, it is necessary to appropriately adjust the requirements between personas and consider values. For this reason, we devised a regional persona relationship model based on the idea of organizational personas proposed in the past (Kondo 2009), as shown in Fig. 4. Figure 5 shows the application of this model to Shimane's "High School Attraction Project" as a successful case study example. Both of these clearly state requirements in the cycle of human-centered design, but we believe that such a visualized model is effective in creating solutions that mutually satisfy these requirements.

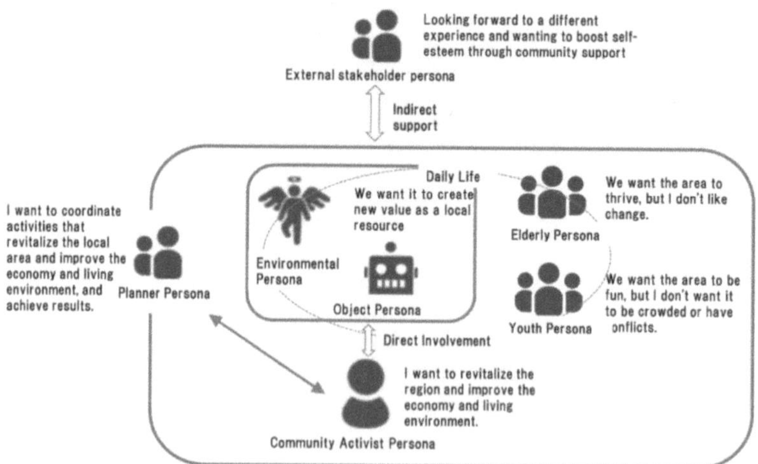

Fig. 4. Regional persona relationship model.

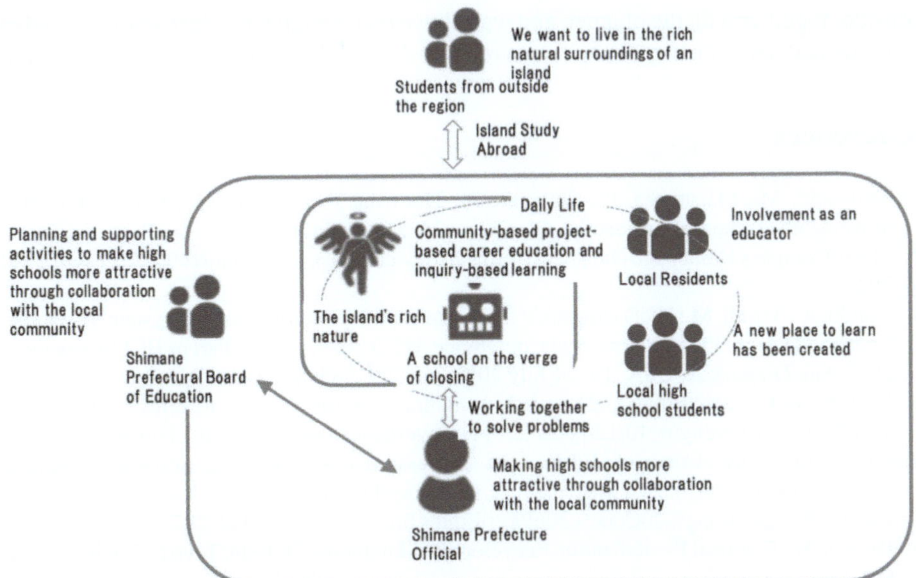

Fig. 5. Shimane's "High School Attractiveness Project".

4   Proposal for Ethical Considerations for Regional Revitalization

In order to revitalize the region, some kind of change will occur that will affect the entire persona of the region that has been described so far. As an ethical approach for information systems that utilize the human-centered design cycle, developers have the following guidelines:

Pursue the best interests of the "public", "customer", and "employer".

Ensure that the "product" meets the highest possible standards.

"Judgment" should maintain integrity and independence.

"Management" should support an ethical approach and make decisions as a team based on the four ethical principles (respect for self-determination, beneficence, non-maleficence, fairness, etc.).

We believe that similar ethical considerations are necessary in regional revitalization using the cycle of human-centered design. Although we strive to maximize the profits distributed among each stakeholder, profits cannot always be measured by economic indicators, and even in qualitative cases such as human relationships and liveliness, some quantitative indicators should be set and fairness should be considered at the design stage. There is no standard for the outcome of revitalization, which corresponds to a "product," as there is for software, but it will be necessary to prevent problems from occurring by considering the public interest as well as the risks of accidents and disasters.

Finally, how to follow the four ethical principles (respect for self-determination, beneficence, non-maleficence, fairness, etc.), which are an ethical approach between stakeholders, is something that the team involved in human-centered design should consider together with the planner, and we believe that it would be effective to proceed by visualizing it using the regional persona relationship model assumed in this presentation.

References

1. Taniguchi, M., Matsunaka, R., Shibaike, A.: Does the social capital support "new public" movement? (Japanese). Infrastruct. Plan. Rev. **25**, 311–318 (2008)
2. SDGs Compass Homepage (Japanese). https://sdgs-compass.jp/column/1997. Accessed 1 Feb 2025
3. Kondo, A., Yoshii, M.: HCD case study for the information security training system. In: Human Centered Design: First International Conference, HCD 2009, Held as Part of HCI International 2009, San Diego, CA, USA, 19–24 July 2009, pp. 979–985. Springer, Heidelberg. (2009)
4. University of Tokyo "Ethics and Law in Information Systems" (Japanese), https://ocw.u-tokyo.ac.jp/lecture_files/engin_10/12/notes/ja/011_Governance.pdf. Accessed 1 Feb 2025
5. Meiji University. Code of Ethics and Professional Practice for Software Engineering. (Japanese). https://www.isc.meiji.ac.jp/~ethicj/Japanese%20Translation%20of%20Software%20Engineering%20Code%20of%20Ethics.htm. Accessed 1 Feb 2025
6. Hisashi, K.: Regional Revitalization Encyclopedia (Japanese), 2nd edn. Toyo Keizai Inc., Tokyo (2016)
7. Nobutaka, I.: Let's connect with the local community! (Japanese). Shizuoka Shimbun., Tokyo (2019)

From Concept to Impact: Risk Communication Methods for DNA Data Sharing

Lipsarani Sahoo[1(✉)], Elham Al Qahtani[3], Yousra Javed[2], and Mohamed Shehab[1]

[1] University of North Carolina Charlotte, Charlotte, USA
{lsahoo1,mshehab}@charlotte.edu
[2] Illinois State University, Normal, USA
yjaved@ilstu.edu
[3] University of Jeddah, Jeddah, Saudi Arabia
eaalqahtani@uj.edu.sa

Abstract. This paper presents a multi-phase participatory design study aimed at developing effective methods for communicating the risks and benefits of genetic data sharing. The study involved designing and evaluating various risk communication methods, with informational videos and infographics being preferred by participants. The informational video proved more effective in enhancing content recall and influencing participants' reluctance to share DNA data, with 77.1% of video participants unwilling to share their DNA in an open genealogy database, compared to 64.2% in the infographic group. This suggests that video-based communication may better convey the complexities of genetic data sharing, including privacy concerns and ethical considerations. The findings highlight the importance of multi-sensory engagement in risk communication strategies, which can be leveraged by developers and policymakers to improve public awareness and informed decision-making regarding genetic privacy.

Keywords: DNA data · Participatory designing · Co-designing · DNA Privacy · risk communication · Genetic testing · Online data Sharing · Genetic data privacy

1 Introduction

The increasing popularity of at-home DNA testing and online genetic data-sharing platforms presents significant privacy concerns. DNA data, as a unique identifier, not only reveals personal information but also exposes familial relationships and health predispositions. Risks such as third-party access, data breaches, and law enforcement usage of genetic data underscore the need for effective risk communication strategies to help individuals make informed decisions about sharing their genetic information [6, 15]. Therefore, it is vital to educate individuals about the potential risks and implications of sharing their genetic information. This suggests the need to create an effective risk communication method to enable users to make informed choices while sharing their DNA data. To address this gap, a study is needed to design and develop an effective method of risk communication to help users understand both the benefits and risks

M. Kurosu and A. Hashizume (Eds.): HCII 2025, LNCS 16332, pp. 396–416, 2026.
https://doi.org/10.1007/978-3-032-12385-5_25

before they decide to share their genetic data. We performed a multi-phase participatory design study in which the participants are involved in the design process to help ensure the results meet the needs and expectations of the stakeholders. Our study consisted of three phases, with the goal of understanding and gathering requirements and content to effectively design risk communication messaging, and to involve the users in creating and developing these methods. These phases are described below:

1. **Need-Finding and Co-Design:** We aimed to understand people's thoughts on genetic data sharing and the factors they consider when sharing their genetic data online with private companies. We also explored users' preferences for communicating associated risks and benefits. Specifically, we investigated which risks and benefits users seek to understand and how they trade off privacy for benefits. Additionally, we gathered their preferences on the time spent learning about these risks and benefits and the stage of site registration for presenting this messaging. Participants suggested video messaging, infographics, and interactive surveys/wizards as effective methods. We conceived five messaging methods: Personal story video, Conversational story video, Informational story video, Infographic, and Wizard.
2. **Design Iteration:** We collaborated with users to iterate, improve, and enhance the designs based on their feedback from the first phase. Participants reviewed all five designs and provided feedback on relatability, enjoyability, ease of understanding, and engagement. We then refined the designs to incorporate user input and eliminated the three least effective and preferred methods.
3. **Design Comparison:** We tested the final two designs against each other to determine the most effective method for communicating the risks and benefits of genetic data sharing. This phase focused on comparing users' understanding, recall of information, and intention to share genetic data after encountering the message.

2   Participatory Design in Risk Communication

Participatory design (PD) is a well-established approach in human-computer interaction (HCI) for creating user-centered solutions. It involves stakeholders throughout the design process, ensuring that the final product meets their needs and expectations. Studies have demonstrated the efficacy of PD in fostering stakeholder engagement and generating effective designs for complex challenges, including privacy and risk communication [2,3,5,8,10,11,13,16,17]. Previous research highlights the challenges of communicating risks associated with emerging technologies, emphasizing the need for methods that balance usability, comprehension, and engagement [5]. For instance, a study on wildfire smoke risk communication used PD to develop and revise communication strategies for hard-to-reach populations, demonstrating the approach's effectiveness in addressing diverse needs [19]. Similarly, a scoping review identified models for participatory design in pandemic communication, underscoring the importance of community engagement in public health emergencies [4]. PD has been applied to various domains, including privacy and risk communication. For example, a participatory approach was used to design a privacy-enhancing instant messaging app, where users' feedback was integral to developing effective privacy features [14]. The user-centered design approach, popularized in the 1980s by Donald Norman, laid the groundwork for participatory design methodologies [13]. This approach emphasized addressing users' needs and desires to ensure usability, thereby enhancing product effectiveness, efficiency, safety, and success [2,7,16]. This mindset values participation and engagement from all stakeholders, making it ideal for designing risk communication strategies for online DNA data sharing [5,8,10,11].

In conclusion, the adoption of participatory design in this study is based on its established efficacy and adaptability in involving stakeholders throughout the design process. This approach ensures that the developed risk communication strategies are effective, user-centric, and reflective of the diverse needs and insights of all stakeholders involved. The broad acceptance and application of PD across various domains underscore its value and relevance in addressing complex challenges, such as those associated with online DNA data sharing risks.

3   Phase 1 Need-Finding and Co-Design

To gather users' requirements and content for the risk communication message, we conducted phase 1 of our study. We aimed to understand what and how users would like to be informed about the benefits and risks of sharing their DNA data online. **Study Goals -** Our goal is to gather feedback from participants on: 1) What information to emphasize to highlight the risks and benefits 2) How to deliver this information 3)How long this communication should be.

Content and Scenarios - The slide content and scenarios were inspired by literature reviews and current news related to DNA testing. We created topics summarizing the risks and benefits of DNA data sharing, emphasizing privacy challenges and potential identification risks. Screenshots of the slides can be found in Appendix [1].

3.1   Recruitment and Demographics

We recruited 10 participants through our University's mailing list, complemented by snowball sampling for diversity. The sample included 5 males and 5 females, aged 20 to 55, from various fields such as graphic design, computer science, and health informatics. Each participant received a $10 Amazon gift card. Recruitment continued until we achieved saturation (i.e., no new information emerged). Institutional Review Board (IRB) approval was obtained.

3.2   Procedure and Analysis

We scheduled video interviews via email, using Zoom for all sessions. The semi-structured interviews, lasting an average of 54 min, began with a consent form discussion and an introduction to the research topic. The interview steps were:

- **Step 1**: Collection of demographics (age, gender, profession).
- **Step 2**: Discussion on at-home DNA testing interest and reasons.

- **Step 3**: Presentation of slides on genetic testing risks and benefits to understand user perceptions. Benefits included ancestry insights, finding genetic relatives, health predispositions, and lifestyle choices. Risks included sharing family DNA, potential law enforcement access, genetic discrimination, insurance access, racial profiling, and third-party access.
- **Step 4**: Drawing task to elicit conceptual ideas on design and risk communication messaging. Participants explained their preferred message delivery method and drew their ideas, describing them verbally during the activity.

Though conducted virtually, participants described their drawings in detail (similar to an in-person interview) and talked about it once they shared the picture with us.

3.3   Results

We questioned participants about their experiences, perceived usefulness, and perceived threats of at-home genetic testing and sharing with private companies. Below is a synopsis of their answers.

Experience: All participants were aware of at-home DNA testing and interested in taking one. 90% mentioned the testing procedure, such as sending saliva or swab samples to companies for DNA reports, indicating familiarity with the process.

Perceived Benefits: 80% of participants wanted to take the test to learn more about their ancestry, ethnicity, heritage, find DNA relatives, and understand their health predispositions. They believed this information could help them change lifestyles and prepare for the future.

Perceived Risks: 50% expressed concerns about private companies potentially selling their data or using it without oversight. They also mentioned security issues like data breaches or hacking.

Privacy Trade-off: Despite concerns about hacking and data breaches, 50% were still curious about taking the test to learn about potential health issues and support family members. This suggests that the privacy trade-off for users is gaining health insights for future preparation and family support.

We then showed participants slides illustrating the advantages and risks of sharing DNA data and asked which information should be emphasized to help people make informed decisions. Tables 1, 2 summarize the topics participants suggested highlighting.

We collected participants' suggestions on methods or settings for DNA data sharing platforms to enhance data sharing privacy. Table 3 presents the summary of our findings.

Finally, we collected participants' feedback on methods to deliver these risks and benefits contents. **Story-telling** emerged as a key approach. People described that story-telling videos and info-graphics could be very pleasing, helpful, understandable, or effective ways to pass or convey the message. We compiled all the information about what content, and how long the risk communication strategies should be comprised of. Our findings are summarized in Table 4.

Table 1. Participants' suggestions of the possible risks that must be included in the risk and benefit message

Risks that must be discussed	Percentage of participants
Third party access	100%
Hacking or data breach	100%
Reveal health information about family	100%
Law enforcement access	80%
Employer or insurance access	80%
Genetic discrimination	80%
Involuntary surveillance or Dragged into police investigation	70%

Table 2. Participants' suggestions of the possible benefits that must be included in the risk and benefit message

Benefits that must be discussed	Percentage of participants
Health predispositions	90%
Traits	70%
Know your Ancestry	60%
Wellbeing & lifestyle	60%
Family finding	40%
Genetic medicine	20%
Participate in research	20%

Table 3. Suggestions on Privacy enhancing settings for DNA sharing platforms

Suggestions	% of Participants
Permission of all parties involved before relatives match	100%
Option to allow or not allow to share data with any entities	100%
Option to completely delete data and information anytime	100%
Notify when someone matches more than certain limits	100%
Company ask authorization before someone can see/access contact details	100%
Notifying user when someone else accesses info	100%
Option to set a certain limit of match for access of contact details	100%
Should be asked access each time law enforcement asks for and inform details about the case and reasons for access	100%
Notify about policy updates of the company	100%
Option to auto-delete data after a certain period of time	90%
Ask each time for any research use and inform details of the research and rights of the participant	90%

Table 4. Participants' designs suggestions

Designs suggestions			% of participants
How do they want the info to be comm-unicated?	Watching video	With personal examples/stories	70%
		With data and information	50%
	Info-graphic		70%
	Interactive survey/wizards		20%
	Reading policy		10%
How much time are they willing to spend?	To watch a video	1-2 mins	30%
		2-3 mins	60%
		3-4 mins	10%
	Length of info-graphic	1 standard page (2-3 min read)	50%
		2 standard pages (2-3 min read)	50%

3.4 Implication of Phase 1: Suggestions to Initial Designs

Based on the findings summarized in Table 4, we created the following designs:
Designs

- **Videos**
    - Personal story video - A cartoon character speaking about her own experience of at-home DNA testing highlighting the benefits she got and the risks she discovered.
    - Conversational story video - Two cartoon characters chatting about the risks and benefits of at-home DNA testing.
    - Informational video - All the information about risks and benefits is explained on a whiteboard.
- **Info-graphics** - All the information about risks and benefits is explained in a one-page paper.
- **Wizards / Interactive survey** - Wizard provides information based on the user's choices.

All videos are 2–3 min long. We also designed an infographic page and an interactive survey (wizard) highlighting the benefits and risks suggested by participants in Tables 1 and 2. Our goal was to enhance these materials by gathering user feedback in phase 2 of our study.

4   Phase 2 Design Iterations

4.1   Methodology

We used semi-structured interviews to enhance our initial designs and gather users' thoughts on the risk communication message.

Initial Designs (Version 1): Based on user suggestions from phase 1, we created five initial designs, incorporating the highlighted risks and benefits. Video transcripts are available in Appendix [1]. Below are the design descriptions:

Personal Story Video:

- **Characters/Setting**: A female cartoon character in her living room (informal setting) with a machine-generated voice-over.
- **Main Idea**: The character shares her experiences with at-home DNA testing, discussing benefits like finding DNA relatives and risks realized after sharing her DNA. Refer to the Appendix [1] for the video frame.
- **Reasoning**: 70% of participants suggested that a casual, personal storytelling approach would effectively convey the message.

Conversational Story Video:

- **Characters/Setting**: Two cartoon characters (one male, one female) discussing at-home DNA testing while shopping and dining in a market (informal setting) with machine-generated voice-overs.
- **Main Idea**: The female character introduces the at-home DNA testing kit in a store, explaining its benefits. The male character gets excited about his adopted aunt finding her family. They then discuss and browse the risks of DNA tests while dining. Refer to the Appendix [1] for the video frame.
- **Reasoning**: 70% of participants suggested that casual, conversational scenarios with personal examples would effectively convey the message.

Informational Video:

- **Characters/Setting**: Formal setting with handwriting on a whiteboard, explained with machine-generated voice-overs.
- **Main Idea**: The video presents data on the number of people who have taken the test, discussing benefits and explaining risks with current genetic protection laws. It includes statistics on law enforcement's use of public genealogy databases. Refer to the Appendix [1] for the video frame.
- **Reasoning**: 50% of participants wanted data-driven information about risks, such as law enforcement access and usage statistics. This video is data-focused without personal examples or casual conversation.

Info-graphics: Titled "Benefits and Risks of DNA Data Sharing," this one-page infographic lists all benefits and risks side by side. Users can learn at their own pace by reading. 70% of participants suggested that infographics are an excellent method to outline risks and benefits. Refer to the Appendix [1] for the frame.

Wizards/Interactive Survey: Refer to the Appendix [1] for the screenshots of the wizards. Users are first asked if they want to know about the benefits and risks. Based on their response, they are shown the relevant information or recommended to learn about the benefits and risks first. The wizard provides information based on user choice, giving them control over what they want to know. 20% of participants in phase 1 suggested that wizards/interactive surveys could effectively communicate risks and benefits.

4.2   Recruitment and Demographics

Participants were recruited via the university mailing list. Among the 7 participants, 3 were male and 4 were female, aged 20 to 50. We initially interviewed 7 participants, showing them version 1 designs and incorporating their feedback. Each received a $10 Amazon gift card. The Institutional Review Board (IRB) approved our study.

4.3   Procedure and Analysis

Researchers scheduled Zoom interviews with interested participants. The semi-structured interviews, lasting about an hour, focused on the design's positive and negative aspects and message understandability. The study was approved by the university's IRB. Interviews began with general feelings about the topic, followed by questions on the designs' look, feel, ease of understanding, and enjoyability. Designs were shown in random order to avoid bias. Participants discussed the best and worst parts of each design and provided improvement suggestions. We also collected demographic information.

Based on feedback from the first 7 interviews, we revised the designs, eliminating the three least coherent ones and modifying the remaining ones to create version 2 designs. These were then shown to another 7 participants for further feedback, leading to the final design versions.

5   Design Versions 1 Feedback Results

This section summarizes feedback on versions 1. Informational video was the most preferred, while the Conversational story video was the least liked. Table 5 details the feedback on the personal story video. Participants liked the casual setting and personal examples but disliked the robotic voice, suggesting a human voice and character.

The conversational story video was the least liked, with three participants finding it hard to understand and engage with. This design was eliminated. Six participants preferred the informational video, enjoying the presentation and finding it easy to understand and engaging. Some found the male voice authoritative.

Participants appreciated the briefness of infographics, suggesting the addition of bright colors, data, and figures. Most participants liked the wizard/interactive survey method, finding it engaging and enjoyable. Some suggested adding audio with text and including data and figures. Table 5 shows detailed feedback. Figure 1 presents participants' responses to relatability, understandability, engagement, and enjoyment. Overall, the informational video was the most preferred, followed by infographics, while the conversational story video was the least preferred, followed by the personal story video.

6   Design Versions 2 and Final Designs

The informational video and infographics were the most liked designs by participants. We focused on improving these based on feedback from 7 participants. To enhance the infographics, we updated fonts and colors for visual appeal, shortened the text, and removed the last section for conciseness and clarity. For the informational video, participants requested a female voiceover to remove the authoritarian tone. We used a machine-generated female voice for consistent and engaging narration. Minor improvements were made to enhance user experience and engagement. We collected feedback from another 7 participants on the version 2 designs of the infographics and informational video. The interview included the same questions to gather detailed feedback (see Table 6) on what they liked and disliked about the designs.

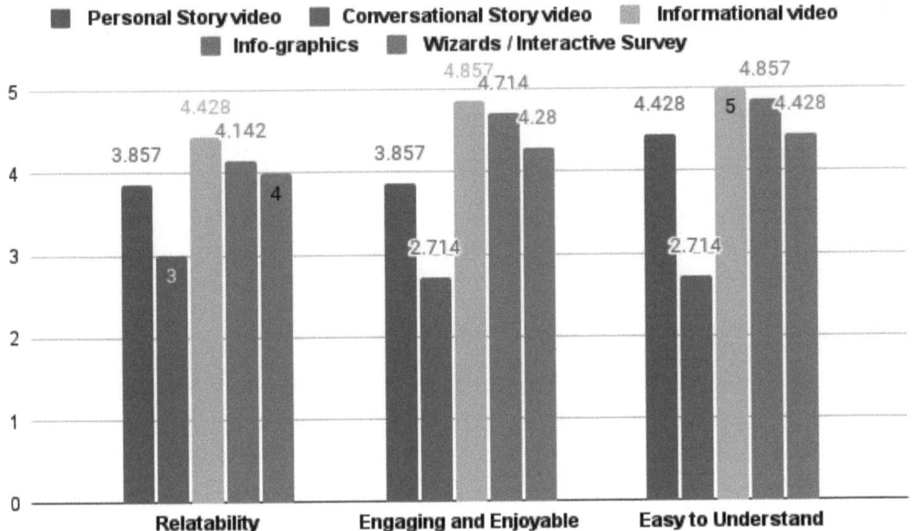

Fig. 1. Participants' feedback On designs: Relatability, Engaging and Enjoyable and Easy to Understand.

Final Designs: Participant feedback was incorporated into the final version of the infographic to provide a clearer and more informative representation of DNA testing and its associated benefits and risks. The infographic begins with general information about DNA testing, noting that over 26 million people have taken a commercial DNA test and that genes are passed down through families. It highlights that sharing DNA data can

Table 5. Participants' feedback and suggestions on "Design Version 1"

Liked (N = 7)	Disliked (N = 7)	Enhancements (N = 7)
Personal Story video		
Casual environment (5)	Robotic voice (5)	Add data as example (5)
Personal examples (5)	Monotonous tone (4)	Pop-up data and figures while explaining (4)
Talked about benefits and risks (4)	No data/evidence (4)	Add more movements (2)
No authoritative figure (3)	White character (2)	Natural/human voice (2)
		Replace the character (2)
Conversational Story video		
Every day or causal environment (3)	No data/evidence (3)	Add data as example (4)
Personal example (1)	Robotic voice (3)	Pop-up data and figures while explaining (3)
Talked about benefits and risks (1)	Could not connect (3)	Use real humans (2)
1 male and 1 female (1)	Expressions (2)	Natural/human voice (2)
Informational video		
Presentation (6)	Authoritarian voice (2)	Change the voice (4)
Data and evidence (6)	Lack of suggestion on "what to do next?" (1)	Use female voice (2)
Talked about benefits and risks (4)		Use characters (2)
Transitions (4)		Add suggestion for people (1)
Info-graphic		
Brief and coherent (5)	Colors and graphics (2)	Add bright colors (2)
Good colors (5)	Last section is long (2)	Shorten some text (2)
Talked about benefits and risks side by side (5)		Add some data and figures (1)
Not overwhelming (3)		
Wizard/Interactive Survey		
Brief and coherent (6)	No data/evidence (3)	Add data and figures (3)
Good colors (5)	No audio (2)	Add suggestions on what users should do (2)
Presented both benefits and risks side by side (5)		Add audio (2)
Easy to keep up with the pace (5)		
Not overwhelming (3)		

Table 6. Participants' feedback and suggestions on "Design Version 2"

ENHANCEMENT FEEDBACK (n = 7)	
Info-graphics	Informational Video
Add more context on DNA and DNA testing (7)	Used a human voice for better engagement (7)
Add examples of risks and benefits, such as traits and ancestry (5)	Slow down the animation to improve comprehension (7)
Improve color scheme (4)	Balanced the content to avoid bias towards risks or benefits (3)
Replace/remove technical terms like "haplogroup" with simpler language (3)	Remove the use of hands in the video (3)

reveal information about family members' DNA without their consent, and that over 70% of people of European descent can be identified through a family member's DNA test. To provide more context, the infographic includes additional information about at-home DNA testing to help readers unfamiliar with the concept. Specific examples of benefits and risks are provided, such as identifying lifestyle factors that can be modified (e.g., avoiding alcohol if you have alcohol reflux). Benefits are highlighted in green, while risks are highlighted in red. The background color was changed to a white and light blue scheme for better readability. Technical terms like haplogroup were replaced with simpler language. Overall, the updated infographic incorporates participant feedback to offer a clearer and more informative representation of DNA testing and its associated benefits and risks.

7 Phase 3 Design Comparison

During Phase 2, we evaluated and compared three designs in terms of ease of use, engagement, relatability, and recall. To further investigate their effectiveness, we conducted a between-subject study to determine which design was the most effective, understandable, and helpful in aiding users' comprehension of the risks and benefits of sharing DNA data. We also gathered insights on potential improvements.

Our research questions were:

- RQ1: Which design(s) did users find the easiest to understand and recall most effectively?
- RQ2: What areas for improvement can enhance the designs' effectiveness and user experience?

By addressing these questions, we aimed to gain insights into the effectiveness of the designs and gather suggestions for enhancing their quality and user experience.

7.1 Methodology

We conducted a between-subject study with 55 participants, sourced from social networks and the university research pool, using the Qualtrics survey platform for efficient data collection and analysis. Participants were first queried about their familiarity with at-home DNA testing and public genealogy databases. We then provided a concise explanation of these concepts to ensure a foundational understanding. Website prototypes resembling actual at-home DNA testing sites and public genealogy databases were created as visual aids. After examining the prototypes, participants were assigned to either the infographic or informational video design group. Participants answered questions to evaluate their understanding and interpretations of the assigned design. This provided insights into their comprehension and the meaning derived from the information. Following the design assessment, participants completed a questionnaire covering ease of understanding, content recall, and intention to share DNA data, providing quantitative data on their experiences and perceptions. Finally, participants provided feedback on the designs, sharing thoughts and suggestions for improvements. This feedback was crucial for refining and enhancing the designs' effectiveness and user experience. section Evaluation This section discusses the results of evaluating both risk communication methods using two participant groups (each exposed to a single method).

7.2 Demographics

Eligible participants were 18 years or older, with no prior involvement in genetic data research. Institutional Review Board (IRB) approval was obtained. Participants were recruited via the university, flyers, and Craigslist. Meetings were conducted on Zoom, and consent was obtained before each session (which was recorded). Participants received a \$7 Amazon gift card. The average study duration was 45 min. There were 110 participants, with each group comprising 55 participants. Chi-Square test was conducted to assess the demographic characteristics of our sample.

In terms of gender, 40.6% participants were identified as male, while 55.4% were female. Our findings revealed no significant differences between the two groups. There was no significant disparity in terms of gender distribution ($\tilde{\chi}^2 = 2.3$, p = .5). In terms of age distribution, the majority of our participants (79.2%) fell within the 18–29 age range. Additionally, 11.9% were between 30–39 years old, and 5.9% were aged 40–49. Our analysis did not yield any significant differences in age distribution between the groups ($\tilde{\chi}^2 = 9.5$, p = .05). Moreover, only 16.8% of the participants identified themselves as Hispanic, Latino, or Spanish. Among the remaining participants, the majority (52.5%) identified as White/Caucasian, 22.8% as Southeast and Southwest Asian, 7.9% as Black/African American, 3% as East/central Asian, 3% as Middle Eastern/North African, and 3% as Native American/Alaska Native. The Chi-Square test did not reveal any significant differences in ethnic or racial composition between the groups ($\tilde{\chi}^2 = 6.5$, p = .3). Regarding the highest level of education attained, 38.6% of the participants had completed some college/associates' degree/technical degree, 25.7% held a graduate or professional degree, and 18.8% had obtained a high school degree or equivalent. The Chi-Square test did not find any significant differences in educational attainment between the groups ($\tilde{\chi}^2 = 2.1$, p = .7).

7.3   Evaluation of Risk Communication

The results of the study are presented in the form of participant responses to various statements related to the info-graphic and video designs. The responses were measured on three criteria: a) Easy to understand and use b) Content recall c) Sharing intention.

Easy to Understand and Use: To evaluate the participants' comprehension and usability, we adopted the SUS scale questions [12]. The responses were measured on a Likert scale, with higher scores indicating a stronger agreement with the statement. The mean (median) scores for each statement and the associated statistical test results were computed.

Participants' perception of the complexity of the message was measured using the statement "I found the [message] unnecessarily complex." The info-graphic design received an average score of 2.1 (with a median score of 2), while the video design received an average score of 1.9 (with a median score of 2). Statistical analysis using the U-test revealed no significant difference between the two designs (p = .49). These results suggest that participants did not perceive a significant disparity in complexity between the info-graphic and video designs. Participants' perception of the ease of understanding the message was evaluated using the statement "I thought the [message] was easy to understand." The info-graphic design received a mean score of 4.1 (with a median score of 4), while the video design received a mean score of 4.2 (with a median score of 4). The results of the U-test indicated no significant difference in the perceived understanding between the two designs (p = .35). This suggests that participants did not perceive a substantial distinction in the ease of understanding between the info-graphic and video designs.

Participants' perception of the need for technical support to understand the message was assessed using the statement "I think that I would need a technical person's support to understand the [message]." Both the info-graphic and video designs received low mean scores, with 1.8 (with a median score of 2) for the info-graphic design and 1.7 (with a median score of 2) for the video design. The results of the U-test indicated no significant difference in the perceived need for technical support between the two designs (p = .95). This suggests that participants did not consider either design to require extensive technical assistance for comprehension.

Participants were asked to rate the integration of risk and benefit messages in the design using the statement "I found the risk and benefit information in the [message] was well integrated." For the info-graphic design, the mean score was 4.0 (with a median score of 4), while for the video design, the mean score was 4.1 (with a median score of 4). The U-test results showed no significant difference in the perceived integration between the two designs (p = .59). This indicates that participants did not perceive a substantial disparity in the degree of integration of risk and benefit messages in the info-graphic and video designs. The statement "I thought there was too much inconsistency in the [message]" received mean scores of 2.1 (median of 2) for both the info-graphic and video designs. The U-test results suggest no significant difference in perceived inconsistency between the two designs (p = .37).

Participants' perception of how quickly most people would understand the message was captured by the statement "I imagine most people would understand the [message] very quickly." Both designs received mean scores of 4.0 (median of 4) for this statement. The U-test results indicate no significant difference in participants' expectations of quick understanding between the two designs (p = .75). The statement "I found the [message] very cumbersome to understand" received a mean score of 2.2 (median of 2) for the info-graphic design and 1.9 (median of 2) for the video design. The U-test results suggest no significant difference in perceived level of cumbersome understanding between the two designs (p = .21).

Participants' confidence in understanding the message was measured by the statement "I felt very confident in understanding the [message]." Both designs received mean scores of 4.1 (median of 4) for this statement. The U-test results indicate no significant difference in participants' confidence levels between the two designs (p = .553).

For the statement "I needed to learn a lot of things before I could understand the [message]," the mean score was 2.0 (median of 2) for the info-graphic design and 1.9 (median of 2) for the video design. The U-test results suggest no significant difference in participants' perception of the need to learn additional things before understanding the message between the two designs.

The participants' ratings on the understandability and usability of the message (video or info-graphics) are presented in Table 7. Utilizing the Mann-Whitney test, we investigated potential differences between individuals who watched a video message versus those who viewed an info-graphic message. However, our analysis did not uncover any significant distinctions between the two groups.

Table 7. Evaluation of informative message between those who watched a video message and info-graphic message including Mean, Median, and Mann-Whitney test value

Statements	Infographic Mean (Median)	Video Mean (Median)	Test Statistic U-test (p)
1) I found the [message] unnecessarily complex.	2.1 (2)	1.9 (2)	1180 (p = .49)
2) I thought the [message] was easy to understand.	4.1 (4)	4.2 (4)	1385 (p = .35)
3) I think that I would need a technical person's support to understand the [message].	1.8 (2)	1.7 (2)	1280 (p = .95)
4) I found the risk and benefit messages in the [message] were well integrated.	4.0 (4)	4.1 (4)	1339 (p = .59)
5) I thought there was too much inconsistency in the [message].	2.1 (2)	2.1 (2)	1389 (p = .37)
6) I imagine most people would understand the [message] very quickly.	4.0 (4)	4.1 (4)	1313 (p = .75)
7) I found the [message] very cumbersome to understand.	2.2 (2)	1.9 (2)	1101 (p = .21)
8) I felt very confident understanding the [message].	4.1 (4)	4.2 (4)	1350 (p = .553)
9) I needed to learn a lot of things before I could understand the [message].	2.0 (2)	1.9 (2)	1215 (p = .68)

Content Recall - Informational Video vs. Info-graphic: In this section we will compare the content recall of the two risk communication methods to understand which method facilitates effective information retention. Table 8 presents details about the percentages of content recall by participants.

Table 8. Evaluation of "Content Recall" between those who watched a video message and info-graphic message

Topic	No Recall		All Details Recall		Test statistics Mann-Whitney U-test (p)
	Video (N = 55)	Infographic (N = 55)	Video (N = 55)	Infographic (N = 55)	
Trait and Wellness	23.63%	36.36%	32.72%	10.9%	1131 (p =.013)
Law Enforcement	20%	38.18%	47.27%	21.81%	1042.5 (p =.003)
DNA Relative Finding	29.09%	43.63%	49.09%	25.45%	1161 (p =.025)
Data Breaches	20%	16.36%	67.27%	56.36%	Not Significant

Recall of Communication about Trait and Wellness - A comparison of datasets from the video and info-graphic responses regarding the "Trait and Wellness" content reveals intriguing patterns. When analyzing the feedback, a large number of respondents from both categories couldn't recall any content, with approximately 24% from the video group and 37% from the info-graphic group answering "none" when asked to recount the information.

Among those who could remember, the information recall appears to be more detailed and specific in the video group compared to info-graphic group. In the info-graphic group, many responses were vague, with only a handful, approximately 11%, remembering key aspects like genetic diseases, alcohol-related traits, and lifestyle factors. In contrast, nearly 33% of the informational video group provided more detailed recollections, mentioning inherited health risks, genetic diseases like sickle cell anemia, and the impact of traits on lifestyle. By conducting Mann-Whitney U-test, we found significant difference between video group and info-graphic group with p value of 0.013.

Additionally, in the info-graphic group, responses were largely generic, with phrases such as "something about alcohol," "traits you may have," and "lifestyle factors." This suggests that while the info-graphic might have engaged the viewers, it didn't necessarily facilitate effective information retention. On the contrary, in the video group, many respondents not only recalled the primary topic of "Trait and Wellness" but also provided specific details like the role of DNA testing in identifying genetic diseases and traits linked to alcohol consumption. These responses demonstrate that video can lead to enhanced recall and understanding of complex topics.

Recall of Communication About Law Enforcement - By analyzing the responses related to "Law enforcement" content from both the video and info-graphic feedback, we found that 19% participants in the video group and 38% in the info-graphic group was lacking retention of information. Among respondents who recalled content, the video group appeared to have a more comprehensive understanding of the topic. Approximately 48% of this group could recite specifics such as law enforcement using DNA databases to solve cold cases, law enforcement's potential use of DNA data for surveillance, the threat of involuntary surveillance, and the possible discrimination due to DNA databases. On the contrary, only about 21% of respondents from the info-graphic group mentioned specifics. By conducting Mann-Whitney U-test, we found significant difference between video group and info-graphic group with p value of 0.003.

The participants' memory of the "Law enforcement" topic shows apparent contrast between the video and info-graphic groups. In the video group, the responses encompassed various aspects, like using DNA databases to solve cold cases and the potential privacy implications of sharing DNA data. The responses demonstrated an understanding of the broad spectrum of legal and ethical issues associated with DNA testing and law enforcement. On the other hand, the info-graphic group responses focused mainly on the potential for involuntary surveillance, with less emphasis on other aspects of law enforcement's use of DNA data. This could imply that the info-graphic was less successful in conveying the complete range of associated issues compared to the video. Overall, we can say video seemed to facilitate better overall understanding and retention of the topic, suggesting it might be a more effective medium for presenting complex issues.

Recall of Communication About DNA Relative Finding - When comparing responses about "DNA relative finding" content, the video and info-graphic groups showed apparent differences in recall ability. About 29% of the video group participants could not recall any content, compared to a considerably more 43% in the info-graphic group, suggesting that the video was more effective at conveying and reinforcing this specific concept. Among those who did recall content, about 49% of the video group could recollect exact aspects, such as finding relatives based on DNA matches.

In contrast, the info-graphic group responses were less precise and mixed. Only about 26% of this group could remember specific aspects. The video group demonstrated a broad understanding of DNA relative finding, encompassing various aspects such as the potential to find global DNA matches and the potential privacy implications related to sharing DNA data. The info-graphic group, on the other hand, mainly focused on the basic notion of finding relatives through shared DNA, with fewer responses mentioning the potential for worldwide connections or the detailed implications of DNA testing. By conducting Mann-Whitney U-test, we found significant difference between video group and the info-graphic group with a p value of 0.025. Thus, the video seems to be more effective in conveying a broad and detailed understanding of "DNA relative finding."

Recall of Communication About Data Breaches - In our review of participant responses about "Data breaches," we found that 19% of those exposed to the video and 15% of those exposed to the info-graphic reported no recollection of the content, suggesting that the info-graphic may be slightly more effective in retention. Among those who did recall the topic, 67% from the video group detailed aspects of data breaches such as hacking risks, DNA data misuse, and potential third-party interference. This suggests a more wide learning of the issue.

In contrast, only about 56% of the info-graphic group could remember specific details about data breaches, especially focusing on risks of hacking and the likely exposure of personal data. The video group showed a greater awareness of potential repercussions of data breaches, such as the potential misuse of DNA data by insurance companies. They comprehended that these breaches could disclose sensitive genetic predispositions with negative impacts. The info-graphic group, while acknowledging the risk of data stealing via hacking, did not expound as much on potential consequences of such breaches. By conducting Mann-Whitney U-test, we did not find significant difference between the video group and the info-graphic group.

In conclusion, although both groups recognized the risk of data breaches in DNA testing, the video group showed slightly deeper understanding of the potential consequences.

Sharing Intention: Furthermore, participants were asked to provide their likelihood of taking an at-home DNA test after viewing the message. Our examination revealed no noteworthy differences between the groups (U = 1019, p = .07). Consequently, we found that 32.5% of participants who viewed the info-graphic message and 37.5% of those who watched the video expressed the likelihood to take an at-home DNA test.

In addition to the above question, participants were asked about their inclination to share their DNA in the Open genealogy database after viewing the message. Similar to the previous analysis, no significant differences emerged between the two groups (U = 1107, p = .15). We discovered that 64.2% of participants who viewed the info-graphic message and 77.1% of those who watched the video responded "No" to this question, indicating their unwillingness to share DNA data in the Open genealogy database.

7.4   Feedback About the Video

Here we list all the positive and negative feedback about the video risk communication method, aimed at understanding viewer preferences and identifying the aspects that made the video an effective risk communication method.

About 85% of the participants, appreciated the use of visuals such as illustrations, graphics, and animations. These respondents found that the use of visual aids, paired with auditory explanations, greatly enhanced their understanding of the material and it helped maintain their engagement throughout the video. The clarity and simplicity of the explanation emerged as another highly valued aspect. Approximately 67% of the participants liked how complex terms and ideas were explained in a simplified, easy-to-understand manner. This was particularly appreciated in the sections where the risks and repercussions of the subject matter were discussed. About 46% of the participants found the overall organization and structure of the video appealing. They liked the logical flow of information, the balance between both the risks and benefits information, and the clarity of points made. A subset of this group specifically appreciated the concise and equal attention given to the pros and cons, aiding in the balanced understanding of the topic. Approximately 46% of the respondents acknowledged the clear audio and the articulate voiceover. Participants found that the quality of the narration contributed to their understanding and overall learning experience. Around 25% of the participants particularly appreciated the historical context provided in the video, especially regarding sickle cell disease among African Americans. They found this perspective valuable for understanding the broader social and racial implications of the subject matter. Additionally, 23% of the respondents applauded the video for being informative and concise, effectively delivering substantial information within a brief time. This kept the viewers engaged, despite the complexity of the topic.

We also delved into areas that viewers found less desirable in the video by asking the question, "What aspects did you not like in the video?" About 14% of the respondents felt that the video was too long and sometimes repetitive, suggesting a need for more concise and streamlined content. Approximately 11% of viewers were not satisfied with the video's audio quality and the narrator's delivery. They commented on the varying volume levels, strange noises, and the narrator's tone of voice and speaking style, which some described as disinterested or lacking confidence. Also, 9% of participants felt that the visuals, particularly the animations, were too simple or not engaging enough. They suggested that more professional, dynamic, and engaging visuals could help maintain viewer interest and facilitate comprehension. Lastly, 7% of viewers thought that the information such as medical terminologies, and acronyms were not adequately explained.

Interestingly, a substantial proportion of respondents (59%) mentioned that they liked all aspects of the video, which could be interpreted as a generally positive reception. In conclusion, while the video was generally well-received, improvements can be made in terms of audio quality, visual presentation, and simplification of complex information. Attention to these details can enhance the effectiveness and reception of the video.

7.5 Feedback About the Info-Graphic

We also aimed to analyze participant feedback on the effectiveness and perceived shortcomings of info-graphic as a tool for risk communication. Respondents' feedback was categorized into positive and negative sentiments, elucidating distinct aspects such as aesthetic appeal, content comprehension, and structural organization. In terms of positive feedback, a significant majority (63%) admired the design of the info-graphic, commending its color scheme, font, layout, and the integration of graphical elements. These features contributed to the aesthetic allure of the info-graphic and facilitated better comprehension of the information. The simplicity of the info-graphic emerged as another liked attribute, appreciated by 59% of the participants. This appreciation was linked to the info-graphic's ability to convey information with clarity and ease, indicating its effectiveness in communication. Moreover, 45% of respondents valued the organization of information in the info-graphic, especially appreciating the clear segregation of sections and the use of bullet points, which augmented readability. A subset of these respondents specifically commended the structure of presenting pros and cons, reinforcing the balanced presentation of information. Impressively, the content of the info-graphic resonated with 79% of the respondents. They found it informative, even learning new information, underlining the educational efficacy of the info-graphic. Some participants particularly valued the incorporation of examples and statistics, accentuating that concrete details promote understanding.

On the other hand, feedback also highlighted areas for improvement. A segment of respondents (22%) found issues with the info-graphic's design, particularly criticizing the font type, size, and aesthetics of figures, which they felt detracted from its professional appeal and readability. Additionally, 19% of participants found the layout and organization too complex and busy, indicating a need for a more streamlined presentation. Finally, 16% of respondents perceived the information as too basic or brief, suggesting a demand for more comprehensive, detailed content.

Interestingly, despite these criticisms, a sizable proportion (36%) of the respondents expressed no objections to the info-graphic, suggesting a general level of satisfaction with its current state. Overall, while the info-graphic demonstrated efficacy as a risk communication tool, feedback suggests room for enhancement, particularly in design aspects, structural simplicity, and depth of content. This would serve to improve the info-graphic's overall effectiveness and appeal.

8 Discussion

The third phase of our research assessed the effectiveness of info-graphic and video formats in shaping participants' comprehension, recall, and DNA data sharing intentions regarding at-home DNA tests and participation in open genealogy databases. Our analysis found no significant differences between the two groups in demographic variables such as age, gender, race, or education level, bolstering the reliability of the comparative evaluations. In terms of risk communication, our analyses revealed no considerable differences in participants' perceptions of complexity, ease of understanding, usability, need for technical support, or comprehension of risk and benefit messages across the two modalities. Both formats were comparably effective in their comprehensibility and perceived complexity. However, participants exhibited noticeable differences in the level of detail recalled. Generally, the video format outperformed the info-graphic in content recall across various topics, such as Trait and Wellness," Law enforcement," and "DNA relative finding." This suggests that the engaging and multi-sensory nature of video presentations may boost information retention, especially for intricate subjects.

When asked about their likelihood of undergoing an at-home DNA test after exposure to the information, participants' responses showed no significant differences across both modalities. However, a larger proportion of participants who viewed the video message expressed reluctance to undergo the test compared to those who viewed the info-graphic message. Similarly, when asked about their willingness to share their DNA in an open genealogy database, a higher percentage of video viewers expressed unwillingness compared to info-graphic viewers, though the difference was not statistically significant. These findings suggest that while both modalities were similarly effective in communicating risk information and influencing participant understanding, the video format might exert a slightly stronger influence in discouraging participants from engaging in at-home DNA testing or sharing their DNA in open genealogy databases. This effect could be due to the video's robust ability to visually and audibly deliver complex information, weave narrative storytelling, and invoke emotional responses [9].

Furthermore, a significant proportion of participants expressed reluctance to partake in the suggested actions (undergoing an at-home DNA test or sharing their DNA in open genealogy databases) after viewing the messages. This could reflect the effectiveness of risk communication in both formats, as they successfully highlighted potential concerns and influenced individual decision-making processes.

8.1 Limitations

This study, despite its valuable insights, has limitations. One key restriction is the sample size and population. The study primarily involved students and university affiliates, limiting the generalizability of the results to broader, more diverse populations. Our sample was mainly young, educated, and likely more technologically adept, which may have influenced their comprehension and reception of the risk communication via info-graphic and video designs. Previous research suggests that age, educational attainment, and digital literacy affect individuals' comprehension and interpretation of health risk information [18]. Thus, our findings may not apply to older, less educated, or less technologically adept populations. Additionally, the small sample size may have affected the statistical power of the study, potentially influencing our ability to detect significant differences in participant responses across the two designs. This limitation may partially explain the lack of statistically significant differences observed in participant perceptions and action inclinations regarding the info-graphic and video designs. Despite these limitations, the study provides important preliminary insights into the comparable effectiveness of info-graphic and video designs in communicating risk information. Further research with larger and diverse populations will be instrumental in refining our understanding of the most effective modes of risk communication for various audiences.

9 Conclusion

In our study, we found that both the informational video and the info-graphic did not significantly change participants' understanding of the topic based on the SUS scale or their interest in sharing DNA data or doing at-home DNA tests. Nonetheless, slightly more participants in the video group (37.5%) compared to the info-graphic group (32.5%) were not interested in doing at-home DNA tests. When asked if they wanted to share their DNA data in the Open genealogy database after viewing the video or info-graphic, the responses were comparable between the two groups. However, more people from the video group (77.1%) than the info-graphic group (64.2%) said 'No,' indicating they did not want to share their DNA. This suggests that the informational video may have been more effective at making people reconsider sharing their DNA than the info-graphic. Additionally, the video group remembered substantially more about the pros and cons of online DNA data sharing than the info-graphic group. Future research should explore the specific elements of video and info-graphic designs that most significantly impact participant understanding and action inclinations. This could provide further insights into optimizing risk communication strategies in different contexts. Furthermore, exploring potential moderators, such as prior knowledge or attitudes towards the topic, may provide a deeper understanding of how different individuals respond to various modes of risk communication.

References

1. Appendix. https://drive.google.com/drive/folders/1UpA-aUACoLLbWPdsjY51juUqhyA-QCEE (2025)
2. Abras, C., Maloney-Krichmar, D., Preece, J., et al.: User-centered design. Bainbridge, W. Encyclopedia of HCI. Thousand Oaks: Sage Publications **37**(4), 445–456 (2004)
3. Chai-Arayalert, S., Suttapong, K., Chumkaew, S.: Design of digital environments to enhance handicraft co-learning experiences. Cogent Bus. Manage. **10**(3), 2286687 (2023)
4. Gerdes, J., Ojedele-Adejumo, T., Buccilli, M.: Using scoping reviews to identify models for participatory design of pandemic communication research. In: Proceedings of the 41st ACM International Conference on Design of Communication, pp. 148–154 (2023)
5. Kang, X., Kang, J., Chen, W.: Conceptualization and research progress on web-based product co-design. In: Informatics, vol. 7, p. 30. MDPI (2020)
6. Kasperbauer, T., Halverson, C., Garcia, A., Schwartz, P.H.: Biobank participants' attitudes toward data sharing and privacy: the role of trust in reducing perceived risks. J. Empir. Res. Hum. Res. Ethics **17**(1–2), 167–176 (2022)
7. Keinonen, T.: User-centered design and fundamental need. In: Proceedings of the 5th Nordic Conference on Human-Computer Interaction: Building Bridges, pp. 211–219 (2008)
8. Krawczyk-Dembicka, E., Urban, W., Łukaszewicz, K.: The study of co-design in the area of manufacturing. Bull. Pol. Acad. Sci. Tech. Sci. **70**(6) (2022)
9. Madhuri, J.N.: Use of audio visual aids in teaching and speaking. Res. J. Engl. Lang. Lit. **1**(3), 108–122 (2013)
10. Masterson, D., Areskoug Josefsson, K., Robert, G., Nylander, E., Kjellström, S.: Mapping definitions of co-production and co-design in health and social care: a systematic scoping review providing lessons for the future. Health Expect. **25**(3), 902–913 (2022)
11. McKercher, K.A.: Beyond sticky notes. Doing co-design for Real: Mindsets, Methods, and Movements, 1st Edn. Sydney, NSW: Beyond Sticky Notes (2020)
12. NN/g: System Usability Scale (SUS). https://www.nngroup.com/articles/measuring-perceived-usability/. Accessed 06 Jul 2023
13. Norman, D.: User centered system design. New perspectives on HCI (1986)
14. Parrilli, D.M., Ogunyemi, A.A., Bauters, M.L.M., Hernández-Ramírez, R.: Designing a communication app for privacy: a scenario-based and participatory approach. In: International Conference on Design and Digital Communication, pp. 369–385. Springer (2024)
15. Sahoo, L., Shehab, M., Qahtani, E.A., Dev, J.: Nobody wants my stuff and it is just dna data, why should i be worried. In: Privacy Symposium: Data Protection Law International Convergence and Compliance with Innovative Technologies, pp. 155–178. Springer (2022)
16. Spinuzzi, C.: The methodology of participatory design. Techn. Commun. **52**(2), 163–174 (2005)
17. Toppenberg, Y.: Moving from designing for to designing with consumers: Utilizing human-centred design approaches to create Facebook advertisements. Master's thesis, University of Twente (2023)
18. Tugut, N., Yesildag Celik, B., Yılmaz, A.: Health literacy and its association with health perception in pregnant women. J. Health Literacy **6**(2), 9–20 (2021)
19. Vien, M.H., Ivey, S.L., Boyden, H., Holm, S., Neuhauser, L.: A scoping review of wildfire smoke risk communications: issues, gaps, and recommendations. BMC Public Health **24**(1), 312 (2024)

Renewable Connect: Empowering Users to Discover and Support Renewable Energy Projects Online

Achhiya Sultana, Md Istiaq Ahmed, Farzana Rahman, Mohammad Shidujaman[(✉)], and Mahady Hasan

Department of CSE, School of Engineering, Technology and Sciences (SETS), Independent University, Bangladesh (IUB), Dhaka, Bangladesh
{achhiyasets,2030096,farzana.rahman,shidujaman,mahady}@iub.edu.bd

Abstract. Renewable energy projects are proliferating all over Bangladesh as a result of the country's urgent demand for sustainable energy alternatives. In order to promote a collaborative effort towards a more environmentally friendly and energy-efficient future, this article proposes a web application that is intended to make it easier to find and support these activities. The suggested platform has an intuitive user interface designed specifically for Bangladesh's distinct socioeconomic environment. By utilizing machine learning techniques and geospatial data, the program provides users with a user-friendly means of investigating and locating renewable energy projects within their local area. Users can learn more about each initiative's overall sustainability, community effect, and technology components by perusing through in-depth project biographies. In addition, the website functions as a platform for crowd sourcing, enabling people and institutions to provide money to initiatives that share their interests and principles. This all-inclusive strategy encourages a sense of ownership and collective responsibility by enabling individuals to actively engage in the nation's transition to renewable energy. With a social networking component, the platform promotes cooperation and knowledge exchange amongst parties. By participating in conversations, exchanging success stories, and benefiting from one another's experiences, users may foster a thriving online community dedicated to promoting sustainable energy practices. Special consideration is paid to regional content, language choices, and internet connectivity issues that are common in Bangladesh in order to guarantee the application's accessibility. The interface is inclusive and broadly adaptable since it is made to accommodate users with different degrees of technical skill. Our goal is to increase the use of renewable energy in Bangladesh by encouraging community involvement, offering financial assistance, and facilitating information exchange through the creation and execution of this online application. The technological architecture, user experience design, and initial results of using the platform in real-world settings are covered in the paper.

M. Kurosu and A. Hashizume (Eds.): HCII 2025, LNCS 16332, pp. 417–427, 2026.
https://doi.org/10.1007/978-3-032-12385-5_26

Keywords: Renewable Energy · Web Application · Sustainable Development · Community Engagement · Bangladesh · Crowdfunding · Geospatial Data · Database · Social Networking

1 Introduction

Bangladesh has experienced a paradigm change in its energy environment in recent years due to a rising realization of how important it is to switch to clean and renewable sources. Since the country is dealing with serious issues including environmental deterioration, energy security, and population growth, it is more important than ever to find creative solutions that incorporate renewable energy.

This article presents a web application that has been thoughtfully designed to tackle the particular possibilities and difficulties that exist in the Bangladeshi setting. Our main goal is to enable people and communities to find, support, and actively engage in renewable energy initiatives by utilizing the power of information technology. The rapid growth of renewable energy projects in Bangladesh calls for a centralized platform that acts as a catalyst for public interaction while simultaneously compiling information on these projects. Our online application offers a technologically innovative and user-friendly solution with the goal of bridging the gap between project creators, possible sponsors, and the larger community.

The idea that sustainable energy transitions are complex social processes involving community engagement rather than just technological undertakings is the foundation upon which this application was developed. We provide customers with an easy-to-use and educational tool for navigating Bangladesh's complex landscape of renewable energy projects by utilizing geospatial data and machine learning techniques.

In addition to serving as an informational resource, the app has a crowdfunding feature that lets users donate money to causes that share their beliefs. This strategy democratizes the process and solves the financial issues that several programs confront, allowing people from all walks of life to actively participate in the nation's transition to renewable energy.

The web application is thoughtfully created with the local environment in mind to enable broad adoption. With inclusion and usability in mind, we tackle language preferences, accessibility issues, and the range of technical literacy levels that are common in Bangladesh.

This paper delves into the technical architecture, user experience design, and preliminary outcomes of deploying the platform. Through this work, we aspire to contribute to the collective effort towards a more sustainable and resilient energy future for Bangladesh, where individuals and communities actively participate in shaping their own environmental destiny.

2 Literature Review

Bangladesh, a South Asian country that is both densely populated and quickly urbanizing, is at the nexus of both urgent environmental concerns and rising energy demand. In this situation, the need for affordable and environmentally friendly energy sources is more pressing than ever. This study of the literature looks at how web applications are developing to make it easier to find and support renewable energy projects in Bangladesh. Early on, the cost of producing renewable energy is significantly greater than that of fossil fuels due to the significant investments required in its development and technological restrictions that necessitate highly capital-intensive approaches [1].

For instance, the renewable energy sector in China has grown considerably more appealing to both local and international investors; over the following four years, from 2018 to 2019 to 2021 to 2022, the nation hopes to raise up to 80 billion [2]. By 2029, the National Development and Reform Commission (NDRC) and the National Energy Administration (NEA) of China intend to invest over 360 billion in renewable energy and generate 13 million employment in the sector. In 2016, there were over 800,000 jobs in the renewable energy sector. China's great potential to significantly enhance production and consumption is a reflection of its commitment to investing in renewable energy.

By 2021, the government wants to have produced 2000 MW of electricity using renewable energy [3]. As of right now, 404 MW of electricity are produced overall from these sources. The new goal for renewable energy would be 10% of all electricity generated by 2021, and by 2030, it would rise to 20%. A 2010 research, for example, estimated that 1.7% of the nation's land is theoretically suitable for grid-connected solar projects utilizing a geographic information system (GIS) [4]. According to the study, the nation has a potential for 50,174 megawatts (MW) of solar electricity, taking into account the annual mean value of solar radiation and the efficiency of solar panels. However, the EU has also introduced the European Green Deal, with the goal of turning the continent carbon neutral by 2050 [5]. In the EU, solar energy is another significant renewable energy source. By 2030, the EU wants to bring the installed capacity of solar energy to 100 GW.

This literature review highlights the growing body of research on web applications designed to assist individuals in finding and supporting renewable energy projects [6]. The reviewed papers cover diverse aspects, including user empowerment, crowd sourcing strategies, user-centered design, social networks, and comparative analyses of different platforms. To sum up, online applications created to support renewable energy projects in Bangladesh present a promising way to tackle the country's energy and environmental issues. The success of these tools depends on a variety of elements, including technological infrastructure and governmental assistance, and they have the ability to increase awareness, promote community involvement, and speed up the adoption of sustainable energy solutions.

3   Problem Statement

The world's transition to sustainable energy requires an easily navigable platform that enables people and organizations to recognize, comprehend, and endorse renewable energy sources [7]. The widespread adoption of renewable energy measures is hampered by the absence of centralized information and support channels. By creating a web-based tool that makes it easier to find renewable energy sources and gives users the knowledge and resources they need to actively support the shift to sustainable energy alternatives, this project seeks to close this knowledge gap [8].

3.1   Why Do We Care About this Issue

- **Environmental Impact:** Addressing the issue of renewable energy is critical for preventing climate change and minimizing environmental damage caused by traditional energy sources.
- **Economic prospects:** renewable energy opens up new markets, job prospects, and economic growth in the clean energy sector.
- **Sustainability:**Transitioning to renewable energy contributes to the long-term sustainability of energy supplies, ensuring a cleaner and more secure energy future.
- **Global Energy Security:** Reducing reliance on finite and geopolitically sensitive fossil fuels adds to global energy security, supporting long-term stability.
- **Plans for Exploration:**Investigate and assemble thorough data on various renewable energy sources, their benefits, and current utilization internationally.
- **Technology Integration:** Investigate cutting-edge technologies in order to create an intuitive and user-friendly web platform for identifying and supporting renewable energy sources.
- **Community Engagement:** Develop community engagement tactics that encourage users to actively participate in discussions, share their experiences, and contribute to the platform's growth.
- **Partnerships and Collaborations:** Form alliances with renewable energy organizations, governmental authorities, and industry players to increase the platform's reputation and access to current information.
- **Education and Awareness:** Create strategies to educate people on the necessity of renewable energy, its environmental impact, and how they can actively participate in the shift.

4   Methodology

To understand the demands of users, project developers, and authorities Fig. 1, we held stakeholder discussions to kick off the development process. User preferences, difficulties, and expectations were shaped in the early stages of the web application's needs by the insightful information obtained from user interviews. A thorough analysis of the market was done to find potential and weaknesses in the current renewable energy platforms [9].

We created an interface that is both aesthetically pleasing and intuitive by utilizing wire frames and prototypes in accordance with UX design guidelines [10]. The integration of geographic data visualization was done to improve the user's capacity to find renewable energy projects [11]. We carefully picked a technological stack for web development, taking into account aspects like cross-browser compatibility, security, and scalability. Personalized project suggestions were generated by integrating machine learning algorithms with mapping libraries to create geospatial functionality [12]. While user acceptability testing solicited user comments on usability and experience, rigorous functional testing guaranteed that each feature operated as intended. Server configuration, smooth database connectivity Fig. 2, and application speed optimization were all part of the deployment process [13]. Because ethical issues were so important, appropriate AI procedures, privacy safeguards, and compliance with applicable laws were all put into place.

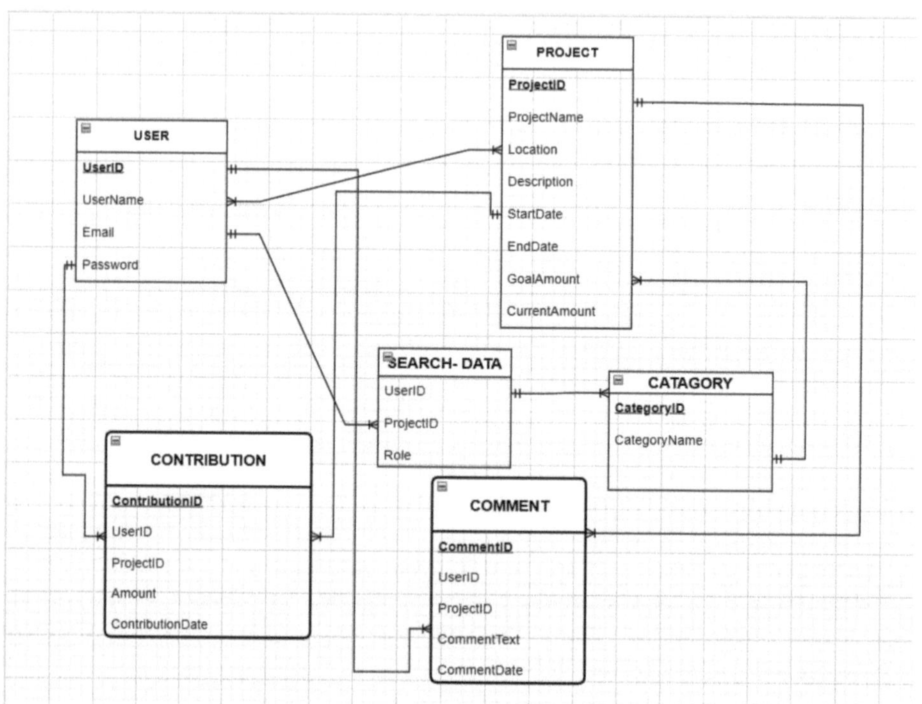

Fig. 1. ERD (Entity Relationship Diagram)

5   Result Analysis

We found a sizable gap in Bangladesh's accessibility and support for renewable energy projects throughout our problem analysis. A lack of centralized platforms is impeding efficient communication between project creators and potential sponsors, according to stakeholder discussions and user interviews. The lack

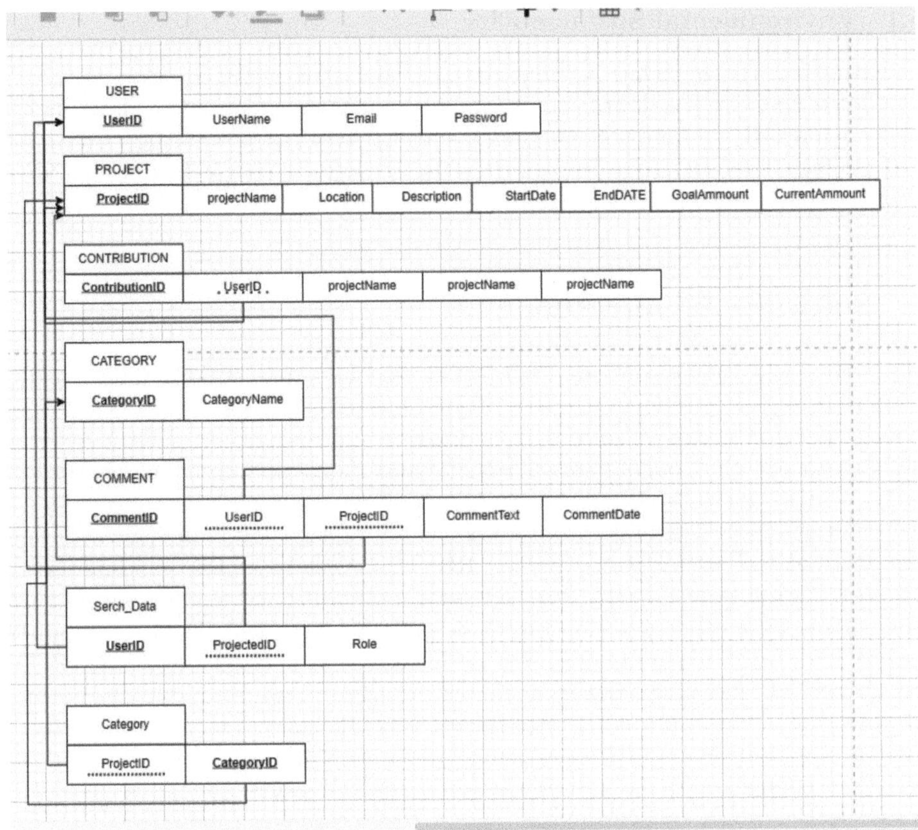

Fig. 2. Schema Design.

of individualized suggestions and user-friendly interfaces in current systems was highlighted by market research [14,15]. The difficulties also include the wide range of technical literacy levels and geographical variations in the Bangladeshi setting. Our online application seeks to resolve these important problems by offering a simplified and inclusive platform for finding and endorsing renewable energy projects.

- **Cost-Benefit Analysis:** Development Costs: $1000000 Maintenance Costs: $12000 Economic Benefits: Increased investments in renewable projects, estimated economic value $1700000.
- **Return on Investment (ROI):** ROI (Return on Investment) Calculation: (Net Benefits/Costs) * 100; Result: Positive ROI of 62%.

5.1   Environmental Sustainability

- **Emission Reduction:** X tonnes of CO_2 emissions reduced.
- **Clean Energy Projects:** 71% of supported projects focused on clean energy.
- **Eco-friendly Features:** Highlight specific features promoting sustainable practices. User Behavior Impact: Positive changes in user behavior contributing to environmental sustainability.

6   Software Architecture

Our web application's software architecture has been painstakingly designed to maximize efficiency, encourage adaptation, and guarantee a flawless user experience. The system is organized into separate modules, embracing a modular design concept that encourages flexibility and makes maintenance chores easier. A centralized database approach, which offers a single platform for effective data storage and retrieval and improves overall information management, lies at the heart of our architecture. We use RESTful APIs to enable communication between various components, fostering interoperability and supporting seamless integration with other systems Fig. 3. Containerization uses Docker containers to provide portability and consistent performance in a variety of contexts. The integration of load balancing systems has resulted in an equitable distribution of workloads, hence improving resource use and efficiency. The design effectively manages asynchronous activities using an event-driven approach, allowing for real-time changes and maintaining system responsiveness. Strong security features, such as data encryption and access restrictions, are included to protect

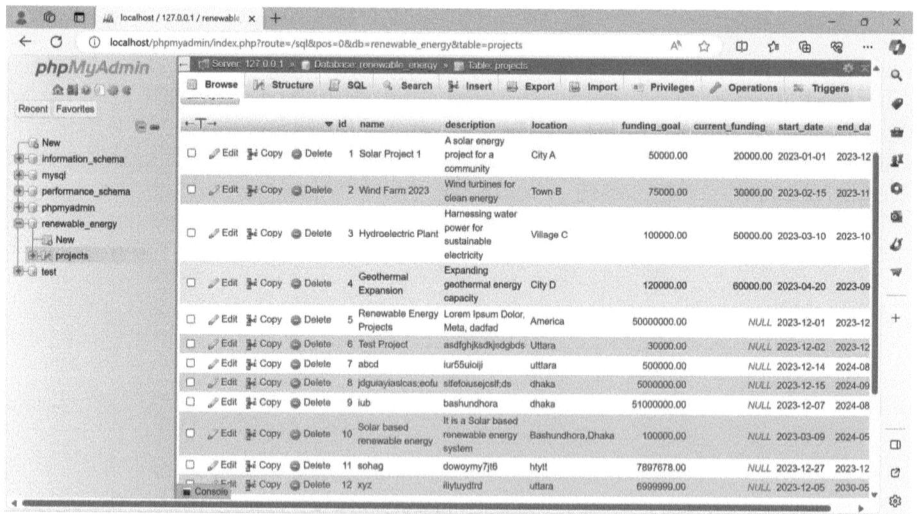

Fig. 3. Xamp Database.

user data, and scalability is attained by a design that allows for horizontal scaling, which allows it to flexibly adjust to different workloads. The design is supported by extensive documentation that offers insightful information on the parts and interactions of the system Fig. 4, enabling efficient maintenance and future growth.

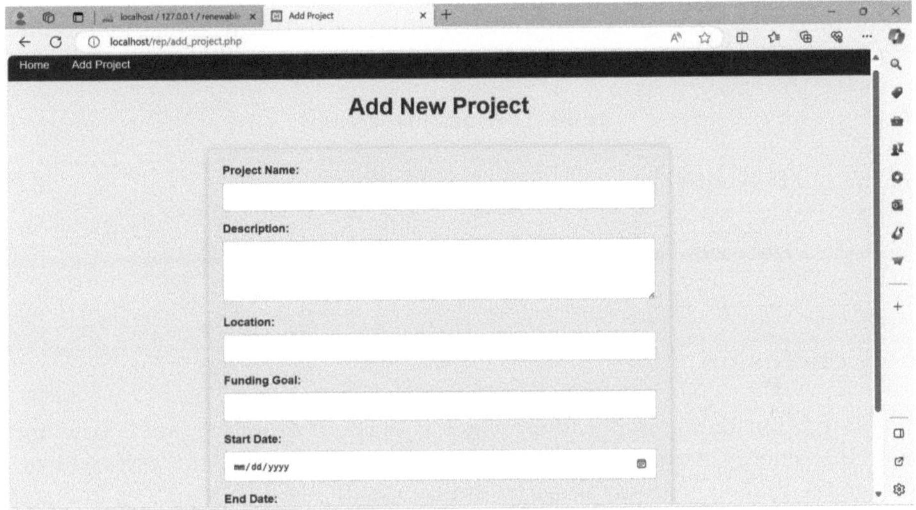

Fig. 4. Add Work UI.

7   Problem Analysis

During the project's early stages, a comprehensive problem analysis was essential in determining the goals and course of our web application. Acknowledging the intricate obstacles linked to the adoption of renewable energy in Bangladesh, we conducted comprehensive stakeholder engagements and user interviews to obtain a refined comprehension of the current problems.

Additional market research identified shortcomings in current systems, emphasizing the requirement for a customized solution. The complexities of the Bangladeshi context—such as disparities in technical literacy and particular geographical factors—became evident as important determinants of our problem analysis. This thorough investigation allowed us to conclude that there is a deficiency in a centralized platform that efficiently links users with renewable energy projects and fosters community support. Our online application's need was further highlighted by the lack of user-friendly interfaces and tailored recommendations.

All things considered, the problem analysis stage set the stage for a solution that not only tackles current issues but also closely matches the unique requirements and dynamics of the Bangladeshi setting, promoting a more comprehensive and effective strategy for supporting renewable energy.

- **Data Privacy and Security:** Handling sensitive data related to renewable energy projects requires robust security measures. Ensuring privacy and protecting against potential cyber threats are essential aspects to address.
- **Data Technical Challenges:** Overcoming complexities in integrating various renewable energy data sources, ensuring data accuracy, and maintaining system scalability can be significant hurdles (Table 1).

Table 1. Renewable Energy

Table Heading	Renewable Energy		
	Solar Energy	Wind Mill	Bio Energy
Discoverd Energy in MW	1200 MW	650 MW	210 MW

8   Conclusion

To sum up, our online application, which is devoted to aiding and encouraging renewable energy projects in Bangladesh, is a big step in the direction of a sustainable and ecologically sensitive future. By doing a thorough examination of the situation, we were able to pinpoint and rectify significant weaknesses in the current platforms, customizing our approach to the particular difficulties that the Bangladeshi environment provided. Our platform's strong foundation is its software design, which prioritizes security, scalability, and modularity to provide maximum performance and flexibility.

Our approach, which includes iterative user feedback loops and stakeholder discussions, is a reflection of our dedication to inclusion, user-centric design, and ongoing development. Our application's software architecture, which is characterized by a modular, scalable, and secure design, is what makes it so successful. Its well-considered architecture guarantees peak performance, future-proofing, and unwavering dedication to data protection. Our approach, which includes user interviews, stakeholder discussions, and iterative feedback loops, highlights our commitment to inclusion, user-centric design, and a continual improvement mindset. The result of these efforts is a web application that encourages community empowerment and involvement while offering a user-friendly interface for finding and supporting renewable energy initiatives.

The successful results of our project's rigorous testing and subsequent implementation demonstrate its potential to have a revolutionary influence on the development of a more sustainable and environmentally friendly world [10]. As a result, our application encourages a sense of empowerment and community participation in addition to offering a user-friendly interface for finding and supporting renewable energy initiatives. The favorable results of testing and deployment highlight the potential contribution of our initiative to Bangladesh's transition to a more sustainable and environmentally friendly energy landscape [11]. In terms of the future, the project provides a basis for continued improvements and ventures into the field of community-driven sustainability and support for renewable energy.

References

1. Gorji, A.A., Martek, I.: Renewable energy policy and deployment of renewable energy technologies: the role of resource curse. Environ. Sci. Pollut. Res. **30**(39), 91377–91395 (2023)
2. Smirnova, E., Kot, S., Kolpak, E., Shestak, V.: Governmental support and renewable energy production: a cross-country review. Energy **230**, 120903 (2021)
3. Islam, M.T., Shahir, S., Uddin, T.I., Saifullah, A.: Current energy scenario and future prospect of renewable energy in Bangladesh. Renew. Sustain. Energy Rev. **39**, 1074–1088 (2014)
4. Alam, S.: Building renewable energy in Bangladesh. The National Bureau of Asian Research (2023)
5. Soava, G., Mehedintu, A., Sterpu, M., Raduteanu, M.: Impact of renewable energy consumption on economic growth: evidence from European union countries. Technol. Econ. Dev. Econ. **24**(3), 914–932 (2018)
6. Bhattacharya, S., Celis, L.E., Chander, D., Dasgupta, K., Karanam, S., Rajan, V.: Crowds of crowds: performance based modeling and optimization over multiple crowdsourcing platforms. Hum. Comput. **2**(1) (2015)
7. Abdul, D., Wenqi, J., Tanveer, A.: Prioritization of renewable energy source for electricity generation through AHP-VIKOR integrated methodology. Renew. Energy **184**, 1018–1032 (2022)
8. Ahmad, T., et al.: Artificial intelligence in sustainable energy industry: Status quo, challenges and opportunities. J. Clean. Prod. **289**, 125834 (2021)
9. Fu, X., Wu, X., Zhang, C., Fan, S., Liu, N.: Planning of distributed renewable energy systems under uncertainty based on statistical machine learning. Prot. Control. Mod. Power Syst. **7**(4), 1–27 (2022)
10. Amin, A., Shidujaman, M., Wang, B.: Improving HCI on cognition for children with intelligent UI/UX. In: Rauterberg, M. (ed.) HCII 2023. LNCS, vol. 14035, pp. 355–366. Springer, Cham (2023). https://doi.org/10.1007/978-3-031-34732-0_27
11. Elsheikh, A.H., Sharshir, S.W., Abd Elaziz, M., Kabeel, A.E., Guilan, W., Haiou, Z.: Modeling of solar energy systems using artificial neural network: a comprehensive review. Sol. Energy **180**, 622–639 (2019)
12. Sultana, A., Islam, M., Hasan, M., Ahmed, F.: Fake news detection using machine learning techniques. In: 2023 IEEE/ACIS 21st International Conference on Software Engineering Research, Management and Applications (SERA), pp. 98–103. IEEE (2023)
13. Higgs, G., Berry, R., Kidner, D., Langford, M.: Using it approaches to promote public participation in renewable energy planning: prospects and challenges. Land Use Policy **25**(4), 596–607 (2008)

14. Song, X., Liu, M., Gong, L., Gu, Y., Shidujaman, M.: A review of human-computer interface evaluation research based on evaluation process elements. In: Kurosu, M., Hashizume, A. (eds.) HCII 2023. LNCS, vol. 14011, pp. 262–289. Springer, Cham (2023). https://doi.org/10.1007/978-3-031-35596-7_17
15. Haque, S., et al.: Automatic product sorting and packaging system. In: 2023 15th International Conference on Intelligent Human-Machine Systems and Cybernetics (IHMSC), pp. 163–167. IEEE (2023)

Correction to: Evaluation of Training Methods for a First Contact Training for Human-Robot Interaction

Erika Rewunow, Ann-Kristin Jaros, Kim Christiane Pfindel, Tamara Schweier, Jonas Birkle, and Verena Wagner-Hartl

Correction to:
Chapter 3 in: M. Kurosu and A. Hashizume (Eds.):
HCI International 2025 – Late Breaking Papers,
https://doi.org/10.1007/978-3-032-12385-5_3

In the original version of the book contained a minor error regarding chapter 3. The author's name Wagner-Hartl was displayed correctly. This has beed corrected.

The updated version of this chapter can be found at
https://doi.org/10.1007/978-3-032-12385-5_3

Author Index